M000102279

Current Studies in
Spanish Linguistics

Current Studies in
Spanish Linguistics

EDITED BY

Héctor Campos and Fernando Martínez-Gil

Georgetown University Press ● Washington, D.C.

COVERS: *Joán Miró / Painting, 1933.* © 1992 Wadsworth Atheneum, Hartford, Connecticut. The Ella Gallup Sumner and Mary Catlin Sumner Collection by kind permission.

Georgetown University Press, Washington, D.C.   20057–1079
Copyright © 1991 by Georgetown University Press. All rights reserved.

Carlos P. Otero holds the copyright to "The cognitive revolution and the study of language: Looking back to see ahead" (pages 3-69 of this volume).

PRINTED IN THE UNITED STATES OF AMERICA
10 9 8 7 6 5 4 3 2 1
THIS VOLUME IS PRINTED ON ACID-FREE ∝ OFFSET BOOK PAPER

Library of Congress Cataloging-in-Publication Data.

Current studies in Spanish linguistics/ Héctor Campos and
Fernando Martínez-Gil, editors
     p. cm.
     ISBN 0-87840-234-9
     1. Spanish language—Grammar.   I. Campos, Héctor.   II. Martínez-Gil,
     Fernando.
PC4105.C87 1992
465—dc20   91-25304

IN MEMORIAM

Osvaldo Jaeggli, 1954-1990

Contents

Foreword

Universal Grammar is a 'theory of the fixed and invariant principles that constitute the human language faculty and the parameters of variation associated with them' (Chomsky 1988: 133). By setting the parameters in one or another way, particular languages can thus be derived from Universal Grammar.

From the time Chomsky developed the notion of 'generative grammar' in his master's thesis, *Morphophonemics of Modern Hebrew* (1951), through Chomsky's (1956) *The Logical Structure of Linguistic Theory* and Chomsky and Halle's *The Sound Pattern of English* (1968), the cornerstones of syntactic and phonological research, to the present, we have moved from a system of descriptive rules to an explanatory system of principles and parameters. Although Chomsky clearly outlined the goals of generative linguistic research in *Aspects of the Theory of Syntax* (1965), it is not until his *Lectures on Government and Binding* (1981) that we find a formal system which is able to account for the logical problem of the acquisition of syntax. Regarding phonological theory, the autosegmental approach of phonological representations, in conjunction with the theories of underspecification and the universal feature hierarchy, have provided more explanatory alternatives to the system of descriptive rules which followed the publication of SPE. Current developments in the theories of syllable structure, lexical phonology, and metrical structure also allow us to get closer to the desired system of principles and parameters.

For the present volume, we have invited scholars in the areas of Spanish acquisition, phonology, morphology, syntax, and semantics who ascribe to a theory of principles and parameters in their research to share their work so that we can appreciate what new insights the perspective of Universal Grammar has to offer to the study of the Spanish language and what these studies themselves have to offer to theoretical linguistics. Many of the topics discussed in this volume failed to be noticed by the traditional grammarians of Spanish. Some topics like clitics and pronouns, or stress and diphthongs, have haunted the Spanish (generative) linguistic literature for the last twenty or more years and still remain at the center of current research, although our understanding of these topics has increased considerably. Some new topics like aspect, tense, phrasal stress, and the prosodic hierarchy are now entering the field. As Popper (1960: 179-80) notes in *The Growth of Scientific Knowledge*, '...the most lasting contribution to the growth of scientific knowledge that a theory can make are the new problems which it raises, so that we are led back to the view of science and of the growth of knowledge as always starting from, and always ending with, problems-problems of an ever increasing depth, and an ever increasing fertility in suggesting new problems.'

This volume is the result of the collective effort of its contributors and we would like to thank all the authors who participated in this project for their warm and encouraging support. The authors served as readers and critics to other works and their collegiality and friendship are reflected in the final version of the works we are presenting here. We would also like to thank Norma González-Catalán, Eric Holt, William Woodard, Bernardo Gárate, Alberto Lanzat and Janalee Burnett, for helping us proofread the different versions of the manuscript: our gratitude also to Dr. John Staczek, director of Georgetown University Press, Dean James Alatis, Assistant Dean Richard Cronin, Thomas Walsh, Ralph Fasold, Patricia Rayner, Patrice La Liberté, the Rev. Richard J. O'Brien, S.J., and the staff at the Dean's office of the School of Languages and Linguistics, for their professional advice and technical support.

We had invited our colleague Osvaldo Jaeggli to send us a collaboration for this volume, but we never got an answer from him. A few weeks later we learned that he was bed-ridden and blind; a few months later he died. Osvaldo was a sharing teacher and friend, who knew how to transmit the love and passion for linguistics. His integrity as a scholar and a human being was truly inspiring. Osvaldo's tragic death is an irreparable loss to us all, but his memory will never abandon us. To Osvaldo Jaeggli we dedicate this volume.

H. Campos

Georgetown University   F. Martínez-Gil

Current Studies in
Spanish Linguistics

SECTION ONE: COGNITION

The cognitive revolution and the study of language: Looking back to see ahead

Carlos P. Otero*
UCLA

0 Introduction. My purpose here is to place the unusual strides recently made toward a deeper understanding of language within a more general context so that we can better appreciate their place in the history of ideas, and their ramified and far-reaching implications.

Three fundamental puzzles have presumably intrigued humans from time immemorial: the nature of the universe, the nature of life, and the nature of human nature. It is of some interest for the student of language (and, more generally, cognition) that most of our current understanding of all three puzzles--some of the most remarkable leaps in the history of science--was developed only after 1900. Since the beginning of the century the extent of our scientific understanding is such that no human being, no matter how gifted or privileged, is able to master it all. This fact immediately brings to mind the ancient argument, of which St. Augustine gives a version in *The City of God*, that since civilization is still progressing (if not taking off), humans could not have been around all that long.[1]

---

* I have drawn freely from a draft of Otero (forthcoming a) and related work, and from drafts of the introductory material for Otero (forthcoming b). I am indebted to Héctor Campos for some stimulating remarks on the general topic of this paper (part of the incitement to write it, for which he is mainly responsible) and for some materials conveniently provided, and to Robert Freidin for having brought Fine's book and Witten's paper on pronominalization to my attention and for a copy of this paper and of some correspondence relating to the 1965 Christian Gauss Seminar in Criticism -- among other things. I'm also grateful to Maria Luiza Carrano for having made some of the references quickly available to me.

[1] St. Augustine, like our grandparents generally (cf. Durrell 1952), accepted a date of about 5,000 B.C. (according to the book of Genesis), rather than some ten billion years ago (see Weinberg 1977, chap. 8), for the creation of the universe. The distinguished physicist Stephen Hawking finds it interesting that 'this is not so far from the end of the last Ice Age, about 10,000 B.C., which is when archeologists tell us that civilization really began' (1988: 7). Needless to say, the Mosaic chronology precluded any understanding of even our earth's past, as had been made clear by James Hutton (1726-1797) and Charles Lyell (1797-1875)--one more case of 'metempsychosis,' to place alongside those of Galileo and Newton (1642), Maxwell and Einstein (1879), Vico and Herder (1744). In Gould's view (1987: 3), John McPhee has provided the most striking metaphor of the 'almost incomprehensible immensity' of the cosmic past ('deep time'): 'Consider the earth's history as the old measure of the English yard, the distance from the king's nose to the tip of his outstretched hand. One stroke of a nail file on his middle finger erases human history.' Cf. Toulmin and Goodfield (1965), Crick (1981, chap. 1).

3

The most profound and reliable knowledge available to us today is then essentially the work of roughly the last three generations of modern scientists (who, of course, stood on the shoulders of giants), out of a total of about thirteen generations (since Galileo). These three and thirteen generations add up to about 0.25% and 1%, respectively, of the roughly thirteen hundred generations since our Cro-Magnon ancestors found themselves (quite abruptly in evolutionary terms, it would appear) standing next to their closest, and by that time already distant, living nonhuman relatives the chimpanzees, among the wild beasts of an inauspicious-looking world, no less than thirty thousand years ago.[2]

The first half of our century contributed what appears to be a definitive leap in our understanding of the cosmos (general relativity is 75 years old), mainly the result of Einstein's unparalleled creativity, and a no less abrupt leap in our understanding of the subatomic puzzles (the new quantum mechanics began to emerge 65 years ago); it was also a period of path-breaking developments in the formal sciences (metamathematics, theory of computation). The advances in physics in turn made it possible, in the third quarter of the century, to bring living organisms under the scope of the physical sciences (molecular biology was born in the Spring of 1953). At exactly the same time, the natural science approach was successfully extended to the study of language and cognition with the emergence of the first elaborate cognitive science (the first version of the proposal was ready for distribution in mid 1955), while the newly developed theory of computation led directly to both computer science and the first phase of mathematical (more precisely, algebraic) linguistics, closely linked at birth. In the fourth quarter of our century, we are witnessing developments which may well lead to a much deeper understanding than was hitherto possible, both of the macrocosmos around us and of some fundamental aspects of the microcosmos

---

[2] Only in recent years have we learned that 'The genetic distance between humans and the chimpanzee is probably too small to account for their substantial organismal differences . . .The average human protein is more than 99 percent identical in amino acid sequence to its chimpanzee homolog . . . By [a standard] criterion, human and chimpanzee mitochondrial DNA's appear identical . . . the nucleic acid sequence difference of human and chimpanzee DNA is about 1.1 percent . . . with respect to genetic differences between species, the human-chimpanzee D value [an estimate of the variability between human and chimpanzee populations] is extraordinarily small . . . humans and chimpanzees have rather similar chromosomes numbers, 46 and 48, respectively' (King and Wilson 1975: 107, 112, 113, 114; see also Wilson 1985. Cf. Otero 1989, n. 69). For Chomsky's view of the emergence of 'homo loquens,' see Chomsky (1970, 1988), Lightfoot (1983: 165-169), Otero (1990), and references therein. Cf. now Bickerton (1990), 'a thought-provoking work' which 'presents a reasoned case that the capacity for language is the distinctive property of human intelligence, and a considered assessment of the problem of accounting for the evolution of this apparently unique natural phenomenon,' in Chomsky's opinion.

of the human brain (perhaps the most complex object in the universe). It is much too early to know for sure whether these developments truly represent a decisive turning point in our understanding of some defining properties of the human species and its place in the universe, as they may very well do. The thought that we may be on the threshold of a new age is hardly original in the 1990s. Thus, in a very small segment of historical time--an infinitesimally minute unit of cosmic time--we have come to understand a great deal of what lies behind two of the three major puzzles (the nature of the cosmos and the nature of life), have developed a model for the study of cognitive domains, and appear to be well on our way to coming up with a profound, if necessarily partial, answer to the question which touches us most directly, namely, the nature of language. This, in turn, means that we are beginning to get the first glimmerings of an answer to the most crucial of all questions: What is the nature of human nature? Just what does it mean to be human? The reason is that the advances in our understanding of language are very real and we can hardly doubt that only through a successful analysis of language can we hope to come to terms with human creativity (in thought or action).

1 Giant steps toward the unity of science. This state of affairs is the more surprising when one considers that it was the new scientific understanding of the atomic structure of all matter that changed everything (except our mode of thinking, as Einstein pointedly observed), and yet the very idea of the atom, which goes back at least twenty-five centuries to the ancient Greek Leucippus and his most famous disciple, Democritus, was not familiar to most scientists until the end of the last century--and even then was not yet universally accepted. Under the influence of the German physicist Ernst Mach (1836-1916), acknowledged by Einstein as one of his four precursors (aside from Newton), many scientists held back from incorporating into their theories anything that could not be observed directly (as the behaviorists were still doing half a century later, we all know now).[3] It is said that what drove the great theorist of heat Ludwig Boltzmann (1844-1906) to commit suicide was that his fellow scientists refused to take his assumption of the atomicity of matter seriously.[4] In fact, Einstein's development away

---

[3] This resistance is the more surprising when one considers that some late nineteenth century physicists, not unlike Aristotle and many other people since ancient times before them, thought they had 'some reason to believe' in 'an aetherial medium filling space and permeating bodies' (in the words of the great Scottish physicist James Clerk Maxwell), a concept which most physicists dropped only early in our century, again under the liberating influence of Einstein's ideas (his special relativity theory in this case).

[4] Weinberg (1983, chap. 1). See Pais (1982: 79ff.) for an overview of the nineteenth century debate among chemists from the vantage point of Einstein's discoveries. Cf. Chalmers (1982).

from his empiricist and positivist beginnings toward the antipositivistic realism of his mature years was not completed until he 'worked out the general theory of relativity,' as he himself noted in 1948 (Fine 1986: 86).

Only after the publication of Einstein's six 1905 papers, in particular the one on the long-known movement of small clumps of matter suspended in solution (Brownian motion), written just before his two famous papers on the special theory of relativity, were some, but by no means all, of the most notorious skeptical scientists--which included the outstanding chemist Friedrich Wilhelm Ostwald (1853-1932)--finally convinced of the reality of the atom.

1.1 From the quantum principle to the structure of DNA. The decisive turning point in the history of the study of the structure of matter (like the rediscovery of Mendel's results, to which we return), came about precisely in 1900.[5] It was in the opening year of the century that a German physicist who was five years younger than Ostwald, one year younger than Saussure, a couple of years younger than Freud, just a few years younger than Ramón y Cajal or Hugo de Vries, and ten years younger than Frege, made a discovery which, in Einstein's view, 'almost entirely conditioned the development of science ever since.' What Max Planck discovered was that light, X rays, and other wave phenomena (including the waves of the tiny electric oscillators inside the atom) could only emit or absorb energy in discrete lumps or packets of a certain size, whose energy is proportional to their frequency. This so-called quantum principle (he dubbed those lumps of energy 'quanta'), together with an equation involving what is now called Planck's constant, was to become the basis for all 20th century research in physics. As Einstein, who had been awarded the Nobel prize for his contributions to quantum theory, was to put it almost half a century later (at the Max Planck Memorial Service), it was the quantum discovery that 'shattered the whole framework of classical mechanics and electrodynamics and set science a fresh task: that of finding *a new conceptual basis* for all physics.'[6]

---

[5] These are not the only two important advances in our understanding of 1900 (the year of *The Interpretation of Dreams*). To mention just one not mentioned below, it was in 1900 that Karl Landsteiner showed that humans differ among themselves, and not only from other species of animal, in their type of blood, a discovery that we can hardly do without now. Later we learned that the differences in the hemoglobin molecules of different mammals, all of which have hemoglobin in the red cells of their blood, are in their amino-acid sequence.

[6] Emphasis added for the benefit of some doubters; cf. the quote in Fine 15-16. Einstein may have found congenial this characterization of physics by Edward Witten, perhaps the most obvious candidate for Einstein's heir apparent (and apparently a much better mathematical calculator than he was): 'Most people who haven't been trained in physics probably think of what physicists do as a question of incredible complicated calculations, but that's not really the essence of it. The essence of it is that physics is about concepts, wanting to understand concepts, the

Moreover, without Planck's discovery it would not have been possible to establish a workable theory of the physics of molecules and atoms, and the energy processes that govern their transformations. This theory finally provided the physical basis for nineteenth century chemistry, which studied the properties of atoms and molecules just at a purely abstract level (much as generative grammar studies the abstract properties of yet unknown neural structures, an analogy to which we return). The first step towards such a physical theory of chemistry was the model of a hydrogen atom proposed in 1913 by the Danish physicist Niels Bohr.

Two years later Einstein, singlehandedly, completed the first of the two major theoretical constructions of twentieth century physics, the theory of the extraordinarily vast (*The Great System of the World* is the title of one of the two works believed to have been written by Leucippus). The masterpiece in which he presented his discovery, *The Foundations of the General Relativity Theory*, was written during the height of World War I (it was finished in late November 1915).[7] Its leading idea is the meaningfulness of Newton's absolute empty space as a physical entity (as Einstein sometimes put it, 'Space is not a thing'), which had already played a key role in the 'special theory' of relativity (1905).[8] Theory had run so far ahead of observation that even Einstein had some difficulty with what for some is the greatest prediction he ever made (in fact, the difficulty led him in 1917 to what he called 'the greatest blunder in my life'): That we live in a expanding universe. The correctness of his prediction was only established in 1929 by the work of the American astronomer Edward Hubble, who was ten years younger than Einstein. The general theory of relativity, which to this day 'is really in its way the most perfect and satisfying of physical theories,' has replaced Newton's theory of universal gravitation, which had reigned supreme for over two centuries.[9]

There is little doubt that Planck's discovery and Einstein's theory represent enormous advances in our understanding. But for all their

---

principles by which the world works. In really fine theories like general relativity there is a well-defined, conceptual formulation, and when you learn it you say 'yes, those concepts are perfect,' and the theory that is based on them is the best embodiment of those concepts' (Davies and Brown, eds., 1988: 90-91; cf. 98).

[7] On November 28 Einstein wrote to a friend: 'During the past month I had one of the most exciting and strenuous times in my life, but also one of the most successful ones' (Pais: 250).

[8] 'Special' because it deals with only one sort of motion: uniform motion with constant velocity in a straight line.

[9] The judgment in quotes is due to Edward Witten (see Davies and Brown, eds., p. 95; cf. above, n. 6). Apparently he is not alone: Many physicists believe it to be 'the most perfect and aesthetically beautiful creation in the history of physics, perhaps of all science' (Bernstein 1973: 72). It has also passed every test, in particular those made possible by the technological leaps of the 1960s and 1970s, with flying colors (Will 1986, Schwinger 1986).

innovations, Planck and Einstein were still, in an important sense, within the 'classical tradition.' To find the real defiers of tradition in contemporary physics, that is, the progenitors of the other major theoretical construction of twentieth century physics, one has to turn to some of their young successors, in particular those who managed to take the intellectual center of theoretical physics away from where it had been for the first quarter of the century.

No one is more representative of these innovators than Werner Heisenberg (1901-1976), best known for his famous uncertainty principle.[10] In the summer of 1925 Heisenberg succeeded in developing a mathematical formalism now referred to as matrix mechanics, based on corpuscular notions, in which Newton's equations of motion are replaced by similar equations between matrices.[11] A few months later (early in 1926) Erwin Schrödinger succeeded in developing an alternative formalism, wave mechanics, based on undulatory notions, and later he was able to prove that his formalism was mathematically equivalent to the earlier formalism developed by Heisenberg.[12] The following year (1927) a student and associate of the great mathematician David Hilbert, John von Neumann (of whom more later), succeeded in constructing a fully rigorous formalization of the new quantum mechanics (although he did not provide some of the required proofs until 1929).[13] This formalization, considered at the time a veritable *tour de force*, turned out to encompass later extensions of the new quantum mechanics, the theory of the extraordinarily tiny.

The consequences of the cascade of developments soon became apparent. In October 1934, not very far from Mussolini's 'oval office,' the Italian physicist Enrico Fermi (born, like Heisenberg, in 1901) and his young

---

[10] In general, quantum mechanics does not predict a single definite result for an observation. Instead, it predicts a number of different possible outcomes with their respective probabilities. Contemporary physicists tell us that it is the best humans can do, which of course does not exclude the possibility that there is a set of laws that determines events completely for some extraterrestrial who could observe the present state of the universe without disturbing it.

[11] The obvious way to measure the present position and velocity of a particle is to shine light on the particle. By Planck's principle, one has to use at least one quantum of light, which is enough to disturb the particle and change its velocity in a way that cannot be predicted. Heisenberg showed that the uncertainty in the position of the particle times the uncertainty in its velocity times the mass of the particle can never be smaller than Planck's constant. This led to the reformulation of mechanics into a new theory called quantum mechanics -- the framework of current quantum mechanics--in the late 1920s.

[12] It is noteworthy that neither of the two men liked the other's theory: Schrodinger was 'frightened away, if not repelled' by the algebraic approach of his German colleague, while Heisenberg referred to the alternative picture of atoms given by the Swiss as 'disgusting'.

[13] From this perspective, the two accounts are but two different representations of one and the same operator calculus in an infinitely dimensional Hilbert space. See Heims (1980: 109-14, 131-34).

collaborators came upon a key laboratory observation 'from which one may well date the effective beginning of the nuclear age' (Holton 1978: 155). By the end of 1938 there was evidence of uranium fission in Hitler's Germany. By January 1939 physicists in the United States had been made aware of the new discovery, which several of them were able to replicate soon after in their own laboratories, and by the end of 1942 the first self-sustaining nuclear chain reaction under the control of humans was produced in one of the first, if not the very first, nuclear reactors, built in Chicago under the direction of Fermi, who had by then emigrated to the United States. In 1945 the atom bomb became a monstrous reality, and before we knew it we were all inexorably in a dramatically new age.[14] To repeat: Everything had changed except our mode of thinking, as Einstein was to put it a few years later.

This is hopefully enough to bring home the fact that our century has witnessed a revolution in physics--in both our understanding of the nature of matter and our view of the cosmos, which are closely related. But this is not the end of the story. By opening the way to the discovery of the physical mechanisms that underlie the processes described by nineteenth century chemists in abstract terms, the development of the new quantum mechanics made physical chemistry possible (as the discovery of the physical mechanisms that underlie the processes described in generative grammar would make neurological linguistics a reality). Physical chemistry in turn opened the way to major advances in the biological sciences.

A recognized prime mover along this direction is the American physical chemist Linus Pauling (born in 1901, like Heisenberg and Fermi). In the very years (late 1920s) in which the new quantum mechanics was being developed, Pauling succeeded in putting the theory of covalent bonding on a secure mathematical footing within the framework of the new physics, although his key paper on the nature of the chemical bond did not see the light until 1931.[15] By 1935 Pauling considered his work on the chemical bond (established by the action of electrons), which was to provide the whole physical basis for present-day chemistry and molecular biology, 'essentially complete.' His classic, and still unrivalled, book on the topic, *The Nature of the Chemical Bond*, a landmark in the history of science, was completed before the end of the decade, roughly at the time of the discovery of nuclear fission. In February 1943 one of the two major progenitors of quantum mechanics, by then a refugee in Ireland, delivered his celebrated public

---

[14] For more on these developments from an illuminating perspective, see Holton (1986, chapter 7) (' "Success sanctifies the means": Heisenberg, Oppenheimer, and the transition to modern physics').

[15] This breakthrough was a crucial step towards what was to follow because of the two types of bonding in chemical compounds, electrovalent and covalent, only covalent bonding is present in the carbon compounds, the molecules of life.

lectures on the physical aspect of the living cell in Dublin, published in 1944 under the title *What is Life?*. This little book of Schrödinger's seems to have appeared at the perfect time to inspire a generation of biology researchers, mostly physicists seeking new pastures in the immediate post-war period. A number of them came to believe that the fundamental molecules of life, the genes, which carry the information necessary for embryological development, could be understood in terms of the newly discovered laws of physics. Schrödinger still assumed, as was common at the time, that genes are made of protein. Before the year was over, the work of Oswald Avery (1877-1955) and his associates at the Rockefeller Institute in New York left no doubt that the hereditary information is actually carried by an acid, deoxyribonucleic acid or DNA for short.[16] At last nucleic acids were taking up their rightful position at the center of the genetics stage.

Once the new discovery began to be assimilated, a reorientation occurred and things moved rather fast. In 1948 Pauling came up with the idea that in a sequence of virtually identical objects in space the change in position from one to the next generates a helix, and by 1951 he had built a particular helical model of amino-acids (the so-called alpha helix) that was later frequently found in the structure of proteins. This, among other developments, led to the discovery of the very structure of DNA less than two years later (1953), 'exactly five hundred years--almost to the day--after the fall of Constantinople' to the Turks, as Gunther Stent has remarked (1978: xi). Just half a millennium after the end of the Dark Ages we were suddenly a giant step closer to understanding the secret of life.

The breakthrough can be dated very precisely: The British former physicist, Francis Crick, and the American biologist, James Watson, the two 'young Turks' who developed the celebrated double-helix model of DNA --'perhaps the most famous event in biology since Darwin's book' according to the most famous account, 'one of the greatest discoveries ever made' in Pauling's view --reported their fresh results in the April 25, 1953, issue of the British scientific journal *Nature*, a couple of months before Noam Chomsky (half a year younger than Watson) became thoroughly convinced that his work on generative grammar was on the right track.[17] Since it was the terse,

---

[16] As Oscar Hertwig, a former student of Ernst Haeckel, had intimated as long ago as 1884 --so far ahead of his time that his suggestion was resoundedly ignored by his fellow cell biologists.

[17] As the numerous references to Pauling in Watson's (1968) account make clear, at least one of the discoverers saw himself in a tight race--trying to 'solve DNA in the same way' and 'beat him at his own game' (see chapters 25 and 7)--with the Cal Tech model builder ('a fabulous chemist,' 'the greatest of all chemists,' 'unquestionably the world's most astute chemist,' 'the world authority on the structural chemistry of ions,' 'the first person to propose something solidly correct about the structure of a biologically important molecule,' 'a great man,' 'a genius

two-page report by Crick and Watson that opened up the era of molecular biology (a new scientific field), it comes as no surprise that the names of the two authors are usually associated with the birth of the physical counterpart of abstract Mendelian genetics (the parallel with the neurological linguistics of the future and generative grammar is perhaps less close than the one with quantum physics and nineteenth century chemistry, but it is instructive). The fascinating story of the discovery is recreated, with unusual literary skill, in Watson's colorful 'personal account' (1968), recently complemented by Crick's far more sober but no less enlightening counterpart (1988).

As soon as the contents of the *Nature* report became known (and they became widely known almost immediately), most biologists interested in the physical mechanism of heredity quickly realized that the time had come to think about genetics in molecular terms. Not only was the era of molecular biology in full swing by then, but its 'classic period' was to be completed by 1965 (with the unraveling of the genetic code), just after a dozen years of feverish activity.[18] We had come a long way since the day in 1865, a mere century before, when Gregor Mendel, onetime abbot of the Augustinian monastery in the Moravian town of Brno, presented his paper ('Experiments on plant hybrids') on the units of heredity later to be dubbed 'genes' before the Brno Society of Natural Science--a piece of deduction so brilliant and

---

of [great] stature,' there is 'no one like Linus in all the world,' ...) whose approach, consciously followed by Watson and Crick, quickly led to the discovery. The main reason why 'the long feared news that Linus [Pauling] now had a structure for DNA,' (ch. 21), 'the Rosetta Stone for unraveling the true secret of life' (ch. 2), failed to materialize ('all too often Linus had gotten there first,' which had been 'most embarrassing for the Cambridge group' [ch. 11], for which he was a sort of Nemesis), may simply have been that he was denied a chance to see the X-ray photographs of DNA taken by Rosalind Franklin in late 1952 (a decisive key to the discovery) because the U.S. State Department had lifted his passport in retaliation for his successful campaign against the testing of nuclear weapons in the atmosphere (which led to his second Nobel Prize, this time for peace, in 1962--he had received the Nobel Prize for chemistry in 1954). 'The failure to let one of the world's leading scientists attend a completely nonpolitical meeting would have been expected from the Russians,' but was received with 'almost complete disbelief' (ch. 17) in London, another sign of the general unawareness of the totalitarian proclivities of the U.S. Department of State, well documented to this day. (Another indication that Pauling takes his responsibility more seriously than most--eventually he left Cal Tech largely because of institutional hostility there to his peace efforts, which continue to this day and spent $18,000 for two newspaper advertisements protesting the Persian Gulf War,' *Los Angeles Times*, Feb 26, 1991, E3)--and that he has great confidence in human rationality, is his 1958 anti-war book--complemented, in his view, by the 1986 one--which in early 1991 has, if anything, greater relevance than at the height of the Cold War, as the picture becomes clearer. Cf. Otero 1991)

[18] For a history of the chief discoveries and an attempt to reconstruct the circumstances of each, see Olby (1974), which has taken the story from the emergence of the idea of macromolecules up to the discovery itself, and Judson (1979), which begins nearer to the discovery and continues until the genetic code was unraveled. See also Cairns, Stent and Watson, eds. (1966).

insightful, and so far ahead of his time, that it went unnoticed by his fellow biologists for 35 years (the partial parallel with generative grammar is suggestive). It was precisely in 1900, the year of the quantum principle, when Mendel's results were achieved independently first in the Netherlands (by Hugo de Vries, the botanist who introduced the crucial idea of a type of change in the genes he called mutation), then in Germany, then in Austria, and then in the United States, England and France, in much the way Mendel had achieved them, in each case by biologists who were aware of the existence of chromosomes, as had become common at the time.

A little over half a century later it was clear that what makes it possible for like to beget like (for all higher plants and animals studied so far, with only minor variations beyond that) is the so-called genetic code (similar in principle to the Morse Code), a little 'dictionary' that relates the four-letter 'alphabet' of the nucleic acids to the twenty-letter 'alphabet' of proteins. A group of three adjacent letters (triplet), called a codon (of which there are 64), codes for an amino-acid (most of which can be coded by more than one codon), and one of three codons stands for 'end of chain.'[19] Once this was understood and the foundations of molecular biology were 'sufficiently firmly outlined,' even Crick would soon be ready to proceed to a far more elusive endeavor: the workings of the brain.

1.2 'The last frontier': A quest for a science of mind. The three decades between the turn of the century and the end of the 1920s are perhaps the most fruitful and turbulent experienced by physics, the very core of the natural sciences. Fundamental physics had been radically modified, leading to hopes for far-reaching unity of science. Notions that were accepted without question in 1900 became barely remembered vestiges of a recent and yet culturally distant past in just a few years. The overall structure of physical science had become greatly simplified. What is more, the very way of approaching the most challenging physical problems had been radically altered.

Beyond this, chemistry was now seen to be essentially a chapter of the unified new theory of quantum mechanics. Thus, the British physicist, Paul Dirac (born in 1902), claimed that his famous relativist quantum equation of the electron (published early in 1928, which makes it a few months older than Chomsky) explained 'most of physics and all of chemistry.'[20] A similar view

---

[19] A succinct description can be found in the Appendix to Crick (1988) or to Crick (1981). Crick is described in the epilogue of Watson's best-seller as 'the acknowledged world leader for the past decade' on 'the nature and operation of the genetic code.'

[20] Dirac's equation led physicist and Nobel prize winner Max Born to tell a group of visitors to Göttingen University in 1928 that 'Physics, as we know it, will be over in six months' (Hawking 1988: 156).

was expressed by his strict coeval Heisenberg in his 1955-1956 Gifford Lectures, published two years later as *Physics and Philosophy: The Revolution in Modern Science*: 'Physics and chemistry have been fused into complete oneness through quantum theory.'

It comes as no surprise to discover that one of the best known physicists of the following generation, Stephen Hawking (born in 1942), tacitly endorses and extends Dirac's and Heisenberg's views in his *A Brief History of Time*: 'We already know the laws that govern the behavior of matter under all but the most extreme conditions,' he writes; 'in particular, we know the basic laws that underlie all of chemistry and biology' (1988: 168). Hawking goes on to reiterate his thesis of 1980 that the end may be in sight for theoretical physics, even though he recognizes that quantum mechanics and general relativity theory are inconsistent (a serious drawback in the so-called grand unified theories of quantum mechanics) and that we still don't know for sure what the ultimate building blocks of nature are.[21] At the beginning of this paper it was pointed out that the discovery of the quantum principle 'set science a fresh task: that of finding a new conceptual basis for all physics,' as Einstein put it. It is only fair to add here that he went on to say that this problem 'is still far from a satisfactory solution,' 'despite remarkable partial gains'--an assessment perhaps essentially not at variance with what he might very well have said many years later, possibly even today, were he alive.[22]

---

[21] Witten does not share Hawking's view (Davies and Brown, eds., 105-6). He would probably agree that 'physics, like science in general, will never become a finished business' (Jammer 1988: 37); it 'is always in the process of going deeper and deeper,' and 'everything you answer leads to the next question, and that'll always be true.' In fact, 'we can't comprehend most of physics, just tiny, little things.' To this day we don't have 'the foggiest idea' of what, say, anti-matter is, so 'even at the most elementary level, the understanding is like a laser that sort of goes through big, dark clouds, and it gives you little points of light here and there.' More generally, 'most of the questions that were asked by the Greeks are in the same state now as they were then;' there is only 'one tiny little area where modern science happened to work.' We still don't have 'the foggiest idea of how you do the simplest things' (e.g., how we tie our shoes), let alone complex ones (how does one construct the next sentence?), to say nothing of true creativity, say, how a great poet writes a masterpiece. Even when we have a complete theoretical understanding, we cannot solve many problems, e.g., the three-body problem. How do three bodies interact according to Newton's laws? Nobody knows, because 3 is too big a number' (Chomsky in Saporta 1990: 37, 34, 32, 38-9), 'and the difficulty increases with the number of the bodies and the complexity of the theory' (Hawking 1988: 168). Furthermore, since the 17th century, when the assumptions of 'constructive skepticism' were developed (Popkin 1979: 48,140; Chomsky 1980: 15-16, 142, 1986a: 240, 1989a), it has been clear that 'whatever evidence we may accumulate in support of some hypothesis, there always exist alternative hypotheses inconsistent with ours but compatible with the evidence' (Chomsky 1980: 258 n. 26; cf. Crick 1988, ch. 6, in particular p. 73).

[22] It would seem that Witten's current view is not unlike Einstein's. For him the most immediate goal is a suitable elaboration of the geometrical ideas upon which Einstein based general relativity such that it would reconcile the theory of gravity with quantum mechanics, still the central problem of physics (see Davies and Brown, eds., 96-7, also Peat 1988: 281, 303f.).

The advances in the biological sciences were made no less quickly. The new field of molecular biology emerged just a quarter of a century after the emergence of the new quantum mechanics. Thus the discoveries of Mendelian genetics were 'accommodated within known biochemistry, eliminating the last vestige of vitalism from scientific biology and offering the hope that the evolution and growth of living organisms might fall within the compass of the unified natural sciences as well' (Chomsky 1989a). The following quote from the recent (1988) 'personal view' by Francis Crick, one of the prime movers, written with 'the end of classical molecular biology' in mind (which for him came in 1966), is perhaps representative:

When I started biological research in 1947 I had no suspicion that all the major questions that interested me--What is a gene made of? How is it replicated? How is it turned on and off? What does it do? --would be answered within my own scientific lifetime. I had selected a topic, or series of topics, that I had assumed would last out my active scientific career, and now I found myself with most of my ambitions satisfied.

On the other hand, some specialists believe that biology today is roughly where physics was in the seventeenth century. It is in any case a fact that embryological development, one of the most intriguing phenomena in the whole of biology, continues to elude genetic and biochemical analysis. Why and how do we get fingerprints, for example? So far nobody has the slightest idea. One of the most advanced claims seems to be that we know the fundamental principles of limb cartilage formation, a discovery facilitated, we are told, by one of the first utilizations of mathematical models in biology.

Nevertheless, the discoveries of the first fifty some years of the twentieth century appear to have provided, in the view of some distinguished scientists, if not final answers, at least far better approximations than we had in 1900 to the answers to two of the three major questions that presumably have intrigued humans from time immemorial: The nature of the universe and the nature of life. It was only natural that by the mid-century the most enterprising researchers would be eager to zero in on the third one: The nature of the most complex object we know of in the universe--and the many wonders associated with it. The human brain was naturally assumed to be 'the next scientific frontier.' The new disciplines which began to appear after World War II 'were to carry us across this frontier,' bringing 'the study of the human mind and all its manifestations in thought and action, judgment and evaluation, creation and understanding,' 'within the compass of the existing natural sciences' (Chomsky 1989a).

Some in fact believed that the required basis had already been laid out-- which was correct, though not in the sense intended. It was correct in the sense that the foundations of the theory of computability, a necessary prerequisite to the serious investigation of the mind/brain, had been firmly established in the 1930s. The work of Bertrand Russell and Alfred North Whitehead, directly inspired in the new logic developed by Gottlob Frege a generation earlier and in Boole's still earlier insights, had culminated with the publication of *Principia Mathematica* in 1910-1913. This was the book that led directly to the research program of the formalists, led by David Hilbert, who were searching for a consistent arithmetical logic that was complete. However, in 1931 the logician Kurt Gödel, a coeval of Heisenberg, Fermi, Dirac and Pauling, published his famous paper on formally undecidable theorems of *Principia* and related systems. His incompleteness theorem, which states that any adequate consistent arithmetical logic is incomplete, suddenly and to everyone's surprise wrecked the formalist program. Gödel showed that it is impossible to demonstrate that an arithmetical logic (admittedly incomplete) is consistent if one uses methods that can be represented in the logic itself. John von Neumann, one of the mathematicians most directly engaged in the formalist program, was apparently also one of the first to quickly understand and accept this result. Just after receiving and reading a letter giving the proof from Gödel (who twenty years later was still for him the 'greatest logician since Aristotle'), he is said to have exclaimed: 'This changes my whole work.'

In the wake of Gödel's paper several mathematical logicians of his generation sought to formalize the notion of an effective procedure--of what could be done by explicitly following an algorithm--which was shown to be coextensive with the notion of general recursive function, the core notion of the theory of computability. This work of the 1930s, which constitutes the mathematical roots of computer science, predates computers by more than a decade.

A central strain of the new theory is the contribution of Alan Turing, who exposed fundamental limits on mechanical computation. Turing's discovery was reinforced by the work of Alonzo Church, Stephen Kleene, and Emil Post on recursive functions and the formalization of mathematical logic. Church developed his lambda calculus (which was to provide the basis for John McCarthy's list processing language, LISP, a favorite of artificial intelligence specialists), Kleene his theory of recursive functions, while Emil Post introduced a system for rewriting strings of symbols which paved the way for the emergence of generative grammar. What is more, all these methods were proven to be equivalent. In particular, in 1936 the proposition was advanced that if a function could be computed by any machine at all, it could be computed by each one of these methods (Church's thesis), and about the same time Turing, building on Post's results, proposed a mathematical system conceptualized as an abstract analogue of a computing machine (later dubbed a Turing machine) which helped chart the limits of the computable.

A particularly important result he obtained is that there exist universal Turing machines, that is, machines which can in principle carry out any computation any Turing machine is capable of carrying out.[23]

An additional contribution to the theory of computation was soon to come from engineering. In his 1938 Master's thesis Claude Shannon explored the similarities between electrical network theory and the propositional calculus and made the observation that the functions of relay switching networks could be represented in the symbolic notation of Boolean algebra.[24] Exactly ten years later he went on to develop the theory of finite-state Markov sources (a Markov source being a type of abstract automata) widely known as the mathematical theory of communication. This theory, which developed the notion of 'information' as a single decision between two equally plausible alternatives (entirely independent from content), was to trigger some of the grandest hopes and expectations of the early postwar years. Around 1950, just as Chomsky entered the scene, it was widely believed that this 'fundamental concept,' which Norbert Wiener took to be on a par with 'matter or energy,' would unify the 'social and behavioral sciences' and permit the development of a solid and satisfactory 'mathematical theory of human behavior' on a probabilistic base.[25] It comes as no surprise that the theory of finite-state machines is one of the 'three models for the description of language' of Chomsky's epoch-making paper of 1956, to which we return.

The notions of intelligent automaton and control mechanism had already been brought together in 1943 in several independent studies by different authors. Perhaps the most important, and certainly the most relevant to our story, was the paper co-authored by Warren McCulloch (a neurophysiologist) and Walter Pitts (a logician whose mental abilities some regarded at the time as on a par with von Neumann's) on the theory of formal neural networks or neural nets, the starting point in the making of logical models for the brain.[26] McCulloch and Pitts showed that the operations of a neuron and

---

[23] For more on this and on what follows, see Denning et al. (1978) and references therein. Cf. Partee et al. (1990).

[24] For Gardner (1985: 144) Shannon's M.A. thesis is 'possibly the most important, and also the most famous, master's thesis of the century.'

[25] Many years later some would still claim that 'information theory opened windows onto a domain of knowledge as broad as nature, as complex as man's mind' (Campbell 1982: 11).

[26] The roots of this work go in fact back to around 1900, the year of the quantum principle and the rediscovery of Mendel's results, when major steps had been taken in revealing the finer details of the human brain. The pioneer Spanish neurophysiologist Santiago Ramón y Cajal (a coeval of Max Planck and Hugo de Vries, as already mentioned) then made available exquisite histological studies of the cortex, revealing its structure as a complex network of nerve cells (neurons) -- perhaps Spain's first contribution to modern science. (Cajal's 'gigantic' *magnus opus* of almost a century ago, the result of applying Golgi's method to 'virtually every part of the

its connections with other neurons (a neural net) can be modeled in terms of logic and that any functioning of the network (in their sense of functioning) 'which can be defined at all logically, strictly, and unambiguously in a finite number of words can also be realized by such a formal neural network.' This 'important result' was the starting point for von Neumann's work on the logical structure of automata, which focused on one of the two 'remaining problems': The question 'whether every existing mode of behavior can really be put completely and unambiguously into words,' a question with 'interesting logical connotations.'[27]

Thus the theory of automata, developed as an independent study at about the same time, was linked at once (and quite properly, in Chomsky's view) to the earlier explorations of the theory of neural networks, which made use of closely related mathematical notions. The notion of automaton (a collection of connected abstract or physical elements computing and transmitting information) was one of the most sustained interests of von Neumann, perhaps the first and foremost computer scientist, who dedicated a considerable effort to formulating axioms and proving theorems about assemblies of simple elements that might in an idealized way represent either possible circuits in human-made automata or patterns in organisms. Among his most original work is his theory of self-reproducing automata, in which he showed that, in principle, it is possible to build machines that reproduce themselves.[28] As is well known, his logical and mathematical investigations coalesced with the technological advances of the 1940s, culminating in the first computers around 1950.

It is less generally known that von Neumann, who for many had one of the subtlest and deepest mathematical minds of the century, differed from almost everyone, in particular from his fellow mathematician and ex-prodigy Norbert Wiener (most readily associated with the development of cybernetics) in that he did not share the widely spread feeling that mathematics, technology and 'behavioral science' were converging on a synthesis that was

---

nervous system,' 'is still recognized as the most important single work in neurobiology' [Hubel 1984; cf. McCulloch 1951: 51,55]. The studies of reflex behavior by a British contemporary of Cajal, Charles Sherrington, had resulted in our first understanding of the points of near contact called synapses.)

[27] The quotes are from von Neumann's Hixon symposium paper (1951: 22-3); see also his unfinished posthumous book on the computer and the brain (1958). The other problem was the problem of nerve physiology.

[28] This theory, developed several years before the discovery of the structure and role of DNA, was consciously modeled on Turing's theory of the 'universal machine,' and 'the principle on which it can be based is closely related to Turing's principle' (von Neumann 1951: 28). Actual electronic computer development sprung as much from von Neumann's work as from the theoretical work of Turing, which is why von Neumann is sometimes taken to be the major figure in the history of computer science.

very simple, very clear, and fully adequate to provide a basic understanding of the fundamental classical questions about the human mind.[29] Von Neumann's qualms about the entire development may not have been entirely unrelated to the fact that some of his colleagues (including Nobel laureates) had the impression that his mind represented a higher stage in human development, further evolved than normal human minds.[30] There was a story that made the rounds about him that he was not a human being but a demigod who had made a detailed study of humans and had come to imitate them perfectly.[31]

And yet it was not John von Neumann's brilliant work that put an emphatic end to the intellectual illusions and inordinate euphoria of the early postwar years and provided a promising alternative no one had thought of.[32] It was the work of a very differently gifted human, a generation younger, who was no less skeptical about the postwar illusions.[33]

---

[29] This is in sharp contrast with the views of some of his epigones of the next generation (one of which, John McCarthy, a leading figure in the field of artificial intelligence, received the Kyoto prize for his contributions to technology the same year the prize was awarded to Chomsky for his contributions to basic science; see note 104).

[30] For a different view, see Casti (1989: 288-9).

[31] See Heims (1980), in particular the beginning of chapter 2.

[32] In Chomsky's view, 'the ideal situation would have been to have someone in 1940 who was steeped in rationalist and romantic literary and aesthetic theory and also happened to know modern mathematics' (1989: 146). Since von Neumann satisfied the second condition, it could be that he did not satisfy the first, if Chomsky's speculation is right. This is of course not the only alternative (see the next note).

[33] This is not to say that von Neumann was sufficiently skeptical about the postwar illusions. Like Wiener, he appeared to believe there was a conceptual framework based on some mathematical ideas for describing aspects of society, except that for von Neumann the cornerstone of this framework was his game theory (rather than Wiener's cybernetics). This was not unrelated to the fact that he ended up being one of the most ardent and pernicious promoters of the atomic (later nuclear) arms race, if not the most ardent and pernicious. In Heims' view, 'his wholehearted endorsement of the nuclear arms race, including the development of what he described as "nuclear weapons in their expected most vicious form," is entirely consistent with his other actions.' He went as far as waving away 'the cancer producing effects of nuclear weapons tests.' There was 'a bitter irony' in his becoming one of the early victims of 'this awful disease,' as he discovered in August 1955, when he was 52. And 'still the United States government depended on his thinking' until shortly before he died on February 8, 1957 (from bone cancer, most probably induced by nuclear radiation exposure). Admiral Lewis Strauss, his immediate superior in the Atomic Energy Commission, describes a meeting which took place sometime after April 1956 at Walter Reed Hospital 'where, gathered around his bedside and attentive to his last words of advice and wisdom, were the Secretary of Defense and his Deputies, the Secretaries of the Army, Navy and Air Force, and all the military Chiefs of Staff.' The contrast of his attitude towards people in power and toward 'the technologies of life and death' and that of Wiener (not to mention wiser attitudes) could not have been sharper (a major theme of Heims' book -- see in particular chapter 12; the quotes are from pages 317, 327, 369-71).

2 One model for the description of cognitive systems. The name of this passionate constructive skeptic (as he turned out to be) was Noam Chomsky. The dominant mood of great expectation and the air of triumphalism in the political culture, as he entered the scene, due in part to the technological euphoria (digital computers were just becoming available), was particularly easy to detect at MIT.[34] This mood was enhanced by the new intellectual tools of information theory, cybernetics, and the behavioral sciences.   When in the Fall of 1955 he joined the faculty of the Modern Languages Department, with a joint appointment in the Research Laboratory for Electronics (RLE),   everyone at M.I.T. was really exuberant about Markov processes.

This feeling was particularly strong among some of his most prestigious colleagues, and none was more prestigious than Norbert Wiener himself (the MIT resident genius who by then was the Institute's pride), co-author of one of the 1943 studies on intelligent automata and control mechanisms alluded to above.   In fact, since 1949 many of the ideas of his cybernetics were being explored in the RLE,   which had evolved out of the wartime Radiation Laboratory. Characteristically, Chomsky does not appear to have been very much bothered by the cybernetics work, which was in a way at the opposite end of what he was doing,   since for him the RLE 'provided a most stimulating interdisciplinary environment for research of the sort that [he] wanted to pursue,' as we can read in the 1973 preface to the published version of the investigation of linguistic theory that he had completed just before becoming a member of the lab.

At least in this one respect Wiener was no exception. Everyone at the time was convinced that Markov sources, which are even narrower (probabilistic features aside) than finite automata, would provide a solution for everything.   It was widely felt that language could be accommodated within this particular type of abstract automata and that the notion of finite discrete source, which seemed to offer a breakthrough, was going to be the fundamental notion in the study of language and mind.

2.1 The rise of language theory as a cognitive science. It was only for this reason that Chomsky started working on the formal properties of automata in the fall of 1955.   Already as a student it had seemed perfectly obvious to him that the idea was extremely naive and unlikely to work. But to give a proof (in a reasonably strict sense of proof) was a different matter.

---

[34] Chomsky (1973: n. 73) has referred to Miller (1951) and to the reports of the 1950 and 1952 speech conferences reprinted in the *Journal of the Acoustical Society of America* 22: 6 (Nov 1950) and 24: 6 (Nov 1952) for 'a clear and accurate picture of the prevailing intellectual atmosphere,' and to Bar-Hillel (1964) for more on this period.

It was only later in the year that he succeeded in doing just that by showing that a generalized form of Markov process that he had developed for the purpose was much too narrow to account for language. A paper on the relative power of grammars of three types which included this rigorous demonstration--his very first contribution to automata theory--became an appendix to one of the ten chapters (ch. 7) of the January 1956 revised version of his extensive study (almost one thousand closely reasoned and highly technical pages), *The Logical Structure of Linguistic Theory*, which he had completed as a Junior Fellow of the Harvard Society of Fellows in the Spring of 1955.

A revised version of this paper was presented the following summer, under the title 'Three models for the description of language,' at a three-day symposium on information theory held at MIT, which was attended by many luminaries of the 'communication sciences,' much in vogue at the time.[35] September 11, 1956, the day Chomsky presented his demonstration at the symposium, was suggested by George Miller in 1979 and adopted by Howard Gardner in *The Mind's New Science: A History of the Cognitive Revolution* (1985) as the birthdate of 'cognitive science'--even though 'it was not formally baptized 'cognitive science' until it was 21 years old.' Both Miller, who was 'one of the most influential figures in this change of course in the study of mind and behavior' (Chomsky 1990c), and Gardner single out two other papers that were featured the same day, one by Herbert Simon and Allen Newell on problem solving (it describes the proof of a *Principia Mathematica* theorem first carried out by a computer program a month earlier) and one by Miller on short-term memory (some limits on our capacity for processing information). Among the other contributors were Claude Shannon, then much admired, who led off the first day with a paper on the zero error capacity of a noisy channel, and the French mathematician M. P. Schützenberger, who presented a semi-group theory of coding.[36]

But presumably the most important reason for choosing September 11, 1956, as the birthday of the cognitive sciences is the novelty and implications of Chomsky's innovative approach. Almost a quarter of a century later, Miller still recalled Peter Elias, a leading information theorist, saying to him that 'other linguists had told him language has all the formal precision of

---

[35] The chair of the organizing committee was Peter Elias, a fellow Junior Fellow of Chomsky's at Harvard also just recruited by MIT (cf. pp. 5, 31 and 140 of the published version of Chomsky 1955-1956), who 'seemed to find no difficulty in being both a leading information theorist and a good friend of Chomsky's' and was perhaps responsible for his being on the program (Miller 1979: 7-8).

[36] Apparently this symposium was the occasion for Chomsky's meeting Schützenberger and the beginning of their collaboration (Miller 1979: 5).

mathematics, but Chomsky was the first linguist to make good on that claim':
'I think that was what excited all of us,' Miller continues:

> We saw the first substantive results from a new field of mathematical
> linguistics, and the formalisms Chomsky used were much more
> important to us than they were to Chomsky .. .. this 1956 paper
> contained the ideas that were expanded a year later in his monograph
> *Syntactic Structures*, which has been generally acclaimed as the
> beginning of an intellectual revolution in theoretical linguistics (1979:
> 8).

There is little question that Chomsky's early paper (he was 26 when he
constructed the proof), perhaps one of the best known by non-linguists
among those he has written, contains the essential elements in his innovative
approach to language.[37] As Justin Leiber writes in his lucid philosophic
overview of Chomsky's thought, 'the basic philosophic and psychological
issues, and Chomsky's way of reasoning about theory, are on the table, at
least in embryo.' (93) Leiber rightly emphasizes that there is little to be said
for the claim of some linguists that 'Chomsky's early work was a
ground-breaking contribution to linguistic theory that can be easily separated
from the 'alien and irrelevant' psychological and philosophic 'speculations' of
his later work.' (94)

To see why even this paper, in isolation from the extensive work which
had preceded it (more on this directly), carries crucial philosophic and
psychological implications, we must consider briefly the reasons for the
fascination with finite-state automata typical of the behaviorists of Wiener's
and Skinner's generation.

One reason, no doubt, was that these devices are so simple that they
lend themselves to characterization in terms of the mathematical theory of
communication. But there was more to it than simplicity. They found the
left-to-right generation of strings attractive (second reason) because it suggests
that we might think of the first word in a derivation as a 'stimulus' which past
'programs of reinforcement' cause the individual 'subject' to 'respond' to by
expecting, in the case of the listener (or adopting, in the case of the
speaker), various possible second words, and we might think of the second
word as a stimulus to the third, and so on.[38] A third reason has to do with

---

[37] It was presented more than a month after *Syntactic Structures*, where it is cited, was
finished (the Preface is dated August 1, 1956).

[38] If the grammar provides only one path, the stimulus could be said to lead to one fixed
response; if there is more than one path, this might be regarded as a complex, weighted
response.

the fact that a finite-state automata derivation of a string does not involve so-called 'non-terminal symbols' (symbols that do not appear in the last line of the derivation), so there is no suggestion of elements that are not characterized in terms of observed behavior (i.e., elements not realized in perceptible sensory events).

Given these properties of the system, if a natural language could be generated by a finite-state automata, it would be reasonable to assume that ordinary native speakers need have nothing more stored in their mind/brains than particular words they have actually memorized and various associations among them, also learned from sequences that the speakers have actually observed. In other words, the theory of finite automata is a precise mathematical characterization of the widespread empiricist doctrine that linguistic behavior is a matter of 'the use of words,' as was then being proposed in descriptive structural linguistics of the Saussurean or Bloomfieldian varieties, in the philosophy of language more or less directly inspired in the work of the later Wittgenstein, and in Skinnerian behaviorist psychology (Chomsky 1973: 6-7). This is why the mathematical theory of communication was generally appealing not only to engineers concerned with the need to ensure accuracy, efficiency, and secrecy in communication channels (the theory had its roots in the military concern with telecommunication during World War II), but also to many linguists, psychologists and philosophers.[39]

These comments are hopefully enough to suggest the range of implications of Chomsky's proof. The fact that it is not too difficult to grasp and that Chomsky lays no great emphasis on it in his writings may easily prove misleading. Leiber is right when he assumes that he is not alone in thinking that 'it is one of the most striking pieces of reasoning in Chomsky's early work' (87)--which Leiber appears to know better than most people. Chomsky's argument shows more than that a natural language system generates an infinite number of sentences--from which it follows that the knowledge a native speaker has of the structure of a natural language cannot be specified except through a recursive computational procedure. From Chomsky's proof

---

[39] Referring to the 1956 symposium, Miller writes that he thinks 'it was unfortunate that Claude Shannon, John Pierce, and others took Chomsky's dismissal of Markovian models as a theory of grammar as if it were a dismissal of those models for engineering purposes. [Chomsky] had no interest in the engineering problem, one way or the other--he simply used Shannon's stochastic approximations to illustrate to information theorists what he was talking about when he talked about grammars. But his remarks were interpreted as an attack on Shannon's model of the source of linguistic messages, and considerable hostility was engendered as a result. Why was it so difficult at the time to see that Shannon had no interest in grammar, and Chomsky had no interest in conserving channel capacity [?]' (1979: 7).

it also follows that the required computational procedure is more powerful than a finite-state device, even though such a device does have the power to generate an infinite number of sentences.[40]   As for the view that a finite-state automaton can serve as a model for the linguistic performance of a speaker or a hearer, it is a virtually empty view.   It is 'merely to say that the user of language is a finitely specifiable organism and that language use can be described as a discrete temporal process,' as Chomsky pointed out in his 1973 preface.   'But from these truisms,' he went on to say, 'it does not follow that the grammar represented in the mind of the speaker-hearer is a 'device' of this character,   and observation of the facts of language shows clearly that it is not.'

Chomsky's 1956 paper then was already an attempt to characterize language capacity on a computational model--a model involving rules and representations which is capable of specifying an infinite range of sentences--a necessary,   but crucially not sufficient,   prerequisite for an account of 'the creative aspect of language use' that every normal speaker exhibits.   But he still had to fight a big and long-lasting battle at MIT; it took time before his ideas began to sink in. (Some would say that the battle is still raging,   at least in the backwoods).   In any event,   after the achievement of the fall of 1955 his review of Skinner's *Verbal Behavior*,   which appeared in 1959 in *Language* and was to prove extremely influential (for some it sounded the death-knell of behaviorism),   could not have been too demanding an effort.

It is important to keep in mind that in the context of the extensive and strikingly original investigation he summed up in *The Logical Structure of Linguistic Theory*,   the 1956 revised version of the appendix was little more than an afterthought.   From today's vantage point it is easy to see that the project he pursued in this unique, epoch-making work was premature and far too ambitious, as he came to realize a few years later (1990b). But the result attained was a precise and highly elaborated theory of generative grammar, including a general discussion of the rigorous theory of representations and rules that he proposed to account for the cognitive domain of human language,   presented there in its fullest and most genuine form.   He had developed the notion of generative grammar in its current sense already in 1949-1951,   that is,   before he was 23,   in his undergraduate master's thesis, *Morphophonemics of Modern Hebrew* (a crucial first step in the path to his first masterwork and his new approach to language structure),   which was to be included as an appendix to chapter 6 of the more comprehensive work but was

---

[40] In Miller's view, Chomsky 'used information theory as a foil for his first public exposition of transformational generative grammar--Shannon's Markovian processes provided the first "model of language" that he discussed' (1979: 7).

omitted from its published version. In fact it was not published until 1979, exactly thirty years after its conception (and it appears to have generally gone unread, despite its crucial importance in the history of generative grammar).[41]

In neither of these two books, as first completed, was there any consideration of finite automata or their 'weak generative capacity' (their capacity to enumerate particular classes of strings). In this most characteristic work of Chomsky's the emphasis was already, as in the 1960s and since, on the investigation of the set of structural descriptions generated by the language system (the linguist's reconstruction of the mental system known by the speaker), not on language as an externalized set of utterances. This crucial shift of focus from behavior and its products to the system of knowledge that enters into behavior was in part obscured by a quirk of publishing history and by some expository passages that were to lead to a considerable amount of misunderstanding, repeated in much subsequent work to this day.[42]

It so happened that, because Chomsky's specifically linguistic work, as developed in his first two books, was too unorthodox to be accepted for publication at the time, his earliest published book-length exposition of generative grammar (and perhaps the most widely known to this day) was essentially a revision of notes for an undergraduate course at MIT, not intended for publication as a linguistics monograph. As in the case of the 1956 paper, this material was presented in a framework suggested by certain topics in automata theory, Markov sources, formal languages, etc., a point of view which was of special interest to MIT students, as it was for the faculty. In these areas the concept of 'weak generative capacity' of a device has a certain relevance, which is why the published monograph departs from Chomsky's earlier and more characteristic work in this respect. It was this slim book (116 pages) that had an immediate and dramatic impact on several

---

[41] The published version differs in interesting ways from the earlier, filed version (presumably more constrained by academic requirements), which in its introductory section attempts to exhibit (1) 'the connection of logic to linguistics' and (2-3) 'the connection (or relevance) of this paper' to logic and to linguistics. It begins as follows: 'This study has its roots in two fields, symbolic logic [added in note: More specifically, the constructional part of philosophy which uses logic as its essential tool] and descriptive linguistics. But the work which constitutes the body of this paper is not an example of what is customarily done in logical construction, nor, for that matter, is it a typical representative of work in descriptive linguistics.' The first reference is to Carnap's *Der Logische Aufbau der Welt* (1928), an author never mentioned in the published version. There is much more to say about these differences, but space does not allow me to go into the topic here, so I will just point out that in the Fall of 1951 Chomsky was still 'very much committed to a research program that had its roots in American descriptive linguistics, in relativistic anthropology, and in a kind of latter-day logical positivism' (Chomsky 1983). Cf. Otero (1985).

[42] See Chomsky (1980, 275 n. 1, 123-8; 1986a, 48 n. 17).

fields and set the study of language on an entirely new course when it appeared under the title *Syntactic Structures* in the spring of 1957--in Holland, like Galileo's *Two New Sciences* (1638) and other unorthodox publications before and after.

Presumably one of the reasons why the nearly 1000-page manuscript of *The Logical Structure of Linguistic Theory* had been rejected when it was submitted for publication over a year earlier was that its striking originality spurred little interest among professional linguists (an article based on the chapter 'Simplicity and the Form of Grammars' that he submitted to the linguistic journal *Word* perhaps in 1954, at the suggestion of Roman Jakobson, had also been rejected, 'virtually by return mail').[43] It was first published (in part) only twenty years after its completion (1975), and for thirty years (until 1985) there was no indexed or paperback edition, although a good number of copies (probably several hundred) of the duplicated 1955 version and the two microfilm copies made by Harvard Libraries (one of the 1955 version and one of the partially edited and revised January 1956 version) have been distributed over the years. This may be a reason why it has only rarely been read with the attention it deserves, or read at all, it would appear, in sharp contrast with Chomsky's famous 1957 book, sometimes referred to as a 'manifesto.' (See 3.2 below.) The point of view developed in the long manuscript of 1955, as in most other writings by Chomsky, is that at an intuitive level, a language is a particular way of expressing thought and understanding the thought expressed, as Sapir had suggested. To know a language is to have mastered this way of speaking and understanding. Essentially the same points are made in *Syntactic Structures*, but not with sufficient prominence, a fact that has undoubtedly been misleading, as already mentioned.

Chomsky's ideas constituted the first major step towards a scientific theory of the mind/brain--the mind being just the brain studied at a particular level of abstraction from physical mechanisms, in this view. To see why, we must be clear about the crucial differences between his ideas and those of his contemporaries. Although he shared with the most advanced of them the demand for rigor and precision, and was as perfectly conversant as Wiener or Shannon and their colleagues with the most recent developments in the formal sciences, and as fascinated by the potentialities and capacities of automata, his approach to the study of the mind and his goals were very different from theirs.

---

[43] For more about what Jakobson's support meant to Chomsky as 'one young student entering the field' at mid-century (even though Jakobson had very little interest in Chomsky's work and regarded it as quite wrong-headed), see Chomsky (1983). Cf. Halle (1987, 1988).

For Chomsky, the complex networks and structures that could be developed by elaboration of the concepts that seemed so promising to many scientists at the time were simply not the structures that in his view had to be postulated to underlie behavior. This applied equally well to stimulus-response psychology (including taxonomic linguistics) and to the mathematical theory of communication or to the theory of simple automata. As he was to put it at Berkeley in January 1967,

> there is no reason to expect that the available technology can provide significant insight or understanding or useful achievement; it has noticeably failed to do so, and, in fact, an appreciable investment of time, energy, and money in the use of computers for linguistic research--appreciable by the standards of a small field like linguistics--has not provided any significant advance in our understanding of the use or nature of language. (1968: 4)

The crucial fact is that behavior involves use of knowledge, and the system of knowledge that underlies behavior is not realized in any direct or simple way in behavior. The theories and models that were developed to describe simple and immediately given phenomena could not incorporate a system of knowledge and belief that, in the case of language--which is at the very center--develops in early childhood. This and other mental systems interact with many other factors to determine the kinds of behavior we observe. We are therefore faced with a problem of quality of complexity, not merely of degree of complexity. The only way out of the *impasse*, in Chomsky's (or Descartes') view, was to postulate 'mind' (an abstract mental level) as an explanatory principle (much as Newton had postulated 'gravity') and to proceed to study its properties and organization. Moreover, there is no reason to expect that the system of knowledge which makes language use possible (a central case) has much in common with the knowledge system for some other cognitive domain (vision, for example). See Chomsky (1980: 39).

Contrary to what empiricists in several fields of human studies were at least implicitly proposing around the mid-century, the study of the mind/brain could then be pursued without departing from the standard approach of the established natural sciences. What was needed was a radical shift in perspective: From the direct study of behavior and its products (then being widely advocated) to systems of mental representation and computation. This amounted to bringing back to life the Cartesian cognitive revolution.

2.2 A lone Cartesian strand in the cognitive revival of the mid 1950s.

Although at the time their authors apparently did not perceive any relation between them, the papers by Chomsky, Miller, and Newell-Simon proposed all three computational models. To get an idea of the progress made in just a few years one has only to compare the 1956 MIT symposium with the 1948 Hixon Symposium on 'cerebral mechanisms in behavior,' held at the California Institute of Technology (Cal Tech for short), closely associated with the emergence and development of molecular biology. To calibrate the advance in our understanding of language in those few years, we may want to place the 'extremely interesting and insightful paper' Karl Lashley presented at the Cal Tech symposium next to the generative grammar of the spring of 1955.[44] For our present purposes it is sufficient to point out that a variety of observations led him to conclude that syntax (i.e., syntactic structure) 'is a generalized pattern imposed upon the specific acts as they occur' ('not inherent in the words employed or in the idea to be expressed'), and that 'there are, behind the overtly expressed sequences, a multiplicity of integrative processes which can only be inferred from the final results of their activity.'[45]

These 'sound and perceptive' conclusions and the 'brilliant critique of the prevailing framework of ideas,' which 'went by unnoticed even in his own university (Harvard), then the leading center of psycholinguistic research,' may represent a crucial step forward for its time and place, but they are also a long way from the specific and carefully elaborated proposals of *The Logical Structure of Linguistic Theory*, which represents a great leap forward, as a comparison with Lashley's extremely narrow and grotesquely primitive approach will reveal at once.[46]

The main thrust behind the research program guiding Chomsky's work, one of the driving forces in an epoch-making shift in perspective barely suggested in Lashley's work, is the computational approach to the study of

---

[44] The quote is from Chomsky (1959: XI).

[45] He also concludes that 'the processes of comprehension and production of speech have too much in common to depend on wholly different mechanisms' (Lashley 1951: 119 [cf. 122], 115, 120), which suggests that he would not have fallen prey to one of the typical misreadings of *Syntactic Structures*. One important observation he makes is that the succession of the finger strokes of a musician is sometimes 'too quick even for visual reaction time;' in rapid sight reading, the notes of an arpeggio 'must be seen in groups, and it is actually easier to read chords seen simultaneously and then translate them into temporal sequence than to read successive notes in the arpeggio as usually written' (1951: 123). Cf. Gardner (1985: 10f.).

[46] The quotes are from Chomsky (1968: 2-3), who apparently never heard Lashley's name during his years at Harvard (1951-1955). Lashley's paper was brought to his attention about ten years after the Hixon symposium by Meyer Schapiro, 'the art historian at Columbia who knows everything about everything' (whom Chomsky knew as a non-Bolshevik Marxist). Lashley's contribution began to be appreciated 'only after his insights had been independently achieved in another context' by Chomsky. After Chomsky's review of Skinner appeared (1959) there was 'something of a Lashley revolution,' his papers were reprinted and 'influenced many in the field' (Chomsky 1968: 3, 1989: 124-5).

mind and its products. The turning point is sometimes referred to as the 'cognitive revolution' (the revolution in the study of cognition), for instance in Howard Gardner's 1985 book, already mentioned. There is little doubt that the new approach to the study of language was a major factor in initiating a change of perspective with regard to the study of human nature and action, and continues to be the prime mover in the study of cognition. But even when this elementary fact is recognized, the picture drawn is often not as clear as it could be.

The term 'cognitive science' means many different things to different people, but there are some identifiable leading ideas and unifying themes. The main one is of course an interest in computational models of mind, as shown in the three papers of the 1956 MIT symposium, the basic thesis being that critical aspects of 'perception, learning, judgement, planning, choice of action, and so on'--what are generally called cognitive processes--'can be illuminated by thinking of them as software problems' (Chomsky 1990d). The general idea is that these processes involve formal operations on symbolic representations carried out by the brain, described at a certain level of abstraction from mechanisms--the level that is taken to be appropriate to formulate principles and explanatory theories--in a manner which is in fact standard scientific practice.

Since the operation may change the mental state, we may distinguish two aspects: if the focus is on the representation produced by the operation, we are studying perception; if the focus is on the change of state, we are studying so-called 'learning.' In fact, when we examine it closely, the change from the initial state to the steady state looks like another aspect of physical growth (undergoing puberty, for example), and probably growth is a better model than 'learning' for the development of cognitive structures in the mind/brain. If the focus is on the states themselves, rather than on the representations or on the state change, we are studying cognitive systems. As objects of inquiry, then, we have the cognitive states themselves (e.g., knowledge of language) and processes of different kinds, including the mapping of signal to symbolic representation (percept) in a given state (e.g., in parsing a sentence), and the state transitions induced by internal maturation or external events (e.g., in language growth).

The general research program remains a promissory note in most domains, but in a few it has been quite fruitful, and in none has it been more so than in the study of language, where many would agree that there has been some substantial progress. This progress is perhaps less surprising when one considers that infinite digital systems are tailor-made for computational approaches (that's what computational approaches are about) and language is an infinite digital system.[47]   It is digital in the sense that, for example, we can have a six word sentence and a seven word sentence, but we cannot have a six and a half word sentence.   And it is infinite because given any sentence one can always form a longer sentence, as every speaker of the language is well aware, and that can go on endlessly.   There is no bound on sentence length, in principle.   In practice, the size of the class of expressions from which normal discourse is drawn,   and which are immediately intelligible and understood,   is so astronomical that for all practical purposes it is infinite (even for simple normal discourse).

At this point it is natural to ask whether it is appropriate to use the term 'cognitive revolution' to refer to the change of perspective with regard to human nature and human action of the mid 1950s,   even in the case of language.   As Chomsky (1987b) has emphasized, the change was in large measure 'a return to earlier concerns and reconstructed earlier understanding, long forgotten, sometimes in new ways,' 'though it was not known at the time, and remains little understood today.' At the center of the composite picture he draws of the fundamental contribution of the parts of Cartesian philosophy that we would today call 'cognitive science' we find the development of a representational-computational theory of mind, particularly in the domains of visual perception and language, which have been central also to the inquiry of the 1950s.   Another cognitive concern, also revived in the 1950s, is the crucial role of innate conditions for the growth of knowledge and understanding (the tendencies and dispositions that Descartes called 'innate ideas').   It was then argued that experience is interpreted not only in terms of ideal forms provided by innate geometry, but also concepts 'determined by the resources of the mind, by virtue of its intrinsic structure, from piecemeal and successive presentations' (1990d).   The Cartesians in fact developed a rather rich form of what much later came to be called 'Gestalt psychology' (Köhler 1947) as similar ideas were rediscovered during this century.

Since there is a considerable overlap between these Cartesian ideas, which were developed and explored in a fairly lucid and thoughtful way in what Chomsky calls 'the cognitive revolution' of the seventeenth and eighteenth century, (including Kant [Chomsky 1980: 35, 247]), and the main

---

[47] Chomsky (1990b). It should also be noted that infinite digital systems are extremely rare in the biological world. In fact the language system may be the only one. There may be no others that did not develop as a by-product of the language faculty (Chomsky 1980a, 1988: 169). Every animal communication system known is either strictly finite (like, for instance, that of the apes) or continuous (for example, the so-called language of the bees) (Chomsky 1968: 61). That's why the development of the language faculty raises interesting questions for the biologist. How could a messy object like the brain (cf. Crick 1988: 6) come up with an infinite digital system? This is the problem of explaining the character of the species, perhaps a question of what is called 'emergence' (see Otero 1990 for discussion).

ideas of 'the cognitive revolution' of the 1950s, they can be naturally seen as two phases of the same advance in understanding.[48] A common feature of both phases is that the imagination of the cognitive scientists was stimulated by the automata of the day. We could then say, in retrospect, that the second phase (including the development of generative grammar) represents a kind of confluence between new technical tools and technical understanding (mathematical ideas that were now available and clear) with ideas and insights attained during the first phase, which until then could be only stated in an intuitive way, not yet as precisely formulated empirical hypotheses that could be evaluated.[49] More specifically, the second phase represents a confluence between new technical understanding about the nature of computation and formal systems that developed largely in the 1920s and 1930s, as we have seen, and that 'made it possible to formulate some old and somewhat vague questions in a much clearer way, so that they could be subjected to productive inquiry in a few domains at least, language being one' (Chomsky 1987b).

This view, however, is misleading in one fundamental respect. Although the new approach to the study of language structure developed within what we are calling the second phase of 'the cognitive revolution' of the 1950s, its interests and assumptions, which were rather disparate from the start, have often diverged from those of other investigations that also make use of computational models of mind. The fundamental divergence can be correlated with the distinction between the natural sciences (physics, biology and psychology in their narrow senses) and formal sciences such as mathematics or computer science. The natural sciences are empirical sciences in that they investigate matters of fact.[50] In contrast, some of the questions studied in the formal sciences (in parts of artificial intelligence, for example) are not questions of psychology. The reason is that they do not involve matters of fact, but rather matters of decision. A typical example is 'Does this program play chess?'[51] Such questions are not susceptible to empirical inquiry, any more than the question of whether an airplane flies in the sense

---

[48] Chomsky refers to what I'm calling the second phase as 'the second cognitive revolution,' with the qualification 'if we may call it that.' Both terminologies ignore of course 'the actual record of erratic leaps, false starts, and all-too-frequent regression' (1987c), and put to the side the fact that even the major contributors to the second phase initially lacked any awareness of the continuity.

[49] For an early discussion from this perspective, see Otero (1970).

[50] For a radically different view of empirical evidence, see, e.g., Haugeland (1979).

[51] 'Understanding Chinese' is no different from 'playing chess' in this respect, and Searle's Chinese Room should be viewed in this light, though it rarely is. See Chomsky (1990d); cf., e.g., Penrose (1989:18f).

in which birds fly is susceptible to empirical inquiry, as Chomsky has repeatedly pointed out (see in particular Chomsky 1979).

For this reason, the purpose of simulation in the natural sciences, at least from the days of Jacques de Vaucanson (1709-1782), the great artificer of the early eighteenth century, is to understand the real systems that are being simulated, not to produce a program that satisfies some performance criterion or operational test. If, for example, both people and a computer program pass some variety of the Turing test for human intelligence (the modern counterpart of the very sophisticated Cartesian test), the crucial question is whether the success of the program tells us anything about humans. The program in itself is of no significance, and of no interest for a natural scientist, unless it helps us understand how a real organism does what it does. A computer program is, after all, 'basically a theory written in odd notation, and we ask the same questions about it that we ask about any other theory.'[52] In sharp contrast with this, in much 'cognitive science' of the second phase simulation is viewed in a way which departs from the cognitive natural sciences in at least this fundamental respect, and from the first phase of the cognitive revolution as well.[53]

This suggests that generative grammar is not just a 'cognitive science,' but a cognitive psychoscience, and that it hopefully represents a fundamental advance toward the cognitive neurosciences of the future. In addition to being the cognitive science most in line with the noncognitive natural sciences, generative grammar is the most successful and advanced one. It also happens to be a fundamental part of the study of human intelligence, which is, perhaps, the central aspect of human nature (of the largely immutable biological characteristics that determine the nature of the human organism).

---

[52] Chomsky (1990e), where the ideas paraphrased in the last two paragraphs are developed more fully. See also Chomsky (1984, 1987a,b, 1988b, 1989a, 1990b); cf., e.g., Clark 1989: 152f.). A similar view seems to be implicit in McCulloch's 1948 comments on von Neumann's blueprint (Jeffress 1951: 32), in contrast with recent developments in 'connectionism' (see Pinker and Mehler 1989; cf. Crick 1988). For a recent computer program of this character, see Dresher and Kaye (1990); see also Kaye (1989). On Jacques de Vaucanson, see Fryer and Marshall (1979), cited in Gardner (1985: 142). By this criterion, artificial intelligence work can be of one of two very different kinds: empirical and non-empirical (cf. Dresher and Hornstein 1976, 1977a,b, Marr 1977, 1982, Marshall 1980b, Longuet-Higgins 1981, Putnam 1988). Among the best examples of the first kind are the work of David Marr and his associates (Chomsky 1980a) and the work of Robert Berwick and his associates (see Barton et al. 1987, Berwick 1991, Fong 1990, and Dorr 1990, the last one being of particular interest in this context).

[53] See standard collective references such as Stillings et al. (1987), Posner, ed. (1989) and Osherson et al., eds. (1990) (also Bever et al., eds. 1984, and Hirst, ed. 1988); readers such as Haugeland, ed. (1981), conceived as a sequel to Anderson (1964), and Block, ed. (1981), the 'closest and most distinguished predecessor' of Lycan, ed. (1990); or monographs such as Hunt (1982), Pylyshyn (1984), Gardner (1985), Baars (1986), Glass and Holyoak (1986), and Johnson-Laird (1983, 1988) (also Bechtel 1988a,b). Cf. Anderson (1964), Harper et al. (1964).

Furthermore, it can contribute to the all important understanding of human nature in another important respect: It furnishes a so far unsurpassed model for studying other domains of the human mind/brain, which might be studied profitably in a similar manner.

Even though the language capacity is unique, it is not the only cognitive capacity in which humans appear to have characteristic and remarkable abilities--abilities that make it possible for them to construct a complex and intricate intellectual system, rapidly and uniformly, on the basis of relatively meager and degenerate evidence.   To illustrate with one of the most extraordinary capacities from a different domain: How can one, after having seen a face from a certain angle, recognize it from another angle, or distinguish one face from a very similar face?   Remarkable geometric transformations are involved in the process, and in fact 'it would be no small task to design a device to match human performance in these respects' (1979: 52).   Could it be that at the level of deep structure a particular face is represented by a single mental entity? If so, would it not be reasonable to suspect, with Chomsky, that 'we even have some innate equipment for processing certain kinds of physical, phenomenal entities, such as faces' (Mehta 1971: 213), and that perhaps 'the theory of face perception resembles generative grammar?' What about our ability to identify three-dimensional objects under various conditions, or our ability to determine the personality structure of another person on brief contact (thus, to be able to guess how that person will react under a variety of conditions), or our ability to handle those branches of mathematics that build on numerical or spatial intuition, or our ability to create dream forms?[54]

If it is true that among the constraints that can be said to constitute human nature there are some that relate to intellectual development and some that relate to moral development (Chomsky 1989: 147), it is only natural to ask: What is the basis for moral judgment? It would surprise no student of Chomsky to discover that it is rooted in human nature. Typically we find some things to be right, others wrong, and over a broad range our judgements converge with those of people from very different cultures. Moral judgement cannot then be simply a matter of convention:

> Growing up in a particular society, a child acquires standards and principles of moral judgment. These are acquired on the basis of limited evidence, but they have broad and often quite precise applicability. It is often though not always true that people can discover or be convinced that their judgments about a particular case

---

[54] See Otero (1989: 46-7). Cf. Marshall (1974), Edelson (1975), Foulkes (1978).

are wrong, in the sense that the judgments are inconsistent with the person's own internalized principles.

The analogy to a speaker's judgement about, say, 'It is I' (if this expression is inconsistent with the speaker's internalized language) suggests itself. We are led then to conclude that

> the acquisition of a specific moral and ethical system, wide ranging and often precise in its consequences, cannot simply be the result of 'shaping' and 'control' by the social environment. As in the case of language, the environment is far too impoverished and indeterminate to provide this system to the child, in its full richness and applicability (Chomsky 1988: 152-3).

Needless to say, our ethical grammar does not ensure that we do the right things any more than our linguistic grammar ensures that we say the right things, a rather obvious point which is apparently less easy to grasp than it would appear (see Otero 1988). If the analogy is legitimate enough, it is then reasonable to speculate that the ethical system that grows in the mind of the child 'owes much to some innate faculty, and just as it is possible to study the range of humanly attainable languages, with some success, it may be possible to study the range of ethical systems.'

Another possible analogue to the case of language is 'our comprehension of the social structures in which we live:'

> We have all sorts of tacit and complex knowledge concerning our relations with other people. Perhaps we have a sort of 'universal grammar' of possible forms of social interaction, and it is this system which helps us to organize intuitively our imperfect perceptions of social reality (Chomsky 1979: 69).

It might then also be possible to study the social structures in which humans can live and function, given their intrinsic capacities and needs (including the capacity for having decent social relations, which perhaps would lead to some new form of society), in a way analogous to the study of language, so as to construct a cognitive science of our development as members of human society.[55]

---

[55] This science in turn might allow us to go on to 'project a concept of social organization that would -- under given conditions of material and spiritual culture -- best encourage and accommodate the fundamental human need -- if such it is -- for spontaneous initiative, creative work, solidarity, pursuit of social justice' (1970: 23; also 1973: 405, and 1987c: 155).

The same is true of our ability to create art forms resting on mental principles of form and organization that 'are only in part subject to human choice' (1988: 152). In fact, the most developed 'application' of the one model for the description of cognitive systems in the Cartesian tradition is 'a generative theory of tonal music.'[56] An even more obvious analogue to our language capacity is our comprehension of literary structures, a unique manifestation of our ability to create art forms resting on principles of form and organization that are closely related to the principles of language, hence to our intellectual development more generally. As argued in A. W. Schlegel's *Die Kuntslehre* (1801), literary forms are unique among art forms in that its very medium, language, is 'a system with unbounded innovative potentialities for the formation and expression of ideas.' Literary creativity is thus related to the creative aspect of language use, which under certain conditions of form and organization constitutes literary art.[57] No wonder the ideal situation for the invention of generative grammar 'would have been someone in 1940 who was steeped in rationalist and romantic literary and aesthetic theory and also happened to know modern mathematics.'[58]

Other aspects of human psychology and culture might, in principle, be studied in a similar way, and some already are (visual perception, for example).[59] Thus transformational grammar provides a suggestive model for the description of other aspects of mental development as particular subcases of physical growth. Needless to say, the point is not to try to work within the Chomskyan framework, but to take for granted the necessity of working on the Chomskyan analogy. There is no reason to expect to find the same representations and the same principles in different mental modules (growth of linguistic judgment, moral judgment, artistic judgment and other types of cognition we can readily identify). It is not at all unreasonable, however, to search for a more abstract relation between two systems such as those underlying mental activities as different as language and dreams. In fact, such a discipline (a cognitive theory of symbolic function) 'may not lie very far

---

[56] See Lerdahl and Jackendoff (1983), condensed in Jackendoff (1987, ch. 11).

[57] The quote is from Chomsky (1966: 18). See now Kiparsky (1988); cf. Tsur (1983). In Kiparsky's view (1983: 36), 'Jakobson's achievement in poetics is to have explicated and vindicated in a deep sense the view expressed by Paul Valery's *dictum* that "literature is, and cannot help but be, a kind of extension and application of certain properties of language".' (See also Lodge 1972: 254, 256-7.)' Cf. Henkel (1990).

[58] This is the opinion of someone that should know (Chomsky 1989: 146, 132; cf. n. 32 above). It should perhaps be mentioned here that the concept of 'organic form' (opposed to 'mechanical form') had an impact well beyond literature (cf. Ritterbush 1972).

[59] See Chomsky (1973: 405, 1987c: 155), Marr (1977: 130; 1982: 28), Jackendoff (1987, chs. 9 and 10).

beyond the horizons of current inquiry,' in Chomsky's view. 'Perhaps it may be possible,' Chomsky continues,

> to sketch the bare outlines of a general cognitive psychology that will attempt to determine the structural properties of specific 'mental organs' and their modes of integration, and to propose biological universals governing these systems, thus laying the foundations for a significant theory of human [mental growth] in various domains. Conceivably, the full range of questions on the nature of function, structure, physical basis, and development in the individual and the species may be open to investigation in coming years, for various components of the human mind. With the dramatic successes of the biological sciences in the past generation, it is perhaps not too much to hope that some of the classical questions concerning the nature of the human mind and its products may also be assimilated to the general body of natural science in the years that lie ahead.[60]

3 Scientific discovery and cultural underdevelopment. If we now ask how our understanding of particular domains has advanced over the past 35 years, it is immediately obvious that generative grammar set the study of language on an entirely new course and, as a result, a good deal has been learned about the fundamental questions of cognitive linguistics in the span of one generation. Furthermore, the current state of our understanding of mental cognitive structures and processes involved in the use of human natural language is far deeper and far broader today than it was 15 years ago, let alone 40 years ago. This advance has few parallels in the history of rational inquiry. Does this mean that there is yet a third major strand in the dramatic scientific progress of the twentieth century, not unlike the leaps in our understanding of physics and biology? (Leucippus' other title was *On the Mind*.) The answer is clearly no if we think in terms of similar levels of understanding (generative grammar does not have the intellectual depth of general relativity or quantum physics), but it is less obvious if we think in terms of actual and potential advance in understanding in a crucial and, until recently, inexpugnable domain. (Cf. Cohen 1985)

For our present purposes it is enough to point out that it was the naturalistic cognitive revolution of the mid 1950s in linguistics that opened up the way to the recently developed principles-and-parameters approach to

---

[60] Chomsky (1980: 252-254). Discussions about the direction and goals of the cognitive sciences should perhaps be placed in this context. For a recent, and quite instructive one, see Anderson (1989), Miller (1990). Cf. Newmeyer (1983), Wasow (1989).

language theory.[61] This represents 'a qualitative advance over earlier approaches,' 'a very radical departure from the tradition of study of language over the past several thousand years.'[62] Even Chomsky, who is not inclined to use the term 'revolution' lightly, is willing to admit that this break may be a revolutionary one.[63] The new comparative understanding of languages, which in its present form was simply inconceivable a mere decade ago, is clearly a direct outgrowth of the generative grammar of the mid 1950s, an initial phase which with the benefit of hindsight can be seen, without much exaggeration (the crucial difference is that generative grammar tried to account explicitly for the linguistic intuitions of the intelligent reader), as a sophisticated reconstruction and development of the best ideas of traditional grammar.[64] We can ask whether there was a better way to get where we are, but it is undeniable that the actual way has been remarkably successful.

Was the modern reconstruction of traditional grammar in the early 1950s really revolutionary?[65] It was certainly nothing like the seventeenth century scientific revolution, the one major revolution of which it is one more outgrowth. We may still ask whether the emergence of generative grammar as an outgrowth of the scientific revolution of the seventeenth century is no more revolutionary than, say, plate tectonics. The most obvious answer is that plate tectonics is not a 'life science,' let alone a 'human brain science,' hence no step toward the 'next scientific frontier,' as described above. A definitive step toward this frontier was the rise of Descartes' epoch-making theory of perception, so we may ask how generative grammar compares with that. A hardly questionable fact is that Descartes' theory has still to bring the field close enough to 'the first real 'scientific revolution' outside of the natural sciences,' as the principles-and-parameters theory is said to be doing.[66] It also seems beyond question that the cognitive linguistics of the mid 1950s

---

[61] Chomsky (1981, 1986a,b, 1988c), and references therein.

[62] Chomsky (1982b: 89; 1989: 501). See also Chomsky (1989: 592-3).

[63] 'If there has been anything which deserves to be called a revolution, which I doubt, it was around 1980. Everything before then was formalizing old intuitions, opening up new data' (Saporta 1990: 38).

[64] This is perhaps one reason why old fashioned traditional grammarians appeared to have less trouble with Chomsky's early model than the professional linguists (the structural linguists). Traditional grammarians seemed to find something familiar in it, the strange notation notwithstanding. What puzzled traditional grammarians no less than professional linguists was precisely the attempt to account explicitly for the linguistic intuitions of the intelligent reader, for them an arcane question about something as simple and 'obvious' as the fact that apples fall down and not up. See below.

[65] There is an extensive literature on this topic, which is beyond the purview of this paper. Cf. Newmeyer (1986a) and references therein; also Koerner (1989, in particular ch. 8) and Pollock and Obenauer, eds. (1990).

[66] The quote is from Chomsky (1989: 396). See also Chomsky (1982a: 40).

represents a real breakthrough for the natural sciences since Galileo and Newton, given that before Chomsky no one had even come close to extending the application of the natural science approach to the study of the mind/brain. In any event, we can safely say that generative grammar was innovative enough to tax the capacity of assimilation of many people at the time and since, including not only some of the most reputed humanists and linguists of the day, but also many luminaries in a variety of disciplines (even sophisticated ones such as biology or philosophy).[67] A comparison with the more developed natural sciences may help to place the achievement in the proper perspective.

3.1 Generative grammar as a natural science: An instructive analogy and a revealing synchrony. A close analogy to generative grammar is provided by nineteenth century chemistry. As Chomsky has repeatedly suggested, we might think of nineteenth century chemistry as a study of the properties of then unknown physical mechanisms, framed in terms of such abstract notions as chemical elements, valence, organic molecules, the Periodic Table, and so on, this abstract study setting the stage for subsequent inquiry into the 'more fundamental' entities that exhibit the properties that are formulated at the abstract level of inquiry.

The discovery of the chemical structure of an organic compound may serve as an illustration. In 1825 Michael Faraday determined that a volatile aromatic liquid later named benzene contained only carbon and hydrogen, in equal proportions. Benzene posed a major theoretical problem for chemists because of its unusual properties, but until Friedrich August Kekulé (1829-1896), the theoretician of the molecular structure of organic compounds, appeared on the scene, organic chemists were working in the dark since they did not have much of an idea of the molecular structures of the substances they worked with.

For example, in 1828 Friedrich Wöhler (1800-1882) had shown that urea was different from ammonium cyanate, although both contained carbon, hydrogen, oxygen, and nitrogen in the ratio of 1:4:1:2 (they were said to be 'isomers,' compounds made of equal parts), but no one understood the different way in which the same number of the same atoms were connected (as no one before our time understood the different way in which the same

---

[67] See Chomsky (1982a, 1982c). Cf. Luria (1973), Piattelli-Palmarini (1980), Delbrück (1986), among others. As Sol Saporta (outstanding among the few) has written, commenting on Chomsky's preference for using the term 'revolution' in 'a rather strict sense,' 'however we choose to characterize the debate between structuralists and generative grammarians in the late fifties, the differences were absolutely fundamental, and the fact that relatively few linguists made the switch reflects the radical difference in the underlying assumptions, assumptions which were, indeed, incompatible' (1990: 35-36).

number of the same words are connected in the two alternative structures of *Flying planes can be dangerous*).

The molecular formula of benzene was known to be C_6H_6, but no chemist had been able to suggest a suitable structural formula for it before 1865, the year Kekulé finally succeeded. The solution was 'only a consequence, and a very obvious consequence' of what 'we now call valence and structural theory' (Kekulé), which had first appeared to him in 'dream forms' and have since been of enormous value in the development of science. The two basic ideas embodied in the dream forms were 'chain' and 'cycle,' which led Kekulé to propose a cyclic structure with the six carbon atoms in a ring and one hydrogen atom attached to each. Since there are just three valence bonds (represented by the lines) from each carbon atom to two other carbon atoms and to a hydrogen atom, he inserted alternating double bonds between the carbon atoms to account for the 'unused valences,' as follows:

Unsurprisingly, not every chemist accepted and appreciated the ring structure, although sensible objections were rarely raised at the time. Perhaps the most sensible one was that the two 'isomers' predicted by the theory do not exist. To account for this systematic gap Kekulé proposed that a ring structure such as the one represented above rapidly interchanges the double and single bonds between the carbon atoms of the ring. Many other possible structures for benzene were proposed before the end of the nineteenth century, but 'none withstood the tests of experimental evidence as well as the Kekulé structure':

Kekulé's view of the structure of benzene and of the thousands of related aromatic compounds resembles the modern view, which is based on the quantum mechanical concept of the electronic linking of atoms, although electrons (much less quantum mechanics) were not known until years after.[68]

If we replace 'quantum mechanics' by 'cognitive neurosciences,' the analogy between organic chemistry and generative grammar becomes fairly obvious. As mentioned in the first section, organic chemistry developed abstract representations of complex molecules in terms of elements of the Periodic Table, valences, ring structures and so on long before the quantum physicists were able to show, in the late 1920s, that there really are things in the natural world that have the properties attributed by chemists to molecules. It was then 'realized that the combining power of atoms and, in fact, all the chemical properties of atoms and molecules are explicable in terms of the laws governing the motions of the electrons and nuclei composing them.'[69] But this achievement would not have been feasible even in the twentieth century without the information provided beforehand by chemistry (without the help of structural representations the physicists would not have known what to look for).

Likewise, without information about the mental representations and computations postulated by the empirical psychosciences--the most advanced of which appears to be generative grammar--the brain scientist would not know what to look for, let alone how to find it. We could then say that the cognitive psychosciences (the study of computational-representational theories of mind and their role in action and understanding) should serve as a guide to the future cognitive neurosciences (in particular, neurolinguistics), providing them with some conception of the properties that the mechanisms sought must satisfy, the way chemistry served as a guide to quantum chemophysics.[70] Furthermore, it should be immediately obvious, as sometimes it is not, that the advance in our scientific understanding brought about by quantum mechanics has not diminished at all the validity and utility of the chemical level of analysis; for one thing, chemistry still allows us to calculate the interactions of atoms without knowing the internal structure of an atom's nucleus.

---

[68] Roberts (1989: 80). As pointed out there, 'the development of not only dyes, but also drugs such as sulfanimide and aspirin, high-octane gasoline, synthetic detergents, plastics, and textile fabrics such as Dacron--all are outgrowths of the aromatic chemistry for which Kekulé laid the foundation by his formula for benzene.'

[69] Pauling & Wilson (1935: 1). For an extremely lucid presentation of this 'modern alchemy,' see Gamow (1961, ch. 7).

[70] They are already guiding some of the best initial steps toward that future. See Grodzinsky (1990), an important and promising recent contribution, which 'marks a significance advance' in the efforts to illuminate 'questions of major importance concerning language structure' 'by carefully designed studies of deficit' (Chomsky).

Similarly, chances are that some grammatical principles can only be formulated at something like the level of generative grammar, so such a level is not likely to be superseded even if the neurosciences eventually succeed in identifying the brain mechanisms involved in having or knowing a human language. One thing that is clear is that a physical system can be studied at several levels of abstraction from mechanism, and priority is on the side of abstract study. It is simply not possible to identify the specific features of the physical mechanisms of the brain that realize the properties postulated in the abstract study without first discovering what these properties are. In fact, at the time generative grammar emerged most people found it hard to believe that brain structure has anything to do with language, as we will see after we take a look at an instructive 'laboratory experiment' contrived by history since the 1950s, which again will hopefully help to place things in the proper perspective.

Oddly enough, the rise of the first cognitive science is simultaneous with the rise of molecular biology. It was precisely in 1953, a couple of months after the discovery of the structure of DNA, that at some point in a stormy crossing of the Atlantic--on an old tub that had been salvaged after being sunk by the Germans during the war--a seasick 24-year-old graduate student of the University of Pennsylvania and Junior Fellow of the Harvard Society of Fellows abandoned any remaining hope that the proposals of the linguists of Wiener's and von Neumann's generation could be made to work and decided to turn his attention entirely to the problems of generative grammar, in theory and application. Soon after he started to write *The Logical Structure of Linguistic Theory*, bringing together the work he had begun on various aspects of generative grammar, 'but now with conviction as well as enthusiasm' (1973: 33).

The phase this work opened, with ideas substantially improved from about 1960, when it began to become clear that a language is not a rule system (and with the investigation of historical antecedents, until then unknown to Chomsky, already in progress), is associated with *Aspects of the Theory of Syntax*, published in 1965, simultaneously with James Watson's celebrated *Molecular Biology of the Gene*, Chomsky (born on 7 December 1928 in Philadelphia) being only eight months younger than Watson, a native of Chicago. As mentioned above, 1965 was the year when the final codons of the genetic code were assigned, bringing to completion the 'classical' theory. At the time the few practicing molecular biologists knew all the known important facts about the gene, which were not very many (what was then known about DNA and RNA could easily be explained to beginning college students), and most of them would have agreed that 'in outline, the basic ideas of molecular biology were largely correct' (Crick), an assessment that, in a way, seems equally applicable to the basic ideas of the 'standard' theory of generative grammar. It was also possible for the handful of generative grammarians of the mid 1960s 'to teach from zero to current research within a term or a year or so' (Chomsky 1982a: 52). Five years later, when the second edition of Watson's book appeared, the number of molecular biologists was rising rapidly. The fact that 'it was still quite uncertain if the future would be as intellectually meaningful as the years just after the discovery of the double helix' (Watson) did not seem to have much effect on the emerging popularity of the cutting edge of biology. For generative grammar, 1970 was the year in which 'Conditions on transformations,' a turning point in the history of ideas, was written, but the cutting edge of psychology was anything but popular, to say nothing of the still widespread appeal of 'the linguistic wars,' exponent of some of the worst tendencies of 'generative semantics,' which, in an astonishing cultural regression, 'set out to capture [the relation between form and content] in as direct (and therefore in as an intuitively plausible, or commonsensical) way as possible.'[71]

Happily for molecular biology, the worries about its future did not last long. By the time the third edition of Watson's book was published in 1976, recombinant DNA procedures had given humans the power to clone genes and a new era of molecular biology was soon in full swing. For generative grammar, 1976 is the year of *Essays on Form and Interpretation*, the book that introduced the emerging conception of the logic of natural languages, a not quite expected dramatic advance (see Otero 1986: 190) in our understanding of the most characteristically human faculty--a watershed that was to be associated, one year later, with the emergence of GLOW (Generative Linguistics in the Old World), unquestionably an organization of scientists and for scientists, which since then has made available an escape hatch, across countries, from local anachronistic constraints.

By the time the fourth edition of *Molecular Biology of the Gene* (1987) was first contemplated as a future project, it had become clear that 'writing it would be beyond the capacity of any one scientist' (it actually took five) and 'it would be a formidable undertaking to keep the book within a manageable length,' since 'DNA can no longer be portrayed with the grandeur it deserves in a handy volume' (Watson). Correspondingly, it would already have been

---

[71] In 1968 'there was hardly a syntactician who was not committed to, or at least attracted to, this new model,' and it was not until 1972 that everyone 'began to abandon ship' (Newmeyer 1980, 2nd ed: 101, 117). From Chomsky's perspective the history of linguistics would have been more rational if the position of generative semantics had developed before the language theory of the 1950s. In fact, a review of Cartesian linguistics (Brekle 1969) implies that the Port Royal grammar is more directly an antecedent of generative semantics than of the *Aspects* theory (Newmeyer 1980: 151n). Cf. Chomsky (1972), Katz and Bever (1976), Otero (1987), Kiparsky (1988: n.9).

a formidable undertaking to keep within manageable length a comprehensive treatment of the theory of the LAD (Language Acquisition Device) expounded in *Knowledge of Language* and *Barriers*, both published in 1986 (and both still short of the theory first outlined in the 'Economy' paper in 1988), and its application to a variety of languages. The overviews of those years, admirable as they are, do not appear to be a match for Watson et al. as a systematic exposition in which the LAD is 'portrayed with the grandeur' with which they portrayed DNA.

A less surprising similarity between the emergence of the two contemporary disciplines is that both sprang from the confrontation of two different and often opposed traditions, in line with A. N. Whitehead's observation, in his *Introduction to Mathematics* (1911), that 'novel ideas are more apt to spring from an unusual assortment of knowledge--not necessarily from vast knowledge, but from a thorough conception of the methods and ideas of distinct lines of thought.' Thus, molecular biology sprang from the confrontation of Mendelian genetics, which by the 1950s had become an outstanding biological discipline, with biochemistry, while generative grammar sprang from the confrontation of a synthesis of traditional grammar and structural linguistics with the theory of computation (recursive function theory), a branch of mathematics developed by the late 1930s.

The similarities are less striking than the differences, however. The creation of molecular biology required the efforts of a motley group of Europeans (mostly, the most obvious exceptions being perhaps Linus Pauling, James Watson and Seymour Benzer). In particular, the discovery of the DNA double helix, due mainly to the close collaboration of Francis Crick and James Watson, is really the result of work involving very directly five scientists (the other three being Pauling--'the greatest of all chemists'-- Rosalind Franklin and Maurice Wilkins). In sharp contrast, the discovery of generative grammar, which can be said to have gained a definitive lease on life at about the same time, was due to a single individual working in almost complete isolation.

This is the more remarkable when one considers that in the first case it was a one-shot, almost overnight, affair, which took two pages of *Nature* (pp. 737-8) to explain. The investigation of DNA was comparatively simple and the problem of its structure could be and was discovered by the method of trial (model-building). As Judson points out, even the structure of a protein (an enzyme, for example) would have been a thousand times more difficult than DNA to solve (1979, 22-3). In contrast, Chomsky's discovery required very sophisticated analysis and theory construction, later summed up in a massive, mostly highly technical, typescript almost one thousand pages long. The bulky study from which *Syntactic Structures* was essentially excerpted (except for the somewhat misleading additions mentioned above) is then 'the more amazing in sweep and complexity in that it represents the largely solitary creation of a wholly new way of doing linguistics, and of new areas in linguistic research'--as well as a model for the cognitive sciences, as we have seen.[72]

This is the more surprising when we consider that the difficulties posed by the study of cognition were considerably greater. Not only is there a considerable gap in the degree of complexity of the two aspects of biology under study (the human brain being the most complex object we know of in the universe), but there are also ethical barriers to the direct investigation of humans. We are just civilized enough not to be able to deal with humans the way we deal with fruit flies and other defenseless organisms. If we were not, 'we might very well proceed to inquire into the operative mechanisms by intrusive experimentation, by constructing controlled conditions on language growth' (Chomsky 1980: 197).

Another difference worthy of note is that the achievement of a single American working in almost complete isolation is not associated with one of the oldest and most prestigious European university cities, but with Philadelphia, and then Cambridge, Massachusetts; not with the long collective effort of an institution in the tradition of the Cavendish Laboratory, a cradle of both modern physics and molecular biology, but with no institution at all during the first crucial years and afterwards with an MIT prototype cross-disciplinary organization housed in Building 20, one of the barracks left over from World War II.

It is at least ironical that this unique American contribution to knowledge which was to have an impact all over the world was essentially the work of someone quite at odds with the leading American intellectuals of the moment, who were just beginning to overcome the inferiority complex towards Europe typical of the preceding decade, as Chomsky pointed out in a 1986 interview in Madrid.[73] It seems reasonable to suspect, as he does, that the

---

[72] The quote is from Leiber (1975: 109). Leiber draws a parallel between Chomsky's innovations and 'Einstein's scientific revolution' (19-22). In one of the best studies of Einstein's life and work, which takes him to be 'by far the most important scientific figure of this century,' it is pointed out that, in some respects, his 'oeuvre represents the crowning of the work of his precursors, adding to and revising the foundations of their theories,' and that in this sense he is not a pioneer, but 'a transitional figure, perfecting the past and changing the stream of future events' (Pais 1982: 15).

[73] For a similar observation from a different perspective he referred to a passage of Norbert Wiener's autobiography which describes a Harvard mathematician ('perhaps the chief representative of the German tradition in American mathematics,' in Wiener's view) who imitated his Göttingen masters even in the most minute mannerisms. 'The chief representative of the German tradition in American mathematics, having studied in Göttingen, where he married a German girl,' writes Wiener, 'brought back the determination to live in America the life of a German professor' (1956: 30).

importance accorded immediately after World War II to behavioral science and the mathematical theory of communication, which was thought to offer a key to the human sciences, was in part due to the eagerness to overcome this complex of intellectual inferiority ('a really pathological one, particularly in places like Cambridge'). It was tempting to pretend that outside the United States there was nothing of value once Europe had been destroyed and the United States had shown a great military and technological capacity, particularly in war technology (a source of boundless pride again in early 1991). It is of some interest that as a student Chomsky was never assigned anything European by his teachers except some work by Carnap, and that only because of its relation to Quine's ideas (cf. note 41).

Another contrast between molecular biology and the cognitive psychology initiated by generative grammar is that the former is just another advance (albeit a very important one) in what might be called a (strictly) Galilean research program for the natural sciences, whereas the latter represents a new breed of natural science which extends and makes innovative use of the 'Galilean style,' namely, cognitive natural science, something in a way new under the sun at the time, and specifically language theory, possibly a very central field in the study of humans.[74] It is this advance in the study of cognition, sometimes referred to as the 'cognitive (science) revolution'--the unstated assumption is that there is no comparable 'volitive science revolution'--that began in the realm of ideas a few months before 1950 and got into high gear in 1953 (the year the DNA double helix was discovered). In contrast, molecular biology has yet to make a contribution to the study of cognition.[75]

Finally, molecular biologists 'solved all the mysteries in terms of classical models and theories, without forcing us to abandon our intuitive notions about truth and reality,' in the words of a prominent molecular biologists who, like Crick and many others, had begun as a physicist:

> In people who had expected a deep solution to the deep problem of how in the living world like begets like, it raised a feeling similar to the embarrassment one feels when shown a simple solution to a chess

---

[74] It could be that the uniqueness of human life essentially derives from the (possibly unique) human capacity to deal with discrete infinities through recursive rules, as manifested in the capacity to construct an unbounded range of expressions (Chomsky 1982a: 20,22; see also 1980a). See note 2.

[75] One could imagine, with Chomsky (1982: 23), that 'the biology of 100 years from now is going to deal with the evolution of organisms the way it now deals with the evolution of amino-acids, assuming that there is just a fairly small space of physically possible systems that can realize complicated structures.'

problem with which one has struggled in vain for a long time. (Delbrück 1986: 237)

In contrast, it would come as no very great surprise if we were to discover that the physical sciences as they are currently understood are not capable of incorporating and accounting for the properties and principles that are discovered in the study of language and mind (which depart sharply from the conventional beliefs prevalent in the 1950s), just as, for example, Cartesian mechanics could not account for the motions of the heavenly bodies, as was shown by Newton, and just as nineteenth century physics could not account for the properties of the chemical elements. It may also turn out to be the case that some of the problems of language and mind lie beyond the scope of human intelligence so there will never be a 'volitive science revolution.'

3.2 The reception of generative grammar: A crucial difference between the sciences and the humanities. Not only was generative grammar something new under the sun, but it was also something that went against the grain of received wisdom. This radical departure from generally accepted beliefs lies no doubt at the root of the resistance it triggered on the part of many, including of course those who have always found it difficult to open their minds to trail-blazing ideas.

Immediately after the emergence of molecular biology, a well-known biochemist (Arthur K. Fritzmann) is said to have proclaimed, as if speaking for his colleagues, 'We're all molecular biologists now' (Crick 1981: 178). The contrast with the early reception of generative grammar, the first, all-important step towards a far-reaching biology of the language faculty, could not have been greater. Chomsky's work encountered fierce resistance among 'the establishment.' As a result, not only did the new discipline not become widely known almost immediately, but, even today, it is not widely known among many people who study or teach language or languages, only a few of whom appear to be prepared to think about language acquisition in Chomskyan terms, a fact perhaps not unrelated to the underdevelopment of linguistics as a professional field with respect to biology in the 1950s and since.[76] The seemingly immediate success of *Syntactic Structures* (1957), due in part to Robert Lees' thorough review (published concurrently in *Language*), a success which was very real at some level, may easily be misleading.

---

[76] For a glimpse of what can be expected of the study of language among non-specialists, see Strozer (1990) and Renzi (1988).

Contributing to this success was a supportive environment, but the support was to be found mainly in psychology, engineering, mathematics, etc. Indeed, the better portion of Chomsky's earliest work appeared more in publications devoted to mathematical, psychological, logical, or philosophical studies (the Institute of Radio Engineers proceedings, *American Documentation, Information and Control*, etc.) than in publications aimed primarily at professional linguists, as Lieber (109), among others, has noted. Similarly, the talks he gave were almost always in departments of engineering, psychology, or philosophy (or such affairs as the Christian Gauss Seminar in Criticism lectures at Princeton in 1965, part of which quickly became *Cartesian Linguistics*--see below).[77] Among linguists, however, the reaction in the early years ranged from indifference to hostility (mainly real hostility):[78] Great hostility with regard to the work on phonology (where the efforts were concentrated when he appeared on the scene), either hostility or total incomprehension with regard to the general picture (which was well beyond their purview), and indifference for the most part with regard to the work on syntax, a field which until then had not received too much attention (presumably because of the difficulties it presented, which no one before Chomsky had been able to overcome).[79] There were a few exceptions (very few), the main one being Yale, where Bernard Bloch, a person of real integrity, was supportive, though he was the first to admit that he did not know what Chomsky was talking about (which was also true of most professional linguists, although not everyone was so ready to admit it).[80]

At another time or place it would have been natural to suppose that the purpose of the two conferences at the University of Texas in the Spring of 1958 and the Spring of 1959 was to give a fair hearing to a new and possibly promising conception of language theory and its application to the analysis of English, but in fact the 1958 conference was called to kill the 'heresy' before

---

[77] This is one of the differences with Sapir's work, which provides a good point of reference. See Darnell (1990), 'an account not only of Sapir's life but of a whole era in American intellectual history' (William Bright) and Koerner, ed. (1984), which includes Zellig Harris' review of Sapir's *Selected Writings* (cf. Chomsky 1973, n. 16). See also Hymes and Fought (1981). Cf. Halle (1988).

[78] Chomsky, who apparently has never had much interest in the profession, seems to have regarded this reaction of hostility, indifference and incomprehension on the part of the leading lights of linguistics of Jakobson's and Harris's generation (Hill, Hockett, Joos, Smith, Trager, Twaddell, to mention only some who were close to the center of things), as natural and not very interesting. Cf. Newmeyer (1986).

[79] Furthermore, the work on syntax was easily misinterpreted, with transformations regarded as just another device in the descriptive armory, more in line with the work of Harris (which had developed quite different concepts).

[80] It is no accident that Chomsky's only technical article in *Language* appeared in the Bloch memorial volume.

it got off the ground (as the participants were well aware). The 1958 papers were not published until 1962 (and it was quite difficult to gain the editor's permission to have Chomsky's syntax paper included also in the Fodor and Katz anthology) and the 1959 papers have never been published.[81] In fact, Chomsky's 1959 paper, 'Transformational basis of syntax,' which, in spite of its title, included a start on *The Sound Pattern of English* (and presumably triggered greater fears because it dealt with phonology), has never been published and appears to have vanished.[82]

Another opportunity missed was the 1962 meeting of the International Congress of Linguists. Chomsky was invited only after Zellig Harris had turned down the invitation, and apparently was not very eager to be part of it, but he ended up presenting a major paper that turned out to be a turning point in the history of generative grammar (the initial germ of the research program which was to lead to the principles-and-parameters modular theory, which in fact amounts to a discovery procedure, 'a scientific advance of the highest importance' that seemed to be 'hopelessly out of the question' at the time).[83] In any case, his appearance set off waves of irrational hysteria. As often happens, some of the participants, including a variety of European professors, were apparently more concerned with defending what they took to be their territory than with any intellectual issues.[84]

The wider picture is not much better. Although some of the most important work that Chomsky has done is his undergraduate thesis, *The Morphophonemics of Modern Hebrew* (1949, elaborated in his M.A. thesis of 1951, with further revisions before the year was over), and *The Logical Structure of Linguistic Theory* (completed in 1955-6), he doesn't seem to have

---

[81] Although everyone understood that the proceedings were to be published (which is why Chomsky submitted a detailed and extensive paper on generative phonology), the organizer apparently decided not to publish them. (It is of interest that it was Chomsky's paper on phonology, not his paper on syntax, that was unceremoniously suppressed.) The published version of the 1958 exchanges between Chomsky and his seniors, which is extremely illuminating (and gives clues to his stature that are hard to miss), makes the loss all the more regrettable.

[82] The only extant copy which is available to interested readers appears to be the one in the library of the Department of Linguistics at Yale, presumably placed there by Bloch, which is missing one page. The only published record is Chomsky and Halle (1960).

[83] The quotes are from Chomsky's response to Haas (pp. 996-7 of the *Proceedings*), the context being the following: 'As I tried to make clear in my paper, a discovery procedure would constitute a scientific advance of the highest importance . . . My view is not that development of a discovery procedure would be uninteresting, but rather that it is, for the present, hopelessly out of the question, and that we do not know enough about language structure to pose this problem seriously.'

[84] Considering his priorities, and not seeing a real reason to expect much difference the next time around, Chomsky recently turned down an invitation to speak at the 1992 meeting.

made any serious effort to have them published.[85]   But since he did run off several dozen copies of *LSLT* and sent them around, it may have been read in a kind of underground.   By how many people was the nearly one thousand page highly technical typescript seriously read at the time or later? It is a fair guess that the number was not vast.   This is not to say that it was completely ignored. One professional linguist who apparently read it during the 1950s with the attention it demands was Robert Lees, after he was at MIT, and there may have been other readers in the 1950s.   Since then there were of course more, particularly after it was published.[86]   Since LSLT   was published (in part) only in 1975 and *MMH* did not appear until 1979, it is clear that the major work Chomsky did in the early and mid-1950s was out of the field for many years at the very least.   In fact, LSLT continues to be generally unknown, it would appear, although perhaps less so than *MMH*.[87]

The resistance to his work on the history of ideas, particularly *Cartesian Linguistics* (1966), was even more irrational, and it might be instructive to try to understand why.   In early 1964 Chomsky was invited by R. P. Blackmur (apparently at the suggestion of Edward Cone, Department of Music, and Richard Rorty, Department of Philosophy) to give the 1965 Christian Gauss Seminars in Criticism lectures at Princeton (Harry Levin and I. A. Richards had given seminars in recent years).   He was asked to 'put together [his] interest in formal logic and the analysis of syntax with some relation to literature,' but he didn't think that he was 'in a position to say anything significant relating to literature' and proposed instead 'the topic of structure of language and philosophy of mind, and, in particular, to try to develop some notions that were extensively discussed in the seventeenth through early

---

[85] Apparently he didn't care very much. Although in the 1950s and the early 1960s publication was difficult for him, it was of course not impossible.

[86] There was at least one paper by a senior linguist, long forgotten, which obviously borrowed from the unpublished work, but without reference--and without showing much understanding of the terms and notions borrowed.

[87] One telling example referred to in Chomsky (1981, ch. 2, n. 120) may serve as a perhaps not untypical illustration of the interest this *magnum opus* has generated so far, which is the more surprising when one considers that it 'retains so much current relevance after all these years, something that can be said for few other linguistic publications since, and a tribute to the rigor, breadth and insight of this book' (Heny 1979); in its author's view, it contains 'just about everything' he did before the 1970s (Chomsky 1989: 129), part of it somewhat premature. As for *MMH*, suffice it to say that the algorithm for evaluating two theories in the same notation by counting the features continues to be associated with work by Morris Halle which was published many years later.

Beyond linguistics the story is not without surprises. An exceptionally perceptive observer has remarked that 'The reception of modern syntactic theory by the (other) psychological sciences constitutes a fascinating, albeit bizarre, chapter in the history of intellectual endeavor' (Marshall 1990; see also Marshall 1977, 1980a, 1981, 1987).

nineteenth centuries, though rarely since.'[88] What he intended was 'to elaborate some themes that were fairly topical in the seventeenth and eighteenth century' and that he thought could be 're-opened in a useful way' then, namely, 'questions about the implications for the study of mental processes of what can be discovered about the structure of language (in a rather broad sense of this last term).' He wanted 'to discuss the history of this question, to the extent that [he was] able to, and to try to evaluate the possible modern contributions (in philosophy, linguistics and psychology) to its clarification and solution.'[89] This proposal was very well received and the six lectures, under the general title 'Concepts of language: The evolution of general linguistics since the seventeenth century,' began on Thursday, Feb 25, at 8:30 P.M. (an hour's talk followed by an hour's discussion), and ended on April 8, 1965. Twenty days later he had already 'written up some material on just the historical part' and expected to 'publish it soon as a monograph of some sort (it is of an unfortunate length, too long for an article and too short for a book).'[90]

The available evidence suggests that the audience included very sophisticated people and that the lectures were well received. Cone was among those impressed by their success: 'It's almost unheard of for a man to keep his entire audience through all six sessions. Your ideas are still resounding through the halls of the Philosophy Department here. Please come again!'[91] Not a hint here of what was to come.

Why, then, did some custodians of the 'history of linguistics' (as they understand it) go berserk when *Cartesian Linguistics* appeared?[92] Whatever the general shortcomings of the academic professions are (turf-protection, for example), they do not seem to provide a complete explanation in this case, since other work which is not shown to be wrong doesn't trigger similar hysteria (and even when the work is shown to be wrong, there is no reason to be hysterical about it). There seems to be something more, and even if a component may have to do with the place of linguistics in the academic profession scale (as reflected, for example, in what some journals are open

---

[88] The date of Blackmur's letter is March 12, 1964, and that of Chomsky's reply is April 13.
[89] Letter of June 16, 1964.
[90] Letter of April 28, 1965, to Cone by Chomsky, who notes that he 'enjoyed the seminars very much and found them very profitable.' The book appeared in mid 1966.
[91] Reply of May 1, 1965 to Chomsky's letter. It should be added that a good part of the audience (most of it distinguished faculty in the humanities) could not really follow the new material about history of ideas, so after a couple of lectures, Chomsky switched to something lighter.
[92] At least one 'respected scholar' virtually pleaded with Chomsky that he stop working in the area when they met by chance on the steps of the British Museum (Saporta 1990:31). For a very different reaction of a respectable philosopher, see Bracken (1970).

to), a not small part may have to do with the 'history' part of the 'history of linguistics.' It is not difficult to see why.

Two very different approaches to history may be identified. In one we set events up 'in implied comparison with the present day,' assuming that an idea or ideal 'can be proved to have been wrong by the mere lapse of time.' It is 'part and parcel' of this approach to history that 'it studies the past with reference to the present,' the historian standing 'on the summit of the twentieth century.'[93] Since a feature of this approach is that it hypothesizes about courses of development in the past on the basis of the empirical evidence presently available, which is not unlike making predictions about courses of development in the future on the basis of the empirical evidence presently available, we may refer to it as the postdictive approach (rather than whig or whiggish, as some, misleadingly, call it). For anyone interested in postdiction, only from an up-to-date perspective is it possible to make sense of history and to develop historical understanding. Consider one example: the significance of the 'discovery' of America and the subsequent subjugation and near extermination of the American Indians may presumably be assessed better in 1991 than in 1891, in 1891 better than in 1791, in 1791 better than in 1691, in 1691 better than in 1591 (cf. Otero 1989: 53f). The thesis is, if anything, truer of intellectual history, which may be profitably seen as an integrated retrospective or retrojection of the work of key contributors: Newton's work can be assessed better after 1915 than before 1905, Mendel's work can be assessed better after 1953 than before 1944, and so on.

The postdictive approach to history 'is not by any means the one which the historical specialist adopts at the precise moment when he is engaged upon his particular research.' At least some specialists are likely to prefer 'the microscopic view of a particular period' ('nothing less than the whole of the past, with its complexity of movement, its entanglement of issues, and its intricate interactions') to the 'bird's-eye view of the whole' sought by the historian aiming at retrojection, 'which is so different from the story that the [data processor] has to tell,' not being 'in possession of a principle of exclusion which enables him to leave out the most troublesome element in the complexity' of human change.

Could it be that 'all history must tend to become more whig [read: retrojective] in proportion as it becomes more abridged' (more generally, that 'there is a tendency for all history to veer over into whig [read: retrojective]

---

[93] Butterfield (1931: 105, 106, 11, 13); cf. Gould (1987: 4-5). Butterfield's view of history is very different from the interpretation of history with the benefit of hindsight ('*storia a ritrosso*') advocated in Giovanni Papini's *Gog* (pp. 47-52), which appeared in English translation also in 1931.

history') and that for some reason 'it has been easy to believe that Clio herself is on the side of the whigs [read: retrodictors]'?[94] It is in any case a fact that Chomsky's approach to history (linguistic or otherwise) is avowedly and unabashedly retrojective. He thinks that 'it is possible to turn toward earlier stages of scientific knowledge and by virtue of what we know today, to shed light on the significant contributions of the period in a way in which the most creative geniuses could not, because of the limitations of their time.' This was precisely the nature of his interest in Descartes and 'in the philosophical tradition that he influenced, and also Humboldt, who would not have considered himself a Cartesian.' In his research on the topic he was basically looking for what has value to him in the seventeenth century, 'that value deriving in large measure from the contemporary perspective with which he approaches' the evidence.[95]

It goes without saying that this type of investigation can only be carried out by researchers who have assimilated the contemporary perspective in several 'disciplines' (in our case, linguistics, psychology and philosophy at the very least), which takes considerable time and effort to prepare for, and even then it is hard work. It is much easier to be a 'scholar' in a narrowly-defined and vacuous 'specialty' without the 'interference' of 'outsiders.' Such a scholar can be far more concerned with dates, editions, punctuation, borrowing, easily detectable connections and factual details than with the all important nature of new ideas and their implications. If one has to understand the nature and implications of the writings of the past, to start thinking hard about significant questions and even to come up with some ideas, one type of scholarly game is quickly over--which is perhaps one reason why the

---

[94] Butterfield (1931: 14, 15-16, 19, 28-29, 7, 6, 8). It is generally easy for the 'children' of the Enlightenment, which with its concept of 'progress' (perhaps its dominant theme) questioned and challenged 'the belief in god-given dynasties and feudal hierarchies, with their emphasis on the status quo,' a development which matched 'the erosion in the natural sciences of the belief in a steady-state world' (Mayr 1982: 323). Those whose roots are in the pre-Enlightenment may find it less easy.

[95] Chomsky (1979: 77-78); for more on the topic, see the confrontation of Chomsky's and Foucault's ideas in the transcript of the 1971 Dutch television broadcast included in Elders (1974).

As is to be expected, the retrojective reading of the past sometimes requires a measure of interpretive license. For example, since in Humboldt's day means were lacking for a clear expression of the fundamental insight that a human language is not a set of constructed objects (utterances), but a process of generation, and that language makes infinite use of finite means, only with some interpretive license can we understand him to be saying, with as much clarity as the limitations of his time permitted, that a language is what is now called a generative procedure.

intellectual level of some reactions to Chomsky's historical investigations has been so dismal and their moral level so pitiful.[96]

A similar explanation for some of the seemingly incomprehensible misunderstandings may be derived from a crucial difference between the sciences and the humanities.   Chomsky does approach the questions he studies differently than many other researchers,   and very differently than ordinary scholarship generally does,   but that is because much scholarship, sometimes even among self-styled linguists/scientists,   tends to be irrational (cf. Botha 1989).   Simply put,   he approaches historical questions (linguistic or nonlinguistic) essentially as he would approach his scientific work (see N. Smith 1989).

In true scientific inquiry (in fact,   in any kind of rational inquiry, including the natural sciences),   productive people try to identify and come to understand major factors and see what can be explained in terms of them. They anticipate that there will always be a periphery of unexplained phenomena (a range of nuances and minor effects that require auxiliary assumptions) which should be very sharply separated.   In this sense, Chomsky is the paradigmatic rational inquirer.   He is clearly among those who always searches for the guiding principles,   the dominant structures,   the major consequences.   In order to do that,   he of course has to put aside a lot of tenth-order effects,   all within a fairly narrow range,   which he thinks are predictable from the major factors.   If one reads the documentary record critically,   it is possible to find those major factors (sometimes prominently displayed,   sometimes partially hidden,   but still they can sometimes be isolated,   documented,   illustrated in historical practice and verified) and to discover that other things follow from them.

Needless to say,   this is not the method of humanistic scholarship.   The typical humanist tends to move in a very different direction.   Oversimplifying somewhat to bring out the main point,   one could say that for the humanist every fact is precious and must be placed alongside every other fact--which is a sure way to guarantee that one will never understand anything.

In contrast, Chomsky does not think rational inquiry is different outside the natural sciences,   as already mentioned; in fact,   he suspects that if the sciences had not gone beyond the stage of much humanistic scholarship,   they would not have reached even the level of Babylonian astronomy.   Archimedes could already do much better than that,   but the real breakthrough came with the Galilean revolution in the seventeenth century,   a new way of looking at

---

[96] Chomsky has understandably been 'sort of put off by the field' (1982a: 37). For some enlightening discussion of one of the most obtuse reactions, 'full of outrageous lies' (Saporta 1990: 31), see Bracken (1984, ch. 7); cf. now the introduction to the 1988 translation of Humboldt (1836). Regrettably, limitations of space do not allow me to go into the topic here.

phenomena involving abstraction and idealization in which for the first time the facts are only of instrumental interest. This was in sharp contrast with centuries of natural history, which includes the humanities, in which the phenomena are of interest in themselves, each one being treasured by itself. Those unacquainted with the natural science approach of Galileo and those standing on his shoulders can easily get the impression that Chomsky is drawing the lines too sharply when he writes on the history of linguistics, that his reconstruction is black-and-white--which is exactly what he is trying to do. That is what it means to try to identify major dominant effects and put them in their proper place, while minor modifications are put to the side, where they belong. The point is to try to understand hidden structures and principles.[97]

From this perspective we can also begin to understand other aspects of the reception of generative grammar. We can begin to understand, for example, why linguistics in the modern sense, which was new and innovative a generation ago (a new direction which soon attracted very bright students), developed in an institution (MIT) without big vested interests in the humanities.[98] Or why it could penetrate institutions such as Vincennes, Tilburg, and so on, but not Harvard, Yale or Princeton (Princeton not until very recently, and the change may be credited to pressure from its outstanding Department of Philosophy) or the universities of Amsterdam, Tokyo, and so on.

We can also begin to understand why the first real breakthrough in our understanding of language in the history of ideas, only a generation ago (recall that the most profound and reliable knowledge available to us today is essentially the work of roughly the last three generations of modern scientists, out of a total of about thirteen generations since Galileo, out of roughly 1,300 generations since our Cro-Magnon ancestors), has received

---

[97] See Chomsky (1990a), Saporta (1990). As Einstein was well aware, 'The more primitive the status of science is, the more readily can the scientist live under the illusion that he is a pure empiricist.' (Pais 1982: 14).

[98] See Saporta (1990: 29). One of the brightest students attracted by the new ideas about language was Edward Witten, a Brandeis history major whose 'real interest, however, was linguistics' (Cole 1987). In 1970, the very year in which, presumably unknown to him, what was to become the binding theory was first committed to paper (although not published until 1973 --see Lasnik 1989, ch. 1), and many years before he was to become one of the foremost physicists of our time (see notes 6, 9, 21 and 22), Witten completed a 139 page paper on pronominalization, apparently not accepted for publication by a prestigious journal at the time, which is interesting to read in the light of later developments (that is, from a retrojective viewpoint).

such scant attention among language teachers and literary scholars.[99] This is the more remarkable in view of the level of confusion exhibited by 'critical theory' in the 1980s.[100] The most superficial contact with Chomsky's work is sufficient to understand that a theory of literature (or a theory of music, or a theory of the visual arts) has to do with a domain of knowledge, while 'criticism' has to do with the study of performance, that is, the use of knowledge (involving freedom and creativity), a far more complex enterprise of which the cognitive theory is only a part. A less superficial exposure to Chomsky's work would lead the literary theorist or critic to distinguish sharply between the language system proper and what we might call the conceptual system, a distinction that is absolutely necessary to discuss questions of interpretation in a serious way.[101]

4 Conclusion. Aristarchus of Samos, who developed quite advanced ideas on the movement of our planet almost 23 centuries ago (more than 18 centuries before Copernicus), was apparently the first to maintain that the Earth rotates and revolves around the Sun, and for that Cleanthes the Stoic

---

[99] Cf. Kiparsky (1983). For Kiparsky (36-38) one of the barriers is that 'the literary scholar has traditionally felt comfortable only with the particular characteristics of individual and traditional styles on the one hand and with non-empirical, purely conceptual reasoning on the other. There is no room in between for empirical theories, systems of abstract hypotheses that interact to predict particular testable consequences.' (See also Hayes 1984: 922). A particularly revealing case that is hard not to mention in this context is Piera's brilliant doctoral dissertation (1980)--see Hayes (1988), Kiparsky (1988), Kiparsky and Youmans (1989)--which apparently has not made the slightest dent in the study of Spanish poetry.

[100] A considerable regression with respect to the 1890s and following decades, it appears (see, e.g., Pomorska et al., ed. 1987; see also Erlich 1955, Lodge 1972, among other studies). Cf. Hobbs (1988).

[101] Even Lacan, who failed to recognize even the existence of the language system, points out that little can be expected of Freud in this domain, given that he didn't have an adequate theory of language, unaware that his own theory of language is not much of an improvement (cf. Edelson 1975). For Chomsky's assessment of Lacan's and Derrida's writings, see Chomsky (1989: 310-11, 1989b) and Saporta (1990).

It is true that this line of reasoning would lead us to conclude that much of contemporary philosophy is part of the humanities. Although the power of Chomsky's arguments against positions with more popularity than intrinsic merit (if he is on the right track) would appear to be difficult to ignore outside the humanities, it has been essentially ignored by every philosopher he has criticized (Quine, Davidson, Putnam, Dummet and other epigones of Wittgenstein) and by many others (cf. Choe 1987), as has his brilliant and extremely original radical reconstruction of Cartesian thought (see Webelhuth 1986). His own empirical investigations (not to be confused with philosophical reflections) on language and interpretation (see Chomsky 1988a; also, 1968, enlarged ed., 1969, 1975, 1976a, 1980) have also been essentially ignored, although there are notable exceptions (cf. George, ed., 1989, A. Smith 1989), perhaps the most recent of which is Neale (1990). This topic, however, is beyond the scope of this paper. For some general remarks, see Otero (1988); see also note 12 of Hornstein's paper in Kasher (1991).

wanted him indicted for impiety. Nothing of the sort has been triggered by the emergence of generative grammar, which goes to show that the world has not stood still during the last 23 centuries. However, since the development of civilization is not yet at an end in early 1991 even outside Mesopotamia, St. Augustine's conclusion that humans could not have been around all that long does not seem to have lost any of its persuasiveness.

In fact, a close reading of Chomsky suggests a way of sharpening the classical argument presented in *The City of God*. His conception of the mind/brain leads naturally to the idea that the course of intellectual history is a direct reflection of the nature of human intelligence. It may be no accident that the level of Euclid's geometry was attained 19 centuries earlier than the level of Galileo's mechanics, which in turn was attained 3 centuries earlier than Kekulé's organic chemistry and Mendelian biology, in turn attained almost a century earlier than generative grammar. Furthermore, in any field that has shown some progress, it appears that at particular moments things converge and we sometimes speak about a scientific revolution: a certain level of understanding is achieved and a certain range of problems are alive and challenging, and suddenly many people will get the same idea or similar ideas as to how to change perspective so as to reach a new understanding.[102]

---

[102] However, this does not seem to be applicable to the early history of generative grammar. (I once asked an extremely gifted linguist who has been described as a clone of Chomsky whether he thought that he would have been able to discover generative grammar if Chomsky had not appeared on the scene, and he reacted as if I had asked him whether he thought that he could find the fountain of youth.) Only in recent years does it appear to be true (in fact, in recent years some of the most careful students of Chomsky's work have repeatedly come up with new and intriguing ideas before he did, something rather rare earlier).

On the other hand, much of what was well understood in Chomsky's early writings on generative grammar (the cognitive science context is a little broader than in 1955, and there were a few terminological changes but basically no conceptual change) has often been greatly misunderstood since then. For example, the 'metarules' of current Generalized Phrase Structure Grammar (GPSG) are not unlike transformations, except that they presuppose that phrase structure is assigned to a complex expression, whereas generative grammar assumed (tried to prove in fact) that it is a mistake to assign phrase structure to a complex expression because it is given automatically by the operation that forms the complex expression (one of the early arguments in the field, which is not insignificant, and appears to be right in an important way). Another example is that it is not a fact that sentences are necessarily readily parsable (there is no necessary relation between parsability and the nature of language), hence this cannot be a 'condition on grammar,' as proposed in GPSG (cf. Chomsky 1982a).

In contrast, an early idea that is extremely obscure and wrongheaded and has been long abandoned is still widely used as if it were well understood, and continues to mislead researchers into all sorts of pointless directions. This is the notion of 'grammatical sentence,' which was seriously investigated only in *LSLT* within a framework of assumptions that were very quickly shown to be erroneous. Unaware of this, many researchers still assume that it is a problem for a theory of language if it allows sets of expressions which have the wrong formal properties (they

It also may not be accidental that some humans have begun to speak about a 'crisis of modernism,' 'marked by a sharp decline in the general accessibility of the products of the creative minds, a blurring of the distinction between art and puzzle, and a sharp increase in "professionalism" in intellectual life,' before we can speak of a scientific theory of literature, for example, and, most regrettably, before we have managed to develop social institutions which at long last allow humans everywhere to create 'free from physical need' and 'in freedom from such need.'[103]

Perhaps it is not a pure accident that part of the subject matter of Galilean physics and its extensions has existed since the big bang, the subject matter of Kekulé's organic chemistry and Mendelian biology has existed only during the last three or four billion years, and the subject matter of generative grammar and neurolinguistics (the human brain) might not have been around in its present form for more than a few tens of thousands of years.

But Cleanthes reaction to the great discovery of Aristarchus of Samos, unwittingly echoed by millions of human beings since that discovery was made (and continued to be echoed even after the Copernican revolution and its aftermath) suggests that a new idea of a truly creative individual mind, no matter how original and innovative, is only a necessary requirement for general cultural advance, not a sufficient one. Also necessary is the development of a new general attitude on the part of many people, something which can only be brought about by a fairly general understanding and internalization of the new idea. Both the new idea and the new general understanding provide precise measurements of the degree of advancement of civilization, but along two different (though not unrelated) dimensions, an observation which suggests two different senses of 'revolution' and a perspective over scientific progress that might shed some light on what the recent discoveries about language may mean in the history of our culture.

It does not seem unlikely that modern generative grammar is among the contributions with great potential for advancing the course of civilization. Actually, the way in which language theorizing has been pursued has recently

---

are not context-free, or recursive, or even recursively enumerable), because of its implications for parsability and learnability.

All these appear to be cases of intellectual history having undergone a serious regression in a relatively short time span (the issues were very explicit and clear in *LSLT*, but have been totally confused and have led to many problems since then), but the list does not pretend to be exhaustive. A related observation is that Chomsky showed from the very beginning a command of the work of his immediate main predecessors that, to my knowledge, has not been surpassed, or even equaled, by any linguist or philosopher with respect to Chomsky's work.

[103] Chomsky (1975: 125). The last two expressions are part of a quote from Marx in which Chomsky sees an echo of Wilhelm von Humboldt's writings. Cf. Stent (1978, ch. 10).

been moved forward on two occasions, a quarter of a century apart: In the early fifties, the study of language was put on a new, technically sophisticated and solidly founded course, though still within essentially traditional lines; in the earliest eighties a far more radical departure from the achievements of the past was brought about.[104] As a result, linguistics may be to the twentieth century what Galilean mechanics was to the seventeenth century (Chomsky has repeatedly been referred to as the Galileo of the cognitive sciences).[105]

It is not difficult to point to nontrivial differences between these two stages in the history of discovery, but they are not unrelated to the fundamental difference between the two disciplines, which from today's vantage point is easier to characterize. Of the two, only the study of language involves the study of the human mind/brain, the most complex object we know of. In the central part of this study (including language) it is not possible to go very far without postulating mental representations and computations, while there is no need for postulating such representations in the study of gravitation or biological reproduction. Furthermore, the linguistic representations and computations are an index of human intelligence, hence of our essential humanity.

A sophisticated account of language such as the one made possible by Chomsky is then bound to have a revolutionary impact far beyond linguistics, something he appears to have been well aware of from very early on. All along he has also been the first to see and write extensively about the general implications of the new ideas and the results obtained pursuing them, in particular their implications for fields in which language figures prominently.[106]

---

[104] This has begun to be recognized well beyond the confines of linguistics. In 1984 Chomsky was the recipient of the American Psychological Association Distinguished Scientific Contribution award ('for enlarging our definition of scientific psychology' and for demonstrating that 'an understanding of grammar must be central to any serious understanding of the human mind' and showing 'psychologists how such understanding can be achieved and developed') and in 1988 he was awarded the Kyoto Prize (some $350,000) in the field of basic sciences. Cf. Horgan (1990).

[105] One would not expect that an immunologist, for example, would pay much attention to a linguist's work, and even less that he or she would write about the 'generative grammar' of the immune system, a system which offers a striking parallelism with Chomsky's view of the conceptual system. Cf. Jerne (1967, 1985), Chomsky (1980:136f), and for more extensive discussion Piattelli-Palmarini (1986); see also Piattelli-Palmarini (1988).

[106] Presumably, some of the problems still blocking this impact 'will simply resolve themselves over the next few years by the replacement of old people by younger people . . . Max Planck is supposed to have said that he didn't intend to convince his colleagues but only their graduate students and that the future of the field would be determined by that. Such a remark is probably appropriate to many fields' (Chomsky 1989: 94). Cf. Jackendoff (1988), Freidin, ed. (1989).

Given all this and what has been achieved in just a few years, there seems to be real grounds for considerable optimism about the prospects that lie ahead for the study of language and mind, and more generally for the study of cognitive systems of the mind/brain of which language is a fundamental essential component, in the human species. As for the promise of the work that lies immediately ahead, a comparison with biology may again be helpful. It is no secret that the biological sciences are well beyond their infancy even though a number of potential contributors may have unfortunately vanished en route over the Bermuda triangle that so often proves irresistible to James Watson's class of 'cantankerous fools who unfailingly backed the wrong horses.' What's more, 'perhaps the most impressive aspect of current biology is its unification,' according to a standard history of the field, since 'virtually all the great controversies of former centuries have been resolved' and 'there is far more mutual understanding than prevailed even twenty-five years ago.'[107]

Will something analogous be true of linguistics and, more generally, cognitive psychology, including non-trivial parts of the humanities and the social sciences, in the not too remote future? It would be foolhardy to hazard a prediction. What can perhaps be safely said is that the chances for that to happen will be greatly enhanced if Bertrand Russell's recipe for longevity no longer goes unheeded and the exercise of exceptional care in the selection of one's ancestors ceases to be a privilege of the very few.

References

Anderson, A. R., ed., 1964. Minds and Machines. Englewood Cliffs, N.J.: Prentice-Hall. (Contemporary Perspectives in Philosophy Series.)
Anderson, S. R. 1989. Review Article on Johnson-Laird 1988, Language 65, 800-11.
Baars, B. J., ed., 1986. The Cognitive Revolution in Psychology. New York: The Guilford Press.
Bar-Hillel, Y. 1964. Language and Information: Selected Essays on their Theory and Application. Reading, MA: Addison-Wesley; Jerusalem: The Jerusalem Academic Press Ltd.
Barton, G. E., R. C. Berwick, and E. S. Ristad. 1987. Computational Complexity and Natural Language. Cambridge: MIT Press.
Bechtel, W. 1988a. Philosophy of Mind: An Overview for Cognitive Science. Hillsdale, New Jersey: LEA. (Tutorial essays in cognitive science series.)
Bechtel, W. 1988b. Philosophy of Science: An Overview for Cognitive Science. Hillsdale, New Jersey: LEA. (Tutorial essays in cognitive science series.)

---

[107] Watson (1968, ch. 2), Mayr (1982: 131). The recent links established between genes and disease appear to be opening a new era in medicine ('the genetic age,' as a cover story in *Business Week* [May 28, 1990] dubbed it), with a number of ethical and social consequences.

Bernstein, J. 1973. Einstein. New York: The Viking Press. (Modern Masters)

Berwick, R. C. 1985. The Acquisition of Syntactic Knowledge. Cambridge: MIT Press.

Berwick, R. C. 1987. Principle-based Parsing. MIT Artificial Intelligence Laboratory. A.I. T.R. No. 972.

Berwick, R. C. 1991. Principle-based Parsing and Rule-based Parsing. In Shieber, Sells and Wasow, eds. (Revised and expanded version of Berwick 1987)

Berwick, R. C., and S. Fong. 1990. Principle-based Parsing: Natural Language Processing for the 1990s. In Winston and Shellard, eds.

Berwick, R. C., and A. Weinberg. 1984. The Grammatical Basis of Linguistic Performance. Cambridge, Mass.: MIT Press.

Bever, T., J. J. Katz, and D. T. Langendoen, eds., 1976. An Integrated Theory of Linguistic Ability. New York: Thomas Y. Crowell.

Bever, T., J. M. Carroll, and L. A. Miller, eds., 1984. Talking Minds: The Study of Language in Cognitive Science. Cambridge, Mass.: MIT Press.

Bickerton, D. 1990. Language and Species. Chicago: The University of Chicago Press.

Block, N. 1990. The Computer Model of the Mind. In Osherson and Smith, eds., 247-89.

Block, N., ed., 1981. Readings in Philosophy of Psychology. Cambridge, Mass.: MIT Press. (2 vols.)

Botha, R. P. 1989. Challenging Chomsky: The Generative Garden Game. Oxford: Basil Blackwell.

Bracken, H. M. 1970. Chomsky's Variations on a Theme of Descartes. Journal of the History of Philosophy 8, 180-92. (Review of Chomsky 1966.)

Bracken, H. M. 1984. Mind and Language: Essays on Descartes and Chomsky. Dordrecht: Foris.

Brekle, H. E. 1969. Review of Chomsky, Cartesian linguistics. Linguistics 49, 74-91.

Butterfield, H. 1931. Whig Interpretation of History. London: G. Bell and Sons.

Cairns, J., G. S. Stent, and J. D. Watson, eds., 1966. Phage and the Origin of Molecular Biology. Cold Springs Harbor, N.Y.

Campbell, J. 1982. Grammatical Man: Information, Entropy, Language, and Life. New York: Simon and Schuster.

Casti, J. L. 1989. Paradigms Lost: Images of Man in the Mirror of Science. New York: William Morrow and Co. (Paperback ed., Nov. 1990.)

Chalmers, A. F. 1982. What Is this Thing Called Science?: An Assessment of the Nature and Status of Science and its Methods. 2nd ed. University of Queensland Press. (1st ed., 1976.)

Choe, H. S. 1987. On the Debate Between Putnam and Chomsky. MIT Working Papers in Linguistics 9, 41-63.

Chomsky, N. 1951. Morphophonemics of Modern Hebrew. University of Pennsylvania Master's thesis. (Published in 1979 by Garland Publications in its series 'Outstanding Dissertations.')

Chomsky, N. 1955-56. The Logical Structure of Linguistic Theory. University of Chicago, 1975. (Paperback edition, 1985, with an index by Jan van Voorst.)

Chomsky, N. 1956. Three Models for the Description of Language. I.R.E. Transactions on Information Theory IT-2, 113-24. Reprinted, with corrections, in Luce, Bush and Galanter, eds., 1965, vol. 2. 105-24.

Chomsky, N. 1957. Syntactic Structures. The Hague: Mouton.

Chomsky, N. 1959. Review of Skinner, Verbal behavior. Language 35, 26-58. (Reprinted in Fodor and Katz, eds., 1964, and, with a preliminary note of great interest, in Jakobovits and Miron, eds., 1967)

Chomsky, N. 1964. Current Issues in Linguistic Theory. The Hague: Mouton.

Chomsky, N. 1965. Aspects of the Theory of Syntax. Cambridge, Mass.: MIT Press.

Chomsky, N. 1966. Cartesian Linguistics: A Chapter in the History of Rationalist Thought. New York: Harper and Row. (Reprinted by University Press of America in August 1983)

Chomsky, N. 1968. Language and Mind. New York: Harcourt, Brace and World, Inc. (Enlarged ed., 1972)

Chomsky, N. 1969. Some Empirical Assumptions in Modern Philosophy of Language. In Morgenbesser et al., eds., 260-85. (The better known first part of this paper appeared in Synthèse 19 (1968), 53-68, under the title 'Quine's empirical assumptions,' with a reply by Quine, 274-83; cf. 299-301)

Chomsky, N. 1970. Language and Freedom. Abraxas: A Journal for the Theoretical Study of Philosophy, the Humanities and the Social Sciences 1:1 (Fall 1970), 9-24; also in White and Newman, eds., 1972. Reprinted in Chomsky 1973, 387-408 and in Chomsky 1987c, 139-55.

Chomsky, N. 1971. Problems of Knowledge and Freedom: The Russell lectures. New York: Pantheon.

Chomsky, N. 1972. [Interview (November 3)]. In Parret, ed., 27-54.

Chomsky, N. 1973. For Reasons of State. New York: Pantheon.

Chomsky, N. 1973a. Introduction to the published version of Chomsky 1955-56.

Chomsky, N. 1975. Reflections on Language. New York: Pantheon.

Chomsky, N. 1976a. The Ideas of Chomsky [interview]. In Magee, ed., 1979, 202-23.

Chomsky, N. 1976b. Noam Chomsky's Views on the Psychology of Language and Thought [interview]. In Rieber, ed., 1983, 29-63.

Chomsky, N. 1979. Language and Responsibility. Based on conversations with Mitsou Ronat [Jan 1976]. Tr. from French by J. Viertel. New York: Pantheon.

Chomsky, N. 1980. Rules and Representations. New York: Columbia University Press.

Chomsky, N. 1980a. The New Organology. Behavioral and Brain Sciences 3, 42-61.

Chomsky, N. 1981. Lectures on Government and Binding: The Pisa lectures. Dordrecht: Foris. (Corrected edition, 1982)

Chomsky, N. 1982a. The Generative Enterprise. A discussion with Riny Huybregts and Henk van Riemsdijk [1979-1980]. Dordrecht: Foris.

Chomsky, N. 1982b. Some Concepts and Consequences of the Theory of Government and Binding. Cambridge, Mass.: MIT Press.

Chomsky, N. 1982c. A Note on the Creative Aspect of Language Use. The Philosophical Review 41, 423-34.

Chomsky, N. 1983. [Roman Jakobson: Homage and Reminiscence.] In Halle, ed.,

Chomsky, N. 1984. Modular Approaches to the Study of Mind. San Diego State University. (First Distinguished Graduate Research Lecture, Nov. 17, 1980)

Chomsky, N. 1986a. Knowledge of Language: Its Nature, Origin, and Use. New York: Praeger.

Chomsky, N. 1986b. Barriers. Cambridge, Mass.: MIT Press.

Chomsky, N. 1987a. Language in a Psychological Setting. Tokyo: The Graduate School of Languages and Linguistics, Sophia University. (=Sophia Linguistica 22)

Chomsky, N. 1987b. Generative Grammar: Its Basis, Development and Prospects. Kyoto University of Foreign Studies. (Studies in English Linguistics and Literature, Special Issue)

Chomsky, N. 1987c. The Chomsky Reader. New York: Pantheon.

Chomsky, N. 1988. Language and Problems of Knowledge. Cambridge, Mass.: MIT Press.

Chomsky, N. 1988a. Language and Interpretation: Philosophical Reflections and Empirical Inquiry. Lecture delivered at UCLA, January 1988 (to appear in the University of Pittsburgh Series on Philosophy and Science).

Chomsky, N. 1988b. Prospects for the Study of Language and Mind. Lecture delivered at the International Workshop on The Chomskyan Turn, Tel Aviv University, April 11, 1988. In Kasher, ed.

Chomsky, N. 1988c. Some Notes on Economy of Derivation and Representation. Paper delivered at UCLA on January 29, 1988, and revised in September. Now in MIT Working Papers in Linguistics 10 (1989), 43-74. Also in Freidin, ed., 1991, 417-54.

Chomsky, N. 1989. Language and Politics. Edited by Carlos P. Otero. Montreal, Canada: Black Rose Books.

Chomsky, N. 1989a. Language and Mind. Darwin Lecture, Darwin College, Cambridge, January 1989.

Chomsky, N. 1989b. An Interview. Radical Philosophy 53 (Autumn), 31-40.

Chomsky, N. 1989c. Mental Constructions and Social Reality. Paper presented at the Groningen conference on Knowledge and Language, in May 1989.

Chomsky, N. 1990a. Interview Conducted by Adam Jones at MIT on February 20, 1990, Latin American Connexions (Vancouver).

Chomsky, N. 1990b. Language and the Cognitive Sciences. Lecture at Carleton College, Feb 23, 1990.

Chomsky, N. 1990c. On Formalization and Formal Linguistics. Natural Language and Linguistic Theory 8, 143-7.

Chomsky, N. 1990d. Accessibility 'in Principle'. The Behavioral and Brain Sciences, forthcoming.

Chomsky, N. 1990e. Language and Cognition. Welcoming address, Conference of Cognitive Science Society, MIT, July 1990.

Chomsky, N., and M. Halle. 1960. The Morphophonemics of English. MIT RLE Quarterly Progress Report 58, 275-81.

Chomsky, N., and M. Halle. 1965. Some Controversial Questions in Phonological Theory. Journal of Linguistics 1, 97-138.

Chomsky, N., and M. Halle. 1968. The Sound Pattern of English. New York: Harper and Row. (Paperback ed., Cambridge, Mass.: MIT Press, 1991, with a Preface dated August 1990)

Clark, A. 1989. Microcognition: Philosophy, Cognitive Science, and Parallel Distributed Processing. Cambridge, Mass.: MIT Press.

Cohen, I. B. 1985. Revolution in Science. Cambridge, MA: Harvard University Press.

Cole, K. C. 1987. A Theory of Everything. The New York Times Magazine, Oct. 18, 1987.

Corson, D. J. 1980. Chomsky on Education. The Australian Journal of Education 24, 164-85.

Crick, F. 1981. Life Itself: Its Origin and Nature. New York: Simon and Schuster.

Crick, F. 1988. What Mad Pursuit: A Personal View of Scientific Discovery. New York: Basic Books.

D'Agostino, F. 1986. Chomsky's System of Ideas. Oxford: Clarendon Press.

Darnell, R. 1990. Sapir: Linguist, Anthropologist, Humanist. Berkeley, CA: University of California Press.

Davies, P. C. W., and J. Brown, eds., 1988. Superstrings: A Theory of Everything? Cambridge: Cambridge University Press.

Delbrück, M. 1986. Mind from Matter?: An Essay on Evolutionary Epistemology. Edited by G. S. Stent et al. Introduction and overview by G. S. Stent. Palo Alto: Blackwell Scientific Publications, Inc.

Demopoulos, W., and A. Marras, eds., 1986. Language Learning and Concept Acquisition: Foundational Issues. Norwood, N.J.: Ablex.

Denning, P. J., J. B. Dennis and J. E. Qualitz. 1978. Machines, Languages, and Computation. Englewood Cliffs, NJ: Prentice-Hall.

Dieltjens, L. 1971. Rule-governed-creativity: An Analysis of the Concept in the Work of N. Chomsky. Leuven, Belgium: Institute of Applied Linguistics.

Dorr, B. J. 1990. Machine Translation: A Principle-based Approach. In Winston and Shellars, eds.

Dresher, B. E., and N. Hornstein. 1976. On Some Supposed Contributions of Artificial Intelligence to the Scientific Study of Language. Cognition 4, 321-98.

Dresher, B. E., and N. Hornstein. 1977a. Reply to Schank and Wilensky. Cognition 5, 147-50.

Dresher, B. E., and N. Hornstein. 1977b. Reply to Winograd. Cognition 5, 377-92.

Dresher, B. E., and J. D. Kaye. 1990. A Computational Learning Model for Metrical Phonology. Cognition 34, 137-95.

Durrell, L. 1952. A Key to Modern British Poetry. [London:] P. Nevill. (1st American ed., University of Oklahoma Press)

Edelson, M. 1975. Language and Interpretation in Psychoanalysis. New Haven, CT.: Yale University Press.

Elders, F., ed., 1974. Reflexive Water: The Basic Concerns of Mankind. Ontario, Canada: J. M. Dent and Sons.

Erlich, V. 1955. Russian Formalism: History, Doctrine. The Hague: Mouton. (2nd, revised ed., 1965; 3rd ed., 1980)

Fabb, N., D. Attridge, A. Durant, and C. MacCabe, eds., 1988. The Linguistics of Writing: Arguments between Language and Literature. New York: Methuen.

Fine, A. 1986. The Shaky Game: Einstein Realism and the Quantum Theory. Chicago: The University of Chicago Press.

Fodor, J. A. 1983. The Modularity of Mind: An Essay on Faculty Psychology. Cambridge, Mass.: MIT Press.

Fodor, J. A., and J. J. Katz, eds., 1964. The Structure of Language: Readings in the Philosophy of Language. Englewood Cliffs, N.J.: Prentice-Hall.

Fong, S. 1990. The Computational Implementation of Principle-based Parsers. Doctoral dissertation, MIT Department of Electrical Engineering and Computer Science. (To be published by MIT Press)

Foulkes, D. 1978. A Grammar of Dreams. New York: Basic Books.

Freidin, R., ed., 1989. A Mirror on the Mind: Chomsky's Revolution in the Study of Language. A Festschrift for Noam Chomsky on the occasion of his 59th birthday . . . from the Members of Freshman Seminar 102, Princeton University, Fall 1987.

Freidin, R., ed., 1991. Principles and Parameters in Comparative Grammar. Cambridge, MA: MIT Press.

Fryer, D. M., and J. C. Marshall. 1979. The Motives of Jacques de Vaucanson. Technology and Culture 20, 257-69.

Gamow, G. 1961. One, Two, Three,..., Infinity: Facts and Speculations of Science. New York: Dover, 1988. (1st ed., 1947.)

Gardner, H. 1985. The Mind's New Science: A History of the Cognitive Revolution. New York: Basic Books. (Reprinted in 1987, with a new epilogue by the author)

Garrido, M., ed., 1989. Lógica y lenguaje. Madrid: Tecnos.

George, A., ed., 1989. Reflections on Chomsky. Oxford: Blackwell.

Glass, A. L., and K. J. Holyoak. 1986. Cognition. New York: Random House. (2nd ed.; first published in 1979.)

Gould, S. J. 1987. Time's Arrow, Time's Cycle: Myth and Metaphor in the Discovery of Geological Time. Cambridge, Mass.: Harvard University Press.

Grodzinsky, Y. 1990. Theoretical Perspectives on Language Deficits. Cambridge, Mass.: MIT Press.

Halle, M., ed., 1983. A Tribute to Roman Jakobson, 1896-1982 [held on Nov. 12, 1982]. Berlin, New York, Amsterdam: Mouton.

Halle, M. 1987. Remarks on the Scientific Revolution in Linguistics, 1926-1929. In Pomorska et al., eds., 95-111.

Halle, M. 1988. The Bloomfield-Jakobson Correspondence, 1944-1946. Language 64, 737-54.

Harper, R. J. C., C. C. Anderson, C. M. Christensen, and S. M. Hunka, eds., 1964. The Cognitive Processes: Readings. Englewood Cliffs, N.J.: Prentice-Hall.

Haugeland, J. 1979. Understanding Natural Language. Journal of Philosophy 76, 619-32. Reprinted in Lycan, ed., 1990.

Haugeland, J., ed., 1981. Mind Design: Philosophy, Psychology, Artificial Intelligence. Cambridge, Mass.: MIT Press. (6th printing, 1988)

Hawking, S. 1988. A Brief History of Time: From the Big Bang to Black Holes. New York: Bantam.

Hayes, B. 1984. Review article on D. Attridge, The Rhythms of English Poetry. Language 60, 914-23.

Hayes, B. 1988. Metrics in Phonological Theory. In Newmeyer, ed., Volume II, 220-49.

Heims, S. J. 1980. John von Neumann and Norbert Wiener: From Mathematics to the Technologies of Life and Death. Cambridge, Mass.: MIT Press.

Heisenberg, W. 1958. Physics and Philosophy: The Revolution in Modern Science. Introduction by F.S.C. Northrop. New York: Harper and Row.

Henkel, J. 1990. Linguistic Models and Recent Criticism: Transformational-generative Grammar as Literary Metaphor. PMLA 105, 448-63.

Heny, F. 1979. Review of Chomsky 1955-56, Synthèse 40, 317-52.

Hirst, W., ed., 1988. The Making of Cognitive Science: Essays in Honor of George A. Miller. Cambridge: Cambridge University Press.

Hobbs, J. R. 1988. Against Confusion. Diacritics 18, 78-92. Reprinted in Hobbs 1990.

Hobbs, J. R. 1990. Literature and Cognition. Stanford: Center for the Study of Language and Information.

Holton, G. 1978. The Scientific Imagination: Case Studies. Cambridge: Cambridge University Press.

Holton, G. 1986. The Advancement of Science, and its Burdens. Cambridge: Cambridge University Press.

Horgan, J. 1990. Free Radical: A Word (or Two) about Linguist Noam Chomsky. Scientific American, May, 40-42 and 44. (Cf. A. Huffman's letter in SA, Feb 1991, p. 10, and G. Harman's reply)

Hubel, D. H. 1984. The Brain. In The brain. Scientific American Offprint. (From The brain. A Scientific American Book. New York: W. H. Freeman, 1979)

Humboldt, W. von. 1836. On Language: The Diversity of Human Language-Structure and its Influence on the Mental Development of Mankind. Translated by Peter Heath with and introduction by Hans Aarsleff. Cambridge: Cambridge University Press, 1988. (Texts in German Philosophy series.)

Hunt, M. 1982. The Universe within: A New Science Explores the Human Mind. New York: Simon and Schuster.

Hymes, D., and J. Fought. 1981. American Structuralism. The Hague: Mouton.

Jackendoff, R. 1987. Consciousness and the Computational Mind. Cambridge, Mass.: MIT Press.

Jackendoff, R. 1988. Why are They Saying these Things about Us? Natural Language and Linguistic Theory 6, 435-42.

Jakobovits, L. A., and M. S. Miron, eds., 1967. Readings in the Psychology of Language. Englewood Cliffs, N.J.: Prentice-Hall.

Jammer, M. 1988. The Problem of the Unity of Physics. International Journal on the Unity of the Sciences 1, 13-37.

Jeffress, L. A., ed., 1951. Cerebral Mechanisms of Behavior: The Hixon Symposium [Sep 20-25, 1948]. New York and London: Hafner. (Facsimile, 1967.)

Jerne, N. K. 1967. Antibodies and Learning: Selection versus Instruction. Quarton et al., eds.

Jerne, N. K. 1985. The Generative Grammar of the Immune System. Science 229 (13 Sep), 1157-9.

Johnson-Laird, P. N. 1983. Mental Models: Towards a Cognitive Science. Cambridge, Mass.: Harvard University Press.

Johnson-Laird, P. N. 1988. The Computer and the Mind: An Introduction to Cognitive Science. Cambridge, Mass.: Harvard University Press.

Judson, H. F. 1979. The Eighth Day of Creation: Makers of the Revolution in Biology. New York: Simon and Schuster.

Judson, H. F. 1980. The Search for Solutions. New York: Holt.

Kasher, A., ed., 1991. The Chomskyan Turn. Oxford: Blackwell.

Katz, J. J., and T. J. Bever. 1976. The Fall and Rise of Empiricism. In Bever, Katz and Langendoen, eds., 11-64.

Kaye, J. 1989. Phonology: A Cognitive View. Hillsdale, N.J.: LEA. (Tutorial essays in cognitive science series.)

King, M.- C., and A. C. Wilson. 1975. Evolution at Two Levels in Humans and Chimpanzees. Science 188 (11 April), 107-16.

Kiparsky, P. 1983. Roman Jakobson and the Grammar of Poetry. In Halle, ed.,

Kiparsky, P. 1988. On Theory and Interpretation. In Fabb et al., eds.

Kiparsky, P., and G. Youmans. 1989. Rhythm and Meter. San Diego: Academic Press.

Köhler, W. 1947. Gestalt Psychology: An Introduction to New Concepts in Modern Psychology. New York: Liveright. (Undated paperback ed., New American Library.)

Koerner, E. F. K., ed., 1984. Edward Sapir: Appraisals of His Life and Work. Amsterdam/Philadelphia: John Benjamins.

Koerner, E. F. K. 1989. Practicing Linguistic Historiography: Selected essays. Amsterdam, Philadelphia: John Benjamins.

Koerner, E. F. K. 1989a. The Chomskyan 'Revolution' and its Historiography: Observations of a Bystander. In Koerner 1989. 101-46.

Koerner, E. F. K., and M. Tajima, eds., 1986. Noam Chomsky: A Personal Bibliography 1951-1986. With the collaboration of C. P. Otero. Amsterdam, Philadelphia: John Benjamins.

Lashley, K. S. 1951. The Problem of Serial Order in Behavior. In Jeffress, ed.,

Lasnik, H. 1989. Essays on Anaphora. Dordrecht: Kluwer.

Leiber, J. 1975. Noam Chomsky: A Philosophical Overview. New York: St. Martin's Press.

Lerdahl, F., and R. Jackendoff. 1983. A Generative Theory of Tonal Music. Cambridge, Mass.: MIT Press.

Lightfoot, D. 1983. The Language Lottery: Toward a Biology of Grammars. Cambridge, Mass.: MIT Press.

Lodge, D., ed., 1972. 20th Century Literary Criticism. London and New York: Longman. (1983 reprint.)

Longuet-Higgins, H. C. 1981. Artificial Intelligence -- a New Theoretical Psychology? Cognition 10, 197-200.

Luce, R. D., R. R. Bush and E. Galanter, eds., 1965. Readings in Mathematical Psychology. New York: John Wiley and sons.

Luria, S. 1973. Life: The Unfinished Experiment. New York: Charles Scribner's.

Lycan, W. G., ed., 1990. Mind and Cognition: A Reader. Oxford: Basil Blackwell.

Lyons, J. 1977. Noam Chomsky. Rev. ed. New York: The Viking Press. (1st ed., 1970)

McCulloch, W. S. 1951. Why the Mind Is in the Head. In Jeffress, ed.,

Magee, B., ed., 1979. Men of Ideas: Face to Face with Fifteen of the World Foremost Philosophers. New York: The Viking Press.

Marr, D. [1945-1980]. 1977. Artificial Intelligence: A Personal View. Artificial Intelligence 9, 37-48. Reprinted in Haugeland, ed., 1981. 129-42.

Marr, D. 1982. Vision: A Computational Investigation into the Human Representation and Processing of Visual Information. San Francisco: Freeman.

Marr, D., and T. Poggio. 1977. From Understanding Computation to Understanding Neural Circuitry. Neurosciences Research Program Bulletin 153, 470-88.

Marr, D., and H. H. Nishihara. 1978. Visual Information Processing: Artificial Intelligence and the Sensorium of Sight. Technology Review 81, 2-23.

Marshall, J. C. 1974. Freud's Psychology of Language. In Wollheim, ed., 349-65.

Marshall, J. C. 1977. Minds, Machines and Metaphors. Social Studies in Science 7, 475-88.

Marshall, J. C. 1980a. The New Organology. The Behavioral and Brain Sciences 3, 23-5.

Marshall, J. C. 1980b. Artificial Intelligence -- the Real Thing? The Behavioral and Brain Sciences 3, 435-7.

Marshall, J. C. 1981. Cognition at the Crossroads. Nature 289 (12 Feb), 613-4. (Review of Piattelli-Palmarini, ed.)

Marshall, J. C. 1987. Language Learning, Language Acquisition, or Language Growth? in Modgil and Modgil, eds., 41-9.

Marshall, J. C. 1990. Foreword to Grodzinsky 1990.

Mayr, E. 1982. The Growth of Biological Thought: Diversity, Evolution, and Inheritance. Cambridge, MA: Harvard University Press.

Mehta, V. 1971. John Is Easy to Please. New York: Farrar, Straus and Giroux.

Miller, G. A. 1951. Language and Communication. New York: McGraw-Hill.

Miller, G. A. 1979. A Very Personal History. Occasional Papers 1, September 1979. (Talk to Cognitive Science Workshop, MIT, 1 June 1979) Cambridge, Mass.: MIT Center for Cognitive Science.

Miller, G. A. 1990. Linguists, Psychologists, and the Cognitive Sciences. Language 66, 317-22.

Modgil, S., and C. Modgil, eds., 1987. Noam Chomsky: Consensus and Controversy. New York, Philadelphia and London: The Falmer Press. (Falmer International Master-Minds Challenged: 3)

Morgenbesser, S., P. Suppes and M. White, eds., 1969. Philosophy, Science and Method: Essays in honor of Ernest Nagel. New York: St. Martin's Press.

Neale, S. 1990. Descriptions. Cambridge, MA: MIT Press.

Newell, A., J. C. Shaw and H. A. Simon. 1958. Elements of a Theory of Human Problem Solving. Psychological Review 65, 151-66. Reprinted in Harper et al., eds., 1964.

Newmeyer, F. 1980. Linguistic Theory in America: The First Quarter-century of Transformational Generative Grammar. New York: Academic Press. (Revised ed., 1986)

Newmeyer, F. 1983. Grammatical Theory. Chicago: Chicago University Press.

Newmeyer, F. 1986. The Politics of Linguistics. Chicago: Chicago University Press.

Newmeyer, F. 1986a. Has There Been a 'Chomskyan Revolution' in Linguistics? Language 62, 1-18.

Newmeyer, F., ed., 1988. Linguistics: The Cambridge Survey. Cambridge: Cambridge University Press.

Olby, R. C. 1974. The Path to the Double Helix. Foreword by Francis Crick. Seattle: University of Washington Press.

Osherson, D. N., ed., 1977. Natural Connectives: A Chomskyan Approach. Journal of Mathematical Psychology 16, 1-29.

Osherson, D. N. 1986. Systems that Learn: An Introduction to Learning Theory for Cognitive and Computer Scientists. Cambridge, Mass.: MIT Press.

Osherson, D. N., S. M. Kosslyn, and J. M. Hollerbach, eds., 1990. Visual Cognition and Action: An Invitation to Cognitive Science, Volume 2. Cambridge, Mass.: MIT Press.

Osherson, D. N., and H. Lasnik, eds., 1990. Language: An Invitation to Cognitive Science. Volume 1. Cambridge, Mass.: MIT Press.

Osherson, D. N. and E. E. Smith, eds., 1990. Thinking: An Invitation to Cognitive Science. Volume 3. Cambridge, Mass.: MIT Press.

Osherson, D. N., and T. Wasow. 1976. Task-specificity and Species-specificity in the Study of Language: A Methodological Note. Cognition 4, 203-14.

Otero, C. P. 1970. Introducción a la lingüística transformacional: Retrospectiva de una confluencia. México: Siglo XXI. (6th revised ed., 1989.)

Otero, C. P. 1984. La revolución de Chomsky: Ciencia y sociedad. Madrid: Tecnos.

Otero, C. P. 1985. Filosofía del lenguaje. In Garrido, ed.

Otero, C. P. 1986. [Background and Publication History of the Dissertations Written under the Supervision of Noam Chomsky, 1964-1986.] In Koerner and Tajima, eds., 183-204.

Otero, C. P. 1987. Chomsky's View of Semantics and Orwell's Problem. In Aspects of Language: Studies in Honour of Mario Alinei. vol. II (Theoretical and Applied Semantics) ed. by N. van der Sijs et al., Amsterdam, Rodopi, 357-71.

Otero, C. P. 1988. Review of D'Agostino 1986. Mind and Language 3, 229-42. (Reprinted, with all pages in the correct order, on pages 306-19.)

Otero, C. P. 1989. Introduction and Notes to Chomsky 1989.

Otero, C. P. 1990. The Emergence of 'Homo Loquens' and the Laws of Physics. Behavioral and Brain Sciences 13, 747-50.

Otero, C. P. 1991. Noam Chomsky. Contemporary American Activists: Biographical Sourcebook, 1960 onward, ed. by D. De Leon. Westport, CT: Greewood Press, forthcoming.

Otero, C. P. forthcoming a. Chomsky's Revolution: Cognitivism and Anarchism. Oxford: Blackwell.

Otero, C. P., ed., forthcoming b. Noam Chomsky: Critical Assessments. London: Routledge. (5 vols.)

Pais, A. 1982. 'Subtle is the Lord...': The Science and the Life of Albert Einstein. Oxford University Press.

Parret, H., ed., 1974. Discussing Language. The Hague: Mouton.

Partee, B. H., A. ter Meulen and R. E. Wall. 1990. Mathematical Methods in Linguistics. Dordrecht: Kluwer.

Pauling, L. 1939. The Nature of the Chemical Bond and the Structure of Molecules and Crystals: An Introduction to Modern Structural Chemistry. New York: Cornell University Press. (3rd ed., 1960; 11th printing, 1989.)

Pauling, L. 1947. General Chemistry: An Introduction to Descriptive Chemistry and Modern Chemical Theory. San Francisco: W. H. Freeman. (2nd ed., 1953.)

Pauling, L. 1958. No More War! London: Gollanz. (25th anniversary edition, New York: Dodd, Mead, 1983.)

Pauling, L. 1986. How to Live Longer and Feel Better. New York: Freeman.

Pauling, L., and E. B. Wilson. 1935. Introduction to Quantum Mechanics with Applications to Chemistry. New York: Dover, 1985.

Peat, F. D. 1988. Superstrings and the Search for the Theory of Everything. Chicago/New York: Contemporary Books.

Penrose, R. 1989. The Emperor's New Mind: Concerning Computers, Minds, and the Laws of Physics. Oxford: Oxford University Press.

Piattelli-Palmarini, M. 1986. The Rise of Selective Theories: A Case Study and Some Lessons from Immunology. In Demopoulos and Marras, eds., 117-30.

Piattelli-Palmarini, M. 1988. Evolution, Selection and Cognition: From 'Learning' to Parameter Setting in Biology and in the Study of Language. Ms., Center for Cognitive Science, MIT, Sept.

Piattelli-Palmarini, M., ed., 1980. Language and Learning: The Debate between Jean Piaget and Noam Chomsky. Cambridge, Mass.: Harvard University Press.

Piera, C. 1980. Spanish Verse and the Theory of Meter. UCLA doctoral dissertation.

Pinker, S., and J. Mehler, eds., 1989. Connections and Symbols. Cambridge, Mass.: MIT Press. (= Cognition: International Journal of Cognitive Science 28)

Pollock, J.-Y., and H. G. Obenauer, eds., 1990. Linguistique et cognition: Réponses à quelques critiques de la grammaire générative. Université Paris VIII. (= Recherches Linguistiques 19)

Pomorska, K., E. Chodakowska, H. McLean, and B. Vine. 1987. Language, Poetry and Poetics: The Generation of the 1890s: Jakobson, Trubetzkoy, Majakovskij. Berlin, New York, Amsterdam: Mouton.

Popkin, R. H. 1979. The History of Skepticism from Erasmus to Spinoza. Berkeley, CA: University of California Press.

Posner, M. I., ed., 1989. Foundations of Cognitive Science. Cambridge, Mass.: MIT Press.

Putnam, H. 1988. Much Ado about Not Very Much. Daedalus, Winter, 269-81. (Special issue on Artificial Intelligence.)

Pylyshyn, Z. W. 1984. Computation and Cognition: Toward a Foundation for Cognitive Science. Cambridge, Mass.: MIT Press. (Paperback edition, 1986; 5th printing, 1989.)

Quarton, G. C., T. Melnechuk and F. O. Schmitt, eds., 1967. The Neurosciences: A Study Program. New York: Rockefeller University Press.

Reiber, R. W. (with G. Voyat), ed., 1983. Dialogues in the Psychology of Language and Thought: Conversations with Noam Chomsky, Charles Osgood, Jean Piaget, Ulric Neisser, and Marcel Kinsbourne. New York: Plenum.

Renzi, L., ed., 1988. Grande grammatica italiana di consultazione. Bologna: Il Mulino. Volume I.

Restak, R. M. 1979. The Brain: The Last Frontier. An Exploration of the Human Mind and our Future. Garden City, NY: Doubleday.

Ritterbush, P. C. 1972. Organic Form: Aesthetics and Objectivity in the Study of Form in the Life Sciences. In Rousseau, ed.

Roberts, R. M. 1989. Serendipity: Accidental Discoveries in Science. New York: John Wiley and Sons.

Rousseau, G. S., ed., 1972. Organic Form: The Life of an Idea. London: Routledge.

Salkie, R. 1990. The Chomsky Update: Linguistics and Politics. London: Unwin Hyman.

Saporta, S. 1990. Society, the University and Language: An Interview with Noam Chomsky. Crítica: a Journal of Critical Essays, 2:2, 19-42.

Schwinger, J. 1986. Einstein's Legacy. New York: Scientific American Library.

Shieber, S., P. Sells and T. Wasow, eds., 1991. The Processing of Linguistic Structure. Cambridge, Mass.: MIT Press.

Sperber, D., and D. Wilson. 1986. Relevance: Communication and Cognition. Oxford: Blackwell. (Reprinted in 1988 by Harvard University Press.)

Smith, A. 1990. Review of George 1989. Mind and Language 5, 174-85.

Smith, N. 1989. The Twitter Machine: Reflections on Language. Oxford: Blackwell.

Stent, G. S. 1978. Paradoxes of Progress. San Francisco: Freeman.

Stent, G. S. 1980. Introduction to his edition of Watson 1968.

Stich, S. 1983. From Folk Psychology to Cognitive Science. Cambridge, Mass.: MIT Press.

Stillings, N., M H. Feinstein, J. L. Garfield, E. L. Rissland, D. A. Rosenbaum, and S. Weisler and L. Baker-Ward. 1987. Cognitive Science: An Introduction. Cambridge, Mass.: MIT Press. (3rd printing, 1989.)

Strozer, J. R. 1990. Non-native Language Acquisition from a Principles and Parameters Perspective (this volume).

Toulmin, S. and J. Goodfield. 1965. The Discovery of Time. New York: Harper and Row. (Phoenix ed., 1982.)

Tsur, R. 1983. What is Cognitive Poetics? The Katz Research Institute for Hebrew Literature. Tel Aviv University. (Papers in Cognitive Poetics, 1)

von Neumann, J. 1951. The General and Logical Theory of Automata. In Jeffress, ed.

von Neumann, J. 1955. Mathematical Foundations of Quantum Mechanics. Princeton, N.J.: Princeton University Press.

von Neumann, J. 1958. The Computer and the Brain. New Haven: CT.: Yale University Press.

Wasow, T. 1989. Grammatical Theory. In Posner, ed.

Watson, J. D. 1968. The Double Helix: A Personal Account of the Discovery of the Structure of the DNA. Text, commentary, reviews, original papers. Ed. by Gunther S. Stent. New York: Norton, 1980.

Watson, J. D. 1976. Molecular Biology of the Gene. 3rd. ed. Menlo Park, CA: Benjamin/Cummings. (1st ed., 1965; 2nd, 1970)

Watson, J. D., N. H. Hopkins, J. W. Roberts, J. A. Steitz, and A. M. Weiner. 1987. Molecular Biology of the Gene. Menlo Park, CA: Benjamin/Cummings. (Revised and greatly expanded co-authored new ed. of Watson 1976)

Webelhuth, G. 1986. Cartesian Philosophy in the Study of Language. University of Massachusetts M. A. Thesis.

Weinberg, S. 1977. The First Three Minutes: A Modern View of the Origin of the Universe. Bantam. (Updated ed., Basic Books, 1988)

Weinberg, S. 1983. The Discovery of Subatomic Particles. Scientific American Library.

Wexler, K. 1978. Review of John Anderson, Language, Memory and Thought. Cognition 6, 327-51.

White, G. A., and C. Newman, eds., 1972. Literature in Revolution. New York: Holt.

Wiener, N. 1956. I am a Mathematician: The Later Life of a Prodigy. Garden City, NY: Doubleday.

Wilson, A. C. 1985. The Molecular Basis of Evolution. Scientific American 253, 164-73.

Witten, E. 1970. Pronominalization: A Handbook for Secret Agents. Unpublished ms.

Will, C. M. 1986. Was Einstein Right?: Putting General Relativity to the Test. New York: Basis Books.

Winston, P. H., and S. A. Shellard, eds., 1990. Artificial Intelligence at MIT: Expanding Frontiers. Cambridge, Mass.: MIT Press.

Wollheim, R., ed., 1974. Freud: A Collection of Essays. Garden City, NY: Anchor Books Doubleday.

Non-native language acquisition from a Principles and Parameters perspective

Judith R. Strozer *
University of Washington

0 Introduction.   It is not a new idea that the recently developed Principles and Parameters (P&P) approach to language theory (Chomsky 1981, 1986a,b, 1988b, and references therein) represents 'a very radical departure from the tradition of study of language over the past several thousand years' (Chomsky 1989: 501).   In sharp contrast with traditional grammar, the new theory presents a radically new way of understanding the nature and 'acquisition' (growth) of a first language and it makes possible a deeper study than possible heretofore of a central cognitive structure.

It also makes possible refined or entirely new 'applications'.   One of these is a far more sophisticated study of nonnative language acquisition (NNLA) than was conceivable before the 1980s.[1] It seems that, at long last, it has become possible to take a fresh look at the fundamental issues raised by NNLA and to examine from a new perspective problems of language acquisition and language teaching that have resisted insightful treatment or have not been investigated at all.

To this day perhaps the most detectable influence of generative grammar on language teaching has been of a negative character: The evidence it provides in support of innate knowledge, and the related emphasis on freedom of choice and creativity, has been used as a helpful resource against

---

*This paper is a revised and updated version of Strozer (1987), which began as an extended comment on two then recent papers: Clahsen & Muysken (1986) and its critique by duPlessis et al. (1987). Since then, Clahsen & Muysken (1989) have revised their views along lines that appear to converge to some extent with the view presented here. A similar position is adopted in Hilles (1989).

I have benefited from many discussions of the topic with Carlos Otero, who has also provided a running commentary on the successive versions.

[1] This terminological innovation appears to be unavoidable. The terms 'second language acquisition'/ 'second language learning' can be quite misleading. From the perspective adopted here, the crucial distinction is between what Chomsky calls growth of language (first, second, third, or *n*th), that is, the process by which a child develops native or perfect mastery of a language, and what I am calling nonnative acquisition of a foreign language (second, third or *n*th) after the critical period. The term 'acquisition' seems preferable to 'learning' to refer to the process of developing an imperfect, but sometimes remarkably proficient, mastery of a foreign language, which the postulated limited availability of the LAD makes possible. This usage of the terms 'acquisition' and 'learning' is not to be identified with that of Krashen (1982) (see Gregg 1984: 79-80 *et passim*). Cf. Salkie (1990: 22-23).

behavioristic approaches to language learning -- a resource which can still be used to good effect, one may add. As Cook reports (1988: 171-72), 'the negative use of Chomsky's creativity argument is widespread among language teachers up to the present day and is still cited in Stern (1983), Harmer (1983), Howatt (1984) and Richards and Rodgers (1986), to take a small sample of methodological texts, none of which cite any work by Chomsky later than 1968.'

However, a crucial, if not often clearly articulated, question has always been the role of the genetic endowment in nonnative language acquisition, more precisely, the role of the language faculty or Language Acquisition Device (LAD), a particular version of Universal Grammar (UG) being simply the linguist's theory of this human cognitive system. As Cook goes on to say, 'if the students' minds were equipped with an ability to acquire language, a LAD, the best course of action for the teacher is the *laissez-faire* approach of supplying sufficient samples of language for LAD to make use of; students would acquire language much better without teacher interference.' In fact, the very limited, unsystematic, and impoverished primary linguistic data that are sufficient for the child should be sufficient for the adult speaker under the assumption of full availability of the LAD. One of the purposes of this paper is to suggest that this is no longer a very plausible hypothesis, if it ever was (see section 2.3).

To be sure, the question of the role of the LAD in NNLA continues to be a central one. As duPlessis et al. (1987) put it, in their critique of Clahsen and Muysken (1986), 'UG or not UG, that is the question.' It comes then as no surprise that there has recently been much debate over whether the LAD is available in nonnative language acquisition. This appears to be a welcome development, since it might contribute to a better understanding of what is at issue and it might lead to a deeper understanding of the nature and growth of language by opening a new window on the study of unconscious linguistic knowledge and on the process of acquisition. Hopefully, it could even have a beneficial impact on the teaching of foreign languages.

The new work on the nature and development of NNLA with a central interest in explanation has a very short history.[2] Among the earliest and

---

[2] Cf. Rutherford (1988: 404-405): 'L2 [second language] acquisition study would be difficult to trace back more than perhaps fifteen years. Moreover, this brief history is one that is characterized, until only two or three years ago, largely by exclusively data-driven descriptive work . . . It is essentially a record of research 'in need of', if not implicitly 'in search of', theories of L2 acquisition within which to accommodate and account for the data being described . . . There is a fundamental distinction to be drawn, however, between the kind of research just described and particular kinds of L2 acquisition study that have begun to emerge within the last two or three years.' Cf. Broselow (1988), Flynn (1988), the editors' Introduction to Flynn and

most extensive contributions based on the P&P framework are those of Flynn (from 1980 on) and Liceras and White (from 1983 on, in the wake of White's 1982 book on language acquisition). Some of the most interesting papers have appeared in a new journal, *Second Language Research*, founded in 1985. Of special interest in this context is that perhaps the earliest book-length monograph is on *The Spanish Nonnative Grammar of English Speakers* (Liceras 1986), and that Spanish is one of the languages more often studied and mentioned. Perhaps the most representative collections of papers from the new perspective to date are the ones edited by Flynn and O'Neil (1988), essentially a revised and expanded version of the proceedings of a conference held at MIT in October 1985, and Gass and Schachter (1989). A general introduction and overview recently became available (White 1989).

A convenient point of departure for this paper is provided by two extreme and contradictory positions: the one presented in Clahsen and Muysken (1986) and the alternative defended in a reply by duPlessis et al. (1987). The first paper claims that there is no reason to believe that UG plays any role in NNLA, a thesis which the reply attempts to refute. The counterclaim is that the thesis that UG is not available is false. The critics distinguish between two alternatives:

(i) L1 [first language] and L2 [second language] acquisition are alike, with UG mediating both in identical fashion, and

(ii) the interlanguages of L2 learners fall within the range of grammars permitted by UG, but UG does not operate in identical fashion in L1 and L2 acquisition.

The latter is the alternative duPlessis et al. (1987: 57) argue for. In their view, 'adults may initially assume the wrong parameter settings for the L2, either because of misleading properties of the L2 input or because they transfer settings from the L1,' so that 'there will be intermediate stages in L2 acquisition when the adult learner shows evidence of having set only some of these parameters appropriately.'

In what follows, as in Strozer (1987), it is suggested that neither of the two extreme positions has been established, that there is strong evidence against the claim that UG plays no role in NNLA, and that the counterclaim appears to be implausible. What seems to be at issue is not so much whether

---

O'Neil (1988), Lightbown and White (1987), Newmeyer (1987), Newmeyer and Weinberger (1988), and references therein. It is interesting to compare what was seen as 'new frontiers' in NNLA fifteen years ago (cf. Schumann and Stenson 1974) and now (cf. Gass and Schachter 1989).

the LAD is involved in nonnative language acquisition (it seems reasonable to assume that it is, since there is a *prima facie* case for the assumption, as we will see), but rather the nature and extent of this involvement.

In this paper I suggest that a reasonable alternative to the contradictory theses of these two articles is readily available within the P&P framework. The first step is to break the question 'UG or not UG?' into two subquestions:

> (Q1) Are the invariant principles of UG operative in the process of non native language acquisition?

> (Q2) Can the parameterized principles be fixed once more for a new language after the critical period?

I also suggest that a negative answer to the question of whether the parameters can be appropriately set by the adult acquirer would appear to carry significant implications for the design and execution of a successful foreign language program. Sections 1 and 2 address each of these two purposes in turn. The main topics of the first section are the implications of the critical period hypothesis (1.1), the relation between the existence of invariant principles and the logical problem of NNLA (1.2), and the relation between two instantiations of parametrized principles and some properties of NNLA (1.3). The topics discussed in the second section are the relation between language theory and the choice of a method of instruction (2.1), the relation between scientific grammars and pedagogic grammars (2.2), and a range of options for language programs (2.3). The paper closes with a brief conclusion.

1 Language acquisition after the critical period. The basic fact to be addressed in the investigation of Q1 and Q2 is that all normal children are totally successful at acquiring the language or languages of their communities, while most adults do not succeed in developing a native-like mastery of a single foreign language.[3] Some would claim that no adult is likely to be totally successful as a foreign-language acquirer, the existence of exceptional

---

[3] Child-adult differences in language acquisition have been widely discussed (cf. the 1982 collection by Krashen et al. and references therein). Bley-Vroman (1989) identifies nine fundamental characteristics of foreign language learning, among them lack of general guaranteed success, general failure (aside from rare exceptions), wide variation in success, course, strategy, and goals, fossilization, need for instruction and negative evidence, and lack of clear grammaticality judgments. It is well known that immigrant children acquire the indigenous language more easily, rapidly, and thoroughly than their parents, who are not always less intelligent or resourceful than their offspring.

individuals (Obler 1987, Obler and Fein forthcoming) notwithstanding.[4] 'We say that a child of five and a foreign adult are on their way towards acquiring English,' writes Noam Chomsky (1988a), 'but we have no way to designate whatever it is that they *have*'; 'the child, in the normal course of events, will come to *have* English (at least partially and erroneously), though the foreigner probably will not.'[5] It is, in any case, uncontroversial that presently available tools reveal no relevant differences in degree of success in the acquisition of a native language among children, whereas the differences between any two post-pubescent acquirers can be considerable, even vast. This sharp disparity, which is somewhat paradoxical (the greatest success is achieved by the least developed organisms, which are in fact less capable at most things than adult organisms), demands explanation.[6]

1.1 Some implications of the critical period hypothesis. An explanation for the sharp disparity between acquisition of language in childhood and later in life was not an issue when behaviorism was the order of the day. Most psychologists of the 1950s held, with Skinner, that language acquisition (more generally, acquisition of any kind) is a question of drive and reinforcement contingencies, while others held that it is a question of talent.[7] Interest in behaviorist approaches dropped off rapidly with the emergence of generative grammar (Chomsky 1957), the revival of a notion of localization (traceable to the pioneering ideas of Franz Joseph Gall), and the related idea of 'cerebral dominance' (Penfield and Roberts 1959), which converged with the notion of a LAD. The convergence was soon to be exploited by Lenneberg, who in his 'major study of language and biology (1967), now recognized as a classic in the field' (Chomsky 1980: 185), argues forcefully for a 'critical period' for language acquisition.[8] According to the Critical Period

---

[4] Not everyone agrees. For example, Gregg writes (1984: 81): 'Of course, some adults do attain native-speaker competence in a second language, and of course such competence is largely unconscious; no one has ever denied this.' He stresses, however, the need 'to explain just why it is that so few adults successfully acquire a second language' (1984: 80).

[5] It is interesting to compare the quoted remark with a similar one he made two years earlier: 'When we ask what language a child of five, or a foreigner learning English, is speaking, . . . we say that the child and foreigner are "on their way" to learning English, and the child will "get there," though the foreigner probably will not, except partially' (Chomsky 1986c: 1). Cf. Chomsky (1986a: 16).

[6] It is characteristic of humans to have evolved a strikingly longer period of infancy than other species, which has been taken to suggest that this period may have singular adaptive value (cf. Turkewitz and Kenney 1982).

[7] Among these, there were some who made considerable efforts to quantify language aptitude in order to provide a reliable measure for predicting success in the classroom (see Neufeld 1978 for a brief overview).

[8] For a brief reassessment a few years later, see Lenneberg (1971).

Hypothesis (CPH), some specific growth can only take place in the maturing organism during a particular time span (a very early one). As Lenneberg put it in a concise summary (1967a) of his book,

> all the evidence suggests that the capacities for speech production and related aspects of language acquisition develop according to built-in biological schedules. They appear when the time is ripe and not until then, when a state of what I have called 'resonance' exists . . .
>
> Language development thus runs a definite course on a definite schedule; a critical period extends from about age two to age 12, the beginning and the end of resonance.

Two dimensions of the hypothesis as understood by Lenneberg are of particular interest here.[9] One may be dubbed 'the use it or lose it hypothesis' or 'the exercise hypothesis': During an early period of their life, humans have a capacity for mastering languages; if the capacity is not exercised during this period, it is lost. A clear endorsement of this dimension of the CPH is given by Chomsky (1988: 179) in the Managua lectures. He begins by offering what he takes to be a parallel case as illustration: There is a certain age at which a pigeon has to fly, but if it is kept in a box beyond that age (beyond 'maybe two weeks or so') and then is let out of the box, it will never be able to fly.[10] Chomsky goes on to say that 'it is very probable that language is something like that': 'Something must happen to the brain about the time of puberty.'[11] A study approximating a direct test of this dimension of the CPH is that of a Los Angeles woman referred to as 'Genie' in the literature, deprived of language experience until age 13, who was not able to learn even the rudiments of the 'computational system' of a first language after puberty (Curtiss 1977, 1988; cf. Chomsky 1980: 57).

The second dimension of the CPH may be called 'the maturational decline hypothesis': During an early period of their life, humans have a capacity for mastering languages; if the capacity is exercised during this period, it begins to decline when the period is over. As Lenneberg (1967: 176) put it, 'automatic acquisition from mere exposure to a given language seems to disappear after this age and foreign languages have to be taught and learned through a conscious and labored effort'; in particular, 'foreign

---

[9] For a related, but not identical, view, see Johnson and Newport (1989: 63-65).

[10] Another possible illustration, perhaps more widely known, would be the critical period for the cat visual system, as described in a much admired 1963 paper by Hubel and Wiesel.

[11] This is, of course, a sort of educated guess, since nobody knows much about the matter at present.

accents cannot be overcome easily after puberty.' This, of course, is not to deny that 'a person can learn to communicate in a foreign language at the age of forty' (and presumably later). The remarks by Chomsky quoted at the beginning of this section (to the effect that the child, 'in the normal course of events,' will come to *have* a native language, 'though the foreigner probably will not') appear to be an expression of a similar view. The claim seems to be that there is something special about a child which makes it perfectly natural not only for a first language, but also for a second or a third or an *n*th one, to 'grow' (Chomsky's term) in its brain. This special capacity of the child is not available after a certain (early) maturational stage.

Lenneberg's hypothesis has triggered much controversy, and even disparagement, in the intervening years, in spite of the fact that 'it is in accord with results from other behavioral domains in which critical periods have been hypothesized' (Johnson and Newport 1989: 95), but no one appears to have come up with a plausible alternative to a critical period for language acquisition extending from infancy to some prepubescent stage.[12] In fact, the evidence accumulated in the last twenty years, including evidence from the study of acquisition of American Sign Language and from the study of NNLA (Johnson and Newport 1989: 61-68), provides considerable support for it.[13] The results now available suggest that 'entirely non-maturational

---

[12] Cf. Walsh and Diller (1981: 3-5), which assumes that there is 'overwhelming behavioral evidence' that the views presented in Penfield (1953, 1964) and Lenneberg (1967) are not correct and purports 'to explain biologically why children sometimes appear to be the better language learners when adults in fact are superior in most respects.' See now Gleitman (1986), Newport (1990). What has not received support from subsequent work is the particular neurological mechanism Lenneberg proposed to explain the critical period (cf. Krashen 1975, 1981). Also, it has been suggested that the gradual decline in the capacity for NNLA 'begins well before puberty,' but 'it also appears that this early decline is small, and that another more major change occurs around puberty.' In a particular study of first language growth distinguishing 'native learners' (exposed to American Sign Language from birth by their deaf parents), 'early learners' (first exposed to ASL between the ages of 4 and 6), and 'late learners' (first exposed to ASL at age 12 or later), the '4-6 age group scored consistently, although not always significantly, below native performance'; in a particular study of NNLA, 'the age 3-7 group scored at ceiling.' 'Further research is therefore necessary to determine with certainty the exact point at which a decline in learning begins for second language acquisition' (Johnson and Newport 1989: 96). Interestingly, there appears to be 'a consistent decline in performance over age for those exposed to the language before puberty, but no systematic relationship to age of exposure, and a leveling off of ultimate performance, among those exposed to the language after puberty' (Johnson and Newport 1989: 79; cf. Harley 1986).

[13] The failure of ultimate attainment characteristic of NNLA (in most cases at least), and in particular the fact that 'transitional grammars' or 'interlanguage grammars' (Selinker 1972) often fossilize (Tollefson and Firn 1983) in a state that bears little resemblance to the ultimate target language, could perhaps be counted as additional evidence for the CPH. See 1.3.

explanations for the age effects would be difficult to support' (Johnson and Newport 1989: 91).[14]

An explanation for the sharp disparity between acquisition of language in childhood and later in life is available in terms of P&P theory, which sheds much light upon a plausible specific interpretation of the CPH, which properly understood is not at odds with the possibility that some aspects of the LAD remain active after puberty.[15]   As in the study of first language growth, in the study of foreign language acquisition the crucial question is what it is that is acquired (knowledge or competence), which is rarely addressed in NNLA research. The term 'competence' is frequently used, but 'unfortunately the distinction between ability and knowledge has all too often been blurred, with a concomitant loss of clarity and coherence' (Gregg 1990: 20).

1.2   Invariant principles and the logical problem of NNLA.   The fact that adult acquirers are rarely, if ever, fully successful in their attempts to develop a native-like mastery of a foreign language is, of course, perfectly consistent with the idea that there is a 'logical problem of NNLA' (White 1985b).   Although the knowledge internalized by advanced adult acquirers reflects their experience in some manner, they appear to know things about the foreign language beyond their experience.   It is natural to see here a case of 'Plato's problem' and one might wonder to what extent it overlaps with the case of 'Plato's problem' presented by first language growth.   It is reasonable to assume there is some overlap.   Like first language growth, adult language acquisition poses in a sharp and clear form 'the problem of 'poverty of stimulus', of accounting for the richness, complexity and specificity of shared knowledge given the limitations of the data available,' in Chomsky's words. A great many cases have been given over the years to illustrate this fundamental problem.   Perhaps the most familiar one is the structure-

---

[14] This is not to say that experiential and attitudinal variables play no role whatsoever, only that they cannot explain the disparity between child and adult at issue. The obvious question is: Why are such variables of no significance in first language growth? Needless to say, the contrary view has never lacked advocates, the latest reference that has come to my attention being Salkie (1990: 92-93). Cf. Gregg (1984: 90ff). It goes without saying that the CPH is not incompatible with the hypothesis that the differences between the special talents and attitudes of two particular individuals might help explain the disparity in their success as adult language acquirers. Nor is it inconsistent with a number of other ideas found in the literature, for example, the idea that the 'successful learners' -- 5 percent, according to an often cited article in the field (Selinker 1972, Jordens 1987) -- employ a set of strategies that is quite different from the set employed by all others.

[15] Experimental evidence is still to come. There are few studies on 'the competence ultimately achieved in the second language' and 'none of these directly examined grammatical competence in the second language' (Newport 1990: 18); for a review of the literature, see Johnson and Newport (1989).

dependence of rules, 'the fact that without instruction or direct evidence, children unerringly use computationally complex structure-dependent rules rather than computationally simple rules that involve only the predicate "leftmost" in a linear sequence of words,' to quote Chomsky again (1986a: 7).[16] It appears that we can substitute 'adult acquirers' for 'children' in the quote without changing its truth value. Thus, no speaker of Spanish capable of constructing minimally appropriate mental representations experiences much difficulty with the fact that the question corresponding to (1) is (2b), not (2a).

(1)   El estudiante que es reflexivo es estudioso.
        'The student who is thoughtful is studious.'

(2) a. *¿Es el estudiante que reflexivo es estudioso?
        'Is the student who thoughtful is studious?'

    b. ¿Es el estudiante que es reflexivo estudioso?
        'Is the student who is thoughtful studious?'

Another case is provided by the binding theory, as illustrated in (3) and (4).

(3) I wonder who [the men expected to see them].

(4) [The men expected to see them].

As Chomsky points out, both (3) and (4) include the clause given in brackets, but only in (3) may the pronoun be referentially dependent on the antecedent 'the men'. Numerous facts of this sort, he goes on to say,

> are known without relevant experience to differentiate the cases. They pose a serious problem that was not recognized in earlier work: how does every child know, unerringly, to interpret the clause differently in the two cases?; why does no pedagogic grammar have to draw the reader's attention to such facts (which were, in fact, not even noticed until quite recently ...)? (Chomsky 1986a: 8)

---

[16] Perhaps it should be mentioned in passing that the first empirical study of this question, with 3-5-year-old children (Crain and Nakayama 1987), was carried out almost 30 years after the completion of Chomsky's *The Logical Structure of Linguistic Theory*, which is somewhat surprising, given the often heard complaint that the results of early generative grammar had little to offer the experimental psychologist.

The same is essentially true of a foreign speaker of English who has attained a certain level of proficiency in the language.

Both principles, structure-dependence and binding, are exemplified in the sentences of (5) and (6) (needless to say, in the first example the person who jumped may be Juan, while in the second example the person who jumped cannot be Juan).

> (5) Cuando saltó, Juan sonrió.
> 'When he jumped, John smiled.'

> (6) Saltó, cuando Juan sonrió.
> 'He jumped, when John smiled.'

Or in the sentences of (7), which are structurally very different.

> (7) a. El estudiante que escribió el ensayo lo distribuyó.
> 'The student who wrote the essay distributed it.'

> b. El estudiante que lo escribió distribuyó el ensayo.
> 'The student who wrote it distributed the essay.'

Again, a foreign speaker of Spanish with a certain level of proficiency in the language does not find it especially difficult to see that *lo* 'it' refers to (is referentially dependent on) *el ensayo* 'the essay' in both (7a) and (7b).

A more subtle point can be made with examples (8) through (11):

> (8) John ate an apple.

> (9) John ate.

> (10) John is too stubborn to talk to Bill.

> (11) John is too stubborn to talk to.

If we were to interpret (10)-(11) on the analogy of (8)-(9), it should be that (11) means that John is so stubborn that he (John) will not talk to some arbitrary person. But, as Chomsky notes, the meaning is in fact quite different, namely, that John is so stubborn that some arbitrary person won't talk to him (John). Again, he goes on to say, this is known without training or relevant evidence; what is more, children do not make errors about the interpretation of such sentences as (10)-(11), 'and if they did, the errors would largely be uncorrectable.'

What is crucially important for our purposes is that, at least to a considerable extent, the same is true of the fluent nonnative speaker, a fact that can be readily explained by assuming that the invariant principles of language (which didn't come to mature in Genie's brain, it appears) continue to play a role beyond the critical period. Furthermore, the properties of (10) and (11) reappear in their Spanish translation, as we would expect, but with an additional twist, to which we return in 1.3.

The conclusion that nonnative language acquisition is in some important respect not unlike first language acquisition (cf. Berwick 1985, Hyams 1986) does not lack antecedents in the area of foreign language acquisition research.[17] The evidence adduced in support of a claim of this nature comes from the similarities observed in the process of learning a foreign language by native speakers of very different languages, contrary to what the assumptions of the 'contrastive analysis' approach--which postulated the effect of 'interference' and tried to relate specific difficulties to particular features of the student's native language--would lead us to believe. A counterclaim of the critics of contrastive analysis was that the acquisition of at least some elements of a particular target language by speakers of a number of diverse languages proceeds in the same order regardless of the specific properties of those elements in the native language of the acquirer and the degree to which they differ from their counterparts in the target language (cf. Krashen 1981: 51ff.) In addition, it was observed that there is sometimes great similarity among the errors made by speakers of very different languages in the process of studying a particular target language (say, English, the most intensely researched case). This similarity, and the specific types of error patterns, suggest that some errors are not entirely due to specific differences between the native language of the acquirer and the target language, contrary to what the 'contrastive analysis' approach predicts.[18]

More recent studies within the new framework by Felix, Flynn, White, and others (some included in Flynn and O'Neil 1988 and Gass and Schachter 1989) have attempted to show that adult acquirers are sensitive to the effects of subjacency, directionality, and proper government (among others), in

---

[17] See Flynn (1987), and section 2.2, for discussion. Cf. Kellerman and Sharwood Smith (1986); Odlin (1989).

[18] From the perspective of the P&P framework, the contrastive approach, properly understood, may be indispensable, aside from the fact that few have ever doubted that it can shed light on, for example, the difficulties Spanish speakers experience with stop sounds at the end of the word or with contrasts such as 'beat'/'bit', 'sip'/'zip', 'bowel'/'vowel'. Cf. James (1971) (and more generally, Nickel 1971) and James (1980).

ways that cannot be explained in terms of simple inductive learning strategies from surface data or in terms of explicit teaching.[19]

In evaluating this type of work, we must be careful not to be misled by irrelevant factors. Consider the two Spanish sentences in (12a) and (12b), which differ only in the presence or absence of *el* 'the', the masculine singular form of the definite article.

(12) a. Lamento haber perdido la clase.
'I regret having missed the class.'

b. Lamento el haber perdido la clase.
'I regret (the) having missed the class.'

Some speakers of Spanish take the two forms as alternative expressions of something like the meaning conveyed by the English gloss, and some linguists are no more able to find any essential difference between them (see Plann 1981 for discussion). However, many of the native speakers who share this belief would readily find the second of the questions in (13) less acceptable than the first.

(13) a. ¿Qué lamentas haber perdido?
'What do you regret having missed?'

b. *¿Qué lamentas el haber perdido?
'What do you regret (the) having missed?'

Are adult acquirers of Spanish capable of this type of deeply rooted discrimination at some point in their development? Suppose a preliminary exploration suggests that the answer is negative at a particular level of proficiency. The result may still be perfectly consistent with the thesis that the invariant aspects of subjacency are accessible to language users after the critical period. The judgment failure may simply show that the acquirers are not or not yet capable of assigning examples such as (13b) the underlying structure assigned to it by native speakers. Presumably, if they were, their reaction would be analogous to the reaction elicited by some other violation

---

[19] The earliest study about the availability of subjacency (as understood before Chomsky 1986b) in NNLA is Ritchie (1978), which suggests that Japanese subjects learning English do not violate the principle (cf. Rutherford 1984). (Gregg 1984, n. 7, finds it 'quite possible' that errors such as *The student of chemistry is older than the one of physics* 'can be explained without having to claim that UG is being violated,' a conjecture that is likely to have wide application.) Results about the effects of subjacency interpreted as showing the opposite are reported in Johnson and Newport (1990).

of the Complex Noun Phrase island constraint (e.g., by the unacceptable *¿Qué lamentas el hecho de haber perdido? 'What do you regret the fact of having missed?'). In other words, invariant principles are expected to yield the right results only when applied to the mental representation of an appropriate 'structural description' of the sentence at issue (in our case, a structure which presumably includes a silent noun analogous to hecho).[20]

Summing up section 1.2, we may say that the thesis that at least some invariant principles of the LAD remain active after the critical period appears to be a highly plausible one. There is no obvious better alternative to explain facts such as those briefly reviewed above. Recent work suggests that the thesis is true, although we may still be far from knowing to what extent. It seems a fair guess that stronger evidence is obtainable and perhaps will soon be available.

1.3 Parametrized principles. Turning now to the claims about 'parameter resetting' in the course of NNLA, it is natural to ask how persuasive they are.

The first thing that one should keep in mind in evaluating such claims is that even if it were to be shown that the output of an adult acquirer is indistinguishable from the output of native speakers, it would not follow that the parameters of the foreign language have been set in the mind/brain of the adult acquirer, let alone that they have been fixed exactly the way they are fixed in the mind/brain of the native speaker. As is well known, radically different grammars can generate identical outputs. It follows that 'correctness' of output is not a sufficient basis to conclude that the parameters of the language under consideration have been set in the mind/brain of the adult acquirer in a native-like fashion. The most that can be claimed is that the output of the adult acquirer is consistent with such a conclusion. To go beyond this, the study must be carried out in far more indirect and subtle ways than have been used so far. A description of properties of some output and a description of a system of unconscious knowledge not unlike the system of a native speaker are very different things.

A second, no less obvious point is suggested by the fundamental difference between the generative procedure of a native speaker of a particular language L and a successful translation skill of an individual from a particular language L' to L. It is important to keep in mind that although such a skill (equivalently, a machine translation program) could be developed in principle, it would not necessarily provide insight into our understanding of the native speakers' knowledge or of their use of their knowledge.

---

[20] The importance of phonological representations in the theory of foreign language phonology is stressed in a forceful and illuminating way in Ard (1989).

With these preliminary observations in mind, consider a basic systematic difference between languages such as English or French and so called 'Null Subject' (or 'Pro-Drop') languages such as Spanish or Italian. As is well known, *arrived yesterday (John)* is inadmissible in English, while its counterpart *llegó ayer (Juan)* is common in Spanish. From a contrastive analysis point of view, it would be natural to hypothesize the overuse of pronominal subjects by anglophone students of Spanish, as was in fact done in the first contrastive grammar of Spanish for English students (Stockwell, Bowen, and Martin 1965). This prediction, however, does not seem to be correct. Since, on the other hand, hispanophone students of English tend to underuse pronominal subjects, we may be tempted to conclude that we have 'very indirect support for the hypothesis that acquisition to omit the subjects is easier than acquisition to put them in obligatorily' (something still to be established); but is it reasonable to go on to say that the difference between the two languages 'does not pose a sufficiently serious problem for the English speaker learning Spanish to warrant comment' (Phinney 1987: 232) or that 'resetting the pro-drop parameter from English and French to Spanish is not difficult with respect to null subjects'. (Liceras 1989: 126)?[21] Some skepticism seems to be in order. Consider again examples (10) and (11), repeated here for convenience:

(10) John is too stubborn to talk to Bill.

(11) John is too stubborn to talk to.

As mentioned above, the properties of these examples reappear in their Spanish translation, as one would expect, but with an additional twist. The Spanish string can have either the sense of (10) or the sense of (11), as (14) shows:

(14) Juan es demasiado terco para hablar con él.
    'John is too stubborn to talk to (him).'

Similarly, when the finite subjunctive form *hable* 'that he may talk' is substituted for the infinitive *hablar* 'to talk' as in (15), the sentence can translate as either (16a) or (16b).

---

[21] Liceras (1989: 129) goes on to conclude that her results 'provide evidence for the unmarked status of the pro-drop option,' but she does not elaborate. She is aware (n. 3) that her conclusion is inconsistent with the subset principle, since the Spanish system is the less constrained (cf. Dresher and Kaye 1990: 166). Relevant recent discussion can be found in Bloom (1990), Valian (1990), and references therein. See also Kean (1986).

(15) Juan es demasiado terco para que hable con él.
Juan is too stubborn for that talk (SUBJ.) with him.

(16) a. John is too stubborn for him to talk to him.

b. John is too stubborn to talk to him.

But (17) only has the sense of (16a).

(17) Juan es demasiado terco para que él hable con él.
Juan is too stubborn for that he talk (SUBJ.) with him

Now we can ask whether the contrast between (15) and (17) 'warrants comment' and the answer seems to be that the question has not even been raised. It would also be interesting to know whether nonnative speakers of Spanish such as those studied by Phinney and Liceras have native mastery of expressions with overt and silent subject pronouns of the type investigated in Larson and Luján (1990). Examples (18a) and (18b) show the contrast between an obligatory silent pronoun (18a) and an optional silent pronoun (18b) (italics indicate identity of intended coreference).

(18) a. Cuando *pro/*él* trabaja, *Juan* no bebe.
'When he works, Juan doesn't drink.'

b. Cuando el director insiste en que *pro/él* trabaje,
Juan no bebe.
'When the director insists that he work,
John doesn't drink.'

The contrast is perhaps even clearer in the two mini-discourses of (19) and (20), which exemplify an interesting and not immediately obvious parallelism between the two languages (capitals indicate contrastive emphasis).

(19) a. ¿Quién cree Juan que ganará el premio?
'Who does John think will win the award?'

b. *Juan* cree que **pro/él* ganará el premio.
'John thinks *he/HE will win the award.'

(20) a. ¿Qué cree Juan que obtendrá en el concurso?
'What does John think he will get in the competition?'

b. *Juan* cree que *pro/*él* ganará el premio.
'John thinks he/*HE will win the award.'

Again, correctness of output, hard to attain as it might be, is by itself no guarantee of unconscious knowledge of the language analogous to the knowledge of the native speaker.

In an earlier study, Liceras found that 'verb-subject inversion and *that-t* effects did not have the same status as null subjects in the respective interlanguages', but drew the reasonable conclusion that 'this is not evidence against the possible relationship among the three properties' (1989: 114, 129). If the three properties followed from one and the same parameter, the absence of one of them from the output may be reason enough to conclude that the value of the parameter has not been fixed. The close inter-relationship of these or other properties would in any case offer a better chance to determine whether nonnative language acquirers succeed in fixing the value of the relevant parameter. In the case under consideration, other properties have been proposed (in addition to missing subjects, free inversion of subject, and apparent violations of the so-called *that-t* filter), including empty resumptive pronouns in embedded clauses, long wh-movement of subject (Chomsky 1981,section 4.3), and so-called 'Clitic Climbing', as recently argued by Kayne (1989).

If Kayne is on the right track, the reason why there is no French analogue (21c) to the Spanish example (21a) or the Italian example (21b) is the same reason why there is no Modern French analogue of *llueve/piove* 'rains'.

(21) a. Juan los quiere ver.

b. Gianni li vuole vedere.

c.* Jean les veut voir.
'Juan/ Gianni/ Jean wants to see them.'

Linguists are not in agreement about the underlying structure of this class of sentences. It has recently been argued (Picallo 1990), on the basis of data from Catalan, that their underlying configuration, in relevant respects, is essentially as follows (with TP in place of Picallo's IP, to use the same notation that will be used in (22).

(22)   TP (=Tense Phrase)

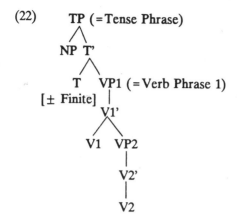

Now consider Spanish ambiguous strings such as the one in (23).

(23) El niño lo puede beber.
   'It is possible that the child drinks it.'
   'The child is able to drink it.'

Picallo proposes that in the underlying structure associated with the first sense (possibility), the finite form of the modal verb *poder* is generated under T and *beber* 'to drink' under V1 (in which case the VP2 subtree is not part of the configuration), while in the underlying structure associated with the second sense (ability) only the tense specification is generated under T, the infinitival form of *poder* being generated under V1 and later adjoined to T, and *beber* is generated under V2. If this proposal, or a proposal of a similar nature, turns out to be on the right track, then it is easy to see that to establish that the 'pro-drop' parameter has been set at the Spanish value by the postpubescent language acquirer will be no simple matter. Still, we are far from having exhausted the complexities of this aspect of Spanish. In particular, nothing has been said so far about the generation of the subject and related problems (cf., for example, the French data analyzed in Sportiche 1988 with the wider range of options available in Spanish.)

   The nature of these and other facts suggests the need for more indirect and subtle ways of gaining reliable information. In the case of the family of phenomena under consideration, the output is complex enough to make it possible to test the ability of the adult acquirers to derive facts that they might not be consciously aware of, including those in (24).

(24) a. La caja que contiene el paquete es redonda.
'The box that contains the package is round.'
'The box that the package contains is round.'

b. ¿Qué caja contiene el paquete?
'Which box contains the package?'
'Which box does the package contain?'

c. ¿Qué caja dices que contiene el paquete?
* ¿Qué caja dices contiene el paquete?
'Which box do you say contains the package?'
'Which box do you say the package contains?'

Nonnative speakers of Spanish who have properly 'reset' the 'pro-drop' parameter at the Spanish value should at least be able to detect the ambiguity in each of the examples in (24) and to provide appropriate interpretations. They should also be able to determine that (25b) is no less grammatical than (25a).

(25) a. Creo que los estudiantes están contentos.
'I believe that the students are happy.'

b. Los estudiantes creo que están contentos.
'The students I believe that they are happy.'

Many other types of tests can be devised to delve deeper, but this brief sample is perhaps sufficient to give an idea of what is at issue. There are, of course, many other possibilities which have not been tried, each of which could provide crucial evidence as to whether the parameter has been properly 'reset' at the Spanish value by an adult speaker. It should also be kept in mind that evidence against the possibility of 'resetting' in the case of a single parameter not transparently reflected in the output may be enough to cast serious doubts about 'resetting' in general for the adult acquirer(s) involved. One would not expect to find that a speaker failed to fix one of the parameters of his/her native language but succeeded in fixing all the others.

As an illustration, consider a precisely defined parametric option in the light of recent discussion of a major systematic difference between English and Romance first characterized in Emonds (1978). If the proposal in Pollock (1989), refined and developed in Chomsky (1988b), and insightfully criticized and revised in Iatridou (1990), is on the right track, the relevant structure of a sentence, technically a TP, in English or French, may be represented as in (26) (some phrase nodes such as NegP or the nodes immediately dominating Adv need not be present).

(26)

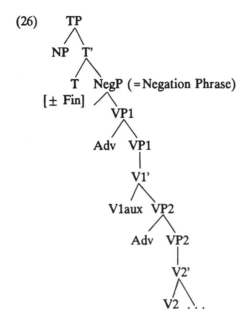

The part of the proposal that is relevant to the point to be made is that Adv(erb) is generated in the same underlying positions in English and French, and presumably in Spanish and other languages as well (different classes of adverbs have different base-generated positions). The disparity in the surface positions of adverbs in English and French is claimed to be due to a difference in the movement of the verb: Every French verb moves past the adverb to its left, leaving behind a trace *t*, and adjoins to the finite tense node [T, +Fin], thus explaining the contrast in outputs, as in (27).

(27) a. John often kisses Mary.

  b. Jean *embrasse* souvent *t* Marie.

In English, on the other hand, only auxiliary verbs adjoin to T, which explains the structural parallelism in (28).

(28) a. John *has* often *t* kissed Mary.

  b. Jean *a* souvent *t* embrassé Marie.

The basis for this contrast between English and French is argued to be the value (+ or -) of a parameter P: French finite Tense is strong (i.e., [+P]), while English finite Tense is weak (i.e., [-P]), and weak T elements block the transmission of the thematic properties of a main verb to its trace, while a strong T element does not. Therefore only nonthematic verbs will move toward T in English.

We can now ask whether the output of highly accomplished anglophone speakers of French who rarely or never make a mistake when using examples such as (27b) and others involving the same parameter, provides evidence that their unconscious knowledge of French derives from having fixed P at value [+], and the opposite for highly accomplished francophone speakers of English.[22] It is immediately obvious that more than mere strict 'correctness' of the output is required to make a positive answer plausible. After all, strict 'correctness' of output (no easy matter in this case if the language acquirer is to go beyond the above examples to encompass the full range of facts) can be obtained resorting to very different strategies.[23]

Anglophone speakers of Spanish have to deal with additional differences, since Spanish lines up with French when there is no auxiliary, as in (27c), but differs from both French and English (cf. 28) in not favoring the French/English word order and in allowing linear orders not allowed in English or French in examples such as the following (cf. Zagona 1988):

(27) c. Juan besa a menudo a María.
   Juan kisses often María
   'Juan often kisses María.'

(29) a. ?* Juan ha a menudo besado a María.
   Juan has often kissed María

  b. Juan ha besado a menudo a María.
    Juan has kissed often María

  c. Juan a menudo ha besado a María.
    Juan often has kissed María

  d. Juan ha besado a María a menudo.
    Juan has kissed María often

---

[22] The picture is of course more complicated, as is to be expected, but the present sketch is enough for our purposes.

[23] For example, place an adverb of class C after a finite main verb or after a finite form of *avoir* 'to have', and other rules of thumb that native speakers don't have to resort to. Cf. Gregg (1984: 83-84).

e.   A menudo Juan ha besado a María.
      Often Juan has kissed María

It is a fair assumption that the choice among these options is a principled one for native speakers. Can the same be said about those that most successfully learned Spanish late in life, even in their teens?

Summing up section 1.3, we may say that the thesis that adults are capable of parameter fixing in the process of NNLA has not been demonstrated. Furthermore, it does not appear to be plausible.[24] The failure of ultimate attainment characteristic of many, perhaps most (if not all), adults, and in particular the fact that 'interlanguage grammars' often fossilize in a state that bears little resemblance to the ultimate target language, suggests that a form of the Critical Period Hypothesis that places the burden of explanation on the unavailability of parameter fixing after a certain stage of maturation (certainly after puberty) appears to be quite plausible in the light of the evidence now available.[25] Needless to say, this conclusion does not commit us to positing 'general learning strategies,' as proposed by Clahsen and Muysken (1989). Obviously, the mind has capacities beyond the language faculty (Chomsky 1975: 210), and 'language-like systems might be acquired through the exercise of other faculties of mind, though we should expect to find empirical differences in the manner of acquisition and use in this case' (Chomsky 1980: 28).

---

[24] A simpler case to explore may be the acquisition of the stress system of a particular language, for example, the acquisition of the English stress system by speakers of Spanish. It has been argued that all of the stress patterns that occur in a set of data from hispanophone speakers of English taken to be representative 'can be generated by the target stress system' under the hypothesis that 'second language learners fail to apply rules of rime extrametricality that are highly marked in their native language' (Mairs 1990: 281). One could adopt an approach along the lines of that in Dresher and Kaye (1990) and try to show that each of the required parameters has been appropriately fixed by the adult learners.

[25] If it is true of the LAD in general that at least some of its principles 'remain active in adult acquisition, while parameter-changing raises difficulties', as the work of Flynn on NNLA suggests to Chomsky (1988c: n.6), 'then the steady state would be the state where all parameters are fixed,' in which case the distinction between perception and acquisition (which the Cartesians failed to distinguish) 'might be a matter of some subtlety.' Chomsky (1988b, n. 23) has also noted that 'there are empirical consequences to these assumptions,' since 'they entail that at the steady state attained in language acquisition,' the LAD invariant principles are 'wired-in,' and 'remain distinct from language-particular properties,' hence distinct from 'the acquired elements of language, which bear a greater cost.' As he put it a few months later (1989a),

It seems that invariant principles of language count as 'less costly' than those that reflect particular parametric choices. Intuitively, it is as if the invariant principles are 'wired in' and therefore less costly than language specific properties. If this is correct, then in the steady state of mature knowledge of language, there must still be a differentiation between invariant principles of the biological endowment and language-specific principles.

2 Implications for language teaching. Since a principled way of teaching a foreign language must be based on some understanding of the nature of language that is at least on the right track, linguistic theory may have implications for the design of a language program, of which at least some are 'perhaps of a rather negative sort' (Chomsky 1989: 108): If the underlying view of language structure is irredeemably wrong, if the concept of language assumed is diametrically opposed to a reasonable one, the method of instruction can do more harm than good.

It is then natural to turn at this point to a major theorist who 'used to be a language teacher for children and also for college students' (Chomsky 1989: 274; cf. 502) and 'was able to develop a number of very strong claims about acquisition simply by stating the problem' in the way he did; in fact, his model of language, generative grammar, 'is really no more (or less!) than a description of the problem of language acquisition' (Gleitman and Wanner 1982: 7).

2.1 Language theory and method of instruction. Immediately after noting that a child is something like a pigeon that will never be able to fly if kept in a box beyond a certain age at which pigeons have to fly (beyond 'maybe two weeks or so') and that 'very probably' human language is not unlike bird flying in this respect (see section 1.1), Chomsky goes on to draw the conclusion that

> For the language teacher, that means that you simply cannot teach a language to an adult the way a child learns a language. That's why it's such a hard job. (Chomsky 1988: 179)

This consequence of the CPH suggests that he is not an advocate of the 'natural method' in any form that ignores crucial changes in the brain between the early years of childhood and later years (cf. Whitaker 1978, Albert and Obler 1978, Obler 1988). We also know that he is strongly against the method called 'pattern practice', in which a certain linguistic pattern is just repeated over and over again. As is well known, this was a direct outgrowth of behavioristic psychology (including linguistics). A quote from Bloomfield's *Outline Guide for the Practical Study of Foreign Languages*, published in 1942, may serve as illustration:

> It is helpful to know how language works, but this knowledge is of no avail until one has practiced the forms over and over again until he can rattle them off without effort. Copy the forms, read them out loud, get them by heart, and then practice them over and over again day after day, until they become entirely natural and familiar. Language learning is overlearning; anything less is of no use.

Bloomfield's treatise, which provided only a point of departure, was to guide the theory and practice of language teaching for decades.   The following echo (to mention just one) appears in a treatise in its wake written by a professor of foreign language education at Yale almost a quarter of a century later (Brooks 1964):

The single paramount fact about language learning is that it concerns not problem-solving, but the formation and performance of habits. The learner who has been made to see only how language works has not learned any language; on the contrary, he has learned something he will have to forget before he can make any progress in that area of language.

For a behaviorist, language learning 'is kind of like catching a ball or something like that' (Chomsky 1988: 181), a view which leads naturally to 'pattern practice' as a method of instruction. Not surprisingly, the model was not successful. The most obvious reason for the failure appears to be that such 'pattern practice' is extremely boring:

Learning doesn't achieve lasting results when you don't see any point to it. Learning has to come from the inside; you have to want to learn. If you want to learn, you'll learn no matter how bad the methods are... And if you use methods which are designed to ensure that no sensible person could possibly pay attention, then there's no hope. (Chomsky 1988: 181-82)

A particularly illuminating assessment of this method of foreign language instruction is to be found in a 1968 interview in which Chomsky stresses that it is 'a very bad way, certainly an unprincipled way, to teach language' because the underlying view of language structure is 'entirely erroneous.' It is 'based on the assumption that language really is a habit structure, that language is a system of skills and ought to be taught by drill and by the formation of stimulus-response associations,' hence it is not 'a method that is based on any understanding of the nature of language' (Chomsky 1989: 108-9).   This is a case in which psychologists and linguists 'have caused a good deal of harm by pretending to have answers to [the relevant] questions and telling teachers . . . how they should behave' (Chomsky 1988: 180).
    Underlying this assessment is the belief that our understanding of the nature of language seems to show quite convincingly that, contrary to what is assumed in a behavioristic approach, 'with its emphasis on habit and skill and pronunciation ability,' 'language is not a habit structure'; rather, 'it has a kind of creative property and is based on abstract formal principles and operations of a complex kind' (Chomsky 1989: 109,108). As Chomsky put it

in the closing words of his celebrated address at the Northeast Conference on
the Teaching of Foreign Languages in August 1965, 'research in the coming
years . . . will show that certain highly abstract and highly specific principles
of organization are characteristic of all human languages, are intrinsic rather
than acquired, play a central role in perception as well as in production of
sentences, and provide the basis for the creative aspect of language use.' It
is ideas such as these that 'may have some potential impact on the teaching
of language.' In the 1968 interview, he went on to express the feeling that

> from our knowledge of the organization of language and of the principles
> that determine language structure one cannot **immediately** construct a
> teaching program. All we can suggest is that a teaching program be
> designed in such a way as to give free play to those creative principles
> that humans bring to the process of language-learning, and I presume to
> the learning of anything else. I think we should probably try to create **a**
> **rich linguistic environment** for the **intuitive heuristics** that the normal
> human automatically possesses. (Emphasis supplied.)

Summarizing, we may say that what Chomsky was advocating a quarter
of a century ago was a principled teaching program, based on some
understanding of the nature of language, which relies and counts mostly on
the student's mind and goes some way toward creating 'a rich linguistic
environment for the intuitive heuristics that the normal human automatically
possesses.' In section 2.2, we consider one possible way of contributing to
bringing about a particularly rich linguistic environment.

2.2 Scientific grammars and pedagogic grammars. As is well known,
Chomsky has repeatedly emphasized that 'the concerns of traditional and
generative grammar are, in a certain sense, complementary.' A representative
recent characterization is the following:

> A good traditional or pedagogical grammar provides a full list of
> exceptions (irregular verbs, etc.), paradigms and examples of regular
> constructions, and some general observations about the form and
> meaning of expressions. But it does not examine the question of how the
> reader of the grammar uses such information in attaining the capacity to
> form and interpret new expressions . . . With not too much exaggeration,
> one could describe such a grammar as analogous to the data presented
> to a child learning a language. Generative grammar, in contrast, was
> concerned primarily with the intelligence of the reader, the principles and
> procedures brought to bear to attain full knowledge of a language.
> (Chomsky 1986a: 6-7; cf. 1980: 237)

The foregoing discussion suggests that from the perspective of the Principles and Parameters theory a good pedagogical grammar will differ from both a traditional and a generative grammar. It will differ from a generative grammar in assuming that at least some of the invariant principles of language need not be specified in detail, since they will be automatically provided by the LAD. But, crucially, it will differ from a nongenerative grammar in that it will provide a pedagogically appropriate but full account of the significant differences between the native language of the student and the target language. In particular, it will systematically present and draw the student's attention to many simple facts illustrating differences between the two languages that are not found in even the most compendious traditional or teaching grammars, or were not even noticed until quite recently.

This will be particularly true of the facts that can be traced to the effects of the parameters. The so-called 'rules' of traditional grammars are really only hints that presuppose that the acquirer already knows the basic structure of language, and they don't have much to say about the effects of the values of the parameters, which cannot be taken for granted by a pedagogic grammar. In the case of the study of a foreign language, an up-to-date pedagogic grammar will attend to the parametric differences between the target language and the native language of the acquirer, thus showing considerable factual overlap with a more technical and perhaps wider ranging comparative grammar.[26] It would seem that only such a parametrically oriented grammar can provide a reliable basis for either successful textbooks or the design of informed and carefully planned language teaching programs of foreign languages. With not too much exaggeration, one could describe such a pedagogic grammar as analogous to the data used by the linguist studying the language.

To illustrate briefly, a pedagogic grammar of Spanish has to incorporate somehow the information that would allow the student to derive only the non-starred examples of (30)- (31) (Campos 1986: 356).

(30) a. Es obvio que necesita gafas.
'It's obvious that he/she needs glasses.'

b. Que necesita gafas es obvio (=30a)
'That he/she needs glasses is obvious.'

---

[26] For a very impressive early attempt at an up-to-date reference grammar for native speakers, see Renzi (1988). The contributors to the first volume (of three planned) are P. Benincà, A. Calabrese, M. Castelli, G. Cinque, P. Cordin, L. Frisson, A. Giorgi, G. Longobardi, A. Marcantonio, M. Nespor, L. Rizzi, G. Salvi, and M. Scorretti.

(31) ¿Pepe necesita gafas?   'Does Pepe need glasses?'

   a. Es obvio que necesita.   'It is obvious that he needs.'

   b. *Que necesita es obvio.   'That he needs is obvious.'

It should also incorporate crucial facts about the *ser/estar* 'to be' contrast, a hallmark of Spanish (and a few other Romance languages). For example, recent work (Torrego 1989, Strozer 1989) suggests that there is a close interrelation between this contrast and the properties of individual-level/stage-level predicates (independently discovered). Consider examples (32) -(34).

(32) a. * Ana es orgullosa de su triunfo.
         'Ana is (*ser*) proud of her triumph.'

   b. Ana está orgullosa de su triunfo.
       'Ana is (*estar*) proud of her triumph.'

   c. Ana es/está orgullosa.
       'Ana is (*ser/ estar*) proud.'

(33) a. Ana es merecedora de su triunfo.
         'Ana is (*ser*) deserving of her triumph.'

   b. *Ana está merecedora de su triunfo.
       'Ana is (*estar*) deserving of her triumph.'

   c. *Ana es/está merecedora.
       'Ana is (*ser/ estar*) deserving.'

(34) a. Ana parece lista.
         'Ana seems clever/ready.'

   b. Ana me parece lista.
       'Ana seems clever/*ready to me.'

An even more subtle point is suggested by the observation that the Portuguese structural equivalent of (35) is ambiguous and can be disambiguated by pseudo-clefting, as in (36) (Raposo and Uriagereka 1990: 531).

(35) Encontramos a Luis cansado.
'We found Louis tired.'

(36) a. Lo que encontramos allí __ fue a [Luis cansado].
'What we found there __ was Louis tired.'

    b. A quien encontramos __ [cansado] fue a [Luis].
'Who we found __ tired was Louis.'

In (36a), where *[Luis cansado]* is a small clause and *cansado* is a stage-level predicate, we find a state of affairs: that of Louis being tired; in (36b), where *[cansado]* is a secondary predicate, specifically an individual-stage level predicate, we find an individual who is tired. One may suggest that there is still another (third) interpretation: In (36b) (minus *allí*), *cansado* can be understood as 'tiresome', perhaps a less shiftable instantiation of an individual-level predicate. Compare the contrast in (37), noticed by Torrego (for Castillian Spanish).

(37) a. Juan parece cansado.
'John seems tired/tiresome.'

    b. Me parece cansado hablar con tanta gente.
'It seems tiresome to talk to so many people.'

    c. Es/*está cansado hablar con tanta gente.
'It is (*ser/ *estar*) *tired/tiresome to talk with so
many people.'

It is true that a specific language teaching program cannot be directly derived from even the most illuminating results of the comparative study of the native language and the target language, but such results could at least provide boundary conditions for the range of empirically based programs with a fair chance to achieve a considerable level of success. It is hardly in doubt that, other things being equal, a teacher who is thoroughly familiar with what is known about the subject matter will be able to do a better job than one who is not. The students invariably benefit from the preparation and knowledge of their teachers, consistently reflected in the information they provide. Adult language acquisition is no exception. The little relevant information available suggests that the proper use of grammatical knowledge (not necessarily overt in the teaching) can make a contribution to successful teaching (cf. Roca 1979). In particular, it can contribute to making the subject interesting. As Chomsky has stressed again and again, 'at any level, from the nursery to graduate school, teaching is largely a matter of encouraging natural development,' so 'the best *method* of teaching is to make it clear that the subject is worth learning, and to allow the child's or adult's natural curiosity and interest in truth and understanding to mature and develop' (Chomsky 1989: 502). Surprising properties such as the one exemplified in (37) are likely to be of interest to some language students.

In this context, it seems clear that the *laissez-faire* approach to teaching referred to at the beginning of this paper is quite inappropriate. If it is true that the parameters for a new language cannot be fixed after the critical period, there is no similarity between the child and the adult acquirer with respect to the range of data needed to learn the language. Rather, the similarity in range of data is between the adult language acquirer and the linguist, who is in need of far more evidence, and far more sophisticated information, than that provided by the primary linguistic data. No language program involving English and French, for example, will deserve high marks if it does not include an appropriate number of carefully selected and selectively contrasted 'minimal pairs' such as those in (28) and (27). More generally, the differences between French and English that Kayne and others have been writing about since the early 1980s, which are interesting in themselves, can only help the French textbook writer. The same could be said of recent work on other Romance languages, the ones more relevant in this context.[27] It would seem that the preparation of language materials that meet the standards that can now be envisioned--standards already much higher than what was barely conceivable in the late 1970s, a not insignificant fact--will require both far more solid linguistic knowledge and more considerable pedagogical sophistication than a generation ago. The informed and responsible language teacher is likely to welcome these developments and to build on them.

We have seen that there are two classes of facts which need not be learned by the child. The first class, discussed in section 1.2, includes knowledge which is innate and completely independent of experience. The second class, discussed in section 1.3, is automatically derived once the value of each parameter has been fixed, but choosing the proper value for each parameter requires linguistic experience even in native language acquisition. For example, once the parametric values have been fixed, the facts

---

[27] See, in particular, Belletti and Rizzi (1981) and subsequent work by them and others. Among the book-length studies, Burzio (1986), for example, contains a wealth of data that a textbook writer may find helpful, and so does Zagona (1988).

exemplified in (21) do not have to be learned by the native speakers of Spanish/ Italian and French, respectively; they follow from the values of the parameters in each of the languages. The situation appears to be different, however, in NNLA. This is a problem for both the student and the teacher. On the other hand, the facts derived from innate knowledge need not be taught in any case.[28]

2.3 A range of options for language programs. What is it, then, that the postpubescent language student has to learn? It is clear that a necessary step for everyone is to learn the lexical items of the language and their properties. This would be an impossible task for anyone not born with a conceptual system in place. Fortunately for every human, to a large extent this task seems to reduce to 'a problem of finding what labels are used for preexisting concepts, a conclusion that is so surprising as to seem outrageous but that appears to be essentially correct nevertheless' (Chomsky 1988: 134). The family resemblance between the labels of the native language of the student and the target language seems to facilitate the task, possibly giving an advantage to the adult.[29] However, the fact is that the postpubescent student will be no match for the child along other dimensions. We all know about 'foreign accents',[30] perhaps due to changes in the brain (Penfield 1953), but this doesn't seem to be the only disadvantage of the adult. Just think that at age 3 or earlier a native speaker of English may exhibit a command of the verb-particle construction that will forever elude even highly proficient adult acquirers, and may matter-of-factly correct, instantly and unhesitantly, the errors of the grown-ups.

This first necessary step may be close to being a sufficient one for those interested just in 'communication'. It is no secret that 'we can often make out what is said in a foreign language when we can identify some of the words, impose a thematic and aitiational structure and use contextual cues, even without much knowledge of the grammar,' a feat which in some ways is

---

[28] For examples from Spanish, see Chomsky (1988: 16, 24f, 45, 63f, 91, 99, 111f, 119, and passim).

[29] For example, the difference in maximum lengths of intensive language courses (e.g., 20 weeks for German, Spanish, Italian, or French, 24 for Dutch, Swedish, or Portuguese, 44 for Russian, Arabic, or Japanese) at the Foreign Service Institute of the U.S. State Department (Odlin 1989: 39) seems to reflect in part the proportion of cognate vocabulary and the transparency of the relation.

[30] It has been repeatedly observed that although adults can often communicate in a foreign language, native-like pronunciation is virtually unattainable after puberty, if not years earlier (cf. Seliger et al. 1975, Broselow 1987). Scovel (1969) discusses the notable case of Joseph Conrad, who acquired English as a young adult well enough to become a major English fiction writer without ever overcoming his nonnative (Polish) accent.

not unlike 'normal comprehension under noisy conditions in our own language' (Chomsky 1980: 56). But in the case of foreign-language acquirers, this success would surely not lie in their possession of knowledge of the language that they hear, apart from peripheral aspects, a fact some foreign language teachers and researchers tend to forget.

Another aspect of the language both the child and the adult must learn is the irregularities (Chomsky 1980: 238), although, again, child and adult may learn them in very different ways. This is likely to be true also of the morphological regularities.

Both the child and the adult face a similar problem of language acquisition. They both have to internalize a system that accounts for the distribution of ungrammaticality (*) in cases such as those exemplified above and numerous other instances (in fact, an infinite number of them), well beyond the sample the child is exposed to or the adult is exposed to. In other words, the paradigms of interrelated facts must be derivable from a simple set of principles that ideally should be internalized by language acquirers if they are to go beyond the utterances they memorize and those they appear to construct 'by analogy' with those they are exposed to.[31] To carry out this task, they both have to rely heavily on the inborn invariant principles of language.

At this point the similarities appear to end. It is an indisputable fact that all normal children are perfectly capable of unconsciously determining the values of the languages of their communities, without training or instruction. In sharp contrast with this, adults appear to encounter insurmountable difficulties when they stubbornly try to duplicate the effortless feat of the child. The research now available does not offer much reason to suppose that it is possible to set the values of the parameters for another language after childhood, even with the help of negative evidence (correction) and other resources not available to the child (see 1.3). The well-known facts in section 1.1 suggest that only a brain undergoing early maturation makes linguistic parameter-setting possible. Extremely accomplished language acquirers report that their mastery of a foreign language differs in nontrivial ways from their mastery of their native languages, and presumably there is much they are not aware of. To give just one example, for students interested in more than 'communicating' (cf. Gregg 1984: 83, 1990: 35), it may not be a secret that the type of sentence exemplified in (38) is admissible in Spanish, or that it is not admissible in French, but being error-free on this score is a far cry from their representing and computing the structure

---

[31] Recall (1.2) that the appeal to 'analogy' is quite misleading and that even identity fails to give the right results in some of the paradigm examples above and innumerable other cases.

underlying (38a) or the structure underlying (38b) as a native speaker does (see Kayne 1990).

(38) a. Juan no sabe si ir al cine.

   b. *Jean ne sait si aller au cinéma.

   'John doesn't know whether to go to the movies.'

This is not to deny that the output of some of the highly accomplished foreign language acquirers may be difficult to distinguish from that of a native speaker, and may even be superior to the output of the native speaker in some way (richness of vocabulary, effectiveness of expression, and so on). Clearly, not all native speakers of English come close to matching the achievement of Joseph Conrad, for example. But even in the best cases, nonnative performance is likely to involve a great deal of conscious or half-conscious 'patchwork' on the part of the speaker, who, for all we know, is using strategies and auxiliary routes that the native speaker does not have to resort to. This appears to be related to the fact that adults acquire languages in ways at great variance with the course of native language acquisition, or so it seems (cf. Van Naerssen 1980), not to mention the well-known fact that when we learn a foreign language, we tend to concentrate on the respects in which it differs from our own.

It is precisely at this point that a good pedagogic grammar, based on the best available linguistic research, can be the most helpful. There is much that the student-teacher team can do to smooth what otherwise could turn out to be a very rough and not very rewarding ride. First and foremost, the teacher can begin by providing a carefully selected and properly graded pool of reliable and revealing facts, as needed for further advancement, including 'input either in the form of grammar teaching, or correction, or other forms of emphasis on particular structures' (White 1987c: 108) geared toward further goals. This may, in fact, be 'a teacher's most important job' (Gregg 1984: 94). At the very least, the adult's data base must contain revealing evidence for the conscious mind about the parametric properties that are unconsciously known by the native speaker. To be concrete, part of the challenge for the teacher of Spanish to speakers of English is to open the way to some generative system of knowledge (presumably not isomorphic with that of the native speaker) from which such facts as those exemplified in (15) and (17) are derivable. It would seem that linguistic research can make a contribution here. This expectation is not inconsistent with an awareness of the limits of well-established theory in fields such as psychology and linguistics. Recall Chomsky's 1966 assessment, which cannot be lightly dismissed:

The applications of physics to engineering may not be seriously affected by even the most deep-seated revolution in the foundation of physics, but the applications of psychology or linguistics to language teaching, such as they are, may be gravely affected by changing conceptions in these fields, since the body of theory that resists substantial modification is fairly small.

Still, much progress has been made in the last quarter-century, particularly in the last decade, and the avenues recently opened appear to hold a great deal of promise.

There is nothing negative or pessimistic about the conclusion that a foreign language can be acquired only through persistent study, and that a teaching program can provide only necessary but not sufficient help. A high level of success in this enterprise, after years of sustained effort, is, in a way, a far greater individual achievement than coming to master a language natively. A human language is a system of remarkable complexity, but coming to have native mastery of it is not something that the child does; rather, it is something that happens to the child, any normal child (Chomsky 1988: 134). In contrast, the challenge posed by a relative mastery of a foreign language, which involves will and deliberate choice, is met with a high degree of success only by some. Paraphrasing Chomsky (1975: 4), we may say that to come to know a foreign language is an extraordinary intellectual achievement for a brain not especially designed for postpubescent language acquisition even with the help of extended exposure, negative evidence, and specific training. Relative mastery of a foreign language appears to go even a step further than relative mastery of, say, mathematics or physics through conscious and sustained effort (there are students who are quite successful in mathematics or physics and total failures in the study of a foreign language, we may note in passing). In the case of a foreign language, conscious knowledge is at most a first step (Gregg 1984: 81), since 'there is no reason to believe that a person could consciously master a grammar as a guide to behavior'; rather, 'people learn language from pedagogic grammars by the use of their unconscious universal grammar (and for all we know this may be unavoidable in principle)' (Chomsky 1975: 248, n.24). Thus every fluent speaker of Spanish unconsciously knows, without having to learn it from a book, that (2a) is not the question associated with (1), or that Spanish sentences such as (5)-(6) have the properties determined by the binding theory. And were speakers to be made conscious of principles that lead to these results, 'there is little doubt that these principles could not be consciously applied in real time, to "guide" performance' (1975: 249). Since this is also true of the parametrized principles for native speakers, which we are assuming cannot be determined after the critical period, post-pubescent language students must find a way of applying, in real time, the alternative systems they use, perhaps based in part on what they consciously know, which 'will be a rather ill-defined and, perhaps, a scattered and chaotic subpart of the coherent and important systems and structures' (Chomsky 1975: 165) that they unconsciously know.

A possible bonus of the type of language study which takes advantage of some of the results of comparative language research now available is that it may shed considerable light on one's own language. It is a common idea, sometimes attributed to Goethe, that those who know only their own language do not 'know' their language, or at least they are not consciously aware of many of the fascinating particular properties of the language they speak natively. Comparative study of two languages at some level of sophistication provides an understanding of how language works, which might shed much light on one's native language, hence on whatever the student ends up doing in life. As Edwin Williams has put it, 'Leonardo da Vinci learned anatomy in order to paint better; when you understand the internal structure of something, you can do more with it.'[32]

The already available results of research on the nature of language make it possible for the creative language teacher, and more generally the educator, to aim at a higher goal. It could be argued that the study of mathematical logic and the study of scientific grammar should be at the core of any well-designed curriculum. If a person unaware of the Copernican revolution is not considered 'educated', why should a person who is unaware of the revolution in our understanding of language be considered 'educated' in the 1990s? Chomsky elaborates on this theme in a letter to a teacher, written March 4, 1984:

> I don't see how any person can truly be called 'educated' who doesn't know the elements of sentence structure, or who doesn't understand the nature of a relative clause, a passive construction, and so on. Furthermore, if one is going to discuss literature, including here what students write themselves, and to come to understand how it is written and why, these conceptual tools are indispensable.
>
> For this purpose, I think traditional grammar so-called (say, the grammar of Jespersen) remains today a very impressive and useful basis for such teaching. I can't see any reason for teaching [behavioristic] structural grammars of English, or for teaching transformational grammar **in the manner of some instructional books that I have seen** (I really don't know the literature very well at all), which simply amount to memorizing meaningless formulas. (Emphasis supplied.)

---

[32] Quoted in *Princeton Weekly Bulletin* 80: 6, 22 Oct, 1990, p. 2.

These observations may come as something of a surprise to those given to quoting out of context the following remark from his 1966 'famous and influential address' (Stern 1983: 327) at a conference of foreign-language teachers: 'I am, frankly, rather skeptical about the significance, for teaching languages, of such insights and understanding as have been attained [up to 1966] in linguistics and psychology' (Chomsky 1966: 43). But as has been occasionally pointed out (e.g., in Diller 1978: 139), this is just one more instance in which Chomsky urges people to be cautious and skeptical of presumed expertise, and to think, assess, evaluate and decide for themselves. 'Teachers, in particular,' he stresses in the same address, 'have a responsibility to make sure that ideas and proposals are evaluated on their merits, and not passively accepted on grounds of authority, real or presumed.' 'The field of language teaching,' he continues,

is no exception. It is possible--even likely--that principles of psychology and linguistics, and research in these disciplines, may supply insights useful to the language teacher. But this must be demonstrated, and cannot be presumed. It is the language teacher himself who must validate or refute any specific proposal. There is very little in psychology or linguistics that can be accepted on faith.

In other words, teachers 'must certainly draw what suggestions and hints they can from psychological research, but they will be well advised to do so with the constant realization of how fragile and tentative are the principles of the underlying discipline' (Chomsky 1966: 45-46). As he put it twenty years later,

People who are involved in some practical activity such as teaching languages, translation, or building bridges should probably keep an eye on what's happening in the sciences . . .
I think it's a good idea to pay attention to what [linguistics] is doing and to see if it gives you some ideas that might enable a translator or teacher to do better, but that's really for the person involved in the practical activity to decide. . .
The proper conclusion, I think, is this: Use your common sense and use your experience and don't listen too much to the scientists, unless you find that what they say is really of practical value and of assistance in understanding the problems you face, as sometimes it truly is. (Chomsky 1988: 179, 180, 182).

Beyond this goal, the contemporary study of language can provide students with a way to understand how science works that could also be used to advantage in the teaching of foreign languages. All students have command of a huge mass of very puzzling facts about the language they speak, which they can compare or contrast with the facts of the target language. There are now explanatory theories of a rather nontrivial sort that explain some of these facts, and do so 'without resort to higher mathematics or other conceptual tools not available to the student (or teacher, generally).' Using this rarely exploited possibility, the student might be introduced into 'the marvelous world of inquiry in which one learns to wonder about the nature of what seem, superficially, to be obvious phenomena, and to ask why they are the way they are, and to come up with answers,' 'an experience generally lacking in the study of the sciences unless the instruction is done really superlatively well.' It is easy to see that these are all 'reasons for studying contemporary grammar--as a branch of science, which deals with questions of central human concern and which happens to be fairly accessible, as compared, say, with quantum physics' (Chomsky 1984).

A superb language teacher could aim at an even higher goal. Cognitive grammar can be taken as a model for other cognitive sciences, thus offering a difficult-to-match point of entry into the study of the human mind. This is an entirely new opportunity, undreamed of just a generation ago. It would be a great pity if today's students continue to leave the university as unaware of the ground-breaking discoveries of the second half of our century as their parents did. The challenge and the accomplishments of the study of language are both very real. If the study of language is to return gradually 'to the full scope of its rich tradition,' some way will have to be found 'to introduce the students to the tantalizing problems that language has always posed for those who are puzzled and intrigued by the mysteries of human intelligence' (Chomsky 1966: 595).

3 Conclusion. The thesis that at least some invariant principles of the LAD remain active after the critical period is a highly plausible one. Recent work suggests that some form of the thesis is true. It seems a fair guess that stronger evidence is obtainable and will perhaps be available in the near future.

On the other hand, the thesis that adults are capable of parameter fixing in the process of nonnative language acquisition (NNLA) has not been demonstrated. Furthermore, it does not appear to be plausible. The failure of ultimate attainment characteristic of adults, and the fact that 'transitional grammars' ('interlanguage grammars') often fossilize in a state that bears little resemblance to the ultimate target language, suggest that a form of the Critical Period Hypothesis that places the burden of explanation on the unavailability of parameter fixing after a certain stage of maturation (perhaps after puberty) appears to be quite plausible in the light of the evidence now available.

If this assessment of current understanding is on the right track, we can derive some implications for language teaching design. On the basis of the foregoing discussion, we would expect that, on the one hand, postpubescent students will not have difficulty with those aspects of a new language they encounter that derive from general unparametrized principles of human language, and, on the other, that they will experience considerable difficulty in the attempt to develop anything approaching native mastery of those aspects which derive from parametrized principles--perhaps the greatest difficulty in those areas in which the parametrization leads to divergent outputs in the native and the target language. This suggests that carefully selected and ordered input may play an especially important role in nonnative language acquisition (NNLA), and that recent advances in comparative grammar may have a contribution to make in the preparation of future textbooks and in the design of carefully planned language programs.

The sharp contrast between the child and the adult on this score also suggests that the data from NNLA will provide a new kind of evidence for the study of language in general, a welcome source of data given the impossibility of direct experimentation on humans to answer the many questions that arise. More than ten years ago it was pointed out that adult language acquisition data provide important evidence to motivate phonological descriptions (Kenstowicz and Kisseberth 1979). We are now beginning to see that the study of adult language acquisition may provide a new kind of evidence in the investigation of the theory of language. Work on NNLA could very well shed light on the nature and structure of the LAD, which is only beginning to be understood; in particular, it may help in our attempts at uncovering possible parametrized principles of grammar. When adult language acquirers come to know more than the linguistic environment has to offer, this may be a hint that an invariant principle is at work. When, on the other hand, adults experience difficulty in acquiring a particular systematic property of a target language, it may be an indication that a parametric difference is at stake, all other things being equal (see Introduction to Flynn and O'Neil 1988, and references therein). Needless to say, specific conclusions must be established on independent grounds, a tall order. Chomsky once remarked that 'for the conscious mind, not especially designed for the purpose, it remains a distant goal to reconstruct and comprehend what the child has done intuitively and with minimal effort' (Chomsky 1975: 4). It is a vast understatement to say at this point (just after a few of the earliest strivings to overcome the new challenge) that it remains a distant goal to reconstruct and comprehend what the postpubescent language-acquirer is capable of doing with enormous effort.

It has sometimes been pointed out that 'applied linguistics' has tended to be more concerned with its 'self-determination' as a discipline than with building bridges between the scientific study of language and the teaching of language. If the foregoing remarks are on the right track, this is about to change, if it is not already changing.   It is no longer utterly unlikely that 'the barriers that have impeded collaboration between theoretical linguists and those engaged in "applied" research will break down in the near future' (Newmeyer 1983: 148).   Hopefully it won't be long before we witness progress in answering questions of great interest to both the researcher and the teacher, and of great benefit to both teacher and student.

References

Albert, M., and L. Obler.   1978.   The Bilingual Brain: Neuropsychological and Neurolinguistic Aspects of Bilingualism.   New York: Academic Press.

Ard, J. 1989.   A Constructivist Perspective on Nonnative Phonology. In Gass and Schachter, eds., 243-59.

Belletti, A., and L. Rizzi.   1981.   The Syntax of *ne*: Some Theoretical Implications. The Linguistic Review 1, 117-54.

Berwick, R. 1985.   The Acquisition of Syntactic Knowledge. Cambridge, Mass.: MIT Press.

Bley-Vroman, R. 1989.   What Is the Logical Problem of Foreign Language Learning? In Gass and Schachter, eds., 41-68.

Bloom, P. 1990.   Subjectless Sentences in Child Language. Linguistic Inquiry 21, 491-504.

Bloomfield, L. 1942.   Outline Guide for the Practical Study of Foreign Languages. Baltimore: Linguistic Society of America.

Brooks, Nelson H. 1964.   Language and Language Learning Theory and Practice. New York: Harcourt.

Broselow, E. 1987.   An Investigation of Transfer in Second Language Phonology. In Ioup and Weinberger, eds., 350-351.

Broselow, E. 1988.   Second Language Acquisition. In Newmeyer, ed., vol 3, 194-209.

Burzio, L. 1986.   Italian Syntax: A Government-Binding Approach. Dordrecht: Reidel.

Campos, H. 1986.   Indefinite Object Drop. Linguistic Inquiry 17, 354-59.

Chomsky, N. 1957.   Syntactic Structures. The Hague: Mouton.

Chomsky, N. 1965.   The Current Scene in Linguistics: Present Directions. Paper presented at the NCTE convention in November 1965. It first appeared in College English 27:8 (May), 587-95. Reprinted in Reibel and Schane, eds., 3-12.

Chomsky, N. 1966.   Linguistic Theory. In R. G. Mead, Jr., ed., Language Teaching: Broader Contexts. (= Reports of the Working Committees, Northeast Conference on the Teaching of Foreign Languages, 1 August 1966.) Menasha, Wis.: George Banta, 43-49. Reprinted in Chomsky 1971, 152-59; also in Lester, ed., 1970, 51-60; 1973, 36-45, and in Oller et al., eds., 1973 (and 1975), 29-35.

Chomsky, N. 1969.   Some Observations on the Teaching of Language. The Pedagogic Reporter 21, 5-6, 13.

Chomsky, N. 1971.   Chomsky: Selected Readings. Edited by J. P. B. Allen and Paul van Buren.   London and New York: Oxford University Press. (= Language and Language Learning, 31)

Chomsky, N. 1975.   Reflections on Language. New York: Pantheon.

Chomsky, N. 1980.   Rules and Representations. New York: Columbia University Press.

Chomsky, N. 1981.   Lectures on Government and Binding. Dordrecht: Foris.

Chomsky, N. 1982.   Some Concepts and Consequences of the Theory of Government and Binding. Cambridge, Mass.: MIT Press.

Chomsky, N. 1984.   Noam Chomsky Writes to Mrs. Davis about Grammar and Education. English Education 16, 165-6.

Chomsky, N. 1986a. Knowledge of Language: Its Nature, Origin, and Use. New York: Praeger.

Chomsky, N. 1986b. Barriers. Cambridge, Mass.: MIT Press.

Chomsky, N. 1986c. Language and Problems of Knowledge. Paper presented at the Madrid Chomsky Symposium, April 28, 1986.

Chomsky, N. 1988. Language and Problems of Knowledge: The Managua Lectures. Cambridge, Mass.: MIT Press.

Chomsky, N. 1988a. Language and Interpretation: Philosophical Reflections and Empirical Inquiry. Paper presented at UCLA, January 28, 1988. To appear in the University of Pittsburgh Series on Philosophy of Science.

Chomsky, N. 1988b. Some Notes on Economy of Derivation and Representation. Paper delivered at UCLA, January 29, 1988. Now in MIT Working Papers in Linguistics 10, 43-74.

Chomsky, N. 1988c. Prospects for the Study of Language and Mind. Lecture delivered at the International Workshop on The Chomskyan Turn, Tel Aviv University, April 11, 1988. In A. Kasher, ed.

Chomsky, N. 1989. Language and Politics. Edited by Carlos P. Otero. Montreal: Black Rose.

Chomsky, N. 1989a. Language and Mind. The 'Darwin Lecture', delivered at Darwin College, Cambridge, January 1989.

Clahsen, H., and P. Muysken. 1986. The Accessibility of Universal Grammar to Adult and Child Learners. A Study of the Acquisition of German Word Order. Second Language Research 2, 93-119.

Clahsen, H., and P. Muysken. 1989. The UG Paradox in L2 Acquisition. Second Language Research 5, 1-29.

Cook, V. J., ed. 1986. Experimental Approaches to Second Language Acquisition. Oxford: Pergamon.

Cook, V. J. 1988. Chomsky's Universal Grammar: An Introduction. Oxford: Basil Blackwell.

Crain, S., and M. Nakayama. 1987. Structure Dependence in Grammar Formation. Language 63, 522-43.

Curtiss, S. 1977. Genie: A Psycholinguistic Study of a Modern Day 'Wild Child.' New York: Academic Press.

Curtiss, S. 1988. Abnormal Language Acquisition and the Modularity of Language. In Newmeyer, ed., vol. 2. 96-116.

Dato, D., ed. 1975. Developmental Psycholinguistics: Theory and Applications. Georgetown University Round Table on Languages and Linguistics. Washington, D.C.: Georgetown University Press.

Diller, K. C., 1971. Generative Grammar, Structural Linguistics, and Language Teaching. Rowley, Mass.: Newbury House.

Diller, K. C. 1978. The Language Teaching Controversy. Rowley, Mass.: Newbury House. (Revised edition of Diller 1971.)

Diller, K. C., ed. 1981. Individual Differences and Universals in Language Learning Aptitude. Rowley, Mass.: Newbury House.

Dresher, B. E., and J. D. Kaye. 1990. A Computational Learning Model for Metrical Phonology. Cognition 34, 137-95.

duPlessis, J., D. Solin, L. Travis, and L. White. 1987. UG or Not UG, That Is the Question: A Reply to Clahsen and Muysken. Second Language Research 3, 56-75.

Eckman, F., E. Moravscik, and J. Wirth, eds. 1986. Markedness. New York: Plenum Press.

Emonds, J. 1978. The Verbal Complex V'-V in French. Linguistic Inquiry 9, 151-75.

Felix, S. 1988. UG-Generated Knowledge in Adult Second Language Acquisition. In Flynn and O'Neil, eds., 277-94.

Flynn, S. 1980. The Effects of First Language Branching Direction on the Acquisition of Second Language. Paper presented at the Winter LSA Meeting, San Antonio, Texas.

Flynn, S. 1981. The Effects of First Language Branching Direction on the Acquisition of Second Language. In W. Herbert and J. Herschensohn, eds., Cornell Workings Papers in Linguistics. Ithaca, New York: Cornell University. 5-63.

Flynn, S. 1983. A Study of the Effects of Principal Branching Direction in Second Language Acquisition: The Generalization of a Parameter of Universal Grammar from First to Second Language Acquisition. Cornell University doctoral dissertation.

Flynn, S. 1985. Similarities and Differences between First and Second-language Acquisition: Setting the Parameters of Universal Grammar. In D. R. Rogers, and J. A. Sloboda, eds., Acquisition of Symbolic Skills. New York: Plenum, 485-99.

Flynn, S. 1987. A Parameter-setting Model of L2 Acquisition: Experimental Studies in Anaphora. Dordrecht: Reidel.

Flynn, S. 1988. Second Language Acquisition and Linguistic Theory. In Newmeyer, ed., vol. 2. 53-73.

Flynn, S. 1989. The Role of the Head-Initial/ Head-Final Parameter in the Acquisition of English Relative Clauses by Adult Spanish and Japanese Speakers. In Gass and Schachter, eds., 89-108.

Flynn, S., and W. O'Neil, eds. 1988. Linguistic Theory in Second Language Acquisition. Dordrecht: Kluwer.

Friedman, S., K. Klivington, and R.Peterson, eds. 1986. The Brain, Cognition, and Education. New York: Academic Press.

Gass, S., and J. Schachter, eds. 1989. Linguistic Perspectives on Second Language Acquisition. Cambridge: Cambridge University Press.

Gleitman, L. R. 1986. Biological Pre-programming for Language Acquisition? In Friedman et al., eds.

Gleitman, L. R., and E. Wanner. 1982. Language Acquisition: The State of the State of the Art. In Wanner and Gleitman, eds., 3-48.

Grimshaw, J., and S. T. Rosen. 1990. Knowledge and Obedience: The Developing Status of the Binding Theory. Linguistic Inquiry 21, 187-222.

Gregg, K. R. 1984. Krashen's Monitor and Occam's Razor. Applied Linguistics 5, 79-100.

Gregg, K. R. 1990. Second Language Acquisition Theory: The Case for a Generative Perspective. In Gass and Schachter, eds., 15-40.

Harley, B. 1986. Age in Second Language Acquisition. San Diego: College Hill Press.

Harmer, J. 1983. The Practice of English Language Teaching. London: Longman.

Hilles, S. 1989. Adult Access to Universal Grammar. UCLA doctoral dissertation.

Howatt, A. 1984. A History of English Language Teaching. Oxford: Oxford University Press.

Hubel, D., and T. Weisel. 1963. Receptive Fields of Cells in Striate Cortex of Very Young, Visually Inexperienced Kittens. Journal of Neurophysiology 26, 994-1002.

Hyams, N. 1986. Language Acquisition and the Theory of Parameters. Dordrecht: Reidel.

Iatridou, S. 1990. About Agr(P). Linguistic Inquiry 21, 551-77.

Ioup, G., and S. H. Weinberger, eds. 1987. Interlanguage Phonology: The Acquisition of a Second Sound System. New York: Newbury House.

Jaeggli, O., and K. Safir, eds. 1989. The Null Subject Parameter. Dordrecht: Kluwer.

James, C. 1971. The Exculpation of Contrastive Linguistics. In Nickel, ed. 1980. Contrastive analysis. London: Longman.

James, C. 1980. Contrastive Analysis. London: Longman.

Johnson, J., and E. Newport. 1989. Critical Period Effects on Second Language Learning: The Influence of Maturational State on the Acquisition of English as a Second Language. Cognitive Psychology 21, 60-99.

Johnson, J., and E. Newport. 1990. Critical Period Effects on Universal Properties of Language: The Status of Subjacency in the Acquisition of a Second Language. Ms., University of Virginia.

Jordens, P., ed. 1987. Interlanguage Development. Dordrecht: Foris.

Kasher, A., ed. 1991. The Chomskyan Turn. Oxford: Blackwell.

Kayne, R. 1981. On Certain Differences between French and English. Linguistic Inquiry 12, 349-71. Reprinted in Kayne 1984.

Kayne, R. 1984. Connectedness and Binary Branching. Dordrecht: Foris.

Kayne, R. 1989. Null Subjects and Clitic Climbing. In O. Jaeggli and K. Safir, eds., 239-61.

Kayne, R. 1990. Romance Clitics and PRO. To appear in Proceedings of NELS 20.

Kean, M. L. 1986. Core Issues in Transfer. In Kellerman, and Smith, eds.

Kellerman, E., and M. Sharwood Smith, eds. 1986. Crosslinguistic Influence in Second Language Acquisition. New York: Pergamon Institute of English.

Kenstowicz, M., and C. Kisseberth. 1979. Generative Phonology. New York: Academic Press.

Klein, W. 1986. Second Language Acquisition. Cambridge: Cambridge University Press.

Krashen, S. D. 1975. The Development of Cerebral Dominance and Language Learning: More New Evidence. In Dato, ed., 179-92.

Krashen, S. D. 1981. Second Language Acquisition and Second Language Learning. Oxford: Pergamon Press.

Krashen, S. D. 1982. Principles and Practice in Second Language Acquisition. Oxford: Pergamon Press.

Krashen, S. D., and L. Galloway. 1978. The Neurological Correlates of Language Acquisition. SPEAQ Journal 21, 21-35.

Krashen, S. D., R. Scarcella, and M. Long, eds. 1982. Child-Adult Differences in Second Language Acquisition. Rowley, Mass.: Newbury House

Larson, R., and M. Luján. 1990. Focused Pronouns. Ms., MIT/University of Texas.

Lenneberg, E. 1967. Biological Foundations of Language, New York: John Wiley.

Lenneberg, E. 1967a. The Biological Foundations of Language. Hospital Practice, December, 59-67. Reprinted in M. Lester, ed., 1970, 3-20.

Lenneberg, E. 1971. Of Language Knowledge, Apes and Brains. Journal of Psycholinguistic Research 1, 1-29.

Lester, M. 1970. Readings in Applied Transformational Grammar. New York: Holt. (Revised edition, 1973.)

Liceras, J. M. 1983. Markedness, Contrastive Analysis and the Acquisition of Spanish Syntax by English Speakers. University of Toronto doctoral dissertation.

Liceras, J. M. 1985. The Value of Clitics in Nonnative Spanish. Second Language Research 1, 151-68.

Liceras, J. M. 1986. Linguistic Theory and Second Language Acquisition. The Spanish Nonnative Grammar of English Speakers. Tübingen: Guntar Narr Verlag.

Liceras, J. M. 1989. On Some Properties of the 'Pro-Drop' Parameter: Looking for Missing Subjects in Nonnative Spanish. In Gass and Schachter, eds., 109-33.

Lightbown, P. M., and L. White. 1987. The Influence of Linguistic Theories on Language Acquisition Research: Description and Explanation. Language Learning 37, 483-510.

Mairs, J. L. 1990. Stress Assignment in Interlanguage Phonology: An Analysis of the Stress System of Spanish Speakers Learning English. In Gass and Schachter, eds., 260-83.

Neufeld, G. 1978. On the Acquisition of Prosodic and Articulatory Features in Adult Language Acquisition. The Canadian Modern Language Review 34, 163-74. Reprinted in G. Ioup and S. H. Weinberger, eds., 321-32.

Newmeyer, F. 1983. Grammatical Theory: Its Limits and Possibilities. Chicago: University of Chicago Press.

Newmeyer, F. 1987. The Current Convergence in Linguistic Theory: Some Implications for Second Language Acquisition Research. Second Language Research 3, 1-19.

Newmeyer, F., ed. 1988. Linguistics: The Cambridge Survey. Cambridge: Cambridge University Press. (4 vols.)

Newmeyer, F., and S. Weinberger. 1988. The Ontogenesis of the Field of Second Language Learning Research. In S. Flynn and O'Neil, eds., 34-45.

Newport, E. L. 1990. Maturational Constraints on Language Learning. Cognitive Science 14, 11-28.

Nickel, G., ed. 1971. Papers in Contrastive Linguistics. Cambridge: Cambridge University Press.

Obler, L. 1987. Exceptional Second Language Learners. Paper presented at Variation in Second Language Acquisition Conference. To appear in conference proceedings.

Obler, L. 1988. Neurolinguistics and Parameter Setting. In Flynn and O'Neil, eds., 117-25.

Obler, L., and D. Fein., eds. forthcoming. The Exceptional Brain: The Neuropsychology of Talent and Special Abilities. New York: Academic Press.

Odlin, T. 1989. Language Transfer: Crosslinguistic Influence in Language Learning. Cambridge: Cambridge University Press.

Oller, J. W., and J. C. Richards, eds. 1973. Focus on the Learner: Pragmatic Perspectives for the Language Teacher. Rowley, Mass.: Newbury House. (2nd printing, 1975)

Pankhurst, J., M. S. Smith, and P. Van Buren, eds. 1988. Learnability and Second Languages: A Book of Readings. Dordrecht: Foris.

Penfield, W. 1953. A Consideration of the Neurophysiological Mechanism of Speech and Some Educational Consequences. Proceedings of the American Academy of Arts and Sciences 82, 201-14.

Penfield, W. 1964. The Uncommitted Cortex: The Child's Changing Brain. The Atlantic Monthly 214, 77-91.

Penfield, W., and L. Roberts. 1959. Speech and Brain Mechanisms. Princeton: Princeton University Press.

Phinney, M. 1987. The Pro-Drop Parameter in Second Language Acquisition. In Roeper and Williams, eds., 221-38. (Paper presented at University of Massachusetts at Amherst. Conference on Parameter Setting in May 1985.)

Picallo, C. 1990. Modal Verbs in Catalan. Natural Language and Linguistic Theory 8, 285-312.

Plann, S. 1981. The Two el + Infinitive Constructions in Spanish. Linguistic Analysis 7, 203-40.

Pollock, J.- Y. 1989. Verb Movement, Universal Grammar, and the Structure of IP. Linguistic Inquiry 20, 365-424.

Raposo, E., and J. Uriagereka. 1990. Long-Distance Case Assignment. Linguistic Inquiry 21, 505-37.

Reibel, D. A., and S. A. Schane, eds. 1969. Modern Studies in English: Readings in Transformational Grammar. Englewood Cliffs, N.J.: Prentice-Hall.

Renzi, L., ed. 1988. Grande grammatica italiana di consultazione, a cura di Lorenzo Renzi, Bologna: Il Mulino. (Vol. I)

Richards, J.C., and T. S. Rodgers. 1986. Approaches and Methods in Language Teaching. Cambridge: Cambridge University Press.

Ritchie, W. C. 1978. The Right Roof Constraint in an Adult Acquired Language. In Ritchie, ed., 33-63.

Ritchie, W. C., ed. 1978. Second Language Research: Issues and Implications. New York: Academic Press.

Roca, I. M. 1979. Language Acquisition and the Chomskyan Revolution. Studia Anglica. Posnaniensia 10, 141-209.

Roeper, T., and E. Williams, eds. 1987. Parameter Setting. Dordrecht: Reidel.

Rutherford, W., ed. 1984. Language Universals and Second Language Acquisition. Amsterdam: Benjamins.

Rutherford, W. 1988. Grammatical Theory and L2 Acquisition: A Brief Overview. In Flynn and O'Neil, eds., 404-16.

Salkie, R. 1990. The Chomsky Update: Linguistics and Politics. London: Unwin Hyman.

Scarcella, R., and S. D. Krashen, eds. 1980. Research in Second Language Acquisition. Rowley, Mass.: Newbury House.

Schumann, J., and N. Stenson, eds. 1974. New Frontiers in Second Language Acquisition. Rowley, Mass.: Newbury House.

Scovel, T. 1969. Foreign Accents, Language Acquisition, and Cerebral Dominance. Language Learning 19, 245-54.

Seliger, H., S. Krashen, and P. Ladefoged. 1975. Maturational Constraints in the Acquisition of a Native-like Accent in Second Language Learning. Language Sciences 36, 20-2.

Selinker, L. 1972. Interlanguage. IRAL 10, 209-31. Reprinted in Schumann and Stenson, eds.

Sportiche, D. 1988. A Theory of Floating Quantifiers and Its Corollaries for Constituent Structure. Linguistic Inquiry 19, 425-49.

Stern, H. H. 1983. Fundamental Concepts of Language Teaching. Oxford: Oxford University Press.

Stockwell, R. P., J. D. Bowen, and J. W. Martin. 1965. The Grammatical Structures of English and Spanish. Chicago: University of Chicago Press.

Strozer, J. 1987. Nonnative Language Learning from a Principles and Parameters Perspective. Ms., University of Washington.

Strozer, J. 1989. *Ser/estar* and Individual-level/ Stage-level Predicates. Paper presented at the South Central MLA, Linguistics Session, New Orleans, October 26-28, 1989.

Tollefson, J., and J. Firn. 1983. Fossilization in Second Language Acquisition: An Inter-Model View. RELC Journal 14., 19-34.

Torrego, E. 1989. Experiencers and Raising Verbs in Spanish. Paper presented at the Second Princeton Workshop on Comparative Grammar, April 27-29.

Turkewitz, G., and P. Kenny. 1982. Limitations on Input as a Basis for Neural Organization and Perceptual Development: A Preliminary Theoretical Statement. Development Psychobiology, 15, 357-68.

Valian, V. 1990. Null Subjects: A Problem for Parameter-Setting Models of Language Acquisition. Cognition 35, 105-22.

Van Naerssen, M. 1980. How Similar Are Spanish as a First Language and Spanish as a Second Language? In Krashen and Scarcella, eds.

Walsh, T. M., and K. C. Diller. 1981. Neurolinguistic Considerations on the Optimal Age for Second Language Learning. In Diller, ed., 3-21.

Wanner, E., and L. R. Gleitman, eds. 1982. Language Acquisition: The State of the Art. Cambridge: Cambridge University Press.

Wheatley, B., A. Hastings, F. Eckman, L. Bell, G. Krukar, and R. Rutkowsky, eds. 1985. Current Approaches to Second Language Acquisition: Proceedings of the 1984 University of Wisconsin-Milwaukee Linguistics Symposium. Bloomington: Indiana University Linguistics Club.

Whitaker, H. 1978. Bilingualism: a Neurolinguistic Perspective. In Ritchie, ed., 21-32.

White, L. 1982. Grammatical Theory and Language Acquisition. Dordrecht: Foris.

White, L. 1985a. The Acquisition of Parameterized Grammars: Subjacency in Second-Language Acquisition. Second Language Research 1, 1-17.

White, L. 1985b. Is There a Logical Problem of Second Language Acquisition? TESL Canada 2, 29-41.

White, L. 1985c. The Pro-Drop Parameter in Adult Second Language Acquisition. Language Learning 35, 47-72.

White, L. 1985d. Universal Grammar as a Source of Explanation in Second Language Acquisition. In Wheatley et al., eds., 43-68.

White, L. 1986a. Implications of Parametric Variation for Adult Second Language Acquisition: An Investigation of the 'Pro-Drop' Parameter. In Cook, ed.

White, L. 1986b. Markedness and Parameter Setting: Some Implications for a Theory of Adult Language Acquisition. In Eckman et al., eds. (Paper presented in 1983), 309-27.

White, L. 1987a. A Note on Phinney. In Roeper and Williams, eds. (Paper presented at University of Massachusetts at Amherst, Conference on Parameter-Setting, May 1985), 239-46.

White, L. 1987b. Markedness and Second Language Acquisition: The Question of Transfer. Studies in Second Language Acquisition 9, 261-86.

White, L. 1987c. Against Comprehensible Input: The Input Hypothesis and the Development of L2 Competence. Applied Linguistics 8, 95-110.

White, L. 1988a. Island Effects in Second Language Acquisition. In Flynn and O'Neil, eds., 144-72.

White, L. 1988b. Universal Grammar and Language Transfer. In Pankhurst et al., eds.

White, L. 1989. Universal Grammar and Second Language Acquisition. Amsterdam/ Philadelphia: John Benjamins.

Zagona, K. 1988. Verb Phrase Syntax: A Parametric Study of Spanish and English. Dordrecht: Kluwer.

SECTION TWO: SYNTAX AND SEMANTICS

Silent objects and subjects in Spanish

Héctor Campos *
Georgetown University

1 Clitics and parasitic gaps. In Chomsky (1982) and in Engdahl (1983) it is argued that a parasitic gap[1] may be licensed only by a wh-trace; hence the contrast between (1a), on the one hand, and (1b,c,d), on the other.

(1) a.   Which report$_i$ did you file t$_i$ without reading e?

    b.   *The report$_i$ was filed t$_i$ without reading e.

    c.   *They filed the report without reading e.

    d.   *They filed it without reading e.

In the examples above NP-traces (1b), R-expressions (1c), and pronominals (1d) do not license parasitic gaps. Chomsky (1982: 44) and Engdahl (1983: 14) observe that a wh-element *in situ* in a echo question reading does not license a parasitic gap in English, either.

(2)   *John filed WHICH ARTICLES without reading e?

We may thus conclude that a parasitic gap is licensed only by an S-Structure wh-trace. Let us call this observation the Parasitic Gap Licensing Condition (PGLC).[2]

(3) Parasitic Gap Licensing Condition (PGLC):

A parasitic gap is licensed by an S-Structure wh-trace.

---

* I would like to thank Carlos Otero, Judy Strozer, and Margarita Suñer for their comments. The errors in the analysis remain, of course, only mine.

[1] The term 'parasitic gap' was posited independently by Engdahl (1980) and Taraldsen (1980). See also Grosu (1980).

[2] Chomsky (1982) and Engdahl (1983) argue that the licensing wh-trace must not c-command the parasitic gap. But see Contreras (1984) for counterarguments. The analysis presented here does not bear on this issue.

The same facts can be observed in Spanish for constructions (1a-c) above. However, the Spanish equivalent of (1d) is possible in Spanish, as shown in (4d).

(4) a. ¿Cuál informe archivaste t sin leer e?
'Which report did you file without reading?'

b. El informe fue archivado t sin leer.
'The report was filed without reading.'

c. *Archivaron el informe sin leer e.
'They filed the report without reading e.'

d. Lo archivaron e_1 sin leer e_2.[3]
It-filed e_1 without to-read e_2
'They filed it without reading e.'

Following Chomsky (1982) and Rizzi (1982), it has been usually assumed that the silent category which appears in the object position associated with the clitic is the pronominal element *pro*, which is licensed by the clitic parallel to the way AGRS[4] licenses *pro* in subject position. If the complement of *archivar* 'to file', e_1, were the pronominal element *pro*, we would expect the Spanish example in (4d) to behave like its English counterpart in (1d). Since only the trace of a wh-element may license a parasitic gap (see (1) above), the grammaticality of (4d) leads us to pursue the hypothesis that e_1 is the trace of a wh-element.

The Parasitic Gap Licensing Condition in (3) requires that a parasitic gap be licensed by a wh-trace in S-Structure. This licensing condition is met in (4a) as the wh-phrase *cuál informe* 'which report' has moved between D- and S-Structure, leaving behind a wh-trace. Parasitic gaps can also be found with silent indefinite object constructions.

(5) ¿Tus padres te mandan dinero? -Sí, siempre me mandan e_1 sin que les pida e.
Your parents you send money? -Yes, (they) always me send e_1 without (I) them ask
'Your parents send you money? -Yes, they always send me (some) without my asking them (for any).'

---

[3] Parasitic gap constructions in Spanish are highly restricted to inanimate arguments:
(i) *Lo_i visitaron e_i sin llamar e.
'They visited him without calling.'
[4] See Chomsky (1989).

In Campos (1986), following Huang (1984) and Raposo (1986), it is argued that the gap corresponding to indefinite objects is a silent operator OP which moves between D- and S-Structure.[5] Thus e_1 is a wh-trace (a variable) in (5) and the PGLC in (3) is satisfied.

However, constructions which involve clitics do not seem to involve movement of the wh-element that we are claiming appears in object position. Consider the examples in (6):

(6) a. Conozco a un muchacho que los archivó e_1 sin leer e_2.
   I know a boy that them filed e_1 without to read e_2.
   'I know a boy that filed them without reading(them).'

   b. No sé quién preguntó por qué José los archivó e_1 sin leer e_2.
   I don't know who asked why José them filed e without to read e.
   'I don't know who asked why José filed them without reading (them).'

The grammaticality of the constructions in (6) contrasts with that of constructions where the parasitic gap is licensed by the trace of a wh-element which has moved.

(7) a. *¿Qué informe$_i$ conoces a un muchacho que archivó t_i sin leer e?
   'What report$_i$ do you know a boy who filed t_i without reading e?'

   b. *¿Qué informe$_i$ no sabes quién preguntó por qué José archivó t_i sin leer e?
   'What report$_i$ don't you know who asked why José filed t_i without reading e?'

(8) a. *(OP)$_i$ Conozco a un muchacho que archiva t_i sin leer e.
   '(OP)$_i$ (I) know a boy who files t_i without reading e.'

---

[5] The evidence for OP is considerable. For Chinese and German, see Huang (1984, 1987, 1989); for Portuguese, see Raposo (1986); for Kinande, see Authier (1988); for French, see Authier (1989b), for Japanese, see Hasegawa (1984/1985, 1988); for American Sign Language, see Lillo-Martin (1985). For an alternative analysis, see Cole (1987). For characteristics of Topic operator, see Authier (1989a).

    b.   *(OP)$_i$ No sé quién preguntó por qué José archivó t$_i$
        sin leer e.
        '(OP)$_i$ (I) don't know who asked why José filed t$_i$
        without reading e.'

    In (7) and (8), the trace licenses the parasitic gap according to the PGLC
in (3). The ungrammaticality of the examples in (7) and (8) follows from
subjacency: the licensing wh-trace and its antecedent are 2-subjacent.[6] Yet the
examples in (6) are grammatical. So, we may conclude that either e_1 is not
a wh-element or that it is a wh-element which does not move. Claiming that
e_1 in (6) is not a wh-element, we would have to posit a new silent category
which could not be a pronominal, an R-expression, or an NP-trace (but see
facts in (1) and (2) above), and which could, at the same time, license a
parasitic gap. However, no such category is found in the actual inventory of
silent categories. We may thus explore the possibility that e_1 is a wh-element
which does not move in the syntax and further explore the possibility of
whether a wh-element *in situ* may license a parasitic gap in Spanish.
    In Spanish, unlike English, a wh-element *in situ* may license a parasitic
gap (cf.2).[7]

    (9) a.   ¿Tú archivaste cuál artículo sin leer e?
            'You filed which article without reading e?'

        b.   ¿Tú mandaste cuál artículo sin revisar e?
            'You sent which article without proofreading e?'

    We see that the PGLC in (3) must be revised in Spanish so as to allow
both for wh-elements and for traces of wh-elements to license a parasitic gap.
Thus the PGLC for Spanish would be (10).

    (10) Parasitic Gap Licensing Condition (PGLC) in Spanish:

        A parasitic gap is licensed by a wh-element *in situ* or by the trace
        of a wh-element.

    A difference between the wh-constructions in English and Spanish is the fact
that in nonecho questions in English the wh-element must obligatorily move

---

[6] See Chomsky (1986).
[7] Notice that if the object is not a wh-element, the parasitic gap is not licensed:
    (i) *Archivaron el artículo sin leer. (=4c)
        'They filed the article without reading.'

to [SPEC,CP] by S-Structure, while in Spanish it may move either in S-Structure or in LF. Thus the constructions in (11) are wellformed without an echo-question interpretation in Spanish.

(11) a. ¿Tú vives dónde?
You live where?
'Where do you live?'

b. ¿Tú sales de la oficina a qué hora mañana?
You leave from the office at what time tomorrow?
'What time do you get off work tomorrow?'

The difference between the PGLC for English, shown in (3), and the one for Spanish, shown in (10), may be related to the different levels in which wh-movement applies in both languages. Further evidence for this claim comes from Japanese, where wh-elements do not move in S-Structure. In Japanese, as in the Spanish examples in (9), a parasitic gap may also be licensed by a wh-element *in situ*.

(12) a. Anata-wa dono reporto-o yomanaide shita no?
You-TOP which report-OBJ without reading file PAST Q?
'Which report did you file without reading?'

b. Anata-wa dono paper-o naosanaide okutta no?
You-TOP which paper without checking sent Q?
'Which paper did you send without checking?'

The facts above seem to suggest that a parasitic gap is licensed in S-Structure and that it must be licensed by a wh-element. Whether it can be licensed by a wh-element or by the trace of a wh-element depends on the syntactic strategy the language employs for wh-movement.

Going back to the examples in (6), we see that the grammaticality of these constructions can be explained if we assume that e_1 is a wh-element *in situ* and if we assume that in Spanish a parasitic gap may be licensed either by a wh-element or by the trace of a wh-element, as suggested in (10).

To account for the parasitic gap in (4d), then, we could assume, following Huang (1982) and Chomsky (1982), that the gap is a silent operator [+WH] OP which is coindexed with a silent topic, as shown in (13).

(13) $[_{TOPIC} X_i [_{CP} [_{IP}$ lo archivaron OP$_i$ sin leer e]]]

$[_{TOPIC} X_i [_{CP} [_{IP}$ (they) it filed OP$_i$ without reading e]]]

As shown in the examples (9) and (12), wh-elements in argument position may license parasitic gaps in Spanish, thus the parasitic gap found in (13) is licensed by the operator OP. The OP operator, being a Topic Operator in Authier's (1989b) sense, moves in LF, thus accounting for the lack of subjacency effects in these constructions.[8] Huang (1984, 1989) argues that the operator would itself be the topic which would be coindexed with a variable in the position of the silent object. Since we have given independent evidence above that wh-elements *in situ* may license parasitic gaps in Spanish, we will continue to assume structure (13) in the following discussion.[9]

Further evidence for our claim that an OP operator *in situ* may license a parasitic gap can be found in Quiteño Spanish. Suñer and Yépez (1988), following Huang (1984), argue that definite object drop in Quiteño Spanish involves a variable which is not the result of movement. These authors, however, also note the existence of parasitic gaps in this dialect.[10]

(14) a. ¿Te permitirán entregar e_1 sin terminar e?
    (They) you will permit to hand-in e_1 without to finish e?
    'Will they let you hand it in without finishing (it)?'

   b. La carta de ese idiota, ahí dejé e_1 sin siquiera abrir e.
    The letter from that idiot, there (I) left e_1 without even to open e
    'That idiot's letter, I left it there without even opening (it).'

Suñer and Yépez (1988: 518) note that these constructions present a problem for their analysis as the test of parasitic gaps is used by Raposo (1986) 'to further the cause of the variable-through-movement proposal, given the analysis that parasitic gaps are sanctioned by a variable created by movement in the matrix.' Thus Suñer and Yépez (1988: 519) are forced to conclude that '...there is no parasitic gap [in these constructions. H.C.] It just happens that the null objects have the same referent.' Such a stipulation is necessary in Suñer and Yépez's system as they are trying to maintain the PGLC which allows only the traces of wh-elements at S-Structure to be licensers of parasitic gaps. No such stipulation is necessary with the analysis presented here if e_1 is a wh-operator and if OP *in situ* may license a parasitic gap, a fact that is

---

[8] The data regarding Topic Operators discussed in Authier (1989b) include movement between D- and S-Structure only. Lasnik and Saito (1987) suggest that this movement may actually be an adjunction to IP. This is compatible with the analysis being presented here.

[9] See Campos (1991) for arguments in favor of an OP which moves in LF versus a variable generated *in situ*.

[10] Examples from Suñer and Yépez (1988: 518).

independently motivated, as shown in the discussion of the Spanish (9) and the Japanese (12) examples.[11]

We thus conclude that constructions which involve a clitic and a parasitic gap are best analyzed as containing an operator OP in the licensing argument position rather than *pro*. In section 2, we will consider whether this analysis can be extended to all clitic constructions, regardless of whether they appear licensing a parasitic gap construction or not.

2 Silent Objects

2.1 Clitics and silent categories. In structure (4d), repeated here as (15a), the clitic refers to a discourse topic. The clitic lacks independent reference. The analysis proposed above can be automatically extended to clitic constructions which are discourse bound and which make reference to an 'understood' topic. The structure for (15b) is shown in (15c).

(15) a. Lo archivaron e_1 sin leer e.
(They) it filed e_1 without to read e
'They filed it without reading (it).'

b. ¿Marta$_j$ conoce a María$_i$? -Sí, Marta la$_{i,*j}$ conoce.
Does Marta$_j$ know María$_i$? -Yes, Marta her$_{i,*j}$-knows
'Does Marta know María? -Yes, Marta knows her.'

c. [$_{TOPIC}$ X_i [$_{CP}$ Marta$_j$ la conoce OP$_{i,*j}$]]
[$_{TOPIC}$ X_i [$_{CP}$ Marta$_j$ her knows OP$_{i,*j}$]]

In (15c), X represents the silent discourse topic, *María*, and following Chomsky (1982) and Huang (1984, 1989), we may assume that it is coindexed with *OP* in LF'. Assuming that the clitic and the element in object position must agree, the clitic *la* 'her' and the element in TOPIC must share the same features. Since the operator is subject to Condition C of the Binding Theory, it must be A-free. This explains the impossible reading in (15c), where *Marta* A-binds the operator. The grammatical reading where OP and the element in TOPIC are coindexed also follows from our system as the latter does not A-bind the former.

---

[11] Farrell (1990) suggests that Suñer and Yépez's data could be analyzed as an instance of *pro*, parallel to the analysis for silent definite direct objects which he motivates for Brazilian Portuguese. Notice, however, that silent objects in Quiteño Spanish license parasitic gaps. If we are to maintain the generalization that only wh-traces or wh-elements license parasitic gaps, then a *pro* in object position would not be possible.

However, it is not the case that clitics are always coreferent with a discourse topic. The clitic in sentence (16) is ambiguous as it may refer either to a discourse topic or to the subject of the main clause.

(16) a. María dice que Marta la conoce.
María says that Marta her knows
'María says that Marta knows her.'

b. [$_{CP}$ *María*$_i$ dice [$_{CP}$ que Marta$_j$ la conoce $e_{i,*j,k}$]]
[$_{CP}$ María$_i$ says [$_{CP}$ that Marta$_j$ her knows $e_{i,*j,k}$]]

If the silent category *e* associated with the clitic in (16b) were OP as in construction (15c), we would expect this construction to be ungrammatical in the reading where the object of *conocer* 'to know' is interpreted as being coreferential with the subject *María*. This reading would be blocked by Condition C, since OP must be A-free. We thus see that *e* in (16b) cannot be *OP* when the gap is interpreted as being coreferential with the subject. In this case, the only silent category that would yield the right binding result is *pro*. If *e* is *pro*, then it would be A-free in its governing category and it would thus be able to refer to the matrix subject *María* in (16b). We may thus suggest that the ambiguity of (16a), repeated here as (17a), be captured by two different representations: as (17b), when the gap is interpreted as referring to a discourse topic, and as (17c), when it is interpreted as referring to the subject.

(17) a. María$_i$ dice que Marta$_j$ la$_{i,*j,k}$ conoce.
María$_i$ says that Marta$_j$ her$_{i,*j,k}$ knows
'María says that Marta knows her.'

b. [$_{TOPIC}$ X_k [$_{CP}$ María$_i$ dice [$_{CP}$ que Marta$_j$ la conoce $OP_{*i,*j,k}$]]
[$_{TOPIC}$ X_k [$_{CP}$ María$_i$ says [$_{CP}$ that Marta$_j$ her knows $OP_{*i,*j,k}$]]

c. [$_{CP}$ *María*$_i$ dice [$_{CP}$ que Marta$_j$ la conoce $pro_{i,*j}$]]
[$_{CP}$ María$_i$ says [$_{CP}$ that Marta$_j$ her knows $pro_{i,*j}$]]

The operator in (17b) is subject to Condition C of the Binding Theory and thus must be A-free. This explains why *OP* may not be coreferential with *Marta*, the subject of the embedded clause, nor with *María*, the subject of the main clause, as both of these arguments are in an A-position. On the other hand, the operator and the silent topic may be coreferential, as the element in TOPIC is not in an A-position. Thus the analysis for clitics when followed by parasitic gaps proposed in section 1 above may be extended to structures which include clitics which refer to a silent or understood discourse topic.

In (17c), on the other hand, the clitic does not refer back to a discourse topic, but to an argument which is outside its governing category. In this case the silent element occupying the object position of *conocer* 'to know' cannot be OP or we would incur into a violation of Condition C of the Binding Theory. If it is *pro*, instead, it must be A-free in the embedded CP domain, and thus it is free to refer to *María* outside its governing category.[12]

We therefore conclude that if the clitic is interpreted as being coreferential with an element in an A'-position, the element in the argument position which is associated with the clitic is an operator OP. Otherwise, it is *pro*.

Our analysis thus makes a prediction. It predicts that a parasitic gap could be found only in a construction where the gap is interpreted as a discourse topic (17b) but not where it may be interpreted as being coreferential to the subject (17c). This is borne out, as shown in (18).

(18) a. ¿Qué hiciste con ese artículo? -Lo$_i$ archivé OP$_i$ antes de leer e.
What did you do with that article? -(I) it$_i$ filed OP$_i$
before of to read e
'Why is this article not marked up? -Because I filed it before reading (it).'

b. *Este artículo$_i$ muestra que lo$_i$ archivé pro$_i$ antes de leer e.
This article$_i$ shows that (I) it$_i$ filed pro$_i$ before of to read e
'This article shows that I filed (it) before reading.'

c. Este artículo$_i$ muestra que lo$_i$ archivé pro$_i$ antes de leerlo$_i$.
This article$_i$ shows that (I) it$_i$ filed pro$_i$ before of to read-it$_i$
'This article shows that I filed it before reading it.'

The construction in (18a) exhibits a parasitic gap and we have argued that there is a operator occupying the object position of *archivé* '(I) filed' which licenses it. In this instance OP is bound by the discourse topic in the topic A'-position; thus no violation of Condition C ensues. In (18b), on the other hand, since the object of *archivar* 'to file' is bound from an A-position, the element occupying this position cannot be *OP* or we would incur into a violation of Condition C. As argued above, the object of *archivar* 'to file' in

---

[12] The question of whether *pro* may also refer to the element in TOPIC will be discussed in section 2.2.

(18b) must be *pro*. But *pro* does not license a parasitic gap. Hence the ungrammaticality of (18b). In (18c) there is no parasitic gap. Instead, a resumptive clitic[13] has been used in the infinitival clause.

This supports our claim that a clitic may be associated either with OP or with *pro*. If the argument position is bound from an A'-position, then the silent category associated with the clitic is *OP*, thus accounting for the fact that a parasitic gap is possible. If the argument position is not bound from an A'-position, then the silent category associated with the clitic is *pro*, thus accounting for the fact that a parasitic gap is impossible.

2.2 Clitics and overt pronouns: Spanish and Chinese. Huang (1984, 1989) has noted that in Chinese the silent category in (19a) must be interpreted as being coreferential with the discourse topic. The structure for (19a) is shown in (19b).

(19) a. Zhangsan$_i$ shuo Lisi$_j$ bu renshi e$_{*i,*j,k}$.
Zhangsan$_i$ say Lisi$_j$ not know e$_{*i,*j,k}$.
'(As for X$_i$), Zhangsan said that Lisi didn't know (him)$_i$.'

b. [$_{TOPIC}$ X$_k$ [$_{CP}$ [$_{IP}$ Zhangsan$_i$ shuo [$_{CP}$ [$_{IP}$ Lisi$_j$ bu renshi OP$_{*i,*j,k}$]]]]]
[$_{TOPIC}$ X$_k$ [$_{CP}$ [$_{IP}$ Zhangsan$_i$ said [$_{CP}$ [$_{IP}$ Lisi$_j$ not know OP$_{*i,*j,k}$]]]]]

Following Authier (1989a), we will assume that OP, being a Topic Operator, moves to [SPEC, CP]. This movement, as argued above, would occur in LF. The ungrammatical readings in (19a) follow from Condition C, as argued above.[14]

We see that Chinese and Spanish can be argued to have the same structure when the silent object refers to a discourse topic. Compare the Chinese example in (19), repeated here as (20a), with its Spanish equivalent in (20b).

---

[13] For resumptive clitics, see Contreras (1991), in this volume.

[14] Huang (1984, 1989) argues that the silent object in (19a) is best analyzed as a variable generated in D-Structure. As argued in Campos (1991), this analysis complicates the grammar since variables are usually generated as a result of Affect α. Huang (1991), however, argues that the silent object in (19a) is not a base-generated variable, but the equivalent of a silent epithet, a [+ pronominal, + referential] element. Since these constructions may license a parasitic gap in Spanish, we will continue to assume that they contain OP in object position rather than a silent pronominal. As Huang (1991: 73, n.9) notes, the variable analysis is not reducible to silent epithets in all cases.

(20) a. $[_{TOPIC}$ X_k $[_{CP}$ $[_{IP}$ Zhangsan$_i$ shuo $[_{CP}$ $[_{IP}$ Lisi$_j$ bu renshi
OP$_{*i,*j,k}$]]]]]
$[_{TOPIC}$ X_k $[_{CP}$ $[_{IP}$ Zhangsan$_i$ said $[_{CP}$ $[_{IP}$ Lisi$_j$ not know
OP$_{*i,*j,k}$]]]]]
'(As for X_k), Zhangsan said that Lisi did not know (him)$_k$.'

 b. $[_{TOPIC}$ X_k $[_{CP}$ $[_{IP}$ Marta$_i$ dijo $[_{CP}$ que$[_{IP}$ Ana$_j$ lo$_k$ conocía
OP$_{*i,*j,k}$]]]]]
$[_{TOPIC}$ X_k $[_{CP}$ $[_{IP}$ Marta$_i$ said $[_{CP}$ $[_{IP}$ Ana$_j$ him$_k$ know
OP$_{*i,*j,k}$]]]]]
'(As for X_k), Ana said that Marta knew (him)$_k$.'

We see that in both constructions OP appears in the object position of the verb *to know*, which accounts for the binding effects noted above. Since the referentiality of the gap can be determined by the syntactic nature of the gap, it is not necessary to assume that the clitic itself has [±anaphor] or [±pronominal] features.[15] The clitic can be analyzed as an object agreement marker in that it indicates the gender, number, and specificity of the object.[16] Huang (1984, 1989) has noticed that in Chinese, while a silent category may refer only to a discourse topic, a lexical pronominal form may refer either to the subject or to the silent topic. This is shown in (21).

(21) a. Zhangsan$_i$ shuo Lisi bu renshi e$_{*i,j}$.
Zhangsan$_i$ said Lisi not knew e$_{*i,j}$.
'Zhangsan said Lisi did not know him.'

 b. Zhangsan$_i$ shuo Lisi bu renshi ta$_{i,j}$.
Zhangsan$_i$ said Lisi not knew him$_{i,j}$.
'Zhangsan said Lisi did not know him.'

Spanish, in this respect, patterns exactly the opposite of Chinese. When no lexical complement appears, the gap is interpreted as being coreferential either with the subject of the matrix clause or with the discourse topic. This is shown in (22).

(22) Juan$_i$ dijo que Pedro lo conocía e$_{i,j}$.
Juan$_i$ said that Pedro him knew e$_{i,j}$.
'Juan said that Pedro knew him.'

---

[15] This has been proposed in Otero (1985) and in class lectures (1981-1986).
[16] See Suñer (1988).

On the other hand, when a pronominal form appears, it must have an antecedent sentence-internally.[17]

(23) Juan$_i$ dijo que Pedro lo conocía a él$_{i,*j}$.
Juan$_i$ said that Pedro him knew e$_{i,*j}$.
'Juan said that Pedro knew him.'

The difference between the Chinese facts in (21a) and the Spanish facts in (22) follows directly from our analysis and they have been discussed above. Following Huang (1984, 1989), we have argued above that the silent element in Chinese (21a) is an operator OP, thus accounting for the binding effects that this construction shows. Regarding the Spanish example in (22), we have argued that the silent category may be either OP or *pro*. It is OP if it is A'-bound; this is the case when the gap is interpreted as being coreferential with the discourse topic. On the other hand, the silent category is *pro* if it is not bound from an A'-position. The fact that in Spanish but not in Chinese the silent category may refer to the matrix subject follows from the fact that Chinese does not allow *pro* in object position, as it has no element to license this, unlike the Spanish clitics which license *pro* in object position, parallel to the way AGRS licenses *pro* in subject position.[18] Both languages may refer to a discourse topic, however, as both languages may have the operator OP in object position.

Consider now the contrast between Chinese (21b) and Spanish (23). Chinese *ta* 'him', similar to the English pronominal 'him', bears the features [+pron, -ana]. By Condition B of the Binding Theory, *ta* and 'him' must be free in their governing category, which in these examples is the embedded IP. Thus these pronominal elements are free to refer to any other element outside the embedded clause provided the features match. Therefore, in (21b), *ta* 'him' may refer either to the subject of the matrix clause or to the discourse topic.

---

[17] *El* 'he' may have a referent outside the sentence only if it is used deictically or contrastively. Thus (ib) cannot be used as an answer to (ia). Instead, a silent category must be used, as shown in (ic).
(i)a. - ¿Pedro conoce a Luis$_j$?
'Does Pedro know Luis$_j$?'
b. -*Yo no sé, pero Juan$_i$ dijo que Pedro lo conocía a él$_j$.
I don't know, but Juan$_i$ said that Pedro him knew him$_i$
'I don't know, but Juan said that Pedro knew him.'
c. - Yo no sé, pero Juan$_i$ dijo que Pedro lo conocía e$_j$.
I don't know, but Juan$_i$ said that Pedro (him) knew e$_j$
'I don't know, but Juan said that Pedro knew him.'
[18] See Chomsky (1982) and Rizzi (1982).

Spanish *a él* 'him' in (23) also bears the features [+pron, -ana]; however, unlike English 'him' or Chinese *ta* 'him', it seems to be a pronominal which requires a sentence-internal antecedent. In this respect, Spanish tonic object pronouns behave like the Greek tonic pronoun *ton ídhios* 'him', as reported in Iatridou (1986) and Enç (1989), while Spanish clitics followed by a gap seem to behave like the Greek clitic *ton* 'him'.

(24) a. O Yiánnis$_i$ théli [i María$_j$ na voithísi ton ídhio$_{i,*j,*k}$]
The Yiánnis$_i$ wants [the María$_j$ SUBJ help him$_{i,*j,*k}$]
'Yiánnis wants María to help him.'

b. O Yiánnis$_i$ théli [i María$_j$ na ton voithísi e$_{i,*j,k}$]
The Yiánnis$_i$ wants [the María$_j$ SUBJ him help e$_{i,*j,k}$]
'Yiánnis wants María to help him.'

Following Enç (1989), we will assume that Chinese *ta*, the Spanish tonic pronoun *a él*, the Greek tonic pronoun *ton ídhios*, and the English pronoun *him* are all [+pronominal]. The tonic pronoun *a él* 'him' in Spanish, like the Greek pronoun *ton ídhios* 'him', is [-L, +B, +pronominal], while the English pronoun 'him' and the Chinese pronoun *ta* 'him' are [-L, -B, +pronominal]. In Enç's system, [-L] means that the element in question is not subject to local licensing conditions (i.e., it is not subject to Condition A); [±B] indicates whether the element in question does or does not need a sentence-internal antecedent that semantically binds it.[19]

Therefore, the difference between Chinese (21b) and Spanish (22) stems from the fact that tonic pronouns in Spanish are [-L, +B, +pronominal] while pronouns in English and Chinese are [-L, -B, +pronominal], a difference among pronominals which has been independently motivated elsewhere.[20]

This characteristic of pronominal elements in Spanish gives further support to our hypothesis that a clitic pronoun may be associated with an argument which is either OP or *pro*. We have argued above that the element associated with the clitic is OP when it is A'-bound and that it is *pro*, otherwise. Thus, consider the ambiguous sentence in (25a).

(25) a. María$_i$ dice que Marta$_j$ la conoce e$_{i,*j,k}$.
María$_i$ says that Marta$_j$ her knows e$_{i,*j,k}$.
'María says that Marta knows her.'

---

[19] In Enç's system, Chinese *ta* 'him' and English *him* would be [-L, +B$_{A'}$] while Greek *ídhios* and Spanish *a él* 'him' would be [-L, +B$_{A'}$, +ID].

[20] Iatridou (1986: 769) proposed a 'Condition D' to account for the behavior of Greek *ídhios* 'him'. Condition D requires *ídhios* to be bound in the whole sentence but free in its governing category. This is captured by Enç's [+B] feature.

b. [$_{TOPIC}$ X_k [$_{CP}$ María$_i$ dice [$_{CP}$ que Marta$_j$ la conoce
  $OP_{*i,*j,k}$]]]
  [$_{TOPIC}$ X_k [$_{CP}$ María$_i$ says [$_{CP}$ that Marta$_j$ her knows
  $OP_{*i,*j,k}$]]]

c. [$_{TOPIC}$ X_k [$_{CP}$ *María$_i$* dice [$_{CP}$ que Marta$_j$ la conoce
  $pro_{i,*j,*k}$]]]
  [$_{TOPIC}$ X_k [$_{CP}$ María$_i$ says [$_{CP}$ that Marta$_j$ her knows
  $pro_{i,*j,*k}$]]]

Since the wh-element in (25b) is subject to Condition C, it may only be bound by the discourse topic in (25b). Hence the reading where the gap is interpreted as coreferential with the discourse topic. Assuming that pronominal elements in Spanish, whether lexical or not, are [-L, +B, +pronominal], we expect them to have a sentence-internal antecedent.[21] Thus *pro* in (25c) must be bound by the subject in (25c). Hence the reading where the gap is interpreted as coreferential with the subject *María*.

Thus our claim that a clitic is associated with OP if the object is bound from an A'-position but with *pro* otherwise follows from our claim that pronominals in Spanish are [-L, +B, +pronominal] and from the fact that the operator OP is subject to Condition C. Then the difference between Chinese (21b) and Spanish (23) follows from the fact that, in Spanish, pronominals (whether lexical or not) are [+B] while in Chinese they are [-B]. The

---

[21] As in Greek, a pronominal may be bound by any matrix clause argument:
  (i)a. O Yiánnis$_i$ ípe ton Cósta$_j$ [oti i María$_k$ aghapá ton ídhio$_{i,j,*k,*l}$]
    '(The) Yiánnis$_i$ told (the) Cóstas$_j$ [that (the) María$_k$ loves him$_{i,j,*k,*l}$]'
  b. Juan$_i$ le dijo a Costa$_j$ [que María$_k$ lo ama a él$_{i,j,*k,*l}$]
    'Juan$_i$ told Costa$_j$ [that María$_k$ loves him$_{i,j,*k,*l}$]'
Both in Greek and in Spanish, when the complement is silent and a clitic appears, the gap can be interpreted as being coreferential to *Yiannis/ Juan*, to *Cóstas/ Costa* or to a discourse topic:
  (ii)a. O Yiánnis$_i$ ípe ton Cósta$_j$ [oti i María$_k$ ton aghapá $e_{i,j,*k,l}$]
    'The Yiánnis$_i$ told Cósta$_j$ [that (the) María$_k$ him loves $e_{i,j,*k,l}$]'
  b. Juan$_i$ le dijo a Costa$_j$ [que María$_k$ lo ama $e_{i,j,*k,l}$]
    'Juan$_i$ told Costa$_j$ [that María$_k$ him loves $e_{i,j,*k,l}$]'
In our analysis these facts follow directly as the gap *e* in (i) and (ii) above may be either OP or *pro*. In the former case, the gap refers to the discourse topic, in the latter one, it may refer to any argument which appears sentence-internally. Notice that there is no c-command condition on the antecedent of *a él* 'him', as the former may corefer to *Costa*, in (iii).
  (iii)a. Juan$_i$ le dijo al padre$_j$ de Costa$_k$ que María lo ama $e_{i,j,k,*l,m}$]
    'Juan$_i$ told Costa$_k$'s father$_j$ that María loves $e_{i,j,k,*l,m}$]'
  b. Juan$_i$ le dijo al padre$_j$ de Costa$_k$ que María lo ama a él$_{i,j,k,*l,*m}$]
    'Juan$_i$ told Costa$_k$'s father$_j$ that María him loves him$_{i,j,k,*l,*m}$]'
Thus the condition on *pro* is that it have a referent sentence-internally rather than it be 'bound' (thus requiring c-command) sentence-internally.

difference between (22) and (23) follows from the fact that silent objects may be OP or *pro*. The fact that a silent object may only be the understood topic in Chinese, while it may be the understood topic or the matrix subject in Spanish, follows from the fact that Spanish allows both *OP* and *pro* in object position, while Chinese only allows OP. If *pro* were the only possible argument associated with a clitic in Spanish (22), then the difference between (22) and (23) would be left unexplained.

2.3 Silent and overt pronouns: on Montalbetti's (1984) OPC. An apparent counterexample for our claim comes from Montalbetti (1984: 94), who proposes the Overt Pronoun Constraint (OPC), shown in (26) below.

(26) Overt Pronoun Constraint. (OPC)

Overt pronouns cannot link to formal variables[22] iff the alternation overt/empty obtains.

The OPC would account for the subject/ nonsubject asymmetry shown in (27) and (28).

(27) a. Nadie$_i$ cree que {*él$_i$,e$_i$} es inteligente.
'Nobody$_i$ believes that {*he$_i$,e$_i$} is intelligent.'

b. ¿Quién$_i$ cree que {*él$_i$,e$_i$} es inteligente?
'Who$_i$ believes that {*he$_i$,e$_i$} is intelligent?'

(28) a. Nadie$_i$ quiere que María hable de él$_i$.
Nobody$_i$ wants that María talk about him$_i$
'Nobody wants María to talk about him.'

b. ¿Quién$_i$ quiere que María hable de él$_i$?
Who$_i$ wants that María talk about him$_i$
'Who wants María to talk about him?'

In (27) a lexical pronoun cannot be bound to the subject of the matrix clause due to the OPC since *nadie* 'nobody' and *quién* 'who' are 'formal variables' and the alternation between an overt and a nonovert form is possible in

---

[22] The notion of 'formal variable' that Montalbetti (1984: 48) adopts is that of Higginbotham (1983) and is shown in (i).
(i) V is a formal variable iff (i) V is an empty category in an argument position; and
(ii) V is linked to a lexical operator in a non-argument position.

subject position. In (28), on the other hand, such alternation is not possible and therefore the variable and the pronoun may be linked.

Montalbetti (1984: 139) argues that we find OPC effects in clitic object constructions. Thus he notes the contrast in (29).

(29) a. Nadie$_i$ cree que Juan$_j$ lo vio {*a él$_i$, e$_i$}.
Nobody$_i$ believes that Juan$_j$ him saw {*him$_i$, e$_i$}
'Nobody believes that Juan saw him.'

b. ¿Quién$_i$ cree que Juan$_j$ lo vio {*a él$_i$, e$_i$}?
Who$_i$ believes that Juan$_j$ him saw {*him$_i$, e$_i$}?
'Who believes that Juan saw him?'

Since *a él* 'him' is [-L, +B, +pronominal], it must be bound sentence-internally. Clearly, the negative word *nadie* 'nobody' and the interrogative *quién* 'who' cannot serve as antecedents for the pronoun *él* 'he' in (29) or we would expect these constructions to be well-formed. The representation that Montalbetti (1984) assigns to (30a) is shown in (30b).

(30) a. *¿Quién cree que Juan lo vio a él?
'Who believes that Juan saw him?'

b. [Quién] [t] cree que Juan lo conoce [a él]?
[Who] [t] believes that Juan him knows [him]?

In (30b) the pronoun *a él* 'him' is linked to the formal variable *[t]*; therefore OPC blocks it. Our analysis must thus explain why the trace of *quién* 'who', which is sentence-internal, cannot serve as an antecedent for the pronominal *a él* 'him'.

Notice, however, that (30a) becomes grammatical if a question word which is more referential is used.[23]

(31) a. ¿Cuál de los muchachos$_i$ cree que Juan lo vio a él$_i$?
Which of the boys$_i$ believes that Juan him saw him$_i$?
'Which of the boys believes that Juan saw him?'

b. Ningún chico$_i$ dijo que Juan lo había visto a él$_i$.
No boy$_i$ said that Juan him had seen him$_i$
'No boy said that Juan had seen him.'

---

[23] See Cinque (1990), Suñer (1988), and Contreras (1991) in this volume.

These facts seem to suggest that the ungrammaticality of the examples in (29) might be due to an incompatibility between the question words *quién* 'who'and *nadie* 'nobody', on the one hand, and the lexical pronoun, on the other. The S-Structure for (31a) is shown in (32).

(32) [$_{C'}$ Cuál de los muchachos$_i$ [$_{I'}$ pro cree [$_{C'}$ que [$_{I'}$ Juan lo vio
      a él$_i$]] t$_i$]]?
      [$_{C'}$ Which of the boys$_i$ [$_{I'}$ pro believes [$_{C'}$ that [$_{I'}$ Juan him saw
      him$_i$]] t$_i$]]?

In (32), the postverbal trace of the wh-element in COMP must be able to serve as an antecedent to the [+B] pronominal *a él* 'him'. Thus the examples in (29) do not really constitute a counterexample to our claim, but rather, their ungrammaticality is due to a specificity compatibility between the wh-word and the [+B] pronominal.

We conclude, therefore, that the position associated with an object clitic in Spanish may be either OP or *pro*. If the gap is bound from an A'-position, it is the operator OP; otherwise, it is *pro*. All of the binding effects will follow from the nature of the element in argument position without having to assume that the clitics themselves are [±anaphor] or [±pronominal]. Clitics in our system are simply object (or subject) markers, reflecting the gender, number and specificity of the complement.[24]

3 Silent subjects

3.1 Silent subjects and Montalbetti's (1984) OPC. In this section we will explore whether the analysis proposed for objective pronominals can be extended to nominative pronominals in Spanish. Consider (33).

(33) a. ¿Luis$_i$ vendrá mañana?
        'Will Luis$_i$ come tomorrow?'

    b. Yo no sé, pero Pedro$_j$ dice que él.$_{i,j}$/e$_{i,j}$ vendrá mañana.
        'I don't know, but Pedro$_j$ says that he.$_{i,j}$/e$_{i,j}$ will-come tomorrow.'

---

[24] See also Suñer (1988).

When the lexical nominative pronominal is used, it may only refer to the subject *Pedro* in (33b), but not to *Luis*.[25] This fact can be explained if the nominative pronominal *él* 'he', like the objective pronominal *a él* 'him', is [-L, +B, +pronominal], and as such, must be bound sentence-internally. When a silent category is used, however, the gap may be interpreted as referring either to the subject *Pedro* or to the discourse topic *Luis*. As for the direct objects discussed in section 2, we may assume that the two readings found with the silent element in (33b) have different elements in subject position, an operator OP and *pro*, as shown in (34a,b), respectively.

(34) a. $[_{TOPIC}$ (Luis)$_i$ $[_{CP}$ $[_{IP}$ Pedro$_j$ dice $[_{CP}$ que $[_{IP}$ OP$_{i,*j}$ vendrá mañana]]]]]
$[_{TOPIC}$ (Luis)$_i$ $[_{CP}$ $[_{IP}$ Pedro$_j$ says $[_{CP}$ that $[_{IP}$ OP$_{i,*j}$ will-come tomorrow]]]]]

b. $[_{TOPIC}$ (Luis)$_i$ $[_{CP}$ $[_{IP}$ Pedro$_j$ dice $[_{CP}$ que $[_{IP}$ pro$_{*i,j}$ vendrá mañana]]]]]
$[_{TOPIC}$ (Luis)$_i$ $[_{CP}$ $[_{IP}$ Pedro$_j$ says $[_{CP}$ that $[_{IP}$ pro$_{*i,j}$ will-come tomorrow]]]]]

In (34a), OP may be coreferential only with the discourse topic *Luis*, which is in an A'-position. The impossibility of *Pedro* and *OP* being coreferential follows from Condition C, as argued above for direct objects. When the subject is *pro*, however, since *pro* is [-L, +B, +pronominal] in Spanish, we must have a sentence-internal antecedent.[26] We thus see that the ambiguity found with the silent category in (32b) can be explained by the fact that either OP, or *pro* may appear in subject position while the only possible reading when the lexical *él* 'he' appears is due to the fact that pronominals in

---

[25] Notice, however, that if the question is (ia), then the pronominal may be used, although marginally.
(i)a. ¿Cuándo vendrá Luis$_i$?
'When will Luis$_i$ come?'
b. ?Pedro dice que él$_i$ vendrá mañana.
'Pedro says that he$_i$ will come tomorrow.'
The relation between focus and pronominals is beyond the scope of this paper. See Larson and Luján (1990), Rigau (1986, 1987, 1988), and references cited therein.
[26] As with direct objects, *pro* may refer to any other noun phrase, provided it is sentence-internal and the features match.
(i) Ana$_i$ le dijo a la hermana$_j$ de Marta$_j$ que pro$_{i,j,k}$/OP$_l$ tenía que estudiar.
Ana$_i$ her told to the sister$_j$ of Marta$_j$ that pro$_{i,j,k}$/OP$_l$ had to study
'Ana told Marta's sister that (she) had to study.'
Where the gap refers to a discourse topic, we find OP in subject position.

Spanish have the feature [+B], which forces them to have sentence-internal antecedents.

If an operator occupies the position of a silent subject, then we expect this operator to be able to license a parasitic gap, parallel to the way an operator in object position licenses a parasitic gap. This is borne out.

(35) a. ¿Qué pasó con el avión? -Explotó antes de hacer revisar.
What happened with the plane? -Exploded before of to-make check
'What happened with the plane? -It exploded before they checked (it).'

b. *El avión explotó antes de hacer revisar.
The plane exploded before of to-make check
'The plane exploded before they checked (it).'

In (35a) the subject is OP, which refers to the discourse topic *el avión* 'the plane'. It is this operator which licenses the parasitic gap in (35a). In (35b), on the other hand, there is no operator, but rather a lexical NP which occupies the subject position. This lexical NP cannot license the parasitic gap, nor can its trace in the object position of *(hacer)-revisar* 'to have checked'. Hence the ungrammaticality of (32b) and the contrast between (35a) and (35b). If the subject of the sentence in (35a) were *pro*, the parasitic gap would not be licensed as pronominals do not license parasitic gaps.[27]

The subject in (35a) is bound from an A'-position by the discourse topic and thus it is OP, as argued above. If it is not bound from an A'-position, the silent subject would then be *pro* and we would expect a parasitic gap not to be possible in this construction. This is borne out.

(36) *Los restos del avión muestran que explotó antes de hacer revisar.
The remains of the plane show that exploded before of to-make check
'The remains of this plane show that it exploded before they checked (it).'

---

[27] Engdahl (1985: 7) notes that a resumptive pronoun in subject position may license a parasitic gap in Swedish.

(i) Det var den fangen som lakarna inte kunda avgora [$_{CP}$ om han$_i$ verkligen var skjuk] [utan att tala med e personlingen]
'This is the prisoner that the doctors couldn't determine if he really was ill without talking to in person.'

The parasitic gap which appears as a complement of *att tala med* 'to talk with' is licensed by the resumptive pronoun *han* 'he'. Engdahl argues that in Swedish, but not in English, resumptive pronouns have the status of variables. Spanish allows silent subjects to license a parasitic gap because OP may appear in subject position in Spanish.

This argues in favor of the two constructions proposed in (34). A silent subject, therefore, parallel to a silent object, may be an operator OP or *pro*. If it is bound from an A'-position, it is OP, otherwise it is *pro*. This suggests, then, that the 'null-subject parameter' is actually the surface form of two different phenomena: the fact that both OP or *pro* are allowed in subject position.

So far, we have been considering subject pronouns in embedded clauses. Is this behavior replicated in matrix clauses? Consider (37).

> (37) a. ¿Trabaja Marta en la universidad?
>   'Does Marta work at the university?'
>
>   b. Sí, ?*ella/e trabaja en la universidad.
>   Yes, ?*she/e works at the university
>   'Yes, she works at the university.'

The use of the pronoun in (37) makes the sentence ungrammatical.[28] This fact would follow from our system of pronominals are [-L, +B, +pronominal]. *Ella* 'she' would not be bound in (37b), hence the ungrammaticality with the pronominal form. We would therefore expect *pro*, if *pro* is also [-L, +B, +pronominal], to be impossible in (37b). Thus the only possibility left is the operator OP, which would be bound by the discourse topic. Then the structure for (37b) would be (38).

> (38) [$_{\text{TOPIC}}$ (Marta)$_i$ [$_{\text{CP}}$ [$_{\text{IP}}$ OP$_i$ trabaja en la universidad]]]
>   [$_{\text{TOPIC}}$ (Marta)$_i$ [$_{\text{CP}}$ [$_{\text{IP}}$ OP$_i$ works at the university]]]

Thus silent subjects in main clauses are the result of having the possibility of an operator OP in subject position, while silent subjects in embedded clauses could be either OP or *pro*. In section 2 the same parallelism was shown for direct objects.

We argued in section 2 that the OP in object position moves in LF, thus accounting for the lack of subjacency effects in those constructions. OP in subject position also seems to move in LF. Consider (39).

---

[28] If the sentence is answered negatively, the use of the pronoun is allowed, however.
  (i) ¿Trabaja Marta en la universidad? -No, (?ella) trabaja en una escuela.
     Works Marta at the university? -No, she works in a school
     'Does Marta work at the university? -No, she works in a school.'
A pronoun may also be used if a specific question is asked.
  (ii) ¿Dónde trabaja Marta? -(?Ella) trabaja en la universidad.
     'Where does Marta work? -She works at the university.'
The relation between focus and pronominals is left open for future research.

(39) ¿Quién te preguntó si sabías cuándo José$_i$ hacía la tarea?
'Who asked you whether you knew when José$_i$ did his homework?'

Luis me preguntó si sabía cuándo *él$_i$/e$_i$ hacía la tarea.
Luis me asked whether (I) knew when *he$_i$/e$_i$ did the homework
'Luis asked me if I knew when he did the homework.'

In (39) the gap may be interpreted as coreferential with the discourse topic *José*. As argued above, we would have OP in subject position A'-bound by the silent discourse topic. If OP moved in (39a), we would obtain a subjacency violation and we would expect the sentence to be ungrammatical. The grammaticality of the sentence when the gap is interpreted as the discourse topic suggests that there has been no movement of the operator OP in S-Structure. As with objects, the operator moves in LF. Notice that a pronominal (whether silent or not) would be ruled out in (39). This is due to the fact that pronominals in Spanish are [+B], as we have argued above. In (39a) the pronominal *él* 'he' (or a silent *pro*) would not be bound sentence-internally when it refers to the discourse topic. Hence the ungrammaticality of the construction in the intended reading. Without the context of the question in (39), the gap may be interpreted as being coreferential with the subject *Luis*. In this case we would have an A-bound *pro* in subject position, as argued above. This supports our claim that either OP or *pro* may appear in subject position. OP appears when the subject is bound from an A'-position, otherwise *pro* appears. If OP appears, movement takes place in LF.[29]

4 Acquisition evidence: L-1 acquisition and the weak Condition B.

Acquisition studies by Jakubowicz (1984), Wexler and Chien (1985), Chien and Wexler (1987), and McDaniel et al. (1990/1991) demonstrate that children obey Condition A at a very early age.[30] Recent research by Crain and McKee (1985, 1987) and McDaniel et al. (to appear) suggests that children at the age of 3 already obey Condition C. However, children seem to experience difficulty with Condition B. Thus English-speaking children sometimes seem to accept the coreference shown in (40), which is not possible in the grammar of an adult speaker.

---

[29] Prepositional pronouns seem to behave differently from nominative or objective pronouns.
(i) Pedro$_i$ le dijo a Luis$_j$ que Carlos$_k$ vivía cerca de él$_{i,j,k,l}$.
Pedro$_i$ him told to Luis$_j$ that Carlos$_k$ lived near of him$_{i,j,k,l}$
'Pedro told Luis that Carlos lived near him.'
Thus prepositional pronouns behave like English or Chinese pronouns (i.e., they bear the features [-L,-B,+pronominal]).
[30] See McKee (1989) for discussion of these studies.

(40) John$_i$ likes him$_j$.

In a very interesting experiment, McKee (1989) compares obedience to Condition B by English- and Italian-speaking children.[31] Italian, like Spanish, has clitics instead of pronouns. McKee used sentences like (41).

(41) a. Lo gnomo lo lava.
   'The gnome him washes.'

   b. Smurfette washed her.

Children have to decide whether the sentences they are presented with are true or false. While one experimenter stages the event that corresponds to one interpretation of the target sentence, the other uses a puppet that watches the event with the child. Then the puppet describes the event and the child must judge whether the puppet's report is a correct or an incorrect description of the event. This truth value judgment task thus assesses whether the child accepts the coreference of the pronoun/clitic with an antecedent.

McKee (1989) reports that 85% of the Italian-speaking children obey Condition B in (41a) by not allowing *lo* 'it' and *lo gnomo* 'the gnome' to be coreferential. In contrast, only 18% of the English-speaking children seem to obey Condition B in example (41b). If the silent object of *lavare* 'to wash' were the silent pronominal *pro*, we would have no way to account for the contrast between Italian- and English-speaking children as we would expect the pronominal element to behave similarly in both instances, unless we made a stipulation that only silent pronominals obey Condition B while lexical pronominals are more erratic, obviously an undesirable stipulation.[32]

The contrast between English and Italian follows directly from our analysis. In (41a), the complement of *lavare* 'to wash' is not a pronominal element, but rather an operator *OP*, as we have argued above. Thus (41a) and (41b) are not expected to behave similarly. In fact, examples like (41a) are expected to obey Condition C.[33]

In spite of the difference between English and Italian regarding intersentential coreference, the results for extrasentential coreference are similar in both languages. Consider (42).

---

[31] See McKee (1989) for discussion of the experiment.
[32] See McKee (1989) for a discussion of the different proposals that have been made to account for this Weak Condition B effect.
[33] McGee's (1989) experiment dealt only with Conditions A and B. Therefore, some further experimentation is needed to corroborate our hypothesis.

(42) a. Dopo che la mucca saltelló, la rana la grattó.
'After the cow jumped, the frog scratched her.'

b. After Tweety Bird jumped over the fence, the little girl kissed her.

In (42a), *la* 'her' may refer to *la mucca* 'the cow' and in (42b), *her* may refer to *Tweety Bird*. McKee reports that 97% of the Italian-speaking children and 93% of the English-speaking children get the coreference right. Our analysis predicts that we have a pronominal element in both cases; thus the similarity in behavior is to be expected.

McKee's experiment needs to be corroborated by Spanish data. If the results were to be replicated, our analysis would offer a direct explanation for the differences and similarities noted between the acquisition of clitics and pronouns in English and Spanish.

5 Conclusion. We have shown here that pronominal elements, whether silent or lexical, are [+B], which requires them to be free in their governing category, but to have an antecedent sentence-internally. We have also shown that the silent element associated with a clitic is OP if it is bound from an A'-position and *pro* otherwise. This analysis thus explains certain differences and similarities between Spanish, on the one hand, and English and Chinese, on the other. The reference phenomena discussed here would remain unexplained if *pro* were the only element which may appear coindexed with a clitic and a discourse topic in Spanish. The relation between focus and pronominals is left open for further research.

References

Authier, J. M. 1988. Null Object Constructions in Kinande. Natural Language and Linguistic Theory 6, 19-38.
Authier, J.M. 1989a. Two Types of Empty Operator. Linguistic Inquiry 20, 117-25.
Authier, J.M. 1989b. Arbitrary Null Objects and Unselective Binding. In O. Jaeggli and K. Safir, eds., The Null Subject Parameter. Dordrecht: Kluwer. 45-68.
Campos, H. 1986. Indefinite Object Drop. Linguistic Inquiry 17, 354-59.
Campos, H. 1991. Preposition Stranding in Spanish? Linguistic Inquiry 22, 741-50.
Chien, Y-C., and K. Wexler. 1987. A Comparison between Chinese-speaking and English-speaking Children's Acquisition of Reflexives and Pronouns. Paper presented at the XII Boston University Conference on Language Development, Boston, MA.
Chien, Y-C., and K. Wexler. 1990. Children's Knowledge of Locality Conditions in Binding as Evidence for the Modularity of Syntax and Pragmatics. Language Acquisition 1, 225-95.
Chomsky, N. 1982. Some Concepts and Consequences of the Theory of Government and Binding. Cambridge: MIT Press.
Chomsky, N. 1986. Barriers. Cambridge, Mass.: MIT Press.

Chomsky, N. 1989. Some Notes on the Economy of Derivation and Representation. MIT Working Papers in Linguistics 10, 43-74.

Cinque, G. 1990. Types of A'-Dependencies. Cambridge, Mass.: MIT Press.

Cole, P. 1987. Null Objects in Universal Grammar. Linguistic Inquiry 18, 597-612.

Contreras, H. 1984. A Note on Parasitic Gaps. Linguistic Inquiry 15, 698-701.

Contreras, H. 1991. Resumptive Pronouns. In this volume.

Enç, M. 1989. Pronouns, Licensing and Binding. Natural Language and Linguistic Theory 7, 51-92.

Engdahl, E. 1980. The Syntax and Semantics of Questions in Swedish. University of Massachusetts, Amherst doctoral dissertation.

Engdahl, E. 1983. Parasitic Gaps. Linguistics and Philosophy 6, 5-34.

Engdahl, E. 1985. Parasitic Gaps, Resumptive Pronouns, and Subject Extractions. Linguistics 23, 3-44.

Farrell, P. 1990. Null Objects in Brazilian Portuguese. Natural Language and Linguistic Theory 8, 325-46.

Grosu, A. 1980. On the Analogical Extension of Rule Domains. Theoretical Linguistics 7, 1-55.

Hasegawa, N. 1984/85. On the So-Called Zero Pronouns in Japanese. In The Linguistic Review 4, 289-341.

Hasegawa, N. 1988. Remarks on Zero Pronominals: in Defense of Hasegawa (1984/85). In W. Tawa and M. Nakayama, eds., Issues on Empty Categories, Proceedings of Japanese Syntax Workshop. Connecticut: Japanese Program, Connecticut College.

Higginbotham, J. 1983. Logical Form, Binding, and Nominals. Linguistic Inquiry 14, 395-420.

Huang, C.T. 1982. Logical Relations in Chinese and the Theory of Grammar. MIT doctoral dissertation.

Huang, C.T. 1984. On the Distribution and Reference of Empty Pronouns. Linguistic Inquiry 15, 531-74.

Huang, C.T. 1987. Remarks on Empty Categories in Chinese. Linguistic Inquiry 18, 321-28.

Huang, C.T. 1989. Pro-Drop in Chinese. In O. Jaeggli, and K. Safir, eds., The Null Subject Parameter. Dordrecht: Kluwer Academic Publishers. 185-214.

Huang, C.T. 1991. Remarks on the Status of the Null Object. In R. Freidin, ed., Principles and Parameters in Comparative Grammar. Cambridge, Mass.: MIT Press. 56-76.

Iatridou, S. 1986. An Anaphor not Bound in its Governing Category. Linguistic Inquiry 17, 766-72.

Jakubowicz, C. 1984. On Markedness and Binding Principles. NELS 14, 154-82.

Larson, R., and M. Luján 1990. Focused Pronouns. Ms. MIT/ University of Texas.

Lasnik, H., and J. Uriagereka 1988. A Course in GB Syntax. Cambridge, Mass.: MIT Press.

Lasnik, H., and M. Saito 1987. Move Alpha: Conditions on its Application and Output. Ms., University of Connecticut.

Lillo-Martin, D. 1985. Two Kinds of Null Arguments in American Sign Language. Natural Language and Linguistic Theory 4, 415-44.

McDaniel, D., H.S. Cairns, and J. R. Hsu. 1990/1991. Control Principles in the Grammars of Young Children. Language Acquisition 1, 297-335.

McKee, C. 1989. A Comparison of Pronouns and Anaphors in Italian and English Acquisition. Ms., University of Arizona. Paper presented at the 14th Boston University Conference on Child Language Development.

Montalbetti, M. 1984. After Binding: On the Interpretation of Pronouns. MIT doctoral dissertation.

Raposo, E. 1986. The Null Object in European Portuguese. In O. Jaeggli and C. Silva-Corvalán, eds., Studies in Romance Linguistics. Dordrecht: Foris Publications. 373-90.

Rigau, G. 1986. Some Remarks on the Nature of Strong Pronouns in Null Subject Languages. In I. Bordelois, H. Contreras, and K. Zagona, eds., Generative Studies in Spanish Syntax. Dordrecht: Foris, 143-63.

Rigau, G. 1987. Strong Pronouns. Linguistic Inquiry 19, 503-10.

Rigau, G. 1988. Sobre el carácter cuantificador de los pronombres tónicos en catalán. In V. Demonte and M. Fernández Lagunilla, eds., Sintaxis de las lenguas románicas. Madrid: Ediciones el arquero. 390-407.

Rizzi, L. 1982. Issues in Italian Syntax. Dordrecht: Foris.

Suñer, M. 1988. The Role of Agreement in Clitic Doubled Constructions. Natural Language and Linguistic Theory 6, 391-434.

Suñer, M., and M. Yépez 1988. Null Definite Objects in Quiteño. Linguistic Inquiry 19, 511-19.

Taraldsen, K.T. 1980. The Theoretical Interpretation of a Class of 'Marked' Extractions. In A. Belletti, L. Brandi, G. Neucioni, and L. Rizzi, eds., Theory of Markedness in Generative Grammar. Pisa: Scuola Normale Superiore di Pisa.

Wexler, K., and Y-C. Chien. 1985. The Development of Lexical Anaphors and Pronouns. Papers and Reports on Child Language Development 24, Stanford University, 138-49.

On resumptive pronouns

Heles Contreras*
University of Washington

1 Types of pronouns. The label 'resumptive pronoun' is used in the literature for forms like the following:

(1) ¿Qué libro te preguntas quién lo_i escribió pro_i?
'Which book do you wonder who wrote it?'

(2) el libro que me pregunto quién lo_i escribió pro_i
'the book that I wonder who wrote it'

(3) Ese libro, me pregunto quién lo_i escribió pro_i.
'That book, I wonder who wrote it.'

The resumptive pronoun is an empty category in the object position of *escribió* 'wrote', presumably *pro*. In (1-3), it is obligatorily coindexed with a clitic, but with certain binders, there is no clitic, as in (4).[1]

(4) Dinero, me pregunto quién tiene *pro*.
'Money, I wonder who has.'

What these pronouns have in common is that they are locally A'-bound, in contrast with the pronouns in (5) and (6), which are locally A-bound.

(5) $Juan_i$ cree que María lo_i odia pro_i.
'John thinks Mary hates him.'

*** I am indebted to H. Campos, V. Demonte, P. Kempchinsky, and M. Suñer for comments on an earlier draft. Remaining errors are my sole responsibility.

[1] Suñer (1988) claims that the clitic is an agreement marker with the feature [+specific]. Although this view is compatible with the facts in 1-4, there are sentences like (i) and (ii) which call it into question.
    (i) A ningún candidato lo entrevistaron.
       'They didn't interview any candidate.'
    (ii) A pocos candidatos los han entrevistado.
       'They have interviewed few candidates.'
I will return to these cases below.

(6) Todo estudiante$_i$ cree que su$_i$ profesor *lo$_i$* odia *pro$_i$*.
'Every student thinks his teacher hates him.'

The pronouns in (6) are sometimes referred to as 'bound pronouns' because their A-binder is a quantifier, which results in the pronoun being a semantic, though not a syntactic, variable.

In this paper, I restrict my attention to resumptive pronouns as in (1-3), and assume the following preliminary definition:

(7) A resumptive pronoun is a locally A'-bound pronoun.

I assume the standard view of local binding, as follows:

(8) x locally binds y iff there is no z such that z binds y, and z does not c-command x.

Two types of resumptive pronoun must be distinguished, depending on whether the A'-binder is an operator or not. In (1), the A'-binder *qué libro* 'which book' is an operator. In (3), an instance of left dislocation, the A'-binder is not an operator. The status of (2) with respect to this distinction will be discussed below in section 7.

Whenever this distinction becomes crucial, I will refer to pronouns in (1) as 'pronominal variables'. Their status as (syntactic) variables derives from the following definition, a modified version of Koopman and Sportiche's (1982):

(9) x is a variable iff (a) and (b)
    (a) x is in an A-position
    (b) x is locally operator-bound[2]

In this paper, I will be concerned with the distribution of resumptive pronouns, especially the subclass of pronominal variables. I will argue that the traditional idea that resumptive pronouns occur inside syntactic islands is basically correct, as long as we restrict this statement to pronominal variables. Assuming that syntactic islands are characterized by (violations of) Subjacency, the following principle suggests itself:

---

[2] Koopman and Sportiche's definition includes (i) as the second condition:
    (i) x is locally A'-bound
According to their definition, both the pronouns in (1) and (3) are variables. As I will argue below, this is not correct.

(10) Anti-subjacency Condition on Pronominal Variables (ACPV)
A pronominal variable must be non-subjacent to its operator.

This paper provides support for such a principle.

2 Some preliminary questions. It is clear from the grammaticality of sentences like (1) that Spanish has resumptive pronouns. Since the English gloss is also grammatical, we have evidence, contra Chao and Sells (1984), that English has resumptive pronouns, and, contra Safir (1986), that English resumptive pronouns are not limited to relative clauses.[3]

Given the distinction between pronominal variables and other resumptive pronouns, and the anti-subjacency requirement which applies to the former, we expect a different distribution for resumptive pronouns like those in (1) and those in (3). Since the resumptive pronoun in (1) is a pronominal variable, we expect it to be limited to occurrence inside syntactic islands. This is correct, as shown in (11).

(11) a. *¿Qué libro$_i$ lo$_i$ compró *pro$_i$* María?
'Which book did Mary buy it?'

b. ¿Qué libro$_i$ no sabes quién lo$_i$ compró *pro$_i$*?
'Which book don't you know who bought it?'

c. ¿Qué libro$_i$ dices que conoces a la autora que lo$_i$ escribió *pro$_i$*?
'Which book do you say you know the author who wrote it?'

In (11b), the resumptive pronoun is inside a wh-island,[4] and in (11c), inside a complex NP. In contrast, there is no island in (11a).
Consider now a resumptive pronoun bound by a non-operator:

(12) a. Esos libros$_i$, María no los$_i$ leyó *pro$_i$*.
'Those books, Mary didn't read them.'

b. Esos libros$_i$, no sé quién los$_i$ habrá leído *pro$_i$*.
'Those books, I don't know who may have read them.'

---

[3] Some speakers consider the English version of (1) and (2) ill-formed, for reasons which are not clear to me. However, sentences like (i) are consistently judged well-formed, in support of the point in the text.
(i) Which book$_i$ do you think that if I read it$_i$ I'll know all about cars?
[4] Following Chomsky (1986a), the embedded CP in (11b) is an inherent barrier. The resumptive pronoun is thus 1-subjacent to the operator *qué libro* 'which book'.

    c. Esos libros$_i$, conozco a la autora que los$_i$ escribió *pro$_i$*.
    'Those books, I know the author who wrote them.'

In this case, the resumptive pronoun may be either subjacent to its binder (12a) or not (12b, c). This justifies restricting the Anti-subjacency Condition to resumptive pronouns which are operator-bound, i.e. to pronominal variables.

3 Islands. In this section, I examine the different contexts where pronominal variables occur in Spanish. This will lead us to a reexamination of the notion Subjacency and its counterpart Anti-subjacency. In particular, we will see that the so-called Subject Condition (Chomsky 1977) should not be subsumed under Subjacency.

    3.1 Complex NPs. We have already seen that pronominal variables inside relative clauses may be bound by an external operator:

(11) c. ¿Qué libro$_i$ dices que conoces a la autora que lo$_i$ escribió *pro$_i$*?
      'Which book do you say you know the author who wrote it?'

This is also true of pronominal variables inside noun-complement structures, as in (13):

(13) ¿Qué libro$_i$ deploras el hecho de que lo$_i$ hayan prohibido *pro$_i$*?
    'Which book do you deplore the fact that they have banned it?'

These facts are compatible with the ACPV, under the standard assumption that the Complex NP Constraint reduces to Subjacency.[5]

    A question arises with respect to structures of type (14), where 'pv' is a pronominal variable, and 't' a wh-trace, both locally bound by the same operator (order irrelevant):

(14) Op$_i$ ... [$_{NP}$ [$_{CP}$ ...pv$_i$...]]... t$_i$...

    It is generally assumed, based on English examples like (15), that such structures, referred to as Weak Crossover cases, are ungrammatical:

---

[5] Under the *Barriers* approach, the CP in a noun-complement structure is a barrier, but not the immediately dominating NP, whereas in a relative clause structure, both CP and NP are barriers. Strictly speaking, then, the resumptive pronoun is 1-subjacent to its operator in (13), while the resumptive pronoun in (11c) is 2-subjacent to its operator. This suggests a relaxation of the ACPV to allow resumptive pronouns to be 1-subjacent to their binders. Further support for this claim will be presented in section 3.2.

(15) a. *Who$_i$ did the woman he$_i$ loved betray t$_i$?

b. *Who$_i$ did the woman that loved him$_i$ betray t$_i$?

The ill-formedness of such structures is attributed to a violation of the Bijection Principle (Koopman and Sportiche 1982) or the Parallelism Constraint on Binding (Safir 1984: 615):

(16) Bijection Principle
There is a bijective relation between operators and variables

(17) Parallelism Constraint on Binding (PCOB)
If O is an operator and x is a variable bound by O, then for any y, y a variable bound by O, x and y are [α lexical].

Either account is compatible with the Antisubjacency Condition. However, there are independent reasons to question both the Bijection Principle and the PCOB. Consider the following examples:

(18) a. ¿Qué puente$_i$ destruyó t$_i$ el ingeniero que lo$_i$ diseñó *pro$_i$*?
'Which bridge did the engineer who designed it destroy?'

b. ¿A qué país$_i$ ofendió t$_i$ la declaración de que su$_i$ gobierno es antidemocrático?
'Which country did the declaration that its government is antidemocratic offend?'

Both the Spanish and the English version of these structures correspond to type (14), and yet they are grammatical. This is a problem for both the Bijection Principle and the PCOB, and it suggests that the reason for the ill-formedness of (15) must lie elsewhere.
Consider (19), structurally parallel to (15).

(19) a. Which famous writer$_i$ did the woman he$_i$ loved betray t$_i$?

b. Which famous writer$_i$ did the woman that loved him$_i$ betray t$_i$?

The difference between (15) and (19) lies in the specificity of the operator. It would appear, then, that the ill-formedness of (15) derives not from the Bijection Principle or the PCOB, which are clearly violated in (18) and (19), but from some as yet unclear requirement relating to the degree of specificity of operators which bind pronominal variables.[6]

In conclusion, a pronominal variable may be bound from outside a complex NP, regardless of whether the operator that binds it also binds a non-pronominal variable. This follows if we adopt the ACPV and reject the Bijection Principle and the PCOB.

3.2 Wh-islands. Consider now pronominal variables inside wh-islands, as in (11b).

(11) b. ¿Qué libro$_i$ no sabes quién lo$_i$ compró pro$_i$?
'Which book don't you know who bought it?'

The structure in question is (20).

(20) [$_{CP1}$ Qué libro$_i$ [$_{IP}$ no sabes [$_{CP2}$ quién lo$_i$ compró pro$_i$]]]

According to Chomsky (1986a), CP2 is an inherent barrier by virtue of being tensed. IP, however, is not a barrier. This entails that the resumptive pronoun is 1-subjacent to the operator *qué libro* 'which book', given Chomsky's (1986a: 30) definition of Subjacency:

(21) x is n-subjacent to y iff there are fewer than n+1 barriers for x that exclude y.

These facts suggest the following modification of (10):

(22) ACPV (revised)
A pronominal variable must be at least 1-subjacent to its operator.

Within the Barriers framework, a tenseless wh-island is weak in the sense that only CP is a barrier. The status of tensed wh-islands is less clear. Chomsky (1986a) suggests that the most deeply embedded IP is an intrinsic barrier in languages like English, whereas in Italian-type languages, the most

---

[6] The following is a reasonable conjecture. Suppose there is a condition on pronominal variables which prevents them from being more specific than their operators. This would account for the ill-formedness of (15), since *who* is specified only as [+human], while *he* and *him* are marked for gender in addition. It is true that *writer* in (19) is not overtly marked for gender either. However, given that gender plays a role in English grammar for the selection of pronouns, it is not unreasonable to assume that nouns are also assigned gender, whether the category is overtly marked or not. Under these assumptions, *he* is a possible variable for *which famous writer*, but not for *who*.

deeply embedded tensed CP has the status of an intrinsic barrier. This means that in English, extraction out of a tensed wh-island would involve crossing two barriers. In Italian type languages, extraction out of a tensed wh-island should involve crossing only one barrier, since presumably the status of intrinsic barrier does not 'reinforce' the barrierhood of CP, which is independently a barrier by inheritance. Under these assumptions, there should not be any contrast between the following two Spanish sentences, while the English glosses should differ:

(23) a. ?¿Qué coche$_i$ no sabes cuándo repararon t$_i$?
'Which car don't you know when they fixed?'

b. ¿Qué coche$_i$ no sabes cómo reparar t$_i$?
'Which car don't you know how to fix?'

In fact, to my ear the Spanish examples differ in the same way as the English glosses do, which suggests that perhaps the 'reinforced' CP barrier in (23a) is stronger than the normal CP barrier in (23b).

With regards to resumptive pronouns, we expect that, given the modified version (22) of the ACPV, they would occur in both types of islands, which seems to be correct, although (24b) may be slightly less acceptable than (24a):

(24) a. ¿Qué coche$_i$ no sabes cuándo lo$_i$ repararon?
'Which car don't you known when they fixed it?'

b. ¿Qué coche$_i$ no sabes cómo repararlo$_i$?
'Which car don't you know how to fix it?'

3.3 Adjunct islands. Extraction out of adjuncts is standardly assumed to violate Subjacency:

(25) *¿Qué escritor$_i$ dices que fuiste a España antes de conocer t$_i$?
'Which writer do you say that you went to Spain before meeting?'

We expect that replacing the trace by a resumptive pronoun would restore grammaticality, and in fact it does:

(26) ¿Qué escritor$_i$ dices que fuiste a España antes de conocerlo$_i$?
'Which writer do you say you went to Spain before meeting him?'

This is further support for the ACPV.

It is well known that adjuncts can contain 'parasitic gaps' (pg), as in (27).

(27) ¿Qué artículos$_i$ archivaste t$_i$ sin leer pg$_i$?
'Which articles did you file without reading?'

Under the null-operator analysis of parasitic gaps (Contreras 1984, Chomsky 1986a), they are non-pronominal variables subjacent to their operator:

(28) Which articles$_i$ did you file t$_i$ without Op$_i$ PRO reading e$_i$?

The parasitic gap, but not the *real* gap, can be replaced by a resumptive pronoun:

(29) a. ¿Qué artículos archivaste sin leerlos?
'Which articles did you file without reading them?'

b. *¿Qué artículos los archivaste sin leer?
'Which articles did you file them without reading?'

c. *¿Qué artículos los archivaste sin leerlos?
'Which articles did you file them without reading them?'

The ungrammaticality of (29b) and (29c) is expected, since they contain a pronominal variable which is subjacent to its operator. The question is why (29a) is not similarly disallowed. If its structure were as in (30), it should be ungrammatical for the same reason that (29b) and (29c) are:

(30) ¿Qué artículos$_i$ archivaste t$_i$ sin Op$_i$ leerlos$_i$?

However, if we assume that nothing forces the presence of a null operator in this structure, the alternative in (31) is available.

(31) ¿Qué artículos$_i$ archivaste t$_i$ sin leerlos$_i$?
'What articles did you file without reading them?'

In this structure, the operator *qué artículos* 'which articles' binds both a trace and a pronominal variable. Since they are respectively subjacent and anti-subjacent to the operator, the structure is well formed.[7]

Another structure relevant to adjunct islands is the following:

---

[7] But below I will argue that Spanish and English C always license a Spec(CP), which dictates adopting structure (30). I have no solution for this conflict.

Another structure relevant to adjunct islands is the following:

(32) a. ¿A quién$_i$ viste t$_i$ antes de que él$_i$ te viera?
'Who did you see before he saw you?

b. ¿A quién$_i$ viste t$_i$ antes de que llegara su$_i$ madre?
'Who did you see before his mother arrived?'

Both the trace and the pronoun are variables, so the structures are predicted to be ill-formed by both the Bijection Principle and the PCOB. The ACPV, on the other hand, correctly predicts their grammaticality, since the trace and the pronominal variable are respectively subjacent and anti-subjacent to the operator.

3.4 The Subject Condition.   Chomsky (1977) has suggested that extraction out of a subject is disallowed by Subjacency.   In the *Barriers* framework, since the subject is not L-marked, it is a blocking category and a barrier, and the IP immediately dominating it is a barrier by inheritance. This accounts for the contrast in (33).

(33) a. *Who$_i$ were [$_{IP}$ [$_{NP}$ pictures of t$_i$] for sale]?

b. Who$_i$ did you sell [$_{NP}$ pictures of t$_i$]?

Given our proposal concerning pronominal variables, (33a) should be grammatical if the trace were to be replaced by a resumptive pronoun. This is not the case, however:

(34) *Who$_i$ were pictures of him$_i$ for sale?

This suggests that either the ACPV is incorrect, or the Subject Condition is not subsumed under Subjacency.   I want to argue for the latter, by showing that in fact there is no Subject Condition.

The evidence comes from observations in Stockwell, Schachter and Partee (1973) and Kuno (1973).   Essentially, what these authors show is that extraction out of a subject is not always disallowed.   In particular, cases like the following seem perfectly well formed:

(35) a. This is a problem to which$_i$ [the solutions t$_i$ by several students] were correct.

b. This is a problem to which$_i$ [several students' solutions t$_i$] were correct.

    c. This is a country on which$_i$ [a book t$_i$ by an Australian author] appeared last year.

    d. This is the conqueror by whom$_i$ [the capture of the city t$_i$] is certain.

Similarly for Spanish:

(36) Esta es la materia en la que$_i$ [la competencia t$_i$ de María] es clara.
'This is the matter in which Mary's competence is clear.'

Given these facts, it is unlikely that the ill-formedness of (33a) can be attributed to Subjacency. I cannot deal with this issue here, but I suggest elsewhere (Contreras 1989) that the main factors relevant to extraction out of Nps in general, subject or otherwise, are the ECP and Chomsky's (1986b) Uniformity Condition on Inherent Case assignment.

An additional argument suggesting that the Subject Condition does not reduce to Subjacency is the following. Consider the possible interpretations of (37) and (38).

(37) [Pictures of everyone] are for sale.

(38) Mary left [before everyone spoke].

(37) is ambiguous. It means either that group pictures are for sale or that for everyone, his or her picture is for sale. (38), on the other hand, has only one interpretation: Mary left at a time prior to the time when everyone had spoken. Thus, if there are three speakers, A, B, and C, who spoke in that order, the sentence is true if Mary's leaving takes place before A speaks, or before B speaks, or before C speaks. Pragmatically, there is something odd if the sentence is intended to refer to Mary's leaving before A spoke, since in that case, there is a more perspicuous alternative:

(39) Mary left before anyone spoke.

Thus, uttering (38) for the intended meaning of (39) violates Grice's (1975) maxim of quantity.

The relevant fact about (38), however, is that, unlike (37), it is not ambiguous, that is, it has no interpretation under which *everyone* has wide scope. Such an interpretation would be identical to that of (39).

The facts in question can be formulated in this way:

(40) a. A quantifier contained in a subject may have wide or narrow scope.

    b. A quantifier contained in an adjunct may only have narrow scope.

I suggest that this distinction can be captured by adopting May's (1977) original proposal that Quantifier Raising obeys Subjacency. This account, however, will only work if the Adjunct Condition, but not the Subject Condition, is subsumed under Subjacency. But his is exactly what we have independently observed above.

A third argument against subsuming the Subject Condition under Subjacency has to do with the relative degree of deviance observed in cases of extraction out of a subject.

The standard assumption is that Subjacency is a 'weak' principle whose violation produces mildly deviant structures. ECP violations, on the other hand, yield strongly deviant structures. This is how the following contrast is accounted for:

(43) a. ?Which car don't you know when they fixed?

    b. *When don't you know which car they fixed?

Since (43a) violates only Subjacency, its degree of deviance is minimal. (43b), on the other hand, which violates Subjacency and ECP, is strongly deviant.

What about the degree of deviance induced by violating the Subject Condition? In some cases, like (35) or (36), there is none, whereas in others, like (33a), the deviance is much stronger than one would expect if only Subjacency were violated. This suggests that if a principle is violated by (33a), it is not Subjacency.

It is beyond the limits of the present article to argue extensively for a revised definition of Subjacency with the desired properties. One possibility, suggested in Contreras (1986), is to base the definition of barrier for Subjacency, not on L-marking as in Chomsky (1986a), but on a different notion which, instead of grouping subjects with adjuncts, groups them with complements. I leave this matter open.

4 Indirect objects. A potential problem for the theory developed here is the behavior of indirect objects (IOs) in Spanish, as in (44).

(44) ¿A quién$_i$ le$_i$ diste un libro e$_i$?
'Who did you give a book to?'

If either the empty category associated with the clitic *le* or the sequence *le...e* is a pronominal variable, structures like (44) clearly violate the ACPV. On the other hand, if IOs are either not pronominals or not variables, there is no conflict. It does not seem fruitful to argue for the non-pronominal status of IOs, since they clearly behave as pronominals with respect to the Binding Theory.

Consider the following structures:

(45) a. María le pegó.
   'Mary struck her/it/him.'

   b. María dice que Juan le pegó.
   'Mary says John struck her/it/him.'

The IO in (45a) is obligatorily disjoint in reference from the subject *María*, while in (45b) coreferentiality is possible. This is exactly what one expects if the IO is a pronominal.

It is possible to argue, however, that IOs are not variables, particularly if they can be shown to belong to the category PP. In this respect, they would behave in the same way as IOs in English. The standard assumption is that S-structure (46) is reconstructed as (47) in LF, and that the variable is the empty category in the latter.

(46) [$_{PP}$ To whom]$_i$ did you talk e$_i$?

(47) [$_{NP}$ Whom]$_i$ did you talk [$_{PP}$ to e$_i$]?

Underlying this analysis is the assumption that only Nps are variables. Clearly, if we adopt this assumption and analyze Spanish IOs as PP, the structures under discussion pose no problem.

Unfortunately, there is no consensus in the literature concerning the categorial status of Spanish IOs. While Jaeggli (1982) and Demonte (1986) argue that they are PP, Strozer (1976) and Suñer (1988) consider them NPs. I cannot give this matter all the attention it deserves here. Should it turn out that IOs are actually Nps, their different behavior with respect to the ACPV would have to be accounted for in a different way. I will, therefore, assume for present purposes that the arguments presented by Jaeggli and Demonte are essentially correct, and that Spanish IOs are of category PP.

5 Partitives. Suñer (1988) notes that partitive constructions like the following admit the presence of a clitic:

(48) a. ¿A cuál de los dos candidatos lo entrevistaron?
     'Which of the two candidates did they interview?'

    b. ¿A cuántas de ellas las interrogaron?
     'How many of them did they question?'

The clitic and its associated empty category are clearly subjacent to the wh-phrases which bind them, in apparent violation of the ACPV. Non-partitive constructions like the following are more problematic.

(49) a. *¿A qué candidato lo entrevistaron?
     'Which candidate did they interview?'

    b. *¿A cuántas pasajeras las rescataron?
     'How many passengers did they rescue?'

Suñer considers them ungrammatical. To my ear, they do not sound totally unacceptable, and the slightly modified versions in (50) sound perfect.

(50) a. ¿A qué candidato dices que lo entrevistaron?
     'Which candidate do you say that they interviewed (him)?'

    b. ¿A cuáles pasajeras dices que las rescataron?
     'Which passengers do you say that they rescued (them)?'

Suñer (1988) attributes the contrast posited between (48) and (49) to a difference in specificity. Under her assumptions, the Spanish direct object clitic is [+specific], and as such it can only corefer with a [+specific] NP. As noted in fn. 1, this hypothesis fails to account for structures like (51), since phrases like *ninguno de los candidatos* 'none of the candidates' cannot be considered specific:

(51) A ninguno de los candidatos lo entrevistaron.
    'They didn't interview any of the candidates.'

If structures like (50) are also well formed, as I believe they are, they constitute an additional problem for Suñer's proposal.

I will suggest following Rizzi (1990) and Cinque (1990), that the relevant feature is 'referentiality', and that wh-phrases and quantifier phrases containing overt Nps or N's can optionally be interpreted as referential. If this interpretation is chosen for (48) and (50), for example, the [clitic...pro] chain is no longer a pronominal variable, but just an ordinary pronoun, and consequently not subject to the Anti-subjacency Condition on Pronominal Variables.

Cinque (1990) suggests that referential interpretation of a wh-phrase is only available when the wh-phrase does not interact with a quantifier, as illustrated by the following examples:

(52) a. *[Quanti pazienti$_i$ ognuno dei medici potesse visitare] non era chiaro neppure a loro$_i$.
'How many patients every one of the doctors could visit was not clear even to them.'

b. [Quanti pazienti$_i$ fossero presenti] non era chiaro neppure a loro$_i$.
'How many patients were present was not even clear to them.'

It is well known that the bound variable interpretation of a pronoun is only available if the pronoun is c-commanded by an operator. Predictably, in (52) the pronoun *loro* 'them' cannot be interpreted as a bound variable, since the operator *quanti pazienti* 'how many patients' does not c-command it. But since in (53) *loro* can corefer with *quanti pazienti*, it must be the case that this phrase is taken to be referential. This is possible, according to Cinque, because in (53) the phrase in question does not interact with a quantifier. Since in (52) it does, the referential interpretation is precluded.

Cinque (1990) points out that his notion of referentiality subsumes Pesetsky's (1987) concept of D(iscourse)-linking, but does not spell out exactly how this happens. I will speculate briefly on how this could be accomplished.

Notice, to begin with, that Cinque's suggestion that quantificational phrases may optionally be considered referential does not extend in a natural way to expressions like *ninguno de los candidatos* 'none of the candidates'. Yet we have seen that phrases like this are compatible with subjacent pronominals, as in (51). A solution to this problem, preserving the spirit of Cinque's proposal, seems to require a mechanism whereby the quantifier is ignored and only the referential part of the phrase (an NP in (48) and (51), and an N' in (49) and (50)) is visible for pronominal coreference. This might be accomplished by reinterpreting the relevant structures as left dislocated constructions in the manner sketched in (54).

(54) a. cuál de los candidatos   → de los candidatos$_x$ [cuál x...]
     which of the candidates → of the candidates$_x$ [which x...]

b. ninguno de los candidatos → de los candidatos$_x$ [ningún x...]
   none of the candidates   → of the candidates$_x$ [no x...]

c. qué candidato   → (en cuanto a) candidatos$_x$ [qué x...]
   which candidate → (as for) candidates$_x$ [which x...]

This might also explain Suñer's judgment that (49) is ungrammatical, on the assumption that it is harder to impose a referential interpretation on N' than on NP (or DP).

These comments are obviously quite tentative, but they seem to point in the right direction.

6 Null operator structures. In this section, I examine null operator structures with respect to the ACPV. I restrict myself to the *tough*-movement construction for purposes of illustration. Consider (55), from Stowell and Lasnik (1987):

(55) John should be easy for his wife to love e.

It is possible to interpret the pronoun *his* as coreferential with *John*. Under this interpretation, the structure is (56).

(56) John$_i$ should be easy Op$_i$ for his$_i$ wife to love e$_i$.

Both *his* and *e* are variables, locally bound by the null operator, and the structure should be disallowed as a Weak Crossover case, in the same way that (57) is:

(57) *Who$_i$ does his$_i$ wife love e$_i$?

In our terms, (55) and (56) violate the ACPV.

The solution to this puzzle, I suggest, lies in Chomsky's (1982) proposal regarding the level at which Predication applies. According to this idea, the coindexation of *John* with the chain headed by the null operator in (56) applies post S-structure. Thus the S-structure configuration for (56) is (58).

(58) John$_k$ should be easy Op$_i$ for his$_k$ wife to love e$_i$.

If ACPV is an S-structure principle, (58) does not violate it, since *his* is not a variable, but a pronoun accidentally coindexed with *John*. This account, however, is not open to (57), hence the contrast.

Stowell and Lasnik (1987) argue against this account of (56), on the basis of structures like those in (59).

(59) a. Which boy$_i$ should be easy to persuade his$_i$ mother to vouch for e$_i$?

b. No boy$_i$ should be impossible to ask his$_i$ mother to talk about e$_i$.

Their claim is that since *which boy* and *no boy* are not referential expressions but quantifier phrases, the pronoun *his* cannot pick up accidental coreference from them. These structures, however, pose no problem for our proposal. Consider (60), the S-structure representation of (59a), according to our assumptions.

(60) Which boy$_k$ t$_k$ should be easy Op$_i$ to persuade his$_k$ mother to vouch for e$_i$?

There is no violation of ACPV, since *his* is not a variable, but a pronoun locally bound by the trace in the matrix subject position. Chomsky's (1982) rule of Predication, a post-S-structure process, equates the indices *i* and *k*. Similarly for (59b), with S-structure (61).

(61) No boy$_k$ should be impossible Op$_i$ to ask his$_k$ mother to talk about e$_i$.

Again there is no violation of ACPV, since *his* is not a variable.

We conclude, then, that these cases are not counterexamples to ACPV, and that no special assumption needs to be made regarding null operators or their variables. In particular, there is no need to posit a new kind of empty category, empty names, as suggested by Stowell and Lasnik (1987).

7 A-binding vs. A'-binding. Several languages have constructions involving apparent resumptive pronouns which violate the ACPV. This is the case in Irish (McCloskey 1989), Welsh (Harlow 1981), Hebrew (Borer 1980, 1984), and Palauan (Georgopoulos 1985). An example from Irish (McCloskey 1989) is (62):

(62) an fear [$_{CP}$ ar bhuail tú é]
the man Comp struck you him
'the man that you struck (him)'

If the structure involves a null operator in Spec(CP), binding the pronoun *é* 'him', it clearly violates ACPV. I will propose that this is not the case. Essentially, this solution will be based on the assumption that Irish, Welsh, Hebrew and Palauan allow 'predicational' structures without null operators, and that the resumptive pronoun in such structures is, consequently, not a pronominal variable. In other words, the structure of (62) is (63), not (64).

(63) [$_{NP}$ [$_{NP}$ an fear]$_i$ [$_{CP}$ ar bhuail tú é$_i$]]

(64) [$_{NP}$ [$_{NP}$ an fear]$_i$ [$_{CP}$ Op$_i$ ar bhuail tú é$_i$]]

Before proceeding with our proposal, let us consider McCloskey's (1989) analysis of the Irish facts. Two preliminary observations are necessary for an understanding of his proposal. First, resumptive pronouns occur only with one of three possible Irish complementizers, which he represents as *aN*. Second, there is a restriction on the occurrence of resumptive pronouns, which McCloskey refers to as the Highest Subject Restriction (HSR), which bans resumptive pronouns from the highest subject position. This is illustrated in (65).

(65) *an fear [$_{CP}$ a   raibh   sé   breoite]
     the man Comp was   he   ill
     'the man that (he) was ill'

McCloskey argues that the resumptive pronouns in (62) and (65) are both bound by null operators, and accounts for the difference in grammaticality in terms of an extension of principle B of the Binding Theory to the A'-system, in the spirit of Aoun and Li (1989). Specifically, he proposes (66).

(66) A pronoun must be A'-free in the least Complete Functional Complex containing the pronoun and a subject distinct from the pronoun.

The relevant domain excludes the A'-binder in (62), but it includes it in (65). Thus, the pronoun in (65) violates McCloskey's revised principle B.

There are theoretical and empirical reasons which argue against this proposal, however. From a theoretical perspective, (66) is not simply an extension of principle B of the standard Binding Theory. Consider (67).

(67) the men$_i$ like [$_{NP}$ their$_i$ pictures]

In Chomsky's (1986b) formulation, the Complete Functional Complex relevant to the binding of the pronoun *their* is the NP *their pictures*, of which *their* is the subject. Crucially, then, the subject required for the identification of a Complete Functional Complex with respect to the principle B of the Binding Theory need not be different from the element being evaluated. For A'-binding, however, the subject must be distinct from the element under consideration. Obviously, McCloskey's proposal is not simply an innocent extension of principle B of the Binding Theory to the A'-system.

Empirically, one problem is that under McCloskey's account, the English counterpart to (62) should be well formed:

(68) *the man$_i$ that you struck him$_i$

This prediction is clearly incorrect.

Another problem is that this account cannot predict the difference reported for Modern Hebrew (Borer 1984) between relative clauses and questions, where only the former allow resumptive pronouns, since the assumed A'-binding facts are the same.

We must, consequently, look for a different solution. In line with current thinking about the range of possible parametric variation, I propose that the difference between English and Irish lies in the lexical properties of the respective complementizers. Adapting Fukui and Speas' (1986) proposal concerning F-features, let us assume that all English (and Spanish) heads of CP have F-features to assign, and that, consequently, the Spec(CP) position is always present.[8] This means that the structure of (68) is (69), which clearly violates ACPV.

(69) *the man$_i$ [$_{CP}$ Op$_i$ that you struck him$_i$]

On the other hand, let us assume that the Irish complementizer *aN* has no F-features to assign, so there is no Spec(CP) position associated with it. The structure of (62) is, then, (63), and no violation of ACPV occurs.

What about the Highest Subject Restriction? The relevant structures are (63) and (70).

(70) [$_{NP}$ an fear$_i$ [$_{CP}$ a raibh sé$_i$ breoite]]

---

[8] This is a modification of Fukui and Speas' proposal, under which only certain functional heads, namely those carrying F-features, license a Specifier position.

If the head NP is considered an A-position, this subject/object asymmetry might be derived from the standard principle B of the Binding Theory. [9] Let us adopt Chomsky's (1986b) version of the Binding Theory, which defines 'governing category' essentially as follows:

(71) The governing category for an expression x is the least Complete Functional Complex containing a governor of x in which x could satisfy the binding theory under some indexing.

According to McCloskey (1989), the underlying structure of Irish clauses is as in (72).

(72)

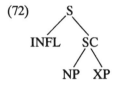

The VSO order is obtained by raising V to INFL. This position governs the subject, and consequently, the governing category for the subject cannot be SC, although SC is a Complete Functional Complex. It must be the next larger Complete Functional Complex. If we assume that the head of a relative clause counts as a subject for determining what a Complete Functional Complex is, we can derive the Highest Subject Restriction: the subject of the SC cannot be coindexed with the head of the relative clause. An object in SC, on the other hand, has SC as the governing category.

Given these considerations, we can now clearly clarify the status of (2) repeated here:

(2) el libro Op que me pregunto quién lo$_i$ escribió pro$_i$
'the book that I wonder who wrote it'

There are two potential binders for the resumptive pronoun, namely the null operator Op or the head NP *el libro* 'the book'. If the occurrence of the null operator is obligatory, as I have proposed is the case for English and Spanish, it must bind the resumptive pronoun; otherwise, there would be vacuous quantification. If this is the case, the resumptive pronoun qualifies as a pronominal variable, and is thus subject to the ACPV. We have seen that this is correct for Spanish.

---

[9] This solution has reportedly been proposed by Huybregts for Modern Hebrew (see Borer 1984: 252, fn 14).

8 Trace spell-outs. Another class of apparent counterexamples to ACPV is that of trace spellouts, which have been reported for Vata (Koopman 1984), Palauan (Georgopoulos 1985), and Hausa (Tuller 1986). I illustrate with Hausa.

According to Tuller (1986), Hausa has two resumptive pronoun strategies, one for escaping Subjacency, and one for escaping ECP. The first of these strategies, I would claim, simply follows from the ACPV. We are now interested in the second, illustrated by the following examples:

(73) a. Waa ka   yi maganaa da *(shii)
        who 2sm   do talk   with him
        'Who did you talk with?'

    b. Waa ka   karanta litaafi *(nsa)
       who 2sm   read   book-of-his
       'Whose book did you read?'

Objects of prepositions, as in (73a), or of nouns (as in (73b)), cannot be null, but must appear as pronouns, in 'extraction' structures. These pronouns are subjacent to their operators, so the structure violates the ACPV.

The solution to this puzzle, I suggest, lies along the following lines. We assume that the label 'trace spell-outs' which has been applied to these resumptive pronouns means that these pronouns are inserted between S-structure and PF. If the ACPV is an S-structure principle, as we have been assuming throughout, there is no violation. This entails that at least the head-government part of the ECP applies to a level between S-structure and PF, which is in agreement with the spirit of the proposal in Aoun, Hornstein, Lightfoot, and Weinberg (1987).

9 Conclusion. In conclusion, we have seen that the distribution of one subclass of resumptive pronouns, namely pronominal variables, obeys a condition of Anti-subjacency. Apparent counterexamples fall into place without special assumptions, once the properties of specific heads of CP are taken into account, and the possibility of trace spellouts, inserted between S-structure and PF, is allowed for.

References

Aoun, J., N. Hornstein, D. Lightfoot, and A. Weinberg. 1987. Two Types of Locality. Linguistic Inquiry 18, 537-78.
Aoun, J., and A. Li. 1988. Minimal Disjointness. Paper presented at the 7th West Coast Conference on Formal Linguistics, University of California, Irvine.
Borer, H. 1980. On the Definition of Variables. Journal of Linguistic Research 1, 17-40.

Borer, H. 1984. Restrictive Relatives in Modern Hebrew. Natural Language and Linguistic Theory 2, 219-60.

Chao, W., and P. Sells. 1984. On the Interpretation of Resumptive Pronouns. NELS 13.

Chomsky, N. 1977. On Wh-Movement. In P. Culicover, T. Wasow, and A. Akmajian, eds., Formal Syntax. New York: Academic Press. 71-132.

Chomsky, N. 1982. Some Concepts and Consequences of the Theory of Government and Binding. MIT Press.

Chomsky, N. 1986a. Barriers. MIT Press.

Chomsky, N. 1986b. Knowledge of Language. New York: Praeger.

Cinque, G. 1990. Types of A'-Dependencies. Cambridge, Mass.: MIT Press.

Contreras, H. 1984. A Note on Parasitic Gaps. Linguistic Inquiry 15, 698-701.

Contreras, H. 1986. Conditions on A'-Chains. Proceedings of the West Coast Conference on Formal Linguistics 5, 29-40. Stanford Linguistics Association. Stanford University.

Contreras, H. 1989. A Modular Approach to Syntactic Islands. Ms., University of Washington.

Demonte, V. 1986. Predication and Passive. In I. Bordelois, H. Contreras and K. Zagona, eds., Generative Studies in Spanish Syntax. Dordrecht: Foris. 51-66.

Fukui, N. and M. Speas. 1986. Specifiers and Projection. MIT Working Papers in Linguistics 8, 128-72.

Georgopoulos, C. 1985. Variables in Palauan Syntax. Natural Language and Linguistic Theory 3, 59-94.

Grice, P. 1975. Logic and Conversation. In P. Cole and J. L. Morgan, eds., Syntax and Semantics vol. 3, New York: Academic Press. 41-58.

Harlow, S. 1981. Government and Relativisation in Celtic. In F. Heny, ed., Binding and Filtering. London: Croom Helm. 213-54.

Jaeggli, O. 1982. Topics in Romance Syntax. Dordrecht: Foris.

Koopman, H. 1984. The Syntax of Verbs. Dordrecht: Foris.

Koopman, H., and D. Sportiche. 1982. Variables and the Bijection Principle. The Linguistic Review 2, 139-60.

Koopman, H., and D. Sportiche. 1988. Subjects. ms., UCLA.

Kuno, S. 1973. Constraints on Internal Clauses and Sentential Subjects. Linguistic Inquiry 4, 363-85.

McCloskey, J. 1989. Resumptive Pronouns, A'-Binding and Levels of Representation in Irish. In R. Hendrick, ed., Syntax and Semantics vol 23. New York: Academic Press. 199-248.

May, R. 1977. The Grammar of Quantification. MIT doctoral dissertation.

Pesetsky, D. 1987. Wh-in-Situ: Movement and Unselective Binding. In E. J. Reuland and A. G. B. ter Meulen, eds., The Representation of (In)definiteness. Cambridge, Mass.: MIT Press. 98-129.

Rizzi, L. 1990. Relativized Minimality. Cambridge, Mass.: MIT Press.

Safir, K. 1984. Multiple Variable Binding. Linguistic Inquiry 15, 603-38.

Safir, K. 1986. Relative Clauses in a Theory of Binding and Levels. Linguistic Inquiry 17, 663-89.

Stockwell, R., P. Schachter, and B. Partee. 1973. The Major Syntactic Structures of English. New York: Holt, Rinehart, and Winston.

Stowell, T., and H. Lasnik. 1987. Weakest Crossover. Ms., UCLA and University of Connecticut. Published in Linguistic Inquiry 22, 687-720.

Strozer, J. 1976. Clitics in Spanish. UCLA doctoral dissertation.

Suñer, M. 1988. The Role of Agreement in Clitic-Doubled Constructions. Natural Language and Linguistic Theory 6, 391-434.

Tuller, L. 1986. Bijection Relations in Universal Grammar and the Syntax of Hausa. UCLA doctoral dissertation.

Temporal and aspectual constraints on predicative adjective phrases

Violeta Demonte *
Universidad Autónoma de Madrid

0 Introduction. After a close look at the standard literature dealing with predicative APs[1] it is possible to assert, I believe, that the core of the discussion regarding their properties, as well as their relevance for the understanding of natural language phenomena, has focused on the syntax of the construction. No central attention has been paid, however, to certain crucial semantic factors which constrain their licensing.[2]

In fact, researchers on the topic of secondary predication have mainly analyzed three questions: (a) the direction (symmetric or asymmetric) of the c-command relation holding between the predicative adjective and its subject (cf. Williams 1980 and Demonte 1988); (b) the underlying structure of subject and object-oriented predicative adjectives, i.e., whether they are or are not both generated under VP, and the precise configuration in which they surface (cf. Williams 1980, Rothstein 1983, Roberts 1988, McNulty 1988, and Demonte 1988); and (c) the categorial nature of the predicate: whether it is a small clause and, if so, what kind of small clause (cf. Williams 1980, Chomsky 1981, and Stowell 1987, among others).

However, the licensing of predicative adjectives is not only formally constrained. As a first hint, observe that the examples in (1) show that a transitive verb such as *conocer* 'to know' appears normally to allow a subject-oriented secondary predicate, while an object-oriented one is precluded in the constructions in which this verb appears.

---

*I want to express my gratitude to Olga Fernández Soriano, Lluisa Gracia, and Avelina Suñer, who made useful observations on an earlier draft of this study. Special thanks are due to Paula Kempchinsky and María-Luisa Rivero, whose deep and insightful referee work undoubtedly contributed to improve this paper. I also gratefully acknowledge the confidence of Héctor Campos. Errors which still remain are all my own.

[1] Mainly, Williams (1980), Rothstein (1983), Demonte (1988), Roberts (1988), and McNulty (1988).

[2] Three brief but important exceptions in this regard are Simpson (1983) on resultatives; Rothstein (1983), which examines the properties which can be characterized through depictive and resultative predicates; and Hernanz (1988), which attempts to account formally for the perfective nature of the adjectives which occur as secondary predicates. Another larger and more recent exception is Napoli (1989). As she asserts, her work 'is in part an attempt to pull linguistic discussions of predication back into the arena of semantics' (Napoli 1989:1) in letting theta-role assignment to be the key to the subject-predicate relationship. In spite of its interest, we will not follow these lines in this work.

(1)a. **Juan** conoció la noticia **divertido.**[3]
'Juan knew the news happy.'

b.*Juan conoció **la noticia cierta.**
'Juan knew the news true.'

Note also that in (2a) and (2b) two verbs of action, both denoting change of state, differ on their possibilities of accepting an object-oriented resultative predicate; moreover, (2c), with a main verb very similar in meaning to that in (2b), seems to have stronger restrictions than the latter for the acceptance of resultatives.

(2)a. Pedro pintó **la casa verde.**
Pedro **la** pintó **verde.**
'Pedro painted the house/it green.'

b.??Pedro construyó **la casa enorme.**
??Pedro **la** construyó **enorme.**
'Pedro constructed the house/it big.'

c. *Pedro edificó **la casa amplia.**
??Pedro **la** edificó **amplia.**
'Pedro built the house/it wide.'

Moreover, it has to be pointed out that examples like (2b) improve in a significant way when the predicative is modified by a degree word like *muy* 'very', *demasiado* 'too much', or similar forms. Nevertheless, cases such as those in (3) have a subtle semantic difference as compared to (2b) and (2c).

(3)a. Pedro construyó **la casa demasiado pequeña.**
Pedro **la** construyó **demasiado pequeña.**
'Pedro built the house/it very small.'

b. Pedro edificó **la casa muy amplia.**
Pedro **la** edificó **muy amplia.**
'Pedro built the house/it very wide.'

---

[3] From here on, I will write in boldface the two items which correspond to the subject and the predicate in the predication relation. In this case, (1a) is an example of a subject-oriented predicative, (1b) is an object-oriented one.

It is my purpose here to explain contrasts similar to those exhibited in (1), (2) and (3). It will be shown that there is a close interrelation between the aspectual class to which the verb belongs and its possibility of co-occurring with certain secondary predicates. More interestingly, the existence of these restrictions and the way they interact with the syntax of the sentences in question will allow us to provide a serious argument in favor of the thesis that knowledge of the lexicon implies knowledge of the structure of a given predicate in terms of the 'sub-events' which it comprises. At the same time, it will also corroborate the supposition that the event structure of a predicate needs to be identified by some syntactic expression, either one element of the thematic structure or a 'special' adjunct.

I will proceed as follows. First, empirical generalizations concerning the distribution of depictive and resultative predicates with regard to verbs classified according to a modified version of Vendler-Dowty's aspectual classification will be delimited and illustrated. Second, following Grimshaw and Vikner's (1989) hypothesis on the substructure of events, it will be shown that object-oriented predicative APs are state predicates modifying the internal or final state of the structure of subevents developed by the verb. More strictly, while depictive predicates 'modify' the internal or medial state, resultative predicates 'express' a final state. In this sense, the presence of a resultative predicative adjective can change the reading of a verb which intrinsically does not define a final state. This contrast will be formally explained, assuming that resultatives are specifiers of VP while object-oriented depictives are adjuncts to the VP. Depictive subject-oriented predicatives, on the other hand, are independent of the event structure as they are generated outside of the VP. Third, following an idea which can be traced to Dowty (1972), arguments will be provided for the conjecture that depictive predicative APs are actually T(ense) P(hrases) dominating an Asp(ect) P(hrase) node; resultative predicates, nevertheless, do not project up to TP but up to AspP. Finally, the way the Tense and Aspect heads of the adjunct predicative adjectives interact with the correlating heads in the matrix sentence will be examined in a preliminary way.

1 The distribution of secondary predicates and the aspectual constraint

1.1 The semantic properties of the predicate. Early studies on secondary predicates, beginning with Simpson (1983) and Rothstein (1983), have made a distinction between so called 'depictive' predicates such as (4) and 'resultative' ones such as (5).

(4)a. **Luis** paseaba **contento**.
  'Luis walked happy.'

b. Enrique bebe **la leche fría.**
'Enrique drinks the milk cold.'

(5) Juan pintó **la casa roja.**
'Juan painted the house red.'

It has also been observed that there is a semantic distinction between these two subclasses of predicates. Resultative predicates appear to refer to final states, or those which show up when a given action is completed (Fabb 1984). In contrast, depictive predicates characterize situations that could be called temporary: they depict the state of the object or entity at the moment the action takes place. Examples (6a) and (6b) are paraphrases of (4a) and (5), respectively, and they illustrate the distinction just made.

(6)a. Luis paseaba cuando/y estaba contento.
'Luis was walking when/and he was happy.'

b. Juan pintó la casa y (como consecuencia de ello) la casa
está roja.
'Juan painted the house and (as a consequence) the house
is red.'

A second semantic property attributed to secondary predicates concerns the necessity of their being [+stative] adjectives with certain associated properties. To be more precise, Rothstein (1983: 153) noticed that the attribute described by the predicate 'must be at the same time an intrinsic property of the subject and a transitory one.' If the property is temporary, we add, it can be characterized as a state. Thus, in (7) (from Rothstein 1983), 'raw' describes an intrinsic and at the same time variable property of carrots, while 'orange' would not be a property describable as transitory, which is the reason for its ungrammaticality.

(7) We eat **carrots raw** / ***orange.**

While denying the idea that the attributed property has to be an intrinsic one, McNulty (1988) reformulates the previous assertion, saying that adjunct predicates attribute, in fact, 'subjective' properties to their subjects (cf. McNulty 1988: chap.4, section 4). Evidence in favor of this idea is provided by (8), where grammaticality increases when the subjectivity of the adjunct predicate is made explicit.

(8) **Mary** left the party ***beautiful** / **more beautiful than
I have ever seen her.**

In sections 2 and 3, I will reconsider this impressionistic approach to the semantic nature of the adjective predicate through its analysis as a Tense Phrase connected in some way to the Tense of the matrix sentence. The properties mentioned by Rothstein and McNulty will follow from this analysis.

A parallel approach to the semantic nature of adjective predicates appears in Hernanz (1988). On the basis of Spanish data, this linguist restates the previous issue establishing that only [+perfective] adjectives can be secondary predicates. She observes that the adjectives which can only be predicated with the Spanish verb *ser* 'to be' are not accessible to secondary predication, as in (9a); on the contrary, those compatible with *estar* 'to be [+state]' are accessible, as in (9b).

(9)a. *__Juan__ habló __temerario__. (cf. *Juan está temerario)
   'Juan spoke brave.'

   b. __Juan__ habló __aburrido__. (cf. Juan está aburrido)
   'Juan spoke boring.'

The generalization that she formulates is that the adjectives lacking the aspectual feature [+perfective] cannot be predicates because they cannot identify (in Higginbotham's 1985 terms)[4] the event argument present in the thematic grid of the matrix term. Hernanz's generalization is interesting in trying to relate the semantics of the predicate to the semantics of the main verb, and in locating the properties of the adjective in a more general framework (i.e., the theory of the functional node ASPECT), but it is not sufficient, in my opinion. Nevertheless, I will be following the spirit of Hernanz's work and I will try to relate the occurrence of secondary predicates to the semantic properties of the main verb. As a minor observation regarding Hernanz's main hypothesis, it has to be said that there are certain intrinsically [- perfective] adjectives which can be predicated secondarily, as in (10). This kind of data suggests that the perfectivity of the adjective (not questionable in general terms) has to be included in a more general context.

(10) José compró __el coche verde__ y lo vendió __marrón__ (i.e., José
    compró el coche cuando era /*estaba verde y lo vendió
    marrón)
    'José bought the car green and sold it brown (i.e, José
    bought the car when it was green and sold it brown).'

---

[4] To be more precise: according to Hernanz the *e* argument of the AP (which is only present when the adjective is [+perfective]) discharges (by identification) on the *e* position of the main verb.

More importantly, this analysis does not account for the sharp difference in productivity between subject- and object-oriented predicates, and predicts that both kinds of predicates will be possible with the same type of verbs, insofar as the predicate takes an *e* argument. This is not the situation as we will show.

1.2 Aspectual classes of verbs and the occurrence of secondary predicates. As I have said, while certain semantic properties of the adjective predicates have been put forward and briefly analyzed, no substantive claims appear in the literature regarding the intrinsic semantic properties of the verbs which co-occur with the various subclasses of predicates, except for tangential observations in Simpson (1983), Demonte (1988), and Rothstein (1983).[5]

In this subsection, I will make explicit certain descriptive generalizations showing that the inherent semantic-aspectual properties of the matrix verbs correlate in a significant way with the possibility or impossibility of occurrence of secondary predicates. At the same time, I will try to incorporate these generalizations within the frame of a plausible hypothesis about the internal structure of the event. In sections 2 and 3, I will elaborate a formal explanation for the facts treated here.

To begin, we need to recall that, traditionally, it has been accepted that a distinction has to be made between Tense or external time (i.e., the time of the situation related to another time, frequently the moment of speaking) and the internal temporality of the situation described by the main verb. This second conception of time in language is what is usually called 'Aspect' or *Aktionsart*.[6] As is well known, this notion covers two different properties of the verbal sequence: the distinction between the imperfective and perfective nature of the action, sometimes marked in the morphology as a feature apparently associated to Tense, as in Spanish; and the fact that verbs, by their inherent meaning, can be described as event, result, or state predicates,[7] or as punctual, continuing, stative or resultative ones.[8] It is also

---

[5] Rothstein (1983: 150) notes that 'resultative predicates are permitted only with verbs which describe a change of state occurring to the patient argument. The predicate describes the state which the verb causes, and predicates this of the object.' Simpson (1983) postulates that only 'change of state verbs' can be constructed with resultative predicates. Demonte (1988: 3) says that 'an adjective is interpreted as a resultative only when it co-occurs with perfective verbs like *pintar* "to paint", *cortar* "to cut", or *cernir* "to sift". Depictives, on the other hand, are found with imperfective verbs like *comer* "to eat"...'. As we will see, none of the previous observations is sufficient to describe the semantic restrictions on the occurrence of resultative and depictive predicates since they are not based on a clear analysis of the character of the verbal action, which appears to play a decisive role in the licensing.

[6] When the two notions are combined, certainly, a move which early structuralists in the Jakobsonian and Slavic tradition do not make.

[7] Cf. Comrie (1976, chap.2) for a distinction along these lines.

commonly accepted that both notions of aspect cannot always be separated in a clear way. Here I will not question in a detailed way this reductionistic approach and I will, in general, consider aspect 'the different ways of viewing the internal temporal constituency of a situation' (Comrie 1976: 3). However, it is the second notion of aspect that I will address. My analysis will show that the tense/aspect distinction perfective-imperfective is connected to other aspects of the syntax of the sentences and that it is not operative in the licensing of predicates.

It was Vendler (1979) who first attempted to separate four distinct subclasses of verbs by their restrictions on time adverbials, tenses and logical statements. He distinguished 'states', 'activities' (sequences of homogeneous intervals), 'achievements' (in fact, achievements without an associated task) and 'accomplishments' (i.e., achievements with an associated task and sequences of heterogeneous intervals). Dowty (1979) extended the characterization of these four aspectual classes of predicates analyzing, in detail, the syntactic contexts in which they occur.[9]

Since I will be using Vendler-Dowty's terminology, although not their core distinctions, I would first like to recall and illustrate the basic axis of their classification. As a matter of comparison and clarification, observe that in this classification what is meant by accomplishment is what Grimshaw and Vikner (1989) name 'constructive accomplishments', namely, those events in which the Theme does not exist until the entire event has occurred. On the other hand, in 'nonconstructive' accomplishments ('destroy', 'record', 'transcribe', or 'break'), which mainly correspond to activities in Vendler-Dowty's framework, the Theme is involved in the activity from the very beginning. Samples of possible members of each class appear in (11):

(11) a. STATES: *saber* 'to know', *poseer* 'to posses', *creer* 'to believe', *desear* 'to wish', *amar* 'to love', *existir* 'to exist', *equivaler* 'to be equivalent', *crecer* 'to grow', *tener* 'to have', etc.

b. ACTIVITIES: *trabajar* 'to work', *caminar* 'to walk', *comer* 'to eat', *escribir* 'to write', *reir* 'to laugh', *comerciar* 'to trade', *pensar* 'to think', *empujar* 'to push', etc.

---

[8] Cf. Bertinetto (1981) for a similar classification.
[9] An insightful criticism of Vendler's aspectual classification is found in Verkuyl (1989). This author shows that Vendler confused some of his criteria: 'he did not distinguish very well between criteria based on (some sort of) agentivity and criteria based on purely temporal properties of situations such as boundedness, uniqueness, etc.' (op.cit.: 41).

c. ACHIEVEMENTS: *reconocer* 'to recognize', *descubrir* 'to find out', *vislumbrar* 'to glimpse', *encontrar* 'to find', *morir* 'to die', *darse cuenta* 'to realize', *alcanzar* 'to reach', etc.

d. ACCOMPLISHMENTS: *construir una casa* 'to build a house', *pintar un cuadro* 'to paint a picture', *hacer una silla* 'to make a chair', *escribir una novela* 'to write a novel', *trazar una línea* 'to draw a line', *correr un kilómetro* 'to run one kilometer', etc.

If we want to propose an approximate definition of these four classes, leading to the criteria on which we will base the characterization of the manner of the action, we could try to represent them through the features [± activity], [± result].   These features imply, on the one hand, that a given event can have or not have a deliberate causation and, on the other, that the developed activity can give or not give a visible result (an object which results from the activity).   Given these features, the verbs in (11) can now be classified as in (12).

(12) a. ACCOMPLISHMENTS: [+activity, +result]

b. ACTIVITIES: [+activity, -result]

c. ACHIEVEMENTS: [-activity, +result]

d. STATES: [-activity, -result]

Departing now from Vendler and Dowty's work, although in the same spirit, I would like to include the impressionistic classification of (12) in a more comprehensive theory of lexical meaning: that which assumes that a semantics based on events is able to apprehend significant generalizations not captured by other traditional approaches to meaning.   I will follow, then, lines traced by Pustejovsky (1988), Grimshaw (1990), and Grimshaw and Vikner (1989) and assume that the analysis of the argument structure of lexical items (mainly of verbs and adjectives) includes the characterization of their event structure in terms of a substructure of events.

Following Pustejovsky (1988), let us assume that the grammar should specify three primitive event types: 'states', 'transitions', and 'processes',[10]

---

[10] According to Pustejovsky, a 'state' 'is an eventuality that is viewed and evaluated relative to no other event. A "transition" is a single eventuality evaluated relative to another single eventuality...[and]... a "process" [is] a sequence of identical eventualities' (1988: 22-23). Verkuyl (1989) develops a 'compositional aspectual theory' which ends up also in an ontological tripartition in which three classes of situational types are distinguished: 'state' (state of no

and let us define these event types as objects with a subevent structure. Approximately, 'states' are obviously the states in (11) and (12); 'processes' roughly correspond to the activities (but these can imply also achievements and non-constructive accomplishments); and 'transitions' include certain achievements and constructive accomplishments. Now, if, by hypothesis, we characterize processes and certain transitions as branching event structures which could include sets of periods (the initial one, an internal sub-period, and a final one), it appears that we have a conceptual basis sufficient to formulate certain empirical generalizations regarding the occurrence of secondary predicates. The distributional rules are shown in (13), (15), and (17), while the relevant examples are shown in (14), (16), and (18), respectively.

(13) Subject-oriented secondary predicates occur in all
       kind of sentences, irrespective of the aspectual properties
       of the main verb.[11]

(14)a. (Yo) vi el cuadro **incómodo.** (state)[12]
        'I saw the picture uncomfortable.'

     b. **Los reyes** se enamoran de sus hijas, las aman
        con látigos de hielo, posesivos, feroces,
        obscenos y terribles... (L.A. de Cuenca). (state)
        'The kings fall in love with their daughters. They love them
        with icy whips, possessive, fierce, obscene and terrible...'

---

change), 'process' (state of change), and 'event' (change of state).

[11] Obviously, there is a general constraint on secondary predication in the sense that only verbs which take subjects that can be attributed a stative property appear in these contexts. For this reason, verbs with expletive subjects or those with propositional subjects are incompatible with depictive predicates:
   (i) *La lluvia (proposition) es imprescindible rápida.
       'The rain is necessary rapid'
[12] See Demonte (1990) for a justification, in line with Lakoff (1970) and Rogers (1972), of the hypothesis that perception verbs divide into two subtypes: statives such as *ver* 'to see' and *sentir* 'to feel', and actives or nonstatives as *mirar* 'to look at' or *palpar* 'to touch'. As a proof of this distinction, observe that the former cannot occur in imperative constructions (see (i)), while the latter can (see (ii)).
   (i) *¡Ve este cuadro!   / *¡Siente esta tela!
       'See this picture!'   'Feel this cloth!'
   (ii) ¡Mira este cuadro! / ¡Toca esta tela!
       'Look at this picture!' 'Touch this cloth!'

   c. **Pedro** ama **deprimido.**   (state)
     'Pedro loves depressed.'

   d. Mientras **alguien** regrese **derrotado** a su cuarto...'
     (L.A. de Cuenca)   (activity)
     'While somebody returns defeated to his room...'

   e. **Luis** siempre trabaja **sonriente.**   (activity)
     'Luis always works smiling.'

   f. **Enrique** se dio cuenta **sereno** de lo complejo de la
     situación. **(achievement)**
     'Enrique realized calm how complex the situation was.'

   g. **Luisa** reconoció **asustada** que su madre había envejecido mucho.
     (achievement)
     'Luisa recognized scared that her mother has gotten much older.'

   h. **El pintor** dibujó una naturaleza muerta **feliz.**
     (accomplishment)
     'The painter painted a still life happy.'

   i. **Los arquitectos** construyeron el puente **deseosos de**
     aliviar los problemas de la zona. (accomplishment)
     'The architects built the bridge eager to alleviate with
     the problems of the area.'

(15) Only verbs of action which denote an internal state (in other
     words, [+activity, -result] verbs, or processes and
     nonconstructive accomplishments) admit object-oriented
     secondary predicates, whether depictives or resultatives.

The corresponding examples are in (16).

(16)a. Colgó **los cuadros juntos.**   (activity, **resultative**)
     '(S)he hang the pictures together.'

   b. Pedro devolvió **el libro roto.** (activity, **depictive**)
     'Pedro returned the book broken.'

c. *María sabe el teorema válido.[13]   (stative, depictive)
'María knows the theorem valid.'

d. *Comprendió la noticia correcta en su formulación.
(achievement, depictive)
'(S)he understood the news correct in its formulation.'

(17) A verb denoting an internal state becomes a verb denoting a final state (i.e., a 'culminating transition' (Pustejovsky 1988), or a constructive accomplishment) when it takes a resultative predicate.

(18)a. Mastica/masticó la carne cruda.   (depictive)
'(S)he chew/chewed the meat raw.'

b. Mastica/masticó la carne chiquitita.   (resultative)
'(S)he chew/chewed the meat very little.'

Observe that (18a) describes an action which can be habitual, while (18b) characterizes one which is completely ended.   Moreover, an important difference between (18a) and (18b) is that the depictive predicate describes a state which is simultaneous (and can be previous or subsequent) to the moment of the action of the main predicate, while the state described by the resultative occurs after the action of the main verb has been developed.   In this line of analysis, 'resultative predication' has to be defined as the expression of a state which follows the almost completion of a change, while 'depictive predication' is the expression of a state which goes along with the affectation of an object.

Note also that a significant implication of (17) is that resultative predicates should not be compatible with constructive accomplishment verbs.

---

[13] Observe that there are many sentences similar to this one (i.e., sentences with a state main verb) which are completely grammatical with a VP internal predicate:
(i) Lo sé contento con la noticia.
'I know him happy with the news.'
(ii) Te imagino severo, un poco triste.' (J.L. Borges)
'I imagine you severe, a little sad.'
(iii) Quiero a Luis destrozado por el recuerdo.
'I want Luis destroyed by the memories.'
They do not represent a problem for generalization (15), however. Note that (ii), for instance, cannot be interpreted as 'I imagine you while you are severe', but it means 'I imagine that you are severe'. It appears, then, that these verbs take a subcategorized small clause but not depictive secondary predicates.

That is, since constructive accomplishment verbs develop an event structure with a final state, a resultative will not be possible in this context. This situation is illustrated in (19a, b). Observe that (19b) is grammatical only when the adjective is interpreted as a manner adverbial; it cannot mean 'He drew the circle until it was distorted'.

(19)a. *Limpió **la camisa blanca.**
     '(S)he washed the shirt white.'

    b. *Trazó **el círculo torcido.**
     '(S)he drew the circle twisted.'

    c. *Pintó **el cuadro colorido.**
     '(S)he painted the picture colored.'

However, there appears to be an important counterexample to the generalization illustrated in (19). As Bosque (1990) has noticed, there is in colloquial Spanish a very productive construction in which, let us say, a cognate participle of the main verb obligatorily preceded by intensifiers like *bien, muy* or *más,* occurs. This cognate participle can co-occur with all kind of verbs:

(20)a. Lavó **la camisa bien lavadita.**
     '(S)he washed the shirt well (washed).'

    b. Trazó **el círculo bien trazado.**
     '(S)he drew the circle well (drawn).'

    c. Haz **la carne muy hecha.**
     'Cook the meat well (done).'

    d. Pica **el tomate más picadito.**
     'Chop the tomato more (chopped).'

    e. Caminó **los tres kilómetros bien caminados.**
     '(S)he (really) walked (the) three kilometers (well walked).'

    f. Pensó **sus palabras muy bien pensadas.**
     '(S)he thought out his/her words very well (thought out).'

    g. Reconoció **sus errores bien reconocidos.**
     '(S)he (really) recognized his/her errors (well recognized).'

I will return to this construction in section 2.1 after considering the underlying representation of resultatives.

Summarizing, it appears that the crucial criterion to establish relevant generalizations regarding the distribution of secondary predicates is the way in which the main verb of the sentence develops its event structure. It is interesting to point out also that the notion of having arrived or not arrived at a final state in the development of a process has a crucial importance in this regard. In this sense, generalizations (13), (15) and (17) do not match one-to-one with any classification in Vendler-Dowty's style. Observe, for instance, that achievements, which standardly describe a momentaneous (result of an) action, are the typical candidates not to accept secondary predication. However, a specific achievement like *encontrar* 'to find', while denoting a sequence of nonhomogeneous states of searching, also accepts modifiers of an internal state: *Encontré el coche roto* 'I found the car broken'. In parallel, a standard (constructive) accomplishment will not accept any predicate denoting a subsequent state (a resultative) unless this state can be interpreted as a modulation of the extent of the event. These were the cases in (3), which we will reexamine in section 2.

In section 2, I will also try to provide a formal explanation for generalizations (13), (15), and (17). I will deduce the fact that only object-oriented predicates are aspectually conditioned from the property of their being generated internally to the VP, becoming in that way strictly related to the subevent structure of the verb. I will also discuss the differences between resultative and depictive predicates and reformulate the traditional view that resultative predication is a lexical process (cf. Simpson 1983), that is, that they are a projection of the subevent structure of the verb and, in this sense, a kind of obligatory adjunct (cf. Grimshaw and Vikner 1989). Subject-oriented predicates, however, are independent of the manner of the action.

2 Resultative and depictive predicates and the structure of event

2.1 Functional heads and the projection of secondary predicates. Let us take from the standard hypothesis on the underlying structure of secondary predicates the idea that the three subclasses of these predicates appear to be adjoined to different nodes of the sentence[14] and that the maximum

---

[14] Roberts (1988) claims that subject predicates are sisters of the subject of the sentence generated internal to the VP; object predicates are under V'.

expansion of a structure with secondary predicates is one equivalent to (21), where the only acceptable order is the unmarked [resultative, depictive of the object, depictive of the subject].

(21)a. Inés$_i$ mastica la carne$_j$ chiquitita$_j$ cruda$_j$ agotada$_i$.
'Inés chew the meat very little raw exhausted.'

I will incorporate to this conception the idea that X-bar projections can be headed by two kinds of heads, lexical and functional ones (Fukui and Speas 1986), and I will also adopt standard proposals regarding the order and dominance of the functional projections within IP. With these provisos, I will slightly depart from the standard hypothesis and claim that secondary predicates are generated in a configuration such as that in (22), which I assume represents the unmarked order in (21).

McNulty (1988) asserts that depictive predicates are both adjoined to VP, subject-oriented adjoined to the upper node (actually they are adjoined to VP'', the maximal projection, V^{n2} being a segment of a maximal projection); object-oriented depictives, on the other hand, are adjoined to V'; resultatives are part of a complex verb and theta-assigning XP's.

Both linguists follow Andrews (1982) in the basic assumption that AP has to be part of VP.

Rothstein (1983) and Demonte (1988) follow the line of Williams (1980) in assuming that subject predicates are not in the VP but are daughters of IP. In the four cases, mutual m-command between the subject and its predicate is satisfied.

(22)

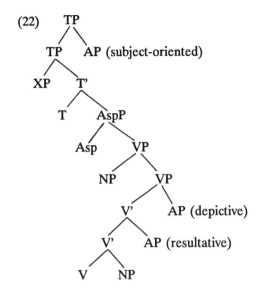

The questions I would like to answer through a configuration like (22), are the following:

(i) How can we deduce that resultative predicates add a final state to the subevent structure of the verb and, in this sense, convert a transitional activity or process verb into an accomplishment one?

(ii) How can we deduce that object-oriented depictive predicates are related to the internal or medial state in the subevent structure of the verb?

(iii) How can we explain that subject-oriented predicative APs are independent of the subevent structure of the verb?

(iv) How is it that both classes of depictive predicative APs are temporally independent while resultative predicates are temporally dependent? (Cf. Roberts 1987, for this distinction) In the same line: is there Tense in predicative APs?

The basic hypotheses encoded in (22) are, first, that D-structure is a projection of the event-argument structure of the verb and that all the members of this structure are linked within the VP through theta-marking, theta-marking taking place under government.[15] In line with Koopman and Sportiche (1989), I also maintain that the thematic subject (or D-structure subject) is the specifier of a V^{n} [16] small clause whose predicate is VP. At the same time, I am assuming, following Fukui and Speas (1986), that

---

[15] See Demonte (1989) for an approach to prepositional verbs along these lines.

[16] Actually, the highest VP in representation (22).

lexical categories can infinitely iterate specifiers as long as those specifiers are fully licensed and can be interpreted at LF.[17]   When the concepts are established in this way, it appears that in the maximal projections of lexical categories there is no distinction between adjuncts and specifiers, and that the notion of base-generated adjuncts becomes not a formal but a semantic notion.   In a stipulative way, I will claim, however, that only the highest specifier (the canonical D-structure subject of the sentence) is an A-position, while the others (the resultative and the depictive) are A'-positions.

Second, I will follow Grimshaw's (1990) supposition that the elements of the event structure are identified through syntactic expressions and, at the same time, that a given argument can encode one or more states of the aspectual substructure.

Third, (22) asserts, that secondary predicates, which are always marked as [+stative], are generated within this structure with a double possibility: they can be specifiers-adjuncts, as assumed in the standard analysis,[18] but they can also develop the subevent structure.   In this second option, they have to appear in the positions relevant for the linking rules.   To be more concrete, I assume that resultative predicates, being the closest-to-the-head right-generated A-bar specifiers of the VP, are the only ones which are accessible to the linking rules.   Obviously, this is the only solution in accordance with a unitary approach to the formal analysis of predicatives. However, there is another possibility, perhaps more perspicuous from a technical point of view.   In fact, it can be thought that resultative predicates occupy the deep-structure position in which usually indirect objects or locative arguments of three-argument taking verbs appear.   Now, if a configuration à la Larson (1988) is adopted, there will then be a way to distinguish structurally between depictive and resultative predicates.   Evidence in support of this supposition comes from the fact that there are no resultatives in constructions with indirect objects, while depictives are possible in such configurations: *Le devolvió el coche roto a María* 'He returned the car broken to María'.   This solution, moreover, is coherent with the idea, sometimes assumed in the literature,[19] that resultatives are subcategorized by certain verbs and should be generated in complement position.   We will leave this dilemma open here.

---

[17] Moreover, according to Fukui and Speas, only specifiers of functional categories can close off projections.

[18] Cf. Chomsky (1986), Demonte (1988), and Rizzi (1990) in this regard. The adjunct condition of secondary predicates explains their behavior under extraction. In the framework adopted here, this behavior will have to be attributed to the number of barriers which are crossed.

[19] See Simpson (1983) and McNulty (1988) in this regard.

Fourth, I also take as a basic hypothesis Tenny's (1988) proposal that internal arguments express a crucial aspectual property of verbs, in that they 'measure out' over time the event described by the verb: 'the verb's direct internal argument may be thought of as being converted into a function of time at some level of representation' (op. cit: 4). I would like to revise and briefly extend this idea and assume that the direct internal argument is the one which delimits the event insofar as it expresses that state which we have called the 'medial' or 'internal' state. The presence of the internal argument marks an end point in time, but its realization does not imply that there cannot be a following state really expressing the closing of the situation. I want to imply, then, that to change a state does not mean to be in a final state. In other words, both activities and nonconstructive accomplishments can affect the object, changing its state, but only constructive accomplishments express directly the existence of this final state. In the sentences of (23), for instance, the presence of the internal argument indicates that the event has a temporal limit; the addition of the phrases in parentheses, however, makes more precise this temporal limit since it manifests overtly the state in which the object affected by the action remains after the action is completely closed.

(23)a. Give a letter (to John).

b. Comer la manzana (masticadita).
'Eat the apple (well chewed).'

c. Cortar el árbol (hasta la mitad).
'Cut the tree (half-way through).'

2.1.1 With these hypotheses in mind, let us return to (22) and consider, first, the licensing of resultative predicates. Suppose that a verb like *masticar* 'chew' is projected from the lexicon as an item with two positions in the event structure: a Cause or initial state and a medial state. If by hypothesis the internal argument is always a projection of the medial state, the direct internal argument will then be the one projecting this position of the event structure in configuration (22). Chomsky (1989) has proposed that the agreement features of the heads are always a reflection of a specifier-head agreement relation. Now if the resultative secondary predicates are in the specifier position of the VP,[20] the stative feature of the predicate will be

---

[20] This is coherent with the notion that predication implies mutual c-command between the subject and the predicate. In this configuration the subject of the predicate, the direct internal argument, does c-command its predicate and vice-versa.

shared, through coindexation, by the verb when Spec-head agreement takes place. This relation of agreement taking place within the VP will modify the reading of the verb which, having projected an internal state, can now add the only one which follows it: the final state. It is obvious that only in an underlying configuration like this can the secondary predicate serve to saturate the event-argument structure since, as is usually assumed, event-argument structure as a whole is projected within the VP. Observe that if the verb had projected the internal argument as a realization of a set of two substates, internal and final (this will actually be the case in the constructive accomplishment constructions), the state indicated by the secondary predicate could not now be added, and ungrammatical sentences such as those in (19) (repeated below as (24)) would appear.

(24)a. *Lavó **la camisa limpia**.
   '(S)he washed the shirt clean.'

   b. *Trazó **el círculo torcido**.
   '(S)he drew the circle twisted.'

   c. *Pintó **el cuadro colorido**.
   '(S)he painted the picture colored.'

The existence of the productive construction with a cognate participle, illustrated through the examples in (20), does not falsify our analysis, however. Notice that this is a construction compatible with all kinds of verbs (irrespective of their aspectual properties) and observe, crucially, that only when the verbs are activities or accomplishments can the cognate participle refer to a final state. Otherwise, they are manner adverbials. In (25) I repeat the examples in (20) and give the relevant interpretation; the new example (25h) shows that this kind of predicate can be also primary.

(25)a. Lavó la camisa bien lavadita. **(accomplishment, resultative)**
   '(S)he washed the shirt well (washed).'

   b. Trazó el círculo bien trazado. **(accomplishment, resultative)**
   'He drew the circle well (drawn).'

   c. Pica el tomate más picadito. **(accomplishment, resultative)**
   'Chop the tomato well (chopped).'

   d. Haz la carne muy hecha. **(activity, resultative)**
   'Cook the meat well (cooked).'

e. Caminó los tres kilómetros bien caminados. (**activity, resultative.**)
'(S)he (really) walked the three kilometers (well walked).'

f. Pensó sus palabras muy bien pensadas. (**state, manner**)
'He thought out his words well (thought out).'

g. Reconoció sus errores bien reconocidos. (**achievement, manner**)
'He (really) recognized his mistakes (well recognized).'

h. El paquete está atado y bien atado. (**copulative, manner**)
'The packet is tied and well tied.'

At this point, it has to be said, however, as a qualification to the implication of generalization (17) (recall the examples in (19)), that even if constructive accomplishments do not accept resultative predicates describing a state different from that described in the main verb, they do accept either resultative cognates or they accept a predicate describing an extension of the final state.[21] The first possibility is illustrated in (25a,b), the second was the case exemplified in (3). In (3) it was shown that the reading of accomplishment verbs with resultative predicate improves when the predicate is modified by a degree adverb. Observe that examples similar to those in (3) can be constructed with verbs like *cortar* 'to cut' or *picar* 'to chop':

(26)a. ??Pica el tomate fino.
'Chop the tomato thin.'

a'. Pica el tomate muy finito.
'Chop the tomato very very thin.'

b. ??Corta la cebolla gruesa.
'Slice the onion thick.'

b'. Corta la cebolla más gruesa.
'Slice the onion thicker.'

The resultatives like those in (3), (25d), and (26a' and b') can now be reinterpreted as the reduplication or extension of a state already expressed by the internal argument. In other words, insofar as a secondary predicate generated within the VP can add a state to the event structure of a change of

---

[21] I owe the second part of this observation to María-Luisa Rivero.

state verb, it can also make more explicit a state already expressed by one of the elements of the argument structure of the verb. Under this condition, the cognate participle construction (which, perhaps, is only an epiphenomenon, and serves various and different purposes) will be apt to be understood as a secondary predicate.

2.1.2 The licensing of the object-oriented depictive secondary predicate proceeds in the normal way. In this configuration the object NP is in a structural relation of mutual m-command (and Spec-head agreement) with the stative predicate, the locality condition that has to be satisfied for the predication rule to apply (cf. Chomsky 1986 and Demonte 1988, among others). The diagram in (27) illustrates the coindexation for predication which results from our proposals in 2.1.1 and 2.1.2:

(27)

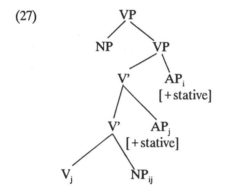

With the proposals developed up to this point, my analysis now has to confront an important problem. It appears that if predicates are VP specifiers, Spec-head agreement between the verb and each of these specifiers will ultimately result in all the specifiers being indexed with each other. This result is in fact desirable[22] with the subject NP and the depictive of the object AP. What is to be avoided, however, is the subject NP and the resultative being coindexed. I think that there is a way to distinguish structurally between the subject specifier and the predicative specifiers: the former, being in a small clause, is adjoined to VP, while the latter are adjoined to V'. Under such conditions, the highest NP under VP will not m-command any

---

[22] Recall that it is usually assumed that object-oriented predicative APs reanalyze with the main verb. With an extended coindexation, the result is that the subject will, in fact, be coindexed with this 'complex' predicate.

of the elements under V' and the structural relation necessary for the predication rule to apply will not be satisfied.

As a tangential but interesting consequence of the previous considerations, observe that the analysis that I have proposed makes a distinction between those aspectual properties related to the perfective-imperfective tense/aspect dichotomy and those linked to the manner of the action, expressed through the sub-event structure in the lexical entry of the verb. My analysis really implies that the AspP in the main sentence is not relevant for predication. This appears, in fact, to be the case: while there are syntactic processes clearly constrained by the perfective-imperfective nature of the action, such as the formation of *se* impersonal sentences (cf. de Miguel 1990), no distinctions in the Tense/Aspect perfective-imperfective area appear to have a role in the licensing of secondary predication.

(28)a. Antiguamente no se llamaba de tú a los padres.
　　　'In old times, parents were not called with *tú*.'

　　b. *Antiguamente no se llamó/ha llamado de tú a los padres.
　　　'In old times nobody called *tú* their parents.'

(29)a. Juan ha comido/come/comió la carne pasada.
　　　'Juan has eaten/eats/ate the meat done.'

　　b. Juan ha clavado/?clava/clavó los clavos juntos.
　　　'Juan has nailed/nails/nailed the nails together.'

　　c. *Juan ha corrido/corre/corrió la carrera fácil.
　　　'Juan has run/runs/ran the run easy.'

The examples in (28) (from de Miguel 1990: 252) show that the perfective or imperfective nature of the event has to combine with the tense/aspectual condition of the verb in order to license the generic interpretation associated with certain of the Spanish impersonal *se* constructions. Thus, (28b) is ungrammatical because the perfective nature of the event voids the generic interpretation which is possible in the imperfective context (28a). The cases in (29) (cf. especially (29c)) show that it is only the aspectual nature of the event, its *Aktionsart*, that constrains secondary predication.

2.1.3 The analysis proposed in (22), on the other hand, distinguishes between subject and object predicates and claims that the former are connected to the TP of the sentence and are independent of the structural context in which elements of the event-argument structure are projected. To be more precise, after being theta-marked, the subject NP under the upper VP specifier in (22) and (27) will have to move to the Spec of IP (more strictly to the AgrSP)[23] in order to receive Case. On its way to this Case position, it will stop in the Spec of TP, where it will be coindexed with the m-commanding predicative AP, thus satisfying the predication rule. This process is illustrated in (30).

(30)

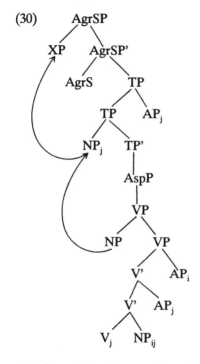

Certain qualifications are in order after the foregoing statement. The simplest one is that since the specifier of the TP is a nonargument position, it can be thought that the thematic subject will not have to stop in this position to satisfy ECP requirements; moreover, it is not clear that anything independent licenses that position. Since I assume that movement out of its VP-internal position is crucial to licensing secondary predication of the subject, we can also think that movement of the subject directly to Spec of

---

[23] As in Chomsky (1989), I assume that AgrSP dominates TP and not vice versa.

AgrSP will license this predication. Note that the predicative AP is assumed to be adjoined to TP and hence not dominated by it (Chomsky 1986). In this situation, the predicative will be in a position of mutual m-command with respect to an element in Spec of AgrSP.[24]

More controversial, in view of standard analyses, is the claim that the predication rule applies once the subject is moved. Recall that in some of these standard analyses of secondary predication (cf. Williams 1980, Rothstein 1983, and Demonte 1988), it was assumed that subject-oriented predicative APs were generated under IP, deep subjects at that time being thought to be also under IP. Now, if, like all the elements of the thematic structure, underlying subjects are VP internal (cf. Fukui and Speas 1986 and Koopman and Sportiche 1989, among many others), the previous assumption will be difficult to maintain if we also want the predication rule to be a kind of theta-assignment, i.e., if we want it to hold only under mutual m-command, which is the step taken, for instance, in Roberts (1988; cf. footnote 14).

Nevertheless, there are empirical reasons which support the idea that the predication rule coindexes subject-oriented predicatives with derived subjects. On the one hand, constituency tests which I will not reproduce here (but see Demonte 1988 against Roberts 1987 and 1988) suggest that subject predicates are outside the VP. More relevant to the present argument is the fact that in Spanish there appears not to be predication when the subject appears inverted (cf. Demonte 1986 in this regard).

(31)a. *Llegó **María cansada**.
   arrived María tired
   'María arrived tired.'

   b. *Ama **Marta derrotada**.
   loves Marta defeated
   'Marta loves defeated.'

---

[24] I owe this suggestion to Paula Kempchinsky.

c. ??Compró **Luisa** la casa **agotada por la discusión.**[25]
bought Luisa the house exhausted by the quarrel
'Luisa bought the house exhausted by the quarrel.'

Let us assume that 'inverted' subjects are sometimes VP internal subjects which haven't been moved to [Spec,IP]. Let us suppose, more strictly, that in null subject languages the subject does not need to move obligatorily in order to receive Case since it can enter in a chain relation with a *pro* element licensed and identified by Agr in the Spec, AgrSP position. 'Inversion' in this sense will be the manifestation of this possibility of null subject languages. Now if this analysis is correct, the examples in (31) suggest that subject-oriented predicative APs are licensed under coindexation with a lexical subject once this is optionally moved to get Case, and are not VP internal. In section 2.2, I will provide independent evidence in support of the idea that they are TP adjuncts.

2.2 Tense and aspect in predicative APs. Traditional in the consideration of secondary predicates is the idea that these structures are in some way related to Tense and are not homogeneous from the temporal point of view. Dowty (1972) was the first to propose that what he calls 'temporally restrictive adjectives' such as those in *The girl married young* or in *John saw Harry alive* (and among which are not included result adjectives such as that in *John shot Harry dead*) were contained in an independent sentence with a tense operator with the same reference as the tense operator in the matrix clause. Following Dowty (1972), Fabb (1984) postulated that postnominal and adjunct APs are clausal constituents with an inflectional element; in these

---

[25] Informants find (31c) considerably better that the two previous sentences. It appears that when the predicative has a modifier, the reading of inverted subject sentences with secondary predicates of that subject considerably improves. The longer the modifier is, the better they sound:
(i) *Llegó **Esther furiosa.**
arrived Esther furious
'Esther arrived furious.'
(ii)?(?)Llegó **Esther muy furiosa.**
arrived Esther very furious
'Esther arrived very furious.'
(iii) (?)Llegó **Esther furiosa con sus colegas.**
'Esther arrived furious with her colleagues.'
So we can conjecture that in sentences like (ii) and (iii), Heavy AP shift has taken place. It is not clear to me, though, how this process interacts with the fact that inverted subjects can be either in their canonical D-structure position or adjoined to the VP if they were previously moved.

constructions, the INFL of the adjunct clause is anaphorically related to the INFL of the matrix.[26]

I will adopt this approach to secondary predicates, revising it, and I will claim that depictive predicates (both subject- and object-oriented) are a TP, while resultative predicates project only as far as AspP. From this conception of both kinds of predicates we can derive why only depictives are anaphoric to the tense of the main sentence (our revision of the previous notion that they are 'temporally independent'), while resultatives can only mean a given result (i.e., a state which starts precisely from the time of finishing of the action of the predicate).

In the following paragraphs I will provide justification for a TP analysis of depictive predicates and at the same time I will show that resultative predicates behave differently in relation to these pieces of evidence.

2.2.1 Negation. As (32) shows, depictive predicates are negated with *no* while the resultatives in (33) are not.

(32)a. María llegó [**no** contenta con lo que había hecho].
'María arrived not happy with what she had done.'

  b. Encontró el coche [**no** destrozado por los ladrones habituales].
'He found the car not destroyed by the usual thieves.'

(33)a.??Guisó la carne [**no** pasada por la parte superior].
'(S)he cooked the meat not done in the upper part.'

---

[26] The AP in *I found the/a man happy with his work* is derived by Fabb (1984) from a configuration like (i).

(i)
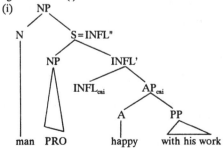

The PRO is controlled by the head of the noun phrase if the clause is a postmodifier, and by the NP if the element is a free adjunct.

b.??Colgó los cuadros [**no** separados de la pared].
'(S)he hung the pictures not distant from the wall.'

To clarify this set of complex data, it is necessary to recall that all kinds of predicatives, as well as prenominal modifiers, can take phrasal or constituent negation. In this situation, illustrated through the examples in (34) and (34'), no contrast such as that in (32)-(33) appears and a contrastive reading is necessarily construed.[27]

(34)a. **María** llegó no (**muy**) **cansada** (sino **disgustada**).
'María arrived not (very) tired (but dissapointed).'

b. Colgó **los cuadros** no (muy) juntos (sino **bien separados**).
'(S)he hung the pictures not (much) together
(but much separated).'

Imperatives also make this difference clear.

(34')a. Bebe **la leche** no **fría** sino **caliente**.
'Drink the milk not cold but hot.'

b. Cuelga **los cuadros** no **juntos** sino **bien separados**.
'Hang the pictures not joined but well separated.'

Aside from the ungrammaticality flavor, observe that the sentences in (32) and (33) have different possible continuations. If, following Klima (1964), we define as instances of sentence negation those structures which permit, among other things, the occurrence of the 'either'-clause, we find again a contrast between (32) and (33) (notice the examples in (35)-(36)). The ungrammaticality of (35) -- where the sentences are conjoined through *y* 'and', and not through *ni* 'neither' -- suggests that the initial negative particle dominates the conjunction of two clausal constituents, since it licenses the polarity item *not...either/ni...tampoco*). The parallel improvement of (36)

---

[27] Obviously, throughout these examples, I am assuming, first, that in contrastive negation constructions, Neg appears independently of Tense and, second, that the predicative in these structures are not TPs but perhaps only APs or AspPs; this assumption calls for a detailed representation of the contrastive negation structures, which I am not providing. Moreover, my argument is circular since I do not have evidence for constituent negation other than the fact that the contrast disappears in these structures, and other proof in favor of this predicative being an AP than the fact that it is allowed in contrastive negation structures. These facts, together with another observation in footnote 28 seriously weaken my argument. I will maintain this claim, however, given that it allows me to show interesting contrasts which need to be explained.

(compared to (33)) may indicate that in resultative structures the negation cannot have scope beyond the adjective phrase because it is not a sentential operator.

(35)a. María llegó **no** contenta con lo que había aceptado
*y/**ni** tampoco con lo que había rechazado.
'María arrived not happy with what she had accepted
nor with what she had rejected, either.'

b. Encontró el coche **no** destrozado por los ladrones
habituales *y/**ni** tampoco por los desagradables vecinos.
'(S)he found the car not destroyed by the current
thieves nor by the horrible neighbors, either.'

(36)a. Guisó la carne **no** pasada por la parte superior y
tampoco por los bordes.
'(S)he cooked the meat not done in the upper part
nor at the edges.'

b. Colgó los cuadros **no** separados de la pared y tampoco
del armario.
'(S)he hang the pictures not distant from the wall
nor from the closet.'

We will now discuss the properties of the configuration in which the nonphrasal negative element can occur. In recent analyses (Zanuttini 1990) it has been asserted that Neg in sentential negation constructions is a functional head which takes TP as its complement. There is certain evidence that this can be in fact the case. It happens, for instance, that negation cannot appear in absolute constructions (see (37)) which are possibly projections of Asp (cf. de Miguel 1990), nor can it appear in imperatives, which lack Tense (cf. Zanuttini 1990; see (38)).[28]

(37) *No visitado el museo, los viajeros regresaron al hotel.
'Not having visited the museum, the travellers returned
to the hotel.'

---

[28] M.L. Rivero (p.c.) has observed that this is not true in many languages: Old Spanish and Bulgarian, for example, where imperatives can be negated. Moreover, there are certain tensed constructions in Old Spanish (*Lerlo ha el libro* 'He will read it, the book', see Lema and Rivero 1989 in this regard) which, however, cannot be negated. These facts suggest, against Zanuttini, a not very clear correlation between TP and Negation.

(38) *No vete de esta casa.
'Not get out from this house.'

Zanuttini (1990), following Kayne (1989), claims that the Neg element, as a sentential operator, occurs only in front of a syntactic representation of Tense and observes that it has to be considered a head because the presence of a negative marker in the embedded clause interferes with the possibility of long clitic climbing.[29]   Note the contrast among *No debo hablarte* '(I) not must speak-to-you', *No te debo hablar* '(I) not to-you must speak' and *Te debo no hablar* '(I) to-you must not speak'.   The explanation for this contrast, according to Zanuttini, is that the clitic cannot move out of a maximal projection which is a sister of *no* because Neg lacks the ability to L-mark its sister constituent which, not being so L-marked, would constitute a barrier to government. If this conception of negation is adequate, it implies that in the constructions in (32) there has to be a TP following the negative marker. In (33), on the contrary, *no* would not be possible because there would not be a syntactic representation of Tense.

2.2.2   Order and occurrence of time and aspect adverbs.   Two relevant lines in the study of adverbs can be traced back to interpretive semantics as well as to the conception which views adverbs as variable-binding operators. Jackendoff (1972) proposes a two-way syntactic classification of adverbs: S-adverbs dominated directly by S and VP-adverbs dominated directly by VP; McConnell-Ginet (1982) distinguishes Ad-verbs, which are VP-internal or subcategorized, from Ad-Sentences, which are external to the VP or Ad-Sentences.   Revising and extending these lines, Rivero (1990) distinguishes subcategorized adverbs, which can incorporate and are like complements of the head of the VP, and adverbs which do not incorporate and are true adjuncts. Manner, Direction, and what she names '*Aktionsart* adverbs' belong to the first subclass, while Aspect and Time adverbs belong to the second. It is the distinction between Aspect, *Aktionsart,* and Time adverbs which concerns here.

To start with, let us recall that the hypothesis that clause structure includes a series of differentiated and syntactically active projections of functional heads allows us to reclassify adverbial constituents and establish differences among them.   Moreover, with the adoption of the hypothesis of the subevent structure of lexical items, we are implicitly assuming that the distinction between a situation seen as 'a whole' vs. 'a continuum' or a situation seen as 'a durative state' vs. 'a series of iterated states' has relevant linguistic consequences.   In fact, the first approach to the description of the

---

[29] This observation was first made in Luján (1978).

situation translates linguistically into the morphological dichotomy perfective-imperfective; the second is lexically inscribed in the subevent structure of the lexical items which, as I have shown, expresses through subcategorization and theta-marking and, as Rivero (1990) has carefully demonstrated, underlies the process of adverb incorporation in certain languages.

Adopting Rivero's distinction between Aspect and *Aktionsart* adverbs, I will include among the class of aspectual adverbs forms such as: *recién* 'just', *ya* 'already', *de una vez* '(all) at once', *hace un momento* 'a moment ago', *todavía* 'still, yet', *continuamente* 'continuously' ; *Aktionsart* adverbs will be *a menudo* 'frequently', *con frecuencia* 'frequently', *dos veces* 'twice', *muchas veces* 'many times', *siempre* 'always', etc.   Of course, items like *ayer* 'yesterday', *hoy* 'today', *mañana* 'tomorrow', *esta tarde* 'this evening', or *anoche* 'last night', are Time adverbs.   As the sentences in (39) illustrate, constraints in the order of occurrence of these listed adverbs in regular sentences with a single predicate suggest that, in fact, the adverbs belong to different projections, that the TP projection dominates AspP, and that *Aktionsart* adverbs are the most embedded ones since they are obviously VP adverbs (from my point of view, now, the preferred order is that in (39c), which would suggest that the *Aktionsart* adverb moves with the V when it raises to INFL).[30]

(39)a. Teresa cantará mañana todavía dos veces.
'Teresa will sing tomorrow still twice.'

b.*Teresa cantará todavía mañana dos veces.
'Teresa will sing still tomorrow twice.'

c. Teresa cantará dos veces mañana todavía.
'Teresa will sing twice tomorrow still.'

The contrast in (40), on the other hand, indicates that depictive predicates (40a, b) allow both classes of adverbs (time and aspect ones) while resultatives (40c, d) allow only aspect adverbs, and it suggests that our hypothesis that depictives are TPs, and resultatives AspPs, can be considered descriptively adequate.

---

[30] Moreover, there do not appear to be constraints on the order between *Aktionsart* adverbs and time adverbs, and again the preferred order is with the former following the verb:
(i) Pedro no bebió esta noche de nuevo ginebra.
'Pedro did not drink tonight again gin'
(ii) Pedro no bebió de nuevo esta noche ginebra.
'Pedro did not drink again tonight gin'
I leave this problem open for further research.

(40)a. Alquila **las casas [ahora ya vacías]**.
'(S)he rents the houses now just empty.'

b. La ansiedad **me** lleva a él **[hoy totalmente rendida]**.
'Anxiety leads me to him today totally exhausted.'

c. Pegó **las hojas [(*ayer noche) completamente juntas]**.
'(S)he stuck the leaves yesterday night totally joined.'

d. Colocó a **la muñeca [(*ayer) parcialmente sentada]**.
'(S)he put the doll yesterday partially seated.'

In this sense, resultative predicates behave as regular perfective adjectives, which also project an AspP, according to Bosque (1990).

(41)a. Un vaso lleno (*esta noche) hasta la mitad.
'A glass filled (tonight) half part.'

b. Una salsa medio espesa (*hasta hoy).
'A dressing half thick (till today).'

2.2.3 Co-occurrence constraints on time adverbs. Dowty (1972) also noticed that a time adverb that occurs in the main clause 'can be moved to the adjective phrase with no change in meaning' (op. cit.: 53). According to him, the sentences in (42) should be synonymous.

(42)a. El sábado encontró **la casa vacía**.

b. Encontró **la casa vacía el sábado**.

'On Saturday he/she found the house empty.'

Observe that in certain cases where there is an adverb modifying the main verb and the depictive AP takes its own time adverb, the predicative reading is not available, as in (43), and the AP is interpreted as a modifier of the noun.

(43) El sábado encontré el coche [robado el domingo].
'On Saturday I found the car stolen on Sunday.'

The examples in (42) and (43) taken together suggest that the Tense nodes of the main clause and the adjunct predicate are related and mutually constrained. The contrasts in (44), moreover, points to the same conclusion: in (44a) there is only a modifier reading, in (44b) the predication interpretation reappears.

(44)a. Hoy tomé el café recalentado ayer.
'Today I drank the coffee reheated yesterday.'

a'.*Lo tomé hoy recalentado ayer.
'I drank it today reheated yesterday.'

b. Hoy tomé **el café caliente aún.**
'Today I drank the coffee still hot.'

b'. **Lo tomé hoy caliente aún.**
'I drank it today still hot.'

The problem with (44a), in contrast to (44b), is that the presence of the adverb *ayer* 'yesterday' indicates that the state described by the predicate has finished before the time of the main action has started; *aún* 'still', on the contrary, says that the state is still active. As we will see, this is the way tense interaction between the verb and the predicative holds.

Recapitulating the facts and discussion of this section, I conclude that the two semantic sub-kinds of predicative APs appear to be a projection of different functional heads: depictive predicates behave as a TP while resultative ones seem to be AspPs. If this conclusion is correct, the inventory of categories which can function as secondary predicates would be in fact reduced. As is well known, although I have constructed my arguments referring only to APs secondary predicates (which appears to be the canonical case), all kinds of projections of lexical heads can show up in this context: in (45a) the predicative is a PP, in (45b) an NP.

(45)a. Dejó a sus hijos [sin dinero por la noche].
'(S)he left his/her sons without money during the night.'

b. Nombró a su caballo [cónsul de Roma].
'(S)he name his/her horse "consul of Rome".'

Within the proposal for which I have provided support, these cases will have to be reformulated to say that these predicatives are projections of a Tense or Aspect head which takes any of the lexical projections as a complement. In view of my proposals, configuration (22) will be as in (46).

(46)

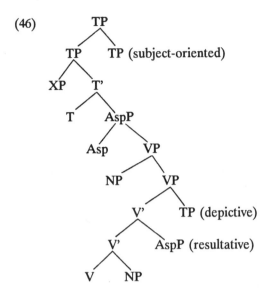

Does this proposal have unexpected implications from a theoretical point of view? I think it does not. It is not surprising, first, that constructions which intuitively are a sort of truncated clause project only part of the nodes of a regular sentence. Second, it is coherent with the conception of grammar as a very reduced set of rules and principles to conclude that the apparently categorically heterogeneous set of secondary predicates is in fact one single construction whose minimal differences (being headed by Tense or by Aspect) follows from other modules of the grammar. From the theory of government it will follow, in fact, that depictives have to be Tense phrases; from the theory of theta-marking we could deduce the aspectual nature of resultatives. I will further extend these considerations in section 3, when speculating briefly on the behavior of Tense in predicative APs.

3   Tense inclusion in predicative APs and other corollaries. I have argued in the preceding section that certain predicative APs are temporal expressions. It is evident, on the other hand, that, similarly to infinitives, they lack the tense features usually associated with finite verbs: they do not refer overtly to past, present, or future. From this fact it follows also that the relation between the predicative TP and the tense of the matrix clause will not be submitted to any identification requirement for tenses such as the Anchoring Principle (cf. Enç 1987) or any other similar requirement.

In her exhaustive study on the syntax and semantics of tense in matrix, complement sentences, and relative clauses, Enç (1987) developed and articulated a set of anchoring conditions which explain why the truth of a tensed matrix sentence is relative to the speech time, and why complement tenses are linked to higher sentences that are linked either to even higher sentences or to the speech time (cf. op. cit.: 642). This linking is the condition which allows what are called 'shifted readings' and 'simultaneous readings' for a given complement tense, namely, a relation of either 'precedence' or 'identity' between tenses. For instance, in a sentence like (47) (taken from Enç 1987: 646) the verb complement in past tense has a shifted reading insofar as the state described by the complement precedes the event described by the superordinate clause.

(47) John heard that Mary was pregnant.

In Enç's system, the shifted reading is obtained by anchoring the complement tense through its Comp. But in sentence (47), there is also a simultaneous reading in which John hears at a past time that Mary is pregnant at the time of hearing. The simultaneous reading is obtained when the complement tense is directly bound.

However, there is nothing equivalent to these two kinds of readings in the relation between the predicative phrase and the matrix tense, even if there is a tense relation between them, as has been frequently claimed. How can this temporal relation be characterized?

Taking the basic notion from Enç (1987), the temporal relation holding between the tense phrases in the constructions under study is one of 'inclusion'. If we assume that predicatives, like the other temporal expressions (tenses and adverbs, for instance), denote intervals, we can characterize the relation between the secondary predicate and the matrix tense, asserting that the interval denoted by the matrix tense has to be included in the interval denoted by the predicate. In other words, a sentence like (48) will be true only if the interval denoted by the main tense is included in the interval denoted by the predicate. Observe that the possible continuations of (48) corroborate this interpretation: the state described by the predicative can begin at the moment in which the main event starts but can also precede it and may or may not follow it, the only condition for the truth of (48) being that the state described by the predicate must have held for some period preceding and extending up to the time of the main action.

(48) Pepe ascendió el Pichincha emocionado,
     'Pepe climbed (the) Pichincha moved,'

     ...pero antes estaba frío de pasiones,
     '... but previously he was cold of passions,'

...tal como venía estando a lo largo del día,
'as he had been (feeling) all along the day,'
...e inmediatamente cambió de humor,
'and immediately he changed his mood,'

...y siguió así durante toda la tarde.
'and he remained in this mood the whole afternoon.'

From the property of being a TP and denoting an interval, the condition of referring only to intrinsic but transitory qualities (recall (7)) will follow.

Let us consider now whether we can formally explain the temporal relation that we are characterizing by assuming this notion of temporal inclusion. In the inclusion relation it is said to be a 'tense' (the one which is included) and an 'antecedence of this tense' (cf. Enç 1987: 651, which follows Partee 1973 and Heim 1982, on these matters); the antecedence has to be interpreted prior to the expression depending on it. According to the procedure set forth in Heim (1982) and adopted again in Enç (1987), 'it will suffice to say that one of the cases where an expression α is interpreted before another expression β is when α c-commands β.' (Enç, 1987: 651).

Now if the procedure established in Heim-Enç's system for the interpretation of the temporal relation of inclusion is the correct one, it is obvious that it does not work in our representation of the syntax of depictive predicates (the one in (22) and (46)), except for the case of subject-oriented depictives. In our representation, the main tense β c-commands the tense in the object-oriented predicative α, but not vice versa, which is the expected relation of c-command.

A possibility which will have to be investigated, but that I will not pursue any further here, is whether depictive object-oriented predicates move in some way at LF in order to have c-command over the main tense.[31]

Regarding the 'temporally dependent' interpretation of resultative predicatives, observe that our conclusion is that this interpretation is not related in fact to tense but to the internal temporality or aspect (or *Aktionsart*) of the predication relation. If the predicate defines a perfective state and if this state can make part of the event structure of the main predicate, it can only be interpreted, as I have said, as a final state. The reading of temporal dependence, therefore, is a collateral reading following from the aspectual properties of the construction, not a central part of the syntax and semantics of resultative predicates.

---

[31] Actually, this is part of Enç's analysis for embedded present complements.

References

Andrews, A. 1982. A Note on the Constituent Structure of Adverbs and Auxiliaries. Linguistic Inquiry 13, 313-17.

Bertinetto, P. 1981. Il carattere del processo ('Aktionsart') in italiano, proposte, sintatticamente motivate, per una tipologia del lessico verbale. Ms., L'Accademia della Crusca.

Bosque, I. 1990. Sobre el aspecto en los adjetivos y en los participios. In I. Bosque, ed., Tiempo y aspecto en español. Madrid: Cátedra. 177-214.

Chomsky, N. 1981. Lectures on Government and Binding. Dordrecht: Foris.

Chomsky, N. 1986. Barriers. Cambridge, Mass.: MIT Press.

Chomsky, N. 1989. Some Notes on Economy of Derivation and Representation. MIT Working Papers in Linguistics 10, 43-74.

Comrie, B. 1976. Aspect. Cambridge: Cambridge University Press.

Demonte, V. 1986. Predication and Passive. In I. Bordelois, H. Contreras, and K. Zagona, eds., Generative Studies in Spanish Syntax. Dordrecht: Foris. 51-66.

Demonte, V. 1988. Remarks on Secondary Predicates. C-command, Extraction and Reanalysis. The Linguistic Review 6, 1-39.

Demonte, V. 1989. Linking and Case. The Case of Prepositional Verbs. In T. Morgan and Ch. Laeufer, eds., Theoretical Analyses in Contemporary Romance Linguistics. Amsterdam: John Benjamins, in press.

Demonte, V. 1990. Transitividad, intransitividad y papeles temáticos. In V. Demonte and B. Garza, eds., Estudios de Lingüística de España y México. México: El Colegio de México, UNAM. 115-50.

Dowty, D. 1972. Temporally Restrictive Adjectives. In J. Kimball, ed., Syntax and Semantics, vol. 1. New York: Seminar Press. 51-62.

Dowty, D. 1979. Word Meaning and Montague Grammar. Dordrecht: Reidel.

Enç, M. 1987. Anchoring Conditions for Tense. Linguistic Inquiry 18, 633-58.

Fabb, N. 1984. Syntactic Affixation. MIT doctoral dissertation.

Fukui, N., and M. Speas. 1986. Specifiers and Projections. MIT Working Papers in Linguistics 8, 173-90.

Grimshaw, J. 1990. Argument Structure. Cambridge, Mass.: MIT Press.

Grimshaw, J., and S. Vikner. 1989. Obligatory Adjuncts and the Structure of Events. Paper presented to the Workshop on Lexical Structure of the Groningen Conference on Knowledge and Language.

Heim, I. 1982. The Semantics of Definite and Indefinite Noun Phrases. University of Massachusetts Amherst, doctoral dissertation.

Hernanz, M. Ll. 1988. En torno a la sintaxis y la semántica de los complementos predicativos en español. Estudi general 8, 7-29.

Higginbotham, J. 1985. On Semantics. Linguistic Inquiry 16, 547- 94.

Jackendoff, R. 1972. Semantic Interpretation in Generative Grammar. Cambridge, Mass.: MIT Press.

Kayne, R. 1989. Null Subjects and Clitic Climbing. In O. Jaeggli and K. Safir, eds., The Null Subject Parameter. Dordrecht: Kluwer Academic Publishers. 239-61.

Klima, E. 1964. Negation in English. In J. Fodor and J. Katz, eds., The Structure of Language. Englewood Cliffs, N.J.: Prentice Hall. 296-323.

Koopman, H., and D. Sportiche. 1989. Subjects. Ms. UCLA.

Lakoff, G. 1970. Irregularity in Syntax. New York: Holt.

Larson, R. 1988. On the Double Object Construction. Linguistic Inquiry 19, 335-91.

Lema, J., and M. L. Rivero. 1989. Inverted Conjugations and V-second Phenomena in Romance. To appear in T. Morgan and C. Laeufer, eds., Theoretical Analyses in Contemporary Romance Linguistics. Amsterdam: John Benjamins.

Luján, M. 1978. Clitic Promotion and Mood in Spanish Verbal Complements. Études Linguistiques sur les Langues Romanes. Recherches Linguistiques à Montréal, vol. 10, Université de Montréal, 103-90.

McConnell-Ginet, S. 1982. Adverbs and Logical Form. Language 58, 144-84.

McNulty, E. 1988. The Syntax of Adjunct Predicates. University of Connecticut doctoral dissertation.

de Miguel, E. 1990. El aspecto verbal en una gramática generativa del español. Universidad Autónoma de Madrid doctoral dissertation.

Napoli, D. J. 1989. Predication Theory. A Case Study for Indexing Theory. Cambridge: Cambridge University Press.

Partee, B. 1973. Some Structural Analogies Between Tenses and Pronouns. The Journal of Philosophy 70, 601-9.

Pustejovsky, J. 1988. The Geometry of Events. In C. Tenny, ed., Studies in Generative Approaches to Aspect. Lexicon Project Working Papers 24. Cambridge, Mass.: MIT Press, 19-40.

Rivero, M. L. 1990. Adverb Incorporation and the Syntax of Adverbs in Modern Greek. Ms., University of Ottawa.

Rizzi, L. 1990. Relativized Minimality. Cambridge, Mass.: MIT Press.

Roberts, I. 1987. The Representation of Implicit and Dethematized Subjects. Dordrecht: Foris.

Roberts, I. 1988. Predicative APs. Linguistic Inquiry 19, 703-10.

Rogers, A. 1972. Three Kinds of Physical Perception Verbs. Papers from the Seventh Regional Meeting Chicago Linguistic Society. Chicago: CLS. 206-22.

Rothstein, S. 1983. The Syntactic Forms of Predication. MIT doctoral dissertation.

Simpson, J. 1983. Resultatives. In L. Levin, M. Rappaport, and A. Zaenen, eds., Papers in Lexical-functional Grammar. Bloomington, Ind.: IULC. 143-57.

Stowell, T. 1987. Small Clause Restructuring. Ms., UCLA.

Tenny, C. 1988. The Aspectual Interface Hypothesis. The Connection between Syntax and Lexical Semantics. In C. Tenny, ed., Studies in Generative Approaches to Aspect. Lexicon Project Working Papers 24. Cambridge, Mass.: MIT Press. 1-18.

Vendler, Z. 1979. Linguistics in Philosophy. Ithaca, N.Y.: Cornell University Press.

Verkuyl, H. J. 1989. Aspectual Classes and Aspectual Composition. Linguistics and Philosophy 12, 39-94.

Williams, E. 1980. Predication. Linguistic Inquiry 11, 203-38.

Zanuttini, R. 1990. Two Types of Negative Markers. To appear in Proceedings of NELS 20.

On the characterization of a class of ditransitive verbs in Spanish

Paula Kempchinsky*

University of Iowa

0 Introduction. One of the most productive lines of research in generative syntax over the last decade has been the attempt to derive the particular properties of the complementation structure of lexical heads from more general aspects of linguistic structure such as the direction of Case assignment and theta-role assignment, the interaction between Case assignment and theta-role assignment, and the interaction between lexical structure and syntactic mapping. One set of verbs in Spanish whose lexical and syntactic properties have resisted easy elucidation is the class of ditransitive verbs exemplified in (1).

(1) a.   {Hemos **obligado** a los estudiantes/ Los hemos obligado} a que asistan a la clase.
'We have obliged the students/ them (ACC) that (they) attend the class.'

b.   {**Convencí** a mi amiga/ La convencí} de que debía consultar con un médico.
'I convinced my friend/ her (ACC) that (she) should consult a doctor.'

c.   Lola {**animó** a Pepe/ lo animó} a estudiar lingüística.
'Lola encouraged Pepe/ him (ACC) to study linguistics.'

As we see in (1), the DP complement of these verbs is marked with accusative Case, while the clausal complement appears with a preposition, either *a* or *de*.   Here I will argue that verbs like *obligar* 'to oblige' and *convencer* 'to convince' are generated at D-Structure with an empty verbal head with a VP complement; raising of the lower verb to the higher verbal head produces the observed surface order.

I will proceed as follows. First I will examine various possible D-Structure configurations for these verbs. I will then examine the facts of

***I wish to thank Violeta Demonte and Karen Zagona for their very useful comments and criticisms on the earlier draft of this essay. Among the various informants who I consulted, I would particularly like to thank Pilar García-Mayo. This research was supported in part by an Old Gold Summer Fellowship from the University of Iowa.

extraction out of the clausal complement; I will argue that these facts both allow us to choose among the competing hypotheses and provide evidence for a conjunctive definition of the ECP requiring both antecedent government and lexical government. I will then examine some differences between the complementation structure of these verbs and the double object structure in English. Finally, I will discuss some implications for the theory of lexical representations and universal principles for mapping lexical representations on to syntactic structures.

1 Syntactic properties and possible D-Structure representations

1.1 Two classes of ditransitive verbs. As was shown in (1), the class of verbs being examined here characteristically have an accusative complement and an obliquely marked clausal complement. When pronominalized, this clause usually appears in an oblique form rather than with a clitic, as shown in (2).[1]

(2) a. Los obligamos a ello.
'We obliged them to it.'

b. La convencí de eso.
'I convinced her of that.'

For my purposes here, I will term this set of verbs 'Class 1 verbs.'[2] A representative sampling of this group includes the verbs in (1), as well as *forzar* 'to force', *compeler* 'to compel', and *persuadir* 'to persuade'. This class contrasts with a second class of ditransitive verbs, which I shall term 'Class 2 verbs,' whose DP complement is dative and whose clausal complement is accusative, as shown by the data in (3).

(3) a. Ana les recomendó a sus amigas ver la última película de Almodóvar.
'Ana recommended to her friends to see the latest film by Almodóvar.'

b. Les han mandado construir una nueva carretera.
'They ordered them (DAT) to build a new highway.'

---

[1] For a small group of speakers, pronominalization of the clausal complement with the dative clitic also seems to be possible (cf. *Se lo animó* '(S/he) encouraged him to it').

[2] In an earlier paper (Kempchinsky 1989) I termed this class *obligar*-type verbs, contrasting them with *ordenar*-type verbs. In that paper I included only verbs with subjunctive or infinitival clausal complements, while in the present work I am extending the two groups to include verbs with indicative clausal complements.

c. Les advertimos que el teléfono no funcionaba.
   'We advised them (DAT) that the phone wasn't working.'

d. Se lo recomendó a ellas.
   '(S/he) recommended it (ACC) to them.'

e. Se lo advertimos.
   'We advised it (ACC) to them (DAT).'

Other examples of Class 2 verbs are *aconsejar* 'to advise', *sugerir* 'to suggest', *explicar* 'to explain', *decir* 'to tell', and many others. Indeed, the great majority of verbs in Spanish with clausal complements falls in this class, while Class 1 comprises a quite limited group of verbs.

Obligatoriness of complements differs significantly between the two classes of verbs. While the dative DP argument may be absent with Class 2 verbs, this optionality does not extend to the accusative DP argument of Class 1 verbs.[3]

(4) a. Recomendaron [que viéramos la última película de Almodóvar]
       '(They) recommended that (we) see the latest film by Almodóvar.'

    b. Advirtió [que el teléfono no funcionaba]
       '(S/he) advised/noted that the telephone didn't work.'

(5) a. *Forzaron a [que construyeran una nueva carretera]
       '(They) forced that (they) build a new highway.'

    b. *No pudimos convencer de [que tenemos suficientes fondos]
       '(We) couldn't convince that we have sufficient funds.'

---

[3] There are superficial counterexamples to this claim:
(i) a. La maestra siempre obliga a que le entreguen las tareas.
       'The teacher always requires that (they) hand in the homework to her.'
    b. La propaganda intenta convencer de que se necesitan los nuevos productos.
       'Advertising tries to convince that the new products are needed.'
However, such examples should be analyzed as containing an arbitrary *pro* in object position, following Rizzi (1986). In (ia) this *pro* is coindexed with the *pro* in subject position of the subjunctive clause, explaining the 3rd person plural subjunctive form, since it is 3rd person plural *pro* which may be interpreted as [-definite] (cf. Jaeggli 1986a).

An additional difference between the two classes concerns the related derived nominals. While the nominals of Class 2 verbs may appear with all three arguments corresponding to the verb (descriptively, AGENT, THEME, and GOAL), those corresponding to Class 1 verbs may appear only with the DP and CP complements, excluding the AGENT.

(6) a. Su recomendación a los estudiantes de [hacer los ejercicios]
   'His/Her recommendation to the students to do the exercises'

   b. Mi explicación a los estudiantes de [cómo hacer los ejercicios]
   'My explanation to the students of how to do the exercises'

   c. Nuestra advertencia a los clientes de [que no nos responsabilizamos de daños]
   'Our notice to the clients that we are not responsible for injuries'

(7) a. *Mi obligación de los estudiantes a [hacer los ejercicios]
   'My obligation of the students to do the exercises'

   b. *Su persuasión de su marido de [que debían comprarse una casa]
   'Her persuasion of her husband that (they) should buy a house'

   c. La obligación de los estudiantes de [hacer los ejercicios]
   'The students' obligation to do the exercises'

   d. La compulsión de Ana de [comer demasiados dulces]
   'Ana's compulsion to eat too many sweets'

Parallel examples in English are found in Kayne (1981a).

(8) a. Mary encouraged her husband to get a job.

   b. *Mary's encouragement of her husband to get a job

   c. Mary persuaded John to leave.

   d. *Mary's persuasion of John to leave

In summary, then, Class 1 verbs differ from Class 2 verbs in the following ways: (i) Case marking of the DP and CP complements, (ii) obligatoriness of the DP complement, and (iii) range of associated semantic roles realized within the corresponding derived nominal. The problem then is to determine the D-Structure and S-Structure representations of the complementation structures of these two classes which will account for these properties.

1.2 Assumptions about phrase structure. In proposing and evaluating possible D-Structure configurations for the Class 1 verbs, I will maintain the following working assumptions about conditions on phrase structure. First, phrase structures must obey the binary branching constraint (Kayne 1981a), a crucial constraint in determining the structure of ditransitive verbs. Second, projection of a lexical head may iterate at the X' level, following Fukui (1986) and Speas (1990); however, projection of a specifier closes off the projection at the X" level. Finally, clausal subjects are generated at D-Structure within the lexical projection of the verb (the Lexical Clause Hypothesis) (cf. Fukui 1986, Fukui and Speas 1986, Sportiche 1988, and others).

As a starting point, let us assume that an argument bearing the role of AGENT is base-generated in [Spec,VP] and that an argument bearing the role of THEME is base-generated as the immediate sister of the lexical head. Turning our attention first to the Class 2 verbs, we see that this predicts a D-Structure representation as in (9) for a sentence such as (3a).[4]

(9)

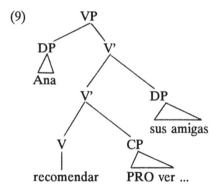

On rather standard assumptions about Case assignment, the argument in [Spec,VP] will raise to the [Spec,IP] position in order to receive nominative Case from INFL, while the CP argument in the sister to V position will receive accusative Case from the V under government. I will assume for Spanish that the dative Case assigned to the DP *sus amigas* 'her friends' is

---

[4] Larson (1988a) and Speas (1990) argue that the theme argument is the sister of V' rather than the sister of the head; this will be discussed in section 4.1.

an inherent Case specified in the verb's lexical entry; we will return to this matter in section 4. I assume that the order V - (dative) DP - CP is derived via extraposition of the CP argument to VP. In the corresponding nominal, of course, the AGENT *Ana* and the clausal complement, presumably a THEME, will receive genitive Case, while the DP complement will retain its inherent dative Case marking (cf. the examples in (6)).

The problematic case, of course, is the structure of Class 1 verbs. A priori, we can distinguish three potential D-Structure representations for this class:

(i) Hypothesis 1: The accusative-marked DP is the direct internal argument of the verb, receiving structural accusative Case, while the obliquely marked clause is an indirect internal argument marked with inherent oblique Case. This hypothesis yields a structure as in (10) for a sentence such as (1c).[5]

---

[5] A variation on this hypothesis is to consider the obliquely marked clause to be not a complement at all, but rather a purpose clause in the sense of Faraci (1974), as proposed by Kempchinsky (1986). However, there is some evidence against this proposal. First of all, purpose clauses, like other adjunct clauses, are optional rather than obligatory. In contrast, the obliquely marked CPs with the Class 1 verbs must generally be present, except in discourse contexts such as (ib).

    (i)   a.   *Forzaron a los prisioneros.
                '(They) forced the prisoners.'
        b.   --¿Quién te animó a venir a EEUU a estudiar?
                'Who encouraged you to come to the U.S. to study?'
                --Fue mi madre quién me animó.
                'It was my mother who encouraged me.'

A more convincing difference between adjunct clauses and the obliquely marked CPs with the Class 1 verbs shows up upon examination of their corresponding nominals. In contrast to Class 1 verbs and nominals, verbs appearing with purpose clause have nominals showing the full range of semantic roles, as evidenced by the data in (ii).

    (ii)   a.   Destruyeron los discos (para dificultar la investigación).
                '(They) destroyed the disks to complicate the investigation.'
        b.   Su destrucción de los discos (para dificultar la investigación)
                'Their destruction of the disks to complicate the investigation'
        c.   Invitamos a ese profesor (a dictar un curso).
                '(We) invited that professor to give a course.'
        d.   Nuestra invitación a ese profesor (a dictar un curso)
                'Our invitation to that professor to give a course'

I will therefore discard the purpose clause variant of Hypothesis 1.

(10)
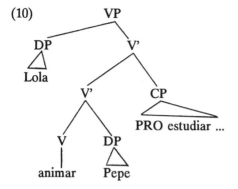

According to this hypothesis, then, the clausal complement of Class 1 verbs has a status akin to that of nominal indirect objects. Evidence in favor of this structure is the fact that some speakers may cliticize the obliquely marked CP with a dative clitic, as shown in (2c).

(ii) Hypothesis 2: The DP and CP complements form a small clause, as proposed by Kayne (1981a) for similar verbs in English.

(11)
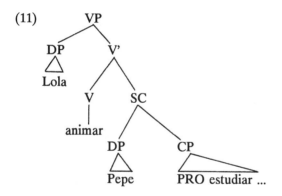

By this analysis, the accusative-marked DP is not an argument of the verb at all, but rather the subject of which the CP is predicated. Assuming a parallel structure for the associated derived nominals, Kayne accounted for the ungrammaticality of examples such as those in (8) by stipulating that N could not govern across a clausal-type boundary. Thus Case assignment to the DP is blocked, on the standard assumption that Case-marking takes place only under government.[6]

---

[6] The same result is obtained under Chomsky's (1986b) proposed Uniformity Condition, according to which an inherent Case assigner such as a N° must govern and theta-mark the Case assignee at D-Structure, and govern the Case-marked category (or its trace) at S-Structure.

(iii) Hypothesis 3: The DP and CP complements are within an embedded VP which is itself the complement to an empty verbal head at D-Structure. Raising of the lexical verb to the higher empty V^0 position, along with movement of the argument in [Spec,VP] to [Spec,IP], produces the S-structure order. This derivation is shown in (12).

(12)

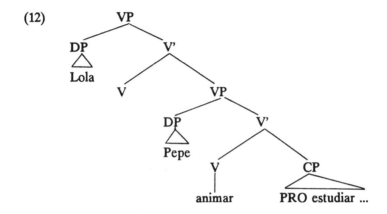

Larson (1988b) and Rochette (1988) propose the structure in (12) for cognate verbs in English and French, respectively, in order to account for control, on the assumption that the (accusative) controller must c-command the infinitival clause at D-Structure. In Kempchinsky (1989) I propose that this structure for Class 1 verbs follows from their general lexical properties, as encoded at the level of lexical conceptual structure (LCS) (cf. Hale and Keyser 1986, 1987). This analysis was motivated in part by a particular analysis of the English double object structure, that of Speas (1990); this will be discussed in section 3.1.

These three proposed structures make different predictions with respect to the extraction properties of the DP and CP complements. In section 2, I will examine the data on extraction out of these complements and will argue that only Hypothesis 3 provides us with an account of these facts.

2 Extraction of adjuncts from subordinate clauses

2.1 Assumptions and definitions. As a point of departure, I will assume the following version of the Empty Category Principle (ECP) (cf. Chomsky 1986a):

Since in the nominal corresponding to (11) the head N governs and theta-marks the entire small clause, but not the 'subject' of the small clause, Uniformity is not met, resulting in a Case theory violation.

(13) ∝ properly governs β iff ∝ antecedent governs or theta-governs β.

Government is sensitive to the notion of 'barrierhood', which in turn, following Chomsky (1986a), is sensitive to the notion of 'L-marking'. The relevant definitions are given in (14) through (17).

(14) **government**

∝ governs β iff ∝ m-commands β and there is no τ, τ a barrier for β, such that τ excludes ∝.

a. ∝ **excludes** β if no segment of ∝ dominates β.
b. β **m-commands** β iff ∝ does not dominate β, and every τ, τ a maximal projection, that dominates ∝ dominates β.

(15) **blocking category**

τ is a blocking category (BC) for β iff τ is not L-marked and τ dominates β.

(16) **barrier**

τ is a barrier for β iff
a. τ immediately dominates δ, δ a BC for β, or
b. τ is a BC for β, $\tau \neq$ IP.

(17) **L-marking**

∝ L-marks β iff ∝ is a zero-level lexical category that theta-marks β, and ∝, β are sisters.

If we take (13) through (17) together, and if 'sisterhood' in (17) is defined strictly, rather than on the basis of maximal projections, the prediction is that extraction out of any complement to a verb other than its most internal argument will result in an ECP violation.[7] Since (13) allows a trace to satisfy the ECP via theta-government, extraction of an object will produce at most a subjacency violation at S-Structure, should more than one barrier be crossed. The trace of an extracted adjunct, on the other hand, will require a trace in [Spec,CP] at both S-Structure and LF to serve as an antecedent governor, and this trace in turn will also need to satisfy the ECP. Thus a clear prediction is made: if a clause is the sister to the verb and therefore L-

---

[7] However, Contreras (1989) argues that L-marking should be extended to include all arguments of a lexical head. See footnotes 23 and 27 below.

marked, extraction of an adjunct out of that clause should result in a well-formed structure. Extraction of an adjunct from a non L-marked clause will always invoke an ECP violation, since the trace in [Spec,CP] will fail to be properly governed. Hence extraction of adjuncts from a subordinate clause should be a reliable test for the complement status of the clause.[8]

2.2 The extraction data. The definitions given in section 2.1 predict that subordinate clauses will fall into two categories in terms of extraction: directly theta-marked complements, i.e., sisters of the head V, vs. all other clauses, whether they be indirectly theta-marked complements, subjects or adjuncts. The data, however, suggest that this categorization is not quite so straightforward. Consider first the cases of object extraction in (18) through (20).

(18) a. Qué libro les aconsejaste [que leyeran [e]]
'What book did you advise them (DAT) that (they) read?'

b. Qué libro les mandaste [leer [e]]
'What book did you order them (DAT) to read?'

(19) a. Qué libro la animaste a [que leyera [e]]
'What book did you encourage her (ACC) that (she) read?'

b. Qué libro los obligaste a [leer [e]]
'What book did you oblige them (ACC) to read?'

(20) a. ?*Qué libro se marchó Ana [sin leer [e]]
'What book did Ana leave without reading?'

b. *Qué libro escribió Pedro el informe [después de leer [e]]
'What book did Pedro write the report after reading?'

---

[8] I am ignoring here Chomsky's proposal that wh-movement may proceed via adjunction to VP, and in fact must do so in order to nullify the barrierhood of VP, a non L-marked category. In most of the examples being discussed here, the hypothesis that VP is a barrier is essentially untestable, since either this barrierhood can be circumvented via adjunction to VP, or at S-Structure VP is in fact L-marked by raising of the lexical verb into INFL (a possibility also discussed by Chomsky). However, Contreras (1989) points out that the possibility of adjunction to VP also leaves open the possibility of adjunction to a PP adjunct, as in the examples of (20), in which case the set of facts subsumed under the Adjunct Condition cannot be accounted for. For the purposes of this article I assume that VP is not a barrier, either as a result of raising of the lexical verb into INFL, or because as a theta-marking category VP is not a blocking category (cf. Contreras *op. cit.* for discussion).

Examples (18a-b) present no surprises; by the proposed structure for Class 2 verbs given in (9), the CP complement is the sister of the verb and so will be L-marked. Hence no barrier is crossed. In contrast, extraction of the objects in the adjunct clauses in (20) can be expected to produce a subjacency violation. Since the adjunct clauses are not L-marked, the PPs heading them will be a blocking category and a barrier; the IP in turn will inherit barrierhood, so that more than one barrier is crossed. The structure for (20a) is given in (21), with the relevant barriers in bold face.

(21) [wh$_i$ [$_{IP}$ ... [$_{PP}$ P [$_{CP}$ ... [e]$_i$ ...]]]]

Let us now examine the sentences in (19) in the light of the three hypotheses. By Hypothesis 1, the CP is not L-marked because it is the indirect internal argument of the verb, rather than a sister in the strict sense. The CP will thus be a blocking category and a barrier, and will transfer barrierhood on to the VP, as shown in (22).

(22) [wh$_i$ [$_{IP}$ ... [$_{VP}$ [$_{V'}$ DP [$_{CP}$ t'$_i$ [... [e]$_i$ ...]]]]]]

This hypothesis thus predicts that object extraction from the clausal complements to Class 1 verbs should be as unacceptable as object extraction from a clausal adjunct, clearly not the right result. The same result obtains with Hypothesis 2, the small clause analysis. The CP is not L-marked by any lexical head, since it is the small clause itself, rather than the CP, which is subcategorized for and L-marked by the V. Consequently, the clausal boundary is both a blocking category and a barrier to extraction. The maximal projection of the small clause will then inherit barrierhood by virtue of dominating a blocking category, as shown in (23).[9]

(23) [wh$_i$ [$_{IP}$ ... [$_{VP}$ V [$_{SC}$ DP [$_{CP}$ t'$_i$ [... [e]$_i$ ...]]]]]]

---

[9] V. Demonte (p.c.) has pointed out that there is another class of Spanish verbs with an accusative DP complement and a clausal complement, with the two complements arguably forming a small clause:
(i) Juan ciñó [[su intervención] [a contestar la primera pregunta]]
     'Juan limited his participation to answering the first question'
(Other examples are *basar-lo en* 'base it on', *reducir-lo a* 'reduce it to' and *dedicar-lo a* 'dedicate it to'.) With these verbs, extraction of an object out of the clausal complement is clearly ungrammatical:
(ii) *Qué pregunta ciñó Juan [[su intervención] [a contestar [e]]]
      'Which question did Juan limit his participation to answering?'
The grammaticality of object extraction thus seems to be a clear diagnostic for distinguishing a small clause analysis from the embedded VP analysis. For another example of a class of small clause complements, cf. Demonte (1989).

Thus neither Hypothesis 1 nor Hypothesis 2 allows a satisfactory account of the examples in (19). What about Hypothesis 3? By this hypothesis, the CP is the direct internal argument of the verb at D-Structure, and is consequently L-marked. If L-marking at D-Structure is sufficient for voiding barrierhood, the grammaticality of these examples is explained. The relevant structure is given in (24).

(24) $[\text{wh}_i [... [_{VP1} V [_{VP2} t_v [_{CP} t'_i [... [e]_i ...]]]]]]$

In (24) the CP, having been L-marked at D-Structure, is neither a blocking category nor a barrier. At S-Structure VP_2 is L-marked by the raised verb, along the lines suggested by Chomsky (1986a) for L-marking of VP by a verb which has raised into INFL, and so it too is neither a blocking category nor a barrier. Thus subjacency is respected and the sentences are ruled grammatical.

A more problematic case is that of adjunct extraction. Consider the data in (25) through (27).

(25) a. Cómo le aconsejaste a Ana [vestirse [e] para la entrevista]
        'How did you advise Ana (DAT) to dress for the interview?'

      b. Con qué receta le recomendaste [que preparara el pollo [e]]
        'With which recipe did you recommend to him/her that (s/he) prepare the chicken?'

(26) a. ??Cómo obligó la madre al hijo a [vestirse [e] para la foto]
        'How did the mother oblige her son (ACC) to dress for the photo?'

      b. ?(?)Con qué receta lo animaste a [que preparara el pollo]
        'With which recipe did you encourage him (ACC) that (he) prepare the chicken?'

(27) a. *Cómo salió Ana de casa [sin vestirse [e]]
        'How did Ana leave the house without dressing?'

      b. *Con qué receta serviste el pollo [después de prepararlo [e]]
        'With which recipe did you serve the chicken after preparing it?'

Again, examples (25) and (27) are straightforward, along the lines of what was sketched above.[10]   In particular, the adjunct status of the infinitival clauses in (27) entails that the PP boundary is not L-marked, preventing antecedent government of the trace in [Spec,CP].   What is surprising is the status of (26).   If the infinitival clauses are L-marked, extraction of adjuncts such as *cómo* 'how' and *con qué receta* 'with what recipe' should be grammatical; if they are not, the resulting structure should be completely ruled out.   What is not expected within the assumptions of the *Barriers* framework is a three-way distinction.[11]   The variation in judgments in (25) through (27) has the flavor of a Subjacency vs. ECP violation; however, by hypothesis the barriers for Subjacency are defined identically to the barriers for government.   Hence extraction of an adjunct cannot violate subjacency without also violating the ECP.   Further, if the ECP is an 'all or nothing condition', then either a trace is properly governed and the principle is respected, or it is not and the principle is violated.

Keeping these considerations in mind,   let us see how our three hypotheses fare with respect to the intermediate status of (26).   By both Hypothesis 1 and Hypothesis 2,   the infinitival clause is not L-marked and hence constitutes a barrier.   Thus antecedent government of the trace in [Spec,CP] is blocked and extraction of the adjunct phrase should be as ungrammatical as in the examples of (27). This prediction seems too strong. On the embedded VP analysis, Hypothesis 3, the CP is L-marked by the V at S-Structure,   and so does not constitute either a blocking category or a

---

[10] If the CP complement of Class 2 verbs is extraposed, as I am assuming is the case at least when the surface order is V-DP-CP, and if the ECP requires both antecedent government and government by a lexical head, as will be argued in section 2.3, then there must be some lexical governor for the trace in [Spec,CP] of the extraposed clause. However, by Chomsky's (1986a) definition of domination, the adjoined clause is not dominated by VP, since it is not dominated by all segments of VP. Hence, V does not m-command the adjoined clause and consequently should not be able to govern it or its specifier. If the V raises into INFL by S-Structure, as proposed by Zagona (1988) and Pollock (1989), then it will in fact be able to govern the trace in [Spec,CP]. Alternatively, it may be the case that a head can govern an adjoined position, given the grammaticality of English examples such as (i).
    (i)   (?) How did you suggest to Ann [that she fix the car [e]]
Government from INFL is presumably not an option in (i), given that the lexical verb in English does not raise to INFL in the syntax.
[11] We will see in section 3.2 that a similar distinction in judgments can be found with English cognates of the Spanish examples. It should be noted here that the degree of acceptance of examples such as those in (26) seems to be sensitive to a number of factors. For most of the speakers I consulted, extraction from an infinitive complement was judged to be more acceptable than extraction from a subjunctive complement, although for one informant these judgments were the inverse. The grammaticality of extraction from the clausal complement also seems to improve if the accusative complement is a clitic rather than a full DP.

barrier. This predicts that extraction of the adjunct phrases should be fully acceptable, on a par with the examples in (25). This prediction seems to err in the opposite direction. What is called for is a reexamination of the formulation of the ECP.

2.3 Evidence for a conjunctive definition of the ECP. To account for the puzzling array of judgments in (25) through (27), I would like to draw on an account of extraction out of English prepositional complements proposed by Johnson (1988). He observed the following contrasts in extraction out of English gerundives.

(28) a. ??Who did you dance [despite [Betsy talking to [e]]]

b. *Who did you dance [despite [[e] talking to Betsy]]

c. Who did you bet [on [Mittie liking [e]]

d. ??Who did you bet [on [[e] liking Mittie]]

In (28a-b) extraction has proceeded out of an adjunct clause, producing a subjacency-strength violation in the case of object extraction (cf. (28a)) and an ECP violation in the case of subject extraction (28b). The Subjacency violation in (28a) implies that there must be at least two barriers between [e] and its antecedent (either in [Spec, CP] or adjoined to VP, on a *Barriers*-style account of movement). Johnson argues persuasively that the subject of gerundive complements to Ps in English is Case-marked by the preposition, and hence presumably governed. He proposes that prepositions are not lexical in the sense relevant to L-marking; hence, the IP complement to *despite* in both (28a) and (28b) is a blocking category and a barrier, from which the adjunct PP itself inherits barrierhood. Of course, in the case of subject extraction as in (28b), one barrier is sufficient to block antecedent government.[12]

Turning to examples (28c-d), Johnson observes that the verb-preposition pair *bet on* may appear in the pseudopassive construction.

(29) That was bet on by all.

---

[12] One aspect of Johnson's analysis which will not be discussed here is that he is led to conclude that the definition of 'barrier' is uniform for subjacency and antecedent government, but not for government by a head. Thus the subject of the clausal gerund in (28a) receives Case under government from the preposition, but the preposition as a nonlexical category does not L-mark the IP, which therefore becomes a barrier to antecedent government.

He assumes that pseudopassives are licensed by verb-preposition reanalysis, which is itself an instantiation of incorporation in the sense of Baker (1988). The structures of (28c-d) and (29) are thus as in (30).

(30) a. That$_i$ was [$_V$ bet on$_j$] [$_{PP}$ [e]$_j$ t$_i$] by all.

b. Who$_i$ did you [$_V$ bet on$_j$] [$_{PP}$ [e]$_j$ [$_{IP}$ Mittie liking t$_i$]]

c. Who$_i$ did you [$_V$ bet on$_j$] [$_{PP}$ [e]$_j$ [$_{IP}$ t$_i$ liking Mittie]]

Since object extraction from the clausal gerund in (28c) does not invoke a Subjacency violation, the IP in the structures in (30) must be L-marked by the complex predicate made up of the verb and the incorporated preposition. Incorporation fails in the adjunct structures of (28a-b) because the resulting trace left by incorporation of the preposition will fail to be properly governed, violating the Head Movement Constraint (ultimately, the ECP).

The puzzling structure, then, is that of (30c). If the IP is L-marked and hence not a barrier, antecedent government of the trace in subject position should be unproblematic. Johnson proposes that the explanation lies in the failure of the subject trace to be lexically governed, since the trace left by incorporation of the preposition is not lexical. Thus, these examples provide further evidence for a conjunctive definition of the ECP; the version proposed by Johnson is given in (31).[13]

(31) A nonpronominal empty category must be properly governed.
   $\propto$ properly governs β iff
   a. $\propto$ theta-governs β, or
   b. i. $\propto$ antecedent-governs β, and
      ii. β is governed by a Lexical governor.

The contrast in ungrammaticality between (28b) and (28d) is now explained: (28d) fulfills the requirement for antecedent government but not lexical government, while (28b) fails to meet either requirement, thereby producing a stronger ECP violation.

The relevance of the above discussion to the Spanish cases being analyzed here is clear. Consider again the range of judgments for adjunct extraction from clausal complements to Class 2 verbs, clausal complements to Class 1 verbs and clausal adjuncts.

---

[13] Various versions of a conjunctive ECP have been proposed; cf. Stowell (1985), Torrego (1985), Rizzi (1986), Aoun et al. (1987), among others.

(32) a. Cómo le has aconsejado/ordenado a Ana [vestirse [e] para la entrevista]
'How have you advised/ordered Ana (DAT) to dress for the interview?'

   b. ?(?)Cómo has animado/obligado a Ana a [vestirse [e] para la entrevista]
'How have you encouraged/obliged Ana (ACC) to dress for the interview?'

   c. *Cómo se marchó Ana de casa sin [vestirse [e] para la entrevista]
'How did Ana leave the house without dressing for the interview?'

The corresponding structures are given in (33).

(33) a. Cómo$_i$ [$_{IP}$ ... [$_{VP}$ V [$_{CP}$ t$_i$ [$_{IP}$ ... [e]$_i$ ...]]]]

   b. Cómo$_i$ [$_{IP}$ ... [$_{VP}$ V [$_{VP}$ t$_v$ [$_{CP}$ t$_i$ [$_{IP}$ ... [e]$_i$ ...]]]]]

   c. Cómo$_i$ [$_{IP}$ ... [$_{VP}$ V ...] [$_{PP}$ P [$_{CP}$ t$_i$ [$_{IP}$ ... [e]$_i$ ...]]]]

In (33a), the trace in [Spec, CP] is lexically governed by the V (*aconsejar* 'to advise', *ordenar* 'to order') and antecedent governed by the wh-element in the highest [Spec, CP]. In (33b), antecedent government of the trace in the lower [Spec, CP] is fulfilled in the same way, but the trace left by raising of the verb to the empty V° position in the higher VP fails to fulfill the requirement for lexical government.[14] Finally, in (33c), the trace in the

---

[14] In fact, it seems that the failure of the verbal trace in (33b) to be lexical in the sense required by the ECP is not due simply to the fact that it is a trace, but rather to the fact that it is the trace of a category which assigns inherent rather than structural Case. If it is true that in languages such as Spanish the verb raises into (tensed) INFL in the syntax (cf. Zagona 1988, Pollock 1989), then even sentences with 'simple' VPs will have a verbal trace at the level of S-Structure, predicting that *every* complement to the verb is an island for extraction. Obviously, this is far too strong a prediction, given the grammaticality of sentences such as (i), from Demonte (1987).
   (i) De quién conoces a [la hija [e]]
       'Of whom do you know the daughter?'
Example (i) contrasts minimally with (ii), in which extraction has taken place out of the internal argument of the pronominal verb *quemarse* 'to get burned'.
   (ii) *De qué mano se quemó [los pelitos [e]]
        'Of which hand did (s/he) burn (nonagentive) the hairs?'

lower [Spec, CP] is neither lexically governed (assuming, with Johnson, that Ps are not lexical governors) nor antecedent governed, since the adjunct clause is not L-marked. One question which needs to be answered here is why the raised V itself does not count as a lexical governor for the trace in [Spec,CP] in (33b). The structure in (33b) is in many ways parallel to an incorporation structure, in which the head X° of a maximal category XP moves into the head position of a Y° governing to XP (Baker 1988). Baker proposes that as a result of incorporation the new complex head governs everything which was formerly in the government domain of the incorporated X° head (the Government Transparency Corollary, GTC). If the GTC extends to the structure in (33b), then the lower VP will be in the government domain of the raised V, which should therefore qualify as a lexical governor for the trace. I assume that this possibility is ruled out by some version of the Minimality Condition (Chomsky 1986a); since the verbal trace is a closer potential governor, it is the only potential governor for the trace, at least for ECP purposes.[15]

Note that by both Hypothesis 1 and Hypothesis 2, neither antecedent government nor lexical government will obtain of the trace in [Spec,CP], since the CP as a non L-marked category constitutes a barrier. Neither of these hypotheses, therefore, will account for the intermediate status of the adjunct extractions in (26). Thus the extraction facts, coupled with the modification of the ECP proposed by Johnson (1988), provide evidence in favor of the embedded VP structure.

3 Lexical representations, Class 1 verbs, and the English double object construction. Given the results of section 2.3, let us assume that the syntactic representation of the Class 1 verbs is indeed that given in (12). The question then is how this structure accounts for the syntactic properties of this

---

In Campos and Kempchinsky (1991), we argue that the theme argument *los pelitos* 'the hairs' is base-generated as the direct internal argument of the verb, receiving inherent accusative Case, while the experiencer argument is base-generated as a sister to V', from which position it moves to [Spec,IP] to receive Case. If extraction out of DP proceeds via the [Spec,DP] position, as has been argued by several linguists (cf. Stowell 1988, Campos 1988, among others), then (ii), like the examples of (26), has a trace in the specifier position of a complement to an inherent Case marker which apparently fails to be head governed in the appropriate way. This inability of inherent Case assigners to govern into the specifier position of their complement is quite plausibly linked to their inability to assign Case to a category which they do not theta-mark. For similar speculations along these lines, see Baker (1988) in his discussion of his proposed 'Non-Oblique Trace Filter'.

[15] If the lack of proper government of the trace in [Spec,CP] is ultimately to be derived from the fact that the verb assigns inherent rather than structural Case to the clause, as discussed in footnote 14, then it may be possible that no appeal to minimality is necessary. I leave this as an open question at this point.

set of verbs which we observed in section 1.1, in particular the Case marking of the two complements and the nature of the corresponding nominals. A full answer to these questions will entail a re-examination of the nature of lexical representations and the principles governing lexicon-to-syntax mapping. This in turn will lead us to a closer examination of the English double object construction and the similarities and differences between this construction and the syntactic structure of Class 1 verbs in Spanish.

3.1 Lexicon-to-syntax mapping. Two well-known facts about the English double object construction are its lexical idiosyncrasy and the observation that the GOAL argument in this construction (descriptively, the first object) bears a greater degree of 'affectedness' with respect to the action expressed by the verb (cf. Oehrle 1976, Larson 1988a, Speas 1990, and references cited therein). Thus in contexts which force the 'affected' reading, only the double object construction is possible.

(34) a. Mary gave John a cold.   (from Green 1974)

b. *Mary gave a cold to John.

Speas (1990) accounts for these two facts by appealing to a view of the lexicon wherein each lexical entry has two levels. The first, the level of lexical conceptual structure (LCS), encodes the meaning of a given verb in terms of variables and primitive semantic functions such as CAUSE, STATE, and the like. LCS representations in turn are projected to the level of predicate argument structure (PAS). The PAS specifies the number of arguments the verb requires, with presumably universal principles determining the appropriate mapping of each argument to syntactic positions. In essence, as Rappaport and Levin (1988) argue, the two proposed levels of lexical representation capture the dual nature of theta-roles: the LCS specifies the content of the semantic roles, while the PAS accounts for the manner of role assignment.

Speas proposes that those verbs which enter both into the double object construction (or so-called dative-shift construction) and the regular V-NP-to-NP construction have two separate LCS representations, with each mapping on to a distinct PAS representation. These are represented in (35).

(35) a. GIVE₁: (nonshifted)

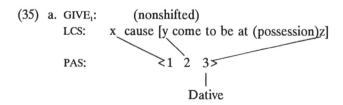

b. GIVE$_2$:   (shifted)

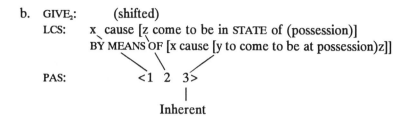

LCS: x cause [z come to be in STATE of (possession)]
BY MEANS OF [x cause [y to come to be at possession)z]]

PAS: <1 2 3>
|
Inherent

Assuming that semantic roles are defined according to positions within the LCS representation, the semantic role of THEME is assigned to the variable occupying the position '___ come to be at' (cf. Rappaport and Levin 1988).[16] Thus in the LCS of (35b) there are two THEMES, the variable z and the variable y. The affectedness of the double object construction is captured by the fact that in the LCS of (35b) this variable undergoes a change of state.

In Speas's account, the PAS representations are derived from the LCS by simply linking variables in the LCS to argument slots in the PAS left-to-right until all variables are linked. In the predicate argument structures in (35), the notation '1' stands for the external argument and the notation '2' stands for the direct internal argument. Notation '3' is the indirect internal argument, linked in both PAS representations to some inherent Case. Speas assumes that one principle of lexicon-to-syntax mapping is that at D-Structure the verb and its indirect argument form a constituent which excludes the direct argument, following Larson (1988a). The PAS of (35b) will therefore yield the D-Structure representation of (36b), while the PAS of (35a) will yield the D-Structure representation of (36a).

(36) a.   b.

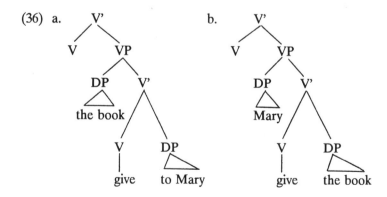

---

[16] This conception of theta roles is very close to that of Jackendoff (1987), who views theta roles as relational notions defined according to positions in semantic conceptual structures. The particular definition of THEME given here can be traced back to Gruber (1965).

The surface order is derived by raising of the lower verb *give* into the higher verbal head, from which position it can assign accusative Case to the higher DP.

I would argue that the change in state reading entailed by the double object construction also holds of Class 1 verbs, in contrast to Class 2 verbs. Consider, for example, *convencer* (Class 1) and *explicar* (Class 2).

(37) a. María convenció a Pepín de [que la luna está hecha de queso]
'María convinced Pepín that the moon is made of cheese.'

b. María le explicó a Pepín [que la luna está hecha de queso]
'María explained to Pepín that the moon is made of cheese.'

To convince someone of the validity of a proposition entails that the second party comes to believe in the truth of the proposition; in contrast, to explain a proposition to someone does not entail that the second party will in fact come to regard this proposition as true.[17] A parallel contrast in entailments can be observed with verbs subcategorizing for embedded imperatives (cf. Kempchinsky 1986), as in (38).

(38) a. Los obligué a que hicieran el trabajo.
'I obliged them that (they) do the work.'

b. Les ordené que hicieran el trabajo.
'I ordered them that (they) do the work.'

To oblige someone to do something implies that the desired action in fact takes place, while to order someone to do something does not necessarily bring about the desired action.[18]

---

[17] An analogous argument was made by Stowell (1981) regarding verbs such as *persuade* and *convince* in English. He further observed that the clausal complements to such verbs are islands with respect to subject extraction. Although I do not find such extraction to be completely acceptable, it is notably better than extraction from an adjunct, cf. the examples in (i).

(i) a. ?Who did Mary convince John [[e] should be the next president of the club]?
b. *Who did Mary leave the party despite [[e] talking to John]?

Assuming that these verbs have the same syntactic structure as that proposed for Class 1 verbs in Spanish--as would be expected given their similar semantic characteristics--the extraction facts follow from the account developed in section 2.3.

[18] Jackendoff (1987) proposes an inference rule to account for, among other things, the fact that a statement of the form in (ia) implies (ib).

(i) a. Bill forced Harry to shut up
b. (At the appropriate time t) Harry shut up

His inference rule takes the form of (ii).

Thus, both Class 1 and Class 2 verbs are characterized semantically as having a clausal complement encoding either propositional knowledge or an indirect imperative and a noun phrase complement representing the person or persons to whom the proposition or imperative is conveyed. In the case of the Class 1 verbs, transmission of this propositional content brings about a changed perception (or state of knowledge) in the hearer. The relevant LCS representations are therefore as in (39), where y corresponds to the clausal complement and z represents the DP complement.

(39) Class 2: x cause [y come to be at (perception) z]

Class 1: x cause [z come to be in STATE (of perception)]

BY MEANS OF [x cause [y come to be at (perception) z]]

The LCS of Class 1 verbs, like that of dative-shifted *give*, contains two THEMES, according to the definition of THEME discussed above. We saw in section 1.1 that one of the differences between Class 1 verbs and Class 2 verbs is that in the case of the former both internal arguments must be present. It is of course characteristic of THEME arguments that they be obligatorily realized; hence the proposed LCS representations account nicely for this distinction between the two classes of verbs.

The above LCS representation for Class 1 verbs will in turn be projected on to a PAS representation, as in (40), yielding the D-Structure representation of (12) above.

(40) x cause [z come to be in STATE (of perception)]

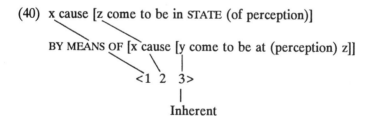

BY MEANS OF [x cause [y come to be at (perception) z]]

<1 2   3>

Inherent

(ii) For an Event of the form [_Event GO (X, [_Path TO (Y)])], there is a point in time t, the termination of the Event. At t, the following holds: [_State BE (X, [_Place AT (Y)])] and for some interval of time leading up to but not including t, [NOT [_State BE (X, [_Place AT (Y)])]

It should be pointed out here that there are a few problematic cases where the entailment differences do not seem as clear-cut as one would wish. It is difficult to see, for instance, the semantic distinction, in terms of entailments, between *animar* 'to encourage' (Class 1) and *aconsejar* 'to advise' (Class 2). Nevertheless, the general correlation is quite strong.

222 / Current Studies in Spanish Linguistics

The above PAS specifies that the position linked to the y variable in the LCS will receive inherent Case from the verb. After raising of the verb to the higher $V°$ position, the DP complement will be structurally Case-marked with accusative Case. Thus the Case properties of the complements of the Class 1 verbs are also accounted for quite straightforwardly.

3.2 Differences with the double object construction. The analysis as developed thus far is appealing in that putatively universal LCS representations appear to underlie the syntactic representations of two different classes of verbs in two different languages.[19] Nevertheless, there are a number of differences between the double object construction in English and the complementation structure of *obligar*-type verbs in Spanish which this account does not predict. First of all, the first object in the English construction cannot be wh-moved or undergo Focus NP shift, while its Spanish counterpart, the DP complement, may undergo such movement.

(41) a. *John sent a letter [every musician in the orchestra].

b. *?John, Mary said that she gave a present.

c. *?Who did Mary say that she gave a present? [20]

(42) a. Obligamos a repetir el curso [a todos los estudiantes que no se habían presentado para el examen final]
'We obliged to repeat the course all the students who had not shown up for the final exam.'

b. ?A varios empleados se ha convencido de que deben quejarse ante el gerente.
'Various employees (one) has convinced that they should complain to the manager.'

c. ¿A quiénes has forzado a que vayan a hablar con el decano?
'Who have (you) forced that (they) go to speak with the dean?'

Second, although English object control constructions for the most part show a surface V-DP-CP structure, differences in the grammaticality of adjunct extraction from the clausal complement parallel the Spanish examples. This

---

[19] Kayne's (1981a) analysis of certain English control verbs, discussed briefly in section 1.2, also drew a parallel between these verbs and the double object construction.

[20] Examples from Larson (1988a).

is illustrated by the examples in (43) through (45), corresponding to the Spanish examples of (25) through (27).

(43) a. How did you advise Ann [to dress for the interview [e]]?

b. What recipe did you recommend [that she prepare the chicken with [e]]?

(44) a. ??How did the mother force her son [to dress [e] for the picture]?

b. ?What recipe did you encourage her [to prepare the chicken with [e]]?

(45) a. *How did you take the car to the garage [for the mechanic to fix [e]]

b. *What recipe did you give the chicken to Ann [for her to fix it with [e]]

This crosslinguistic parallelism could simply be attributed to 'semantics' *grosso modo*, but ultimately these semantic factors should be captured by the appropriate lexical representations, which in turn will affect the syntactic representations. Significantly, those English control constructions which do allow fully grammatical adjunct extraction have a dative-marked controller in the corresponding nominal; recall that Class 2 verbs in Spanish have a dative-marked DP complement and adjunct extraction from the clausal complement is fully acceptable (cf. (25)). In contrast, the English cognates to Spanish Class 1 verbs yield marginal cases of adjunct extraction and do not have a grammatical nominal counterpart with all three of the arguments corresponding to the verb (the cases originally discussed by Kayne 1981a).[21]

(46) a. The general's order to the soldiers to attack

b. The teacher's request to the children to work quietly

c. *Mary's encouragement of her husband to get a job

---

[21] The correlation here is not absolute; two of the ungrammatical English nominal constructions included in Kayne's data are *permission* and *prohibition*, which correspond to Spanish verbs with dative rather than accusative controllers (*permitir, prohibir*).

    d. *My obligation of the students to go to the language lab

There is a third difference, again with respect to derived nominals. While neither the double object construction nor Class 1 verbs have corresponding grammatical nominals with all three arguments, Class 1 verbs do have nominal constructions with the two internal arguments, as we saw above (cf. 7c-d). In contrast, the double object construction does not have any corresponding grammatical nominal at all.

(47) a. *La obligación de la madre al/del niño a/de fregar los platos
        'The obligation of the mother of the child to wash the dishes'

      b. La obligación del niño de fregar los platos
         'The child's obligation to wash the dishes'

      c. *My gift (of) Mary (of) a book

      d. *Mary's gift of a book
         (with the meaning, 'someone gave Mary a book')

Finally, dative-shift is not an option in Spanish for verbs such as *dar* 'to give'; this is not expected if the LCS and PAS representations of Class 1 verbs are otherwise available.

If Spanish verbs such as *animar* 'to encourage', *convencer* 'to convince' and *obligar* 'to oblige' (and their English counterparts) share an abstract semantic representation with English dative-shifted verbs, then the syntactic differences enumerated above must be accounted for. Within our assumptions regarding lexical representations, what these facts indicate is that the English double object construction and the Class 1 verbs in Spanish both have an LCS representation with an embedded predicate. However, the syntactic structure projected from the related PAS is distinct.

3.3   A new account of the English double object construction

3.3.1   Incorporation and Case assignment in the double object construction. I want to suggest here a new analysis of the English double object construction, which in fact draws upon several current analyses. Let us focus first on the general lack of dative-shift in Spanish. As did Larson (1988a), I will draw upon Kayne's (1981b) proposal that dative-shift in English is licensed by the ability of prepositions in English to assign objective rather than oblique Case. Kayne argued that dative-shift involved reanalysis between the verb and the preposition, and that such reanalysis is blocked in languages such as the Romance languages where prepositions assign a Case distinct from the objective Case assigned by transitive verbs. If we interpret reanalysis as an instantiation of verb-preposition incorporation with a phonetically null preposition, following Baker (1988) (cf. section 2.3 above), then we arrive at the structure in (48), as proposed by Baker.

(48) [$_{VP}$ [$_V$ give + $\emptyset_i$] [$_{PP}$ [e]$_i$ Mary] [$_{DP}$ a book]]

Baker proposes that the ungrammaticality of examples such as (41), in which the complement to the empty preposition has been wh-moved, is due to a general filter barring empty categories governed by oblique Case-assigners, his Non-Oblique Trace Filter. At first glance, such a filter seems to account satisfactorily for the resistance of the first object to wh-movement. Nevertheless, to appeal to such a stipulation would in fact be contradictory with the assumption that reanalysis is licensed precisely by the ability of English prepositions to assign objective rather than oblique Case. Furthermore, this account contradicts Baker's own proposal, discussed by Johnson (1988) (cf. examples (29), (30)), that verb-preposition reanalysis in English is an instance of abstract verb-preposition incorporation. Thus the structure of a sentence such as (49a) would be that of (49b), violating the filter.

(49) a. Which horse did you bet on at the race?
      b. [wh$_j$ [... [$_{VP}$ [$_V$ bet on$_i$] [$_{PP}$ [e]$_i$ t$_j$]]]]

Baker's proposal therefore does not yet explain adequately for the facts in (41). Nor does it account for the evidence presented by Barss and Lasnik (1986) indicating that in the double object construction the first object c-commands the second. Finally, this analysis violates the binary branching requirement which I have been assuming as a working hypothesis.

What I would like to propose here is that Baker's essential idea of verb-preposition incorporation is the core of the English double object construction. However, this process takes place in an embedded VP, followed by V' to V reanalysis as proposed by Larson (1988a). Finally, raising of the new complex V to the higher empty verbal head produces the observed surface order. This analysis is sketched in (50).

(50)

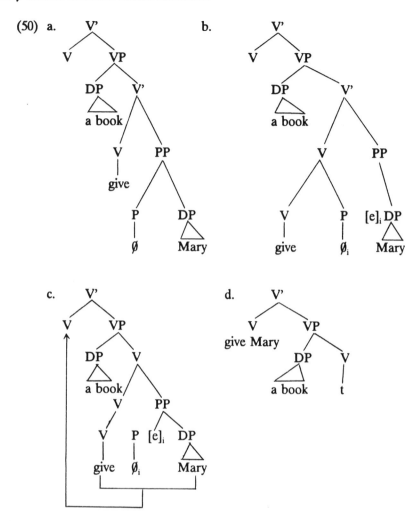

Let us assume that c-command is computed on the basis of the highest lexical node. Then in (50d) the inner object *Mary* c-commands the outer object, since the lexical node V which arose from the process of V' to V reanalysis, c-commands the DP *a book*. We can thus account for the Barss and Lasnik data. To explain the nonextractability of the first object, I will appeal to a general principle against extraction out of a complex word, along the lines of Stowell's (1981) analysis of this construction. I assume that V' to V reanalysis is forced by a general principle requiring adjacency of the incorporated P and its trace at all levels, perhaps for identification purposes.

Baker assumes that the second object (the 'outer object') is assigned (inherent) oblique Case, while Larson assumes that both objects receive objective Case. However, he proposes that of these two instances of objective Case, one is inherent (that assigned to the THEME argument), and the other is structural (that assigned to the GOAL argument). I will assume, contra these two analyses, that both objects receive structural objective Case. Suppose that Case marking is in fact a type of indexing, as proposed by Baker. In (50b) the GOAL argument, *Mary*, is Case-indexed by the complex structure created by V-P incorporation. Following reanalysis (50b) and raising (50c), the new complex V Case-indexes the THEME argument *a book*. I will argue in section 4.1 that in fact there is no inherent Case associated with the double object construction, and it is these special Case-marking mechanisms of the double object construction which allow the representation to meet Case theory requirements.

3.3.2 Explaining the differences. Summarizing to this point then, the S-Structure representation of the double object construction is the structure of (50d), contrasting with the S-Structure representation of the complementation structure of Class 1 verbs, given in (51).

(51)

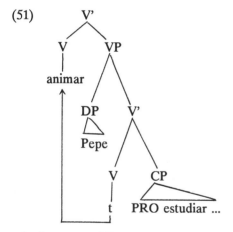

How do these two different structures account for the differences we noted above? I have proposed that the general lack of dative-shift in Spanish is to be attributed to the lack of verb-preposition incorporation in that language, on the hypothesis that this process is licensed in English by the Case-assigning properties of English prepositions.[22] Extraction of the first object in the

---

[22] Obviously, this is too strong an hypothesis as it now stands, since it would predict the nonexistence of verb-preposition incorporation in any language whose prepositions assign oblique Case. Clearly, the vast majority of the languages studied by Baker (1988) with overt verb-preposition incorporation show oblique Case on the objects of prepositions. Perhaps the crucial

double object construction is prohibited by a general constraint against extraction of a subpart of a word. In contrast, extraction of the DP complement of a Class 1 verb is allowed, since this DP is an independent constituent and is properly governed by the raised V at S-Structure. English verbs such as *encourage* and *force* show the same degree of deviance with respect to adjunct extraction because their D-Structure and S-Structure representations are identical to those of their Spanish counterparts; consequently, the trace in [Spec,CP] lacks a lexical governor at S-Structure. Verbs such as 'order' and 'recommend', on the other hand, either have a syntactical representation identical to that of (9), in which case proper government of the antecedent trace in [Spec,CP] follows from the direct object status of the clausal complement, or they are derived as a double object construction. Consider the case of 'order', whose underlying prepositional dative complement shows up in the corresponding nominal, as we saw above. At D-Structure the VP in (52a) will have the representation of (52b), with (52c) showing the corresponding S-Structure configuration.

(52) a. How did the general order the soldiers to attack?

b. $[_{V'e} [_{VP} CP [_{V'} [_{PP} P_\emptyset DP]]]]$

c. $[_{V'} [_V + P_\emptyset [_{PP} [e] DP]] [_{VP} CP t_v]]$

At D-Structure the clausal complement, as a sister to V', is not directly L-marked. However, at S-Structure after V' reanalysis, it is a sister to V°. Thus the CP is not a barrier to antecedent government of the trace in [Spec,CP], which meets the lexical government requirement of the revised ECP in (31) via government by the raised verb.[23]

Finally, we can account for the properties of the derived nominals corresponding to the two constructions on Case-theoretic grounds. Consider first the D-Structure and S-Structure representations of the nominal of the Class 1 verb *obligar* 'to oblige'.

---

factor in the case of English is the lack of overt morphology in the incorporation process; empty prepositions (again in the spirit of Kayne 1981b) are licensed only by identity of Case assignment with verbs. I leave this as an open question here.

[23] If all theta-marked arguments are L-marked, as proposed by Contreras (1989), then the clausal complement in (52) would already be L-marked at D-Structure.

(53) a.   La obligación de Lola de ayudarme
'Lola's obligation to help me'

b. *Mi obligación a/de Lola de ayudarme
'My obligation of Lola to help me'

c.
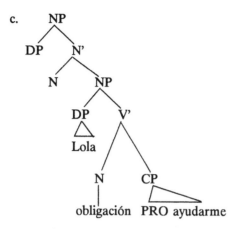

d.
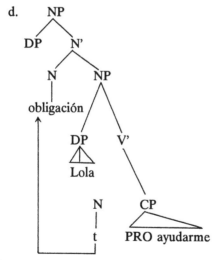

What is immediately obvious from an examination of the structures in (53) is the fact that the DP position corresponding to the AGENT, the specifier of the higher NP, is not governed by the head N *obligación* at D-Structure. Therefore assignment of inherent genitive Case by the head N to the argument in that position will violate the Uniformity Condition of Chomsky

(1986b).[24] Thus the external argument cannot be assigned Case and realization of this argument within the nominal is ruled out. Note that raising of the head N causes no problems for the two internal arguments. The DP complement is clearly governed at both D-Structure and S-Structure. The CP complement is directly governed by the head N itself at D-Structure, and by the trace of the raised N at S-Structure.[25]

What then is the explanation of the complete ungrammaticality of any nominal corresponding to the English double object structure? The relevant D-Structure configuration is given in (54).

(54)

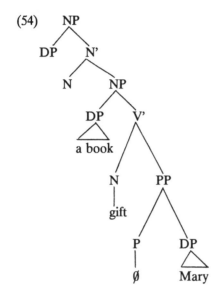

---

[24] Clearly, the proposal that the lexical head does not govern the external argument at D-Structure has important consequences for theta-theory; I will discuss this issue in section 4.1.

[25] Alternatively, we might suppose that there is no raising at all within the nominal. Larson (1988a) motivates raising of the lower V into the higher (empty) verbal head for reasons of tense and Case requirements holding between INFL and V; these presumably would not be relevant in the derived nominal. However, he later suggests that raising of the V is forced by thematic requirements; if no raising occurs, the V will not be associated with the external argument. Given that within the nominal the external argument can never appear, for the Case-theoretic reasons outlined in the text, it is an open question as to whether similar thematic requirements would force raising of the head N. Nevertheless, if the embedded structure is derived from the lexical conceptual structure of the verb and its associated nominal, one would expect that structure to be base-generated for the nominal as well as for the verb. One piece of evidence in favor of raising within the nominal is the fact that this would be the most straightforward way to derive the unmarked order of N-DP-CP.

As with the Class 1 verbs, assignment of inherent Case to the external argument will violate Uniformity. The question then is what blocks Case assignment to the internal arguments. Since by hypothesis all nouns are potential inherent Case assigners, the head N *gift* in (54) should minimally be able to assign (genitive) Case to the DP *a book*, which it governs at both D-Structure and S-Structure. However, at D-Structure the head N does not govern the DP *Mary*, which is within the PP headed by the empty preposition. Assuming that empty prepositions cannot assign Case, the P in (54) will need to incorporate into a Case-assigning head which governs the whole PP. At this point there are two potential explanations: either noun-preposition incorporation is not licensed, because prepositions in English in general do not assign the same Case as that assigned by nouns, or incorporation *is* possible, but Case assignment to the DP will violate Uniformity. By either account, the lack of double object derived nominals finds an explanation.[26]

4.0 Lexicon-to-syntax mapping revisited

4.1 The role of Case. In section 3.1 I argued that Class 1 verbs in both English and Spanish and English verbs entering into the double object construction share a similar LCS representation, repeated below as (55).

(55)   x cause [z come to be in STATE]
         BY MEANS OF [x cause [y come to be at z]]

The D-Structure representations corresponding to this LCS for the two sets of verbs are alike in that the external argument appears in the specifier position of a VP whose head is empty and whose complement is a VP headed by the actual lexical verb and containing the two internal arguments. Such a representation entails that the argument bearing the role of AGENT is not in the government domain of the lexical head at D-Structure; this assumption, in fact, was crucial to the account developed above of the structure of the derived nominals of Class 1 verbs. This, of course, has nontrivial consequences for the Lexical Clause Hypothesis.

Larson (1988a) derives VPs headed by an empty head from what he terms the Single Complement Hypothesis. He proposes that X'-theory limits the number of complements which any given X^0 may take to exactly one, in the

---

[26] To attribute the ungrammaticality of these nominals to Uniformity requires a strict interpretation of this principle, since the (abstract) preposition governs the DP at D-Structure and is part of the complex noun-preposition structure which would arise as a result of incorporation. Note that this account crucially assumes that the preposition in English is not merely a type of Case marker, but also assigns the relevant theta-role to the (dative) argument. See section 4.1 for further discussion of the role of the preposition.

same way that the number of subjects is limited to exactly one. Consequently, the only way to project a VP whose head takes three arguments is for this VP to become the complement within an X' 'shell' whose head is empty and therefore lacking in independent thematic requirements. The specifier position of this shell is thus available for the projection of the third argument, generally the AGENT, by Larson's proposed Thematic Hierarchy and Principle P2 for the mapping of thematic roles to syntactic positions. Raising of the verb will enable the AGENT thematic role to be realized within a projection of the lexical verb.

Speas (1990), on the other hand, proposes that the generation of extra verbal heads at D-Structure is determined by the presence of the CAUSE predicate in the verb's LCS. Consider, for example, the two LCS representations for ergative and agentive 'break', respectively, proposed by Hale and Keyser (1987).

(56) a. y come to have a separation in material integrity ...
(The glass broke.)

b. x cause [y come to have a separation in material integrity ...]
(Floyd broke the glass.)

The LCS of (56b), containing the CAUSE predicate, will project an extra verbal head at D-Structure, while that of (56a) will not. Speas argues that the projection of extra verbal heads therefore follows from lexical requirements in that the argument bearing the role of AGENT is an argument of the higher predicate, while the other arguments are arguments of the lower predicate and hence at D-Structure are within the projection of the actual lexical verb.

Although Speas thus appears to capture an important generalization with respect to the AGENT thematic role, her analysis results in a proliferation of empty verbal heads, since any agentive predicate, not only those with two internal arguments, will project an extra verbal head. What I would like to suggest here is that the projection of such empty heads is limited to those verbs with an embedded causal predicate. Thus, compare the proposed LCS of Class 1 verbs, given in (55), with the LCS of (57).

(57) x cause [y come to be at (perception) z]

The LCS in (57) constitutes the embedded predicate within the LCS of (55), introduced by the relation 'by means of'. Since it is only in the case of verbs with an embedded causal predicate that an extra verbal head will be projected, only with these verbs will the AGENT argument be outside of the government domain of the lexical verb at D-Structure. This therefore explains the limitations on the projection of arguments within the corresponding derived nominal which we observed above. These nominals, unlike those corresponding to simple causative predicates, disallow the projection of the AGENT argument because this argument will be unable to receive inherent Case from the head N.[27]

Now although the D-Structure representations of the two sets of verbs are alike in the projection of the argument corresponding to the x variable in the LCS, they differ with respect to the location of the arguments corresponding to the y and z variables, as shown in (58).

(58)   a.   Class 1 verbs   b.   'Dative-shift' verbs

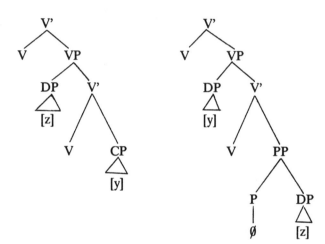

These syntactic differences must be attributable to a distinct predicate argument structure for the two sets of verbs, since it is the level of PAS which mediates between the level of LCS and the syntax.

---

[27] Recall that Hypothesis 1 for the complementation structure of Class 1 verbs was that the clausal complement was projected as an indirect internal argument of the verb, and consequently was not L-marked, on a strict interpretation of sisterhood. If we assume, as proposed by Contreras (1989), that L-marking extends to all theta-marked complements of a head, the extraction facts discussed in section 2.2 do not provide as strong an argument against this hypothesis, although a partial argument remains: Under the revised version of L-marking, extraction of adjuncts from the CP complement would be predicted to be completely acceptable, rather than marginal. Assuming that some explanation could be found to explain these data, Hypothesis 1 still fails to account for the structure of the corresponding derived nominals. Certainly, it is the case that other verbs with both a direct and an indirect internal argument, as well as an agentive external argument, have fully grammatical derived nominals (cf., for example, *enviar* 'to send'/ *envío* 'shipment').

I would like to propose that the level of PAS, contra Rappaport and Levin (1988), does make reference to theta-role labels, where these are defined, as before, according to positions within the LCS. Thus THEME, as we have already seen, can be defined as the variable in the position '/_ come to be at'; AGENT can be defined as the variable in the position '/_ cause'; and GOAL can be defined as the variable in the position '/at __'. I further assume that the variables in the embedded predicate are linked first to the PAS, with the existence of the higher predicate via the notation of bracketing. In the LCS of (55), consequently, the variable z bears two theta-roles, that of THEME and that of GOAL; however, it is the GOAL which actually appears in the PAS, as in (59).

(59) x cause [z come to be in STATE]
      BY MEANS OF [x cause [y come to be at z]]
                    < agent < theme, goal > >

The THEME role is assigned directly by the verb. I propose that the crucial difference between Spanish and English is the way in which the GOAL role is assigned. In Spanish, this role is assigned directly by the verb; the dative *a* is merely a realization of Case. However, in English this role is assigned by the preposition 'to', which therefore must be represented in some way in the PAS. To put it in other terms, 'to' in English theta-marks its DP complement and assigns it (objective) Case, within the government domain of the verb. Dative *a* in Spanish, on the other hand, is merely a realization of inherent Case assigned by the verb which theta-marks the corresponding DP. Support for this proposal comes from an examination of the semantic contribution of 'to' in English versus dative *a* in Spanish. As Larson (1988a: 370) notes, dative 'to' is not unlike other instances of 'to' in its semantic contribution to a sentence, in that it specifies something like 'goal of "motion" along some trajectory or path.' Hence, 'to' cannot appear with an argument receiving the theta-role of SOURCE rather than GOAL.

(60) I bought the car from/ *to John.

In contrast, dative *a* appears with an indirect object theta-marked GOAL or SOURCE; ultimate determination of the theta-role rests with the governing verb.[28]

(61) a. (Le) vendí el coche a Juan.
'(I) sold the car to John.'

    b. (Le) compré el coche a Juan.
'(I) bought the car from Juan.'

In section 3.3, I argued that dative-shift verbs had no specification for inherent Case in their PAS, in contrast to Class 1 verbs, which link the argument position occupied by the z variable to inherent (oblique) Case. Thus the common LCS representation of these two sets of verbs diverges into two distinct PAS representations, shown in (62).

(62) a. x cause [z to come to be in STATE]
        BY MEANS OF [x cause [y to come to be at z]]

    b. $<x \ <z \ y>>$ c. $<x \ < Pz \ y>>$
       |
     Inherent

Now although standard views of syntactic projection assume that the THEME argument is the direct internal argument of the verb, both Larson (1988a) and Speas (1990) assume that the THEME is actually the specifier of the lower VP. As Speas notes, the syntactic projection of the THEME versus GOAL arguments of ditransitive verbs is obviously not a clear-cut matter. On the one hand, the THEME argument is intuitively the direct internal argument of the verb; it is the argument which undergoes passivization in standard ditransitive structures and which can be long wh-moved. On the other hand, attempts to derive relative syntactic prominence of arguments from some type of thematic hierarchy often differ in the placement of THEME vs. GOAL on the hierarchy. THEMES more often than GOALS show up in surface subject position, and so may be considered to be 'higher', while (on standard accounts) THEMES as direct objects are closer to the verb than GOALS as

---

[28] The semantic roles of Spanish indirect objects are discussed in some detail by Strozer (1976), who also argues that Spanish indirect objects are NPs (in current terms, DPs) rather than PPs. Dative *a*, of course, also shows up with benefactive indirect objects, which receive their theta-role from the obligatory dative clitic (cf. Jaeggli 1986b, Kempchinsky 1990). Benefactive datives thus corroborate the idea that the dative *a* serves merely to mark Case.

indirect objects. I propose that in fact the relative syntactic prominence of these two thematic roles is left unspecified by principles of lexicon-to-syntax mapping. Rather, their syntactic projection is determined by the Case properties of the individual verbal head. Consider the abstract structure underlying the D-Structure representations of the two sets of verbs, given in (63).

(63)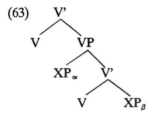

In (65), both XP_α and XP_β must receive Case in some way in order to be theta-marked. The argument in the position of XP_α will be able to receive structural Case from the raised V at S-Structure; however, the argument in the position of XP_β cannot receive Case from the verb if, as Baker (1988) proposes, a given structural Case assigner may assign structural Case to only one Case assignee.[29] For Class 1 verbs, the syntactic mapping is thus relatively straightforward. The CP complement, already linked to inherent Case in the PAS, will map on to the position of XP_β, while the DP complement will be mapped to the position of XP_α, where it will receive structural accusative Case from the raised V at the level of S-Structure.

What about the English dative-shift verbs? A priori, there are two possible D-Structure configurations, shown in (66).

(66) a.   b.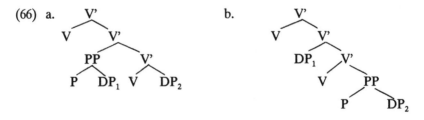

---

[29] Alternatively, this result could be derived if it is true, as Baker also proposes, that verbal traces may not assign structural Case. However, this restriction seems too strong in that it would predict that the trace left by verb movement into INFL would be unable to assign structural (accusative) Case to its direct internal argument. It would also leave unexplained the grammaticality of V fronting in wh-questions in Spanish, which clearly does not result in the lack of accusative Case assignment, even in instances where the accusative-marked object does not receive a theta-role from the verb, as in perception verb complements.

  (i) ¿Cuándo oyó Juan a María cantar?
      'When did Juan hear María sing?'

In (66a), the argument linked to the GOAL thematic role is mapped on to the position of XP_α, with the other internal argument therefore appearing in the position of XP_β. At S-Structure, after raising of the lexical verb to the higher verbal head, DP_2 will be unable to receive Case. Further, the PP will receive accusative Case, violating the Case Resistance Principle (Stowell 1981).[30] Thus this particular mapping from the PAS on to the D-Structure representation will ultimately violate Case theory requirements.[31]

Now consider (66b), in which the argument bearing the GOAL thematic role is mapped on to the position of XP_β, with the THEME argument therefore occupying the position of XP_α. By the analysis outlined earlier, verb-preposition incorporation will license the assignment of objective Case to DP_2. Upon reanalysis and raising, DP_1 will also receive structural Case from the raised verb. As argued earlier, the two processes, incorporation and V' reanalysis, license the two instances of Case-indexing via objective Case assignment, which is otherwise generally prohibited. Thus projection of the two arguments on to these two respective syntactic positions will satisfy the demands of Case theory and ultimately of theta-role assignment.[32]

---

[30] It could be argued that both of these conflicts could be avoided if the verb assigns its accusative Case to DP_2 at D-Structure, so that it is unable to Case-mark the PP at S-Structure even after raising. However, I assume, following Chomsky (1986b), that structural Case may be assigned only at S-Structure and *must* be assigned there; hence, there is no way for the PP to avoid being Case-marked. Even if objective Case is 'pulled apart' into structure objective Case and inherent objective Case, as proposed by Larson (1988a), thereby solving the problem of lack of Case to DP_2, the structural objective Case will still end up being assigned to the PP.

[31] There is, however, at least one class of verbs in English with the abstract LCS representation of (62a) and a PAS like that of (62b), with the y variable linked to an inherent Case. These are the locative variants of the 'spray/load' class of verbs analyzed by Rappaport and Levin (1988), cf. (i).

    (i)   The farmer loaded the wagon with hay.

Because the argument corresponding to the y variable (*hay*) is linked in the PAS either to an inherent Case (realized with the preposition), or perhaps to the preposition itself, it will project to the position corresponding to XP_β in (63). The other argument, lacking inherent Case, must be projected to a position in which it may receive Case, namely, the position corresponding to XP_α. Thus even within one language a given LCS may project to different PAS representations and ultimately to different D-Structure representations.

[32] I argued earlier that verb-preposition incorporation occurs when the preposition is an *abstract* nonlexically realized preposition. The natural question then is what happens when the dative preposition 'to' is base-generated in a structure such as (66b). If V' reanalysis applies (since it is not dependent upon the prior application of incorporation), then the resulting string would be equivalent to one produced by Heavy NP shift, which Larson (1988c) argues is actually a process of 'light predicate raising' produced by V' reanalysis. If V' reanalysis does not occur, then the resulting string would be equivalent to a simple dative structure. However, neither of these orders is compatible with the semantic interpretation of the LCS which has been proposed here for the double object construction:

    (i)   a.   *Mary gave to John the worst cold he's ever had in his life.

4.2   Some final considerations.   The LCS representation of (55) expresses, as it were, the essence of the semantic parallelism between Class 1 verbs and English dative-shift verbs: some entity comes to be in some state (of possession, of perception) because some AGENT brings to them the object possessed or the objected perceived. Minimally, the level of LCS representation is meant to express the number of participants in the action denoted by a given verb; this purpose is indeed met by (55). However, the LCS also needs to express all those aspects of the verb's meaning which are linguistically relevant (Hale and Keyser 1987) as well as, in a sense, mediate between real world knowledge and purely grammatical constraints such as principles mapping specific theta-roles on to specific syntactic positions. Now part of the meaning of verbs such as *obligar* 'to oblige', *forzar* 'to force', *persuadir* 'to persuade' and *convencer* 'to convince' is that the first two express what in previous work (Kempchinsky 1986) I termed 'embedded' imperatives and the latter two express complete propositions. These are linguistically relevant aspects in so far as specific grammatical forms correspond to these two classes (subjunctive clauses, indicative clauses, or noun phrases with propositional content). Therefore these concepts must also form part of the LCS. Furthermore, if the mediating level between LCS and the syntax is the level of PAS, then this information must also be represented in some way at that level. Such considerations would seem to advocate an enriched PAS with at least minimal theta-role labels, rather than just numerical or letter variables. It seems, in fact, that sometimes even these labels are not sufficient. If THEME means '__ come to be at y', where y is state or location, then the label THEME is not sufficient for explaining the constraints on the formation of the English middle (cf. Hale and Keyser 1987: 20). If syntactic categories such as CP and DP are to be predictable from semantic roles, in the spirit of Grimshaw (1981) and Pesetsky (1982), then the notions of 'proposition' and 'imperative' must also be accessible to the syntax and therefore expressed in the PAS. Thus, the lexical representations proposed here for the verbs under study are only a first approximation to their ultimate characterization.

---

b.   *Mary gave a cold to John.

It might be the case that base-generation of the overt dative 'to' in this structure is prohibited by a general principle of recoverability, since the two strings above obscure the LCS from which the syntactic structure was derived. I leave this as an unresolved problem at this point.

References

Aoun, J., N. Hornstein, D. Lightfoot, and A. Weinberg. 1987. Two Types of Locality. Linguistic Inquiry 18, 537-78.

Baker, M. 1988. Incorporation: A Theory of Grammatical Function Changing. Chicago: University of Chicago Press.

Barss, A., and H. Lasnik. 1986. A Note on Anaphora and Double Objects. Linguistic Inquiry 17, 347-54.

Campos, H. 1988. Extraction from NP in Spanish. Romance Linguistics and Literature Review 1, 1-32.

Campos, H., and P. Kempchinsky. 1991. Case Absorption, Theta Structure and Pronominal Verbs. In D. Kibee and D. Wanner, eds., New Analyses in Romance Linguistics. Amsterdam/ Philadelphia: John Benjamins. 171-85.

Chomsky, N. 1986a. Barriers. Cambridge, Mass.: MIT Press.

Chomsky, N. 1986b. Knowledge of Language: Its Nature, Origin and Use. New York: Praeger.

Contreras, H. 1989. A Modular Approach to Syntactic Islands. Ms., University of Washington.

Demonte, V. 1987. C-command, Prepositions and Predication. Linguistic Inquiry 18, 147-57.

Demonte, V. 1989. Linking and Case: The Case of Prepositional Verbs. Paper presented at LSRL XIX, Ohio State University. To be published in C. Laufer and T. Morgan, eds., Theoretical Analyses in Contemporary Romance Linguistics. Amsterdam/ Philadephia: John Benjamins.

Faraci, R. 1974. Aspects of the Grammar of Infinitives and For-phrases. MIT doctoral dissertation.

Fukui, N. 1986. A Theory of Category Projection and its Applications. MIT doctoral dissertation.

Fukui, N., and M. Speas. 1986. Features and Projections. MIT Working Papers in Linguistics 8, 128-72.

Green, G. 1974. Semantics and Syntactic Regularity. Bloomington: Indiana University Linguistics Club.

Grimshaw, J. 1981. Form, Function and the Language Acquisition Device. In C. L. Baker and J. J. McCarthy, eds., The Logical Problem of Language Acquisition. Cambridge, Mass.: MIT Press. 165-82.

Gruber, J. 1965. Studies in Lexical Relations. MIT doctoral dissertation.

Hale, K., and S. J. Keyser. 1986. Some Transitivity Alternations in English. Lexicon Project Working Papers 7, MIT.

Hale, K., and S. J. Keyser. 1987. A View from the Middle. Lexicon Project Working Papers 10, MIT.

Jackendoff, R. 1987. The Status of Thematic Relations in Linguistic Theory. Linguistic Inquiry 18, 369-412.

Jaeggli, O. 1986a. Arbitrary Plural Pronominals. Natural Language and Linguistic Theory 4, 43-76.

Jaeggli, O. 1986b. Three Issues in the Theory of Clitics: Case, Doubled NPs, and Extraction. In H. Borer, ed., Syntax and Semantics, vol. 19: The Syntax of Pronominal Clitics. New York: Academic Press. 15-42.

Johnson, K. 1988. Clausal Gerunds, the ECP, and Government. Linguistic Inquiry 19, 583-610.

Kayne, R. 1981a. Unambiguous Paths. In R. May and J. Koster, eds., Levels of Syntactic Representation. Dordrecht: Foris. 143-83.

Kayne, R. 1981b. On Certain Differences between French and English. Linguistic Inquiry 12, 349-71.

Kempchinsky, P. 1986. Romance Subjunctive Clauses and Logical Form. UCLA doctoral dissertation.

Kempchinsky, P. 1989. An Adjunct Extraction Paradox in Spanish. Paper presented at LSRL XIX, Ohio State University. To be published in C. Laufer and T. Morgan, eds., Theoretical Analyses in Contemporary Romance Linguistics. Amsterdam/Philadephia: John Benjamins.

Kempchinsky, P. 1990. Theta Role Assignment and Proper Government in the Possessive Dative Construction. Paper presented at LSRL XX, University of Ottawa.

Larson, R. 1988a. On the Double Object Construction. Linguistic Inquiry 19, 335-92.

Larson, R. 1988b. Promise and the Theory of Control. Lexicon Project Working Papers 23, MIT. Published in Linguistic Inquiry 22 (1991), 103-40.

Larson, R. 1988c. Light Predicate Raising. Lexicon Project Working Papers 27, MIT.

Oehrle, R. 1976. The Grammatical Status of the English Dative Alternation. MIT doctoral dissertation.

Pesetsky, D. 1982. Paths and Categories. MIT doctoral dissertation.

Pollock, J.- Y. 1989. Verb Movement, Universal Grammar, and the Structure of IP. Linguistic Inquiry 20, 365-424.

Rappaport, M., and B. Levin. 1988. What to Do with Theta-roles. In W. Wilkins, ed., Syntax and Semantics, vol. 21: Thematic Relations. New York: Academic Press. 7-36.

Rizzi, L. 1986. Null Objects in Italian and the Theory of pro. Linguistic Inquiry 17, 501-57.

Rochette, A. 1988. Semantic and Syntactic Aspects of Romance Sentential Complementation. MIT doctoral dissertation.

Speas, M. 1990. Phrase Structure in Natural Language. Dordrecht: Kluwer.

Sportiche, D. 1988. A Theory of Floating Quantifiers and its Corollaries for Constituent Structure. Linguistic Inquiry 19, 425-50.

Stowell, T. 1981. Origins of Phrase Structure. MIT doctoral dissertation.

Stowell, T. 1985. Null Antecedents and Proper Government. In S. Berman et al., eds., Proceedings of NELS XVI. Amherst, Mass.: GLSA, University of Massachusetts. 476-93.

Stowell, T. 1988. Subjects, Specifiers and X' Theory. In M. Baltin and A. Kroch, eds., Alternative Conceptions of Phrase Structure. Chicago: University of Chicago Press. 232-62.

Strozer, J. 1976. Clitics in Spanish. UCLA doctoral dissertation.

Torrego, E. 1985. On Empty Categories in Nominals. Ms., University of Massachusetts at Boston.

Zagona, K. 1988. Verb Phrase Syntax. Dordrecht: Kluwer.

Clitic and NP climbing in Old Spanish

María-Luisa Rivero *
University of Ottawa

0 Introduction. Modern Romance complement clitics are not considered full-fledged syntactic categories. In the Government and Binding literature, this idea corresponds to proposals where they do not project to Xmax in syntax. Thus, Borer (1984) considers clitics spell-out features of the V projecting the VP; for Jaeggli (1986) they are syntactic affixes forming a V° with the V they attach to; for Suñer (1988) they are agreement markers; and for Kayne (1989a) they are X°s which may undergo Head-movement (but see fn. 8).

In contrast, I have argued (Rivero 1986b) that Old Spanish (OSp) complement clitics are phrasal. That is, they project to Xmax in the syntax, and their atonic character makes them phonological (en)clitics, irrespective of the syntactic category of the preceding element. From this perspective, OSp clitics resemble French unstressed subject pronouns, which occupy an NP position in syntax and cliticize to the inflected V in phonology (Couquaux 1986, Kayne 1983, Rizzi 1986).

In this paper, I consider some of the consequences which the diverse nature of Modern Spanish (MSp) and OSp clitics have for clitic climbing. Patterns such as *Yo quiero comerlo* and *Yo lo quiero comer* 'I want to eat it' are attested from the earliest documents. However, within my approach, such apparently identical strings receive different treatments in OSp and MSp. Also, the overall syntax of Climbing exhibits contrasting properties in the two stages. In brief, if modern Climbing is Head-movement, as Kayne argues (1989a), old Climbing is Xmax movement for NPs/PPs and clitics, and the contrast follows from the status of modern and old clitics as nonmaximal and maximal items, respectively.

Previous studies on Clitic Climbing have paid much attention to the structure of the Climbing V and its complement. A prominent idea first seen in Aissen and Perlmutter (1976) and Rizzi (1976) makes Climbing possible when a biclausal structure receives uniclausal treatment. A second approach involves double subcategorization (Strozer 1976, and later work), parallel structures (Goodall 1984), or coanalysis (Di Sciullo and Williams 1987) for climbing Vs, with Climbing occurring with VP rather than clausal

---

*Work for this paper has been partially subsidized by Grant 410-88-0101 from the SSHRCC. I thank M. Morales for help in obtaining OSp materials, and M. Suñer, E. Treviño, and D. Wanner for many suggestions.

structures (Goodall 1984), or coanalysis (Di Sciullo and Williams 1987) for climbing Vs, with Climbing occurring with VP rather than clausal complements, or when the V and Infinitive form a morphosyntactic complex. A third approach assumes uniform biclausal status for Climbing constructions (Luján 1978, Kayne 1989a, among others), and this is also the analysis motivated for OSp herein, which focus on the properties of old clitics, rather than complementation issues.

The paper is organized as follows. Section 1 reexamines and expands arguments for the phrasal status of OSp clitics. Section 2 shows how recent proposals on Negation further motivate the assumed analysis, and establishes similarities between VP-Preposing, the movement of Vmax, and Interpolation, the movement of clitics as Nmax or Pmax, since both are sub-types of focalization.

Section 3 examines Climbing constructions, including Perfect Tenses, proposing that (a) Old Climbing is adjunction of Xmax to I', instead of Head-movement; (b) clitics exit complement clauses through adjunction to IP, making Climbing sensitive to Tense effects; and (c) these properties are partially shared by NPs and PPs. In the old period, Clitic and NP Climbing combine in predictable ways, in view of my hypothesis, giving startling word orders from the perspective of Modern Romance. Also, Old Climbing escapes adjacency requirements, applying across intervening heads, and differs in several respects from Modern Climbing. Old Perfect Tenses share these properties, since the Aux as a climbing V takes a small clause complement.

1 The phrasal status of OSp clitics. In Rivero (1986b), I argued in favor of NP status for OSp clitics such as *lo* 'it', and PP status for *en(de)* 'of it' and *hi* 'in it', items which did not survive beyond the medieval period.

I developed arguments on the basis of (a) the parallel distribution of clitics and complement NPs/PPs, and of (b) medieval doubling constructions, which differ in several respects from (reported varieties of) MSp, which I will not review. Instead, I concentrate on a line of motivation closely connected with the aims of this paper and Climbing, based on 'Interpolation' (and see Gessner 1893, Meyer-Lübke 1897, Chenery 1905, Ramsden 1963 for discussion and examples).

Interpolation refers to the pattern where OSp clitics, unlike modern clitics, are not adjacent to V and appear to its left, preceding one or more intervening phrases, as in (1). Relevant clitics are capitalized, and the material before V is in brackets, for ease of exposition. In the ensuing discussion, I examine the properties of Interpolation central to my purposes.

(1) a. Dixe   que   LO   [yo] avía muerto   Z 75
      I+said that HIM [I] had   killed
      'I said I had killed him'

    b. Este preso que SE [agora] partió ...   es mi amigo   Z 75
      This prisoner who HIMSELF [now] left ...is my friend
      'This prisoner who just left ...   is my friend'

    c. Grant derecho sería   que   me matases ...,
      Big   right   it+would+be that me you+kill

      si ME [de ti non]   guardase   Z 238
      if ME [of you not] protect

      'Your killing me would be quite right..., if I did not protect myself
      from you'

    d. Non vos mengüe en ninguna cosa   que   VOS [a dezir] oviese
      Not you I+missed in no   thing that YOU [to tell] I+had
      'I omitted nothing of what I had to tell you'   Z 222

1.1 The nature of Interpolation. For Chenery (1905), Interpolation is most frequent in the fourteenth century (see also Ramsden 1963). However, its syntax shows similar 'qualitative' properties from the preliterary documents before 1250, to its rapid disappearance after the middle of the fifteenth century. For instance, intervening PPs are less frequent than the interrupting Subjects, or Negations in (1a-c), as shown later; however, this less usual pattern is found (a) quite early, as in (2a-b) from legal texts with no literary aims; (b) in the middle of the period, as in (1c) from circa 1300; and (c) late, (2c-d). Also, Clitic and V may be separated by several 'words' forming a phrase, as in (2), which is found through the relevant period. More importantly, however, patterns where two 'constituents' intervene, as in (1c), (3), and the infinitival clause in (1d), are grammatical all along. For reasons seen in section 2, I treat *no* 'not' as the head of NegP (see Chomsky 1988 for English, Kayne 1989a for Italian and French, Kitagawa 1986 for Japanese, Lema and Rivero 1989a,b for Romance and Slavic, Pollock 1989 for English and French, and Zanuttini 1989 for Italian dialects).

(2) a. El ceruicio queS [dellas] leuantar   DLE 25 (1220)
      The service that-SE [of-them] would+obtain
      'The service one would obtain from them'

244 / CURRENT STUDIES IN SPANISH LINGUISTICS

    b. Con salzes plantados et con fruteros et con quanto
       With willows planted and with fruit-trees and with all

       UOS [en el] damos   DLE 46 (1223)
       YOU [in it] we+give

       'With planted willows and fruit trees and everything in it we give
       you'

    c. Non te es posyble de TE [della] apartar   Cor 167
       Not you is possible of YOU [of+her] separate
       'It is not possible for you to leave her'

    d. Mando al omne que VOS [esta mj carta] mostrara
       I+order to-the man who YOU [this my letter] would+show

       que enplase a todos los que LO [contra ella] fizieren DLE (1140)
       that call to all those that IT [against her] would+do

       'I order the man showing you this letter of mine to
       challenge all those acting against it'

(3) Et si LO [el rey por bien] toviere, mándeme quemar   CD 243
    And if IT [the king for good] had, order-me burn
    'If the king considers it good, let him order that I burn'

1.2 Root and nonroot patterns in Interpolation. Chenery (1905) considers Interpolation a nonroot pattern, and most of its cases are in embedded clauses. However, this aspect follows from an independent restriction on clitics as 'nontonic' phrases, or an OSp manifestation of Wackernagel's law, in terms of syntactic constituency: namely, clitics cannot be initial in the minimal CP containing them (Rivero 1986b,c), requiring a first constituent for well-formedness, such as the Comp in (1a-d), the conditional *si* 'if' in (1c-3), or the wh-phrase *quanto* 'with everything (how much)' in (2b).

    Matrix or independent clauses may show Interpolation, although this is rare, if they contain a CP-initial phrase for clitic support. This is seen in the direct questions in (4), with the wh-phrase in the Spec of CP, or in (5), with the adverbials *nunca* 'never', *nin* 'and not', and *ya* 'already', as CP-initial constituents to satisfy the law (and Ramsden 1963 for additional examples, and Salvi 1989, fn. 6 for Old Portuguese).

(4) a. Por qé ME [non] recudes?   B. Milg. 293c
       Why ME [not] you-answer?
       'Why don't you answer me?'

   b. Dixo Elbet: -Señor, por qué ME LO [non] dices?   CD 284
      Said Elbet: -Sir, why ME IT [not] you+say?
      'Elbet said: Sir, why don't you say it to me?'

(5) a. Elo que yo quis nunca LO [uos] contradixiestes   Alex 2284c-d (0)
       And-this which I wanted never IT [you] contradicted
       'And you never opposed what I wanted'

   b. Nin ME [yo] pornía en tan grandes grandías -dixo ...   Z 156
      And+not ME [I] would+put in such big bigness- he+said ...
      'And I wouldn't consider myself so great -he said...'

   c. Et alo que cosa son los angeles, fijo, ya   UOS [yo]
      And to-the what thing are the angels, son, already YOU I

      dixe quelas preguntas que me fazedes son de muchas
      told that-the questions that me you+make are of many

      sçiencias Juan Manuel, *El libro del Cavallero et del*
      sciences   *Escudero* 470,6 (as cited in Chenery 1905)

      'And as to what angels are, son, I already told you that
      your questions belong to many sciences'

If the items before the Clitic are the first phrase in CP, it follows that the initial Topics in (5a) and (5c) are outside of this CP,   since in Left-dislocations Topics fail to license preverbal clitics, as in (6), where LAS 'them' follows V, rather than precedes it.[1] I assume that Topics attach to S" (and see Rivero 1986b,c).

(6) E estas palabras que dezia el cavallero oyóLAS Grima   Z 63
    And these words that said the knight heard THEM Grima
    'And Grima heard the words the knight said'

Since OSp NP focalization is not a root pattern, as shown in section 1.3, Clitic Interpolation shows no special properties in this area.

1.3 The analysis of Interpolation. In Rivero (1986b), Interpolation is Xmax adjunction to the complement of CP,[2] and seldom, to a lower

---

[1]   For clitics after finite Vs, as in (6), there are many views. In Rivero (1986b), I proposed that OSp head-government is bidirectional, allowing OV and VO basic orders, and did not mention V-raising or Affix-Hopping. Under that view, *oyó las* in (6) is VO, while *las oyó* would be OV, with V canonically head-governing the clitic as NP object in either case; in infinitives, VO and OV alternate both for NPs and clitics, so if V does not move, my proposal accounts for the order (but see Kayne 1989c for the idea that V_{inf} + CL is the result of adjoining V). For finite Vs, my idea can be maintained under an Affix-Hopping analysis, or if INFL can be initial/final, and V raises to it in either direction. Otherwise, orders such as *oyó las* in (6) can be obtained by moving clitic and V to some INFL level, with subsequent finite raising of V to C (Benincà 1983-1984; Adams 1986). However, finite Vs are not the only items raising to C in Old Romance, as seen in Inverted Conjugations (Lema and Rivero 1989a, b), and finite V-movement is only one of the strategies for an initial CP-constituent for clitic support. Also, V could raise to I, with the clitic remaining in VP, or the split AgrP and TP model (Pollock 1989) could provide a location for V higher than the clitic. Salvi (1989) (see also Alemán 1985) has a general rule moving Old Romance clitics to a slot after the first constituent in CP. Interpolation aside, a preferable solution is to attach the clitic to some level of I, with movement of other elements to the Spec-of-CP, C, and IP (by adjunction); such a treatment is unproblematic for main and subordinate clauses alike, since, as Salvi himself observes, Old Romance clitics are not necessarily second in the clause. Rouveret (1987) treats present Portuguese postverbal clitics as syntactic NPs and phonological enclitics. A more problematic idea is to invert clitic around V in main clauses (see Campos 1988 for Modern Gallegan). Also see fn. 2.

[2] As mentioned in Rivero (1986a), my view of Interpolation differs from Meyer-Lübke's (1897) for similar Old Portuguese phenomena. For him, 'clitics' occupy second position under Wackernagel's law (1892). In my analysis, Xmax is focalized, so clitics and tonic NPs alike occupy the same position, which is not a slot for clitics. I use the term 'focus' in a syntactic sense, employing syntactic criteria (word order) to define it, which does not mean that the notion is semantically inert.   Then, (a) OSp Interpolation signals phrasal status and (b) only the restriction against clause-initial position seen as a filter in Rivero (1986b) indicates clitic status (in phonology).   Meyer-Lübke saw both phenomena in the same light. The situation is probably different in languages such as Serbo-Croatian where Interpolation of pronominal/auxiliary clitics signals a second position unique to them. In Old Romance, clitics cannot be first, but they need not be second, along the lines of Mussafia (1886).

projection such as VP. Within *Barriers* (Chomsky 1986: 32), adjunction to IP is disallowed, but Frampton (1990: 53) proposes that canonical head-government overrides this restriction. In my treatment, old clitics as NPs are canonically governed *in situ*, and I° canonically governs VP, so that they can adjoin to IP as assumed. Adjunction to IP relates Interpolation to old Climbing, as argued in section 3.5.

Under this view, if NP-objects can adjoin to the left by focus movement, crossing NegP and other constituents, so can clitics as NPs, if their landing site is not the first position of CP in root and nonroot contexts (remember that 'focus' refers to a CP-internal site, not to a semantic reading). Within this analysis, (7) involves extraction of the (capitalized) object NP (intermediate material other than V is within square brackets). If (emphatic) *él* 'he' is in a focus site in (7a), then the moved NP is adjoined to the complement of CP, that is, NegP. If *maguer* 'although' in (7b) is in C, the displaced object also adjoins to NegP. The same holds for the relatives in (7c-e), with the last showing raising of a Dative. The same analysis serves for the Accusative clitics in the lower clauses in (1-3), as phrasal complements of V; Dative clitics are similar. Then, *Si LO non fezieran* Est.28 'If they did not do it', with Clitic, and *Si A VOS non pesare* Est.28 'If it did not pain you', with Dative PP, are identical.

(7) a. Ca el FIJO NINGUNO [non] ha   Z 199
     Since he SON NONE [not] has
     'Since he has no son at all'

    b. E maguer EL FECHO [non] vieron   Z 59
     And although THE DEED [not] saw
     'Even though they did not see the action itself'

    c. El que OTRO CUIDADO [non] ha sinon apañar aver   CD 294
     The who ANOTHER WORRY [not] has except gather possessions
     'The one whose only concern is to become wealthy'

    d. El que A SI MESMO [non] castiga   Z 270
     The who TO HIMSELF [not] punish
     'The one who does not punish himself'

    e. La razon por que AL FIJO DE SANCTA MARIA [non] dieron
     The reason why TO-THE SON OF SAINT MARY [not] give

     otra muerte sinon de cruz   Est 247
     other death but of cross

     'The reason why Mary's Son was crucified'

For infinitives, (8a) shows movement of the NP-object, crossing NegP, to a position lower than *por* 'for' as Comp. Extraction of the object Clitic is parallel: (8b-c). *Por* must be CP-internal; otherwise, the Clitic would be clause initial, which is not possible.

(8) a. Murieron ... por LENGUA [non] refrenar   Cor 268
       They+died... for TONGUE [not] restrain
       'They died ... for not keeping their mouths shut'

    b. Maldiziendo su conciencia por LA [non] creer   Cor 118
       Cursing his conscience for HER [not] believe
       'Cursing his conscience for not believing her'

    c. Fincava desfaçada de LO [nunca más] ver   Z 404
       Remained hopeless of HIM [never more] see
       'She remained without hope to ever see him again'

The position of the Negation in (7-8) eliminates a treatment of these embedded clauses as OV, that is, V-final in basic structure. Such patterns would be as in (9), which is unusual; more likely, (9) shows constituent, rather than sentential negation, with *non* modifying the PP, and this will be important when discussing Climbing in 3.1. Also, movement to the left need not result in V-final order, as in (7e).

(9) Et que onra et biçio non en una morada biven   Est 186
    And that honor and vice not in a house live
    'Honesty and vice do not live in the same house'

As stated, in root clauses, Interpolated clitics are rare, since they must comply with Wackernagel's law, but their movement properties are those of tonic NPs, as seen in (5) vs (10); in both cases, the object of V lands above the subject.

(10) Et ESTO [El] fizo por su voluntad   Est 228
     And THIS [He] did for his will
     'And he did this willingly'

To summarize, in OSp a phrase may left-adjoin to the complement of CP in root, and nonroot finite/nonfinite clauses. When the rule moves a Clitic (a nontonic Xmax, in my terms), the result is called Interpolation. When it affects a tonic Xmax, no traditional label exists. However, if my proposals are correct, Interpolation of clitics and left-movement of NPs/PPs are the same rule: Move-*alpha* as adjunction to the complement of CP, as in (11). Interpolation is most often found in embedded clauses, because such environment ensures a constituent preceding the adjoined Clitic, so that Wackernagel's law is *ipso facto* satisfied. When a tonic phrase is left-adjoined, no preceding phrase is needed.

(11)

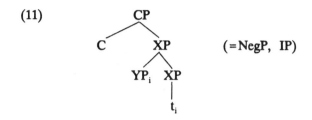

In my analysis, clitics and NPs have underlying sources as canonical complements of V. When they move out of their VP, they adjoin as Xmax, which extends to Clitic and NP Climbing, including Perfect tenses, as argued in section 3.

By contrast, MSp clitics are not phrasal, so they fail to interpolate, making (1-5) distinctly ungrammatical and often uninterpretable to the modern ear. Today, patterns like *Fasta que SE NOS [non] encubra* (Por 53) 'Until we are not harbored' are difficult to process, unless the clitics are replaced in their modern position before V. However, this does not exhaust the differences between the two stages. The movement for tonic complements in (7), (8a), and (10) no longer exists in its general form either. At times, it has been obligatorily replaced by a doubling strategy, as in *El que a si mismo no se castiga* for (7d), or by Left-dislocation, such as *Y esto el lo hizo por su voluntad* for (10), or by focalization, such as *Porque él, hijo no tiene* for (7a).

These options, also found in the medieval period and in all types of clauses, are now restricted to finite clauses.

2 NegP and Interpolation

2.1 Crossing Negation in Interpolation. Elements which most frequently separate a left Clitic and V are Negation and Subjects, as the lists compiled by Chenery (1905) indicate (see also Ramsden 1963 for counts). In addition, Ramsden sees as significant that the interpolated Clitic most frequently follows a Complementizer or a wh-phrase. Let us consider these two aspects in turn, from the perspective of my analysis.

Chenery had at his disposal poor editions, but more reliable newly available medieval texts give similar results. For instance, of the 128 cases of Interpolation I recorded in a recent edition of *El libro de los Estados*, which is an almost exhaustive count excluding some identical examples, 74 or 58% involve *non*, along the lines of (12a), and 45 involve Subjects, as in (12b).

(12) a. Beemos que LO [non] fazen así   Est 45
   We+see that IT [not] do so
   'We see that they do not do it this way'

  b. El sabe que LO [yo] deseo   Est 81
   He knows that IT [I] desire
   'He knows that I desire it'

(a) Interpolation is adjunction to the complement of CP; (b) OSp subjects may be in the Spec of IP in an affirmative clause; and (c) NegP, when present, precedes the finite V, being higher than IP=TP. As a consequence, Subjects or Negation are quite likely to intervene between clitic and V, if Interpolation applies, and V raises to Tense/Agr heading IP (Emonds 1978, Pollock 1989), which accounts for the frequency of the types in (12).[3] I assume that NegP complements CP in negative clauses, while IP is the complement in affirmative ones, with subjects in Spec-of-NegP in the first case, and Spec-of-IP in the second.

---

[3] In my view, the paucity of Interpolation and its restricted nature in other old Romance languages correlates with the differing nature of the clitics. For example, Martineau (1989: 78ff) mentions its extreme rarity in Old French; the few examples where it occurs contain intensifier adverbs separating clitic and V, but it is likely that such adverbs are clitic-like rather than phrasal. In her detailed study of two Middle French texts, she finds only five examples of interpolation in finite clauses. All involve negations, four with *ne* (perhaps a clitic) and one with *pas* as intensifier, so she considers the phenomenon exceptional, not part of the grammar of the period; in particular, Interpolation over subjects is not attested.

These differences, coupled with the grammar of OSp Climbing examined here, make me disagree with Wanner's contention (1987, 1988) that Old Romance clitics are homogeneous in their characteristics, and evolve along parallel lines since Proto-Romance, or earlier. This hypothesis can only be maintained if the distinctions between OSp and Old French clitics in the existing early texts are ignored, for instance. Also, for OSp, the middle of the fifteenth century brings important changes for clitics, in areas not necessarily shared by all Romance languages in their early documented stages: (a) the loss of Interpolation, (b) the disappearance of Inverted Conjugations or analytic Futures/Conditionals, with changes in the nature of Auxiliaries (Rivero 1989), (c) the emergence of clause initial clitics, and (d) the reduction in the number of Vs allowing Climbing. In my view, these changes, in particular (a) and (b), make Spanish clitics come to resemble those of other Romance languages at a much later stage than Wanner's hypothesis allows.

It seems unexpected that old clitics so readily cross Neg, in view of modern Romance, but my analysis predicts that clitics should behave differently in this respect in the two periods.

In MSp, Neg blocks Clitic Climbing (Roldán 1974, Strozer 1976, Luján 1978): *Yo quiero no verla* 'I want not to see her' vs. **Yo la quiero no ver.* For Kayne (1989a), Neg is the head of an intervening phrase as Xmax, blocking the formation of the chain between moved Clitic and trace, which fails to be properly governed. Thus Clitic Climbing as Head-movement across *no* gives an ungrammatical result.

In OSp Interpolation, Negation is often crossed. If the Clitic is an Xmax which adjoins, and the Negation is a head, the result is expected. In that situation, Interpolation shares the properties of Xmax processes such as wh-movement and VP-Preposing, which are possible when a Negation intervenes in the movement path, in Old and MSp alike. OSp wh-movement across NegP is seen in (4). OSp VP-Preposing, or extraction of an Xmax within the complement of a modal V, is shown in (13); the moved VP lands within the complement of CP, higher than the Negation, exactly as interpolated clitics do in many of the previous examples. VP-Preposing is also found in root environments.

(13) Sy ... su vezina   tan fermosa   fuese que DESALABAR SU
     If ... her neighbor so beautiful were that DISDAIN   HER

     FERMOSURA [non] puede   Cor 139
     BEAUTY   [not] can

     'If her neighbor was so beautiful that she could not dismiss her beauty'

For the NP1-NP2-Neg-V order in (7a), with NP1 the subject, and NP2 the object, the NPs may be seen as focalized or adjoined to the complement of CP: NegP; this analysis is possible under the assumption that Neg (and I also) governs bidirectionally in OSp, so that subjects are canonically head-governed and can adjoin to NegP/IP (and see fn. 1; alternatively, a Focus Phrase may contain a base-generated NP1). If a VP is adjoined, rather than an NP, the ensuing pattern is (14a). If a complement Clitic is moved instead of a tonic NP, the ensuing Interpolation is as in (14b-c).

(14) a. Que ninguno FAZER PLASER A DIOS [non] puede   Cor 47
        that no+one MAKE PLEASURE TO GOD [not] can
        'Because no one can give pleasure to God'

b. El mi padre A MI [non] lo troxiere   Cor 209
    The my father TO ME [not] it would + bring
    'My father would not bring it to me.'

c. Que ellos TE [non] digan en que puede finar   Alex 2482c(0)
    That they YOU [not] tell in what can end
    'Let them not tell you how it can end'

Pattern (7a) and the less frequent (14a-c) can be analyzed along parallel lines, involving movement of two Xmax to A-bar sites above Neg, in a not necessarily root context. Notice that OSp *ninguno* 'no one', as in (14a), is not excluded from focus position, as argued in Rivero (1986b) on the basis of doubling constructions. Alternative analyses are obviously possible, such as adjunction of Xmax (VP or PP) to X' (= I' or NegP') rather than X", as seen in section 3 for Climbing. Also, for Rivero (1986b), (14c) was adjunction to a VP containing NegP, with no V-raising to I. Here, I simply wish to emphasize the parallelism in phrasal A-bar extraction for VPs, NPs/PPs, and clitics any analysis must preserve.

2.2 The landing site of Interpolation. Ramsden (1963) observes that interpolated clitics usually follow a Comp or wh-phrase, which makes him consider (14c) and similar patterns anomalous.

If (a) Interpolation is adjunction to the complement of CP, (b) clitics cannot initiate the clause, so that CP must be filled, and (c) CP usually contains C, wh-phrases, or a Preposition in infinitives, this common order follows without stipulation, when the Clitic is the only adjoining phrase.

Also, if the Spec-of-CP can occasionally contain operator-like constituents other than wh-phrases, Interpolation will not necessarily land next to a complementizer or a wh-phrase, and this less frequent situation is shown in (5). See Ramsden for additional examples that he considers anomalous; within my approach, they may be rare but are predicted to be grammatical, a crucial distinction.

We saw that Focus movement can affect two phrases, including a Clitic, so that two patterns are then possible. First, the Clitic may adjoin higher than the other complement, as in (1d), whose relevant portion is repeated in (15). Second, the Clitic may adjoin to the lower site, as in (16), an order Ramsden considers anomalous (see also his examples), but which is well-formed in my approach.

(15) Si ME [de ti non] guardase   Z 238
     If ME [of you not] protect

(16) a. Se de nos TE [non] partes   Alex 133d (0)
     If of us YOURSELF [not] part
     'If you do not leave us'

    b. So cierto que tan buen entendimiento VOS [Dios] dió ...
       I + am sure that so good understanding YOU [God] gave ...

       que entendredes muy bien todas las cosas   Est 16
       that will + understand very well all the things

       'I am sure that God gave you such intelligence that you
       will understand everything well'

In brief, a detailed treatment combined with a precise theory of syntax can account for infrequent patterns which 'recur' in unrelated texts of various types during the period with a common system, such as Old Spanish. Often, the tradition is to note such uncommon examples, and dismiss them as anomalous, case by case, on literary rather than linguistic grounds. I contend instead that they differ minimally from the frequent patterns, once an appropriate analysis is proposed, and that they must have been grammatical for the scribes who copied or modified them, so that it is up to the researcher to discover why they could count as well formed, rather than to simply discard them. Also, manuscripts vary in their versions of a given example, but they tend to reflect grammatical alternatives of the period. The number of erroneous examples outside of the system (ungrammatical sentences) is not as high as the philological tradition based on stylistics and metrics, rather than a theory of grammar, would lead us to conclude.

To summarize, the assumption that old clitics are phrases adjoining to the complement of CP, and cannot be CP-initial because they lack tonicity, accounts (a) for the properties of Old Spanish Interpolation, including its frequent appearance in subordinate clauses or much more rarely in main clauses; and (b) for the parallelism between this Old Spanish phenomenon, and focus movement of NPs/PPs and VPs in the period. In particular, these A-bar Xmax-movements are alike in crossing Negation and Subjects, affecting phrases which often land next to complementizers or wh-phrases.

When comparing the syntax of old clitics and NPs/PPs from the modern perspective, Interpolation is startling, and NP or PP focalization is quite close to what is possible today. However, for Climbing, as shown in section 3, the situation is reversed; here, clitics may behave according to modern expectations, but NPs clearly do not. Within my analysis, the contrasts follow if the modern stage has focalization for phrases (excluding clitics) and climbing for heads (excluding NPs), while the old period treated both movements as phrasal. Viewing old Interpolation and Climbing under

254 / CURRENT STUDIES IN SPANISH LINGUISTICS

this common light provides two sources of evidence for a unitary analysis of old clitics and NPs.

Modern Slavic languages such as Serbo-Croatian, Polish, and Czech have second position constraints for clitics, and Interpolation-like effects. However, there are several reasons not to extend my proposals to Slavic. First, Slavic clitics include pronouns and auxiliaries, do not constitute a well-defined class as to category, and cannot be treated as argument phrases uniformly. Second, Slavic pronominal clitics do not pattern like NPs distributionally; they do not appear to be heads either, as they arguably adjoin to Xmax. Third, Climbing does not exist in Slavic, a difference which precludes parallelisms between clitics and NPs in this area.

3 Climbing in Old Spanish. There have been many approaches to Clitic Climbing in Modern Romance, as mentioned before. Recently, Kayne (1989a) has argued that Modern Romance clitics are X^o or heads, with Clitic Climbing as Head-to-Head Movement, and I will use these proposals as the basis for the comparison with Old Spanish, highlighting differences.

Given my treatment of old clitics, (a) the properties of Clitic Climbing should be different in the two periods, reflecting distinctions between X^o-movement vs. Xmax movement; and (b) old NPs should climb along the lines of old clitics. These predictions are correct, as we shall see.

Old Climbing is adjunction of Xmax to I', the one-bar projection for the Tense + Agreement complex, with clitics escaping complement clauses through adjunction to IP, as argued in section 3.5 for Tense effects. Climbing is attraction to the I-node, but the process cannot be Head-movement, because the items able to climb are phrases; so it must be Phrasal-movement, as argued in sections 3.1.-3.2. The locality effects of old (Clitic) Climbing seen in section 3.3 point toward the same conclusion, as clitics may cross intervening heads when climbing. This analysis extends to Perfect Tenses, as will be seen in section 3.4.

In sections 3.1-3.4, I outline differences between Old and Modern Clitic Climbing, and parallelisms between old Clitic and NP Climbing, and motivate the different facets of the proposed treatment, concentrating on the clitics and their nature.

First, the list of Old Climbing Vs is larger than the modern one, as Wanner (1982) notices (and see Suñer 1980 for a MSp inventory of Climbing Vs), extending to Vs which are not auxiliaries and take propositional complements (contra Napoli 1981 for Italian or Rochette 1988 for Romance). The Old list comprises modals, aspectuals, Vs of volition, thinking, motion, and command with object control (see fn. 8). In my view, this situation eliminates analyses with Old Climbing from 'nonclausal' VP-complements exclusively (against proposals by Strozer 1976, 1981, Zagona 1982, and

Rochette 1988), favoring the biclausal approach with two I-nodes, independently motivated in sections 3.1-3.4 (see also fn. 9).

3.1 Clitic and NP/PP Climbing. In Rivero (1986b), I stated that old Climbing is not only for clitics, but can affect NPs or PPs, as expected from my proposals. Thus, patterns like (17) are very common in Old Spanish, whether early, (17a,b), or late, (17d), but the modern stage disallows such word orders ((17c) is from the edition used in Rivero 1986b, not the one listed later). On the other hand, Climbing patterns like (18) appear identical to present ones, but the overall grammar of Old Clitic Climbing is quite different. I capitalize the climbing phrase.

(17) a. Qui ESTA NUESTRA UENDIDA ...quisiere crebantar... aya
     Who THIS OUR SALE wanted break have

     la ira de Dios   DLE 173 (1224)
     the wrath of God

     'Let the one who wants to break our sale have the wrath of God'

   b. Yo ATI vin buscar   B S. Dom. 341a
     I TO+YOU came look
     'I came looking for you'

   c. Quando tu ALGUNA COSA DESTAS quisyeres saber Cruz 220A
     When you SOME THING OF+THESE wanted know
     'When you would want to know one of these things'

   d. Quando aquel glorioso esposo Jesuchristo LAS SUS
     When that glorious husband Jesus THE HIS

     DIVINALES BODAS quisiere celebrar   Cor 278
     DIVINE WEDDING wanted celebrate

     'When that glorious husband Jesus would want to celebrate his divine wedding'

(18) a. Qui LA quisiere uender al monasterio   DLE 50 (1228)
     Who IT wanted sell to+the monastery
     'Whoever would want to sell it to the monastery'

   b. Antes que LA queria conplir   Cor 271
     Before that IT wanted fulfill
     'Before he wanted to fulfill it'

The examples in (17) are not V-final patterns, in the sense of OV, which would result in *alguna cosa destas saber quisyeres* in (17c). Rather, they display VO, that is, Aux-V order, with extraction of the NP-complement of the nonfinite V to a position below the subject.

In my view, (17-18) show a type of adjunction for old clitics shared by NPs in a restricted way, and absent in present Romance (but see Gueron and Hoekstra 1988) for a similar idea for present clitics): i.e., adjunction to I', the one-bar structure dominating the Tense + Agreement complex. Under this perspective, the schematic derived structure of (17c-d) is (19), with V-raising of *querer* 'to want'. The structure of the complement clause is discussed in section 3.5.

(19)

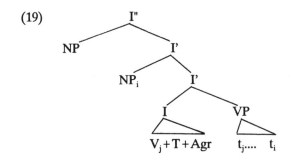

Subjects may be focalized, but I assume that analyses where they are in Spec of IP, as in (19), are also available. Otherwise, Climbing would be identical to the Interpolation/Focus movement discussed previously for (14), with NP_i in (19) adjoined to X", not X' (and likewise for a Clitic).

Although adjunction to X' is disallowed in *Barriers* , Rizzi and Roberts (1989) propose that in French Complex Inversion an NP subject adjoins to C', as movement of a nonhead into a nonhead, with the derived structure of (20) as in (21) (traces are omitted).

(20) Où Jean est-il allé?
     Where John is-he gone?
     'Where has John gone?'

(21) $[_{CP}$ Où $[_{C'}$ Jean $[_{C'}$ $[_{C_0}$ est-il] [allé]]]]]

The old Climbing in (19) is parallel to the X'-adjunction in (21), but an NP-complement moves to I' instead.

Although all phrases may I'-adjoin, NPs/PPs do not move to I' if I" is the complement of NegP, a restriction inapplicable to clitics. I propose that this is due to the different tonicity of these two kinds of phrases, as follows.

Patterns such as *El rey no lo quiere leer* 'The king does not want to read it' are easily found, but the type *El rey no este libro quiere leer* 'The king does not want to read this book' is unattested, and it must have been ungrammatical. I assume that this restriction in word order is phonological, similar in spirit to the constraint for clitics in Interpolation, but it affects *no* instead.

I assume that medieval (sentential) *no*, which heads a NegP c-commanding IP in syntax, must (pro)cliticize to V in phonology. That is, old *no* is a syntactic Xmax, and a phonological proclitic of V. Now, old clitics are also Xmax requiring the support of a(ny) previous element, so they lean on NegP, when following it, and form the complex which becomes proclitic on V. However, since tonic NPs/PPs cannot be enclitic on NegP, they prevent *no* from cliticizing on V, when they appear adjoined to I' in Climbing.

In the same vein, Old Spanish OV patterns fail to contain negations, because a preverbal object would separate *no* and V. In this connection, I am assuming that (9) has constituent rather than sentential negation, with the interpretation: they live *not* in the same house, but in different ones. Thus, the prohibition on NPs adjoining to I' and the restriction against preverbal NP-objects, if there is a negation, are identical. This constraint derives from the proclitic nature of *no*, or the lexical contextual specification that this item must attach to V by PF or phonology. From this point of view, the only item that could intervene between finite V/Aux and its negation would be a V functioning as complement, such as *dezir* 'to say' in (22); but here the negation modifies the embedded V, as the reading shows. I will return to this example in section 3.2.

(22) Todo quanto vos yo digo- et aun lo que se non dezir puede   Est 143
     All what you I tell and even what one not tell can
     'What I tell you and even what can be left unsaid'

Returning to Climbing, a Clitic as phrase has two options when leaving the VP, if negation precedes the finite V or Aux. It may adjoin to I', giving the equivalent of Climbing, as in (23), which looks similar to the modern pattern. Alternatively, clitics may land in an X" higher than I", giving Interpolation, as the examples in (24), which are ungrammatical today. Under parallel conditions, the tonic complement will not end up in I', in view of the requirements of negation, so it will necessarily interpolate across this phrase, as in (25), which today would be deviant, but better than (24).

(23) Dixo que a Dios non LO podría ver omne bivo   Est. 226
     He+said that to God not HIM could see man alive
     'He said that no one could see God while still alive'

(24) a. La ventura de que SE [ninguno non] puede anparar   CD 157
       The fortune of which HIMSELF [no one not] can take
       'The fortune no one can obtain'

     b. Si vieremos ... que SE [non] puede escusar   Est. 35
       If we + saw   that HIMSELF [not] can excuse
       'If we saw ... that he cannot excuse himself'

(25) Que AQUEL TERMINO [non] puede traspasar   Cor 218
     That THAT BOUNDARY [not] can pass
     'That he cannot go beyond that boundary'

In the absence of *non* (and preverbal subjects), NP and Clitic Climbing apply in parallel ways, and can be treated as I" or I' adjunction. NP Climbing, as in (26-27a), and Clitic Climbing, (27b), appear under identical conditions.

(26) a. Quien LO SUO ouier de heredar   DLE 192, 1241
       Who THE HIS had to inherit
       'The one who would inherit what is his'

     b. Coal quiere que ESTA DICHA VINNA ouiere de heredar por
       Who ever that THIS CITED VINE had   to inherit for

       uos   DLE 1272, 126
       you

       'Whoever would inherit this vineyard for you'

     c. Si TIERRAS ovierdes a mandar   Z 261
       If LANDS you + had to manage
       'If you had to manage lands'

     d. Et TODO ESTO puede fazer guardando los diez mandamientos
       And ALL THIS can do observing the ten commandments
       'He can do all this observing the Ten Commandments' Est. 109

(27) a. Los pechos que AMJ ouieren adar daquiadelante   DLE 205
       The taxes that TO + ME had to + give from-now-on
       'The taxes to be given to me from now on'

b. Los pechos que ME aujan adar   DLE 205, 1315
   The taxes that ME had to+give
   'The taxes that they had to give me'

To the modern ear, the word order in (17), (26), and (27a) sounds highly poetic at best, or plain ungrammatical at worst. This is because several factors separate Old and present Spanish, making the two systems different in subtle ways. First, adjunction of an Xmax can now be to a X" site only. Second, Focus movement is now restricted to main clauses or complements of declarative Vs, that is, root-like contexts. Third, definite NPs are now usually associated with Left-dislocation, rather than topicalization/focalization.

On the other hand, examples (18a-b) and (27b) sound grammatical, lexical differences aside, as they can be analyzed as adjunction of a head to a head, i.e., Modern Climbing. However, if the present analysis was retained for the old period, the observed parallellisms between clitics and NPs could not be reflected. Additional differences between Old and Modern Clitic Climbing, seen in section 3.3, lead to separate treatments for the two periods from the perspective of locality, and also to movement across an intervening head.

3.2 NP/PP and Clitic Climbing combined. In section 3.1, it was seen that clitics and tonic complements climb out of their VP through a common rule of adjunction to an A-bar position. However, the tonic complement is more restricted in landing sites than the Clitic because of the phonological properties of negation. Under such analysis, NP and Clitic Climbing should combine, and this is a correct prediction.

First, when the tonic NP/PP adjoins as the external phrase, the result is as in (28); because focalization appears in a root context, and the Clitic is in a position amenable to the present analysis as head, the pattern appears similar to current structures. Second, when the Clitic adjoins an external phrase, and the moved NP/PP is internal, the result is Interpolation, as in (29), which is unacceptable for the modern speaker from the perspective of both extracted phrases. As the configuration is nonroot, the Clitic complies with Wackernagel requirements.

(28) a. E AQUEL VOS abremos a dar por marido   Z 165
       And THAT+ONE YOU will+have to give as husband
       'And we should have to give you that one as husband'

    b. OTRA RAZON TE quiero fazer entender   Cor 246
       ANOTHER REASON YOU I+want make understand
       'I want to make you understand another reason'

(29) a. Si LO EN VOS podiese fallar Z 212
    If IT IN YOU I-could find
    'If I could find it in you'

  b. E bendito sea el nonbre de Dios que VOS TAL CAVALLERO
    And blessed be the name of God that YOU SUCH KNIGHT

    quiso acá enbiar Z 159
    wanted here send

    'Let the name of God be blessed because he sent such a knight to you'

  c. Mas bendito sea el nonbre de Dios que NOS TAN GRAN
    But blessed be the name of God that US SO BIG

    MERÇET quiso fazer Z 322
    MERCY wanted make

    'Let the name of God be blessed because he did us such a big favor'

  d. Todos aquellos que VOS MAL quisieren fazer Z 338
    All those that YOU EVIL would+want make
    'All of those who would want to hurt you'

  e. Los que LO A EL solían mostrar Est 13
    The that IT TO HIM used show
    'Those who used to show it to him'

When negation is present, a tonic phrase must bypass it in Climbing, for the reasons given in section 3.1. The Clitic can also skip the negation along similar lines, as in (30).

(30) Salvo si SE DE EL [non] puede partir Z 328
    Except if HIMSELF OF HIM [not] can part
    'Except if he cannot part from him'

It is not necessary for the tonic climbing phrase to bypass a subject, as adjunction to I' is possible in such a situation, as seen in (17b,c,d). However, adjunction to I" is also allowed for NPs/PPs and clitics under similar conditions, resulting in (31) in a climbing context.

(31) Si BUEN ENTENDIMIENTO LE [Dios] quiso dar para entender
If GOOD UNDERSTANDING HIM [God] wanted give to
understand
'If God gave him a good mind to understand'   Z 335

To conclude, within climbing environments, clitics and NPs combine in
Climbing and Interpolation alike.   This parallel behavior follows from the
hypothesis that both are Xmax adjoining to I' or X".   Thus, climbing patterns
provide additional motivation for the analysis first defended for nonclimbing
constructions, and separate Old and Modern Spanish quite radically.[4]

3.3   Nonadjacency in Old Climbing.   MSp Clitic Climbing must meet
adjacency requirements (Luján 1978, Kayne 1989a, among others), but
Wanner (1982) has observed that Old Clitic Climbing is unrestricted in this
area, which is expected under the analysis I defend.   That is, if the process
is phrasal movement of the adjunction type, it should resemble wh-movement
in freely crossing many types of intervening material.   In this respect, old
and present climbing differ in still another aspect, because interrupting
material was much more varied than at present.   Notice that lack of adjacency
may be problematic for Climbing solutions relying on restructuring, parallel
structures, or coanalysis, but is not symptomatic of phrasal versus head status
for clitics per se; however, we shall see that the nature of the intervening
material in climbing indicates that old clitics are indeed phrasal.
   I begin by showing that, in general, adjacency is not required for old
climbing.   Notice first that NP Climbing is not subject to adjacency either,
as seen in (32).

(32) a. Yo ESSY quiero, madre, rescibir et tomar   B.S.Or 192c
        I THAT+ONE want, mother, receive and take
        'Mother, I want to receive and take that one'

     b. ESPERANÇA deve ome aver que abrá buena çima   Z 57
        HOPE must man have that will+be good peak
        'One must have hope that there will be a good end'

     c. E ESTO pudiéredes vos muy bien escusar si quisiérades   Z 416
        And this could you very well excuse if you-wanted
        'And you could excuse this very well if you wanted'

---

[4] Combinations of Climbing and Interpolation are absent in the Middle French texts studied
by Martineau (1989), as expected. See also fn. 3.

The NP climbs out of its VP across parenthetical material, (a), subjects alone (b), or a combination of subject and adverbial, (c).

Clitic climbing in similar structures is extremely common in the period. The patterns in (33), in chronological order, show climbing across subjects, adverbials, or a combination of both, too. Climbing across parenthetical material appears in (33f) from Wanner (1982), who uses an earlier edition of the *Corbacho* than the one I cite.

(33) a. FueLAS luego guardar con ábito qual suelen los
　　　 He+went-THEM after keep with clothes that use the

　　　 pastores usar　　　　　　　　　　　　　 B.S. Mil 5c-d
　　　 shepherds use

　　　 'After, he went to keep them with clothes like the ones sheperds use'

　 b. Non ME deve el león fazer traición, non LE aviendo yo
　　　 Not ME must the lion make treason, not HIM having I

　　　 nunca errado a él　　　　　　　　　　　 CD 155
　　　 never failed to him

　　　 'The lion must not forsake me, since I have never failed him'

　 c. Asi LOS podemos más aina matar e astragar　 Z 364
　　　 Thus THEM we+can more early kill and destroy
　　　 'This way we can kill them and destroy them earlier'

　 d. Sin buen seso natural non LA puede ome bien aprender
　　　 Without good sense natural not IT can man well learn
　　　 'Without natural intelligence man cannot learn it well'
　　　　　　　　　　　　　　　　　　　　　　 Est 57

　 e. Non LOS querría otro dya más ver　　　　　 Cor 138
　　　 Not THEM wanted another day more see
　　　 'He would not want to see them again another day'

　 f. Sy ... nosotros LO podiéremos, como suso dicho es, fazer
　　　 If . . . we IT could, as above said is, do
　　　 'If we could do it, as said above'　　　　 Cor 49

The examples in (33c,d) show much favored OSp orders, which result from the complementation pattern of *poder* 'can', *dever* 'must', and *querer* 'want'. These Vs take infinitive complements in a VO fashion, but the complement itself is often V-final, with subject, complements, and adverbial modifiers in preverbal position. This order follows if (a) SOV schemes are available, which seems uncontroversial, (b) adverbials appear in the Spec of VP, and (c) infinitives need not undergo V-raising in their embedded clause. As a result, main V and infinitive often are not strictly adjacent, which does not block climbing, as shown.

Perhaps one of the old patterns which better exemplifies the lack of adjacency requisites in Clitic Climbing is the analytic Future/Conditional, seen in some detail in Lema and Rivero (1989a, b). I briefly recall the properties of this construction, I show that clitics attach to its finite Aux, and then turn to its Climbing characteristics.

First, in the analytic/split Future in (34), the clitic is attached to the finite Aux for reasons given below, and the Infinitive climbs to C, in Long Head Movement (LHM) bypassing the Aux. The V-trace in the VP satisfies the ECP, with the moved V in C providing antecedent-government transmitted through the Aux as mid link in an extended head-chain, because the Aux Tense-marks the V it governs, and the two are coindexed. So when V moves to C, a head-chain results (see Lema and Rivero 1990).

(34) a. Et fazerVOS he algunos enxiemplos   Luc 48
And make+TO-YOU I-will some examples
'And I will make some examples for you'

b. $[_{CP}[_{C}fazer_i]$ [vos he $[_{VP}t_i$ algunos enxiemplos]]]

Second, the LHM trigger in patterns like (34) is Wackernagel's law, as Menéndez Pidal (1964-1969) suggests. Recall that old clitics cannot be CP-initial, as mentioned in section 1.2, so movement of V to C provides a constituent within CP preceding the Clitic attached to the Aux. For this thinking to be valid, the Clitic must be with the Aux, as Menéndez Pidal wants, not with the Infinitive, as Staaf (1906) claims. If the Clitic were with the Infinitive, (a) there would be no trigger for the movement, and, (b) with my analysis, (34a) would show VP-Preposing, with V and object NP moving. However, Lema and Rivero (1989a, b) argue that analytic constructions involve Head-movement, showing no properties of VP-Preposing. Thus, the Clitic must be with the Aux for at least two reasons, and I now provide additional justification for this conclusion.

Menéndez Pidal does not motivate his stand, but the evidence is strong, if constructions longer than (34) are considered. Analytic patterns with more than one Aux and one V show two exceptionless properties which support the idea that the Clitic is attached to the finite Aux. First, LHM affects the Aux or V immediately adjacent to the finite Aux: in (35) the underlying sequence is 1. *edes,* 2. *venir,* 3. *dezir,* so the second item moves to C. Second, clitics always precede the finite Aux, even when they originate in the lower V which remains *in situ:* in (35) *me lo* comes from *dezir,* not from *venir.*

(35)   Et venirMELO edes dezir   CD 282
        And come-TO + ME-IT you + will say
        'And you will come to say it to me'

These two aspects show that in analytic patterns, clitics climb to the finite Aux, and precede it. In my terms, they adjoin to I', and are not within the Infinitive Phrase at S-structure. This triggers LHM of the second V/Aux, for a Wackernagel effect for the Clitic, as schematically shown in (36). In contrast with old clitics in Interpolation or Climbing, Lema and Rivero (1989a, b) argue that Vs cannot cross NegP in OSp LHM, a difference which follows from the contrasting movements involved: phrasal for clitics versus head for V.

Old Spanish LHM is identical to movements in several Romance and Slavic languages, with properties determined by UG.

(36)

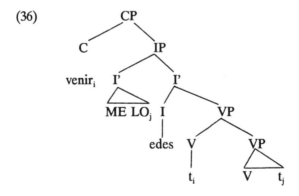

Alternatives to the above proposal appear problematic. First, making the Clitic climb obligatorily, but only to the second V, followed by Preposing of V' with adjoined Clitic, is not a good solution. Under this treatment, Climbing to the mid position must necessarily apply, but for unknown reasons. Also, the movement of middle V and Clitic is unlike VP-Preposing, which affects the main VP, not mid ones in isolation. Second, if the Clitic obligatorily moves to the intermediate V to form a head-unit, against my analysis, subsequent extraction of this complex can be by Head-movement to

C, but then the trigger for LHM is unclear, as there is no prohibition against an initial Aux in Old Spanish.

If clitics are in I' in (36), then old Climbing differs from the present one in several respects. Thus, not only does the drastic dismembering of the mid VP fail to block Climbing, but in addition, adjacency is not satisfied in the analytic constructions in (37-38), with the Clitic climbing from *repentir* to the finite Aux across an adverb, in a structure with the mid Aux in C. In short, there are no clear adjacency requirements in early Spanish, which makes restructuring, parallel structures, and coanalysis proposals for Climbing appear problematic for this old period.

(37) Et del rebatamiento poderVOS yades muy aína repentir   Luc 205
       And of+the anger can+YOURSELF would very soon repent
       'And it could be that you regret your anger very soon'

(38)

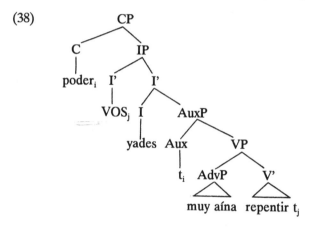

As MSp does not have LHM, the comparison with (36-38) is indirect. However, the two stages differ in relation to VP-Preposing, which is shared and can be contrasted. In the old period, VPs and/or projections of V (see van Riemsdijk 1989 for interesting proposals for the movement of nonmaximal phrases) could be preposed, as in (39), and Climbing was possible, much as in Italian and Middle French (40).

(39) a. E pues yo [gradescer] non VOS LO puedo   Z 362
        And since I thank   not you it can
        'And since I cannot thank you for it'

     b. Si [así fazer] non LO quisiéredes...   DLE 221, 1352
       If [so make] not it you+would+want
       'If you did not want to do it this way'

    c. [En la fenbra fallar] nunca LO podrán   Cor 81
    [In the female find] never it they+can
    'They will never be able to find it in a woman'

(40) a. [Offerte a sua moglie] credo que M ancora non LE abbia
      Offered to his wife I+think that M yet not THEM had
      'I think that M had not offered them to his wife yet'
                                       (Longobardi 1985: 186)

    b. Mais [croire] ne L'osa   CNNA: 1/13
      But [believe] not IT dare   (Martineau 1989: 34)
      'But he did not dare to believe it'

In (39-40), a phrase containing the EC associated with the Clitic next to the finite item is preposed. Thus, these OSp cases escape Connectedness effects, like Italian (Longobardi 1985: 186) or Middle French, with all raising Vs. Longobardi suggests that patterns with VP-Preposing and Climbing undergo Reconstruction (in the sense of Cinque 1982), which interprets left phrases as if they were in the corresponding sentence-internal position. Notice that Reconstruction is equivalent to an inheritance procedure for the moved VP and could apply irrespective of the nature of the Clitic.[5]

    In contrast, MSp allows Climbing out of VPs *in situ* exclusively, as in (41a-42a). If a VP is preposed, Climbing is disallowed with any V: (41c-42c). MSp *haber* disallows VP-Preposing, so the MSp equivalent of (40) is ungrammatical for additional reasons.

(41) a. No LE quiero leer el libro
      Not him I+want read the book
      'I do not want to read him the book'

    b. LeerLE el libro no quiero
      'Read him the book I do not want'

    c. * Leer el libro no LE quiero

---

   [5] Kayne (1989a: 258) suggests that VP-Preposing allows Climbing in Italian because the Aux-cum-Participle structure in (40a) contains no I with intermediate trace in the preposed constituent, and no ECP violation ensues. In Old Romance, VP-Preposing and Climbing combine with all climbing Vs, so this solution does not seem to be available. In addition, for OSp, my treatment of clitics precludes Kayne's approach, so a kind of reconstruction-like analysis may be preferable. Reconstruction is also required for OSp Interpolation and the Binding Theory, as pointed out in Rivero (1986b).

(42) a. Creo que Mario no LOS quiere ofrecer a su mujer
'I think that Mario does not want to offer them to his
wife'

    b.   [OfrecerLOS a su mujer] creo que Mario no quiere

    c. * [Ofrecer a su mujer] creo que Mario no LOS quiere

Thus, MSp patterns (41-42) escape Reconstruction, and are similar in status to operator-like Italian extractions (Rizzi 1976 and his later work), such as clefting, or the Pied Piping in (43).

(43) a. Estas ideas, a hablarTE de las cuales vendré pronto ...
These ideas, to speak-to+you of which I+will+come soon ..
'These ideas, about which I will come to speak to you soon'

    b. *Estas ideas, a hablar de las cuales TE vendré pronto...

The difference between OSp and MSp need not depend on the change in phrasal status for clitics. Italian, Middle French (Martineau 1989), and MSp clitics are not Xmax, but the first two contrast with the second as to Climbing, as we just saw. Also, the distinction cannot lie in the Reconstruction of VP-Preposing exclusively, since NP-movement combined with it gives grammatical results in MSp and Italian (and OSp too), as seen in (44).

(44) a.   Traicionado por su mujer creo que Mario no ha sido nunca

    b.   Tradito da sua moglie credo che Mario non sia mai stato

       'Cheated by his wife, I think Mario has never been'

The above patterns show passivization out of a preposed VP, the context disallowing Climbing in MSp, so Clitic Climbing and NP-Movement differ when the MSp VP is not *in situ*, with the first sensitive to the Connectedness effects discussed by Longobardi (1985). This topic requires further research, but perhaps Kayne's idea for Italian clefting (1989a: 253) can be adopted in a general way for MSp. Namely, in 'VP-Preposing' in (42c) it can be assumed that the infinitival phrase as CP or IP is not L-marked in its S-structure position, and cannot inherit L-marking either. As a result, this preposed clause contains a trace resulting from the movement of the Clitic through the embedded I which is not antecedent-governed.[6]

Returning to Climbing, under restructuring analyses, adjacency is a necessary condition for modern Clitic Climbing, since finite and nonfinite Vs must form the syntactic complex word the Clitic precedes. Although interrupting Adverbs or Complementizer may be part of the restructured complex, dismembered or preposed VPs cannot be. Similar comments apply to parallel structures (Goodall 1984) or co-analysis proposals (DiSciullo and Williams 1987) where Aux and V count as a morphosyntactic complex for Climbing to apply. Again, the previous Italian, Middle French, and Old Spanish examples indicate difficulties for these positions.

Under Kayne's Head-movement analysis, on the other hand, adjacency is not required per se (the same seems to apply to clause union (Aissen and Perlmutter 1976), but how their proposal could extend to (39-40) is unclear to me). Under the Head-movement alternative, the modern Clitic as X^o is unable to bypass a head such as Negation, but it can in principle climb over subjects and adverbials in the movement path, if these are treated as Specifiers and not intervening heads. This can cover sentences such as *No lo puedo ni siquiera pronunciar* 'I cannot even pronounce it', pointed out by Suñer, if *ni siquiera* is in the Spec-of-VP. Likewise, other complements can be bypassed, since they do not interrupt the path in the relevant sense.

Turning to OSp, if Clitic Climbing in (33-39) did not correlate with the parallel NP Climbing in (32), it could still be assumed that clitics move as

---

[6] Contrasts between across-the-board phenomena (Williams 1978) in OSp and MSp could also be attributed to the status of the clitics, but this does not seem correct. Middle French and OSp are similar in sharing some across-the-board patterns, such as (i) and (ii), but have differing clitics. In contrast, no Climbing and two clitics are required (preferred?) in this context at present: (iii).

    (i) No LO podrié nul omne comedir nin asmar   B S Dom 756c
         Not IT could no man consider nor think
         'Nobody could consider it'
    (ii) Elles ne le debveroient faire ou dire   CNNV 63/03
         'They not IT must do or say'   (Martineau 1989)
    (iii) No deberían hacerLO o/ni decirLO
         'They should not do it or say it'

On the other hand, Wanner (1982) cites the interesting example in (iv), which is clearly ungrammatical now. Various kinds of across-the-board Middle French climbings are found in (Martineau 1989), but none of type (iv). If OSp (iv) is not an isolated case, the two old languages could after all differ. Clearly, across-the-board structures require much more study.

    (iv) E por esta razón non LO devía patir nin podía   20R 243:48
        And for this reason not IT must suffer nor could
        'For this reason, he should not and could not have suffered it'

heads, crossing specifiers and complements, but not interrupting heads.[7] Also, parenthetical material could intervene as the result of movement in PF, which would not interfere with head-raising in syntax. Finally, with Reconstruction, the ECP could be satisfied once a VP is repositioned in its internal position.

In this respect, (22), repeated as (45), is important.

(45) Todo quanto vos yo digo- et aún lo que SE [non dezir] puede
All what you I tell and even what SE [not tell] can
'What I tell you and even what can be left unsaid' Est 143

If the second relative clause in (45) is equivalent to the modern *lo que puede no decirse* 'what can be left unsaid', as the meaning suggests, this example shows Climbing across the embedded *non*, the crucial aspect distinguishing phrasal from head movement. Also, Interpolation in the matrix separating Clitic from the Aux is another extraction distinguishing Old and later clitics, or, in this particular case, adjunction from I' to I" within the relative clause.

In conclusion, Old Climbing is not Head-movement, since Phrases climb, and intervening Heads may be crossed.[8]

---

[7] For climbing across subjects, adverbs, and parentheticals in Middle French, see Martineau (1989), who argues in favor of a Head-movement analysis. If her analysis is correct, MFr NegP in (i) must have *ne* as the higher head (as in Italian, or MSp) and *pas* as a lower adverb/specifier (see Kayne 1989a: 243 on Modern French). Otherwise, the climbing clitic would cross Neg as head. In Middle French *pas* is not obligatory, and *ne* carries the force of the negation, so the proposed treatment is viable in principle.

(i) Il ne LE faut pas dire   CNNA 40/77
It not IT must *pas* say 'One must not say it'

Alternatively, it could be that a Neg which does not c-command Tense, that is *pas*, is not an intervening head (Zanuttini 1989), and does not block Climbing. However, if Middle French had switched to the analysis with lower Neg (as in Pollock 1989), the prediction would be that an embedded Neg fails to block Climbing (i.e. *Il le faut ne pas dire*), but this situation seems unattested. In brief, it appears as if in (i) no negation is crossed.

[8] For Kayne (1989a), Modern Climbing does not apply with Object Control, because Head-movement by the clitic is through the embedded I, coindexing the two I-nodes, which are necessarily coindexed with their respective subjects. Within my Old Climbing analysis, this restriction should be inoperative, as Old clitics are not heads moving through I. Then, it becomes tempting to cite the following Old Climbings as support for my treatment, but the conclusion seems hasty, in view of MSp.

(i) a. Yo VOS mandaré dar una de las mias   Z 128
I TO+YOU will-order give one of the mine
'I will order that one of mine be given to you'
b. MandátME dar la nave e a omes seguros   Z 128
Order+ME give the ship and men sure
'Order that the ship and reliable men be given to me'

3.4 Climbing in compound tenses. In OSp, the Perfect Aux *aver* 'to have' shares some of the syntactic characteristics of modals, unlike MSp. First, I have argued elsewhere (Rivero 1989) that inversion of the old Perfect, as in (46a), is similar to VP-Preposing, as in (14a) = (46b), and comparable to German (46c), as in Webelhuth (1985) (and see Koster 1987) for Dutch; but in Lema and Rivero (1990), Perfect Preposing differs from VP-Preposing. In these three cases, the material in brackets does not move as head, in contrast with the V of OSp analytic Futures in (34-37).

Phrasal-Preposing is licensed by modals and aspectuals in OSp, as in Italian. By contrast, MSp *poder* 'can' allows the process, but *haber* 'to have' clearly does not.

Examples such as (i) are also found in MSp (Luján 1978), as in *Se lo mandaré dar* 'I will order that it be given to him', and Kayne suggests that they are hidden causatives with VP-complements. Thus, the relevance of (i) to this argument depends on treating Vs of command as involving Object control in OSp, but not now. However, *mandar* has always taken Subjunctive complements, as in *Manda a Juan que cante* 'Order John that (he) sing', suggesting unchanged clausal complementation and Object control.

That Old Climbing does not require coindexation of Is is seen in clausal causatives. First, since the complement of *fazer* 'make' can be Passive, as in (ii), I suggest that it is clausal. Also, causative Vs have always allowed productive Subjunctive complements, as in *Hace a Juan que cante* 'He makes John sing'.

    (ii) Faze ser sospechados a los leales consejeros   CD 155
         Makes be suspected to the loyal counselors
         'He makes the loyal counselors be suspected'

Second, since *fazer* can be followed by the NP subject of the lower clause, as in (iii), I propose that the embedded I is *in situ*, followed by its VP-complement. Obviously, matrix and embedded I are not coindexed.

    (iii) Et ella faze al omne flaco cavalgar sobre el elefante   CD157
         And she makes the skinny man ride on the elephant

Under the above assumptions, in (iv), Climbing to the matrix causative is out of the embedded VP, with adjunction to the embedded I", as will discussed in section 3.5, and across the embedded subject, in apparent violation of the Specified Subject constraint. However, this subject is a Specifier, so bypassing it is unproblematic, as pointed out before. If Kayne is right that Modern Climbing is impossible when the intervening Is are not coindexed, this should have no effect on OSp Climbing, as clitics do not move through I, and (iv) provides support for this view.

    (iv) E fízoME a un escudero tomar ante si en el cavallo
         And madeME a soldier take before himself in the horse
         et troxiéronme a la çibdat   Z 181
         and brought me to the city
         'And he made a soldier take me in front of him on his horse
         and they brought me to the city'

For MSp causatives, which are sensitive to the Specified Subject Constraint, unlike the old ones, Treviño (1990) proposes a combination of Xmax and X°-movement for complement clitics. They first move to the embedded Spec-of-IP as Xmax, and later climb to the matrix V as heads. Thus, if the embedded subject site is filled in the modern equivalent of (iv), climbing cannot proceed, accounting for the difference in the two periods.

(46) a. Onde, pues que [dicho] avemos de los veniales,
   Whereas, since that [said] we + have of the venial,

   conviene que se diga de los criminales   Set 186
   it + is + convenient that one talk of the criminal

   'Since we have spoken of venial sins, we should discuss
   mortal ones too'

   b. Que ninguno [FAZER PLASER A DIOS] non puede   Cor 47
   That no one [MAKE PLEASURE TO GOD] not can
   'Since no one can give God pleasure'

   c. [Gelesen] hat Hans das Buch nicht
   [Read]   had Hans the book not
   'Hans had not read the book'

(47) a. [Darle alegría a Dios] no puede
   'She cannot give joy to God'

   b. *[Leído el libro] no ha
   'Read the book she has not'

Also, old Perfects show the properties of other climbing constructions: phrases, not just clitics, climb, and intervening material is of the same type. For Napoli (1981), Italian climbing Vs and aspectuals are similar in being auxiliary-like, but in my argumentation the reason why OSp *aver* belongs to the extensive class of climbing Vs is that it is still another V with a propositional complement.

3.4.1 *Aver* and Past Participle Agreement. First, I establish that the Old aspectual Aux *aver* takes a (small) clausal complement,[9] unlike modern *haber*.

---

[9] Climbing across wh-phrases, as in (i) with *por qué* in the Spec of CP, indicates that climbing Vs can take CP-complements. Although Rochette (1988: 227) suggests adjunction to VP for an object wh-phrase in parallel Italian cases, *por qué* in (i) is an adjunct making such a solution unavailable. Patterns such as (i) appear problematic for restructuring via VP-movement, as in Burzio (1986), unless the embedded VP is extracted from a CP toward the right. See section 3.5 for an analysis of this example; see also fn. 11.
   (i) Dizien ... que non GELOS auíen por qué lexar   DLE 238, 1258
   They + said that not TO + HIM-THEM had why lend
   'They said that they did not have a reason to lend them to him'

Participles optionally agree in Gender and Number with objects in Perfect tenses in OSp, so I adopt Kayne's idea (1985, 1989b) that this situation correlates with (small) clausal status for the complement of the Perfect Aux. For French, Kayne proposes that the structure of such a complement is roughly as in (48), and I will suppose the same for OSp, in contrast with MSp.

(48) Paul les$_i$ a [e]$_i$ AGR$_i$ repeintes [e]$_i$
     'Paul has painted them'

To provide an analysis of OSp Participle Agreement is beyond the scope of this paper, so I will outline its general typology, leaving the topic for future research.

First, (capitalized) Object Agreement is found with relativization, (49a), climbing of clitics, (49b), as in Modern French (and see (52) for climbing NPs), and resumptive strategies, (49c).

(49) a. Son los q<ue> ante auemos dichOS   Cruz 156v75
        Are the that before we+have said (m.pl.)
        'They are the ones we said before'

     b. Et estas son las figuras de todas las maneras desta
        And these are the figures of all the manners of+this

        opposition segund las auemos dichAS   Cruz 99v77
        opposition as them we+have said (f.pl.)

        'And these are the figures of all the ways of this
        opposition as we stated them'

     c. Sube una mugier que la ha dexadA su marido   Pic 2r30-1
        Raises a woman that her has left (f.sg.) her husband
        'A woman who was abandoned by her husband appears'

Second, Object Agreement is also observed without apparent movement of the object NP, (50), as in literary Italian, the Italian and Occitan dialects mentioned by Kayne (1989b), and Old French (Dupuis 1989: 203ff).

(50) a. Et auedes perdudOS los parientes et los amigos   Esp II 152v52
        And you+have lost (m.pl.) the parents and the friends
        'And you have lost family and friends'

     b. Tu as oydA la mi oratio<n>   Pic 30r14
        You have heard (f.sg.) the my prayer

c. Et pos q<ue> auemos dep<ar>tidAS estas cosas Ast 8r53
And after we + have discussed (f.pl.) these things

d. Otros muchos logares de q<ue> auemos escriptOS
Other many   places   of which we + have written (m.pl.)

los nombres   Esp I 8v51
the names

'Many other places whose names we did not write'

However,   it is not evident that movement is missing in the above
examples,   as Kayne points out for parallel Modern Romance cases,   and
much depends on a precise analysis.   For instance, if (50) shared the step in
the derivation surfacing as (51)--a small clause with NP in subject position
(= [NP$_i$ Participle e$_i$])--then the agreeing NPs in (50) could have been
extraposed,   or scrambled to the right,   and be outside of the complement,
like those in (49).

(51) a. Delas horas eguales quando ouieres [el ascendente sabudO]
Of + the hours same when you + would + have the ascendent known
'Of the same hours when you would know the ascendent'
                                                 Ast 24v81

b. Et ouo [todas las planetas ayuntadAS]   Jui 200r51
And he + had all the planets joined
'And he joined all the planets'

c. Si ovieras [a mi dexadO solo]   Z 318
If you + had to me left alone
'If you had left me alone'

d. Otra cosa muy aprovechosa por que el non oviesse
Another thing very beneficial for which he not would + have

[nada fecho]   Luc 242
nothing done

'Another very beneficial thing for which he would have done
nothing'

In Modern French (but not Old French,   see Dupuis 1989: 216-19),
patterns with NP objects before Participles are deviant,   and Kayne proposes

that *avoir* is not a Case assigner, with the NP in a caseless position. Then, within this logic, (51) shows that OSp *aver* assigned Case to the NP subject of the small clause, or the embedded Agr.

Phrasal-Preposing correlates with Theta-role assignment by an Aux to its complement in Lema and Rivero (1989a, b), and I have already mentioned that old *aver* is an XP-Preposing Aux. Then it can be concluded that Old Perfect *aver* is a lexical Aux like *poder*, not a functional Aux like Future *a* or Conditional *ia*, from two perspectives: Case and Theta theories. Modern Spanish *haber* is defective on both counts. Having established the status of Old Perfect *aver*, I turn to Climbing.

3.4.2 Climbing with Perfect *aver*. First, Climbing of NPs out of the complement of the Perfect Aux is seen in (52). Since the Participle shows Object Agreement, examples (52b, c, d) are parallel to (50a, d) in this respect also.[10]

(52) a. Et quando ESTO TODO ouieres   fecho, aurás
And when ALL THIS you+would+have done, you+will+have

   acabadA la lámina   Ast 161v11
   finished the page

   'And when you have done all this, you
   will have finished the page'

b. LAS FIGURAS DELA OCHAUA ESPERA auemos todas
THE FIGURES OF+THE EIGHTTH SPHERE we+have all

   nombradAS et dichAS   Ast 18v3
   named and said

   'We have named and mentioned all the figures of
   the eighth sphere'

c. E ESTA RAZON auemos nos esplanadA   Jui 49r74
And THIS REASON have we explained
'And we have explained this reason'

d. Et N<UEST>ROS CAUALLEROS aquí auemos perdudOS
And OUR KNIGHTS here we+have lost
'And we have lost our knights here'   Esp II 89v13

---

[10] Climbing is not obligatory in OSp, but this applies rarely to Perfects. See Gessner (1893: 44) for some examples with the clitic following the Participle.

The combination of NP and Clitic Climbing already seen with *querer* 'to want' is also observed in Perfect Tenses: (53). Participle Agreement is with the Clitic in the first instance, and the NP in the second. As before, I assume that *a ti* 'you' and *me* 'me' in (53a) move out of the complement and adjoin to I'.

(53) a. Dios A TI ME a mostradA   SME 1180
　　　　God TO YOU ME has shown
　　　　'God has shown me to you'

　　 b. AQUESTA SANGRE NOS a El dadA   SME 1270
　　　　THIS BLOOD TO-US has He given
　　　　'He has given us this blood'

Climbing from the complement of Perfect *aver* shows the same absence of adjacency between Aux and V as in previous cases:

(54) a. Estavan los discipulos en uno aplegados, com LOS avié
　　　　Were the disciples in one gathered, as THEM had

　　　　don Christo quand s'iva castigadOS   Loor 154b
　　　　lord Christ when he-left punished

　　　　'The disciples were huddled together, the way Christ had punished them when he left'

　　 b. Et LO auemos nos ya departido ante desto   GE IV 49r56
　　　　And IT have we already discussed before this
　　　　'And we have discussed it already before this'

　　 c. Ya LO he muy bien entendido   CD 298
　　　　Already IT I+have very well understood
　　　　'I have understood it very well already'

Example (54a) shows movement across parenthetical material, (54b) across a subject and an adverb, and (54c) across an adverb. The last two cases make Old Spanish resemble French, as in *Marie lui a déjà parlé* 'Mary has already spoken to him', but there are two major differences. First, French has no *bona fide* Climbing, so compound tenses do not correlate with climbing patterns with modals. Second, Old Spanish NP climbing as in (52-53) indicates phrasal movement anyway. Also, Climbing in Perfects is just like Climbing from other small clauses.

(55) Pora levar el agua a los de iuso, que no LA sabíen hy
For carry the water to the of down, that not IT knew there

nunquas puestA   DLE 182 (1228)
never placed (fem., sg.)

'To carry the water to those who were downwards, who did not
know it (to be) placed there ever'

Finally, Interpolation in Perfects has expected properties.

(56) a. Si ME [yo] oviese llegado al leon   CD 129
If ME [I] had approached to+the lion
'If I had gone to the lion'

b. Estas cosas que ME [vos] avedes dicho   Est 28
These things that ME [you] have said
'These things you have told me'

The above patterns clearly distinguish OSp from MSp, where (a) NPs no
longer climb nor clitics interpolate; (b) Perfect Aux and Participle disallow
intermediate subjects, adverbs, quantifiers, or parentheticals (see Suñer
1987 for discussion); (c) there is no Participle Agreement; (d) nor
VP-Preposing with Perfect Aux.

3.5 Tense effects in Old Clitic Climbing. As shown in fn. 8, and
example (iv) repeated as (57), Old Climbing escapes the Specified Subject
Condition.

(57) E fízoME a un escudero tomar ante si en el cavallo
And madeME a soldier take before himself in the horse

et troxiéronme a la Çibdat   Z 181
and brought me to the city

'And he made a soldier take me in front of him in his horse
and they brought me to the city'

However, it obeys the Tensed-Island Condition, since clitics move out
of nonfinite clauses without exception, as all the previous examples indicate.
Within the analysis proposed here, the [+tense] Comp which disallows
wh-extractions from wh-islands in many languages in Frampton's system
(1990: 61-64) will also prevent Climbing from nonfinite clauses, if clitics can

exit a complement clause only through adjunction to IP, and are barred from moving through the Spec-of-CP (see Chomsky 1986 on finiteness and Subjacency). In this sense, no special conditions are required. First, consider example (i) in fn. 9, repeated as (58).

(58) Dizien ... que non GELOS auíen por qué lexar   DLE 238,1258
     They+said   that not TO+HIM-THEM had why lend
     'They said that they did not have a reason to lend them to him'

If Climbing involves adjunction to the embedded IP, as also required for Interpolation, and subsequent extraction from the CP, bypassing the [-Tense] C and the wh-phrase in the Spec-of-CP in (59), this pattern is similar to wh-extractions from infinitive wh-islands such as *Tomatoes, which I don't know how to plant t,* and may receive a parallel treatment (Frampton 1990: 62).

(59)   V [$_{CP}$ wh-phrase [Comp [$_{IP}$ CL IP]

Namely, Climbing from the IP-adjoined position, parallel to English wh-movement, crosses no barriers, as CP is L-marked and V canonically governs the CL site, allowing subsequent adjunctions, because the [-Tense] C does not create a minimality effect.

Second, if Prepositions such as *a, de,* and *por* head a [-Tense] C, as in (60) or (26), Climbing out of prepositional Infinitives is as in (59) also, minus the wh-phrase (remember that pre-Infinitive clitics, as in (8b), provide evidence that P is CP-internal in infinitival complements). If the adverbial operator is in the embedded Spec-of-CP in (60b), the parallelism is evident, and P-heads are similar to Neg in not blocking climbing.[11] I assume that *auríen* 'they would have' in (60b) is in the matrix C to support the Clitic that lands in the matrix I' (and see fn. 1).

(60) a. Onbres de Antiocho ME andan por matar
        'Men from Antiochia are about to kill me'
                               (Appo 81c as cited by Gessner 1893)

---

[11] Under the assumptions in the text, (i) contains two phrases that adjoin to the embedded IP from inside the lower VP. If I L-marks the VP voiding its barrierhood, as Kayne (1989a) proposes for null-subject languages, adjunction to IP can be in one step. From its IP-adjoined position, the NP *ninguna cosa* adjoins to the complement of the matrix CP, or NegP, bypassing *non*, as discussed previously, while the clitic *le* adjoins to I'. Climbing from the complement clause bypasses *de* in C and *nunq<ua>* in the Spec-of-CP in both instances.
(i) Que NINGUNA COSA non LES he nunq<ua> de demandar DLE 31, 1236
    That NO THING not THEM I+have never of ask
    'That I will not ever have to ask them anything'

b. Et auríen LE [_{CP}much a menudo [_{C'}de [_{IP}t [_{IP} toller t]]]]
'And they would have to take (something) away from him
very often'   Ast 25V18

Third, a [+tense] C induces a Minimality effect, making its CP count as
barrier for the Clitic adjoined to IP, preventing canonical government by the
higher V, and subsequent adjunctions, barring Climbing out of tensed
clauses.

By contrast, extraction of wh-phrases out of finite clauses without
wh-islands is unproblematic *per se*. The same is true of OSp extraction by
focalization, as in (61), with movement of the NP similar to that of the
wh-phrase in *What do you think they did t?*.

(61) a. Una cosa de nuevo querríemos que feziesses t
'One thing again, we would wish you to do'
(Alex 291b as cited by Gessner 1893)

b. Nobleza grande tenían los antigos que auya t el sol más
que las otras planetas   Set 84
'Greater nobility, ancient people thought the sun had,
more than the other planets'

However, clitics fail to move in patterns similar to (59), so it can be safely
assumed that *la querríemos que feziesses t* was deviant. This situation may
appear contradictory in view of my contention that clitics and NPs do not
differ in category, but I attribute the distinction to the pronominal character
of old clitics, which prevents them from occupying positions reserved for
operators. Frampton derives tense restrictions in extraction from wh-islands
from the blocking effect of a [+tense] C in relation to the phrase adjoined to
IP, as we have seen. In his system, wh-phrases move to the Spec-of-CP,
an operator-like position, or adjoin to IP. If old clitics as pronominals can exit their clause through the nonoperator position, or adjunction to IP exclusively, they will always fall under the effect of a [+Tense] C, and be unable
to climb out of a finite clause. Focalizations of nonclitics, on the other hand,
may involve the Spec-of-CP, and be operator-like, escaping finiteness effects
in subsequent movements. Under this view, OSp focalization may be by adjunction to IP, or through the Spec-of-CP, similar to wh-movement in
Frampton's system, but, when a Clitic moves, only the first option is
available, so Clitic Climbing is out of untensed complements exclusively.

Within this analysis, the formal property making an OSp V belong to the
climbing category is its ability to head-govern into the embedded position
adjoined to IP, and this could relate to the nature of the intervening C:
namely, its transparency or its absence.

4 Summary and conclusions. Although OSp and MSp share many apparently identical strings involving Clitic Climbing, they differ as to the overall grammar of Climbing, accounting for numerous unshared patterns. On the one hand, OSp Climbing is Xmax-movement as adjunction, shared by both NPs and clitics. First, their Xmax nature allows clitics to adjoin to the complement of CP (IP in affirmative sentences and NegP in negative clauses), in a process of focalization also shared by complement NPs, and known traditionally as Interpolation. Clitics cannot move to the Spec-of-CP for two reasons: (a) they would be CP-initial, which is impossible; and (b) they would occupy a slot reserved for operators or quantificational items, which clitics are not. Second, clitics climb from embedded clauses through the adjunction site of Interpolation, subject to the Tensed-Island effects resulting from a finite Comp, but escaping Specified Subject phenomena, similar to wh-extractions out of infinitives (i.e., an embedded preverbal subject can be crossed). This option is available to climbing NPs, providing support for the analysis.

On the other hand, MSp clitics do not adjoin as Xmax, so Interpolation, or the focalization NPs and clitics shared in OSp, is absent. Also, if we adopt Kayne's (1989a) proposal for modern Romance, where clitics as heads adjoin to a head, MSp Clitic Climbing should show no phrasal movement properties, and complement NPs should not climb, which seems correct.

References

A. Text editions

Alex, stanza, line (ms.) = El libro de Alexandre, ed. R. S. Willis. New York: Kraus Reprint, 1965.
Ast, ms. page, paragraph, line = El libro del saber de astronomía. In Concordances ... (Kasten and Nitti 1978).
B Milg, stanza, line = Gonzalo de Berceo, Los milagros de Nuestra Señora, ed. B. Dutton. London: Tamesis, 1971.
B S Dom, stanza, line = Gonzalo de Berceo, La vida de Santo Domingo de Silos, ed. B. Dutton. London: Tamesis, 1978.
B S Or, stanza, line = Gonzalo de Berceo, Vida de Santa Oria. In Cuatro poemas de Berceo, ed. C. Marden. Madrid: RFE, 1928.
CD, page = Calila e Dimna, ed. J. M. Cacho Blecua and M. J. Lacarra. Madrid: Castalia, 1984.
Concordances and Texts of the Royal Scriptorium Manuscripts of Alfonso X, el Sabio, ed. L. A. Kasten and J. Nitti. Madison, Wis.: Hispanic Seminary of Medieval Studies, 1978.
Cor, page = Alfonso Martinez de Toledo, Arcipreste de Talavera o Corbacho, ed. J. González Muela. Madrid: Castalia, 1970.
Cruz, ms. page, paragraph, line = Libro de las Cruzes. In Concordances.
DLE, number, year = Documentos lingüísticos de España, ed. R. Menéndez Pidal. Madrid: CSIC, 1966.
Esp I, ms. page, paragraph, line = Estoria de España I. In Concordances.
Esp II, ms. page, paragraph, line = Estoria de España II. In Concordances.

Est, page = Juan Manuel, Libro de los Estados, ed. R.B. Tate and I.R. Macpherson. Oxford: Clarendon Press, 1974.
GE IV, ms. page, paragraph, line = General Storia IV. In Concordances.
Juic, ms. page, paragraph, line = El libro conplido en los iudizios de las estrellas. In Concordances.
Loor, stanza, line = Gonzalo de Berceo. Los loores de Nuestra Señora. In Los himnos.
Los loores de Nuestra Señora. Los signos del juicio final, ed. B. Dutton. London: Tamesis, 1975.
Luc, page = Juan Manuel. El conde Lucanor, ed. J. M. Blecua. Madrid: Castalia, 1984.
Pic, ms. page, paragraph, line = Picatrix. In Concordances.
Por, page = Poridat de las poridades, ed. L. A. Kasten. Madrid: CSIC, 1957.
Set, page = Alfonso el Sabio, Setenario, ed. K. Vanderford. Buenos Aires: Instituto de Filología, 1945. 1984 reprint. Barcelona: Editorial Crítica.
SME, line = La vida de Santa María Egipciaca, ed. M. Angeles Castellanos. Madrid: Real Academia Española, 1964.
Z, page = Libro del caballero Zifar, ed. J. González Muela. Madrid: Castalia, 1982.

B. Studies

Adams, M. 1986. From Old French to the Theory of Pro-drop. Natural Language and Linguistic Theory 5, 1-32.
Aissen, J., and D. M. Perlmutter. 1976. Clause Reduction in Spanish. Berkeley Linguistic Society 2, 1-30.
Alemán, I. 1985. The Position of Clitics in Old Spanish. Cornell Working Papers in Linguistics 7, 1-17.
Benincà, P. 1983-84. Un'ipotesi sulla sintassi delle lingue romanze medievali. Quaderni Patavini di Linguistica 4, 3-19.
Borer, H. 1984. Parametric Syntax. Dordrecht: Foris.
Burzio, L. 1986. Italian Syntax: A Government-Binding Approach. Dordrecht: Reidel.
Campos, H. 1989. Clitic Position in Modern Gallegan. Lingua 77, 13-36.
Chenery, W. 1905. Object Pronouns in Dependent Clauses: A Study of Old Spanish Word Order. PMLA 20, 1-151.
Chomsky, N. 1986. Barriers. Cambridge, Mass.: MIT Press.
Chomsky, N. 1988. Some Notes on Economy of Derivation and Representation. MIT Working Papers in Linguistics 10, 43-74.
Cinque, G. 1982. Constructions with Left Peripheral Phrases, Connectedness, Move- α and ECP. Ms., University of Venice.
Couquaux, D. 1986. Les pronoms faibles sujets comme groupes nominaux. In M. Ronat and D. Couquax, eds., La grammaire modulaire. Paris: Les editions de Minuit.
Di Sciullo, A. M., and E. Williams. 1987. On the Definition of Word. Cambridge, Mass.: MIT Press.
Dupuis, F. 1989. L'expression du sujet dans les subordonnées en ancien français. University of Montreal doctoral dissertation.
Emonds, J. 1978. The Verbal Complex V'-V in French. Linguistic Inquiry 9, 151-75.
Frampton, J. 1990. Parasitic Gaps and the Theory of Wh-chains. Linguistic Inquiry 21, 48-78.
Gessner, E. 1893. Die Spanische Personalpronomen. Zeitschrift für Romanische Philologie 17, 1-54.
Goodall, G. T. 1984. Parallel Structures in Syntax. University of California at San Diego doctoral dissertation. [Subsequently published by Cambridge University Press].
Gueron, J. and T. Hoekstra. 1988. T-chains and the Constituent Structure of Auxiliaries. To appear in the Proceedings of the GLOW Meeting.

Jaeggli, O. 1986. Three Issues in the Theory of Clitics: Case, Double NPs, and Extraction. In H. Borer, ed., Syntax and Semantics 19: The Syntax of Pronominal Clitics. New York: Academic Press. 15-42.

Kayne, R. 1983. Chains, Categories External to S and French Complex Inversion. Natural Language and Linguistic Theory 1, 107-139.

Kayne, R. 1985. L'accord du participe passé en français et en italien. Modèles Linguistiques VII. 73-90.

Kayne, R. 1989a. Null Subjects and Clitic Climbing. In O. Jaeggli and K. Safir, eds., The Null Subject Parameter. Dordrecht: Kluwer. 239-61.

Kayne, R. 1989b. Facets of Past Participle Agreement. In P. Benincà, ed., Dialectal Variation and the Theory of Grammar. Dordrecht: Foris. 85-103.

Kayne, R. 1989c. Romance Clitics and PRO. Paper read at NELS 20.

Kitagawa, Y. 1986. Subjects in Japanese and English. University of Massachusetts, Amherst doctoral dissertation.

Koster, J. 1987. Domains and Dynasties. Dordrecht: Foris.

Lema, J., and M. L. Rivero. 1989a. Inverted Conjugations and Verb-second Effects in Romance. To appear in C. Laeufer and T. Morgan, eds., Theoretical Analyses in Contemporary Romance Linguistics. Amsterdam: Benjamins.

Lema, J., and M. L. Rivero. 1989b. Long Head Movement: ECP vs HMC. North Eastern Linguistic Society 20, 333-47.

Lema, J. and M. L. Rivero. 1990. Types of Verbal Movement in Old Spanish: Modals, Futures, and Perfects. Ms., University of Ottawa.

Longobardi, G. 1985. Connectedness, Scope, and C-Command. Linguistic Inquiry 16, 163-92.

Luján, M. 1978. Clitic Promotion and Mood in Spanish Verbal Complements. Montreal Working Papers in Linguistics 10, 103-90, also in Linguistics 18, 381-484 (1980).

Martineau, F. 1989. La montée du clitique en moyen français: une étude de la syntaxe des constructions infinitives. University of Ottawa doctoral dissertation.

Menéndez-Pidal, R. 1964-1969. Cantar de mio Cid: texto, gramática y vocabulario, 3 vols. 4th ed. Madrid: Espasa-Calpe.

Meyer-Lübke, W. 1897. Zur Stellung der tonlosen Objektspronomina. Zeitschrift für romanische Philologie 21, 313-34.

Mussafia, A. 1886. Una particolaritá sintattica della lingua italiana dei primi secoli. Miscellanea di filologia e linguistica in memoria di N. Caix e U.A. Florence: Canello. 255-61.

Napoli, D. J. 1981. Semantic Interpretation vs. Lexical Governance. Language 57, 841-87.

Pollock, J.- Y. 1989. Verb Movement, Universal Grammar, and the Structure of IP. Linguistic Inquiry 20, 365-424.

Ramsden, H. 1963. Weak-pronoun Position in the Early Romance Languages. Manchester: Manchester University Press.

Rivero, M. L. 1986a. La tipología de los pronombres átonos en el español medieval y el español actual. Anuario de Lingüística Hispánica II, 197-220.

Rivero, M. L. 1986b. Parameters in the Typology of Clitics in Romance and Old Spanish. Language 64, 774-807.

Rivero, M. L. 1986c. Dialects and Diachronic Syntax: Free Relatives in Old Spanish. Journal of Linguistics 22, 443-54.

Rivero, M. L. 1989. Estructura flexional y movimiento(s) de verbo: Futuros, condicionales y perfectos en rumano y español medieval. To appear in Proceedings of the 19th International Congress of Romance Linguistics and Philology, Santiago de Compostela, Spain (August 1989).

Rizzi, L. 1976. Ristrutturazione. Rivista di Grammatica Generativa 1, 1-54.

Rizzi, L. 1986. On the Status of Subject Clitics in Romance. In O. Jaeggli and C. Silva-Corvalán, eds., Studies in Romance Linguistics. Dordrecht: Foris. 391-420.

Rizzi, L., and I. Roberts. 1989. Complex Inversion in French. Probus 1, 1-30.

Rochette, A. 1988. Semantic and Syntactic Aspects of Romance Complementation. MIT doctoral dissertation.

Roldán, M. M. 1974. Constraints on Clitic Insertion in Spanish. In R. J. Campbell, M. G. Goldin, and M. C. Wang, eds., Linguistic Studies in Romance Languages. Washington, D.C. : Georgetown University Press. 124-38.

Rouveret, A. 1987. Syntaxe des dépendances lexicales. Université de Paris VII thèse de doctorat d'Etat.

Salvi, G. 1989. La sopravvivenza della legge di Wackernagel nei dialetti occidentali della peninsola iberica. To appear in Medioevo Romanzo.

Staaf, E. 1906. Etude sur les pronoms abrégés en ancien espagnol. Uppsala: Lundstrom.

Strozer, J. 1976. Clitics in Spanish. UCLA doctoral dissertation.

Strozer, J. 1981. An Alternative to Restructuring in Romance Syntax. In H. Contreras, and J. Klausenburger, eds., Proceedings of the Tenth Anniversary Linguistic Symposium on Romance Languages. Seattle: University of Washington. 177-84.

Suñer, M. 1980. Clitic Promotion in Spanish Revisited. In F. Nuessel, ed., Contemporary Studies in Romance Languages. Bloomington, Ind.: IULC. 300-30.

Suñer, M. 1987. Haber + Past Participle. Linguistic Inquiry 18, 683-89.

Suñer, M. 1988. The Role of Agreement in Clitic-doubled Constructions. Natural Language and Linguistic Theory 6, 391-434.

Treviño, E. 1990. Noncanonical Subjects in Causative and Psych-Verb Constructions. Paper read at the 20th Linguistic Symposium on Romance Languages, Ottawa.

van Riemsdijk, H. 1989. Movement and Regeneration. In P. Benincà, ed., Dialect Variation and the Theory of Grammar. Dordrecht: Foris.

Wackernagel, J. 1892. Uber ein Gesetz der indogermanischen Wortstellung. Indogermanische Forschungen 1, 333-436.

Wanner, D. 1982. A History of Spanish Clitic Movement. Berkeley Linguistic Society 8, 135-47.

Wanner, D. 1987. The Development of Romance Clitic Pronouns. From Latin to Old Romance. Berlin: Mouton de Gruyter.

Wanner, D. 1988. Unstressed Object Pronouns in Old Spanish: NP vs. Clitic Status. Ms., University of Illinois.

Webelhuth, G. 1985. German is Configurational. The Linguistic Review 4, 203-46.

Williams, E. 1978. Across-the-Board Rule Application. Linguistic Inquiry 9, 31-43.

Zagona, K. 1982. Government and Proper Government of Verbal Projections. University of Washington, Seattle, doctoral dissertation.

Zanuttini, R. 1989. Two Types of Negative Markers. North Eastern Linguistic Society 20.

Indirect questions and the structure of CP: Some consequences

Margarita Suñer *
Cornell University

0 Introduction. Spanish indirect questions appear to provide evidence for a doubly-filled Comp since the complementizer *que* 'that' cooccurs with a wh-phrase in (1), and with the question word *si* 'whether/if' in (2).

(1) a. Me preguntaron [que] [a quién] invitarás tú al concierto.
to-me they-asked [that] [whom] will-invite you to-the concert
'They asked me whom you will invite to the concert.'

b. Tartamudeó [que] [cuántos libros] llevaba la niña a la escuela.

3sg-stuttered [that] [how-many books] carried the girl to the school
'S/he asked stuttering how many books the girl carried to school.'

(2) a. Le preguntaron [que] [si] su madre la visitaría la semana siguiente.
to-her they-asked [that] [if] her mother her would-visit the week next
'They asked her whether her mother would visit her next week.'

b. Repitieron [que] [si] los visitaríamos la semana siguiente.
they-repeated [that] [if] them we-would-visit the week next
'They asked repeatedly whether we would visit them next week.'[1]

However, not all verbs behave like those in (1) and (2). *Saber* 'to know', for example, disallows the cooccurrence of *que* + question word (3a), even

---

* I would like to gratefully acknowledge the comments and suggestions made to earlier drafts of this paper by W. Harbert, M. Rivero, and E. Torrego. The present version benefited from the queries posited by an anonymous referee, and from H. Campos's editorial expertise. I also thank all of my informants whose intuitions I could not have done without. As it is customary, all shortcomings must remain my responsibility.

[1] Due to the lack of the 'complementizer + wh-phrase' construction in English, the glosses of the Spanish examples can only be taken as rough approximations. All the verbs that enter into the *que* + wh constructions should be understood as 'ask' modified by the Spanish verb, i.e. 'ask repeatedly', 'ask stuttering', etc.

though it readily accepts one or the other member of the sequence by itself (3b-c).

(3) a. Juana no sabía (*que) [cuándo] visitaría a sus abuelos.
Juana didn't know (*that) when would-visit her grandparents.
'Juana didn't know when she would visit her grandparents.'

b. Todo el mundo sabía [que] Mara se había copiado en ese examen.
'Everyone knew [that] Mara had cheated in that exam.'

c. No sabemos [quién] ganará las elecciones.
'We don't know [who] will win the election.'

My objective here is to find out what the structure for this 'doubly-filled' Comp is in indirect questions, and to explain the contrast exemplified in (1)-(2) vs. (3).[2] In the process of achieving this aim, I provide evidence that wh-initial complements selected by the verbs under discussion must be divided into two: genuine indirect questions (selected by the Spanish equivalents to the *ask/wonder*-type of verb), and semi-questions (selected by the *know/tell*-predicates). Additionally, I maintain that while indirect interrogatives project a double CP structure, semi-questions project a single CP. Their different behavior with respect to extraction from wh-islands in the syntax and at LF further confirms the proposal that indirect interrogatives and semi-questions are not one and the same type of complement. Due to reasons of space, no discussion about the positions that the subject and the verb occupy in the embedded clause is undertaken in this essay.[3]

1 Indirect questions and semi-questions. In what follows, I draw from Plann's (1982) work on verbs of communication. One important generalization that Plann makes is that only those verbs of communication which can take a direct question quote (4a) can receive a true indirect question interpretation for their embedded clause (4b).

---

[2] The projection of the Spanish Comp has received considerable attention within previous frameworks. Demonte (1977) already noticed that the *que* precedes the wh-phrase. Rivero (1980) postulates a three-place Comp, and both Hurtado (1981) and Plann (1982) resort to a recursive Comp. Plann (1982) is the analysis which comes closer to the one argued for in this paper.

[3] This paper is part of a more encompassing project (started in 1986) which explores many facets of the syntax and semantics of indirect questions and semi-questions in Spanish.

(4) a. Juan preguntó/dijo/balbuceó: '¿A quién invitaron?'
Juan asked/said/babbled: 'Whom did they invite?'
(direct question quote)

   b. Juan preguntó/dijo/balbuceó que a quién habían invitado.
Juan asked/said/babbled that whom they had invited.
(indirect question)

Those verbs of communication which do not tolerate a direct question quote (5a) may still take a wh-phrase (5b), but the embedded clause is interpreted as an assertion and not as an indirect question.

(5) a. *Pilar confesó/explicó: '¿A quién protegió José?'
Pilar confessed(=revealed)/explained: 'Whom did José
protect?'
(*direct question quote)

   b. Pilar confesó/explicó (*que) a quién había protegido José.
Pilar confessed/explained (*that) whom José had protected.
(assertion)

Although traditionally the examples in both (4b) and (5b) have been considered to be indirect questions, there are reasons to cast doubts on this premise. Therefore, I keep the label 'indirect question' for the type found in (4b), and I use 'semi-question' to identify that in (5b). The two types do not behave alike in important respects. In addition to the above contrast, another difference is that only the verbs that enter the pattern in (4) permit a 'doubly-filled' Comp (i.e., *que* plus a +wh-phrase); those in (5) reject the *que*. This is Plann's second generalization: for a clause to be interpreted as an indirect question its wh-phrase must be obligatorily preceded by *que* (except for the verb *preguntar* 'to ask').
   A third difference has to do with whether there is a gap in the knowledge of the speaker. In semi-questions, cf. (5b), there is no gap in the knowledge of the speaker; therefore (6) can be felicitously continued by (6a) but not by (6b).[4]

(6) Te digo/confieso/repito cuál es su mayor ilusión . . .
'I tell/confess/repeat to you which is her dearest dream . . .'

   a. . . . dar la vuelta al mundo.
'. . . to go around the world.'

---

[4] Cf. Suñer (1989) for more details.

    b. . . . %pues yo no lo sé.[5]
    '. . . because I don't know it.'

Exactly the opposite happens with indirect questions: (7) may be continued by (7b) but not by (7a), precisely because the speaker is not in possession of the relevant piece of information.

    (7) Te pregunto/repito que cuál es su mayor ilusión . . .
        'I ask/repeat to you that which is her dearest dream . . .'

        a. . . . %dar la vuelta al mundo.
        '. . . to go around the world.'

        b. . . . pues yo no lo sé.
        '. . . because I don't know it.'

Further confirmation for this claim is provided by a syntactic test due to Ross (1971), and cited in Grimshaw (1979). Ross remarks that interrogatives may take appositive disjunctions (8a) but not appositive conjunctions (8b).

    (8) a. Bri preguntó que quién, (o sea) Paco o Pepe, la acompañaría.
        Bri asked (that) who, (namely) Paco or Pepe, would accompany her.

        b. %Bri preguntó que quiénes, (o sea) Paco y Pepe, la acompañarían.
        Bri asked (that) who, (namely) Paco and Pepe, would accompany her.

If the verbs *saber/explicar* 'to know/explain' were to introduce true interrogatives, they should pattern as in (8). That they pattern exactly opposite, that is, that they cooccur with appositive conjunctions and not with appositive disjunctions (9), further confirms our point that these verbs do not select indirect questions but semi-questions.

    (9) a. %Bri sabía/explicó quién, (o sea) Paco o Pepe, la acompañaría.
        Bri knew/explained who, (namely) Paco or Pepe, would accompany her.

---

[5] Since the oddity of this rejoinder is more semantic than syntactic in nature, I use the symbol '%' instead of the usual sign for ungrammaticality.

b. Bri sabía/explicó quiénes, (o sea) Paco y Pepe, la
acompañarían.
Bri knew/explained who, (namely) Paco and Pepe, would
accompany her.

The reasons for this disparity are not hard to find. In (8), Bri does not
know who is going to accompany her, therefore, she cannot identify the
unknown *x* with the exhaustive set of Paco **and** Pepe because of the
contradiction that ensues. The disjunction of Paco **or** Pedro is allowed
because the *x* is not exhaustively identified; it could be one or the other but
Bri is not certain of which one. In (9), the reverse holds. In this sentence
Bri knows who is going to go with her (i.e., there is no gap in her
knowledge), hence, she can positively identify her escorts.

Another important difference between true indirect questions and
semi-questions is that only the latter allow for multiple question words to be
given either a pair list answer, or an individual answer, as shown in (10).
Genuine indirect questions reject the pair list possibility; they accept only the
individual answer (11).[6]

(10) a. ¿Quién sabe/te dijo dónde compró Juan qué cosa?
'Who knows/told you where Juan bought what?'

b. Drea sabe/me dijo dónde compró Juan un reloj, y Rosa
(sabe/me dijo) dónde compró (él) un perfume.
'Drea knows/ told me where Juan bought a watch, and Rosa
knows/told me where he bought (a bottle of) perfume.'

c. Drea lo sabe/me lo dijo.
'Drea does/did.'

(11) a. ¿Quién te preguntó/dijo que dónde compró Juan
qué cosa?
'Who asked/told you that where Juan bought what?'

b. *Drea me preguntó/dijo que dónde compró Juan un reloj,
y Rosa (me preguntó/dijo) que dónde compró (él) un
perfume.
'Drea asked/told me that where Juan bought a watch, and
Rosa asked/told me that where he bought (a bottle of)
perfume.'

---

[6] See Srivastav (1990) for similar claims for Hindi.

    c.   Drea me lo preguntó/lo dijo.
        'Drea did.'

The implication of the above is that wh-phrases in semi-questions can raise at LF to the matrix Comp to produce pair list answers, while wh-phrases inside indirect questions cannot take wide scope over the matrix clause by raising at LF. In effect, indirect interrogatives form islands from which no element appears able to escape. We return to this point in section 5.

In brief, I have argued against the traditional notion that embedded wh-initial clauses under *preguntar/se* 'ask/wonder', as well as under *saber/contar* 'know/tell' matrix verbs, should be considered indirect questions. I have presented five pieces of evidence against this view and in favor of separating genuine indirect questions (introduced by the *ask/wonder*-type of verb) from semi-questions (introduced by the *know/tell*-type).

2 Selectional properties and the 'doubly-filled' Comp effect. The next logical step involves determining the extent of the 'doubly-filled' Comp effect. As already mentioned in section 1, not all verbs of communication participate in the *que* + wh construction. Essentially, there are three verb groups that do.

2.1 *Preguntar/se*. The prototypical verb used to introduce embedded interrogatives is *preguntar/se* 'to ask/ wonder'. It obligatorily selects for such a clause-type (12a); witness the ungrammaticality of (12b).

(12)   a.   Mara me preguntó que qué libros había comprado yo en Rusia.
            Mara asked me that what books I had bought in Russia.

        b.   *Mara me preguntó que yo había comprado muchos libros en Rusia.
            Mara asked me that I had bought many books in Russia.

2.2 Manner of speaking verbs. A second group is constituted by manner of speaking verbs such as *tartamudear* 'to stutter', *susurrar* 'to whisper', *balbucear* 'to babble', *sollozar* 'to whimper', *gritar* 'to shout', and also *contestar* 'to answer.'

(13)   Ani susurró/gritó/contestó que dónde habíamos puesto el dinero.
        Ani whispered/shouted/answered that where we-had put the money.

These verbs, however, select for indirect question only optionally since they also cooccur with *que* clauses (14).

(14)   Susurró/gritó/contestó   que   ya   había   almorzado.
        S/he-whispered/shouted/answered that s/he-had already
        had-lunch.

Of special interest, though, is the fact that in Spanish, manner of speaking verbs, just as their English counterparts, are incompatible with embedded clauses directly introduced by a wh-phrase.   This is another point which argues for differentiating between embedded interrogatives (13) and semi-questions (15).

(15)   *Me susurró/gritó/contestó a quién amaba.
        S/he whispered/shouted to me/answered me   who s/he loved.

2.3 *Decir* and *repetir*. Finally, verbs like *decir* 'to say/tell' and *repetir* 'to repeat' not only cooccur with true indirect questions (16), but also with assertions, whether introduced by *que* 'that' (17a) or by a wh-phrase (17b).

(16)   Dije/repetí que a quién habían detenido.
        I-said/repeated that whom they-had arrested.

(17)   a.   Dije/repetí que llamaron a Juan.
              I said/repeated that they-called Juan.

        b.   Dije/repetí a quién habían detenido.
              I said/repeated whom they-had arrested.

One thing the three sets of verbs clearly show is that Spanish has earmarked a specific construction, the *que* + wh- one, to signal indirect questions unequivocally (thus, syntactically differentiating them from semi-questions). Our immediate task, then is to explore what syntactic structure this construction has.

3 The structure of the *que* + wh- construction. The extension of X-bar theory to the nonlexical categories Det(erminer),   Infl(ection),   and Comp(lementizer) (Chomsky 1986, Fukui 1986, Fukui and Speas 1986, Abney 1987) has the important consequence for our purposes that CP has an internal structure which parallels that of lexical categories.

(18)

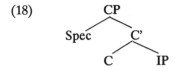

The CP in English, for instance, has a Spec(ifier) position which is the landing site for wh-type elements;[7] and a head, C⁰, which may be occupied by the complementizer (*that* and *for*) or by the fronted finite auxiliary/modal as part of the verb-second effects common in many languages. Crucially, Chomsky (1986) concludes that of the three possible elements that might materialize in pre-IP position, -- a wh-element, the fronted inflected auxiliary/modal (i.e., V_1), and the complementizer itself, -- in effect only two may cooccur. This postulate follows from the fact that only two pre-IP positions are available in CP, the Spec and the head positions, giving rise to the structure in (19).

(19) $[_{CP}$ (+wh) (V_1) IP]

It is obvious that a structure like (18) does not solve the 'doubly-filled' Comp effect that Spanish observes in indirect questions, where the complementizer *que*, a head, precedes the wh-phrase.

Within Fukui's (1986) and Fukui and Speas's (1986) well-argued theory of category projections, functional categories such as Comp and Infl project to the X double-bar level and have a unique Spec position which serves to close off the projection. This means that when the wh-word is in [Spec, CP], given the surface word order, the *que* 'that' must be outside this projection. These facts suggest the structure in (20), in which the *que* is in the head position of the upper CP.

(20)

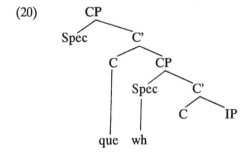

---

⁷ This follows from the version of X'-theory which assumes that Move-α obeys Emonds's (1976) Structure Preserving Hypothesis. It specifies that while X⁰ (i.e., heads) moves to head position, X^max moves to specifier position (Chomsky 1986: 4). This means that the traditional 'movement to COMP' is either movement to C or to the Spec of CP.

One mystery in (20) is the following: what could possibly be in the upper [Spec, CP] position? Is this slot ever occupied by an overt element? Although it appears that the upper Spec position is never taken by an overt element in embedded contexts, it is filled by *cómo* 'how (come)' in the non-embedded surprise type of echo questions which call for explanations, see (21) (cf. Sirbu-Dumitrescu 1988).

(21)   a.   ¿Cómo que adónde van las niñas?   (Ya te lo dije)
            how that where go the girls already to-you it I-said
            'How come that you are asking me where the girls are going?
            (I've already told you)'
       b.   ¿Cómo que dónde lo puso el perro?   (Siempre lo pone en
            el mismo lugar)
            how that where the dog put it (It always puts it in the same
            place)
            'How come that you are asking me where the dog put it?
            (It always puts it in the same place)'

To dispel any speculations that the *cómo que* 'how come' surprise type of echo questions might be derived from the *cómo es que* 'how is it that' construction by deleting the copula *ser* 'to be,' one should take the following into account: First, there is no principled way to explain this assumed copula deletion. Second, while the *cómo que* question may echo, and as such reproduce (cf. (22b)) a direct question (cf. (22a)), the *cómo es que* construction cannot (22c). The latter expression appears to require assertive clauses.

(22)   a.   A-- ¿Dónde vas de vacaciones?
            'Where are you going on vacation?'

       b.   B-- ¿Cómo que dónde voy de vacaciones?   Siempre voy a
            mi casa en la playa.
            'How come that where I go on vacation?   I always go to
            my house at the beach.'

       c.   B-- *¿Cómo es que dónde voy de vacaciones?
            'How is it that where I go on vacation?'

Finally, the discourse situations in which the two constructions are appropriately used are different. One contrastive example suffices; consider (23).

(23)   a. No me quiero casar.
'I don't want to get married.'

b. ¿Cómo es que no te quieres casar?
'How is it that you don't want to get married?'

c. ¿Cómo que no te quieres casar?
'How come that you don't want to get married?'

The utterance in (23a) can be answered with either (23b) or (23c) but the implications are not the same: with (23b), one accepts (23a) but questions the reasons for such a statement; but with (23c), the speaker is expressing incredulity and challenging the premise of (23a). Consequently, the two expressions are not synonymous.[8]

Having discarded the possibility that *cómo que* is derived from *cómo es que*, we conclude that the former provides independent empirical evidence for the projection in (20). I assume that the top [Spec, CP] position in (20) is occupied by a null operator whose function is to mark the whole structure as an indirect question (more about this in section 4).

Before continuing to discuss the structure in (20), I entertain and reject two other alternatives.

(a) Adjunction to IP. One such alternative would maintain that there is only one CP projection with *que* 'that' as head; the fronted wh-phrase would be adjoined to IP, see (24).

(24)

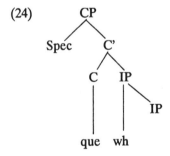

An immediate problem with this structure is that it cannot account for selectional properties. I follow the general Government and Binding framework assumption that the lexical entry of verbs specifies whether or not a given verb can take an indirect question as its complement, that is, the

---

[8] I am indebted to D. Sirbu-Dumitrescu (p.c.) for the second argument, and for discussing the third one with me.

selectional properties of the head of the construction determine the kinds of complements it can accept. In the ideal system where categorial selection is derived from these semantic properties (Pesetsky 1983, Chomsky 1986: 86ff), verbs select semantically for or against an interrogative complement (I return to this topic in section 4). However, in (24) the wh-phrase is not in head position; rather it is an adjoined XP, that is, a maximal projection. Even if a mechanism were to be posited so that this adjoined phrase could count as satisfying selection, it would run against empirical evidence which suggests that adjoined elements are disregarded for selectional purposes. Consider (25), where after the *que*, there appears a (non-wh) XP (in bold) adjoined to the wh-introduced CP.

(25) a. Me preguntaron que a **Juan**$_i$, qué le$_i$ habría prometido el decano.
          They asked me that **to John**$_i$, what the dean could have promised to him$_i$.

      b. Me preguntaron que a **mi hijo**$_i$, dónde lo$_i$ iban a mandar los militares.
          They asked me that **my son**$_i$, where the military were going to send him$_i$.

It is clear that the adjoined XPs above are instances of left-dislocations (note the clitics with which these (definite) phrases are mandatorily coindexed) which do not interfere with the fact that the matrix V requires an interrogative complement.

Consequently, the reasons just presented lead me to reject (24) as a possible structure for indirect questions. [9]

(b) [Spec, IP] landing. The second alternative is made possible by the claim that subjects are generated VP-internally (Zagona 1982, Koopman and Sportiche 1986, 1988, Contreras 1987, Mallén 1988, Sportiche 1988, among many others). I assume that (non ergative) subjects are generated in [Spec, VP]. If so, in a null subject language like Spanish, which does not require the subject to obligatorily move to [Spec, IP] for Case-theoretic reasons (as happens in English), the [Spec, IP] position provides a potential landing site for the fronted wh-phrase, as in (26) (non relevant details aside) (cf. Diesing 1988 and 1990 for Yiddish).

---

[9] This conclusion leaves open the possibility that IP-adjunction of wh-phrases may be used as a escape hatch to surmount wh-island violations; cf. Frampton (1990), and section 5.

(26)

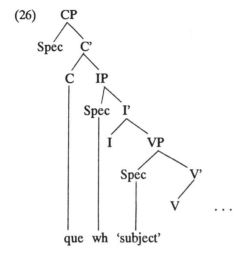

que   wh 'subject'

However (26), besides running into the same difficulties with respect to fulfilling the selectional properties of matrix verbs that (24) encountered, confronts additional problems.

First, although thematic wh-question words (cf. (1)) obligatorily trigger subject-verb inversion, questions with *si* 'whether' (cf. (2)) and the questioning of adjuncts (27) do not (Torrego 1984).

(27)   a.   Me pregunto/digo [que] [por qué] *el gobernador* no firma ese proyecto en ley.
I wonder/say that why *the governor* doesn't sign that project into law.

b.   ¿[En qué medida] *la constitución* ha contribuido a eso?
In what way has *the Constitution* contributed to that?[10]
(Torrego 1984: 106)

---

[10] There are speakers who question the well-formedness of examples like (i) with a preverbal subject.
(i)   ¿Por qué Juan no estudiará?
Why John wouldn't study?
However, I believe this judgment is caused by performance factors having to do with what I label 'balance'. Once the sentence is balanced by lengthening it, the same speakers consider it acceptable.
(ii)   ¿Por qué Juan no estudiará más para la clase de química?
Why John wouldn't study more for the chemistry class?

Considering that a finite V raises to I obligatorily in Spanish,[11] and that the position of the negative element *no* 'not' must be higher than I but lower than the [Spec, IP], the word order in (27) strongly suggests that the (underlined) subject is in [Spec, IP] in this type of example. But, if this is so, the fronted wh-phrase could not be in [Spec, IP] as well.

Second, one of the subdialects of colloquial Caribbean Spanish is well known for requiring obligatory subject-verb word order in questions, even in instances of thematic wh-phrases (28) (cf. Suñer 1986a).

(28) a. Me dijo [que] [cuántas capas] *yo* llevaba debajo.
S/he asked me that how many layers *I* was-wearing underneath.

b. ¿Qué *Iván* dijo de eso?
What *Iván* said about that?

c. ¿Dónde diablos *Juan* lo puso?
Where on-earth *Juan* put it?

Given the obligatoriness of V to I, the implication is that the italicized subjects in (28) must be in [Spec, IP] by S-structure. But since the wh-phrases precede the subjects, they must be in other than [Spec, IP] position.

In brief, if the wh's in instances like (27) and (28) cannot land in [Spec, IP], I see no strong reasons for postulating that wh-phrases might be in [Spec, IP] sometimes, that is, when the subject is not occupying such position. Not only would we be missing the generalization that wh-phrases have a uniform landing site in general Spanish, but we would have to claim that Caribbean Spanish differs from general Spanish precisely in that it does have such a uniform site (i.e., [Spec, CP]).

---

[11] One way to show this is by noticing that VP-adverbs (cf. (i)) and the quantifier *todos* 'all' (cf. (ii)) intervene between the main verb and its complement.
(i) a. Habla *bien* el chino.
s/he speaks *well* Chinese
'S/he speaks Chinese well.'
b. Conocen *perfectamente* sus circunstancias.
They understand *perfectly* their situation.
(ii) Los niños comieron *todos* la sopa.
the children(m, pl) ate *all*(m, pl) the soup
'All the children ate the soup.'
According to Pollock's (1989) analysis, Spanish qualifies as having an Agr rich enough to be 'transparent' to theta-role assignment.

Furthermore, from a conceptual standpoint, Koopman and Sportiche (1988) conclude that [Spec, IP] is an A-position even though it is a non-theta position. This means that if a wh-phrase were to land in [Spec, IP], the wh-would be locally A-binding its coindexed variable in violation of the dictum that variables must be A-bar bound.

In short, empirical and theoretical considerations argue against structure (26) for embedded indirect questions.[12]

To summarize this section, we have examined two possible alternative structures to the projection given in (20), and since neither of them proved empirically and/or conceptually superior to it, we conclude that (20) must be the correct representation for the CP projection of embedded interrogatives in Spanish.

4 Selection revisited. In section 2, the three groups of verbs which cooccur with indirect interrogatives were presented, and in section 3 the CP structure for this type of complement was justified (cf. (20)). What remains to be discussed is how exactly these verbs select for indirect questions *vis-à-vis* the projection in (20) (repeated here for convenience).

(20)

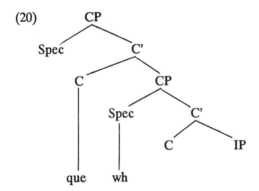

Recall that we are following the common practices of the GB framework in considering that selection is a head-to-head relationship. Therefore, let us posit that the relevant verbs select for a [+wh] complement, as is often done in the literature. One immediate roadblock to this hypothesis is that it falls short of distinguishing between genuine indirect questions and semi-questions, so that, for example, both complements in (29) would be characterized as [+wh] despite their differences pointed out in section 1.

---

[12] The correctness of our argumentation would prevent [Spec, IP] from serving as a escape hatch for wh-movement (contra Lema 1989).

(29) a. Dijeron que qué película ganó el Oscar. (indirect question)
They-said (= asked by saying) that which movie won the
Oscar.

  b. Dijeron qué película ganó el Oscar. (semi-question)
They-said which movie won the Oscar.

In addition, by treating both complements alike, this proposal fails to capture the fact that manner-of-speaking verbs cooccur with embedded interrogatives but not with assertive complements introduced by a wh-phrase (cf. (13) vs. (15)). Consequently, the features [± wh] do not provide a rich enough system to encompass the Spanish data.

One shortcoming with the features [± wh] is that they are used ambiguously in the literature. On the one hand, they are used to signal syntactic cooccurrence, such as that of a verb which tolerates wh-phrases in its embedded Comp; on the other hand, they are used to indicate semantic selection, as in the case of a verb which selects for an interrogative complement. Note that although syntactic and semantic cooccurrence might coincide (e.g., *preguntar/se* 'ask/wonder'), this is not necessarily true in all instances (e.g., manner-of-speaking verbs in Spanish, or the *decir/repetir* 'to say/repeat' usage in both languages, cf. (29b)). In order to avoid this ambiguity, I will use capital [± WH] to indicate semantic selection,[13] but lower case [± wh] to refer to the lexico/syntactic feature. This results in four possible feature combinations (30). The question is: are all of them realized? In other words, what types of complements are predicted to exist?

(30)	Semantic	Syntactic	Complement types
a	+WH	+wh	indirect questions
b	+WH	-wh	*
c	-WH	+wh	semi-questions
d	-WH	-wh	*que/that* clauses

It is obvious that of the four possibilities, only three come true. We could speculate that the slot in (30b) corresponds to yes/no indirect questions introduced by *si* 'if/whether' (cf. (2)), since strictly speaking, Spanish *si* does not have the appearance of a syntactic wh- (or Qu-). However, yes/no indirect questions parallel in all pertinent aspects the *que* + wh construction, crucially they are selected by the same verb groups, cf. (31).

---

[13] This [+WH] semantic feature (in head position) is one manifestation of the 'Q' operator (which I assume to be in [Spec, CP]) postulated in Baker (1970) for matrix questions.

(31)   Drea preguntó/dijo/balbuceó *que si* la podía ayudar (o no).
        Drea asked/said/babbled *that if* I could (or couldn't) help
        her.

Therefore, I assume that *si* is a [+wh] question word which occupies the
[Spec, CP] position. Although a full exposition about Spanish *si* would take
us too far afield, some additional evidence is in order. Note that *si* does in
indirect questions (31) what intonation does in direct questions (32).

(32)   ¿Me puedes ayudar (o no)?
        Can (or can't) you help me?

Hence, *si* appears to be the overt counterpart of the [+Q] null operator of
yes/no direct questions already posited by Baker (1970). For Catalan, Rigau
(1984) also correlates the behavior of *si* with that of other wh-phrases.
Following Huang (1982), she hypothesizes that *si* is an operator moved to
Comp, from where it binds the variable left in Infl. For our purposes, all
that is relevant is that Spanish *si* displays the behavior of a wh-phrase in
[Spec, CP]; whether it is base-generated or moved to [Spec, CP] is not
crucial.[14]

But if *si* indirect questions do not take up the slot in (30b), we are still
confronted with the quandary of explaining the gap in (30b). I do not have
a principled explanation for it; intuitively, though, it seems that a semantic
[+WH], i.e., a question, demands a syntactic wh-phrase because only wh-
phrases act as operators which signal a request for information meant to fill

---

[14] Nothing in the theory seems to prevent base-generation of *si* (provided it binds a variable
in the lower clause). For example, Chomsky (1986: 5) states that the wh-phrases and other
similar elements could either be base-generated or moved to pre-IP position. Sobin (1987)
assumes that English 'whether' occupies the same position as 'that' (i.e., C^0). However, 'whether'
partakes in the quantifier-like properties of other wh-phrases; therefore, it makes sense for it
to be in Spec. Support for this hypothesis can be deduced from the fact that although sequences
of two elements are known to have been permitted (e.g. 'who that'), as in (i), no 'who whether'
attestation has ever been found (Sobin 1987: 53).
(i) Men shal wel knowe [who that] I am. (Middle English; Lightfoot 1979)
Moreover, the contrast between (ii) and (iii) would be hard to explain if both 'that' and 'whether'
were in head position.
(ii)   What did you say [$_{CP}$ t that [$_{IP}$ John bought e]]
(iii)   *What did you wonder [$_{CP}$ t whether [$_{IP}$ John bought e]]
On the other hand, if 'whether' were in [Spec, CP], the landing site in the embedded Comp
would be filled and movement of 'what' to the matrix in (iii) would violate Subjacency.
Kayne (1987) considers Romance *se/si* 'whether' to be in C and not in Spec of CP. For the
disjunctive readings of English 'whether', see Larson (1985).

a gap in the speakers' knowledge. No other phrases seem to overtly carry this function.

With this background we concentrate on the details of semantic selection. The procedure must be something like the following: Whenever one of the *ask*-type of verbs discussed in section 2 selects for an interrogative complement, the [+WH] verbal head requires a [+WH] CP. But if the CP is [+WH], its head must also be so marked because selection is by hypothesis a head-to-head relationship. Thus, the implication is that the [+WH] feature percolates to the head, cf. (33).

(33) V $[_{CP/+WH}$ $[_{C'}$ C°] ...
+WH   +WH

According to the CP projection in (20), the head of C in (33) is the one occupied by *que* 'that', which immediately suggests that the Spanish complementizer, contrary to the general assumption, is [± WH]. Moreover, whenever *que* is [+WH] as in (33), it requires that the head of its complement, the lower CP, be [+WH] also. The complete 'selection chain' is as in (34).

(34) V $[_{CP1/+WH}$ $[_{C'}$ que] $[_{CP2/+WH}$ $[_{C'}$ C°] $[_{IP}$ ...
+WH   +WH   +WH

I do not expect these claims and/or their implications to be uncontroversial; therefore, I clarify several issues. First, let us assume, contrary to (34), that the *que* is always [-WH]. This would have the disadvantage that a selected [+WH] CP would have a nonmatching head--a head which, in addition, would have to select a [+WH] CP$_2$. Obviously, this is not a very desirable result for any framework which postulates selection as a head-to-head relationship. The question is: can the [+WH] *que* select an interrogative complement on its own, that is, when it is not itself selected by the *ask*-type of verbs? Indeed, this appears to be the case. *Que* is commonly used to introduce echo questions as in (35c).

(35) a. A-- ¿A qué hora salimos?
          What time do we leave?

      b. B-- ¿Qué dijiste?
          What did you say?

      c. A-- **Que** [a qué hora salimos]
          That [at what time we leave]

The *que* in (35c) must be [+WH] because the following CP is only interpreted as a(n echo) question and never as a semi-question.[15] In brief, the [+WH] feature of *que* is theoretically and empirically justified.

Second, in (34) the head of CP_2 must also be [+WH] for selection to operate correctly. This suggests that Spanish has a null [+WH] complementizer, as suggested by Platzack (1986) for the Germanic languages.

Third, Spec-head agreement requires matching between the two relevant elements. Thus, since both C heads in (34) are [+WH], their specifiers must carry this feature also. We know that the lower [+WH] feature is satisfied by the wh-phrase moved to the Spec of CP_2. But how is the top [+WH] Spec feature satisfied? Our hypothesis, already mentioned in section 3, is that this position is taken by a null [+Q] operator. That this Spec position is indeed projected is corroborated by Fukui's Functional Projection Theorem. It maintains that the Spec position of a functional category appears only when the functional head has certain features to assign; if the head has no such features, the projection of the functional category stops at the single-bar level. Since the *que* which introduces indirect questions has been shown to be [+WH], it should sanction its Spec position.[16] This null [+Q] operator in the Spec position of CP_1 serves to identify the double CP structure as interrogative. Note that an indirect question is just that: the reproduction or quoting (with the necessary deictic accommodations) of a previously stated direct question (cf. (4) and (31)-(32)). Following Partee (1973), the *que* would be the 'quotation morpheme', while the lower CP would be what is being quoted indirectly. The implication of this argumentation is that while the double CP structure of embedded interrogatives contains two operators (one in each of the Spec positions), the single CP of semi-questions has only one such operator. To avoid possible confusions, allow me to provide the (partial) structures after Move-α has taken place, for indirect questions with their embedded double CP (36) and for semi-questions with their single CP (37).

(36)   Indirect questions

---

[15] For a detailed study of echo questions in Spanish and Romanian, see Sîrbu-Dumitrescu (1988).

[16] Fukui (1986: 55) provides the following table for functional categories in English, where his [±K-assigner] is reinterpreted as [±AGR]:

	C	I	DET
[+AGR]	wh	Tn/AGR	's
[-AGR]	that	to	the

a. Selecting verbs: *preguntar(se)* 'to ask/wonder', *decir* 'to say', *repetir* 'to repeat' (manner of speaking verbs (cf. section 2))

b. V [$_{CP1}$ OP [$_{C'}$ que] [$_{CP2}$ wh-phr [$_{C'}$ C°] [IP ...

c. Mara preguntó/repitió/balbuceó *que dónde* estaba la niña.
Mara asked/repeated/babbled *that where* the girl was.

(37) Semi-questions

a. Selecting verbs: *saber* 'to know', *explicar* 'to explain', *repetir* 'to repeat', etc.

b. V [$_{CP}$ wh-phr [$_{C'}$ C°] [$_{IP}$ ...
c. Mara sabía/explicó/repitió *dónde* estaba la niña.
Mara knew/explained/repeated *where* the girl was.

Formal semantics corroborates this since in this framework, indirect questions are translated by two lambda operators (i.e., $\lambda a \lambda i (\phi)$, i.e., by the function from worlds into propositions (λa), and by the function from world into truth values (λi)), while the translation of semi-questions requires just one lambda (i.e., $\lambda i (\phi)$). A full discussion of this aspect of embedded interrogatives and semi-questions will take us away from our main concern, I direct the interested reader to Suñer (1989) for elaboration.

Having explored and justified selection of indirect interrogatives, one further detail must be addressed before bringing this section to a close. The verb *preguntar/se* 'to ask/wonder' is unique in that it unambiguously selects for interrogatives; thus no confusion with another interpretation is ever possible. Consequently, this verb is the only one discussed which permits the [+WH] *que* to be null while the embedded clause is still interpreted unequivocally as an indirect question (38).

(38) Sam preguntó (que) dónde lo había yo puesto.
Sam asked (that) where I had put it.

With the other groups of verbs, the omission of the *que* would cause the sentence to be interpreted as other than an indirect question, due to the double selection (interrogative and semi-question) proper to these verbs; therefore, the *que* becomes obligatory. That the clauses without the *que* cannot be ambiguously interpreted is explained by the fact that Spanish has developed the *que* + wh construction specifically to introduce nondirect questions.[17]

But why is a [+WH] *que* by itself unable to fulfill the selection requirements of the matrix verb *preguntarse*, that is, why is (39) ungrammatical?

(39)   *Preguntaron [que   Ø   los visitaríamos en enero]
             [+WH]   [+WH]
        They wondered that we would visit them in January.

The answer is simple: a [+WH] *que* demands a [+WH] CP as complement, a condition which is not met in the example above.

5   Wh-island effects.   Given that Spanish verbs of the *ask*-type have been shown to have an embedded double Comp projection (cf. (20)), but that verbs that select semi-questions do not, it is to be expected that some direct consequences should follow from this difference.   This expectation is fulfilled by their disparate behavior concerning extraction from wh-islands in the syntax proper (5.1) as well as at LF (5.2).

5.1   Syntactic wh-islands.   Spanish can violate the wh-island condition under certain circumstances.   Leaving aside factors extraneous to our central quest (for details, see Torrego 1984, Suñer 1987), consider the grammatical examples with embedded semi-questions in (40).

(40)   a.   ¿Quién no recuerdas cuándo llegó a este país?
             who don't you remember when s/he arrived in this country?

        b.   ¿A cuántos te dijeron si había invitado Carlos?
             how many did they tell you whether Carlos had invited?

        c.   ¿A cuáles de ellos sabes quién no les dio una buena recomendación?
             which of them do you know who didn't give them a good recommendation?

---

[17] Girón Alchonchel (1988) states that this use of *que* does not appear in the language until the first half of the thirteenth century. However, M. Rivero (p.c.) cautions that since extensive documents begin only around 1250, the absence of the *que* + wh construction before the thirteenth century could correlate with the paucity of materials.

On the other hand, extraction out of true indirect questions always yields ungrammatical results (41).[18]

(41)   a. *¿Quién preguntaste/dijiste que cuándo llegó a este país?
            who did you ask/said that when s/he arrived in this country?

          b. *¿A cuántos preguntaron/repitieron que si había invitado Carlos?
            how many did they ask/repeat that whether Carlos had invited?

          c. *¿A cuáles de ellos preguntó/susurró que quién no les había dado una buena recomendación?
            which of them did s/he ask/whisper that who hadn't given them a good recommendation?[19]

Since the verb *preguntar(se)* 'to ask/wonder' does not obligatorily require *que* 'that' to precede the wh-phrase, it might be speculated that its omission might influence grammaticality judgments. That this is not the case is shown by (42).

(42)   a. *¿Qué te preguntas dónde compró Luis?
            what do you wonder where Luis bought?

          b. *¿Quién preguntaste si llamó por teléfono?
            who did you ask whether telephoned?

Not even the most favorable context for extraction, that is, extraction from an infinitival interrogative and *que* omission, leads to improved examples (43).

---

[18] Torrego (1984: 114, fn. 25) notes this for the verb *preguntarse* 'wonder' without attempting an explanation.
    For Italian, Rizzi (1982: 51) points out that extraction of an interrogative pronoun from within a wh-island gives variable results (his examples).
    (i)   *Chi ti domandi chi ha incontrato?
         who do you wonder who __ met __?
    (ii) ??Chi non sai che cosa ha fatto?
         who don't you know what __ did __?
    (iii) ??A chi non sai che cosa ho detto?
         to whom don't you know what said __ __?
Note the contrast in judgments between the equivalents of 'wonder' (which selects an interrogative complement), and 'know' (which selects a semi-question).
[19] Example (41c) is grammatical with the higher wh-phrase interpreted (irrelevantly for our purposes) as indirect object of the matrix.

(43) a. *¿Cuántos de estos libros te preguntas cuándo donar?
         how many of these books do you wonder when to donate?

      b. *¿Qué preguntaste si comer?
         what did you ask whether to eat?

I take (42) and (43) as evidence that *que* omission with *preguntar(se)* 'to ask/wonder' does not result in a simplification of the double CP projection in (20), but rather that [+WH] *que* has a null counterpart.

A final contrastive example will further reinforce my point. Chomsky (1986: 25ff), while discussing that CP is not an inherent barrier to movement, cites Torrego's observation that a NP can be extracted from a wh-phrase in [Spec, CP]. This shows that this position is governed by the selecting verb. It is important to us that Torrego's example contains the verb *saber* 'to know' which selects for semi-questions, cf. (44a). Note that the extraction is blocked when the matrix verb selects for indirect interrogatives, as is the case with *preguntar* 'to ask' in (44b).

(44) a. Este es el autor [del que]ᵢ no sabemos
         [CP[qué libros tᵢ] leer]
         This is the author of whom we don't know
         which books   to read

      b. *[de quién]ᵢ preguntaste [CP [que] [CP [cuáles fotos tᵢ]
         vender
         of whom did you ask that which pictures
         to sell

So once again we have proof that the two complement types do not behave alike.

We need to explain this disparity concerning extraction from the two complement types. Let us consider the CP structure for semi-questions (45) first.

(45)   semi-questions

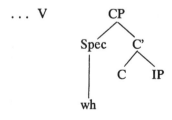

In the *Barriers* model extraction from wh-islands always crosses (at least) one barrier because IP is not L-marked and, therefore, CP inherits barrierhood from it.[20] In what follows, I adopt Frampton's (1990) modifications of the *Barriers* model so that IP adjunction can serve as a possible escape-hatch for wh-phrases provided the adjoined element is licensed by canonical head-government.[21; 22] Due to the obligatoriness of the movement of V to I in Spanish, VP is not a barrier; thus IP does not inherit barrierhood from it. The long-extracted wh- first adjoins to IP which means that, by the segment theory of domination (May 1985, Chomsky 1986), IP does not include the adjoined element; from this position the wh- is free to move directly to the matrix [Spec, CP] without crossing any barriers since CP is theta-governed and L-marked by the matrix verb. We still need to ascertain whether the IP-adjoined *t* is adequately licensed. The Head Government Condition on Adjunction (HGCA) requires that the matrix verb canonically govern this *t*. Since there are no intervening barriers, it does so by definition (46).

(46)   X head-governs Y if X is a head that s-governs Y and there are no nonempty heads that intervene between X and Y.

                                                                          (Frampton 1990: 62)

The trace, however, is not antecedent-governed because the wh-phrase in [Spec, CP] interferes with this government (cf. Rizzi 1990). Consequently, unless the initial *t* is lexically governed in its base-generated position, no extraction out of the wh-island would be possible. The immediate outcome of this is that, although arguments may be so extracted (cf. (40)), adjuncts cannot (47).

(47)   a.   *¿Cuándo no recuerdas quién llegó a este país?
                 when don't you remember who arrived in this country?

---

[20] The following definitions are from Chomsky (1986: 15).
    (i) α theta-govern β iff α is a zero-level category that theta-marks β, and α, β are sisters.
    (ii) α L-marks β iff α is a lexical category that theta-governs β.
[21] See also Fiengo et al. (1988) for an alternative on extraction from wh-islands.
[22] This is Frampton's (1990: 52) Head Government Condition on Adjunction (HGCA):
    (i) A wh-element can only be adjoined to a maximal projection XP from a position that is canonically governed by the head of XP.
Frampton justifies the IP adjunction with parasitic gap phenomena, the *that*-trace effect, and extraction from wh-islands.

    b. *¿Dónde te dijeron a cuántos habían invitado?
        where did they tell you how many they had invited?[23]

In brief, the theory corroborates the empirical fact that long extraction of a
wh-phrase from a semi-question is indeed possible in Spanish (under certain
conditions).

    Let us now consider indirect questions. They have the CP structure in
(20) which, after the IP-adjunction of the wh-phrase, results in (48).

    (48)   indirect questions

$$\ldots \text{V} \quad \begin{array}{c} \text{CP}_1 \\ \diagup\diagdown \\ \text{Spec} \quad \text{C'} \\ | \quad\quad \diagup\diagdown \\ \text{Op} \quad \text{que} \quad \text{CP}_2 \\ \diagup\diagdown \\ \text{wh} \quad \text{C'} \\ \diagup\diagdown \\ \text{C} \quad \text{IP} \\ \diagup\diagdown \\ t_{\text{wh}} \quad \text{IP} \end{array}$$

The reasoning is parallel to that just used for semi-questions except for the
added complication of having a double CP projection. Once the wh- adjoins
to IP, it must jump over this double Comp because the Spec positions are not
available for landing. Can it do so without crossing any barriers? And
would the t_{wh} be head-governed by the *ask*-type of matrix verb? The answer
is negative for both. Let us see why. In (48), the verb L-marks CP_1 but not
CP_2. In turn, CP_1 does not L-mark CP_2 because L-marking depends on being
a lexical category able to theta-govern its complement, a property that *que*
'that' lacks; therefore, CP_2 is a barrier by inheritance (Chomsky 1986); CP_1
becomes a barrier also. This means that the matrix verb is not able to head-
govern t_{wh} for two reasons: (a) the barriers and (b) the intervening head *que*
(by (46)), regardless of whether the head is overt or not (recall examples in
(42)-(43)). Therefore, the impossibility of extraction from genuine indirect
question follows.

    5.2 Wh-islands at LF. When discussing the differences between semi-
questions and indirect questions in section 1, we mentioned that only the

---

[23] Once again the examples are grammatical with the higher wh- as part of the matrix.

former can receive pair-list answers to multiple questions. Examples (10) and (11) are repeated for ease of exposition.

(10) a. ¿Quién sabe/te dijo dónde compró Juan qué cosa?
          Who knows/told you where Juan bought what?

      b. Drea sabe/me dijo dónde compró Juan un reloj, y Rosa
          (sabe/me dijo) dónde compró (él) un perfume.
          Drea knows/ told me where Juan bought a watch, and Rosa
          knows/told me where he bought (a bottle of) perfume.

      c. Drea lo sabe/me lo dijo.
          Drea does/did.

(11) a. ¿Quién te preguntó/dijo que dónde compró Juan qué cosa?
          Who asked/told you that where Juan bought what?

      b. *Drea me preguntó/dijo que dónde compró Juan un reloj,
          y Rosa (me preguntó/dijo) que dónde compró (él) un
          perfume.
          Drea asked/told me that where Juan bought a watch, and
          Rosa asked/told me that where he bought (a bottle of)
          perfume.

      c. Drea me lo preguntó/lo dijo.
          Drea did.

This distribution of the data indicates that while a verb like *know* permits both a wide (49a) and a narrow (49b) scope interpretation, one like *ask* only accepts the second alternative (49b).

(49) a. for which person x and thing y, x V where Juan bought y

      b. for which person x, x V for which thing y, where Juan
          bought y

In essence, LF raising of the relevant wh-phrase to the matrix is blocked in interrogative complements but permitted in semi-question ones. The implication of this finding is that the LF behavior of wh-phrases parallels their syntactic behavior. The ideal situation, then, would demand a parallel explanation.

No problems arise with the pair-list possibility for semi-questions, since we already saw that the CP projection in (45) creates no barriers for extraction, and that the matrix verb canonically governs the IP-adjoined (argument) trace; i.e., there is no ECP violation. However, when considering the structure of indirect questions (48), we discovered that there are two barriers (hence a Subjacency violation), and a failure to head-govern the adjoined trace (hence an ECP violation). The difficulty with this double violation is that the general assumption within GB (e.g., Chomsky 1981 and 1986, Huang 1982, Lasnik and Saito 1984, among others) is that although the ECP operates at the LF level, Subjacency constrains overt Move-α (or the resulting structure) in the syntax proper but not at LF. However, this asymmetry between the syntax and LF remains a stipulation.

Fiengo et al. (1988) (and references therein) hypothesize that although Subjacency operates at LF, its effects are not visible in English (or Chinese) because the whole island adjoins to IP, after which the relevant phrase is able to raise without crossing any barriers. In other words, they derive the lack of 'visible' Subjacency effects from the theory of adjunction and the existence of QR at LF (vs. its absence in the syntax).

The hypothesis that, all other things being equal, no asymmetry with respect to Subjacency should exist between syntax and LF, receives strong support from Spanish. We have seen that while extraction out of semi-questions is permitted at both levels, extraction from genuine indirect questions is blocked in the syntax and in LF. The conclusion can only be that Subjacency is active at both levels because of the barriers that emerge due to the double Comp projection proper to this kind of complement. This outcome explains the absence of pair list answers to multiple questions (11b) with *ask*-type of verbs.

To sum up this section on wh-island effects, we have seen that with respect to extraction from wh-islands in the syntax and at LF, the contrasting behavior of Spanish *ask*-verbs and *know/tell*-verbs confirms our claim that indirect interrogatives and semi-questions should not be considered one and the same type of complement. At the same time, we have shown that each complement type patterns identically irrespective of the level (syntax or LF), a strong indication that the syntax/LF asymmetry with respect to Subjacency is illusory, as Fiengo et al. hypothesized.

6 Conclusion and speculations. The main thrust of this paper has been twofold. First, I have provided evidence showing that the wh- introduced complements under discussion here are of two kinds: true indirect questions and semi-questions. Second, I have argued that their CP projections are different; while semi-questions have the same kind of CP as English does, indirect interrogatives display a double CP projection that arises through selection (as opposed to free recursion). Essentially, Spanish has developed a specific structure, the double CP one, to accommodate the sequence *que* + wh- to signal indirect question complements. This double CP directly accounts for the failure of wh-phrases inside indirect questions to extract, contrary to what happens with those in semi-questions. However, it seems to be the case that languages that do not allow a double Comp projection, such as Italian (recall the examples in footnote 16) and even English in a limited way (50), have more trouble extracting from a wh-clause under *ask/wonder* than under the *know/tell* type of verbs.[24]

(50)   a.   ?*Which papers do you wonder where to file?

      a'.   *Which papers do you wonder where John filed?

      b.   ?Which papers do you know where to file?

      b.'   ??Which papers do you know where John filed?

Furthermore, the contrast between the two V-types is preserved at LF since in English, just as in Spanish (recall (10)-(11)), it is possible to give a pair-list answer to multiple wh-phrases when the matrix verb belongs to the *know/tell*-class (51a), but not when it is *ask/wonder* (51b).

(51)   a.   Who knows where John got what?

      b.   Who wonders where John got what?

If this difference extends to other languages as well, then it indicates that there is a generalization begging to be captured. The question is then how to do this. In what follows, I sketch a tentative proposal.

    Consider that the two verb classes under discussion select for different types of complements: a real question for the *ask*-type vs. a semi-question (i.e., an assertion) for the *know/tell* type. In the ideal system, 'meaning' and 'form' should match up. Spanish manages to approach this ideal system in the realm under discussion because it has a different syntactic structure for each kind of complement. English does not. However, English behaves (cf.

---

[24] The 'ungrammaticality' symbols used in (50) are arbitrary. What is important is that the (a) pair is worse than the (b) one, and that the tensed version in each set is worse than the corresponding infinitival. That tensed complements in English give rise to stronger 'ungrammaticality' judgments than infinitival ones has long been known; see, for example, Chomsky (1986: 37), where the speculation is that 'tensed IP is an inherent barrier (possibly weak) to wh-movement, over and above the system just outlined...'

(50)-(51)) as if it did.   Under the Universal Grammar hypothesis, this situation is not surprising since languages are not expected to vary wildly. One possibility would be to acknowledge the fact that syntactic representations at times poorly correlate with lexical conceptual structure (cf. Hale and Keyser 1988).   Although this is unquestionably true, Spanish gives us proof that the match-up of syntax and semantics is indeed a possibility in this instance. Hence, a more enlightening hypothesis would maintain that English has the same two different Comp projections that Spanish does (i.e., (45) and (20)), except that the double CP structure is not readily apparent in English but only indirectly evident because of its effects, as in (50) and (51).   In other words, English would have the projection in (52) but CP_1 is always empty (perhaps because *that* has no [+WH] counterpart).   However, if selection is indeed a head-to-head relationship, the upper C must be [+WH] agreeing with the null operator.

(52)   V
      ask/wonder CP_1
              Op   C'
                     C CP_2
                  [+WH]   wh   C'
                              C   IP
                           [+WH]

Since the double CP structure in both languages is a matter of selection, no other verbs except for those lexically specified to select indirect interrogatives would be able to appear in the structure in (52).

In brief, I have taken the direct evidence that Spanish provides for distinguishing between two kinds of complements and tentatively extended it to English, where although the overt signals are less transparent, the data in (50)-(51) suggest that this is a reasonable step to take.   Note that my hypothesis, which obviously needs to be further verified, is perfectly consonant with the research plan sponsored by a Universal Grammar vision of the theory of grammar.

References

Abney, S. 1987. The English Noun Phrase in Its Sentential Aspect. MIT doctoral dissertation.

Baker, C. L. 1970. Notes on the Description of English Questions: The Role of an Abstract Question Morpheme. Foundations of Language 6, 197-219.

Chomsky, N. 1977. On WH-Movement. In P. Culicover et al., eds., Formal Syntax. New York: Academic Press. 71-132.

Chomsky, N. 1981. Lectures on Government and Binding. Dordrecht: Foris.

Chomsky, N. 1986. Barriers. Cambridge, Mass.: MIT Press.

Contreras, H. 1987. Small Clauses in English and Spanish. Natural Language and Linguistic Theory 5, 225-243.

Demonte, V. 1977. La subordinación sustantiva. Madrid: Cátedra.

Diesing, M. 1988. Word Order and the Subject Position in Yiddish. NELS 18 (Toronto), 124-40.

Diesing, M. 1990. Verb Movement and the Subject Position in Yiddish. Natural Language and Linguistic Theory 8, 41-79.

Emonds, J. 1976. A Transformational Approach to English Syntax. New York: Academic Press (original manuscript 1969).

Fiengo, R., J. C. T. Huang, H. Lasnik, and T. Reinhart. 1988. The Syntax of Wh-in-situ. WCCFL 7.

Frampton, J. 1990. Parasitic Gaps and the Theory of Wh-chains. Linguistic Inquiry 21, 49-77.

Fukui, N. 1986. A Theory of Category Projection and Its Applications. MIT doctoral dissertation.

Fukui, N., and M. Speas. 1986. Specifiers and Projections. MIT Working Papers, vol. 8, 128-72.

Girón Alchonchel, J. L. 1988. Las interrogativas indirectas en el español medieval. Madrid: Gredos.

Grimshaw, J. 1979. Complement Selection and the Lexicon. Linguistic Inquiry 10, 279-326.

Hale, K., and S. J. Keyser. 1988. Explaining and Constraining the English Middle. Lexicon Project Working Papers 24, 41-57.

Huang, C-T. 1982. Logical Relations in Chinese and the Theory of Grammar. MIT doctoral dissertation.

Hurtado, A. 1981. The Structure of the Complementizer in Spanish. LSRL X. Papers in Romance 3, 123-31.

Kayne, R. 1987. Null Subjects and Clitic Climbing. In O. Jaeggli and K. Safir, eds., The Null Subject Parameter. Dordrecht: Kluwer. 239-61.

Koopman, H., and D. Sportiche. 1986. A Note on Long Extraction in Vata and the ECP. Natural Language and Linguistic Theory 4, 357-74.

Koopman, H., and D. Sportiche. 1988. Subjects. Ms., UCLA.

Larson, R. 1985. On the Syntax of Disjunctive Scope. Natural Language and Linguistic Theory 3, 217-64.

Lasnik, H. and M. Saito. 1984. On the Nature of Proper Government. Linguistic Inquiry 15, 235-89.

Lema, J. 1989. Category Switching: Configurational Effects of Verb Movement. NELS 19, 301-13.

Lightfoot, D. 1979. Principles of Diachronic Syntax. Cambridge: Cambridge University Press.

Mallén, E. 1988. Extraction from DP, Case assignment, and [Spec, IP]. Ms., Cornell University.

May, R. 1985. Logical Form. Cambridge, Mass.: MIT Press.

Partee, B. 1973. The Syntax and Semantics of Quotation. In S. Anderson and P. Kiparski, eds., A Festschrift for Morris Halle. New York: Holt, Rinehart and Winston. 410-18.

Pesetsky, D. 1983. Paths and Categories. MIT doctoral dissertation.

Plann, S. 1982. Indirect Questions in Spanish. Linguistic Inquiry 13, 297-312.

Platzack, C. 1986. Comp, Infl, and Germanic Word Order. In L. Hellan and K. Christensen, eds., Topics in Scandinavian Syntax. Dordrecht: Reidel. 185-234.

Pollock, J.-Y. 1989. Verb Movement, UG and the Structure of IP. Linguistic Inquiry 20, 365-424.

Rigau, G. 1984. De com si no és conjunció i d'altres elements interrogatius. Estudis Gramaticals 1 : Working Papers in Linguistics. Bellaterra: Universidad Autónoma de Barcelona. 249-78.

Rivero, M-L. 1980. On Left-dislocation and Topicalization in Spanish. Linguistic Inquiry 11, 363-93.

Rizzi, L. 1982. Issues in Italian Syntax. Dordrecht: Foris.

Rizzi, L. 1990. Relativized Minimality. Cambridge, Mass.: MIT Press.

Ross, J.R. 1971. Conjunctive and disjunctive questions. Ms., MIT.

Sirbu-Dumitrescu, D. 1988. On the Syntax of Echo-questions in Spanish and Romanian. Paper read at the MLA Convention, December 1988.

Sobin, N. 1987. The Variable Status of Comp-Trace Phenomena. Natural Language and Linguistic Theory 5, 33-60.

Sportiche, D. 1988. A Theory of Floating Quantifiers and Its Corollaries for Constituent Structure. Linguistic Inquiry 19, 425-49.

Srivastav, V. 1990. Hindi WH and Pleonastic Operators. NELS 20.

Suñer, M. 1986a. Lexical Subjects of Infinitives in Caribbean Spanish. In O. Jaeggli and C. Silva-Corvalán, eds., Studies in Romance Linguistics. Dordrecht: Foris. 189-203.

Suñer, M. 1986b. On the Structure of the Spanish CP. Ms., Cornell University.

Suñer, M. 1987. Two Properties of Clitics in Clitic-Doubled Constructions. Forthcoming in J. Huang and R. May, eds., Logical Structure and Linguistic Structure: Cross-Linguistic Perspectives. Dordrecht: Reidel.

Suñer, M. 1988. The Role of Agreement in Clitic-doubled Constructions. Natural Language and Linguistic Theory 6, 391-434.

Suñer, M. 1989. About Indirect Questions. Ms., Cornell University.

Torrego, E. 1984. On Inversion in Spanish and Some of Its Effects. Linguistic Inquiry 15, 103-29.

Zagona, K. 1982. Government and Proper Government of Verbal Projections. University of Washington doctoral dissertation.

The Tobler-Mussafia law in Old Spanish

Dieter Wanner *
The Ohio State University

0 Introduction. A large part of syntactic studies on Spanish, and in particular on Old Spanish, concerns the clitic pronouns.   Important claims of considerable theoretical relevance have been advanced in recent treatments under the perspective of Government and Binding,[1] involving the notion of clitics and its parametric interpretation in synchrony and diachrony.   The major solutions attribute to clitics either NP status, or N status, or a subword level of syntactic representation.   The present contribution focuses on the linearization properties of Old Spanish (OSp.) clitic object pronouns with regard to their host verbs.   The phenomenon is generally known as the Tobler-Mussafia law (TM), a variety of Wackernagel's law (W) specific to a language family.   The paper will present a reconstruction of the essential aspects of clitic linearization, and it will consider the implications of so-called interpolation, of the imperfect adverbial clitic pronouns *y, ende*, and of clitic pronouns depending on nonfinite (nf) verbal forms in Old Castilian.   The arguments purport to establish that TM is not required as a principle of Old Spanish (or Old Romance in general), rather that the effects grouped under the label of TM are a derivative of specific phrase structure constellations combined with Head Movement of the Verb to I(NFL) or C(OMP).   This interpretation depends on the recognition of a specific landing site for the clitic pronouns, i.e. AGR_{int} as an adjunct to INFL', conceived under a modified program of extended clausal architecture (Chomsky 1986, Johnson 1989).   The consequence of this reconstruction is a clear-cut answer as to the nature of clitic elements.   Among the three choices of NP, N, and Spell-Out of AGR, only the X^0 level category of N can hold up to scrutiny.   However, the results impose the view of an extensive area of normal syntactic behavior surrounded by a narrow periphery of untidy situations, loose ends, and contradictory cases.   While the N^0 status of clitics for Old and Modern

---

* The paper has benefited from extensive discussions of phrase structure options with Peter Culicover, Shigeru Miyagawa, Mineharu Nakayama, Pauline Jacobson. The stimulating work by María-Luisa Rivero and her specific comments on earlier versions of the ideas presented here have been essential for the improvement of this paper. All shortcomings are obviously my sole responsibility. For the Old Spanish data, the electronic text editions originating from the Seminary of Medieval Spanish at the University of Wisconsin, Madison, have been utilized where available (Alfonso X, *Estoria de España, General Estoria*; Heredia, *Crónica de Morea, Florilegio*; cf. the References section).

[1] Better, perhaps, Principles and Parameters; the traditional terminology will, however, be maintained here.

Spanish is a secure result, it is also the case that clitic grammar — like other aspects of formal grammar — is not a categorical phenomenon. Rather, its rigidity must be corrected with the more flexible properties of dynamic (production) principles. Formal structural considerations are thus only one aspect of language, and other approaches need to complement the blind spots of an exclusive formalism.

1 Wackernagel's law and the Tobler-Mussafia Law. Wackernagel's Law (as implied in Wackernagel 1892) has been a staple of linguistic descriptions and attempts at explanation in both synchrony and diachrony throughout its existence. In particular in the Romance languages, the last decade has seen numerous appeals to this principle of second position (P2), mainly with regard to the unstressed, clitic object pronouns of the medieval and modern Romance idioms. To a certain extent, this is a curious development, since the predictions of Wackernagel's Law (W) in (1) are not very faithfully observed in some of the languages for which it was originally proposed.

(1) W: Inherently unstressed/unstressable words
   (a) are preferentially found in *Second Position* (P2); and
   (b) specifically, they cannot stand in first position (P1).

While Sanskrit and early Ancient Greek conform to W (1) in a rather predictable way for a range of unstressed elements, Latin texts are riddled with apparent contraventions of unstressed, potentially enclitic elements in nonsecond position (contra (1a)). Part (b) of W (1) is almost always respected (no clause initial *en*clitics, almost by definition), while the exceptions usually concern part (a) requiring enclitics to be in P2. The 'law' thus belongs to the well-known category of tendencies promoted to idealized regularity in the neogrammarian tradition.

In an interesting twist, the ensuing Romance languages all developed a class of clitic object pronouns which in their medieval phases obey W (1b) strictly. In its medieval Romance guise, W (1b) is known as the Tobler-Mussafia law TM (2).

(2) TM   Unstressed object pronouns cannot stand in absolute initial position in the sentence.[2]

---

[2] As in the case of Wackernagel's Law, TM (2) has not been formulated in exactly these concise terms, and in the further evolution of research it has come to cover a wider array of cases. TM (2) represents the case TM I of Mussafia (1886), i. e., absolute initial position (equal to Ramsden's class XIII); cf. Wanner (1987: 155-65) for a reconstruction of the various treatments.

In their further evolution, the Romance idioms have emancipated themselves from TM (2) in the transition to Renaissance and modern language forms. The demise of absolute application of TM (2) ranges from about 1300 A.D. for Old French to the seventeenth century for European Portuguese, with its clear obsolescence since the fifteenth and sixteenth centuries for the other Romance languages.

Again, the narrow law TM cannot have universal validity since it is broken in subsequent developments. Compared to W, the case for clear diachronic development without internal rupture of typology is nearly airtight for TM, since it is an evolution which can be observed very closely in the rich textual documentation throughout the history of a number of Romance languages. Gradually, the absolute prohibition of TM is given up without any attendant explanatory developments. During the entire period of its validity, TM applies only to a designated set of unstressed object pronouns; other unstressed elements akin to object clitics (even if formally and etymologically identical to them, e.g., the definite articles) do not fall under its provision. TM is a language-specific, lexically controlled principle, with a considerable general appeal, since it is repeated in so many other Romance languages and also beyond the narrow Romance circle (e.g., in Byzantine/Medieval Greek with a closely parallel history, but no relevant genetic relation to Late Latin; cf. Joseph 1978). Other languages are known to have a very strict interpretation of both parts (a) and (b) of W, e.g., Serbo-Croatian (Browne 1974), Czech (Toman 1972), Pashto (Tegey 1977), and beyond Indo-European in, e.g. Luiseño (Steele 1978), with visible concentration of applicable clitic elements in P2.[3] But again, the wider context of clitic phenomena reveals such utterance-defined P2 (according to W (1a)) to be not more than one parametric setting of options (cf. Klavans 1985 for details). TM is subsumed under W, and this principle W is in turn part of a wider range of clitic settings. TM appears thus as a language-specific instantiation of a broad pattern of clitic options anchored in UG.

2 Limitation to Old Spanish. It is thus evident that W is not a component of Universal Grammar by itself. It is more profitable to understand it as a theorem to be derived from more basic notions, in such a way that its widespread occurrence, its sometimes erratic applicability, and its inherent ambiguities receive a true explanation. The notion of P2 must be specified, for any given language and class of clitics, in terms of constituent level (morpheme, word, phrase, clause). While the range of elements affected by W is rather narrow cross-linguistically, due at least in

---

[3] If W (1) is strictly observed, the two parts (a) and (b) are redundant, since (a) subsumes (b).

part to prosodic reduction with concomitant semantic/pragmatic restrictions on clitics, there may be significant differences from language to language. The choice may include some or all members of one or more of the groups of auxiliary verbs, certain sentence scope adverbs, different classes of pronouns and other types of elements. The severity with which the principle controls surface manifestations is basically indeterminate and dependent on accidental factors. In most renditions, W consists of a curious mix of phonological, morpho-lexical, and syntactic features which seem to run counter to the generally accepted separation of linguistic components. The common assumption that W applies to so-called clitic elements is not of much help since there is a definite lack of understanding of what it means for an element to be a clitic. This loosely structured category typically refers to the same mix of ingredients from various linguistic components, and the exact contents of components seems to vary from language to language (cf. Zwicky 1985 for a battery of diagnostics for cliticness and a wide range of phenomena).

In the present situation, the parameters are set in such a way that the relevant form class for OSp. is the usual unstressed object (clitic) pronouns *me, te, se, lo, la, le, se, nos, os, los, las, les* (plus some morphosyntactic variants, usually affected by apocope). The principle in question for Old Spanish reduces to W (1b) = TM (2). The narrow circumscription of the field of investigation will permit a deeper penetration of the local issue of what the labels TM and clitic mean in more systematic terms.

3 Two dimensions of TM in Old Spanish

3.1 Negative filter. In the perspective of recent research on the Romance languages, the most likely form of W/TM is that of a negative filter prohibiting elements marked as clitics from occurring in sentence-initial position, where clitic tentatively refers to Arguments of a hierarchical status lower than NP, appearing in the derivation somewhere between SS and PF. A particular formulation (Rivero 1986, Wanner 1990) describes the phenomenon as a contact reaction with a left CP boundary.

(3) TM $*[_{CP} \emptyset \text{ cl}$ where $\emptyset$ designates a phonologically null string spanning structurally complex arrangements, including $[_{C'} [_{IP}$, any lexically nonfilled nodes such as $[_C \text{ e }]$, and/or structurally required empty categories such as pro.

The actually observed appearance of the clitic in second position in enclisis to the initial verb must be due to principles other than TM; TM is not a movement rule, but a negative filter. In the context of the systemic properties of PF rules, of which very little is known, TM is not a stylistic rule in any relevant sense: optional, subject to expressive purposes, etc. Thus TM cannot fall under the class of reordering processes of the type Scrambling, i.e., reordering of maximal and nonmaximal projections outside of the requirements of Government, Adjacency, etc. The effect of TM is not a relatively free reordering of constituents, but rather the elimination of a specific structure. TM could not be maintained as a positive template either. The alternative TM^{pos} (4a) is contradicted by all clitic occurrences outside of P2, yet these are normal configurations for OSp. (4b). The only valid prohibition is against utterance-initial clitics, standing in P1 (4c).

(4) a.   TM^{pos} $[_{CP}$ V - cl ...   or $[_{CP}$ X - cl ... obligatory

    b.   *$[_{CP}$ XP ... XP cl - V ...   predicted ungrammatical, but a regular option

    c.   *$[_{CP}$ cl - V ...   ungrammatical, not observed

Rather, the meaning of TM as a reordering rule is a conditional: if V is CP initial, and if V has a clitic associated with it, then the arrangement of the group {V, cl} is enclitic, /V - cl/, and cannot be proclitic /cl - V/, as in (4c). Nothing is thereby said about the noninitial position of V as in (4b).

3.2   Elements affected by TM.   The form of TM combines a phonological expression — the null-string between $[_{CP}$ and the clitic — with a syntactic category, CP. The complex condition is predicated of a class of elements, the clitics, which are prosodically marked by absence of lexical stress; they correlate this restrictive property with the syntactic status of being less than a maximal projection, incorporated into another constituent, while displaying the Argument function typically associated with a maximal projection (NP). Membership in this class is idiosyncratic and lexically determined; cf. the difference between Spanish and Catalan with regard to the oblique clitics Cat. *hi, en* 'there; of it, whence'. These (Old and Modern) Catalan oblique pronouns are regularly clitics like the direct/indirect object pronouns/anaphors, and they cluster freely with them. But the corresponding OSp. forms *y, en(d(e))* are frequently not on a par with the other clitics (cf. below, section 9). For the remainder, the class of clitics is coherent, comprising in all Romance languages, in principle, the nonemphatic object pronouns for direct and indirect object, [±anaphoric], for all three persons and both numbers.[4]

4 Previous interpretations of W/TM

4.1 W as a trend. Some deeper insight must be gained on what the term 'clitic' in TM, or the loosely used clitic of many linguistic discussions, really means. The combination of formal opacity of the statement of TM and terminological vagueness about its key term *clitic* precludes an understanding of the nature and *modus operandi* of TM.[5]

For Wackernagel (1892) only 'enclitic' is a useful term, designating such lexical elements (particles, e.g. S-attitudinal adverbs, pronouns of 1st and 2nd person) as would displace their (potential) lexical stress on the preceding lexical element in Ancient Greek and other classical languages. The stress retraction, clearly marked in the Alexandrine accentual writing system for Greek (Laum 1928), gave these elements the name of *enklitikói* 'leaning-on (the preceding word)'. The traditional understanding of W, in particular Wackernagel's own, is in the form of a positive output filter of variable applicability. Such enclitics are attracted to - in certain linguistic stages of Ancient Greek (etc.) even forced into - the second clause slot (P2) which was assumed to be accentually weak by nature. There are two underlying properties explaining W in its form (1). The enclitics are accentually weak in the clause context, 'leaning on' the preceding word, and the clause contains one specifically weak position, P2, which attracts accentually nonprominent elements, in particular enclitics, but also accidentally unstressed words such as the nonfocused verb of the clause (and here, in particular, auxiliary and other restricted forms). W (1) can thus be understood as a prosodic-lexical coanalysis of the syntactic string (5).[6] Example (5c) shows a lexical category in the position [S, X^n], while (5d) illustrates the phenomenon with a phrasal category PP.[7]

---

[4] Minor deviations do exist, e.g. the Italian problem clitic *loro*, the Piedmontese and Rumanian selective enclitics, or the complete absence of all clitic object pronouns in modern Surselvan, with the sole remnant of a single anaphoric clitic form for all reflexive functions *sa*. Rumanian in addition has auxiliary verbs which are interspersed with pronominal clitics.

[5] While this could lead into an unfortunate terminological regression if pursued systematically in the full breadth of Zwicky (1985), a look at how the term has been used in essential treatments of TM for Msp. and Osp. is necessary.

[6] The formulae w^* and cf^* refer to the possible accumulation of unstressed elements in P2. S, w mark rhythmically strong and weak elements, respectively.

[7] The Latin adverbs *autem, enim, vero* etc. are typically clitic items appearing in second position, showing parallel behavior to pronominal clitic occurrences; cf. Hofmann and Szantyr (1972: 398-401).

(5) a. prosody (template)   ##   S   w˙   ...

    b. syntax   [$_{CP}$ X^n cl^* ...

    c. [$_{NP}$ magnos$_i$ **vero** usus$_i$] adfert ad navigia facienda (Cicero, *De nat. deor.* II.152)
great truly utility it-brings to ships building
'it [wood] is truly useful for ship building'

    d. [$_{PP}$ a Balbo] **autem** animadvertisti credo quam multa dicta sint (ib. III.4)
by Balbus but you-noticed I-believe how much said be
'You did notice, I believe, how much had been said by Balbus'

W includes a crucial time dimension in that it is a more regularly observed condition of older language phases (both in Greek and in Latin, but then again in Late Latin; cf. Wanner 1987: chap. 5). In actual Greek documents, especially of a highly stylized nature, and of classical and Hellenistic provenance, its precepts are not necessarily observed. In addition, the term cl^* originally must have referred to any constituent level $Y^{n_,}$ provided it was prosodically (and discourse dynamically) weak. This original view of W is couched in terms which make it a nonuniversal, family-specific property resting on the language-specific trait of Ancient Greek enclisis (extendible to Sanskrit, Latin, and other IE languages and branches), and on the (otherwise rather hypothetical) family-specific prosodic template of a weak P2 in Indo-European.

4.2 Rhythmical explanation. The ensuing investigative phases (clearly preestablished in Wackernagel 1892) led to consideration of the clitic properties in Balto-Slavic languages, of the V2 phenomenon mainly in Germanic, but also Old French (cf. among others Thurneysen 1892), and the pronominal clitics of the Romance idioms; the latter are all connected with the concept of TM. The Romance pronominal clitics were actually recognized in their systematic behavior before Wackernagel (1892), in the well-known famous series of publications Tobler (1875, 1889), Mussafia (1886, 1898), and Meyer-Lübke (1897), establishing the (sub)family regularity of the Tobler-Mussafia law for the medieval Romance languages. The main trend in understanding the phenomenon of the disallowed clitic pronoun in absolute clause-initial position has been prosodic ('rhythmical'), in parallel to Wackernagel's assumption that P2 in IE is a weak position; cf. the above template (5a). The clitic pronouns of Romance, originating from unstressed Latin pronouns (e.g. ME:, TE:) and distal demonstratives (e.g. ILLE, ILLA), would have acquired standard stresslessness by the time of

Old Romance documentation (demonstrably before 800 A.D. given the eighth century *Parody of the Lex Salica*).[8] W (1b) thus becomes a property of obligatory character, requiring the inherently unstressed clitic to shun initial position, i.e., TM (2). The readily available P2 accommodates the forms, so that TM now reestablishes itself as a negative filter at PF (due to its access to prosodic information), operating in the context of an initial V. Prosody must be supplemented by lexical and/or syntactic information, since other (fully and near-) identical and typically unstressed forms do not share the prohibition against initial occurrence (e.g. /prep + NP/, /det + N'/, /c + subordinate clause/, /prep + infinitive/, /gerund/). Only pronouns of internal argument status, plus two oblique functions (locative/comitative IBI:, and genitive/separative/partitive INDE) are clitics, but definitely no external argument (subject) or other oblique pronouns. The applicable class must therefore be specially marked for cliticness, since it is not a natural grouping. The domain of the prohibition must be stated by referring to the V as the clitic host, i.e. the strong P1 term X^n of (5b). The purely rhythmical understanding of TM for this complex situation is unsatisfactory; the wild constructs of rhythmical conditions which would permit the specific facts to be explained are also quite suspect. The most recent such interpretation is found in Ramsden (1963: 112-33).

4.3 Difficulties with negative filter. While Wackernagel's original insight may have been on the right track, the further Romance development of investigation (up to and including Ramsden 1963) represents a dead end for a genuine understanding of the problem. The renewed interest in clitic studies within transformational and contemporaneous frameworks constitutes a step ahead. The acceptance of a category label of clitic is the evident Achilles heel of this perspective, even though the classification may be refined, e.g. into simple vs. special clitics (Zwicky 1977). Simple clitics are prosodically reduced, but as a given constituent, they are syntactically left *in situ*, as opposed to special clitics that show syntactic displacement with regard to the position normally occupied by its nonclitic X^{max} counterpart. Since these are only prototypical situations, clitics turn out to be almost as multifaceted as the range of phenomena and languages covered. Any property elevated to universal importance for defining clitics can be shown to

---

[8] This curious parodistic text, preserved in an eighth century manuscript, contains the first attestations of the Romance definite article and 3rd person pronouns deriving from Latin ILLE not only in their Romance function, but in their typically apheresized form *la, los,* etc.; cf. Beckmann (1963), Wanner (1987: 120n). The stresslessness of these forms in their prior evolution from 'ILLA, 'ILLOS is uncontroversial, since the parallel stressed forms yielded *'ella, 'ellos* with full preservation of the etymological material and prosodic pattern of penultimate stress.

be nonessential in at least one situation, leading to a view of clitics as a superclass. As such they may offer prototypical instantiations, responding to a range of parametrized settings and creating a fine weave of possible clitic phenomenology (Zwicky 1985), or they may consist of a relatively solid but not inalterable core of more important clitic properties (Wanner 1987: 462-79).

Such approaches require clitics to be seen as language specific, responding to universal tendencies with a particular parameter setting for language L_i. The formulation of TM as in (3) is deceivingly universal. It looks nonspecific only because it states a negative condition over a phonological zero (by definition language nonspecific). But TM requires an exact description of the class of applicable clitics and structures, for which OSp. will be a case study.

The concept of a negative filter applicable at PF is highly questionable for reasons of learnability. The effect of such a filter is to block a given configuration from appearing on the surface. The only evidence available for this blockage by fiat (instead of as a consequence of interactive positive principles) is the systematic gap in the surface data: a classical case of negative evidence not admissible in a realistic analysis (the old *argumentum e silentio*). The rewriting of the negative filter in a positive version (as in (4a) above) is specious since it undergenerates the admissible structures seriously. It is only an attempt at salvaging the negative filter by a technicality. In this context, it is quite evident that TM for the medieval Romance languages is a suspect principle. It will be argued that it can be dispensed with under a specific interpretation of the effective phrase structure configuration of these languages, i.e., if they contain a separate target node $AGR_{int(ernal)}$ for Agreement phenomena relating to VP internal arguments.

5 Nature of Old Spanish clitics

5.1 Different theoretical conceptions. Modern Romance clitic object pronouns (in all languages and dialects that still have them) are regarded by consensus as properly 'clitics'.[9] They essentially receive three treatments. Two analyses attribute to them the status of a nonmaximal projection, either as a lexical Head moved from a maximal projection into the domain of another Head in syntax, the so-called Head approach (Kayne 1989 for French), or as excrescences of AGR originating from specific spell-out rules,

---

[9] This is not the case for 'subject clitics', which differ according to their syntactic origin, e.g., as full NPs for ModFr. vs. AGR manifestations for certain Northern Italian dialects (Brandi and Cordin 1989). I will not consider subject clitics here due to limitations of space; the complex issue of the pro-drop parameter requires a much more extensive treatment.

but not subject to syntactic movement, the so-called Spell-out analysis (Borer 1984). In a third approach, OSp. clitics are treated (in Rivero 1986) as NPs in all respects except their phonetic surface manifestation, differing thereby from their modern Romance counterparts; this analysis will be referred to as the NP view.[10]

5.1.1 The Head approach sees clitics as originating in A-position of their appropriate NP; the sole lexical material of this maximal projection, the nominal clitic element, moves by Head movement to the V of its government domain, and on to I, where I is sufficiently 'strong' to L-mark the VP (with finite verbs, producing proclisis, e.g. *te llamo más tarde*; not with nonfinite I in French *pour* [$_I$] [$_{VP}$ *bien le faire*]]; but yes in Italian, and thus also in Spanish *para hacer* [$_I$ *lo* + I] *bien*, yielding enclisis). The movement path does not include the normal VP, IP adjunction of maximal projections, but rather the lexical Head positions of V and I (Kayne 1989: 239-43).

5.1.2 The Spell-out solution postulates a basic structure of [$_V$, αCase] which spells out the necessary features for clitic pronoun identification by an inflectional rule as [$_V$ [$_{cl}$ α Case, β gender, γ number, δ person]]; the portion [$_{cl}$] is an affix, and as such it does not satisfy subcategorization requirements; rather the clitic, standing in A-bar position, properly governs the coindexed NP complement of form [$_{NP}$ e] (Borer 1984: 37-41).

5.1.3 According to Rivero (1986: 774-75), OSp. clitics (referring to a period between 1100 and 1450) are not clitics in a syntactically relevant sense; rather they are clitics in PF only, while their status throughout the syntactic derivation is that of a maximal projection, NP.[11] She characterizes the

---

[10] Two other technical solutions have been provided, which seem to fall under the more general heading of the AGR centered clitics. In Jaeggli (1986) clitics are syntactic affixes on the Verb, forming with this host an X° category, e. g., [$_V$ cl [$_V$]] for proclisis. Suñer (1988) uses the notion of agreement marker; this differs from the Spell-out solution only by the mechanism through which these elements come into existence in syntax. Since these two proposals evidently aim at a situation with fully categorical clitic elements, in the same way as the Spell-out approach, they cannot add much light to the Medieval Spanish situation. In this linguistic phase, the clitic nature is not yet established at such a near-morphological level, as the discussions in Rivero and in this paper underline. The finer technical distinctions of a syntactic affix or agreement marker, as opposed to an element spelled out from syntactic features under AGR, do not have crucial impact and will be disregarded. Rather, the discussion will center on the distinction between NP and N status of clitics.

[11] The *communis opinio* of traditional historical linguistics deals with these elements as 'clitics' in the same (pretheoretical) sense as in Modern Spanish. Another clitic approach described in detail in Kayne (1975) for French attributes full NP status to them, originating them in regular A-position and moving the (downgraded?) lexical NP in the form of the clitic element to its

difference between the OSp. clitics and the modern Spanish true clitics as in (6). (6a) represents the structures in the sense of Borer 1984 with the link between the clitic and the empty category. In (6b), the A-position is that taken by the NP containing the *clitic* form, and no other empty position is required or allowed in this set-up.

(6) a. [s [NP ellos] [VP [V' [V lo$_i$ entendieron] [NPi e]]]] MSp.
'they understood it'

b. [s [NP ellos] [VP [V' [NP lo] [V entendieron]]]] OSp.

Positions in which clitics are found in an OSp. utterance must therefore be positions in which NPs can occur by virtue of general movement rules for maximal projections and equally general restrictions on such movement imposed by one or more modules of grammar. So far, the so-called clitic object pronouns of OSp. are nothing more than unstressed pronominals and anaphors, akin to unstressed object pronouns in a language such as English. If pronouns such as *her* in *I saw her* [r] *yesterday at the bank* are clitics, then this is so only in a phonological sense of simple cliticness (Zwicky 1977, 1985). OSp. clitics become clitics only after syntax, in PF. Since they do obey TM,[12] TM must be a rule of the PF branch, applicable after the syntactic rules, perhaps at the early stages of phonological interpretation, when prosodically weak NPs (or also other constituents, depending on the language) are readjusted to reduced status. At this point, the syntactic constraints, in particular the Theta-Criterion and the Extended Projection Principle, have no further validity, so that the NP can now cease to fulfill a role as maximal projection. This downgrading marks the ex-NP with the (diacritic) property of 'cliticness' which will subject it automatically to any later clitic specific conditions, principles, and processes such as TM (3).

5.1.4 The essential aspect of a true clitic can thus be a (nominal) lexical element of nonmaximal projection status, regardless of its syntactic enveloping structure. In OSp., the newly created PF clitic is the reflex of a Head, the Head N (or Det) of the NP appearing in clitic form. In Modern Spanish, the clitic can be interpreted as a Head (along the lines designed in Kayne 1989 for Modern French), moved by Head Movement to AGR and

---

appropriate preverbal position. This solution is no longer favored in general, and specifically, not available in the Government and Binding framework of recent years.

[12] This is so according to every account in more recent work, regardless of theoretical perspective, e.g., Menéndez Pidal (1944.I: 402-12), Ramsden (1963: 117-27), Alemán (1985), Barry (1987), Rivero (1986, 1991).

combining there with the verbal word into a morpholexical unit, the clitic being prosodically subsumed in the complex word. For OSp. vs. MSp., this analysis locates the essential Head-only status of the clitic already in syntax for the modern stage, but it might relegate it to PF in the Medieval language. Clitics in the Spell-out approach (Borer 1984) can be viewed as nonmaximal projections, in this case not even having syntactic status as such. Their prosodic properties are immaterial since they will be regulated by the word level principles dealing with the clitic and its host as a unit. Such clitics acquire a rather morphological aspect, quite far removed from the syntactic properties of the medieval (non-)clitics.

5.2 Importance of lefhand CP periphery. The Romance clitics, whether OSp. unstressed object pronouns or truer Modern Spanish instances of this label, contain a prosodic element of nonprominence, either by losing prosodic individuality, as in the OSp. NP analysis, or by not being able to realize it, as in the Head proposal, or by not pertaining to a category of stressable items, as in the Spell-out approach. In the Head and Spell-out proposals the syntactic dimension is responsible for the prosodic consequence of nonprominence, while for the NP approach, the prosodic downgrading is not a corollary, but a cause in its own right. The causes of cliticization are thus distinct, which the analysis chosen by Rivero claims as central; the surface manifestation is, however, basically nondistinct in the two classes of clitics.

In fact, the OSp. clitics differ in only two essential respects from the Modern Spanish ones, i.e., linearization with the verb, as expressed by the applicability of TM (3) in the Medieval language, and possible separation from the verb (cf. section 8 for discussion of Interpolation). TM (3) as a filter applicable to a language with PF cliticization (OSp.) must be a phonological rule, if any separation of modules is to be maintained. Syntax is characterized by NP status of eventual clitics, yet cliticization is only effective in the phonological component, and only then can TM (3) be applied. In the given formulation, TM (3) contains the appropriate phonological variable $\emptyset$, which may span different structural levels. This condition is not immediately expressible in syntax, so it seems to be well placed here. On the other hand, the syntactic boundary condition [$_{CP}$ is a nontrivial syntactic description, in that it must carefully distinguish between CP level constituents and all constituents hierarchically below CP, i.e., C', IP, I', VP, etc. Only the phonologically null left periphery of a CP produces a filter violation, circumvented by the /V-cl/ enclisis so typical of the Medieval Romance languages. This CP peripherality is not only given at the absolute left edge of the utterance in which the CP clause occurs. There may be preceding material in the same utterance, e.g., a preceding sentence-scope adverb, subordinate clause, or an NP/PP in TOP (essentially any adjunction to CP).   In all these cases,   enclisis will be observed as regularly as when the {V, cl} group is additionally utterance initial.   If TM (3) as a PF rule,   within the subcomponent for filters,   is basically phonological in nature, it cannot at the same time be syntactically steered, unless one is willing to assume considerable cross-reference between two separate modules of grammar.   This modular autonomy seems to be endangered by the given analysis, unless prosodic rules can be shown to require this kind of syntactic information independently.   The metrical grid at the phrase level is certainly conditioned by syntactic arrangements, but it is questionable whether the fineness of the required syntactic distinction between CP and C', etc. can be presupposed as otherwise necessary for phonological rules.

Notice that the syntactic CP boundary is not coextensive with the phonologically comprehensible condition of absolute utterance-initial position. While the left-hand CP boundary will frequently coincide with a marked intonational break, perhaps even with an actual pause before it, this is not a requirement in the presence of a [$_{CP}$ bracket, as the MSp. intonation for coordinate conjunction demonstrates: *las saludó y ellas le echaron una sonrisa* 'he greeted them and they smiled back at him': ['jejas] with glided [j] for the conjunction *y* /i/.   The same phonological conditions can safely be attributed to OSp., where metrical patterns treat *e(t)* = /e/, /i/ (and prevocalic [j]) as a proclitic to whatever it coordinates, yet it causes a following group {V, cl} to appear in enclitic arrangement, indicating an intervening CP boundary: *et* [$_{CP}$ V - cl ...] (cf. section 6.5).

5.3 Diachronic progression: NP - Head- Affix. From a descriptive point of view, the two essential structural features of TM (3) are uncontroversial, i.e., the phonological null string and the left-hand CP boundary condition. In a first move, the observational need for TM (3) will lead the investigation of the further properties of such a filter (cf. section 6), while keeping in mind the uneasiness about such a negative output filter.   The central question is the intersection of TM with the three major approaches to clitics, NP vs. N vs. affix status.   In principle, the argumentation takes the following shape with regard to the three options.

Overall research results militate for a rather strict separation of modules, so that the consequences of the NP approach together with TM (3) are highly unwelcome.   First, the phonological null string in TM (3) should be reinterpreted in a purely syntactic dimension.   The phonological condition is overextended in view of the surface ambiguities of coordinate conjunction and abstract vs. lexical null categories.   Second, the natural move then is to question the assumption that the clitics become such only in PF after passing through syntax as maximal projections nondistinct from other NPs.   If the clitic condition were fulfilled at some stage in syntax, then the syntactically sophisticated content of TM (3) is guaranteed to obtain at the appropriate level. As a consequence of these two reanalyses, the filter (in the form of its structural equivalent) may apply at a syntactic level where its syntactic relevance is sustainable.

The syntactically weakest approach of the morphological spell-out rule is not sufficient to account for the surface data of OSp. In particular, in interpolation (cf. section 8) such clitics are separated from the host verb, i.e., from the presumable AGR location. This indication of possible independence of clitics is contrary to the characteristics of a segment spelling out inherent V features.

The intermediate formulation of Head movement may be an adequate compromise view if reinterpreted in a diachronic sense of progressive clitic development from NP to N, i.e. Head, and ultimately to pure affix status. Such a solution appears to have a number of advantages over the more extreme approaches. By associating the clitic not necessarily with the V, but rather with the AGR portion of I (Kayne 1989: 240), it becomes possible to understand interpolation without losing the explanation of the overwhelming V-centeredness of OSp. clitics. Modular separation is left intact. The solution can refer to a (partly) lexically determined class of clitics (inclusion or not of the oblique pronouns *y*, *ende*). Finally, it provides for an intuitively more appealing parametric setting uniting OSp. with MSp. – both have similar types of clitics – as opposed to the other grouping of OSp. with (Late) Latin. Late Latin, and even more so Early and Classical Latin, did not have anything approaching the old or modern Romance clitic pronoun systems. NP status corresponds to the pre-clitics of Late Latin, and the major parametric switch occurs with the onset of the Romance languages (presumably already in the preliterary phases), when the clitics have dropped to Head status and thereby are a syntactic phenomenon; the final evolution to true affix status (as implied by the Spell-out approach) is still not fully reached even in the modern Romance languages.

It will be interesting to probe the evidence adduced for the NP status of unstressed object pronouns in OSp. in detail to assess the identity of TM (3) between syntactic and phonological. Section 6 contains a description of the Tobler-Mussafia law and its effect on OSp. clitic object pronoun location. An additional clitic linearization principle is needed to account for the context following a subject NP (section 7). Interpolation as a central case of divergent views on OSp. clitics comes under scrutiny in section 8, where it is argued that the facts point to a further additional principle of clitic linearization, different from both TM (3) and subject-induced enclisis (section 7). The clitic status of the two adverbial/oblique pronominals *y* and *ende* is rather controversial. These elements show a pattern of collocation somewhat distinct from that of more central OSp. clitic pronouns and represent a true halfway solution to cliticness (section 9). Section 10 investigates the linearization properties of clitics with nonfinite verb forms, concluding that the structural solution expressed in expanded phrasal architecture, i.e., the special AGR$_{int}$ node, is inappropriate for nonfinite host verbs. The scalar arrangement of decreasing cliticness between definite articles, object clitic pronouns, oblique pronominals and full NPs can then motivate a nondichotomous view of the status of the standard OSp. clitic pronouns (section 11).

OSp. clitic pronouns thus appear as word level units in the process of shifting from syntactic status of maximal projections to that of lexical form and eventually to near-inflectional element. Wackernagel's law, for the history of the Romance languages in the guise of the Tobler-Mussafia law, is a series of reinterpretations organizable into three layers: (a) prosodic downgrading of argument NPs, (b) syntactic connection between clitics and their host V, and (c) progressive substitution of morphological principles for syntactic ones. These three phases roughly correspond to the three structural options for clitics in syntax as NPs, as Ns, and as affixes.

6 Detailed consideration of TM

6.1 Clitics as NPs. The mechanics of TM (3) (repeated here for convenience) and the principle's effect on OSp. object clitics are rather well known.[13]

(3) TM   *[$_{CP}$ ∅   cl   where ∅ designates a phonologically null string spanning structurally complex arrangements, including [$_{C'}$ [$_{IP}$, any lexically nonfilled nodes such as [$_C$ e], and/or structurally required empty categories such as *pro*.

The CP boundary is essential in its hierarchical level. Assuming a clausal architecture containing the maximal projections of [$_{CP}$ ... [$_{PolP}$ ... [$_{AgrP}$ ... [$_{TnsP}$ ... [$_{VP}$ ...]]]]] (cf. Pollock 1989, Johnson 1989), together with their intermediate and lexical levels, the only left-hand boundary condition of relevance for enclitic linearization is CP: a clitic in contiguity with [$_{CP}$ will produce ungrammaticality, i.e. there are no clitics in absolute initial position, nor in utterance-internal, but CP-initial location; cf. (7).

---

[13] Cf. Wanner (1990), Barry (1987), Alemán (1985), Ramsden (1963), Menéndez Pidal (1944.1: 402-12) as principal sources.

(7) a. Echos doña Ximena / en los grados delant el altar (PMC 327)
        (*se echo ...)
        threw-herself lady Ximena on the steps before the altar

    b. et desque sopo que el infante entraua en caualgada, enuiol su
        fijo con dozientos caualleros (Fern. §1043, 726a22) (*le envio...)
        and as soon as he-found-out that the infante was-entering in
        cavalry [formation], he-sent-him his son with two-hundred
        knights

The only way a clitic could possibly be in such initial position is if [Spec, CP],
C, [Spec, PolP], and Pol are lexically unspecified. Thus TM (3) can have
an effect only for root clauses (empty C) without a fronted subject NP,
another clause internal argument NP, or a filled PolP (*no(n)*). The V comes
to stand in initial position in such constructions thanks to the unfilled C node,
mediated by V-to-I and I-to-C Head movement. Specifically, the movement
has to take V from its base position as Head of VP to TnsP, uniting it with
the Tense constituent, and the amalgamated [V+Tns] Head moves up to
AgrP to become [[V+Tns] AGR] for full finite inflection, which now shifts
into C position given the empty (or absent) PolP[14]; cf. (8).

(8) $[_{CP} [_{C'} [_C [[V+Tns] AGR]]_{i+j+k} [_{AgrP} e_{i+j+k} [_{TnsP} e_{i+j} [_{VP} e_i]]]]]]$

     e.g. [[habl$_V$ + a + ba$_{Tns}$] n]

Under the NP proposal, the clitic pronoun which needs to be prevented
from ending up in first position is a NP base generated in internal Argument
position with the verb, moved through adjunction sites (on VP, AgrP) to the
left of the V and to the right of a potential PolP element *no(n)* or a lexical
subject NP in [Spec, IP] position. This will produce the normal proclitic
pattern of the noninitial {V, cl} group (9a, b). At the same time it also

---

[14] The question as to whether an affirmative clause has a lexically empty PolP or whether it
does not contain the projection of PolP at all is as yet unsettled. Modern Spanish affords one
argument for the possible presence of PolP in all clauses, negative as well as affirmative, since
a reinforcing affirmative particle *sí* appears optionally in the slot of the negative element *no*: *Mi
abuela sí lo cree* 'my grandmother *does* believe it' (cf. *Mi abuela no lo cree* 'my grandmother does
not believe it'). PolP may thus enter into play also for affirmation, not only negation, an
important support for the semantic motivation of this construct. On the other hand, it is still
possible that PolP is only projected when it is lexically specified (e.g., *no*, *sí*), rather than being
a regular feature of all clauses which will receive lexical or zero specification according to the
case.

creates the enclitic string characteristic of TM (3) if the V complex can be raised to C in the absence of a subject NP or negation. If OSp. clitics are NPs in status everywhere in syntax and LF, general restrictions on landing sites for NP movement by adjunction could prevent the preverbal appearance of such clitics in PF (according to Rivero 1986). Raising the complex [[V + Tns] AGR] into C leaves the adjoined AgrP clitic to the right of the verb, in a position which will produce automatic enclisis; cf. (9c).

(9) a. $[_{CP}[_{C'}[_{C} C][_{NP} NP] [_{AgrP} [_{NP} cl_n] [_{AgrP} [V+Tns]_{i+j} AGR [_{TnsP} e_j [_{VP} e_i e_n]]]]]$

b. $[_{CP} [_{C'}[_{C} C][_{PolP} neg [_{AgrP} [_{NP} cl_n] [_{AgrP} [V+Tns]_{i+j} AGR [_{TnsP} e_j [_{VP} e_i e_n]]]]]$

c. $[_{CP} [_{C'}[_{C} [[V+Tns] AGR]_{i+j+k} [_{AgrP} [_{NP} cl_n] [_{AgrP} e_k [_{TnsP} e_j [_{VP} e_i e_n]]]]]]$

The open position [Spec, CP] is apparently not reachable for the NP-cl in the presence of the fully specified C. So far, TM (3) is no more than a nonsystematic description of the convergence of independent and general restrictions.

A serious difficulty of this approach is the distinction between regular NPs and NPs which will become clitics in PF. An utterance initial preverbal lexical NP is in no way restricted from appearing in the language. This is especially true for nonemphatic subjects. In the structure sketched in (9a), the difficulty is checked by the assumption that a subject NP would occupy the (empty) position [Spec, AgrP],[15] while the eventual clitic NP lands in the Agreement constituent. This is, however, not a necessary situation, since in OSp. lexical object NPs may appear in fully utterance initial position without difficulty (cf. (19a) *la mano*$_{DO}$ *l*$_{cl\,IO}$ *va besar*). They are prevented from this only in the case that they take the morphophonological shape of clitic pronouns in PF (*$*la$_{cl\,DO}$ al Çid$_{IO}$ va besar*), a condition which cannot happen to subject NPs. The difficulty is thus how the true lexical NPs are distinguished from the NPs representing eventual clitics, if both entities are syntactically nondistinct. It is evident that the approach identifying NPs and clitics in syntax crucially requires the PF filter TM (3) to sort out the good from the bad string arrangements.

---

[15] Equivalent to [Spec, IP] in regular terms.

6.2 Clitics as heads. The position taken here is that the eventual clitics are already clitics in syntax, so that the dilemma of filtering out only the appropriate ones does not exist in postsyntactic derivation. As a consequence, the filter TM (3) is not needed on this count for a solution which recognizes clitics as syntactic phenomena. If clitics in Old Spanish are taken to be syntactic phenomena, either as downgraded original X^0 Heads, or as some consequence of Spell-out processes, they presumably find their place under the AGR node. Under the assumption of the same kind of V movement to C (cf. (8)), the structure in (10) would yield correct results of enclitic pronouns on the initial V.

(10) $[_{CP} [_{C'} [_C [[V + Tns] \, AGR + cl_a]_{i+j+k+n} [_{AgrP} e_a \, e_k [_{TnsP} e_j [_{VP} e_i \, e_a]]]]]]$

TM (3) can be dispensed with in this view. But the assumptions about Head movement need repair for the clitic aspect in structures where the V is not raised to C and remains in AGR. If AGR can be viewed as the external layer of the verbal inflection, i.e., [[V + Tns] + AGR] according to morpho-phonological sequencing of endings as in MSp. $/habla_V - ba_{Tns} - mos_{ps/nr}/$, then the object clitic as a reflection of the internal Arguments is always predicted to be enclitic as in (10). The external agreement features (with the subject) incorporate morphologically into the V word, thus not permitting any other position for the less morpheme-like clitics than outside the V word, and specifically to the right of it as enclitic.[16] This is a rather artificial problem, deriving from the so far uncontested assumption that AGR is a unitary node for agreement purposes. But the double orientation of agreement, toward the external Argument obligatorily (person/number endings), and toward the internal Arguments optionally (clitic pronouns), suggests that the node should be reduplicated in a more advanced clausal architecture. (11a) simply extends the approach taken above. The reformulation of (11b) provides a different status for the new constituents as optional X^0 elements in adjunction to I'.

(11) a. $[_{CP} \cdots [_{PolP} \cdots [_{AGRintP} \cdots [_{AGRextP} \cdots [_{TnsP} \cdots [_{VP} \cdots]]]]]]$

   b. $[_{CP} \cdots [_{IP} [_{X'} Spec] [_{I'} Pol [_{I'} AGR_{int} [_{I'} [_I AGR_{ext} + Tns/Md]]]]$
   $[_{VP} \cdots]]]$

---

[16] Under the assumption of free order between the clitic, i. e., the internal argument of the verb, and the verbal complex, as it is proposed in Rivero (1986) for the NP-cl view, both enclisis and proclisis can be produced. But in this case there is a need for an additional principle responsible for the choice of correct linearization. TM (3) will not be equal to the task making a further language-specific principle necessary.

The architectural dissolution of I by PolP, AgrP, TnsP is not necessarily a positive development. The alternative structure (11b) will be adopted here whereby IP is retained as the enveloping structure of the simple clause, and the polarity and internal agreement phenomena represent I' adjunctions, while subject agreement, tense, and modality constituents fall under the unitary label of I. In this way, the linear sequence of these constituents is preserved as a hierarchical layering; the optionality of polarity and internal agreement elements is appropriately expressed, and the IP remains intact for traditional subject position.[17] The newly structured string of (11b), as well as the stacked maximal projections of (11a), permits the representations in (12), with observed normal surface order *neg > cl > V*.

(12) a. $[_{CP} \dots [_{PolP} \text{neg} [_{AGRintP} cl_k [_{AGRextP} [V+Tns] AGR]_{i+j} [_{TnsP} e_j [_{VP} e_i \ e_k]]]]]]$

b. $[_{CP} \dots [_{IP} \dots [_{I'} [\text{neg}] [_{I'} [cl_k] [_{I'} [_{I} [V+Tns] AGR_{ext}]_{i+j} [_{Tns} e_j]][_{VP} e_i \ e_k]]]]]]$

It is obvious that the novel X^0 elements, Pol, AGR_{int}, AGR_{ext}, and Tns of (11b), (12b) are not all of one type, since they show rather distinct properties of what elements they allow to attach to them by Head movement. The properly verbal parts for AGR_{ext} and Tns translate into morphologically incorporated elements at the PF level, i.e., obligatory endings, while the negative and pronominal elements corresponding to Pol and AGR_{int} retain some word status as clitic elements, i.e. optional bound words. In this perspective the old unity of INFL has really given way to an array of potentially separate phenomena, with wide morphological implications.

This effect is not confined, however, to the approach treating clitics as syntactic phenomena; it characterizes as well the NP solution in its diachronic extension: the NP clitics will eventually need to be allowed as real syntactic clitics, hosted by AGR_{int} in Modern Spanish from the sixteenth century on. The difference between the two approaches consists in the chronological deployment of the AGR_{int} constituent sometime between Late Latin (fourth

---

[17] Other options, e.g., grouping all these elements under I, or some intermediate solution, could be envisaged in a discussion more focused on these problems. The essential decision here is to retain IP as a traditional category and to deny the status of maximal projection for the negation and internal agreement slots, recognizing their special nature.

century) and early Modern Spanish (sixteenth century). For the NP approach, the crucial moment is at the end of this period, during the fifteenth century; for the Head approach, the AGR_{int} slot is already effective by the tenth century for the earliest OSp. documentations.

The Head Movement analysis of OSp. clitics, as shown in (11b), (12b), foresees two distinct movement paths based on the syntactic properties of the Head to be moved and of the available landing sites. A V^0 will be raised to Tns, AGR_{ext}, and to C if applicable; Tns and AGR_{ext} are verb-compatible nodes which accept a moving Head even though they contain previous material (the tense, mood, aspect and subject reference materials). On the other hand, C rejects Head movement with prior occupation of the landing site (a complementizing element, even if in [Spec, C] such as WH forms); but C is compatible with, or neutral with regard to, a verbal element. Head Movement to C is blocked by intervening maximal projections (e.g., subject NP in [Spec, IP], PolP if it is a maximal projection) and negation even if only an X^0 level element; it is also blocked if C is previously filled. The intertwined paths of Head Movement for the N^0 clitic is coded into AGR_{int}, under avoidance of the intervening V^0 node.[18] AGR_{int} is the only noun-compatible landing site, and it is the closest one in the movement path of the clitic (thus, the subject position is not reachable by the clitic, since it is farther away in [Spec, IP]. AGR_{int}, like Tns and AGR_{ext} , is fully transparent for Head Movement of a nonnominal element, e.g., V^0. The negative element in Pol, if present, acts as a blockage for Head movement of V^0 and N^0, so that only postsyntactic principles (a stylistic rule; cf. section 8) can overcome this obstacle. Once a Head element has landed in a site, it is amalgamated with any admissible preexisting material in this location (e.g., verbal inflection) and will undergo further Head movement only as an expanded unit.

The external argument reference is an indisputable fact of all OSp. and MSp. finite verb forms, with their inflectional endings faithfully indicating person and number; hence AGR_{ext} is an essential component, and a co-occurring subject NP constitutes no problem whatever (cf. (13)). On the other hand, in Modern Spanish the reference to internal arguments via clitics (so-called clitic doubling) is obligatory only in specified cases and for given dialects (in principle for [+human, +specific] IO); in the case of DOs it is an optional property for [+human, +definite/specific] NPs, and it is

---

[18] If VP has underlying free order, the V^0 node need not intervene between the syntactic origin of the clitic as DO/IO of V and its landing site to the left of I. However, for the modern Romance languages with fixed underlying order V > O, the avoidance of the V^0 landing site remains unchanged as a requirement. The Modern Spanish or French clitics are not tied up with verbal inflection in the same way as the subject reference endings. An intermediate stage of syntactic amalgamation with the external agreement material is thus not justified.

unacceptable for [−human] and/or [−definite/specific] NPs with Accusative Case (cf. (14)).[19] For the Medieval language, the doubling construction is never obligatory, but it is more freely possible for the constructions involving a [−animate] or [−specific/definite] DO or oblique NP (15), where the modern language registers an ungrammaticality (cf. Rivero 1986: section 3).

(13) a. ({yo, tú, él, ella, nosotros/as, etc. }) vendía + {∅, s, ∅, mos, ys, n}

     b. (yo) vend + o, ({ tú, él, ella, nosotros/as, etc. }) vende + {s,∅, mos, ys, n}

(14) a. *(le$_i$) dimos un precioso regalo a su hija$_i$/a ella$_i$
      IO, [+hum, + spec (+pron)]
      'we gave a great present to her daughter/to her'

     b. no (?le$_i$) haríamos esta confianza a cualquiera$_i$
      IO, [+hum, -spec]
      'we would not make this confidence to just anyone'

     c. *(le/lo$_i$) vimos a él$_i$ DO, [+hum, +spec, +pron]
      'we saw him'

     d. (le/lo$_i$) saludamos a Juan$_i$ DO, [+hum, +spec, +pron]
      'we said hello to John'

     e. (*le/lo$_i$) dibujé este árbol$_i$/éste$_i$ DO, [-hum, +spec, ± pron]
      'I drew this tree/this one'

(15) a. que cate ... que merescimiento et que servicio ha fecho et quales$_i$ los$_i$ puede fazer de alli adelante (Juan Manuel, *Lib. Estados* 156.27, = Rivero 1986:794, ex. (50))
     that he-watch ... what merits and what services he-has done and which-ones (them) he-can do from there onward

---

[19] For this question, cf. Jaeggli (1982), Suñer (1988) in addition to standard language descriptions, e.g., the quantified observations in Keniston (1937b) for MSp., Keniston (1937a) for the sixteenth century, or the finer distinctions in Fernández (1951).

b. las cosas en que$_i$ non se podría y$_i$ poner consejo ninguno
    (from Gessner 1893:20, = Rivero 1986:794, ex. (51a))
    the things in which no one could (there) put advice any

As a consequence, neither OSp. nor MSp. presents doubling data which permit a clear answer to the question of the presence or absence of AGR$_{int}$. The exceptions to obligatory projection of AGR$_{int}$ in Modern Spanish are considerable, at any rate, enough to invalidate any comprehensive claim for truly morphological status of MSp. clitics (so-called objective conjugation of other syntactic frameworks; cf. Heger 1966). The wider availability of clitic doubling in OSp. alternatively should support the view that OSp. clitics are actually more likely to be clitics in syntax, if not morphology, permitting clitic and NP to be distinct, though possibly concurrent, representations of an argument. The impossibility of clitic doubling in specific contexts of MSp. (e.g. (14e)) indicates that the clitic in MSp. has Argument function, at least sometimes, so that the duplication with a coreferential NP in normal Argument position leads to ungrammaticality. Since the OSp. data are more liberal in this respect (15), even in situations where no independent Case marker (such as *a* for IO and [+human] DO) is available, a NP analysis of OSp. clitics requires that the lexical NP appear as a Case-less adjunct NP, while the cl NP has Case and satisfies the Theta grid (cf. Rivero 1986: §3.1). The consequence of this move is that the arguments for the NP analysis thus lose most of their value, since now clitics can appear essentially in any position, and may even be doubled up in D-structure. They thereby render the Theta Criterion basically empty, unless some independent formal correlate can be established to make the liberal system somehow finite and thus learnable. For the Head approach, such doubling is due to the presence of a NP in A position, combined with exceptional Head Movement of a copy of the Head. The double occurrence of lexical material to fill one Theta grid slot creates difficulties for both approaches; but it weakens the NP hypothesis of clitics considerably, since it allows for unrestrained NP generation without identifiable function in the clause.

6.3 TM as corollary of head analysis. The need for TM (3) under the NP approach to OSp. clitics can be eliminated in the Head perspective through the assumption of a separate syntactic slot for Agreement expression of internal arguments, i.e., a slot for clitic elements. This is a desirable consequence, since the negative filter TM (3) presents difficulties with learnability requirements. Furthermore, the postulation of this agreement property (AGR$_{int}$) is independently required in the development to Modern Spanish, regardless of the Medieval clitic pronoun view adopted.

To return to the interpretation of TM (3), the two main avenues of understanding, the NP vs. the Head/Spell-out approach, can well be differentiated in terms of their adequacy for a systematic interpretation of TM (3). For the Head proposal, TM (3) is unnecessary due to general principles, the presence of a node AGR_{int} as landing site for Head clitics, and under the specific assumptions of V-to-(Tns-to-AGR-to-)C raising (morpheme surface order) with empty C. The normal proclitic pronouns in noninitial position find an explanation again through the AGR_{int} slot. For the NP approach, TM (3) is a requirement to block eventual utterance-initial clitics in PF (while such regular NPs may occur in this configuration, yet cannot be differentiated in syntax from eventual clitics). The special position AGR_{int} is not (yet) available for preverbal NP-clitics *ex hypothesi*. Furthermore, the mere reliance on free and optional adjunction cannot guarantee the normally obligatory proclitic arrangement of the {V, cl} group.

For both types of clitic understanding, TM (3) (or its general underlying principle) is a reduced version of W (1), covering only the negative condition against P1 clitics (1b). Neither approach attributes significance to the positive stipulation of Wackernagel's law, i.e., the tendency of clitics to appear in P2 (cf. (1a)), even though this is a frequent surface arrangement. If P2 for OSp. object clitics is the frequent result of NP movement or of the position of AGR_{int} in the string in OSp., this is by sheer coincidence and not because P2 represents an operative target in OSp. Such clitic pronouns are only accidentally in P2. But consistently they are found contiguous to the verb (but cf. section 8), proclitic or enclitic to it, even if this should mean a place further to the right than P2. In the remainder of this paper, TM (3) (or the TM effect) will be a cover term for the analysis proposing AGR_{int} as a relevant site for object clitics, as elaborated here in sections 6.2 and 6.3. Wherever necessary for clarity, the more complex AGR_{int} structures will be indicated; otherwise the TM (3) term will be used for ease of reference.

6.4 Factors determining clitic linearization. The larger picture of clitic linearization in OSp. needs to be considered under the postulation of the two clitic constructs, NP or Head. For the Head proposal, the V centeredness of these clitics is a direct consequence of the assignment of clitics (in S-structure) to AGR_{int}. For the NP view, the contiguity between V and clitic is only accidental, a consequence of the rich topography of NP landing sites around the S-structure V position in I (AGR_{ext}) or C. These targets to the immediate linear right and left of the raised V depend on the liberal availability of adjunction to all types of constituents, maximal as well as nonmaximal projections, and projections of lexical as well as nonlexical categories, as the discussion in Rivero 1986 makes clear.

The two hypotheses thus make different claims about the overt distribution of OSp. clitics. The NP approach foresees such clitics also in isolation from the verb, in structures where either the V fails to be raised to C (clauses with some preverbal, clause-internal constituent, e.g., the subject NP), or where the NP-cl adjoins to a constituent higher than AGR_{int} (e.g. to I' at level Pol, to C' or CP). These predictions are claimed to be significantly fulfilled in Rivero (1986, 1991) by the phenomenon known as Interpolation; cf. (16).

(16) a. si **lo** tu por bien touiesses & lo mandasses; matariemos nos estos x<r>i<sti>anos que son aqui contigo (EE103vb)
          if it you for good would-hold and would-order would-kill we these Christians that are here with-you

      b. este Rey don Alffonso mantouo so Regno muy bien por conseio de los sabios por quien **se** el guiaua (EE100vb)
          this king Don Alfonso ruled his kingdom very well by advice of the wise-men by whom himself he directed

The pronouns *lo* and *si* are said to be adjoined to IP in both cases, so that the order $[_{CP}$ (Spec) (C) $[_{IP}$ clitic$_i$ $[_{IP}$ subject - X - verb ...e$_i$...]]] will result without difficulty by NP movement of clitic$_i$ into an A-bar position. The interpolation phenomenon is discussed at some length in section 8.

In the remainder of this section, the focus is on the overwhelming majority of cases in which V and clitic are contiguous, forming a group {V, cl} with varying linearization. TM (3) (as a corollary of its underlying mechanism of V-to-C raising) makes crucial reference to $[_{CP}$. In the context of $[_{CP}$, only /V-cl/ sequences will be observed. The nonoccurrence of /cl-V/ sequences in given string types in OSp. can thus be taken as an indication of the presence of a left-hand CP boundary immediately before the {V, cl} group. This occurs in the situations of (17), illustrated in (18); cf. Wanner (1990) for a more extensive discussion of this question.

(17) a. absolute initial {V, cl}
      b. after a finite subordinate clause plus {V, cl}
      c. after a nonfinite subordinate clause plus {V, cl}
      d. after a subject or object NP of the matrix clause, followed by a finite/nonfinite subordinate clause plus {V, cl}
      e. after a sentential adverb or adverbial phrase
      f. after a topicalized internal argument NP (with resumptive clitic pronoun strategy)

g. after a topicalized non-argument NP (resumptive pronominal phrase optional)

h. after a root clause coordination with *e, mas*

(18) a. [$_{CP}$ Vansele acogiendo / yentes de todas partes (PMC 403)
go-refl-to him gathering people from all sides
'people are gathering around him from everywhere'

b. mas por que me vo de tierra / [$_{CP}$ dovos .l. marchos (PMC 250)
but because refl. I-go from land I-give-you 50 marks
'but because I am leaving my country, I give you 50 marks'

c. Roy Diaz Çid estando en Saragoça, [$_{CP}$ allegosse a ell muy grand gentio (PCG890.559b46)
Roy Diaz Cid being in Zaragoza came-refl to him very great crowd
'while Roy Diaz Cid was in Zaragoza, there came to him many people'

d. mio Çid quando los vio fuera / [$_{CP}$ cogios commo de arrancada (PMC588)
my Cid when them he-saw outside he-took-refl as of upstart
'when my Cid saw them outside, he positioned himself as for a retreat'

e. Despues [$_{CP}$ fuesse esse rey de Denia pora Tortosa (PCG890.560a23-4)
after went-refl this king of Denia to Tortosa

f. Al rey de Valencia [$_{CP}$ plogol desto quel enuio dezir el rey de Denia (PCG890.560a20)
to-the king of Valencia pleased-him of-this what-him sent say the king of Denia
'the king of Valencia was pleased with what the king of Denia sent to tell him'

g. Con aqueste aver / [$_{CP}$ tornan se essa conpaña (PMC 484)
with these goods return-refl this group

h. et acogieron quanto y fallaron, et [$_{CP}$ tornaronse con todo a
su hueste (PCG1041.725b9-11)
and they-took whatever there they-found and returned-refl
with all to their force

The structural representations of these strings therefore need to contain the
crucial CP boundary, allowing the verb to raise to C to the left of AGR$_{int}$,
as indicated schematically in (18).

Any other configuration will not by itself produce enclisis (but cf. section
7) in the group {V, cl}. This refers in particular to preposed constituents
from the VP or more peripheral oblique functions, to moved wh-phrases (in
questions and relatives, root or subordinate level), VP internal adverbs,
coordination of nonroot clauses and VPs (or even IPs) at any level, and most
subject NPs; cf. (19).

(19) a. [$_{CP}$ la mano$_i$-l ban besar e$_i$ (PMC 298)
the hand-him going to-kiss

b. [$_{CP}$ en vida$_i$ nos faz juntar e$_i$ (PMC 365)
in life us make get together

c. ¿[$_{CP}$ Que$_i$ uos diremos e$_i$? (PCG1044.727a34)
what to-you will-we-say

d. deziendoles palabras [$_{CP}$ con que$_i$ les fazie perder el espanto
e$_i$ (PCG1044.726b50-1)
telling-them words with which them he-made lose the fright

e. / [$_{CP}$ assi$_i$ lo an todos ha far e$_i$ (PMC 322)
so it have all to do

f. [$_{CP}$ onde [$_{VP}$ te ruego] e [$_{VP}$ te conseio] que te non vayas
(PCG59.43a46-7)
whence you I-beg and you I-advise that refl not you-go
'whence I beg and advise you that you not go'

g. [$_{CP}$ [$_{NP}$ yo] vos daria buen cavallo et buenas armas, et una
espada a que dizen Joyosa (PCG598.341a28-30)
I you would-give good horse and good weapons and a sword
to which they-say Joyosa

The implications for the two clitic approaches are parallel, *mutatis mutandis*. For the Head proposal, it is essential to postulate the left-hand CP boundary as indicated in (18), and to presume it removed from the V in the contrastive cases of (19). The independently needed presence of AGR$_{int}$ will then correctly prevent all inadmissible proclitic arrangements of {V, cl} from originating. The extended cost for this analysis is the postulation of the CP boundaries on the root clause portions in (18); this means that the left-hand constituents − adverbial subordinate clauses, topicalized NPs, sentence scope adverbs − are adjoined to CP, while the partially same elements in (19) are clearly internal to the same minimal CP of the group {V, cl}.

The NP-cl proposal needs to operate with the same assumptions as in (8), section 6.1, that [Spec, CP] is not available for the moved NP-cl due to Binding restrictions under Government, and that this extends to other moved Xps from VP origin (i.e., (19)). The structures of (18) could then use [Spec, CP] for the left-hand constituent, or else adjunction to CP, predicting necessary enclisis in {V, cl} in either situation due to the empty C.[20] As before, the stipulation of TM (3) is required for the NP-cl approach to assure that a syntactically unmarked NP-cl cannot appear contiguous to its left CP boundary, a position a regular NP can occupy without difficulty; cf. the ungrammatical (20b) as opposed to the normal (20a) = (19a).

(20)   a.   [$_{CP}$ [$_{NP1}$ la mano] [$_{NP2}$ l] ban besar]   = (19a), NP$_1$,
        NP$_2$ equivalent in
        syn-

       b.   *[$_{CP}$ [$_{NP2}$ l(e)]] [$_{NP1}$ la mano] ban besar]   tax with inverted
                                                                order of NPs

6.5 Effect of *e(t)*. The distinction between root clause and subordinate clause coordination (cf. (18h) vs. (19f)) is a clear indication that the conjunction (mostly *e(t)*, *y*) is not located in C, since this would leave unexplained the strict encliticization for {V, cl} in root clauses. For the Head approach, a left-hand CP bracket is inevitable in (21a), while its absence is crucial in (21b).

(21)   a.   et [$_{CP}$ [$_{C'}$ [$_{C}$ acogieron$_i$] [$_{IP}$ e$_i$ quanto y fallaron]]], et [$_{CP}$ [$_{C'}$ [$_{C}$
        tornaron$_j$][$_{IP}$ [$_{AGRint}$ se] e$_j$ con todo a su hueste]]] (= (18h))

---

[20] If [Spec, CP] is excluded as an A-position, it appears that TM (3) as an actual principle of grammar could operate on a lowered threshold level of the left-hand boundary, i. e., C' instead of CP. However, the proposal does not work out, as discussed at length in Wanner (1990).

b. $[_{CP} [_{PP}$ onde$]$ $[_{C'} [_{C}$ $Ø_c$ $]$ $[_{IP} [_{IP} [_{I}$ te ruego$_i]$ $[_{VP}$ e$_i]]$ e $[_{IP} [_{I}$ te conseio$_j]$ $[_{VP}$ e$_i]]$ $[_{CP}$ que te non vayas y esperes tiempo$]]]]]$ $(=(19f))$

c. $[_{CP} [_{PP}$ onde$]$ $[_{C'} [_{IP}$ te ruego$]$ e $[_{IP}$ te conseio $[_{CP}$ que te non vayas y esperes tiempo$]]$

This structure allows the TM (3) effect to regulate the observed {V, cl} arrangements appropriately. The NP-cl view, short of postulating also TM (3) as implied above, will need to rely on a difference in the C for the two situations. In root clauses with empty C the V raises to C, thus preventing a NP-cl from standing to the left of it; in subordinate clauses, the C must be filled or absent as a position to prevent the same effect from taking place. Given the examples, C could only be filled by a lexically specified null-C in (21b), as opposed to the empty C slot of (21a). If there is no C slot at all, as in (21c), a proclitic result from {V, cl} can also be expected.

6.6 Null complementizer. The question of null complementizer vs. empty C position has one further point of interest. The root clause C is normally empty of true complementizing material (and is thus available as a landing site for the Head-moved V), while in subordinate clauses this position is (almost) always lexically filled (*que* plus assorted elements in [Spec, C] position). In the situation of subordinate clause coordination above, and marginally with a rare example of absent subordinating conjunction as in (22), the observed result is proclisis of {V, cl}. On the other hand, in root clauses the absent C never produces proclisis (in a way comparable to the coordinate conjunction cases of 6.5). Both clitic approaches are led to make a distinction between the empty C slot — for the root clause C — and the null complementizer element present in the subordinate clause.

(22) a. $[_{CP} ... [_{CP}$ C $[_{IP}$ cl - V ... $]]]$

b. $*[_{CP} ... [_{CP}$ Ø $[_{IP}$ cl - V ... $]]]$ predicted as ungrammatical based on TM (3), but solely grammatical

c. $[_{CP} ... [_{CP}$ Ø $[_{IP}$ V - cl ... $]]]$ predicted as grammatical, but not observed

d. donde creo [$_{CP}$ te llevo ya embuelto (Cel 148)
whence I-believe you I-carry already wrapped
'for which I gather that I have you already caught in the
web'

The problem is minor in terms of its textual prominence; the strings of type (22d) are nearly unattested in typical OSp.[21]

6.7 pro as a lefthand environment.

Empty positions vs. null elements provide one more interesting interaction with the linearization of {V, cl} which may prove important for an understanding of the TM (3) effect. OSp. is an undisputed null-subject language, with the external argument represented by *pro*.[22] If subject NPs of OSp. originate in [Spec, IP] position, they can express the SVO characteristics of the language adequately. For S-structure, the V will have moved to I (AGR) for lexical subjects, protecting the /NP {V, cl}/ string from the effect of TM (3), thus permitting proclisis [$_{CP}$ NP cl-V ...]. If the subject is *pro*, this is an empty category of specified status, not just an empty position as the root clause complementizer. But unlike the subordinate clause empty complementizer [$Ø_c$], *pro* does not have the effect of disabling the application of TM (3): otherwise it would be necessary to find clear cases of utterance-initial clitics. This is a situation which is not encountered before the fifteenth century.

There are two possible solutions. Either *pro* can participate with the lexical subject NPs in free postposition to the right of the verb, thus permitting the verb in S-structure to occupy the C slot only when *pro* is postverbal; this would produce enclisis in {V, cl} for verb-initial utterances

---

[21] This is a result of the lack of a lexical null complementizer in most idiolects of OSp. The question needs further study for the history of Spanish; for Italian, with extensive presence of a null complementizer in various functions, cf. Wanner (1981). The oldest example known to me at this point of a grammatical string type (18b) needs to be qualified further. The text is later than what is normally taken to be the limit of Old Spanish; the *Celestina* dates from around 1500 and in many respects represents a language closer to MSp. than a work from the early or middle fifteenth century, e.g., the *Corbacho* (still squarely medieval in its linguistic typology). In spite of this relativization, the syntax of clitic pronouns in the *Celestina* follows the medieval pattern of TM (3) completely for absolute initial position (Keniston 1937a: §5.412) , and variably for CP internal boundary locations and after *e* (Keniston 1937a: §5.3, 5.18, 5.412) in parallel to sixteenth century texts in general. The proclitic arrangement of (22d) carries a respectable frequency of 96 tokens in 16 texts (from a total of 30 possible texts). This feature seems to be a rather late development.

[22] While there is some controversy as to the identity of the null subject in technical terms — pro and PRO being the contenders — this question does not affect the further discussion; the arbitrary choice of *pro* in what follows does not prejudice the argument in any way known to me.

due to the flat structure order V > AGR$_{int}$, or *pro* is viewed as a truly abstract empty category without blocking effect for Head movement of the verb to C, producing the familiar enclitic pattern in the regular way, without the contortions of a variably shifted abstract category *pro*. This second option appears more appealing in the context of the typology of empty syntactic slot [$_C$ Ø], abstract empty category *pro*, lexically empty concrete element [$_C$Ø$_C$] and the syntactically relevant position AGR$_{int}$ as clitic landing site, as discussed here.

7 Enclisis after subject NP. I have argued elsewhere (Wanner 1990) that TM (3) cannot account for all enclitic occurrences in the {V, cl} group, since a considerable class of examples throughout the history of OSp. shows optional enclisis after a lexical subject NP; cf. (23).

(23) a. los moros e las moras / bendiziendol estan (PMC 541)
'all the Moors are blessing him'

b. el prior entendiolo que eran enbargados (Berceo, *S. Dom.* 135c)
the prior understood-it that they-were baffled

c. Et ellos partieron se con sus huestes cada uno a su parte (PCG293.175b48)
and they left refl with their forces each one to his side

d. e el bienauenturado rey don Alonso pusose de ynojos (Alf XI 354.17)
and the very-fortunate king Don Alonso put-himself of knees
'and King Alfonso, much favored by fortune, fell to his knees'

There is no motivated way to bring the TM (3) derived mechanism of a left-hand CP boundary into play to explain the unexpected encliticizations. The placement of the relevant subject NPs to the left of the matrix CP implies discourse dynamic prominence of a topical nature, predicting that only emphasized topical subject NPs would cause this encliticization. But this is not the case; rather the examples show a predilection for nonemphatic topical subjects to have this effect, while all focused and many emphasized topical subjects combine with expected proclisis; cf. (24).

(24) a. Rey, Dios te defenda que non fagas tal fecho (Berceo, *S. Dom.* 145d)
king God you may-defend that not you-do such act

b. el diablo **lo** urde que trae grand enganno (Berceo, *S. Dom.*
152b)
the devil it instigates who brings great deception

c. Un sueño**l** priso dulçe (PMC 405)
a dream-him took sweet
'he fell into a sweet dream'

d. Señor, yo **te me** conozco por rey y muy pecador (Alf XI 354.24)
Lord I to-you myself avow as king and great sinner

Subject status of the NP is essential, since any other Case function will not
produce this kind of additional encliticization; e.g., preverbal object NPs
always combine with proclisis (25a), if they are not marked by the resumptive
pronoun strategy, which leads to enclisis with an initial {V, cl} group; cf.
(25b,c).[23]

(25) a. oro e tus e mirra / **te** offreçieron commo fue tu veluntad (PMC
338)
gold and incense and myrrh to-you they-offered as was your will

b. çiento moros e çiento moras / quiero **las** quitar (PMC 534)
a-hundred Moors (m) and a-hundred Moors (f) I-want them
leave
'I want to leave behind two hundred Moors, men and women'

c. Y el a las niñas / torno **las** a catar (PMC 371)
and he to the girls he-turned them to watch
'and he looked again at the girls'

The mismatch between structural implication by an additional [$_{CP}$
boundary and the reality of the discourse situations argues for the postulation
of a separate minor process of encliticization in the context of an immediately
preceding subject NP; cf. (26).[24]

---

[23] In (25c) the preposed subject *el* does not have the force to pull the clause together into
a single IP constituent.

[24] An alternative analysis could propose an option for the subject NP to be located in [Spec,
CP]. The following C would have to be lexically specified as empty and accessible (against
normal root clause behavior in WH situations) to allow the V to raise to C. If this is not a
motivated analysis, clitic encliticization in this context must be a stylistic reordering rule, as
proposed here.

(26) Subject Induced Enclisis (SIE)

NP$_{su}$ [$_{I'}$ [$_{I'}$ cl - [$_{I}$ V] ...] -> NP$_{su}$ [$_{I'}$ [$_{I}$ [$_{I}$ V - cl] ...]] optional,
stylistic rule

It is equally impossible to account for this phenomenon without some
additional machinery in both types of clitic approaches. TM (3) is irrelevant
due to the inconsequential difference between /subject cl-V/ and /subject
V-cl/ in motivated configurational terms; thus the Head approach needs to
add to the arsenal of encliticization devices. The rather massive evidence in
favor of the (interpreted) principle TM (3) makes it impossible to tamper with
its formulation, e.g., by lowering the threshold value of intervention to C'
from CP (cf. fn. 20 and Wanner 1990 for discussion). The NP-cl hypothesis
cannot invoke any independently motivated restriction on adjunction to IP
with subject NPs in place, since for the majority of examples exactly this
adjunction site must be chosen for the NP-cl to yield the normal proclitic
versions. Subjet Induced Enclisis (26) is an independent phenomenon with
its own diachronic trajectory, expanding throughout the thirteenth century and
receding in the fifteenth century, rather unaffected by other developments of
clitic and other syntax. Its formulation in (26) as a phenomenon concerning
derived structure (after V Movement) includes crucial reference to the direct
contiguity between the subject NP and the verbal complex (e.g., no
intervening negation possible).

To sum up the results obtained so far, TM (3) is an observational
constant of OSp. syntax. The Head proposal, with its independently needed
stipulation of a syntactically relevant position AGR$_{int}$ in adjunction to I', can
dispense with TM (3) as a language-specific (or universal) principle. In its
place the more general and independently motivated principles of Head
movement (for the clitic as N^0 to AGR$_{int}$, and for the verb as V^0 to I or C).
The NP-cl view requires the principle as such regardless of other parameters;
it is needed to constrain the output of otherwise free adjunction of NPs to
various constituent levels wherever these NPs correspond to eventual clitics;
such restrictions do not seem to fall out from other considerations. The
advantage of the NP hypothesis is only apparent. The considerations
surrounding root vs. subordinate clause coordination, and divergent properties
of different null elements, apply equally well to the two approaches, *mutatis
mutandis*. The apparently free variation of enclisis/proclisis after subject NPs
offers some additional support to the non-NP view of OSp. clitics. For the
Head proposal, the reference to the essential ingredients, a subject NP
standing next to a {V, cl} group, is naturally given, since clitics are
identified as such throughout the derivation. Under the NP hypothesis, the
phenomenon would have to be left to chance regulation, given the
impossibility of identifying the clitic element anywhere before the PF

component of stylistic rules.[25]   The stipulated phonological nature of a macroscopic reordering rule parallel to SIE (26) is at least questionable. The Head proposal fares better by being able to circumvent the questionable negative filter TM (3) with the AGR_{int} position.   While this is a direct complication of clausal architecture compared to the Late Latin situation (presumed in the NP-cl approach), it is fully needed as soon as the NP-cl phase changes into the Modern Spanish Head (or Spell-out) situation.

8   Interpolation

8.1   Predictions of different interpretations. The question of the nature of clitics in the context of TM (3) receives some differential light from Interpolation (cf. (16) in section 6.4 above for an initial example).   In the Spell-out approach, object clitics are totally tied to AGR_{int}, thus bound to the verb licensing the theta grid of the clause.   Any separation of the clitic from the verb by elements other than clitics needs an extra principle in this view. Furthermore, it would inappropriately need to elevate a morphological element to syntactic status.

On the other hand, the strength of the NP-cl hypothesis is the correct prediction that NP-cls do not need to be placed with the verb, and that all sorts of material can intervene between the clitic and the verb, of different length and constituency; cf. (27).

(27) a. que **la** tu des a mi (SME 382)
          that it you give to me

     b. ca **le** non tomaria dende nada (Cron. 1344 429.24)
          then of-him not they-would-take from-there nothing

     c. ca sy**la** yo avn non veo yo morre (SME 494)
          then if-her I still not see I will-die

Across the various centuries of OSp. documentation, all kinds of discontinuous arrangements between V and cl are found, giving support to the idea that the clitic positions come about by NP movement, since lexical NPs seem to have the same distribution as surface clitics. The only price to pay for this parallelism is the claim that OSp. clitics are not clitics in syntax,

---

[25] Free NP movement of a NP-cl is not equivalent to SIE (26), since the factual limitation to specific enclisis on the verb, and no further-reaching rightward movement, is not naturally expressible in this framework. Lexical NPs have obviously full freedom of rightward movement.

but actual NPs; the rest seems to follow from standard stipulations of NP behavior in various affected modules.

The Head approach, however, is also in a position to explain the phenomenon of interpolation, since the N-to-AGR$_{int}$ Head movement does not contain an intermediate step of N-to-V movement (contra Kayne 1989; cf. section 6.2 above). In other words, the clitic in surface position is in principle not associated with the V, but with a portion of the larger INFL context, i.e., an adjunct of I'. Through obligatory V-to-I Head movement, the Tense and AGR$_{ext}$ material will be syntactically associated with the lexical V and morphologically amalgamated with it. Separation between I and its left adjunct AGR$_{int}$, i.e., interpolation, is in principle imaginable in the Head proposal through a syntactic shift of AGR$_{int}$. The relevant clitic element has lexical status as N^0 and is only indirectly associated with INFL proper. As a consequence, the Head approach is more accommodating than the exclusive Spell-out solution which does not admit of any Interpolation in a natural way, but Interpolation nevertheless does not come as an equally natural consequence as for the NP hypothesis.

8.2 Extent of interpolation. There are, however, some questionable aspects in the proposed adaptability of the NP approach to Interpolation. The distribution of NP-cls is skewed by not including any occurrences further to the right of the verb than immediate contiguity; i.e., all postverbal clitics are enclitics on the verb. This property is not shared by lexical NPs which may, in fact, be located away from the verb, since, as Rivero (1991) demonstrates, contiguity is not required in OSp. for Case assignment from the verb to the NP; cf. (28a,b), the reconstructed normative clitic versions (28d,e), and the unobservable (28c) for (28b).

(28) a. E desque las bodas fueron fechas, guisaron todos quatro sus huestes muy grandes (PCG293.175b36)
       and after the wedding was made prepared all four their forces very great
       'and after the wedding was over, all four assembled great armies'

      b. en tal que no ouiesses tenido en to poder mi cuerpo$_i$ (PCG 59.41b21-2)
       in such that not you-had held in your power my body

      c. *en tal que no ouiesses tenido en to poder lo$_i$ right separated clitic

      d. en tal que no lo$_i$ ouiesses tenido en to poder   regular proclisis

e. en tal que lo$_i$ no ouiesses tenido en to poder   optional   interpolation (left
separation)

Second, while the material intervening between the V and a left-hand clitic is in principle unrestricted, the inverse angle of observation focusing on the distance of the clitic from the left-hand clause boundary reveals that such a clitic, when separated from its verb, appears in classical Second Position P2: after an overt element in C and/or [Spec, C]. With the exception of some hapax-like constructions (cf. (29)), the separated clitic does not appear outside of P2 with regard to the C of its clause, and thus outside of a subordinate clause.

(29) a. si buen entendimiento **le** Dios quiso dar para entender (Zif 335, quoted in Rivero (1991), ex. (31)) (expected: si (**le**) buen entendimiento Dios (**le**) quiso dar)
if good sense to-her God wanted to-give to understand

b. e o quier que la noviella siempre **la** el veye e la tenie ante los ojos o quier que se el tornasse (GE IV.6.23) (expected: e o quier que la noviella siempre el **la** veye)
and where ever that the young cow always her he saw and her held before the eyes where ever that refl he turned

Third, a serious question must be raised about the overall picture of OSp. clitic syntax as it derives from an approach employing free NP movement for NP-cl placement vis-à-vis the observed reality of the language. On an impressionistic level, OSp. resembles Modern Spanish where clitics are associated with the verb. The cases of interpolation are always in the minority, in most texts they are hardly visible. This slanted distribution toward 'regular' clitic behavior, i.e., clitic syntax compatible with the Head approach, cannot be overlooked. What is ultimately at stake in the serious observation of the surface appearance of a language is learnability.

8.3   Interpolation in its historical development. The array of known data about interpolation - mainly the two studies by Chenery (1905) and Ramsden (1963: 134-158), in addition to Rivero's (1986, 1991) observations - demonstrate clearly that the theoretically complex options of 'free' NP-cl placement[26] are broader than their actual effect. The patterns are almost

---

[26] 'Free' in the sense that the restrictions imposed on adjunction for NP movement are extremely liberal, not really eliminating any imaginable position outside the range of TM effects.

exclusively restricted to the schema (30a), where the string types (30b, c), with the clitic neither in P2 after a C element nor in contiguity to the verb, are virtually absent.

(30) a.　　[$_{CP}$ C cl XP* V ...]

b. ?? [$_{CP}$ C XP cl XP* V ...]

c. ?? [$_{CP}$ XP* cl XP V ...]

　　If the crucial intermediate cases do not have any practical weight for OSp., then the specific interpretation of the NP-cl proposal loses its essential support against an alternative analysis. The alternative is that object clitics attached under AGR$_{int}$ can be subjected to an additional minor rule preventing them from being in contact with the verb and repositioning them under C. This extended Head movement of N=cl from AGR to C has various properties of a stylistic rule of an optional nature. It introduces a formal variation in a certain contrast to the principles of syntax at S-structure (moving a Head over a specified Head or maximal projection, mostly negation, a short adverb or the subject). For the Head movement proposal, Head movement from the DO/IO position to AGR$_{int}$ cannot cross a properly projected PolP, nor can the V-to-I-to-C Head movement do so. This explains the obligatory outcome /neg - cl - V/ in the absence of Interpolation. The fact that Interpolation lets the clitic jump over this negation requires that Interpolation be a different process from the one which effects regular clitic placement and Verb raising, i.e. Head movement.

　　The relatively unnatural character of the interpolation process derives from the inherent contradiction between the conscious and expressive purpose of stylistic rules of the reordering type, and the inexpressive character of the clitic elements affected. But the surface effect of clearly manifest variation is what maintains this process as a viable stylistic rule, like SIE (26).

　　Keeping in line with normal stylistic rules, the actual distribution of Interpolation is heavily steered by nonautomatic quantitative patterns across texts, authors, and periods. An impression of this development can be gained from the graphics in figure I. The three curves, elaborated on the materials collected by Chenery (1905), show the percentage of interpolation cases with regard to the totals of three subclasses of interpolated materials, (a) negation, (b) subject, and (c) adverbs. The 'other' cases (d) do not allow easy tabulation; cf. (31).

(31) a. [C neg V ...], i.e., [C cl neg V ...]　　interpolated;
　　　 [C neg cl V ...]　　　　　　　　　　　 normal
　　　 Et ella dixo que **lo** non farie ca non lo avie mester (EE f102v1)
　　　 and she said that it not she-would-make since not it she-had need

b. [C subj V ...], i.e., [C cl subj V ...]   interpolated;
   [C subj cl)V ...]   normal
   conseio de los sabios por quien se el guiaua (EE f100v2)
   advice from the wise-men by whom himself he oriented

c. [C adv V ...], i.e., [C cl adv V ...]   interpolated,
   [C adv cl V ...]   normal
   El rey Abenhut de que uos ya contamos (PCG 1042.725b22)
   the king Abenhut of whom to-you already we-told

d. [C X^n V ...], i.e., [C cl X^n V ...]   interpolated;
   [C X^n cl V ...]   normal
   Mas ta<n> grand fue el miedo de todos aquellos quel aquello
   oyeron dezir que ... (EE f103v) X^n = DO NP
   but so great was the fear of all those that-to-him that heard say
   that ...

The left-hand element is (almost) always a subordinating conjunction (C). While this is not an exhaustive listing of cases, it accounts for over 80% of the examples collected by Chenery, thus representing the diachronic trajectory of this phenomenon.[27]   It is visible that the second half of the thirteenth century is the period of development of this feature, that it continues strong in the fourteenth century, but with the falling tendency throughout the fifteenth century.   By the sixteenth century, the idealized beginning of postmedieval, later, Modern Spanish, it has disappeared from the language.   The individual text measures show considerable discrepancy for a similar period of time, but the three curves indicate a comparable frequency for the three Interpolation contexts in a given text.

---

[27] The other cases are less apt for quantitative consideration due to their sporadic distribution. For a more complete account of the categorizations of Chenery (1905); cf. Ramsden (1963). The *exordium* in Chenery's materials, the left-hand element on which the interpolated clitic depends, shows a near 100% adherence to some C (or [Spec, C]) element, i.e., a conjunctive element of flat structure: *que, si, quando,* etc. This gives considerable weight to the restrictive formulation (32b) of Interpolation.

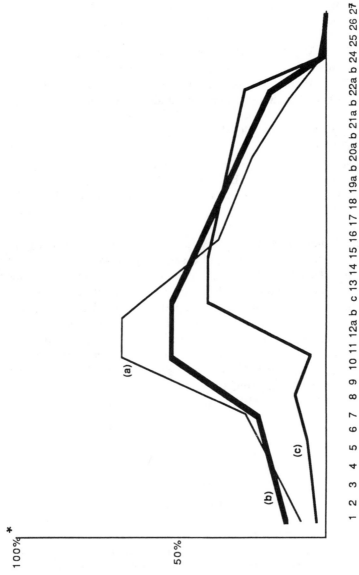

FIGURE I. Development of interpolated elements according to Chenery 1905

* % interpolation of total for elements (a) subject, (b) negation, (c) adverb.

Approximately chronological list of texts considered in data represented in FIG I (for full bibliographical identification, cf. Chenery 1905):

13th century
1 = Poema de mio Cid
2 = Santa María Egipciaca
3 = Apolonio
4 = Berceo, Milagros
5 = Alexandre
6 = Fernán González
7 = Catón
8 = Poemas
9 = Documentos
10 = Infantes de Lara
11 = Conquista de Ultramar

15th century
18 = Pedro de Luna
19a = L. de enxiemplos, ms Paris
19b = L. de enxiemplos, ms Madrid
20a = 4 doctores de Sa. Eglesia
20b = Iosaphat e Barlaam
21a = Amadís de Gaula
21b = Sergas de Esplandión
22a = Almela, *Compendio*
22b = Historia abad Montemayor

14th century
12a = Juan Manuel, Coza
12b = Juan Manuel, Cavallero Esc.
12c = Juan Manuel, Patronio
13 = Libro de buen amor
14 = Poema de Alfonso XI
15 = Rimado de Palacio
16 = Poema de José
17 = Visión de Filiberto

16th century
24 = Celestina
25 = Juan Valdés, Diálogo
26 = Lazarillo de Tormes
27 = Fray Luis de León

This diachronic development is interesting in the specific sense that interpolation is not an archaic feature of OSp. clitic pronouns inherited from the previous Late Latin conditions. In Late Latin, Wackernagel's law W (1a) plus (1b), i.e., preferable positioning of clitics in P2 (and not to the V) regardless of other conditions, can still be observed as a tendency. The virtual nonexistence of this pattern in the earlier OSp. documents casts a heavy doubt on the continuity of this condition between Late Latin and later Medieval Spanish. Interpolation is a process which takes places within the context of the Old Romance TM (3) effect. In this view, it appears justified to postulate the second clitic specific process (32), Interpolation, in contrast to the imprecise assumption of the sole relevance of NP movement for the distribution of clitic pronouns in OSp.

(32) Interpolation (Inpol)

    a. $[_{CP} ... [X^n] ... AGR_{int} ... V ...] --> [_{CP} ...[_X n [X^n] [AGR_{int}]_i]... e_i ... V ...]$ stylistic, optional

    b. $[_{CP} ... [C] ... AGR_{int} ... V ...] --> [_{CP} ...[_C [C] [AGR_{int}]_i]... e_i ... V ...]$ stylistic, optional

The AGR_{int} constituent is thereby moved to adjoin a preverbal left-hand element of some X-bar projection level. In this form, Interpolation (32a) is fully general and can produce all possible patterns. It fails, however, to capture the strong preference for a C to be the effective left-hand element. While the practical restriction of the material intervening between the clitic and the verb is a consequence of the preverbal syntax of OSp. − negation, (mainly unstressed) subject pronouns, short adverbs, preposed object NPs are typically found in this way − the condition on the left-hand element does not fall out from other factors. The stipulation of the normative C (or [Spec, C]) element in (32b) is too exclusive for the very few, but *bona fide* examples like (29),[28] but this configuration alone can explain the standard phonetic encliticization of the moved clitic into the host element.

The claim of this analysis is that Interpolation is a superimposed phenomenon on top of the basic syntactic mechanisms responsible for clitic regulation. The devices needed so far under the Head hypothesis are thus:

(33) Syntax   base generation as N^0 in normal argument position, plus Head movement to AGR_{int} by S-structure

     Stylistic   optional: encliticization after subject NP, R (26) SIE

---

[28] An alternative to outright Interpolation (32) is the hypothesis that the interpolated pronouns are in fact no longer clitics and have regained (or never lost) full NP status. In this way the analysis of Rivero (1986) would enter into full vigor for these instances. The exceptionality of the Interpolation cases would thus derive from the change in syntactic status by the clitic, i.e., an ondulation N -> NP -> N or cl. The argument is not very convincing, since the deviation through NP status is only motivated by an unexpected occurrence in the string of these relatively few cases; their referential properties and phonetic shape are as much clitic (or nonclitic, as the view may be) as all the other clitics found in contiguity to the verb. A third interpretive option is equally unsatisfactory as long as examples of type (29) need to be accounted for. In this view, Head movement of the clitic N^0 would apply further, exceptionally, to let the clitic reach the already filled C position. C would thus act as a permeable element for the content of AGR_{int}. This is in itself exceptional, since a V could never be raised to C under these conditions; furthermore, the sudden transparency of the intervening negation for Head movement would also need to be marked. Again, this is not a better solution than the outright movement rule (32), which has the advantage of declaring the phenomenon as stylistic and thus potentially distinct from standard syntactic restrictions.

optional: repositioning of cl (usually to enclisis with
C), R (32b) Inpol

PF   --

For the NP view, the AGR_{int} position is superfluous, but in turn it requires
the postulation of TM (3) as a concrete filter at PF.   The NP=cl approach
does not need to specify the Interpolation rule (30), since it is seen as a
consequence of NP movement.[29]   While such a NP could reach the [Spec,
CP] position, a move which would produce clause/utterance-initial clitics,
TM (3) will eliminate such occurrences in PF.   But what this restriction on
the process responsible for Interpolation means is that there is a crucial
difference between NPs and eventual NP=cl.   NP=cls are additionally
restricted in their freedom of movement, while NPs are not (admitting
rightward separation from V, CP initial position).   NP=cls appear in an
overwhelming majority (90-95%, frequently even 100% of text frequency,
depending on period and author/text/type of discourse) in arrangements
which distinguish clearly between NPs and NP=cl (only NP=cl between neg
and V) or which favor clitic interpretation in a straightforward Modern
Spanish sense, along the lines of the Head or Spell-out approaches.[30]

9 The two clitics *y* and *ende*

9.1 Special linearization conditions. The picture of OSp. clitic pronoun
behavior turns out to be quite complex, and it becomes increasingly
questionable whether a single classification of clitics as NPs, Ns, or subword
items can do justice to the complications of placement and linearization
encountered in sections 7 and 8.   In fact, one typical Medieval class of
variably stressed, unstressed, or clitic pronominals has only been mentioned

---

[29] Negation needs a special treatment: NP and NP=cl can cross it (= Interpolation). But for
the position between negation and V, a NP is admitted only if it is NP=cl. In Rivero (1991)
the restriction is handled as a condition on *no(n)* to be proclitic on the verb. The problem
demands some adjustment.

[30] Another approach to the surface effect of Interpolation could explore the options of a
parametrization of the expanded I-region of the clause. The order PolP > AgrP > TnsP is not
universally assumed; for Johnson (1989) TnsP dominates the entire complex, while the Romance
data require PolP to be over the others; the relationship between AgrP and TnsP is equally
ambiguous. Languages seem to differ in their choice of order of these elements (in some kind
of connection to the morphological principles governing inflectional word constitution). Thus
OSp. could differ from MSp. in terms of a parameter setting for the order of I-subcomponents.
But even under the assumption of this parametrization, Interpolation can only be accommodated
as far as the interpolated element is the negation. There is no easy extension of this analysis to
subjects, adverbs, and other materials. Again, Interpolation remains without real explanation.

in passing, and it is generally avoided in the recent literature. The adverbial pronouns *y* '(to) there; locative' (basically, *a/en* + NP) and *ende* 'from there; separative; partitive; genitive' (basically, *de* + NP) are frequent in the texts from the thirteenth to the fifteenth century, but they distinguish themselves from regular object clitics by apparently unpredictable placement and linearization behavior. They frequently resemble normal clitics in terms of their placement to the verb (34a, b), but sometimes they appear to have full PP status, even with discourse connected emphasis. This includes CP initial position (34c,d) and rightward separation from the verb (34e), options which do not exist for normal object clitic pronouns. Of the cases which are contiguous to the verb, about one-half follow regular clitics in terms of linearization (as for (34a,b), (35a), perhaps also (34f)); sometimes they even form clusters with other clitics (35b,c). The other half occupy immediately postverbal position (35d,e), sometimes contrasting with a preverbal normal clitic pronoun on the same host verb (35f).

(34) a. derribo del muro todo lo que y dexara su padre (EE 98v1)
     he-destroyed of-the wall all that which there had-left his father

   b. Mas fue y muy mal espantado por un gran roydo (EE 97v1)
     but he-was there very badly frightened by a great noise

   c. // i estauan doña Ximena / con cinco dueñas de pro (PMC 239)
     there stood doña Ximena with five ladies in-waiting

   d. et y lo fallaredes todo (Juan Manuel, *Caballero y escudero* 19.5)[31]
     and there it you-will-find all

   e. & faze a los om[n]es la malazon tan fuerte que muere[n] los omnes **ende** (EE 97v2)
     and he-makes to the people the illness so strong that die the people of-this

   f. el fue y con su cuerpo mismo (EE 98r1)
     he went there with his body same
     'he went there himself'

---

[31] The normal clustering is *lo - y*, and *et* does not allow proclitics to follow it in root clause conjunction (cf. 6). The two properties strongly indicate that *y* in this example is a regular PP, including emphasis to account for its marked CP initial position.

(35) a. & todo lo al que y fallaron (EE 98r2)
and all the other which there they-found

b. quanto se y fizo despues (EE 105r2)
how-much one there did afterwards

c. & quemaron los y cerca de las puertas dell Alcaçar (EE 101r2)
and they-burned-them there close to the doors of-the castle

d. a Roy blasquez que fallo y (EE 96v2)
to Roy Blasquez whom he-found there

e. Mas fue muy mal espantado por un grand roydo que firio y cerca
dell (EE 97v)
but he-was very badly frightened by a great noise that hit there
close to-him

f. & venir te a ende periglo & crebanto (EE 103v2)
and come-to-you has from-there danger and ruin
'and you will receive from it danger and damage'

Given the wide range of placement and linearization options for y and
ende, it will not be possible to recognize the presence of the two stylistic
processes of Subject Induced Enclisis (26) and Interpolation (32) without
considerable ambiguity. The postverbal y in (35f) may be due to the
preferential enclisis of the adverbial pronominals, or it could represent
enclisis due to SIE (26) after the subject pronoun el.[32]

9.2 Variability of clitic status. Two case studies reveal the inherent
variability of clitic status for y, ende (cf. also Badia Margarit 1947). In a
typical thirteenth century Castilian prose text, the Estoria de España
(1270-72), the above picture of y, ende applies directly. For a fourteenth
century text of a different dialectal extraction (Aragonese), the Florilegio by
Heredia, the two pronouns are found exclusively as normal clitics on a par
with the object clitics. This difference between Estoria de España and the
Florilegio is not attributable to diachronic evolution, whereby these pronouns
would have achieved clitic status by the fourteenth century, while before they

---

[32] Since Interpolation (32) is a clitic specific phenomenon affecting AGR_{int}, it may not
surprise that it will not be visible on the not-really-clitic elements y, ende, frequently found
outside the AGR_{int} position. This could be developed into an interesting proof that Interpolation
is not a good argument for NP status of clitics after all.

were still more like NPs. On the contrary, in Castilian the two pronouns were already on the decline in the fourteenth century, further accelerated in the fifteenth century, finally to disappear in the sixteenth century.[33] We will show that the two dialects represent two different solutions of clitic formation for the two pronouns.

9.3 Two case studies.

9.3.1 The selection from EE comprises nine thousand words (ff. 96-105 of ms. E of the Cámara Regia, contemporary with the composition of the work). The 38 occurrences of *y*, and the 12 instances of *ende* fall into the following categories of placement and linearization (36).

(36) *y*

	#	%	%root	#root	#subord
en-norm	15	40	93	14	1
en-except	13	35	8	1	12
pro-norm	10	27	0	0	10
pro-except	-	-	-	-	-
exc-exc	-	-	-	-	-
Totals	38	100%		15	23

---

[33] *y* is only preserved in a lexicalized form *hay* 'there is/are' from *ha* + *y*; *ende* continues as a strong oblique pronoun in a few set phrases, e.g., *por ende* 'therefore' in Msp. -- The dialectal difference is significant since the phenomenon of oblique pronominals of the type *y*, *ende* is widespread in the Romance languages, corresponding to the French *y*, *en* and the Italian *vi/ci*, *ne*. The French and Italian type is fully integrated with the other non-oblique object clitic pronouns (standard clustering, identical linearization and placement properties). For the Ibero-romance subfamily, the *y*, *ende* type is fully functional in the French and Italian sense in Catalan *hi*, *en*; and since the earliest texts from the 11th c. The presence of *y*, *ende* decreases as one moves from East to West in the Northern Iberic Peninsula, Catalan > Aragonese > Riojano > Castilian > Leonese > Galician (cf. Badia Margarit 1947). The crucial transition zone is Aragonese for the modern language (fixed presence of *hi*, *en* in Catalan, increasingly weak reminiscences in Aragonese from East to West as the Catalan typology recedes before the Castilian overlay); in the Middle Ages Castilian and Leonese were the turning point with indecisive formation of *y*, *ende* clitics, as demonstrated in the 13th c. text of *Estoria de España*.

ende

	#	%	%root	#root	#subord
en-norm	5	42	100	5	0
en-except	4	33	(25)	1	3
pro-norm	2	17	(0)	0	2
pro-except	-	-	-	-	-
exc-exc	1	8	(0)	1	0
Totals	12	100%		7	5

en   enclisis (en-norm = normal enclisis according to general predictions; en-except = exceptional enclisis)

pro   proclisis (pro-norm = normal proclisis according to general predictions; pro-except = exceptional proclisis)

exc-exc   exception to clisis (not contiguous to verb or interpolated according to Interpolation (30))

The two pronominals *y, ende* in EE show preponderant clitic properties of placement to their host verb (100% for *y*, over 90% for *ende*). About two-thirds of the cases fall under the regular principles of linearization depending on TM (3), or alternatively its structural correlate of AGR_{int}, optional SIE (26), and coordinate conjunction. The remaining third manifests encliticization (en-except) to the verbal group regardless of the left context (linear or structural). Notice that there are no instances of exceptional proclisis (which would represent anti-TM cases such as (34a) or the absent cases of Interpolation). The one instance of noncontiguity (exc-exc) depends on emphatic word order (V as preposed focus), i.e. example (34e). There is a clear preference for pro-norm arrangements in subordinate clauses (all pro-norm instances for *y, ende*) vs. indifferent distribution of enclisis (en-norm, en-except) in root and subordinate clauses. Encliticization is 'normal' for root contexts (due to TM, SIE and coordination conjunction, a corollary of TM), while in subordinate clauses almost any enclisis needs exceptional motivation. The presence of varied and strong tendencies toward enclisis concerns the root clauses; and these contain (almost) exclusively enclitic instances of *y, ende*. In the subordinate clause, the enclitic preference of *y, ende* is effectively counteracted by the virtual absence of encliticizing forces for regular object clitics. The forms *y* and *ende* have acquired progressive clitic traits, and they will thus be undergoing the pressure toward default proclisis typical of subordinate clauses.

If Interpolation is allowed to apply vacuously to put a clitic element in preverbal position regardless of its distance from the verb, then the subordinate clause procliticizations of *y, ende* (the cases pro-norm of (36)) can be expressed in the following way. The forms *y, ende* are lexically specified as enclitics (if they are not tonic); as such they respond to the one clitic-specific principle which eliminates postverbal enclitics, i.e., Interpolation (30). This principle applies with higher probabilities in subordinate clauses, anchored in the minimal host class of C(onjunction). No new principle is needed beyond the additional class of lexically specified enclitics *y, ende.*[34]

9.3.2 The picture in the *Florilegio* by Heredia is different. The text of about twenty four thousand words contains thirty occurrences of *y, hi,* and fifty instances of *ende* (which has different manifestations, *ende, ne,* and in fixed combination with a pleonastic reflexive, *sende* and *sen*). The placement and linearization distribution is simpler than in EE; cf. (37).

(37)

	y				
	#	%	%root	#root	#subord
en-norm	4	13	100	4	0
pro-norm	26	87	18	5	21
pro-except	-	-	-	-	-
Totals	30	100%		9	21

	ende				
	#	%	%root	#root	#subord
en-norm	4	8	(50)	2	2
pro-norm	44	88	75	33	11
pro-except	2	4	(100)	2	0
Totals	50	100%		37	13

Practically all instances are interpretable as pronominal clitics, and they also follow the linearization patterns of the object clitics. The lexical specification of enclisis is not part of the Aragonese clitics *y, ende/ne* as it is of their Castilian counterparts. The two exceptional proclitics pro-except concern the context after root level coordination (38a) and after root level subject NP with relative determination (38b), which always required enclisis in other texts.

---

[34] This is a situation not unknown from other instances. Modern Italian has the normal object clitics with basic proclitic arrangement, vs. the one lexical enclitic *loro* which is, however, never proclitic, since Modern Italian has no parallel to Interpolation (32) (cf. Rizzi 1982, Wanner 1977).

(38) a. et abagatan ende comio et [CP ne fizo comer a su gent (Flor 33r2)
and Abagatan of-it ate and of-it he-made eat to his people

b. et [CP todos los moros [CP qui pudien escapar del poder delos
tartres] sen fuyen en egipto] (Flor 32r)
and all the Moors who could escape of-the power of-the Tartars
refl-from-there fled to Egypt

But the {V, cl} grouping is fully preserved even in this more advanced
procliticization. In this Aragonese text sample, the heavy preponderance of
proclisis for *y, ende/ne* over their enclisis is purely a function of the different
clitic system found in this text: the TM effect is basically operative for both,
but neither SIE (26) nor Interpolation (32) appears to belong to the grammar
of this dialect/idiolect, so that the many encliticizing forces characteristic of
the *Estoria de España* are absent.[35]

9.4 Lexical clitics. The Heredia text shows a compact clitic syntax for
y, ende, supporting the view of these pronouns as true clitics. The
Alphonsine text, on the other hand, requires a finer gradation between full
NP and clitic, so that the regular components *y, ende* of this OSp. dialect
can be differentiated from the object pronouns as less systematically
developed clitics, and from regular NPs by the reduced freedom of
movement. It is evident from this account that the clitic specification must
be available at the lexical level (object pronouns vs. oblique pronouns, and
both types of clitics vs. regular NPs). Therefore, the specification of
cliticness is available in syntax in the form of a lexical marking to account for
the considerably distinct properties of NPs vs. clitics in placement and
linearization. The additional class of para-clitics *y, ende* makes this even
more essential. Only an approach accommodating cliticness in syntax can do
justice to this situation, i.e., the Head solution as against the NP proposal.
In addition, it is necessary to stipulate lexical classes of clitics to distinguish
between *y, ende* and object clitics.

10 Clitic linearization with nonfinite forms. An additional area of
concern for clitic behavior relates to the non-finite verb forms as host. This
aspect is not normally treated in the recent literature, and it receives only

---

[35] While *y* has a single Aragonese form [i], graphically *y, hi* the type *ende* appears here under
two guises: full *ende* and reduced *ne*. Both derivations from Latin INDE have alternate
manifestations with an amalgamated reflexive, i.e., *sende* full and *sen* reduced. But the
phonological difference does not translate into a difference in outright cliticness; these forms are
all N⁰ in AGR_int.

intermittent attention in previous studies (e.g., Ramsden 1963: 103-11, 179-85). The difference between finite (fn) and non-finite (nf) clitic linearization constitutes a problem for all approaches to clitics, since apparently identical string configurations produce different {V, cl} sequences, depending on the finiteness of the host verb. The nf forms show a clear preference for enclisis of the object pronouns. The present treatment can only point out the major features of the question, and in a rather schematic way.

10.1 Facts. The three form types of interest are the past participle (ppl), the gerund (ger) and the infinitive (inf).[36] They can occur in the basic frames of (a) absolute constructions (without syntactically governing auxiliary/ modal/ aspectual verb), (b) [aux + ppl] as compound tense or passive construction, (c) [aux + ger] for aspectual expression, (d) [modal/aspectual + inf] for varied meanings of relative semantic union between V_1 and V_2, (e) other [V_1 + inf], (f) [V_1 + c + inf] - these three (d), (e), (f) for verb complementation -,[37] (g) [prep + inf] for infinitival and (h) for gerundial adverbial use; cf. the schematic examples in (39). The synopsis also indicates the clitic linearization pattern found with regard to the nf forms in OSp. (omitting interpolation).

(39)

	Function	Form	String	Clisis	Schematic example
a.	absol	nf	ppl - cl	en	*dicholo*
			ger - cl	en	*diziendolo*
			inf - cl	en	*dezirlo*
b.	cpd, pass	aux+ ppl	*ppl-cl/*cl-ppl	-	**ha dicholo/ lo-dicho*
			R:{aux, cl} ppl	en/pro	*lo ha/halo fecho*
c.	aspect	aux+ ger	(aux ger - cl)	(en)	*está diziendolo*
			R:{aux, cl} ger	en/pro	*lo está/estalo diziendo*

---

[36] The present participle (prpl), e.g. *faziente*, is found in Berceo and other texts with clearly Latinizing or Arabicizing tendencies; the form is otherwise not native in Osp. (or Modern Spanish) as a verbal form, only as an adjective or noun, e.g. *diferente* 'different', *cantante* 'singer'.

[37] Structure (e) is also appropriate for subject complement clauses which are typically found in extraposed position.

d. mod/asp   mod/asp   (m/a inf - cl)   (en)   *quiere fazerlo*
            +inf

                       R:{m/a,   cl} inf en/pro   *lo quiere/*
                                                quierelo fazer

e. compl V_1+ inf V_1 inf - cl   en   *cuida fazerlo*
                        (V_1 cl - inf)   *pro   *cuida lo-fazer*
                        R:{V_1,   cl} inf   en/pro   *lo cuida/cuidalo*
                                                 fazer

f. compl V_1 c+ inf V_1 c inf - cl   en   *insiste en fazerlo*
                        (V_1 c cl - inf)   (pro)   *insiste en lo*
                                                 fazer
                        R:{V_1,   cl} c inf en/pro   *lo insiste/*
                                                insistelo en fazer

g. adv compl   p + inf   p inf - cl   en   *para fazerlo*
                           p cl - inf   pro   *para lo fazer*

h. adv ger.   ger   (*en*) ger - cl   enc   (*en*)
                                                    faziendolo

Comments: R: Placement scope on V_1 (corresponding to clitic raising)
              No intervening constituents or inversion of $V_2 V_1$ considered
              here (for neg, cf. (41))
              /V cl V/ surface string always ambiguous where no other
              considerations are applicable
              (en), (pro) indicate infrequent occurrence

There is not only a linearization question for {nf, cl}, but also one of placement for the constructions with two verbal elements (b-f). The scope of the linearization principles may be on V_2, the nf form, or it may be on V_1 (fn or nf, with varying context). Since the clitic pronouns represent arguments of V_2, the shift to V_1 is the well-known phenomenon of Clitic Movement (CM). For the auxiliary construction (b), CM is inevitable; for the modal/aspectual strings (c) it is highly regular, but non-CM cases occasionally do occur. With other complementation structures (e) and (f), regardless of the presence or absence of a complementizing element C, both CM and non-CM configurations are expected, even though the CM result can be viewed as normal in most instances. For present purposes, only the non-CM renderings are of interest, because only here does the question of linearization of an object clitic with the nf verbal host arise. The relevant constructions show a clear preference for enclitic pronoun arrangements, i.e. exclusively for (a), (c), (d), and (h), while for (e) and (f) proclisis is a weak option (rare in the texts). Only the adverbial complementation [prep - inf] shows appreciable proclisis, but not the parallel gerundial cases (h).

10.2 Structural predictions. It is immediately evident that the normal syntactic representations make different predictions for clitic linearization in the context of the principles discussed so far for fn verb hosts; cf. the sketches in (40). If the intervening negation *no(n)* is taken into further account, the patterns of (41) emerge.

(40) fct	string	Clisis	Prcpl	Observed
a. absol	$[_{CP} ...[_{CP} [_C nf]_i - cl ...ei...] ...]$	en	TM	= en
b. cpd	—			—
c. asp	$[_{CP} ...V_{asp} [_{CP} [_C ger]_i cl ...ei ...]...]$	en	TM	= en
d. m/a	$[_{CP} ...V_{m/a} [_{CP} [_C inf]_i cl ...e_i...]...]$	en	TM	= en
e. compl	$[_{CP} ...V_1 [_{CP} [_C inf]_i cl ...e_i...]...]$	en	TM	= en
f. compl	$[_{CP} ...V_1 [_{CP} [_C] cl inf ...] ...]$	pro	(dflt)	≠ en,(pro)
g. adv	$[_{CP} ...[_{PP} p [_{CP} [_C inf]_i cl ...e_i...]]$	en	TM	≠ en, pro
h. advger	$[_{CP} ...[_{PP} (p) [_{CP} [_C ger]_i cl ...e_i...]]$	en	TM	= en

(41) fct	string	clisis	prcpl	observed
a. absol	$[_{CP} ...[_{CP} neg cl nf ...] ...]$	pro	dflt	? ??
b. cpd	—			—
c. asp	$[_{CP} ...V_{asp} [_{CP} neg cl ger...] ...]$	pro	dflt	? ??
d. m/a	$[_{CP} ...V_{m/a} [_{CP} neg cl inf ...] ...]$	pro	dflt	? ??
e. compl	$[_{CP} ...V_1 [_{CP} neg cl inf ...] ...]$	pro	TM	? ??
f. compl	$[_{CP} ...V_1 [_{CP} [_C c] neg cl inf ...]...]$	pro	(dflt)	≠ en, pro
g. adv	$[_{CP} ...[_{PP} p [_{CP} neg cl inf ...]...]]$	pro	TM	≠ (en),pro
h. advger	$[_{CP} ...[_{PP} (p) [_{CP} neg cl ger ...]...]]$	pro	TM	= pro

In principle, the structural approach predicts enclisis for all cases in (40) due to the applicability of the TM effects, a corollary of the AGR_{int} position; the nf V_2 always represents a CP in its own right. Only in (40f) is it impossible for the nf to raise to its governing C, since this constituent is previously filled by the complementizing preposition. In the same logic, the presence of a preverbal negative element must lead to proclisis in all cases of (41), since V-(to-I)-to-C Head movement is blocked by the intervening negation as a lexical element (if not a maximal projection).[38]

The predictions are precise and nontrivial in syntactic terms; the data show a clearly distinct situation; the predictions are thus falsified and the analysis is put in doubt. First, all three cases of (40e,f,g) exhibit enclisis, combined with minoritarian proclisis (40f), and for adverbial clauses even

---

[38] Most negative structures are not easy to document in the extant texts, as is indicated by the notations in (41).

with considerable frequency of proclisis (40g). Second, the structural analysis predicts invariable proclisis on the nf form in the presence of a preverbal negation, as in (41). This is in keeping with the finite verb situation where negation always requires proclisis (as long as interpolation does not intervene). The data for the nf forms contrast with the deductions by showing preferential enclisis, except for the adverbial (41g) and gerundial (41h) with preferred proclisis. Again, the problematical predictions are well motivated within their frame of reference; thus the underlying analysis must be modified, relativized, or abandoned.

10.3 Limitations of structural predictions. It might be possible to take advantage of the shared element PRO of the three affirmative constructions (40e,f,g) to accommodate the varying enclisis. As nonfinite CPs, they all contain PRO as their subject expression in [Spec, IP] position; cf. (42).

(42) String   TM prediction   Other predictions
a. $[_{CP} ...V_1 [_{CP} \emptyset [_{IP}$ PRO nf ...]]]   TM $\supset$ en   SIE(26)$\supset$ pro/en
b. $[_{CP} ...V_1 [_{CP}$ c $[_{IP}$ PRO nf ...]]]   TM $\supset$ pro   SIE (26)$\supset$ pro/en
c. $[_{CP} ...V_1 [_{PP}$ p $[_{CP} \emptyset [_{IP}$ PRO nf.. TM $\supset$ en   SIE (26)$\supset$ pro/en

Enclisis on the infinitives in (42a-c) takes place in the context of an immediately preceding subject expression, PRO. It is thus possible to attribute this enclisis to SIE (26). While the TM effect is sufficient to explain (42a,c) for the enclitic results, enclisis in (42b) can only derive from an additional principle such as SIE (26). The special CP internal conditioning of SIE is thus able to explain the nondifference between adverbial and complement structures with or without complementizing preposition. SIE depends on the preceding subject and not on any more distant element or structural property. In such an interpretation, PRO (at least in (42b)) must count as a lexically specified element (different from the lexically invisible pro; cf. 6.7). As such, it can also explain the variable proclisis found in this context, since SIE is an optional process. For the same reason of variable proclisis against the predictions of the TM effect in (42a,c), SIE may be seen as applicable to all three types of structures in (42), uniting the structural divergence under the identity of the constant element PRO.

The solution disappears, however, through the realization that it cannot accommodate the cases under (41), i.e., the preverbally negated structures. The noncliticizing effect of *no(n)* cannot be modified here, if it is to retain its central and uncontroversial role in the finite {V, cl} situations. In addition, a certain distributional difference must be accounted for between the adverbial and complement cases, given the higher probability of proclisis with the adverbial complements. This is not available to the SIE solution without additional machinery and/or ad hoc imposition of probabilities, i.e., a performance-oriented steering of phenomena dependent on competence.[39]

10.4 Variable situation. Another approach for the nf forms can be attempted via an independently needed differentiation of INFL, specifically for Tense and AGR_{ext}. For finite forms, the raising path of V determines the enclitic/ proclitic arrangement in the {V, cl} group; cf. (43a) vs. (43b), and also (10), (12).

(43)   a. $[_{CP} [_C V+T+A_x] [_{IP} [_I [_{Ai} cl [_{Ax} e_i [_T e_i]]]] [_{VP} e_i ...]]$

--> V > cl

b. $[_{CP} ([_C c]) [_{IP} ([_{NP} x]) ([_{Pol} neg]) [_I [_{Ai} cl$
$[_{Ax} V+A_x+T [_T e_i]]]][_{VP} e_i ...]]$

--> cl > V

The absence of lexically filled preverbal elements (other than the object clitic in AGR_{int}) allows the V+I complex to reach C in (43a); the presence of one or more such elements in (43b) blocks this same super-raising, and the V+I complex remains in the highest accessible position of AGR_{ext}. The raising of V into the I domain is required by the morphological facts. The same treatment applies also to the OSp. imperative forms which do not exhibit any particularity with regard to clitic linearization.[40] For the nonfinite verb forms, the full raising to C should take place in exactly the same way, i.e.,

---

[39] An interesting typology of pre-{V, cl} elements would result from the validation of the PRO solution: enclisis (due to the TM effect) would invariably result from actual absence of material between $[_{CP}$ and {V, cl}, or presence of a nonlexical empty category, including a pro subject; the subordinate PRO, however, would produce enclisis directly through the optional intervention of SIE, even though more frequently than does a lexical subject or subject pronoun (furthermore, in a subordinate clause, which is otherwise exceptional); preverbal negation definitely blocks encliticization by the TM effect, as will any other CP internal element preceding the {V, cl} group. In the same vein, the earlier distinction (section 6.6) between the lexical zero complementizer $[_C Ø_e] = X^0$ and the absence of a complementizer $[_C Ø]$ must be taken into consideration with its differential effect on the TM syndrome (enclisis if the C is empty, e.g., in root clauses; proclisis with a lexically specified zero complementizer in subordinate clauses). From the above discussion it is evident that the encliticization effect as such does not always depend on a single structural item, but sometimes also on the string configuration, so that these factors of encliticization are hierarchically ordered.

[40] The complications introduced by SIE (26) and Interpolation (32) do not require any specific treatment here, since they are only superimposed on the basic mechanism of TM and its structural underpinnings.

wherever no preverbal element (such as neg, c, adv) appears;[41] cf. (44), strictly parallel to (43).

(44)   a. $[_{CP} [_C nf+\overset{\curvearrowleft}{T}+A_x] [_{IP} PRO [_I [_{Ai} cl [_{Ax} e_i [_T e_i]]]] [_{VP} e_i ...]]$

        --> V > cl

     b. $[_{CP} ([_C c]) [_{IP} PRO ([_{Pol} neg]) [_I [_{Ai} cl$
        $[_{Ax} nf+A_x+T [_T e_i]]]] [_{VP} e_i ...]]$

        --> cl > V

The difference between fn and nf INFL would have to consist in the possibility that with nf the need for super-raising to C does not exist obligatorily; this would produce the minoritarian, but still possible, proclitic arrangements. If this effect is expressed in the structure of the INFL for nf, it would require some weakness for purposes of Government in the chain formation between INFL in C and its trace in I. OSp. nf forms contain some Tense indications (ppl vs. ger/inf), so that the specific property needs to reside in AGR_{ext}, the subject reference suppressed as a morphological form. It could be speculated that AGR_{ext} in C could not govern its trace in $[_{AGRext}]$, thus blocking super-raising. The problem with this solution is that the blocking effect needs to be optional and frequently flexible, responsive to a number of secondary conditions, e.g., the adverbial complement showing considerably more proclisis than the verbal complement, even though the structural predictions by themselves foresee obligatory enclisis for adverbial complements, and similarly, standard proclisis for verbal compiements introduced by a complementizing preposition.

     The difficulties with attributing the nf behavior to differential properties of INFL (finite) vs. INFL (nonfinite) are compounded by the fact that Interpolation still needs to be recognized as a separate phenomenon. The inclusion of clitics under the structural portion of I requires the separation of cl from AGR_{int} under I' for Interpolation, in such a way that the verbal inflection can still proceed as normal $([V+T+AGR_{ext}])$. The nonfinite problem is larger than a simple structural modification, especially since it is characterized by variability. Such context-free variation is not generally captured by structural solutions, which necessarily contain an inherent rigidity.

---

[41] PRO, which might be viewed as partially responsible for encliticization with nf forms, evidently does not block super-raising (nor does the usual clitic in AGR_{int}; cf. section 6.2).

10.5   Historical vacillation.   It is interesting to note that the linearization question with nf verb forms does not have a true historical trajectory: the situation at the beginning of the thirteenth century (e.g. in the *Poema de Mio Cid*) is not distinct from the modern pattern of strict enclisis with nf forms. The intermediate appearance of proclisis in different contexts (cf. the range indicated in the tables in 10.2,   10.3) is only parenthetical, unsystematic and astructural.   The appearance of proclisis in PMC is exclusively tied to the verse end where the enclitic pronoun would have destroyed the assonance scheme (45a).   In the middle of the verse, only enclisis with nf forms is documented (in sufficient quantity to represent the true linguistic condition of the language of the author); cf. (45b).   An apparent verse internal proclisis (45c) is rather a case of rare interpolation as with finite forms.

(45)   a.   Vera Remont Verengel / tras quien vino en alcança // oy
                   en este pinar de Tevar / por toler **me** la ganançia (PMC
                   998-9)
                   will-come Remont Verengel after whom he-came in
                   pursuit today in this pine woods of Tevar to take-away
                   from-me the gain

         b.   Las azes de los moros / yas mueven adelant // por a mio
                   Çid e a los sos / a manos **los** tomar (PMC 700-1)
                   the battle-orders of the Moors already-themselves move
                   ahead for to my Cid and to the his-folks at hands them
                   to-take

         c.   si **nos** çercar vienen / con derecho lo fazen (PMC 1105)
                   if us to-encircle they-come with right it they-do

In the Alphonsine prose (second half of thirteenth century), especially the *Estoria de España,* enclisis is normative for infinitives and affirmative gerunds (46a),   while only negated gerunds show proclisis (regularly) (48b).   This distribution is quite expected on the basis of the structural considerations in (41).

(46)   a.   ante que ueuir assi ueyendo **la** perder (EE 101v2)
                   before than to-live so seeing her be-lost

         b.   Empos esto Çulema non **se** fiando en los de Cordoua salio
                   se de la Çibdad (EE 101v1)
                   after this Çuleman not himself trusting in those of Cordova
                   left refl from the city

The *Cavallero Zifar* (about 1300/10, but in a fifteenth century manuscript) shows considerable proclisis, but in variation with enclisis in most cases. The gerund is enclitic (with or without introductory *en*) unless negated, i.e., as in (46). For the infinitive, proclisis is preferred if there is a preposition introducing the nf form, but this applies to complementizing prepositions (47a) as well as to adverbial prepositions (47b), so that there is a need for readjustment of the adverbial string if the structural solution of (41) is to be maintained. In all cases of complementation and adverbial complement there are also enclitic instances, regularly if no preposition precedes (47c), otherwise less frequently than proclisis in the same situation (47d).

(47)   a.   e toviese guisado de **lo** complir (*Zif* 107)
            and might-have managed to it accomplish

       b.   mas querria **lo** conosçer por **le** fazer onra (*Zif* 99)
            but he-would-want him to-know to him make reverence

       c.   deven **los** omes sufrir**se** (*Zif* 107)
            must the people suffer-for-themselves

       d.   en **vos** querer poner en coraçon de conosçer**vos** (*Zif* 98)
            in you wanting to-put in heart to know-yourselves

For the Aragonese texts of Heredia (*Crónica de Morea, Florilegio*), enclisis is actually the only option found with nf forms. While it may be that the negative gerund continued even here with proclisis,[42] the negative infinitive at least appears with enclisis *el sagrament de no dizir lo a tu* (Mor b411-18) 'the oath not to tell you about it'. The situation of the fifteenth century (e.g., the *Corbacho*) stresses the importance of proclisis with adverbial complements (*et por me enojar lo fizo* Cor 611.54 'and to spite me he did it') and a few verbal complements introduced by a complementizer, while enclisis is otherwise standard (except for the negated gerund). By the sixteenth century, the picture has not really changed, as reflected in the *Celestina* and as recorded in Keniston (1937a: chap. 9.2). Enclisis is overwhelmingly more

---

[42] No example was found; but the somewhat younger Castilian Enrique de Villena shows exclusive enclisis, even for negated gerunds.

frequent in all situations than proclisis (1143 examples in 30 texts according to Keniston 1937a); the only hold-out positions for sporadic proclisis are the negated gerund and infinitive (24 examples in 6 texts), the WH constructions of relatives (9 examples in 7 texts) and indirect interrogatives (3 examples in 3 texts), and most visibly, the complements (adverbial or verbal) introduced by a preposition (108 examples in 16 texts). None of the proclitic instances excludes enclisis, not even negation. The array of structures allowing proclisis does not constitute a syntactic class of string configurations, and the grouping of enclitic contexts (obligatory and optional) results in the morphological classification of the nonfinite verb forms, which has been generalized for the modern language.

10.6 A possible solution. The linearization properties of nf forms escape a neat formal solution ever since the thirteenth century. The most promising approach up to this point is to assume enclisis as basic since the inception of true OSp. documentation; proclisis represents an external overlay, conditioned in part by structure (negation) and in part by surface constitution (after preposition, regardless of adverbial or complementizing structure), but in all cases regulated by stylistic preference and individual parameters. The option of more or less unmotivated proclisis is clearly documented in the *Poema de Mio Cid* with the metrical ploy of avoiding enclisis in the verse end due to assonance. The constitution of proclisis at any time during OSp. could be guaranteed by analogical extension from the interplay of enclisis and proclisis with finite forms. The astructural distribution of proclisis (adverbial vs. complement clauses) justifies the invocation of a surface principle such as analogy.

A formal foundation for the entire story can be found in the hypothesis that the difference between finite and nonfinite forms must nevertheless lie in the constitution of their respective INFL regions. The crucial constituent (portion) AGR_{int} is a property of fn forms only, because the complexity of external and internal agreement expression occurs only here. The nf forms lack the external subject reference by definition. As a consequence, the clitic specific node AGR_{int} developed only where necessary, for fn forms with a functional AGR_{ext} node (48a). The AGR field for nf forms is not overloaded and can accommodate the internal argument reference of the clitic in its standard form and position (48b). The difference between AGR_{ext} and AGR_{int} appears now more clearly. AGR_{ext} belongs to a true INFL range, and it requires the verb to raise as far as its position to assure proper agreement expression on the morphological level (48a). On the other hand, AGR_{int} is a more syntactic constituent, in addition an adjunct to true INFL material, and thus optional as opposed to the obligatory AGR_{ext} (48b). It follows from this foundation that for nf forms AGR will consist of internal object reference only in the absence and in the actual place of subject reference, thus with standard enclisis of the pronoun.

(48)a.$[_{IP}$ $[_{I'}$ AGR_{int} $[_I$ AGR_{ext} $[_T$ $]$ $]$ $]$ $[_{VP}$ V ... $]$ $]$ $]$ -->
$[_{IP}$ $[_{I'}$ AGR_{int} $[_I$ $[_{AGRext}$ $[V + T]_{i+j}$ $+AGR]$ $[_T$ e_{i+j} $]]$ $]$ $[_{VP}$ e_i ... $]$ $]$ $]$ =
cl - [V + finite inflection] (without V-to-C Raising)

b. $[_{IP}$ $[_{I'}$ $[_I$ AGR [T]] $[_{VP}$ V ... $]$ $]$ $]$ -->
$[_{IP}$ $[_{I'}$ $[_I$ $[_{AGR}$ $[V + T]_{i+j}$ $+AGR$ $[$ e_{i+j} $]]$ $]$ $[_{VP}$ e_i ... $]$ $]$ $]$ =
[V + non-finite inflection + cl] (without AGR_{ext} materials)

The difference between nf and fn linearization behavior of clitic pronouns in OSp. is thus a consequence of the variable projection of a separate constituent acting as a landing site for such clitics, present in finite forms due to the overload of AGR by subject reference material, absent in nonfinite forms due to the lack of morphological subject reference. This AGR_{int} adjunct to INFL has configurational properties, since the Head movement Raising process of the V complex (V plus AGR_{ext} plus Tense (Mood, Aspect)) leaves it intact in place. When V-to-C applies, the object clitic constituent AGR_{int} remains stable, thus producing the differential enclisis (with V-to-C movement) vs. proclisis (without this Raising due to a blocked path or filled C), as discussed above. For nonfinite forms, this cannot take place, since the sole AGR constituent contains the internal reference material, the clitic, and it is part of the INFL constituent proper, thus eventually integrated into the morphology and not subject to a configurational differentiation.

In this view, the occasional to rather frequent proclisis of the object clitic with nf forms after a preposition or negation is a secondary phenomenon due to flat structure string analogy. The preceding element (prep, neg) acts as the traditional C element of subordinate clauses in filling P1, thus allowing (attracting) the clitic into its preverbal second position by analogy with finite subordinate clauses. The astructural properties of this proclisis, and its rather unpredictable appearance in the texts (as discussed above), mark it as a stylistically guided phenomenon indicative of analogy.

There is a previous analysis available for the nf problem area. It assumes a parallel approach for fn and nf constitution of INFL, both projecting the optional AGR_{int} in adjunction to I proper. Here fn and nf forms should exhibit the same syntactic variability of linearization due to application or not of V-to-C Raising. The contradictory linearizations (characterized above as astructural) need to find a motivation in another corrective process, Subject Induced Encliticization (26) triggered by the syntactically visible PRO. But it has been pointed out above that this solution suffers from serious drawbacks, so that the invocation of SIE (26) does not constitute more than an ad hoc device without any predictive power. The structural solution with a constituent AGR_{int} appearing only for finite forms appears better adapted to the requirements of the data, if the analysis is in general to be maintained on a structural/configurational level.[43]

10.7   Status of Agr(int).   Returning to the larger question of the syntactic status of OSp. clitic object pronouns, it is apparent that neither of the two principled solutions, clitics as NPs or as Head Ns (or even as Spell-out elements of AGR), has particular insights to offer about the situation with nonfinite forms, and that, on the contrary, they cannot accommodate the unmistakably refractory data in any meaningful way. The interpolation phenomena (cf. (45c)) may give some support to NP status; the proposed morphological integration of clitics with nf forms under an undivided AGR indicates the relevance of the AGR Spell-out approach, while the

---

[43] Interestingly, the modern situation is not much more transparent (and receives equally scant attention). While the basic situation is comparable – a principle to fix the scope on V_1 or V_2 (with slightly different conditions), plus a general condition of encliticization to nf forms, without any variation for preceding *c, neg* or adverbial conjunction – the problem now is the imperatives. Affirmative command forms, regardless of left context and irrespective of whether they are imperatives proper or subjunctives, require enclisis in Modern Spanish, while the negative commands, all of subjunctive form, require proclisis. In this last aspect, they seem to follow the inevitable Medieval proclisis with *no(n)*. In the modern requirement of enclisis for affirmative commands, the Medieval encliticization effect of TM (3) is continued in a categorical extension of prototypical CP initial position for commands. All of this holds true in spite of the complete dissolution of the TM effect several centuries previously.

The modern situation of fn, nf verb forms with clitics can be described by a battery of simple linearization conditions (ii) belonging to a morphological component and applying in the order given:

   (i) syntax   scope determination (V_2 vs. V_1 or V_{1+2})
   (ii) morphology   (a) nonfinite   enclisis
                      (b) *no* {V, cl} proclisis
                      (c) imperative   enclisis
                      (d) default   proclisis

These four principles are applicable only to unspecified groupings of {V, cl}; as soon as the linearization aspect is specified for a given instance, it becomes immutable; i.e., there is no reordering of clitics, only one simple order specification per derivation. The given set of principles is not the only possible one; the other ones are, however, not more intuitive or formally better. They all stumble over the affirmative imperative cases (or inversely, over the negated nonfinite forms; cf. (iic) or (iia), given (iib)). This is a frequent problem in the modern Romance languages; it is, e.g., repeated in Italian and further complicated there by optional enclisis/proclisis with negative imperatives, behaving ambiguously according to their function or form (infinitive for 2 sg, or special imperative = finite form for 2 pl). No deeper meaning can be discerned in this distribution; and it is difficult to attribute much more systematicity to the variable Medieval situation of OSp. The integration of this flat structure description with a deeper understanding of the overall nature of Modern Spanish clitics—from syntax to phonology —still awaits a comprehensive study.

interpolation phenomena (cf. (45c)) may give some support to NP status; the proposed morphological integration of clitics with nf forms under an undivided AGR indicates the relevance of the AGR Spell-out approach, while the general clitic behavior with nf and fn forms points toward Head status in a syntactically identifiable string position, AGR_{int}.

The historical-evolutionary point of view may prove helpful at this juncture. The unmistakable NP nature of Latin pronouns (with occasional PF clitic reduction) gives way to a downgrading of the maximal projection to a lower level, e.g., Head status. This takes place over time during Late Latin and preliterary Romance. The process progresses with differential speed for finite clauses and nonfinite clauses. The absorption of the N^0 element into the nf INFL was facilitated by the absence of overt subject reference material and by the normal Latin object reference (for subject function) for infinitives in the widespread *accusativus cum infinitivo* constructions, generally saved into the Romance languages as Clitic Raising (cf. Wanner 1987: chap. 7). The relative independence of argument reference in finite clauses leads to the half-way solution of a separate landing site (AGR_{int}) for these no longer maximal projections with syntactic properties, but also with clitic characteristics. This is the situation of OSp., with all its inherent contradictions of an unfinished system. The further history of Spanish draws the somewhat awkward AGR_{int} constituent (as adjunct to I') progressively into the INFL domain, similar to the status of the nf clitic site AGR under INFL. The Modern Spanish phenomenon of clitic doubling with most internal argument positions is the direct expression of this progressive morphologization of the syntactic clitic phenomenon. It has not yet reached its stable and invariable condition of regular object conjugation, but it may be approaching it progressively. To the extent that clitic doubling is not normative in all cases, the AGR_{int} constituent has not yet been integrated into INFL, perhaps as $[_I \ AGR_{int} \ [_I \ AGR_{ext} \ T]]$. The larger scope diachronic trajectory is by definition structurally imprecise, since it must bridge the configurational discontinuities. In turn it manages to tie together the atomistic aspects of structural precision which cannot accommodate the fluctuations of the data. The two views (and perhaps also other ones) are necessary as complementary perspectives on a highly complex phenomenon central to the reconstitution of Latin syntax as Romance.

The best that can be done for the situation of OSp. nf forms at this point is to give a succinct description of the facts deriving from two independent scalar parameters: (a) verb scope and (b) strength of P1; cf. (49).

(49)a. V_1 scope strength   compound tense > aspectual gerund
                                  > modal/aspectual V > other V_1

b. CP internal strength of P1 negation > preposition (adverbial complementizer) > preposition (complementizer) > $\emptyset_C$[44]

V_1 scope determination is a fact of the language—imprecise, variable, but still continuing in the modern idiom and across the Romance languages (other than French). V scope is semantic in nature (cf. Napoli 1981, Wanner 1982b, 1987: chap. 7), while P1 strength is a lexical-syntactic constraint overriding purely structural constellations, e.g., the inclusion of the adverbial complementizing prepositions under possible P1 elements akin to neg, in spite of the clear structural CP barrier intervening between V_2 and this preposition. The P1 parameter thus presupposes a certain readjustment of the string, equating the adverbial complementizing preposition with the infinitival complementizing preposition.

Associated with appropriate probability indices, left undetermined for the purposes of this study, and interacting freely for each component aspect, the two scalar parameters can produce frequential distribution effects close to the textual observations. What remains to be explained is the nature of these constraints and their learnability. Since they can be observed in similar form in Older Italian and other dialectal or historical Romance idioms, they must represent some linguistically interpretable generalization; since they do not characterize the oldest phases of Spanish or Italian in the same way as they do the later texts from the late thirteenth to the fifteenth, the P1 strength constraint can be viewed as a superimposition over a more pristine, simpler situation, a reinterpretation which derives from the variable interaction of two or more contradictory local ordering principles, as sketched in section 10.7.

The nf verb forms fail to endorse any of the clitic views espoused so far in the recent theoretical literature; they constitute an interesting challenge for a more adequate analysis.

11 Conclusions. If it is not possible to assign cliticness parametrically, how many distinctions in cliticness are really necessary? A general survey (Zwicky 1985) or a loose net of clitic-like properties (Wanner 1987: chap. 9) would predict the possible distinction of an indefinite number of degrees and kinds of cliticness, as many as there are combinatorial variants of feature specifications. It is unlikely that a single language at one point in time would employ more than a minimal number of significant class distinctions between clitics$_a$ vs. clitics$_b$ vs. clitics$_c$, etc. In Old Castilian, the essential distinction

---

[44] Cf. Modern (European) Portuguese, traditionally described in terms of standard enclisis, with various items acting as *attractors* of clitic pronouns into proclisis in a {V, cl} group. This applies very strongly to the negation *não*. Cf. Wanner (1982b), Sampaio Dória (1959).

is between the regular object/indirect object clitics and the oblique/adverbial pronouns, both contrasting with normal NPs. This three-way distinction refers to one coherent class of syntactic manifestations, all of which can express the role of arguments. If true NPs/Pps do not show any restriction with regard to positioning—they can appear in what seem to be clitic positions, other than between negation and V (Rivero 1986, 1991)—their status as maximal projections will be sufficient to predict this pattern, together with the relatively great freedom of constituent arrangement in OSp. (an undisputed fact, e.g., expressed through the stipulation of an unordered constituent pattern within VP; Rivero 1986, Wanner 1990). The distribution of 'regular' clitics and that of the *y, ende* type requires special statements (placement to the verb, linearization, clustering, conformity with TM (3)) which do not apply to NPs, and some of which must differentiate between regular (direct and indirect object pronouns) and particular clitics (*y, ende*). This may be a lexical matter, given the small closed set of forms involved; but as such, clitics (in whichever categorical imperfection) emerge as entities distinct from NPs already in syntax.

At the clitic end, the typology might be continued for OSp. with the definite article. This (lexically determined) form is always syntactically cliticized to a more nominal element, with the two arguable exception types /art + prep/ and /art + rel. conj./, i.e. *el de* and *el que*, where the article-like form acquires lexical status for prosodic purposes (it is stressable and carries weak deictic force, optionally reinforced to a true demonstrative *aquel de, aquel que*). The article, however, does not belong to the same kind of form class as the regular object pronoun clitics, in spite of their etymological identity,[45] and it is not a clitic in a relevant sense; in particular, the article is not affected by the TM (3) effect or any similar restriction. It can stand only in NP initial position, and thus also in absolute initial clause position, in spite of its being a prosodically weak element, like the object pronoun clitics. The article's property is to be prosodically incorporated into the NP and to be invisible as a phonological clitic to a PF principle such as TM (3). For historical purposes, the article in its Late Latin precursor phase did have one more clitic property, that of variable linearization to the N' (cf. Wanner 1987: ch. 3, Aebischer 1948, Kurzová-Jedličková 1963). In an overall view, it is possible to place the four classes on a scalar parameter of cliticness, from near-complete cliticness of the definite article[46] to

---

[45] The articles *el, los, la(s)* are adjectival derivations of Lat. ILLE, ILLA, etc. 'that (one)', while the (3rd person nonreflexive) clitics *lo(s), la(s), le(s), -l, l-* are their pronominal continuations; cf. Wanner (1987:chap. 3).

[46] Cf. also the different, less explicit clitic nature of the indefinite article, e.g., disallowed as a clitic in Harris (1983).

374 / Current Studies in Spanish Linguistics

considerable cliticness of regular OSp. object clitics to variable cliticness of the oblique pronominals *y,* *ende* to the complete noncliticness of NPs as normal maximal projections. Interestingly enough, this gradation corresponds directly to the diachronic development of OSp. clitics, from Late Latin NP to variable clitic (indirectly attested in late Latin texts for object pronouns, and directly for OSp. *y,* *ende*) to majority clitics (OSp. object clitics) to exclusive clitics (OSp., MSp. articles, MSp. object clitics). The different degrees of cliticness are endowed with nonobvious properties, such as the (observational) obeyance of a filter TM (3), or the relevance of the additional clitic principles of Subject Induced Enclisis (26) and Interpolation (32). A purely general treatment of cliticness at PF, without differentiation of lexical groups, will not be able to explain either the synchronic conditions of OSp. nor the previous and ensuing diachronic development of the different classes of clitics: rapid consolidation and de-syntactization of the article, slow categorical (near-)completion of object clitics, and loss of an incipient clitic category at the end of the Medieval phase.

In summary, three phases of syntactic status for clitic pronouns can be presented in the following way.

(1) In Early and (spontaneous) Late Latin, full stressed NPs are prosodically reduced in nonprominent contexts, in particular the nonemphatically used deictic pronouns (e.g., ILLE). Such weakened and lexically skeletal elements are attracted to P2, as foreseen by W (1). A typical clause arrangement leaves such nonemphatic deictics as DO, IO in preverbal position, Latin being a nonrigid V final language. At the same time, emphasized internal Arguments tend to be placed in postverbal (focus) position with increasing frequency and regularity in Late Latin.

(2) The grammaticalization of this trend yields in a covert proto-Romance/spontaneous Late Latin phase the array of typical structures $[_{CP} \text{V - cl} \dots]$, $[_{CP} \text{X cl V} \dots]$, and $[_{CP} \text{X cl Y V} \dots]$ as opposed to truly full NPs in $[_{CP} \text{V} \dots \text{NP} \dots]$ and $[_{CP} \text{X V} \dots \text{NP} \dots]$. The distinction indicates a different status for the elements bravely designated as clitics in opposition to the full NPs; the clitics can be viewed as lexical heads of their respective NPs, having lost their syntactic independence as maximal projections, but still being able to function as argument place-holders in conjunction with an appropriate syntactic prop-up, the verb. The unit creation between clitic and V is essential to offset the loss of syntactic freedom of the Argument; the N^0 level element is more or less tightly incorporated into another X^0 category, yielding the effect of Head movement in derivational terms. The surface effect is encliticization/procliticization of the N to the V according to the syntactic string context; this is due to the halfway-house solution of an AGR_{int} landing site with syntactic, i.e., configurational effect for finite verb forms. This phase may roughly correspond to the Medieval Romance languages, where

a certain syntactic leeway of such clitics is still preserved, tentatively identifiable with their intermediate N^0 status.

(3) With the total loss of prosodic identity for the incorporated clitics, these elements also forego their lexical identity and become more affix-like (without reaching this condition categorically), thus associated with the INFL node (the appropriate AGR portion) of the overall verbal expression. The originally syntactic determination of linearization between clitic and verb changes now into a rather morphological process, akin to the principles responsible for the build-up of morphosyntactic endings for tense, mood, and aspect (T), and person and number (AGR_{ext}). The post-Medieval Romance clitic pronoun systems are the expression of such a grammar.

The three phases are sketched in idealized terms; the transitions must be viewed with a considerable leeway, and the internal consistency of any one phase may be less than perfect (especially between the more advanced Medieval and early modern cliticization phases (2) and (3)).

The structural perspective of this investigation reveals itself to be limited in its significance, since it alone cannot overcome the difficulties and apparent contradictions in the data. A considerable amount of consolidating work lies ahead for the already heavily expanded field of clitic studies.

References

A. Text editions

Alf XI = Gran crónica de Alfonso XI (1344). In R. Menéndez Pidal, ed., 1966. Crestomatía del español medieval. 2.410-414. Madrid: Gredos [location by /chap.no. of original, page.line of ed./].
Berceo, S. Dom. = Gonzalo de Berceo, La vida de Santo Domingo de Silos. Edited by B. Dutton. London: Tamesis, 1978 [location by /stanza.verse/].
Cel = Fernando de Rojas, La Celestina, edited by D. S. Severin. Madrid: Cátedra, 1988 [location by page].
Cor = Alfonso Martínez de Toledo, Corbacho. In R. Menéndez Pidal, ed., 1966. Crestomatía del español medieval. 2.609-15. Madrid: Gredos [location by /chap. no. of original, page.line of ed./].
Crón = Crónica de 1344 (Segunda crónica general). In R. Menéndez Pidal, ed., 1966. Crestomatía del español medieval. 2.429-33. Madrid: Gredos [location by /chap. no. of original, page.line of ed./].
EE = Estoria de España. Edited by R. Menéndez Pidal. 1955. Primera crónica general de España. 1-615 (1:passim, 2:321-349). Madrid: Gredos. 2 vols. [location by /ch. # of original, page. column.line of edition/].
Fern = Crónica particular de Fernando III. Edited by R. Menéndez Pidal 1955. Primera crónica general de España. 1029-1135 (2.713-774). Madrid: Gredos. 2 vols. [location by /chap. no. of original, page.column.line of edition/].
GE = Alphons X the Learned of Castile. General Estoria. Part IV. ms. (transcription University of Wisconsin, Seminary of Medieval Spanish Studies) [location by folio, side, column].

Flor.= Juan Fernández de Heredia (1310?-1396). Florilegio. ms. (transcription University of Wisconsin, Seminary of Medieval Spanish Studies) [location by folio, side, column].

Mor = Juan Fernández de Heredia (1310?-1396). Crónica de Morea. ms. (transcription University of Wisconsin, Seminary of Medieval Spanish Studies) [location by folio, side, column].

Luc = Don Juan Manuel, Libro de los enxiemplos del conde Lucanor et de Patronio, edited by J. M. Blecua. Madrid: Clásicos Castalia, 1982 [location by page].

PCG = Primera crónica general de España. Edited by R. Menéndez Pidal. 1955. Primera crónica general de España. 616-1028 (2.349-713). Madrid: Gredos. 2 vols. [location by /chap. no. of original, page.column.line of edition/].

PMC = Poema de Mio Cid. Edited by C. Smith. Madrid: Cátedra, 1987 [location by verse of edition].

SME = Alvar, Manuel. 1970-1972. Vida de Santa María Egipciaca. Estudios, vocabulario, edición de los textos. Madrid: CSIC (Clásicos hispánicos) 2 vols. [location by verse].

Zif.   = Libro del caballero Zifar. Edited by Joaquín González Muela. Madrid: Clásicos Castalia, 1982 [location by page].

B. Studies

Aebischer, P. 1948. Contribution à la protohistoire des articles *ille* et *ipse* dans les langues romanes. Cultura neolatina 8, 181-203.

Alemán, I. B. 1985. The position of clitics in Old Spanish. Cornell University Working Papers in Linguistics 7, 1-17.

Badia Margarit, A. M. 1947. Los complementos pronominalo-adverbiales derivados de IBI e INDE en la Península Ibérica. Revista de Filología Española, Anejo 38.

Barry, A. K. 1987. Clitic pronoun position in 13th century Spanish. Hispanic Review 55, 213-20.

Beckmann, G. A. 1963. Aus dem letzten Jahrzehnt des Vulgärlateins in Frankreich. Zeitschrift für romanische Philologie 79, 305-34.

Borer, H. 1984. Parametric Syntax: Case studies in Semitic and Romance languages. Dordrecht: Foris.

Brandi, L., and P. Cordin. 1989. Two Italian Dialects and the Null Subject Parameter. In O. Jaeggli and K. J. Safir, eds., The Null Subject Parameter. Dordrecht: Kluwer. 111-42.

Browne, W. 1974. On the Problem of Enclitic Placement in Serbo-Croatian. In R. D. Brecht and C. V. Chvany, eds., Slavic Transformational Syntax. Ann Arbor: Dept. of Slavic Languages and Literatures, University of Michigan. 36-52.

Chenery, W. H. 1905. Object Pronouns in Dependent Clauses: A Study in Old Spanish Word Order. PMLA 20, 1-151.

Chomsky, N. 1986. Barriers. Cambridge, Mass.: MIT Press.

Fernández, S. 1951. Gramática española. vol. I: Los sonidos. Los nombres y pronombres. Madrid: Revista de Oriente.

Gessner, E. 1893. Das spanische Personalpronomen. Zeitschrift für romanische Philologie 17, 1-54.

Harris, J. W. 1983. Syllable Structure and Stress in Spanish: A Nonlinear Analysis. Cambridge, Mass.: MIT Press.

Heger, K. 1966. La conjugaison objective en français et en espagnol. Langages 3, 19-39.

Hofmann, J. B. and A. Szantyr. 1972. Lateinische Syntax und Stilistik. Munich: Beck (Handbuch der Altertumswissenschaft, II.2.2)

Jaeggli, O. 1982. Topics in Romance Syntax. Dordrecht: Foris.

1991-92
Seattle Youth
Symphony Orchestr.

50th Anniversary

SEATTLE YOUTH SYMPHONY

Performance Dates:
Sunday Afternoons:
November 24, 1991
March 8, 1992
May 10, 1992

All performances
Seattle Center Opera House
For info, call or write
11065 5th NE Suite E
Seattle, WA 98125
To order call (206) 362-2300
1 p.m. - 5 p.m. Weekdays

For Families & Friends

2 For 1

SEATTLE YOUTH SYMPHONY
is pleased to offer you a
FREE TICKET
ENJOY ONE COMPLIMENTARY TICKET
WHEN A SECOND TICKET OF EQUAL OR
GREATER VALUE IS PURCHASED.

Valid thru October 1992   **215**
(Not valid with any other Coupon, Promotion or Sale)

Non–Transferable / Cash Value 1/20th Cent

SKATE KING

*"Family Roller
Skating Center"*
Fun for everyone!
Get the whole family out
for an evening of skating.
A night to remember for everyone!

641-2046
2301 140th N.E.
Bellevue
852-9371
10210 S.E. 260th
Kent

For Families & Friends

2 For 1

(Skate Rental Extra)
(Not Good for Special Events)

skate king
is pleased to offer you
FREE ADMISSION

**Valid for One Complimentary Admission
when a Second Admission of Equal or
Greater Value is Purchased.**

Valid thru October 1992   **216**
(Not valid with any other Coupon, Promotion or Sale)

Non–Transferable / Cash Value 1/20th Cent

Jaeggli, O. 1986. Three Issues in the Theory of Clitics: Case, Double NPs, and Extraction. In H. Borer, ed., Syntax and Semantics 19: The Syntax of Pronominal Clitics. New York: Academic Press. 15-42.

Johnson, K. 1989. Clausal Architecture and Structural Case. Ms., University of Wisconsin-Madison

Joseph, B. D. 1978. Morphology and Universals in Syntactic Change: Evidence from Medieval and Modern Greek. Bloomington: Indiana University Linguistics Club.

Kayne, R. S. 1975. French Syntax: The Transformational Cycle. Cambridge, Mass.: MIT Press.

Kayne, R. S. 1989. Null Subjects and Clitic Climbing. In O. Jaeggli and K. J. Safir, eds., The Null Subject Parameter. Dordrecht: Kluwer. 239-61.

Keniston, H. S. 1937a. The Syntax of Castilian Prose. Chicago: University of Chicago Press.

Keniston, H. S. 1937b. Spanish Syntax List. New York: Holt.

Klavans, J. L. 1985. The Independence of Syntax and Phonology in Cliticization. Language 61, 95-120.

Kurzová-Jedličková, H. 1963. Die Demonstrativa im Vulgärlatein. Acta Antiqua Academiae Scientiarum Hungaricae 11, 121-43.

Laum, B. 1928. Das alexandrinische Akzentuationssystem. Paderborn: Schöningh.

Menéndez Pidal, R. 1944. Cantar de mio Cid. I: Crítica del texto, Gramática. Madrid: Espasa-Calpe.

Meyer-Lübke, W. 1897. Zur Stellung der tonlosen Objektspronomina. Zeitschrift für romanische Philologie 21, 313-34.

Mussafia, A. 1886. Una particolarità sintattica della lingua italiana dei primi secoli. In G. I. Ascoli et al., Miscellanea di filologia e linguistica in memoria di N. Caix e U. A. Canello. Florence: LeMonnier. 255-61.

Mussafia, A. 1898. Enclisi o proclisi del pronome personale atono quale oggetto. Romania 27, 145-6.

Napoli, D. J. 1981. Semantic Interpretation vs. Lexical Governance. Language 57, 841-87.

Pollock, J.- Y. 1989. Verb Movement, Universal Grammar, and the Structure of IP. Linguistic Inquiry 20, 339-63.

Ramsden, H. 1963. Weak-pronoun Position in the Early Romance Languages. Manchester: Manchester University Press.

Rivero, M. L. 1986. Parameters in the Typology of Clitics in Romance and Old Spanish. Language 62, 774-807.

Rivero, M. L. 1991. Clitic Climbing and NP Climbing in Old Spanish. (In this volume)

Rizzi, L. 1982. Issues in Italian Syntax. Dordrecht: Foris.

Sampaio Dória, A. de. 1959. Sintaxe de pronomes. São Paulo: Ed. Nacional.

Steele, S. 1978. The Category AUX as a Language Universal. In J. H. Greenberg et al., eds., Universals of Human Language. Stanford: Stanford University Press 3. 7-45.

Suñer, M. 1988. The Role of Agreement in Clitic-doubled Constructions. Natural Language and Linguistic Theory 6, 391-434.

Tegey, H. 1977. The Grammar of Clitics: Evidence from Pashto and Other Languages. University of Illinois doctoral dissertation.

Thurneysen, R. 1892. Zur Stellung des Verbums im Altfranzösischen. Zeitschrift für romanische Philologie 16, 189-307.

Tobler, A. 1875 (=1912). Review of J. Le Coultre, De l'ordre des mots dans Chrétien de Troyes. Vermischte Beiträge zur französischen Grammatik 5. Leipzig: Hirzel. 395-414.

Tobler, A. 1889. Vermischte Beiträge zur französischen Grammatik, 10. Zeitschrift für romanische Philologie 13, 186-91.

Wackernagel, J. 1892. Über ein Gesetz der indogermanischen Wortstellung. Indogermanische Forschungen 1, 333-436.
Wanner, D. 1977. On the Order of Clitics in Italian. Lingua 43, 101-28.
Wanner, D. 1981. Surface Complementizer Deletion: Italian *che* ~ ∅. Journal of Italian Linguistics 6, 47-82.
Wanner, D. 1982a. Pragmatics and Syntax in Portuguese Clitic Placement. In J. Lantolf and G. Stone, eds., Current Research in Romance Languages. Bloomington, IN.: Indiana University Linguistics Club, 194-206.
Wanner, D. 1982b. A History of Spanish Clitic Movement. In M. Macauley et al., eds., Proceedings of the 8th Annual Meeting of the Berkeley Linguistics Society. Berkeley: Berkeley Linguistics Society, 135-47.
Wanner, D. 1987. The Development of Romance Clitic Pronouns: From Latin to Old Romance. Berlin: Mouton de Gruyter.
Wanner, D. 1990. Subjects in Old Spanish: Conflicts between Typology, Syntax and Dynamics. To appear in: P. Hirschbühler et al., eds., Proceedings of LSRL XX. Amsterdam: Benjamins.
Zwicky, A. M. 1977. On Clitics. Bloomington: Indiana University Linguistics Club.
Zwicky, A. M. 1985. Clitics and Particles. Language 61, 283-305.

Perfective *haber* and the theory of tenses

Karen Zagona*
University of Washington

0 Introduction. The analysis of perfect tenses illustrated in (1), compared with simple tenses in (2), has played a central role in investigations seeking to develop a theory of Tense for natural language.[1]

(1) a. Los estudiantes han leído eso.
the students have + PRES read that
'The students have read that.'

   b. Habíamos corregido los ejercicios a las tres.
have + PAST + 1stPL   corrected the exercises by three o'clock
'We had corrected the exercises by three o'clock.'

(2) a. Los estudiantes leen eso.
the students read-PRES that
'The students read/are reading that.'

   b. Corregimos los ejercicios a las tres.
correct + PAST + 1st PL the exercises by three o'clock
'We corrected the exercises by three o'clock.'

As observed by Hornstein (1981), perfect tenses are problematic for theories of tense which analyze 'tenses' themselves (eg., PAST, PRESENT, FUTURE) as the primitives of the theory. While the representation of simple tenses in (2) is straightforward, Hornstein argues that such theories, including Tense Logic and Generative Semantic approaches, can only represent perfect tenses through recursion of tense operators or predicates. For example, a generative semantic analysis of (1b) would be shown in (3), details aside.

---

*I wish to thank Magui Suñer, Judith Strozer, Carlos Otero, and Heles Contreras for helpful comments on an earlier draft of this paper. All remaining errors are, of course, my own.

[1] There is also a third form, the future perfect:

   (i) Los niños se habrán despertado para las nueve.
   the children will have awoken by three o'clock

This paper will examine the interaction of present and past tenses with perfective *haber*, and will not be concerned directly with the future tense. For discussion of future interpretation, see Zagona (1989).

(3)

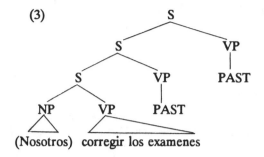

(Nosotros) corregir los examenes

Hornstein notes that, although such a representation is adequate to express the interpretation of the past perfect, it is formally too powerful as a mechanism for describing the tenses of natural languages. Since the mechanism which achieves the interpretation is recursion of the tense predicate, and there are no bounds on recursion, it is predicted that the number of possible tenses is infinite. Consequently, such theories fail to explain the absence of iterated tenses as in (4).

(4) Past Past Past Past ...

They therefore fail to account for the acquisition of tenses for particular languages, since UG provides no constraints on the notion 'possible tense'.

For these reasons among others, generative studies of the grammar of tense (Hornstein 1977, 1981; Enç 1987, Zagona 1988b, 1989) have adopted approaches which analyze 'times' as the basic entities of tense analysis, and TENSE as a relation between times. In one such approach, following Reichenbach (1947), Hornstein (1977) proposes that there are three times which are necessary for characterizing tenses: S (the moment of speech), R (reference time), and E (the time of the event). There are two operations which relate times: 'linearity' (represented by __) and 'associativity' (represented by ,). The former operation characterizes a precedence relation between two times and the latter is simultaneity or cotemporality. The temporal representation of (1) - (2) would be as shown in (5) - (6).

(5) a. Present Perfect: E __ S,R

     b. Past Perfect: E __ R __ S

(6) a. Present: S,R,E

     b. Past: E,R __ S

The interpretation of (5a) is that the event precedes the moment of speech and reference time, and the latter two are cotemporaneous. In (5b), the event precedes the reference time, which in turn precedes speech time. In (6a), the three times are all associated, and in (6b), the reference time and event are linearized relative to speech time. This type of framework is more explanatory than those mentioned above, since it permits the grammar to delimit the number of 'times' which are available in UG to a small number, so that the number of tense relations in a given structure is also restricted, and the theory approaches the degree of restrictiveness necessary to account for the acquisition of tenses.

In the following sections, I will compare the Reichenbachian analysis of Hornstein (1977, 1981) with the analysis of 'Temporal Argument Structure' (TAS) of Zagona (1988b), examining each with respect to their ability to account for properties of perfect tenses. Section 1 will introduce the framework of TAS, noting the crucial differences with the account described above. Sections 2 and 3 will argue that the TAS model is better able to account for distinctive properties of perfect tenses, including (a) their interaction with lexical aspect, (b) the interpretation of durational adverbs and (c) the interpretation of the 'immediacy' of the event. Section 4 concludes the discussion with a reexamination of the goal of restrictiveness for theories of tense.

1 Temporal argument structure

1.1 Syntactic realization of 'times'. It is proposed in Zagona (1988b)[2] that the basic entities referred to as 'times' are syntactically realized as (temporal) arguments selected by the [±TENSE] features of INFL. The complement of INFL, VP, is theta-marked[3] with an internal temporal role (EVENT),[4] and an external role (SPEECH TIME) is realized in the Spec of

---

[2] The core concept of the TAS framework, the notion that 'times' are temporal arguments of a clause, is introduced in Zagona (1988b). Further development of the framework, including syntactic reflexes of temporal arguments and examination of construal of tenses is found in Zagona (1988a, 1989, in press).

[3] The notion of theta-marking of VP by INFL is introduced in Chomsky (1986), although the nature of the role is not specified. For discussion, see Zagona (1988b, chapter 3).

[4] The term EVENT to describe the internal temporal argument of the clause is adopted from the Reichenbach (1947) framework, and is not meant to distinguish aspectual subclasses (e.g., 'activities' versus 'states').

CP.[5] The temporal representation of simple tenses such as (7) is shown in (8).

(7) Marta   cantó.
    Marta   sing + PAST
    'Marta sang.'

(8) $[_{CP}$ T-Arg $[_{IP}$ Marta $[_{I'}$ [Agr [+ TNS]] T-Arg (= VP)]]]
                                        [+ PAST]

In (8), *T-arg* in CP is Speech-time and VP is the syntactic category that is interpreted as the event of the clause. This interpretation derives from the assignment of a temporal theta-role to VP. The feature [+ PAST] is a Case-like feature assigned by [+ TENSE], which temporally identifies the Event VP.

Notice that in (8), there are only two temporal arguments: the Event and Speech-time. This analysis, which follows from the absence of a syntactically realized third argument, is captured in terms of the lexical properties of [±TENSE], which is analyzed here as transitive. By contrast, perfect tenses are analyzed as involving a third temporal argument in addition to the two shown in (8). Let us adopt the term 'reference point' of the Reichenbachian framework as a term for the role assigned to the VP dominating *haber* 'to have' in (9). The temporal argument structure for (9) (details aside) is thus as shown in (10).

(9) Juan había cantado.
    Juan have + PAST sung
    'Juan had sung.'

I assume that temporal features, including the referential index and temporal role of Speech-time do not interfere with other elements that move to the Spec of CP. Since 'times' are a type of entity with the special property of being ordered, it is reasonable to suppose that both the type of role and the type of index involved are distinctive, and that principles of grammar such as the Theta-criterion are sensitive to the distinction.

For a different approach to temporal arguments, see Enç (1987). Enç's analysis permits Comp to bear a temporal (referential) index, although Comp is analyzed as a Spec of IP, rather than as an independent argument.

(10)

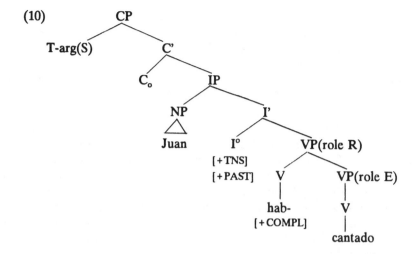

In (9), INFL (i.e., [±TENSE]) assigns the role R to its complement (headed by *haber* 'to have') and *haber* in turn assigns the role E to its complement.

A central claim embodied in this approach is that a 'time' cannot constitute part of a logical form unless a temporal role is assigned to a syntactic constituent, and is thus an argument. In other words, temporal arguments are subject to the Theta-criterion and Projection Principle. It is thus clear why there is no Reference-argument in (8): there is no VP which is present to bear the role R, therefore (unless R is an 'implicit' argument) it plays no part in the interpretation of the simple tenses.[6]

This approach utilizes theta-theory to limit the number of times that are available to tense theory, and also relates the appearance of temporal arguments to properties of individual lexical items. The argument structure selected by heads is shown in (11).[7]

(11) a. [±TENSE]   E, S (Ext)   (e.g. (8) above)

b. [±TENSE]   R   (e.g. (10) above)

c. *haber:*   E, S (Ext)   (e.g. (10) above)

---

[6] Note that INFL could not assign the role R to its complement if *haber* 'to have' is not selected, since in this case, INFL does not select an external argument (the roles S and E are assigned by *haber*), and the clause would have no temporal construal.

[7] The categorial selection of the internal roles, which is not marked in (11), is understood to be VP.

As shown in (11a,b), [±TENSE] may assign the roles: S and E, or it may assign the role R (selecting *haber*), and *haber* in turn selects S (which raises to CP) and E. It is notable that the Tense features of INFL and *haber* have in common the ability to take temporal arguments. However, they differ with respect to the ability to assign a feature [±PAST] to license a temporal argument. I return to this point in section 2.3.

1.2 Construal of tenses. Rather than assuming that construal derives exclusively from two semantic operations, 'linearity' and 'associativity', the TAS approach includes a syntactic component which contributes to construal by subjecting temporal arguments to Binding Theory. This is a natural extension of Binding Theory on the assumption that temporal arguments are analogous to standard arguments in their referential status, since it is to be expected that conditions on coreference are expressible in Binding terms. The features [+PAST] and [-PAST] assigned by INFL are the basis of the feature complexes [±Anaphor], [±Pronominal], stipulated as shown in (12) and (13).[8]

(12)   [+PAST] = [-Anaphor], [-Pronominal]

(13) a. [-PAST] = [-Anaphor], [+Pronominal]

   b. [-PAST] = [+Anaphor], [-Pronominal]

   c. [-PAST] = [-Anaphor], [-Pronominal]

The feature [+PAST] implies a precedence relation between a temporal argument and Speech-time (i.e., 'linearizes' it from Speech-time), and this argument therefore cannot be understood as anaphoric to Speech-time. Consequently, I take [+PAST] arguments as name-like, and assume that they are subject to Principle C. On the other hand, [-PAST] may receive any of the interpretations in (13), depending on syntactic conditions. I will focus here on (13a) and (13b),[9] but first a word of explanation of (13c). Following

---

[8] An additional [-PAST] possibility, discussed in Zagona (1989) is: [-Anaphor], [-Pronominal], for future readings of present and future tenses. Like past tense, future readings are name-like, in that they are disjoint from Speech-time. However, unlike past tenses, future readings are proposed to require an A-bar binder. They are thus analogous to variables with respect to binding.

[9] The missing specification: [+Anaphor], [+Pronominal] is not available for internal temporal arguments, since these are always governed by INFL. It is standardly assumed that the features [+Anaphor] [+Pronominal] can only be attributed to the ungoverned element PRO, since any governed element with those features would result in a Binding contradiction. If PRO

Zagona (1989), I assume that 'future' interpretations are available for [-PAST] inflected arguments if the event is A-bar bound by a modal or modally construed constituent (such as a future adverb). Being A-bar bound, the event is the equivalent of a variable, and is well-formed if it bears the feature specification in (13c).[10]

1.2.1 Construal of Simple Tenses. Returning to (13a)-(13b), consider the interpretations of (14)-(15).

(14) a. John sings.   (Generic-present; *present-moment event)
     b. Juan canta.   (Generic-present; present-moment event)

(15) a. John is singing.   (Present-moment construal)
     b. Juan está cantando.   (Present-moment construal)[11]

The generic reading of (14) does not mean that the event of singing takes place at the moment of speech, but rather at some unspecified time(s). The construal of (14a) must express this, since English present tense does not have present-moment readings. I take the generalization underlying the generic present to be a pronominal-like reading, where the event may refer to any time, just so it does not refer to speech time. In other words, the Event-argument satisfies Principle B. Principle B is satisfied if the Event argument is free in its governing category. This will be true if IP is the minimal category containing a governor for the Event-VP (INFL) and an accessible subject (Tense features).

The present-moment reading of (14b) and (15) does assert that the event takes place at Speech-time, and in this sense is claimed here to be [+Anaphoric]. This reading is obtained if the Event-argument of the clause satisfies Principle A, requiring that it be bound (by the external argument, Speech-time) within its minimal governing category. As proposed in Zagona (in press), the contrast between English and Spanish with respect to the

---

had a governor, it would have a governing category, and would then be forced to satisfy both Principle A and Principle B of the Binding Theory.

[10] The hypothesis that the fundamental tense distinction is [± PAST] is proposed in Otero (1974), which utilizes both purely temporal features and aspectual features (perfectivity) to characterize Spanish tenses. That analysis similarly captures the advantages of both Jesperson's and Reichenbach's insights.

[11] Note that the progressive construction may also have a non-present-moment interpretation in the presence of adverbs:
   (i) Marta está estudiando física este trimestre.
      'Marta is studying physics this quarter.'
The interpretation of (i) does not imply that Marta is necessarily studying at the present moment.

availability of this reading can be related to the possibility of V-movement to INFL by S-structure. Since Spanish permits V-movement, it may be supposed that Principle A is satisfied by, in effect, expanding the governing category for the event VP. The structure after movement is shown in (16).

(16) $[_{CP}$ T-arg C° $[_{IP}$ Juan V+INFL $[_{VP}$ t_v . . .]]]

The Event-argument (chain) now consists of V°+INFL-VP. The closest governor is C°, and within CP there is a potential binder, so Principle A can be satisfied. The event is now construable as cotemporaneous with Speech-time.[12]

Further evidence for a configurational basis for construal is the interpretations of (15a,b) as present-moment events. In these cases, V-movement to INFL is available in both languages, and as in (16), the Event argument has CP as a governing category, so that Principle A can be met.

A central claim of the analysis described above is that the construal of tense does not derive directly or exclusively from specification of [±PAST], as in the Reichenbachian framework.[13] Instead, [±PAST] are handled as syntactic features which have a binding-theoretic interpretation, as illustrated in the examples (14) - (16). Empirically, this analysis is supported by the fact that [-PAST] inflection does not have a unique interpretation (S, R, E) and by the fact that the interpretation(s) available in a particular structure (and language) appears to be determined configurationally, as is expected if Binding Theory is relevant.

1.2.2 Construal of perfect tenses. A second claim which follows from the TAS approach is that perfect tenses are not 'double' tenses, but are instead complexes of two distinct relations: a 'tense' (a 'time' which has a binding-theoretic interpretation in relation to Speech-time) and a second

---

[12] Although no main verbs move to INFL in English, State predicates are understood as true at Speech-time (e.g., *That box contains your papers.*). Zagona (in press) argues that the manner in which this reading is derived must be distinct from that of activities. States are true at 'every' moment in their interval, while activities may have gaps or interruptions in the activity during the interval at which the predicate holds.

[13] To be precise, it is the 'Basic Tenses' of Hornstein's analysis which have interpretations exclusively determined on the basis of [± PAST]. Basic tenses can be operated on by Adverb Rules, so that a certain range of change from the Basic Tense Structure is permissible. For example, to derive the future reading for (i), the adverb 'tomorrow' linearizes R, E from S, as shown in (ii).

(i) Mary leaves tomorrow.

(ii) S,R,E <u>tomorrow</u> ->   S __ R,E

                         tomorrow

relation (between R and E), claimed here to be an 'aspectual' relation. In other words, the verb *haber* 'to have', which selects an Event-argument, does not assign the feature [±PAST] to that argument. Rather, it assigns an aspectual feature [+COMPLETED]. This analysis follows from the TAS framework on purely syntactic grounds. To illustrate, consider the alternative hypothesis, according to which *haber* not only selects an Event argument as its complement, but also assigns an inflectional feature [+PAST] which licenses that complement (allowing it to satisfy Binding Theory) relative to Speech-time. Under such an analysis, *haber* would be identical in properties to the [±TENSE] features of INFL, and it would be expected that clauses of the type in (17) would be well-formed.

(17) *Juan comido.
     'Juan eaten.'

In (17), a [+Finite] INFL assigns the feature [+PAST] to its Event argument, and that complement is realized as the participial suffix *-ido*.[14]

Let us specify in further detail the nature of the interpretation of [+COMPLETED].[15] The claim underlying the use of this aspectual feature rather than the 'tense' feature [+PAST] is that while the latter linearizes the entire event relative to Speech-time, the former aspectual feature implies only that 'one aspect' of an event is linearized with respect to Reference-time. The contrast is illustrated in (18).

(18) a. Juan lo vio.
       Juan it see + Pret. + 3rd.sg.
       'Juan saw it.'

     b. Juan lo veía.
       Juan it see + Imperf. + 3rd.sg.
       'Juan was watching/looking at it.'
       'Juan used to see it.'

     c. Juan lo ha visto.
       Juan it have + Pres + 3rd.sg. seen
       'Juan has seen it.'

---

[14] See Zagona (1988a,b) for further syntactic arguments that the participial inflection is not identical to [+ PAST].

[15] M. Suñer (p.c.) suggests that the appropriate feature is [+PERFECTIVE], insofar as [+COMPLETED] is often understood to imply that the entire event is terminated. As the discussion in the text indicates, this generalization is not correct for the relation between Reference-time and the Event expressed by the participle.

In (18a) and (18b), the entire event of Juan's seeing or watching precedes the moment of speech, such that if Juan also sees it now, this seeing is construed as a distinct event. As observed by Bull (1968), only one aspect of the event of (18c) is necessarily prior to the [-PAST] Reference-time. There are two forms of evidence in support of Bull's observation. First, sentences like those in (18) can be completed as shown in examples (19) - (21).

(19) Susana lo buscó,
    a. pero no lo encontró.
    b. *pero no lo encuentra.
    'Susana looked for it,
    a. but didn't find it.
    b. *but doesn't find it.'

(20) Susana lo buscaba,
    a. pero no lo encontró.
    b. *pero no lo encuentra.[16]
    'Susana was looking for it,
    a. but she didn't find it.
    b. *but she doesn't find it.'

(21) Susana lo ha buscado,
    a.   *?pero no lo encontró.[17]
    b.   pero no lo encuentra.
    'Susana has looked for it,
    a.   *?but didn't find it.
    b.   but she doesn't find it.'

With verbs such as *buscar* 'to look for', which have no inherent termination, the present-perfect event of (21) is understood as perduring to the present, while this is not possible in (19) and (20), since both the Preterite and Imperfect are [+PAST], i.e., the entire event precedes (is disjoint from) the present.

---

[16] M. Suñer (p.c.) observes that a present tense may complete (20) in examples such as the following:
    (i) Susana lo buscaba, pero no lo encuentra/va a encontrar porque yo lo escondí.
    'Susana was looking for it, but she doesn't/won't find it because I hid it.'
It seems to me that the 'not finding' in (i) must be understood as an event which is independent of Susana's searching, and instead is a consequence of the hiding of the object. If correct, this implies that the searching need not be understood as continuing to the present.

[17] The continuation in (21a) is expected to be grammatical for speakers for whom the present perfect may have a reading analogous to the preterite, as in French and Italian.

A second type of evidence, as Bull notes, is that construal of the perfectivity of the event is determined by aspectual properties of the participle. The manner in which aspectually distinct verbs affect construal of the perfect tenses is illustrated in (22) - (23).

(22) a. Marta lo ha/había comido.
'Marta has/had eaten it.'

b. Marta se ha/había levantado.
'Marta has/had gotten up.'

c. Los niños lo han/habían encontrado.
'The children have/had found it.'

(23) a. Marta lo ha/había amado.
'Marta has/had loved him.'
b. Marta ha/había escrito poemas.
'Marta has/had written poems.'

c. Su esposo le ha/había obligado a hacer las compras.
'Her husband has/had obliged her to do the shopping.'

In the examples in (22), the final or terminative aspect of the event is completed, and thus the entire event is completed. These sentences exemplify 'desinent' verbs, while the sentences in (23) exemplify 'non-desinent' verbs.[18] The latter examples, like (18c) and (21b), assert either that the beginning of the event or some part of the event is completed, but not that the entire event is completed.

Returning to the comparison with Hornstein's analysis, recall the basic tense structure for Perfect tenses given in (5), and repeated here as (24):

(24)   a. Present Perfect: E _ S, R
        b. Past Perfect: E _ R _ S

The analysis in (24) has the characteristic that it treats the 'completedness' in examples (22) -(23) as linearized, in the same way that the event of past tenses is linearized for examples like (17a) and (17b), whose basic Tense Structure is repeated as (25).

---

[18] For this distinction, Jespersen (1924: 287) adopts the terms 'conclusive' and 'non-conclusive'; Bull (1968) adopts the terms 'cyclic' and 'non-cyclic', and also cites Bello's terms 'desinent' and 'non-desinent'. For further references and discussion, see Jespersen (1924: 273ff).

(25) E, R __ S

Although there is a formal difference of location of the Reference Point in (24a) *versus* (25), the theory, (a) does not provide any semantic correlate to this difference, and (b) does not express the fundamental distinction between the 'entirety' of an event preceding Speech-time and an 'aspect' of an event preceding the Reference point. By contrast, the claim that the relation between *haber* 'to have' and its past participle is aspectual rather than tense-like, does express the distinction.

1.3 Summary and comparison. The framework of TAS, which analyzes 'times' as temporal arguments of a clause, differs from the Reichenbachian framework in several respects. First, as discussed in section 2.1, the availability of 'times' for construal is restricted by Theta-theory, so that the Reference point is an entity for construal of perfect tenses, but not simple tenses. In the Reichenbachian framework, all tenses are complexes of the three times, and there is consequently no formal distinction between simple and compound tenses.

Second, the TAS framework permits application of Binding theory as an element in tense construal. Since 'times' are arguments, it is expected that coreference between temporal arguments should be subject to syntactic constraints, as is the case for standard arguments. This claim permits an explanation for the range of interpretations available for [-PAST] tenses, and for the generalization that the interpretation in particular cases appears to be purely syntactic (configurational) in character. By contrast, the Reichenbachian framework of Hornstein (1977, 1981) associates an interpretation with tense morphology itself. This predicts that each tense should have a unique interpretation, insofar as the structure is not altered by the addition of other constituents such as adverbs.

Third, the Reichenbachian framework described here analyzes perfect tenses as double tenses, in the sense that the relation between S and R is of the same 'type' as the relation between R and E. The TAS framework distinguishes the 'tense' relation between times from the 'aspectual' relation which obtains between R and E. It was argued that this generalization accounts for the fact that the aspectual relation of 'completedness' is not a relation between two temporal arguments, but rather between a temporal argument (Reference-time) and an aspect of the event.[19]

---

[19] I assume lexical aspect to be represented as temporal features (e.g., [± Durational], [± Inceptive]) associated with V^0 or V'. See Zagona (1988b, appendix to chapter 3) for further discussion.

Sections 3 and 4 will present further arguments for the TAS framework with respect to analysis of perfect tenses. Section 3 considers the construal of temporal adverbs, and section 4 examines the nature of the 'immediacy' of Present-Perfect events.

2 Adverb construal. As noted above, the TAS and Reichenbachian frameworks differ in the nature of the relation that is asserted to hold between the Reference-time and the Event of Perfect tenses. The Reichenbachian framework linearizes the Event, so that it precedes the Reference point in perfect tenses, in exactly the same manner in which the Event precedes Speech-time in a simple past tense.

(26)   a. Simple Past: E, R __ S

       b. Present Perfect: E __ S, R

       c. Past Perfect: E __ R __ S

In both (26a) and (26c), the Event is linearized relative to S, S,R or R. By contrast, the TAS framework analyzes the relation as an aspectual relation between the Reference point and an aspect of the Event. This is illustrated in (27), adopting the terminology of Hornstein's analysis for comparison.

(27)   a. Simple Past: E __ S

       b. Present Perfect: E $<+C>$ R, S

       c. Past Perfect: E $<+C>$ R __ S

The construal of the [+COMPLETIVE] symbol $<+C>$ in (27b), (27c) is that one aspect of E precedes R. It is argued here that the construal of adverbs supports the latter analysis.

2.1 A rule of adverb construal. Let us begin by reviewing Hornstein's (1977) analysis of adverb construal. It is proposed that adverbs may modify either the Reference point or the Event, as shown by the ambiguity of (28).

(28) La secretaria había salido a las tres.
     'The secretary had left at three o'clock.'

In (28), either the secretary's leaving occurs at three o'clock, or the secretary's leaving is prior to three o'clock. For each interpretation, the adverb is associated with one of the two times. This is accomplished by adding the adverb to the basic structure for Past Perfect, deriving the representations in (29).

(29) a. E _ R _ S three o'clock -> E _ R _ S
                                            three
                                            o'clock

    b. E _ R _ S three o'clock -> E _ R _ S
                                            three
                                            o'clock

Since both R and E may take adverbs, as shown in (29), and since the relation between R and E in the past perfect is the same as the relation between E and S in the simple past tense (E,R _ S), it is expected that the same range of adverbs and the same range of interpretations should obtain in both cases.

Recall that by contrast, the TAS analysis posits an aspectual relation between aspectual *haber* 'to have' and the Event: *haber* assigns a feature [+COMPLETED], which modifies an aspect of the Event, rather than the whole event. Since the relation between Speech-time and Reference-time is of a different character from the relation between Reference-time and the Event, the TAS analysis predicts that adverbs should not behave or be interpreted identically in the two cases. The reading on which *a las tres* 'at three o'clock' modifies R (corresponding to (29a)) is shown by the structure in (30).

(30)

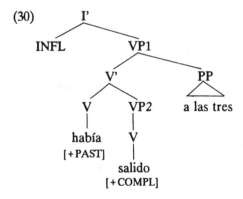

In (30), the adverb modifies the time R, so Reference-time is 'three o'clock', and an aspect of the Event of leaving is completed relative to R. Because *salir* 'to leave' is a desinent verb, the aspect which is picked out as completed is its termination, and the entire event is consequently understood as completed, by inference.[20]

The reading on which the secretary's leaving is at three o'clock is derived by generating the adverb as an adjunct of VP_2, as shown in (31).

(31)

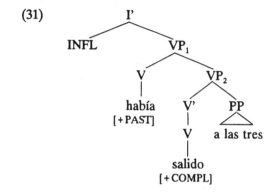

In (31), the adverb modifies the event, so leaving takes place at three o'clock. As in (29), the terminative aspect of the event is completed at the Reference-time, which is therefore understood as prior to three o'clock. The Reference-time is also prior to Speech-time by the feature [+PAST].

We have seen that both analyses derive the two readings of (28) by associating a temporal adverb with Reference-time or the Event. The analyses differ both in the manner in which the interpretation is derived, and in their predictions for nondesinent verbs and for nonpunctual adverbs. The Reichenbach framework predicts that interpretations should be identical in relevant respects to those described above for three other cases: present perfect events should be analogous to (29a); desinent and nondesinent verbs should pattern alike; and punctual and durational adverbs should pattern like durational adverbs in relevant respects. The TAS framework predicts that nondesinent verbs should not pattern like desinent verbs with respect to the first reading, since nondesinent verbs will not invite the inference that the entire event is completed. It also predicts that past and present perfect events should pattern differently, since in each case, completedness is relative to R, but the two differ as to whether R is identified as Speech time

---

[20] The claim that the event of leaving is completed 'by inference' in (30) is supported by comparison with nondesinent verbs in parallel structures. Consider (i):

    (i) La campana había sonado a las tres.
       'The bell had rung at three o'clock.'

On the reading parallel to (30), with 'three o'clock' modifying R, the bell is understood to have begun ringing prior to three o'clock, but the termination of the event may or may not have occurred prior to R.

or as past time. As for durational adverbs, the Reichenbach framework predicts a possible interpretation as in (29a) for verbs which accept durational adverbs. This prediction is not made by the TAS framework, since the event of past perfects is not claimed to be linearized relative to R. In the following discussion, I will show that with respect to each of these predictions, the TAS framework provides the correct generalizations. We begin by examining the construal of punctual adverbs with additional verbs in simple and compound past tenses in 2.2, then consider durational adverbs in 2.3.

2.2 Punctual adverbs. Punctual adverbs are interpreted differently depending on whether they modify an event in the Preterit or the Imperfect past, as illustrated in (32)-(33).

(32) a. La campana sonaba a las tres.
'The bell was ringing/used to ring at three o'clock.'

b. Se ruborizaba a media noche.
'(S)he was blushing/used to blush at midnight.'

c. Estaba allí a las dos.
'(S)he was there at two o'clock.'

d. Salía a las nueve.
'(S)he was going out/used to go out at nine o'clock.'

e. Llegábamos a la una.
'We were arriving/used to arrive at one o'clock.'

(33) a. La campana sonó a las tres.
'The bell rang at three o'clock.'

b. Se ruborizó a medianoche.
'(S)he blushed at midnight.'

c. Estuvo allí a las dos.
'(S)he was there at two o'clock.'

d. Salió a las nueve.
'(S)he went out at nine o'clock.'

e. Llegamos a la una.
'We arrived at one o'clock.'

In each of the examples in (32), the adverbs describe a time during the interval of the event. For example, in (32a) the ringing of the bell continues for some length of time, one moment of which is three o'clock; similarly in (32b) for blushing, etc. In (33), the event is not understood as ongoing at the specified time, but neither is it a purely 'punctual' event. Rather, the adverb modifies one aspect of the event: either its inception, as in (33a) - (33c) or its termination, as in (33d,e). The determination as to which aspect of the event is picked out by the adverb is determined by properties of the verb. 'Desinent' verbs (see 1.2.2) are understood to terminate at the time specified by the adverbs; nondesinent verbs are understood to begin at the time specified by the adverb.

The Reichenbachian framework predicts that perfect tenses should pattern with one or the other of the simple tenses in interpretation of punctual adverbs relative to R or S,R in past and present perfect tenses. As the examples in (34) show, punctual adverbs are not felicitous with the present perfect when the adverbial is taken to denote a unique time.[21]

(34) a. ??La campana ha sonado a las tres.
          'The bell has rung at three o'clock.'

      b. ??Se ha ruborizado a medianoche.
          '(S)he has blushed at midnight.'

      c. ??Ha estado allí a las dos.
          '(S)he was there at two o'clock.'

      d. ??Ha salido a las nueve.
          '(S)he has left at nine o'clock.'

---

[21] There are several points to be taken into account with respect to the examples in (34). First, as H. Contreras (p.c.) notes, these examples are grammatical on a reading where the adverb does not denote a unique time, and the statement has a habitual reading. I assume that in these cases, the adverb invokes a contrastive reading. For example, (34a) would mean that at three o'clock today the bell did not ring, but that it has rung on other days at three o'clock.

Second, as C. Otero (p.c.) notes, for some speakers examples (34a,b and d) are acceptable in certain contexts. For example, (34a) is acceptable if the sentence is uttered the same day on which the bell has rung at three o'clock. By contrast, (i) is ungrammatical:

(i) *Ayer la campana ha sonado a las tres.
    'Yesterday the bell has rung at three o'clock.'

The analysis developed in the text predicts the status of (i), but provides no immediate explanation for the relative grammaticality of the above-mentioned text examples under the specified conditions.

Finally, the examples in (34) are expected to be fairly acceptable for speakers for whom the present perfect freely replaces the simple preterite (as in French and Italian). However, according to Bull (1968), punctual adverbs are not felicitous with the preterit interpretation, even for such speakers.

e. ??Hemos llegado a la una.
'We have arrived at one o'clock.'

The first point to be noted in connection with the examples in (34) is that their status relative to (32)-(33) is not predicted by the Reichenbach framework. Since in both cases the Event is linearized, it is expected that the adverb rules should treat both cases alike. The issue which remains mysterious for the Reichenbach framework is why there should be a difference between the two structures in (35a), (35b) with respect to punctual adverbs:

(35) a. E, R __ S   (Past)

b. E __ S, R   (Present Perfect)

Informally stated, the generalization which appears to be missed in the Reichenbachian framework is that punctual adverbs modify past times which are linearized from Speech-time by the tense feature [+PAST], and that this tense-type relation does not hold in the Present Perfect, contrary to (35b). Instead, as is implied in the TAS analysis, only one aspect of the event of a present perfect tense is construed as [+COMPLETED] in relation to the time R, and furthermore, the event is not in a temporal (i.e., linearized) relation to Speech-time. In the TAS framework, the status of the examples in (34) is accounted for by the absence of a tense-like relation between S and E. The Event is, in effect, an unspecified interval, one aspect (moment) of which precedes R. Since the event itself taken as a whole is unspecified as a time relative to Speech-time, a punctual adverb has no [+PAST] temporal argument to modify.

Consider now the parallel examples of (36) in the past perfect.

(36) a. La campana había sonado a las tres.
'The bell had rung at three o'clock.'

b. Se había ruborizado a las ocho.
'(S)he had blushed at eight o'clock.'

c. Había estado allí a las dos.
'(S)he had been there at two o'clock.'

d. Había salido a las nueve.
'(S)he had left at nine o'clock.'

e. Habíamos llegado a la una.
'We had arrived at one o'clock.'

Of the examples in (36), only (36d) and (36e), with desinent verbs, are transparently ambiguous. The nondesinent verbs in the first three examples are construed as having the event occurring at the time specified by the adverb. The alternative reading, where the Reference-time is modified by the adverb, and the event is completed, or prior to that time, requires the addition of a second adverb, as in (37).[22]

(37) a. La campana ya había sonado a las tres.
'The bell had already rung at three o'clock.'

b. Ya se habían ruborizado a las ocho.
'They had already blushed at eight o'clock.'

c. Ya había estado allí a las dos.
'(S)he had already been there at two o'clock.'

The distinct interpretations of [±Desinent] Events is predicted by the TAS framework, since only one aspect of the Event is claimed to be completed relative to the Reference-time. The addition of *ya* 'already' as a modifier of the Event in the examples in (37) adds an additional specification of completedness to the Event. The Reichenbach framework, as discussed above, predicts that all the examples in (36) should be ambiguous, since the Event is, in all cases, analyzed as linearized relative to R. Furthermore, it predicts that the adverb *ya* in (37) is redundant, rather than being necessary for construal of the second reading of the examples with non-desinent verbs.

To conclude this discussion, we have seen that two of the respects in which the Reichenbach and TAS models make distinct predictions for construal of perfect tenses have provided support for the TAS framework. First, the TAS model correctly predicts that punctual adverbs cannot modify the Event of a present perfect tense, since completedness of the event is evaluated relative to R, which is itself construed as Speech-time. Second, the TAS framework correctly predicts the nonambiguity of nondesinent Events with a single punctual adverb in the past perfect. The Reichenbach framework incorrectly predicts that nondesinent and desinent events should have identical potential for ambiguity. We will see in section 2.3 that the

---

[22] Hornstein (1977) follows Braroe (1974) in claiming that adverbs 'add to' temporal interpretations, rather than modifying readings which are already inherent in basic tense structures. In view of this claim, the fact that the second reading for past perfect nondesinent verbs is available only if an adverb such as 'already' is introduced, supports the contention that the Event of the past perfect is not inherently linearized relative to Reference-time, as claimed in the Reichenbach framework.

construal of durational adverbs provides additional evidence for the TAS framework with respect to the construal of perfect tenses.

2.3 Durational adverbs. Durational adverbs such as *(por) dos horas* '(for) two hours' describe the duration of past events, as illustrated in (38) and (39) for Preterit and Imperfect past tenses.

(38) a. Estuvo allí dos días.
'(S)he was there for two days.'

b. Cantamos por tres minutos.
'We sang for three minutes.'

c. Trabajaron por veinte horas.
'They worked for twenty hours.'

(39) a. Vivíamos en México tres meses y en Chile dos.
'We used to live in Mexico for three months, and in Chile for two.'

b. Hacíamos las compras por seis meses, y luego las hacía él por seis.
'We used to do the shopping for six months, then he did it for six.'

c. Parecía cansada por varias horas.
'She seemed tired for several hours.'

Although durational adverbs in (38)-(39) modify the duration of the event itself, rather than an aspect of the event, the adverb is nonetheless sensitive to aspectual properties of the event. Desinent verbs, or verbs understood punctually, are either ungrammatical, as in (40a), or have a distinct reading, as in (40b,c).

(40) a. *Terminó el trabajo (por) un momento.
'(S)he finished the job (for) a moment.'

b. Salió por media hora.
'(S)he left for half an hour.'

c. Se levantó una hora.
'(S)he got up for an hour.'

In (40b) and (40c), as in the English equivalents, the adverb does not modify the event, but rather an interval following the event of getting up or going out.[23]

One contrast in interpretation between the readings of (38) and (39) follows from the difference in interpretation between Preterit and Imperfect. In the examples in (38), the event is understood to be ended at the end of the time specified by the adverb. In the Imperfect, the events described are 'habitual'. Despite these differences, both tenses have the property that the durational adverb describes an interval of the event, and that interval is linearized with respect to Speech-time. That is, in neither case is the interval of the event understood as perduring to Speech-time.

With respect to the last point, consider examples (41) and (42) in the Past Perfect:

(41) a. Había estado allí dos días.
          '(S)he had been there for two days.'

      b. Habíamos cantado por tres minutos.
          'We had sung for three minutes.'

      c. Habían trabajado por veinte horas.
          'They had worked for twenty hours.'

(42) a. Habían vivido en México tres meses.
          'They had lived in Mexico for three months.'

      b. Había hecho las compras por seis meses.
          '(S)he had done the shopping for six months.'

      c. Había parecido cansada por varias horas.
          'She had seemed tired for several hours.'

As these examples show, durational adverbs have a distinct interpretation in perfect tenses from their interpretation in simple past tenses: in these examples, the duration of the event is understood as ending at the Reference-time. That is, unlike the simple past tenses, where an unspecified

---

[23] This point is noted in Bull (1968). Alternatively, the event in (40b,c) could be analyzed as the time interval of 'being out' or 'being up', and the action of going out, getting up, would then be the inception of the event. This analysis has the appeal of permitting a unified treatment of durational adverbs as modifying the duration of the event itself in every case. However, given the completedness of *salir* 'to leave' in the past perfect (discussed in sections 3.1 and 3.2), and following Bull (1968), I will assume that verbs like *salir* 'to leave' and *levantarse* 'to get up' are desinent.

interval intervenes between the event and Speech-time, the perfect tenses are *not* construed as involving an interval between the event and the Reference-time. In other words, the simple tenses exhibit the interpretation of linearization, while the past perfect does not.

The TAS framework predicts the distinct interpretations of simple and perfect tenses, since only the syntactic feature [+PAST] linearizes an Event, while the feature [+COMPLETED] linearizes an aspect of the Event relative to the Reference-time.[24]

2.4 Summary. To summarize the argument of this section, we have compared the Reichenbach and TAS models with respect to three predictions concerning adverb construal in simple versus perfect tenses. The Reichenbach model, which analyzes perfect tense as 'double' tenses, predicts that simple and perfect tenses should pattern alike, while the TAS model predicts that they should pattern differently, since in the simple tenses, the Event is linearized by the feature [+PAST], while in the latter, only an 'aspect' of the event is linearized, by the feature [+COMPLETED]. With respect to (a) punctual adverbs with past versus present perfect events, (b) the interpretation of punctual adverbs with desinent versus nondesinent events, and (c) the construal of durational adverbs in simple and perfect tenses, the predictions of the TAS framework are supported, and the properties of perfect tenses are accounted for.

3 Present relevance of the present perfect. One of the informal generalizations that has been assumed to characterize the present perfect versus the past tense concerns the 'immediacy' or present relevance of the perfect tense. For example, Bull (1968) maintains that the present perfect is used to describe events which immediately precede the present, where there is no interval between the event and its perception at speech time. Bull cites the contrasts in (43) as examples.

(43) a. ¡Cuidado! Nos ha visto. (*Nos vio.)
'Careful! (S)he has seen us.' (*(S)he saw us.)

---

[24] The fact that the Reference-time is understood as the end-point of the Event does not follow in any obvious way from the TAS framework (although it is compatible with the model, as we have shown to be the case for the Reichenbach framework). Although the formalism remains for future research, it appears that the generalization which should be expressed is that, like punctual adverbs, durational adverbs must be interpreted relative to times which are marked on the time-line. The durational adverb modifies the interval relevant for the completedness relation, defined by the aspect of the event completed and the time of its evaluation R. The latter is thus the endpoint, by virtue of being the evaluation time for completedness.

b. ¡Dios mío!   Qué he hecho?   (*Qué hice?)
'My god!   What have I done?   (*What did I do?)

Bull attributes the distinct interpretations of the present perfect and past to the presence or absence of an interval between the event and speech time. In the situations expressed in (43), there is no interval between the event and the time of speaking. The past tense does imply such an interval, and hence cannot be used in these situations.

Let us compare the Reichenbach and TAS analyses with regard to this generalization. The TAS framework directly expresses the distinction between the present perfect and the past tense with respect to the attribution of an interval. The present perfect always lacks such an interval, since neither Reference-time nor the Event is 'linearized' or [+PAST]. The past tense is linearized from Speech-time, and the existence of an interval between the two times is possible, and perhaps the norm in the absence of any modification.

Again adopting the notation of Hornstein's (1977) analysis, the Reichenbach framework analyzes the event of both tenses as linearized:

(44) a. E,R __ S (Past)

      b. E __ S,R (Present Perfect)

However, the Reichenbachian analysis might be said to express the distinction between immediacy and remoteness by the position of the Reference-time in the present perfect versus the past. If so, then the generalization underlying the immediacy/remoteness contrast is not correctly expressed in terms of the presence or absence of an interval as claimed by Bull.

Let us consider an alternative hypothesis, based on a well-known contrast noted for English in (45).

(45) Einstein lived/*has lived in Princeton for years.

In (45), the present perfect cannot be used once Einstein is no longer alive. This contrast suggests that the source of the immediacy requirement is either a semantic or pragmatic existential requirement for the subject of the clause. However, examples like (46) show that this is not strictly so.

(46) Galileo has been exculpated by the Pope.

What appears to distinguish the felicitous use of the present tense in (46) from its impossibility in (45) is that the subject of the sentence in (46) has undergone a change of state as a consequence of the event, and the state holds of the present time. The same reading in (45), where Einstein is, at

Speech-time, in a state with respect to living in Princeton, can only lead to the conclusion that Einstein is still alive. Rather than being ungrammatical, this is pragmatically excluded.

Assuming this generalization to be relevant, let us return to the issue of the representations in (44). The issue which arises is whether the notion of 'result state' can be appropriately captured in the Reichenbachian framework, which analyzes R as present in the representation of all tenses. There appear to be two options: either R always represents a result state, or it represents a result state only when associated with S, as in (42b). If R were to always represent a state, which is evaluated according to its associative or linear relations to other times, it would be expected that the result state reading should hold for the past tense as well, and the contrast between the two tenses in (45) is then unexplained. On the other hand, if it were stipulated that R represents a result state only when it is associated with S, the solution would be *ad hoc*, and it would fail to capture the similarity between the present perfect and the past perfect with respect to the result state reading.

The TAS framework captures this distinctive property of the perfect tenses naturally. First, since the Reference-point is present only when it is selected by INFL, i.e., in perfect tenses, such a contrast in interpretation is expected. Second, the nature of the contrast is also naturally expressible, if *haber* 'to have' is analyzed as a stative verb. In this case, the completedness relation between an aspect of the event and the state derives a 'result state' reading. The fact that this state holds at either the present (present perfect) or a time in the past (past perfect) follows directly from the fact that the Reference-time is temporally identified by the feature [±PAST] assigned to it by INFL.

4 Conclusions. The notion of times as entities, and of tenses as relations between times was proposed in Jespersen (1924). Jespersen proposed to analyze all tenses as binary, involving 'Past' and 'Future' moments relative to the moment of speech. Reichenbach (1947) argued that a binary analysis of tenses was inadequate to express the properties of perfect tenses, and proposed a model in which all tenses are analyzed as complexes of the three times, 'Speech-time', 'Reference-time' and 'Event-time'. The TAS framework discussed here, with constraints which follow from independent principles of grammar, such as Theta-theory and Binding Theory, is intermediate between the two traditional approaches mentioned above. It shares with Reichenbach the claim that perfect tenses are analyzed as involving three times (or temporal arguments). However, simple tenses must be analyzed as involving only two times, unless there is empirical evidence for asserting the presence of a third temporal argument. The discussion of section 3 has argued that in fact the Reference-point is not present in simple tenses, given the contrast between simple and perfect tenses with respect to the 'immediacy' or result state reading. The TAS framework thus shares Jespersen's analysis of simple tenses as binary, in the sense that only two times are involved in their construal. It also shares with Jespersen the view that tenses are binary in the sense that a relation of [±PAST] only holds between Speech-time and one temporal argument: the event of a simple tense, and the Reference-time of perfect tenses. Section 2 above argued that the relation between Reference-time and Event-time of perfect tenses should not be analyzed as a 'linearized' or [+PAST] relation, but rather as an aspectual relation between one aspect of the event and the 'Reference-time'.

If an approach of this type is correct, it provides the basis for a theory of tenses which is both rich enough to characterize the range of tense and tense-aspect relations in language, as well as the range of interpretations associated with each, and at the same time sufficiently restrictive so as to account for the acquisition of tense, given the poverty of stimulus which exists in primary linguistic data for tenses, as Hornstein (1981) notes.

References

Braroe, E. 1974. The Syntax and Semantics of English Tense Markers. Monographs from the Institute of Linguistics, University of Stockholm.
Bull, W. 1968. Time, Tense, and the Verb. Berkeley, CA: University of California Press.
Chomsky, N. 1986. Barriers. Cambridge, Mass.: MIT Press.
Enç, M. 1987. Anchoring Conditions for Tense. Linguistic Inquiry 18, 633-57.
Hornstein, N. 1977. Towards a Theory of Tense. Linguistic Inquiry 8, 521-77.
Hornstein, N. 1981. The Study of Meaning in Natural Language: Three Approaches to Tense. In N. Hornstein, and D. Lightfoot, eds., Explanation in Linguistics. London: Longman. 116-51.
Jespersen, O. 1924. The Philosophy of Grammar. London: George Allen and Unwin.
Otero, C. P. 1974. Introducción a Chomsky in Estructuras Sintácticas por Noam Chomsky. Mexico City: Siglo XXI. ix-lvi.
Reichenbach, H. 1947. Elements of Symbolic Logic. New York: Macmillan.
Zagona, K. 1988a. Proper Government of Antecedentless VP in English and Spanish. Natural Language and Linguistic Theory 6, 95-128.
Zagona, K. 1988b. Verb Phrase Syntax: A Parametric Study of English and Spanish. Dordrecht: Kluwer Academic Publishers.
Zagona, K. 1989. Non-isomorphism of Morphological Tense and Temporal Interpretation. In K. Kirchner and J. Decesaris, eds., Proceedings of the 17th Meeting of the Linguistic Symposium on Romance Languages. Amsterdam: Benjamins. 477- 92.
Zagona, K. forthcoming. Binding and Construal of Present Tense. In C. Laeufer, and T. Morgan, eds., Proceedings of the Nineteenth Linguistic Symposium on Romance Languages. Amsterdam: Benjamins.

SECTION THREE: PHONOLOGY AND
                MORPHOLOGY

The alternating diphthongs of Spanish:
A paradox revisited

María Carreira*

University of Southern California

0 Introduction. This paper presents an analysis of the alternating diphthongs of Spanish ([je]~[e], [we]~[o]) that derives the monophthongal forms from sequences of two vocalic elements. This proposal generates the above alternations from general properties of the system of diphthongs in Spanish. In doing so, it goes much further than its immediate goal of explaining the behavior of [je] and [we]. This proposal also accounts for the absence of [ow] and [wo] in Spanish and provides an analysis that extends, with minor modifications, to Italian.

The presentation of this analysis will take the following form. Section 1 presents the facts as well as the paradox regarding stress and diphthongization discussed in Harris (1985). Section 2 presents background information about the distributional properties of the diphthongs of Spanish. Section 3 reviews Harris' (1985) analysis of the alternating diphthongs of Spanish. It will be argued that such an analysis not only fails to account for significant data but also makes predictions that are contrary to Spanish syllable structure. Section 4 presents an alternative analysis. It is my contention that the alternating diphthongs derive from a sequence of a high vowel and an empty V-slot. Subsequent to syllabification and various feature filling processes, these sequences become {wo} and {je}.[1] In unstressed syllables, {je} and {wo} contract to [e] and [o], respectively. In stressed syllables {wo} changes to [we] due to a surface ban on tautosyllabic sequences of [+round] segments, as shown in section 5. Finally, in section 6 I present a sketch of how the proposed analysis presented can be modified to account for a similar--though not completely identical--phenomenon in Italian.

1 The facts. In this section I show that unstressed [je] and [we] do not appear in certain environments, arguing that earlier analyses that assign a special structure to the alternating diphthongs have no way of explaining the systematic absence of unstressed [je] and [we] from these environments.

The following alternations are observed in Spanish: [o]~[we], [e]~[je]. The distribution of the diphthongs is restricted to stressed syllables. In

---

* Many thanks are due to J. Harris, J. I. Hualde, M. Kenstowicz, and H. H. Hock. All errors, of course, are strictly my own. 'Este trabajo está dedicado a la memoria de mi madre.'
[1] Braces are used to distinguish an intermediate stage in the derivation of the diphthongizing mid vowels from their surface representations which, as customary, are enclosed in brackets.

unstressed environments a mid vowel appears that agrees in backness with the glide in the stressed variant.[2]

(1) o/we: Venez[w]éla   'Venezuela'   d[w]érmo   'I sleep'
            Venezoláno   'Venezuelan'   dormír   'to sleep'

     e/je: v[j]éjo   'old'   p[j]érdo   'I lose'
            vejéz   'old age'   perdér   'to lose'

Harris (1985) identifies two additional alternations [i] ~ [je], and [u] ~ [we]. However, since these only occur in a single lexical item each (*jugar* 'to play', *j[w]ego* 'I play', and *adquirir* 'to acquire' *adqu[j]ero* 'I acquire') I do not propose a distinct underlying representation for them. It is my claim that these lexical items are exceptional with respect to monophthongization, one of the processes that affect unstressed [je] and [we].

A more pressing problem with the alternating diphthongs concerns their effect on stress. Prevocalic glides in the penultimate syllable of a word always block antepenultimate stress. For example, in *Venez[w]éla*, the presence of a rising diphthong in penultimate position determines the location of the stress. Main stress cannot appear on the antepenultimate syllable because of the branching structure of the penultimate syllable. However, the structure of the penultimate syllable, that is, the fact that it bears the diphthong [we] instead of the vowel [o], depends on stress. This is because the diphthongs [je] and [we] only appear in syllables that have been stressed at some point in the derivation. Thus, it appears that in forms like *Venez[w]éla* stress depends on the structure of the alternating syllable, but the structure of the alternating syllable depends on stress. This problematic ordering relation between stress assignment and diphthongization is observed in Harris (1985). This 'paradox' represents an important issue that my analysis must adress.

Another important fact that we must bear in mind is that unstressed mid vowels do not necessarily have diphthongal variants in stressed environments. That is, it is not possible to predict whether a root with a mid vowel in an unaccented syllable will have a diphthong in a morphologically related form that has the relevant syllable in a stressed position. This is illustrated in (2):

(2) comér   'to eat'   podér   'to be able to'
     cómo   'I eat'   p[w]édo   'I am able'

     pesár   'to weigh'   pensár   'to think'
     péso   'I weigh'   p[j]énso 'I think'

---

[2] I will indicate phonological stress rather than orthographic stress to facilitate the discussion. I have also chosen to preserve Spanish spelling in all cases except those where it might interfere with the presentation.

However, with few and systematic exceptions, it is the case that accented [je] and [we] appear as [e] and [o], respectively, when destressed. This is generally true because [je] and [we] are the only diphthongs of Spanish whose distribution is limited to stressed syllables. Thus, while there exist minimal pairs such as *volár* 'to fly'/ *v[j]olár* 'to violate' and *v[j]ajár* 'to travel'/ *bajár* 'to descend', no such contrast exists with [je] and [we].[3] That is, in the infinitival form, where the accent is always on the final syllable, there are generally no roots that bear the above diphthongs. Malkiel (1966: 432) states:

> The entire edifice of the Spanish language is characterized by the limitation of its characteristic diphthongs *ie* /je/ and *ue* /we/ to the stressed syllable. Predictably, where in the process of extracting one word from another through some morphological device--inflectional or derivational-- the place of the original word stress is shifted, *ie* yields to *e* and *ue* to *o*, as in *hierro* 'iron' beside *herrero* 'blacksmith' and *cuero* 'rawhide, leather' beside (mass-noun) *corambre* 'hides, skins'. Exceptions exist, but they are few and narrowly circumscribed.

This generalization is summarized in (3):

(3)   The dipthongs /je/ and /we/ bear the main stress of a word.

The following are exceptions to the above generalization. Some of these are found in Malkiel's article, others are my own.
(i) Unstressed [je] and [we] may appear across morpheme and word boundaries: *cár[j]+e* 'cavity' and *tén[w]+e* 'tenuous', *su olvído → s[w]olvído* 'his forgetfulness' *metrópoli extranjéra → metropol[j]extranjéra* 'foreign metropolis'.
(ii) These diphthongs may also surface in unstressed environments if the roots in which they appear are followed by certain suffixes. The diminutive *-(c)ito*, the pejorative *-ucho*, and the superlative *-ísimo*, always bear main stress. Nonetheless, these suffixes do not trigger monophthongization of [je] and [we]:

(4)	a.	b.	c.	d.
	vejéz 'old age'	v[j]éjo 'old man'	v[j]ejíto 'little old man'	v[j]ejísimo 'very old'
	novedád 'novelty'	n[w]évo 'new'	n[w]evecíto 'a little new'	n[w]evísimo 'very new'

---

[3] Orthographic *v* and *b* are pronounced the same way in Spanish. Both segments represent voiced bilabial obstruents.

(iii) Infinitives that have been formed from a noun or an adjective by affixation of the prefix *a-* may also bear [je] and [we] in unstressed position:

(5) m[w]éble/a + m[w]eblár   'furniture'/'to furnish'
     d[j]éstro/a + d[j]estrár   'dexterous'/'to train'

Like the examples in (4), these words have the property of being derived from lexical items that had the diphthong in a metrically strong position early in its derivation. A very small number of verbs that are derived from nouns may appear without the characteristic marker *-a*. Often, these words are highly colloquial and restricted in use. The following example is a term used in rural areas in Argentina: *ʃ[w]éte/ʃ[w]eteár* 'horsewhip/to horsewhip'.

(iv) The last systematic exception to the generalization that the diphthongs [je] and [we] only appear in stressed syllables is found in lexical items where unstressed [we] has a tautosyllabic [k] (orthographic *c*) in onset position: *frec[w]entar* 'to attend', *ac[w]educto* 'aqueduct', *sec[w]estrár* 'to kidnap'. However, as will be seen in section 2, there's reason to think that the sequence [kw] forms a complex segment. Since the sequence [we] does not form a rising diphthong when the segment [k] precedes it, words like *frec[w]entar* and *ac[w]educto* do not violate the generalization that there are no unstressed rising diphthongs of the form [we].

Let us summarize our findings regarding the environments that are exceptional with respect to Malkiel's generalization. First, it is most importantant to note that some suffixes allow [je] and [we] in unstressed syllables. These are the diminutive and superlative suffixes, as well as the prefix *-a*. Second, although the tautomorphemic sequence [kwe] often appears in unstressed syllables, there is evidence that the phonemes [k] and [w] form a complex onset. The sequence [we] in such cases does not have a similar structure to that of other diphthongs of Spanish. We will examine its unique structure in section 2.2. And third, and most important, heteromorphemic [je] and [we] freely appear in unstressed syllables. Therefore, any generalization to be made regarding the absence of [je] and [we] in unstressed syllables must be restricted to tautomorphemic instances of these diphthongs.[4]

---

[4] This situation might reflect a representational difference between adjacent identical feature values that are heteromorphemic and those that are within the same morpheme. It is my hypothesis here that at some point in their derivation the alternating diphthongs share the same instantiation of the feature back (as in (i)), in contrast with two consecutive instantiations of [back] that are singly linked to the skeletal tier (as in (ii)):

(i)   [α back]   (ii)   [α back]   [α back]
       / \ | |
      V   V   V   V

In addition to the morphemes mentioned above, there are other suffixes that allow the diphthongs to surface in unstressed position. The roots in (6a) undergo monophthongization with certain morphemes (6b), but not with others (6c).

(6)

a.	b.	c.
m[w]éble 'furniture'	mobil[j]ár[j]o 'suit of furniture'	m[w]eblísta 'maker'
c[w]énto 'story'	contar 'to tell a story'	c[w]entísta 'storyteller, gossipy'
h[w]élga 'rest, strike'	holgár 'to idle'	h[w]elguísta 'striker'
f[j]ésta 'party'	festejár 'to party'	f[j]estéro 'jolly, merry'
p[w]éblo 'town'	poblac[j]ón 'population'	p[w]ebléro 'pertaining to a town'
h[w]érta 'vegetable garden'	hortaliza 'vegetable'	h[w]ertéro 'vegetable gardener'
v[w]élo 'fullness, flare'	volánte 'ruffle'	v[w]elúdo 'full (said of a garment)'
c[w]éro 'rawhide'	corambre 'hides, skins'	c[w]erúdo 'heavy skinned'
ab[w]élo 'grandfather'	abolorio 'ancestry'	ab[w]elástro 'stepgrandfather'
f[j]éra 'wild animal/fierce'	feróz 'ferocious'	f[j]eréza 'fierceness'

The double association of the feature back in (i) is one of the properties that contributes to monophthongization. This being the case, one could argue that the reason why heteromorphemic [je] and [we] fail to monophthongize is because in their representation each [back] autosegment is linked to different vowel. This situation might result from the failure of the OCP to apply across morpheme boundaries. Clearly, the effect that an intervening morpheme boundary has on the diphthongs [je] and [we] is an issue that demands further study.

The situation is further complicated by the fact that some of the above morphemes, as well as others that have not been mentioned, do not exhibit a uniform behavior with respect to the alternating diphthongs. In some words they trigger monophthongization while in others they allow [je] and [we] to appear in unstressed syllables. The examples in (7) show that the same suffixes that fail to trigger monophthongization in (6) have the opposite effect for certain lexical items. Thus items (7a-c) contrast with the first three sets of examples in (6c). For the remaining data, the examples on the left contrast with those on the right.

(7) a. d[j]énte/dentísta   h[j]érba/herbísta
'tooth/dentist'   'herb/herbalist'

b. b[w]éy/boyéro   h[j]érro/herréro
'ox /ox driver'   'iron/blacksmith'

c. c[w]érno/cornúdo   f[w]érza/forzúdo
'horn/horned, cuckold'   'strength/husky'

d. m[w]éble/am[w]eblár   c[j]érto/acertár
'furniture/to furnish'   'certain /to guess right'

b[w]éno/bondád/ab[w]enár   pr[j]éto/apretár
'good/goodness/to pacify'   'dark/to tighten'

e. osár[j]o/h[w]esóso   m[j]él/melóso
'ossuary/bony'   'honey/ mellow'

f. mostrár/m[w]estrário   h[w]éso/osário
'to sample/sample book'   'bone/ossuary'

g. tesón/t[j]esúra   t[j]érno/ternúra
'firmness'/stiffness'   'tender/tenderness'

h. vejez/v[j]ejón   p[w]érta/portón
'old age/oldish'   'door/ gate'

The examples mentioned in (7), as well as those given in (6), do not exhaust the list of morphemes that are exceptional with respect to the alternating diphthongs of Spanish. A classification of all such morphemes however, would take us far from the topic at hand. Though I do not attempt such a task, it is important to recognize the existence of three distinct classes of morphemes. Some morphemes never trigger monophthongization. The diminutive and the superlative suffixes are members of this class (henceforth, class 1). Suffixes like -*ista* and -*ero* represent another class (class 2). These morphemes trigger monophthongization in some roots that have the alternating diphthongs but not in others. The third class (class 3) consists of suffixes that always trigger monophthongization of [je] and [we]. The suffixes -*al*, -*dad*, -*c[j]ón*, and -*il* belong in this class.[5] As the examples in (8) illustrate, other diphthongs appear with these suffixes in numerous lexical items.[6]

(8) -*al*: bon[j]atál, d[j]alectál, p[j]ornál, c[w]aresmál, d[j]ocesál
-*dad*: s[w]avidád, infer[j]oridád, inv[j]olabilidád, anc[j]anidád
-*ción*: v[j]olac[j]ón, g[w]arnic[j]ón, pers[w]as[j]ón
-*il*: g(w)adaníl, p[j]oneríl

Having identified a class of suffixes that consistently triggers monophthongization of [je] and [we], we are now ready to test an important hypothesis regarding the nature of the alternating diphthongs. A crucial assumption of previous analyses has been that the alternating diphthongs of Spanish are somehow different from other diphthongs. An unstated corollary of this assumption is that there are two different structures underlying the surface sequences [je] and [we]. One of these structures undergoes

---

[5] It has generally been assumed that suffixes that trigger monophthongization are added at the first level of the lexical phonology, before the initial assignment of stress. Since these suffixes are subsequently stressed, they keep primary stress away from the alternating diphthong in the root. This triggers monophthongization of [we] and [je] in words like *bondád* (*b[w]éno*) and *pernil* (*p[j]érna*).

It has also been assumed that the restriction that triggers monophthongization of unstressed [je] and [we] shuts off at the noncyclic levels of the phonology. Consequently, when stress is shifted form alternating diphthongs at any time after this restriction becomes inoperative, they will not undergo monophthongization. If we accept this, we must assume that class 1 suffixes such as -*ito* and -*ísimo* are added at a noncyclic level of the phonology of Spanish, when the restriction against unstressed [we] and [je] no longer applies. For this reason, the stress shift that accompanies the suffixation of these items will not trigger monophthongization of the alternating diphthongs.

The existence of a group of Spanish suffixes which exhibits characteristic behavior both of class 1 and class 3 suffixes has gone unnoticed until now. The situation created by these suffixes is similar to that which exists in English with the suffix -*al*. The stress pattern of this suffix, as well as its ability to attach to nonwords, suggest that it is affixed very early in the phonology of English. However, the fact that -*al* may follow -*ment*, i.e. *governmental*, a suffix which is added in a later level of the phonology, contradicts the previous claim and suggests that -*al* affixation takes place rather late. The ambivalent nature of the suffix -*al* has spurred a number of analyses (see Selkirk 1982 and Halle and Vergnaud 1988).

[6] The suffix -*il* is not as productive as the other suffixes given here. For this reason I have only been able to give two lexical items that have the relevant diphthongs.

monophthongization in unstressed environments. The other one is no different from that of other diphthongs of Spanish and consequently is not subject to stress–triggered alternations.

A different proposal regarding the alternating diphthongs is that there is only one underlying representation for the sequences [je] and [we] and that monophthongization is a function of the conditions that apply to these sequences. This analysis predicts that given the same conditions, all [je] and [we] sequences will behave alike. This prediction radically differentiates our proposal from that of previous analyses.

Of course, all proposals about the alternating diphthongs of Spanish must restrict the domain of monophthongization. But analyses that posit a different structure for the diphthongs that alternate predict that within the same environment we should find surface manifestations of the two underlying sources of [je] and [we]. In environments where all alternating diphthongs monophthongize, there should be unstressed sequences of [je] and [we] that escape monophthongization because they have a similar structure to that of the rest of the diphthongs of Spanish.

We have identified a class of suffixes (class 3) that consistently triggers monophthongization in all words that have the alternating diphthongs. If our hypothesis is true, namely, if there is a single underlying source for all surface manifestations of [je] and [we], then we predict that there should be no unstressed [je] and [we] in all words with these suffixes. If the alternative hypothesis is correct, then we should be able to find both alternating and nonalternating instances of [je] and [we]. Those that have a structure similar to that of other diphthongs should not be affected by stress. The rest should surface as monophthongs in unstressed syllables.

To the best of my knowledge, there is only one root with the diphthong [je] that fails to monophthongize when in combination with a class 3 suffix: *qu[j]etac[j]ón* 'the act of quieting down.'[7] There are two instances of [we] that appear in unstressed position with a class 3 suffix: *cr[w]eldád* 'cruelty' and *p[w]eríl* 'puerile'.

Now, let us consider how the contrasting hypotheses account for these facts. The proposal that there are two underlying representations for [je] and [we] must consider it accidental that among the words formed with a class 3 suffix all but three roots have the alternating diphthongs [je] and [we]. The

---

[7] Other words that appear to go against this generalization are *amb[j]entál* 'environmental', *p[j]edád* 'piety', and *oriental/orientación* 'oriental'/'orientation.' Closer inspection of these items reveals, however, that the segments that form the diphthongs above are not tautomorphemic. The root in *amb[j]entál* is *ambi-*. This morpheme appears in words like *ámbito* 'ambit.' *P[j]edád* derives from *pío* 'pious.' The [e] in *p[j]edád* is an epenthetic vowel that appears between every stem-final [i] and the suffix *-dad*: *séri+o/ser[j]edád* 'serious'/'seriousness', *vári+o/var[j]edád* 'various'/'variety.' Similarly, *oriental* contains the root *ori* also found in *oriundo* 'native.'

proposal that posits only one underlying representation for all surface manifestations of [je] and [we] must assign exceptional status to *qu[j]etac[j]ón*, *cr[w]eldád* and *p[w]erfl*. Hence, the difference between these proposals with respect to the above facts comes down to two contrasting claims regarding what is outstanding about [je] and [we]. In order to differentiate between these claims we must examine the distribution of [je] and [we] in other environments. I have chosen three-syllable words with tautomorphemic diphthongs in the antepenultimate syllable. The reason for this is that antepenultimate stress is one of the most marked stress patterns in Spanish. Despite this, when the diphthongs [je] and [we] appear in the antepenultimate syllable of words that have no other suffix but a classmarker, they are always stressed. This does not happen with the other diphthongs of Spanish.[8]

(9)

d[j]éresi+s	'diaeresis'	murc[j]élag+o	'bat'
m[j]ércole+s	'Wednesday'	p[j]élag+o	'high sea'
t[w]étan+o	'marrow'	m[w]érdag+o	'mistletoe'
h[w]érfan+o	'orphan'	c[w]évano	'large basket'
d[j]amánt+e	'diamond'	d[j]adém+a	'tiara'
D[j]onís[j]+o	'Dyonisius'	m[j]opí+a	'nearsightedness'
v[j]olént+o	'violent'	alíc[w]ot+a	'in equal parts'
G[w]antánam+o	(a place)	j[w]anét+e	'bunion'

To restate our findings, [je] and [we] are always stressed when they appear in words that have no suffix other than a classmarker. The other diphthongs of Spanish are not subject to this restriction. Unlike our previous observation regarding class 3 morphemes, this generalization admits no exceptions.

Having identified an environment in which it is possible to make a generalization that applies to all instances of [je] and [we], it is now possible to choose between the proposals presented regarding the structure of alternating diphthongs. Only the analysis which claims that there is a single underlying representation for all surface manifestations of [je] and [we] can explain the systematic absence of such diphthongs from the class of words that have no suffixes other than a classmarker. Under the alternative analysis, the absence of unstressed [je] and [we] from certain environments where other unstressed diphthongs appear is purely accidental.

---

[8] I have purposely excluded from this table any examples that have tautosyllabic high vowels. The reason for this is that we will examine the structure of high vowel sequences in a subsequent discussion. Putting aside the question of what structure should be assigned to such sequences, it is possible to get tautosyllabic high vowel sequences in unstressed position: *suicída* 'suicide'.

In view of the superiority of the first analysis in accounting for the distribution of [je] and [we], I will assume that all tautomorphemic instances of these diphthongs have a similar underlying structure. I will also assume that monophthongization is triggered by conditions that apply to the diphthongs [je] and [we] at specific stages of their derivation. This is an assumption that all analyses of the alternating diphthongs must make. However, in previous analyses, monophthongization applies only to diphthongs that have a structure that is unique to the alternating diphthongs. In the present work I claim that monophthongization affects tautosyllabic sequences that have the normal structure of other rising diphthongs of Spanish. This brings us to our third point: although [je] and [we] have a structure that is similar to that of other rising diphthongs, I will show that their feature composition at a certain point in the derivation is different from that of other diphthongs of Spanish. This difference makes them susceptible to monophthongization.

This is the line of argumentation that will be pursued here. In my account of the alternating diphthongs of Spanish, I propose an analysis that explains the absence of unstressed [je] and [we] in the relevant environments. In addition, I address the issue of why only rising diphthongs are subject to stress triggered alternations. Before proceeding with these issues, however, it is important to spell out my ssumptions regarding the structure of Spanish diphthongs.

2 The diphthongs of Spanish

2.1 The structure of Spanish diphthongs. In Carreira (1989, 1990) I argue that rising diphthongs are derived from a sequence of an unstressed high vowel and an onsetless syllable. This process eliminates the syllable node and the V-slot originally associated with the high vowel. It then links the [+high] vocoid to the following V-slot and it incorporates the floating consonant(s) into onset position. This process results in a 'light' diphthong.

(10)   Contraction:

$$[+high] \quad [\alpha high] \qquad\qquad [+high] \quad [\alpha high]$$

$$C \quad V \qquad V \quad \rightarrow \quad C \quad V$$

$$\sigma \qquad \sigma \qquad\qquad\qquad \sigma$$

Condition: [+high] is unstressed

Thus, I will assume here that rising diphthongs are derived via Contraction. It will also be my contention that, unlike rising diphthongs,

Spanish falling diphthongs are 'bi-skeletal.' There are two main arguments in favor of this last point. First, VG rhymes have a duration that is nearly identical to that of VC rhymes. Rising diphthongs, on the other hand, pattern like V rhymes in their duration. Second, VG rhymes cannot be followed by a tautosyllabic segment. GVG and GVC rhymes, on the other hand, are perfectly acceptable. If we assume that the Spanish rhyme follows the nearly universal limit of two elements from the skeletal tier, then the incorporation of an additional segment to a VG rhyme will be ruled out. In contrast, the incorporation of a coda to a GV sequence is acceptable because rising diphthongs are 'mono-skeletal' structures. The structure of falling diphthongs is given in (11):

(11)

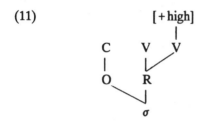

The details of these and other arguments are outlined in Carreira (1990). In section 2.2 I examine the distribution of diphthongs in Spanish.

2.2 The distribution of Spanish diphthongs. On the surface, Spanish appears to have a completely symmetrical system of rising diphthongs. The front high vowel can combine with all other vowels but itself to form a rising diphthong. The same appears to be the case for the high back vowel:

(12) p[j]áno   'piano'   ad[w]ána   'customs'
      pim[j]énto   'pepper'   p[w]érta   'door'
      p[j]onéro   'pioneer'   S[w]íza   'Switzerland'
      tr[j]únfo   'victory'   c[w]óta   'cuota'
      *[ji]   *[wu]

Closer inspection reveals, however, that the diphthong [wo] is unusual in a number of significant ways:

1. Tautomorphemic instances of [wo] are always preceded by the segment [k] (orthographic *c*) in onset position, e.g., *c[w]óta*. No such restriction holds for the other diphthongs.

2. With respect to stress, [wo] is abnormal on two counts. While all other prevocalic glides in penultimate position block antepenultimate stress, [wo] does not appear to do so, e.g., *a.lí.cwo.ta*. Second, while prevocalic glides in word-final position generally do not allow stress to appear in the

antepenultimate syllable, [wo] does not have that effect, e.g., *ven. trí. lo. c[w]o*. The fact that [wo] has no bearing on stress suggests that the glide in words like alíc[w]ota and ventríloc[w]o is not in the rhyme but in the onset of the syllable in which it appears. In addition, the fact that tautomorphemic [wo] is always preceded by the sound [k] suggests that the glide forms a special bond with [k] that is not possible with other segments. Of course, this reflects the historical source of the segment from Latin labiovelars. In view of these facts, I will assume that instances of [wo] that are preceded by a velar consonant represent a complex onset followed by a vowel [o]. Words like *alíc[w]ota* and *ventríloc[w]o*, then, do not contradict my claim that the tautomorphemic rising diphthong [wo] does not exist in Spanish.

The representation of the sequence [kwo] in words like *ventríloc[w]o* is given in (13a). This structure is contrasted with (13b), proposed for rising diphthongs in Carreira (1989, 1990).

(13)   a.   k w o   b.   m j a
              \ / | | \|
              O   R   O   R
               \ /   \ /
                σ   σ

Not only is tautomorphemic [wo] ruled out in Spanish, but certain heteromorphemic sequences of these vocoids are systematically eliminated when they arise from morpheme concatenation. As examples in (14) illustrate, stem-final /u/ in noun forms is deleted when the class marker -o follows.

(14)   act[w]ár   act[w]ac[j]ón   act+o   (*actu+o)
       'to act'   'performance'   'act'

       habit[w]ár   habit[w]ál   hábit+o   (*habitu+o)
       'to get used to'   'habitual'   'habit'

       punt[w]ár   punt[w]ac[j]ón   punt+o   (*puntu+o)
       'to punctuate'   'punctuation'   'point'

The importance of these facts is that they illustrate a general intolerance in Spanish towards the diphthong [wo]. This exclusion has received little or no attention in recent generative studies of Spanish syllable structure (see Harris 1983, Selkirk 1984, and Morgan 1986).

The diphthong [ow] creates a gap in the inventory of falling diphthongs that is analogous to that of [wo] in rising diphthongs. While all other falling diphthongs exist in numerous lexical items, to the best of my knowledge the sequence [ow] appears in only one word in Spanish: *bo[w]*. This lexical item is a borrowing from Catalan whose existence and meaning is not known to most speakers of Spanish. The word represents a type of fishing net that is dragged between two boats. The diphthong [ow], however, is very common in Galician and it is found in some Galician names that are heard throughout the Spanish–speaking world: *Souza, Bousoño, Outeiro, Ourense*. I believe, however, that these words are felt to be foreign. Alarcos-Llorach (1967: 145) states: 'Podría eliminarse [ow] que aparece, fuera de un par de términos no castellanos, sólo señalando límite entre unidades morfológicas o léxicas: firmó un cheque.' Similarly, in *Esbozo de una nueva gramática de la lengua española* (1973: 50, fn. 36), the Real Academia Española states that [ow]: 'es extraño a la fonética castellana y sólo se encuentra en voces de origen gallego o catalán.' As is the case with [wo], the absence of [wo] from the inventory of Spanish diphthongs is something that has gone unnoticed in recent generative studies.

The absence of diphthongs of the form [wo] and [ow] suggests the existence of a ban in Spanish on sequences of tautosyllabic segments that are [+round, +back]. Constraints that rule out tautosyllabic sequences that agree in the value of either of these features appear to be common across languages. Chinese, for example, rules out tautosyllabic sequences of vowels that agree in the value of the feature [back]. This constraint disallows [wo], [ow], and [je] along with other diphthongs (see Chung 1988). Christdas (p. c.) reports that in Tamil the vowels /o, u/ do not occur in underlying representations after the back glide /w/, and the front vowels /i, e/ do not occur morpheme-internally after the front glide [j].

It will be my hypothesis that a similar constraint applies in Spanish to rule out the surface manifestation of monomorphemic [wo]. I argue that the source of the [we]/[o] alternation is the diphthong {wo}. Before proceeding with this analysis, however, we need to examine previous proposals regarding the alternating diphthongs of Spanish.

3 Previous analyses. The outstanding contribution of Harris (1985) is that it addresses the ordering paradox between stress assignment and diphthongization. Previous solutions had not recognized this problem. Harris (1969), for example, differentiated alternating mid vowels from nonalternating ones by means of the feature [tense]. In an earlier analysis, Foley (1965) proposes that the alternating diphthongs derive from /e:/ and /o:/. Neither one of these proposals succeeds at explaining how the monophthongal variant blocks antepenultimate stress from penultimate position.

Harris (1985) deals with the stress problem by means of the representations in (15). In this analysis, the alternating diphthongs consist of a mid vowel followed by an empty position. This empty skeletal position is assigned to the rhyme headed by the mid vowel. Since the representations have a branching rhyme, it follows that words with alternating diphthongs in penultimate position will block antepenultimate stress. With this, Harris (1985) eliminates the stress paradox of the alternating diphthongs.

(15)

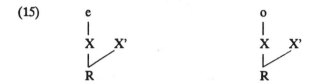

(X' = a skeletal position associated with no features)

The empty skeletal position in the structures above triggers a series of rules that lead to diphthongization. A rule of diphthongization associates the feature [-consonantal] (annotated as V) to the empty skeletal position in the rhyme of a stressed syllable, as in (16a). A typical derivation is given in (16b) (*R = a stressed rhyme):

(16) a. Diphthongization

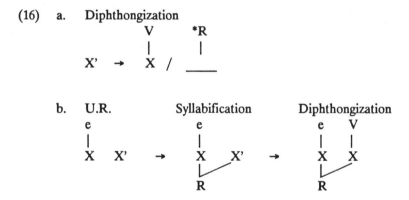

      b. U.R.   Syllabification   Diphthongization

Diphthongization allows a rule of Default to supply the features of the vowel [e] to any empty V position.

(17) Default:

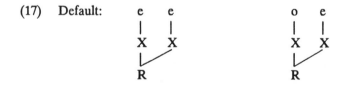

Next, there is a readjustment rule that shifts the head of structures in (17)

to the right. The claim made here is that between adjacent vowels of equal height, the second vowel will always be more sonorous and hence will be given nuclear status.

(18)   Readjustment:

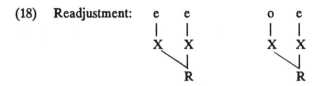

Following this step, there is a rule that raises the left component of the structures in (18), yielding the correct surface forms:

(19)   Raising:

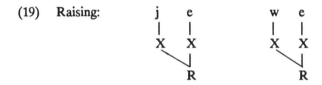

In unstressed syllables the rule of diphthongization does not apply. As a result, Default fails to supply the empty position with feature values. The skeletal slots that remain unassociated to a segmental matrix are then deleted by a universal convention.

According to Harris, the only language-particular process that applies in the above derivation is the restriction of diphthongization to stressed rhymes. This restriction is crucial to the analysis because Diphthongization is what allows the vowel [e] to appear in stressed syllables. An X-slot that is not marked as [-cons] does not qualify for Default assignment. Without melodic content, such a slot does not surface. However, as the examples in (20) show, in Spanish, default assignment of the vowel [e] is not limited to stressed environments:

(20)   a.   esféra, espermatozóo
       b.   árbol + es, abertúra

In the examples in (20), the role of the default vowel is to allow a consonant that would otherwise be unsyllabifiable to be adjoined into the syllable headed by the epenthetic vowel. When the Default rule functions like this, the vocalic quality of the segment introduced by Default is completely predictable from the environment since only the insertion of a vowel produces a syllabifiable sequence of segments. In the structures in (15) there is nothing that mandates that the segment that fills that empty position must be a vowel. A consonant could very well appear in this position since VC rhymes are perfectly grammatical in Spanish. What Harris's rule of diphthongization does, then, is to artificially create the environment for default assignment. By further restricting diphthongization to stressed syllables, Harris moves away from the usual role that the Default rule plays in Spanish--that of rescuing segmental material that is otherwise unsyllabifiable. This strategy results in an undesirable complication for Spanish phonology. Two rules of diphthongization must be formulated; one which inserts the appropriate value of the feature [consonantal] to a skeletal slot depending on syllable structure and stress (as in (16)); and the other which applies as a repair strategy (as in (20)).

A second problem with the solution at hand is that it fails to explain how the sequence of a mid vowel followed by an empty skeletal slot is ever parsed into the same syllable by the rules of syllabification in Harris (1983: 23). This work establishes a basic rhyme template which consists of a [+syllabic] segment and a following optional [-syllabic] segment. A glide may be adjoined to the left of this structure, and the phoneme /s/ may be adjoined to the right. Crucially, three-segment rhymes that start with a vowel (a [+syllabic] element) must end in /s/. VGN, VGL, and VGO rhymes are considered ungrammatical, as are all other vowel-initial rhymes that consist of three segments.[9] We know, however, that the alternating diphthongs may appear in nasal-final and liquid-final syllables: *p[w]erta, p[w]ente, m[j]el, p[j]enso*. Harris's analysis of the alternating diphthongs requires that such syllables be represented as in (21):

(21)   p[w]erta/portal   p[j]enso/pensar

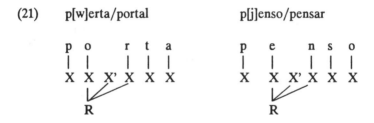

The structures in (21), however, violate the syllable templates proposed for Spanish by Harris (1983). Specifically, they contain two postvocalic segments, the last of which is not an /s/. Thus, the analysis of alternating diphthongs given in Harris (1985) generates structures that are ruled out by the rules of syllabification in Harris (1983). In order to make this analysis compatible with Spanish syllable structure, we would have to allow rhymes of the form VXC and stipulate that their distribution is restricted to alternating

---

[9] Except, of course, for a handful of well-known exceptions: *ve[j]nte* 'twenty', *cla[w]stro* 'cloister', *a[w]nque* 'even though', etc.

diphthongs. This last condition is necessary in order to rule out ungrammatical rhymes like *eir, oin, uil*, etc. Aside from the obvious complications that this move introduces, this stipulation poses serious problems for acquisition.

A related problem appears when we consider the claim that between vowels of the same height it is always the right one that is more sonorous and consequently the one that becomes the head in Spanish. The behavior of tautosyllabic sequences of nonidentical [+high] vocoids reveals that this claim does not always apply. In stressed syllables [ju] alternates with [iw], and [wi] alternates with [uy]. Thus, while the analysis of alternating diphthongs mandates that between vowels of the same height the right one always function as the head, the behavior of diphthongs with two high vowels fails to support this claim.

In addition to these difficulties, the solution outlined in (21) faces several external problems. First of all, Harris (1985) offers no explanation for why it should be the case that the diphthongs [je] and [we] are the only diphthongs of Spanish that are systematically absent from unstressed syllables. If the alternating diphthongs arise from the representations in (15), it follows that there should be other [je] and [we] diphthongs that arise from the underlying representations /je/ and /we/. These diphthongs should not undergo monophthongization in unstressed environments because they do not have the appropriate structure. However, there are almost no instances of unstressed [je] and [we] in words formed with a class 3 suffix and in roots that are followed by a classmarker.

Another problem with the solution presented by Harris is that it fails to extend to a closely related language like Italian, which has the alternations [je]/[e] and [wo]/[o]. In order to account for these alternations by means of the same analysis we would have to claim that Italian has two epenthetic vowels: [e] and [o]. However, as the following examples illustrate, it is the vowel [i] that usually functions as an epenthetic segment in Italian:

(22) Spagna   in Spagna   →   in [i]Spagna
      'Spain'   'in Spain'

      per Spagna   →   per [i]Spagna
      'for/through Spain'

Without epenthesis, it is not clear how Harris's analysis could extend to Italian. And yet, the many similarities between Spanish and Italian, not only in the pattern of alternating diphthongs but also in the phonologies at large, would seem to demand solutions that are minimally different. In section 6 of this paper, I discuss how the analysis proposed here accounts for the Italian facts with minimum modifications. I now present my analysis.

4 The paradox revisited

4.1 Preliminaries. We have seen that the diphthongs [je] and [we] in Spanish require a representation that not only accounts for their pattern of alternation but also explains their restricted distribution to stressed environments. We have also seen that the tautomorphemic sequence [wo] is limited in its distribution to syllables having the segment [k] in onset position. No other rising diphthong of Spanish is subject to a similar restriction. Three rising diphthongs, then, appear to be problematic for Spanish: [je], [we], and [wo]. The first two differ from the last not only in that they have monophthongal variants in unstressed environments, but also in that they contain the default vowel of Spanish, [e].

When considering what the structure of the alternating diphthongs must be, the simplest analysis that comes to mind is one which posits an underlying representation that is similar to that of the surface forms in stressed syllables: {je} and {we}. If we try to characterize what is unique about these two sequences we find that it is not the relationship that holds between the two members of the diphthong that sets these sequences apart from other rising diphthongs. Instead, it is the presence of the vowel [e].

Therefore, if we posit an underlying representation of the alternating diphthongs that consists of a high vowel followed by [e], (i.e., /ie/ and /ue/) we have to stipulate that it is the presence of the vowel [e] that triggers monophthongization in unstressed syllables. Crucially, it is not possible to formulate monophthongization as a process that applies to vowel sequences that stand in a certain relation to each other. This is because the constituents of [je] do not bear the same relation to each other as those of [we]. The segments in [je] agree in the value of the feature [back]. Other rising diphthongs with this property are [wa] and [wo]. The constituents of [we] disagree in the value of [back]. The diphthong [jo] shares this property.

Thus, an analysis of the alternating diphthongs of Spanish that posits /je/ and /we/ as the underlying source of the alternations cannot explain monophthongization in terms of the relation that exists between the segments that form the diphthong. Such an analysis commits us to a version of monophthongization that is driven by the presence of the vowel /e/.

However, there is no apparent reason why /e/ should trigger monophthongization when it appears in an unstressed rising diphthong. The segment does not cause any alternations when it surfaces in falling diphthongs (*pé[j]ne/pe[j]nár*) or when it appears across a morpheme boundary and is preceded by a high vocoid (*cári+e* 'cavity').

Another problem with this analysis is that it fails to say anything about the absence of [wo] in the system of rising diphthongs. This is a particularly glaring deficiency in view of the fact that the segments that form the diphthongs [je] and [wo] stand in a similar relation to each other. Having stipulated that it is the presence of the vowel [e] rather than the relationship that holds between the segments that causes monophthongization, it is unclear why both [je] and [wo] have a limited distribution, though of different kinds. For these reasons, I reject an analysis that posits the underlying sequences /ie/ and /ue/ as the source of the alternating diphthongs of Spanish.

Let us now consider /ie/ and /uo/ as possible underlying structures for the alternating diphthongs. The appeal of an analysis that posits these sequences is that it can explain monophthongization in terms of a process that affects unstressed rising diphthongs whose members share the features [round] and [back]. We have already seen that diphthongs of this type are ruled out in a number of languages. It is also the case that restrictions that limit the distribution of marked structures such as these to metrically weak positions are not uncommon across languages. My hypothesis, then, is that monophthongization in Spanish works as a repair strategy on 'short' tautomorphemic diphthongs that are unstressed and whose components share the value of the feature [back]. This hypothesis not only provides a more explanatory account of monophthongization, but it also explains the absence of [wo] from stressed environments.

In spite of its appeal, this analysis faces two drawbacks. First of all, it must explain how the sequence [wo] surfaces as [we] in stressed syllables. We have seen that there exists a restriction in Spanish against the diphthongs [wo] and [ow]. This restriction could trigger the change from {wo} to [we].

A more serious drawback facing an analysis that posits /uo/ as the source of the [we]/[o] alternation is that it fails to explain what happens to the underlying sequence /ue/. If the source of the [we]/[o] alternation is /uo/, then there must be surface [we]'s that do not alternate because they derive from the underlying sequence /ue/. However, as we have seen, there are certain environments where unstressed [we] does not appear. This would suggest that all surface manifestations of tautomorphemic [we] have identical underlying representations. The hypothesis that posits the sequence /uo/ as the underlying source of the [we]/[o] alternation has no way of explaining the distributional gaps of [we].

In sum, the two analyses we have considered thus far are incapable of accounting for the full range of facts. The solution I would like to propose is one which incorporates ideas from both analyses. This solution relies on a theory of underspecification that allows the existence of segments that are completely unspecified for place of articulation features. Like Harris (1985), I propose that the alternating diphthongs have in their underlying representation an element from the timing tier that is unspecified for place of articulation features. The [je]/[e] alternation is represented underlyingly as the front high vowel followed by a [-cons] slot containing no place-of-articulation features (i.e. /iV/). Similarly, the source of the [we]/[o] alternation is /uV/. My proposal differs from that of Harris (1985) in how the unspecified segments in these sequences are syllabified and assigned place-of-articulation features. I now turn to these issues.

5.2   Syllabification and feature assignment.   The theory of underspecification presented in Archangeli (1984, 1988) is one in which only the bare minimum of information is present in underlying representations. This minimally specified phoneme inventory contains a segment which receives all of its features by rule. The quality of this phoneme is language specific. With respect to Spanish, the claim is made that the maximally underspecified vowel is /e/.

Archangeli (1984) proposes the underlying representations for the vowels of Spanish shown in (23):

(23)   i   e   a   o   u

High   +   +

Low   +

Back   +   +

In a five-vowel system like that of Spanish the value of the feature [back] always agrees with that of [round] for all vowels but /a/. However, since /a/ is uniquely specified as [+low], we do not need to specify values for both features to distinguish the rest of the vowels. Steriade (1987) argues that when there is a choice, [round] is the redundant feature and [back] is present underlyingly. Following this, I will assume that in Spanish the feature [back] is present underlyingly, while the values of [round] are introduced via complement rules of the form: [αback] → [αround].

Let us assume that the diphthong [je] is represented underlyingly as in (24a). Tentatively, let us also assume that surface [we] is represented as the high back vowel followed by a maximally underspecified [-cons] segment, as in (24b).

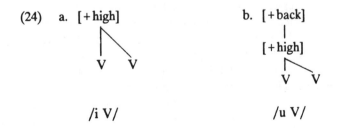

(24)   a. [+high]   b. [+back]
                                               |
              V   V   [+high]

                                               V   V

             /i V/   /u V/

Two questions arise about these representations: (i) How do the initial rules of syllabification parse the above sequences? and (ii) Is it possible for this segment to receive place of articulation features from a process other than Default assignment?

Regarding the first question, the assumption in Harris's analysis is that the sequences in (24) are parsed into the same rhyme. This syllabification is what subsequently allows default assignment and diphthongization to apply. However, in section 3 we saw that for lexical items *p[j]erdo* and *p[w]ente* there is no way to include the high vowel, the unspecified segment, and a following consonant in the same rhyme without exceeding the one segment limit that is imposed on postnuclear position. We have also seen that prevocalic glides exhibit no cooccurrence restrictions with onset segments and appear in syllables with the maximum number of onset segments. These facts strongly suggest that prevocalic glides do not appear in onset position.

If the high vowel and the following segment cannot share the same rhyme and the high vowel cannot appear in onset position, then the two segments must be parsed into separate syllables. This is, in effect, the representation that the CV (Steriade 1984) rule will assign to such sequences.

(25)

CV rule:

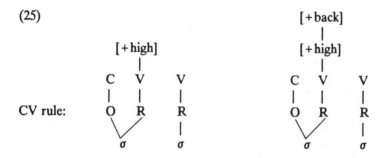

The left-to-right application of the CV rule creates a CV syllable from the consonant-high vowel sequence. The maximally underspecified V is then parsed as a separate rhyme. The result is that both the high vowel and the unspecified V are parsed as syllable heads.

In Harris's (1985) the unspecified V is assigned the features of the default vowel [e]. However, there is another option that is not only theoretically feasible but is actually attested in Spanish. Segments that lack melodic content can acquire feature values from an adjacent segment via spreading. This option is exercised by syllable-final nasals in nonvelarizing dialects. Nasal assimilation is one of two feature-filling processes that are available to syllable-final nasals. The other possibility is for nasals to acquire feature values via rules of default. When there is a choice, however, nasal assimilation is preferred over default assignment. For example, the underlying representation /kaNpo/ surfaces as [kampo] rather than *[kanpo]. This means that nasal assimilation precedes and bleeds default assignment of the features [+anterior, -labial] for nasals.

In the absence of evidence to the contrary, it is logical to assume that the same feature-filling processes that are available for consonants are also available for vowels. This assumption is supported by spreading processes in other languages.

Hayes (1989: 18) proposes that the way in which 'empty prosodic positions are provided with segmental content forms part of syllabification. For example, the syllable-forming rules for an individual language may specify that empty prosodic positions are syllabified by spreading from the preceding vowel (as in Latin and most dialects of ancient Greek)....' If spreading is included in the syllabification mechanisms of a language, then feature-filling via spreading should always take precedence over default assignment.

Let us assume, then, that the empty nuclear positions in (24) may acquire features from the adjacent vowel. Given a choice between feature-filling via harmony and feature-filling via redundancy rules, let us also assume that the former prevails. These two assumptions find support both in Universal Grammar and in the behavior of syllable-final nasals in Spanish.

The grammar of Spanish, however, disallows long tautomorphemic segments. Thus, *[u:], *[i:], *[pp], *[dd] are ungrammatical when they are morpheme internal. This means that the kind of harmony that applies between a partially specified segment and a maximally unspecified segment must be constrained so as not to result in a root geminate. The underspecified segment, therefore, must receive only a subset of the adjacent vowel features that are present at the time when spreading takes place.

Let us now consider how harmony can supply values to the [-cons] segment that follows each of the high vowels in (24). The vowel /i/ in (24a) only has the feature value [+high] present in its underlying representation. It cannot share this specification with the following vowel since this would result in a long segment. Consequently, the unspecified vowel that follows /i/ in (24a) must rely on redundancy rules to supply feature values of the epenthetic vowel.

The unspecified vowel that follows /u/, on the other hand, may receive feature values via spreading. The vowel /u/ bears two feature specifications underlyingly: [+high] and [+back]. Either one of these but not both may spread over to the adjacent V. If [high] spreads, we get [+high, +back] followed by [+high]. After redundancy rules apply, this yields the vowel sequence [ui]. If, on the other hand, it is the feature [back] that spreads, the resulting sequence is [+high, +back] followed by [+back] or [uo]. In terms of what we want to accomplish, the sequence [uo] represents a better result. The monophthongization of /uo/ to [o] is entirely analogous to the change of

/ie/ to [e]. In view of these facts, let us now consider how the operation of spreading can be formulated so that only [+back] participates in the process.

The overwhelming number of studies done on segment geometry suggest that [high] and [back] are daughter nodes of the Dorsal articulator node (see Sagey 1986 and Clements 1985). If we accept this view, then we must stipulate that only the feature [back] may spread. This is a drawback for my analysis since it introduces an arbitrary restriction. There is, however, an alternative theory of segment geometry which argues for a representation of the features [back] and [high] that allows a well-motivated account of why spreading should be restricted to the feature [back]. In view of what it can accomplish for my analysis, I will now consider such a theory.

Archangeli (1985) makes the claim that Universal Grammar anchors the feature [back] on [high] and [high] on the core skeleton. If this is the case, then [back] should be able to spread independently of [high], but not vice versa. Notice that if [high] spreads to the adjacent V, the value of the feature [back] will also be shared by both positions. This results in a long vowel (26a), an ungrammatical structure in Spanish. If, on the other hand, the feature [back] associates to the unspecified vowel, the result does not violate the constraint against geminates since the segments do not share all of the features present.[10]

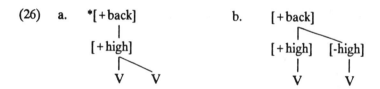

(26) a. *[+back]   b. [+back]
           | /‾‾
        [+high]   [+high] [-high]
         /‾‾‾\ | |
        V   V   V   V

Since the unspecified vowel is only allowed to receive one of the features of the adjacent vowel, it must be the feature [back] that spreads. Such a process results in the following structure.

(27)   [+back]
           /‾‾‾‾‾\
        [+high] [-high]
          | |
          V   V

The structure in (27) contains adjacent segments that share the feature [back]. The first segment bears the feature values that identify the vowel /u/. The

---

[10] Since [back] cannot anchor on the skeletal tier directly, I assume that [-high] is inserted before the feature [back] can spread to the unspecified vowel from the preceding segment.

second segment is associated to [+back]. This is the specification that the vowel /o/ bears in its underlying representation. Thus, the result of applying harmony to a structure like (27) subject to the constraint that a long segment may not be created, is the sequence [uo]. This is a desirable consequence for my analysis since it takes us a step closer to providing a uniform account of the monophthongization of the alternating diphthongs of Spanish.[11]

---

[11] Despite its attraction, this analysis of harmony faces a potential drawback. The organization of the features [high] and [back] suggested by Archangeli predicts that the feature [high] should never spread independently of [back]. This is because the feature [back] is anchored to [high]. Therefore, any association to [high] will also include [back]. This prediction is not borne out for all languages. Though rare, it is not impossible to find languages where [high] spreads independently of [back]. For these languages the features [high] and [back] cannot be organized as in (27). Archangeli (1985) cites two of these languages: Menomini and Montañés. The latter is a particularly troublesome example for us in view of the fact that Montañés is very closely related to standard Spanish and is spoken in Spain. The fact that the feature [back] cannot be anchored to the feature [high] in Montañés suggests that a similar situation might hold for Spanish. If the features [high] and [back] are not represented as in (27), they must be represented in one of two possible ways: either each of the features is on a different plane (as in i), or [high] is anchored on [back] and [back] is docked to the skeletal tier (as in ii). In either case there is no reason why [high] should not participate in harmony:

Archangeli (1985) claims that there is evidence that in languages like Montañés the features [high] and [back] are represented as in (i) rather than as in (ii). This multiplanar representation represents the marked option. The rarity of rules that spread [high] independently of [back] reflects this fact. In order for the language learner to acquire a marked structure such as this, the theory of learnability mandates that there be triggering evidence that alerts the learner to the need to deviate from the structure prescribed by Universal Grammar. In the absence of any such evidence, the less marked representation will be chosen by the learner. In Montañés, for example, the existence of harmony rules that affect [high] independently of [back] provides the language learner with evidence that the features [high] and [back] are not organized as in (27). However, unlike Montañés, Spanish has no processes that manipulate the feature [high] independently of [back]. All the evidence available to the learner of Spanish is consistent with the representation in (27). Consequently, there is no reason to assume that in Spanish [high] and [back] will not be organized in the least marked way.

Thus, the rare existence of harmony systems where [high] spreads independently of [back] does not constitute evidence against the organization of features proposed in Archangeli (1985). Universal Grammar prescribes that [back] is anchored to [high]. For languages such as Montañés there is evidence that triggers the change from an unmarked representation of these features to a multiplanar one. In the absence of such evidence , however, the structure prescribed by Universal Grammar will be chosen. Since Spanish has no phonological processes that manipulate [high] independently of [back], I will assume that these features are represented as in (27). This representation, along with the ban against root geminates, commits us to a version of harmony that spreads only the feature [back]. This version of spreading transforms the underlying sequence /uV/ into {uo}.

Let us now consider how the empty V slot in the sequence /iV/ acquires its features. The table of underlying feature values given in (23) shows that the front high vowel is distinguished from other vowels by a single feature value: [+high]. If this feature spreads to the adjacent V, a long segment will be created. Since long tautomorphemic segments are ruled out in Spanish, the underspecified vowel in the underlying sequence /iV/ cannot acquire the value [+high] via spreading. Therefore, Default assignment will supply this segment with the features [-high, -back, -low]. The resulting sequence will be interpreted as {ie}.[12]

We are now a step closer to my goal of providing a well-motivated account of monophthongization. The underlying representation /iV/ becomes {ie} as a result of Default assignment. Harmony transforms the sequence /uV/ into {uo}. Both {ie} and {uo} will qualify for Contraction and surface as {je} and {uo}, respectively, provided that the high vowel in each sequence is unstressed. The resulting diphthongs are unique in that they consist of segments that agree in the value of the feature [back].

It is my contention that this property makes them susceptible to monophthongization. This being the case, three fundamental questions arise: (a) Why is it that the only diphthongs that are affected by this restriction are those that agree in the value of the feature [back]? (b) Why is this restriction operative only on unstressed syllables? (c) Why aren't falling diphthongs subject to the same constraint? We start by addressing this last question.

4.3 Why are alternations of Spanish limited to rising diphthongs?

Recall that Contraction affects a sequence of two adjacent vowels, the first one of which is unstressed and [+high]. The process eliminates the syllable node and the skeletal position of the high vowel. The floating vowel associates to the following V-slot, creating a 'light' diphthong in the sense of Kaye (1985). Falling diphthongs, on the other hand, are 'bi-skeletal' in structure. Each of the elements of such a structure has its own V-slot.

If we assume that a one-to-one association between members of different tiers is the unmarked option, then we must agree that rising diphthongs represent a more marked structure than falling diphthongs. This is because

---

[12] I will assume that the Shared Features Convention (Steriade and Schein 1986) yields the following structure:

in a rising diphthong two feature matrices share a single V. Rising diphthongs whose members share a feature have a doubly linked V and a doubly linked feature matrix. For this reason, feature sharing represents a greater burden or complexity on rising diphthongs than on falling ones. This is illustrated in (28) by contrasting the structure of the diphthong {je} to that of {ej}.

(28)   {je}   {ej}

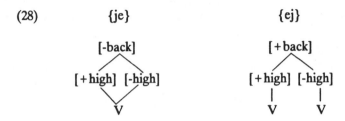

We are now ready to answer the question raised at the beginning of this section. The reason why only rising diphthongs are subject to stress-triggered alternations is that the restriction that triggers the alternations targets only multiply linked structures such as that on the left-hand side in (28). Lesser complex representations are not affected by the ban on shared feature matrices. This ban applies only to unstressed segments that are anchored to the same V position.

Falling diphthongs that share a feature value have a structure that is similar to that of nasals which assimilate to the point of articulation of a following consonant. Such structures have a one-to-one association between the root tier and the melodic tier. Rising diphthongs, on the other hand, consist of two root nodes linked to a single V. For these structures, a shared feature matrix represents a complexity that is not tolerated in unstressed syllables.

We have now isolated the crucial variables in stress-triggered monophthongization. First, the segments that form the diphthong must share a feature value. It is not clear at this point whether this condition applies only to the feature [back] or whether it is a more general ban that applies to all shared feature values. And second, the segments that share this feature value must also share a skeletal position. When these conditions are realized in a metrically weak position, monophthongization results.

It is important to point out that the lack of stress-dependent alternations among the falling diphthongs is a purely accidental phenomenon in Harris (1985). This analysis recognizes four types of alternations, namely, [je]~[e], [je]~[i], [we]~[o], and [we]~[u]. Each of these diphthongs is represented, respectively, as /eX/, /iX/, /oX/, and /uX/ (i.e., a vowel followed by an empty skeletal slot). Given these underlying representations, the apparent monophthongization of the alternating diphthongs is really the deletion of the X-slot. According to Harris, this deletion takes place in unstressed syllables because in this environment the X-slot fails to qualify for Default assignment. Since the segment will not be assigned features, it will not surface. Crucially, stress is what ultimately determines whether or not the empty skeletal slot will surface. This condition has the undesirable consequence that it makes it theoretically possible for there to be stress-triggered alternations among the falling diphthongs.

In order to see how this is possible, let us reverse the order of the underlying sequences proposed by Harris. That is, let us assume that the empty skeletal position precedes, rather than follows, the nonlow vowel: /Xe/, /Xi/, /Xo/, and /Xu/. In that case, we should expect the sequences /Xi/ and /Xu/ to give way to the following alternations: [ej]~[i], [ew]~[u]. The diphthongal variant should appear in stressed syllables, where Default assignment can apply to the empty X-slot. In unstressed syllables, only the specified vowel should surface since the X-slot will not receive any features. This kind of alternation, however, does not exist in Spanish. Falling diphthongs are not subject to stress-triggered alternations. In order to rule out this possibility from Harris's analysis, we need to stipulate that an empty skeletal slot cannot precede a vowel.

In my analysis, monophthongization is triggered by the structural complexity of rising diphthongs that share a feature value. Falling diphthongs lack this complexity because they are bi-skeletal.

4.4 Why are unstressed syllables subject to monophthongization? Restrictions that limit the distribution of more marked structures to stressed syllables are not uncommon across languages. In English, the full range of vowels is not realized in unstressed syllables. Catalan, a language closely related to Spanish, shows the vowel distribution in (29) (capitals stand for lax vowels):

(29)   stressed syllables   unstressed

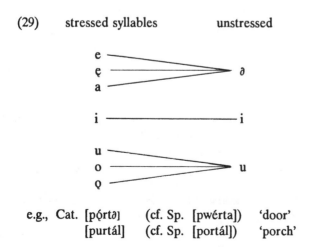

e.g., Cat. [pórtə]   (cf. Sp. [pwérta])   'door'
      [purtál]   (cf. Sp. [portál])   'porch'

The examples in (29) are of particular importance for my analysis. In Catalan, the [pɔ́rtə]/[purtál] alternation is triggered by a restriction on the type of vowels that may appear in unstressed syllables. Syllables that do not bear stress exhibit a reduced number of vowels. The fact that monophthongization in Spanish applies in the same environment where Catalan shows a reduction of vowel types supports my view of monophthongization as a process of simplification. Monophthongization simplifies a structure that is too complex for an unstressed syllable by reducing the number of association lines.

The change that takes {je} to [e] and {wo} to [o] can be expressed in a number of ways. One possibility is to delink the association between the left component of the diphthong and the skeletal position and to allow Stray Erasure to eliminate the floating melodic material. Delinking the left component preserves the head of the syllable at the expense of the glide. In the case of {je} this will yield [e], and in the case of {wo} the result will be [o].

Another way to account for the monophthongization of {je} and {wo} is to view it as a process that fuses the constituents of the diphthong to a single segment. In the theory of 'Charm and Government' (Kaye, Lowenstamm, and Vergnaud 1985), the process involves fusion of the High line. The glide part of the structure serves as the operator and the mid vowel serves as the head. The hot feature [-high] is preserved on the head. The value of the feature [back] remains the same since both segments undergoing fusion have the same value for this feature. The process is illustrated in (30):

(30)

	-back +high	-back -high	→	-back -high
	I	E	→	E
	↑	↑		
	operator	head		
	↓	↓		
	+back +high	+back -high	→	+back -high
	U	O	→	O

I will not choose here between an analysis of monophthongization based on fusion versus one based on the delinking of the glide. What is important for my purposes is that the mechanics of monophthongization can be handled without complications in either analysis. This is possible because the vowel sequences that underlie our representation of the alternating diphthongs of Spanish are different from the sequences that appear on the surface. If the underlying source of the alternating diphthongs were [je] and [we], we would have no way of expressing monophthongization as a uniform process that affects these sequences and excludes others.

We are now ready to answer the third and final question: Is the restriction that causes monophthongization triggered only by the feature [back] or is it triggered by the sharing of any feature?

4.5 Shared feature matrices in unstressed rising diphthongs. Let us begin by restating the problem at hand. It has been my claim that rising diphthongs that share the value of the feature [back] are subject to monophthongization in unstressed syllables because they exceed the maximum number of associations allowed. This being the case, we predict that any other unstressed rising diphthong whose constituents agree in the value of any other feature should also be subject to monophthongization since they too will exceed the maximum number of associations allowed.

Of course, not all surface sequences that share a feature value have this value present in both segments at the time the constraint against shared feature values is operative. Roca (1986) presents evidence that monophthongization is limited to the cyclic phonology. Consequently, shared feature values that are introduced at noncyclic levels will not be banned from unstressed syllables. According to Steriade (1987) and Archangeli (1984), 1988), in a triangular vowel system such as that of Spanish, the vowel [a] is uniquely specified as [+low] in the underlying representation. Other features are not assigned to this segment until the noncyclic levels of the phonology. The only feature of [a], then, that is present at the time when the restriction against shared feature values applies is [low]. Therefore, we must exclude from consideration the diphthong [wa].

There are, however, two diphthongs whose constituents share a feature value at the cyclic levels of the phonology--these are the diphthongs consisting of the two high vocoids: [ju] and [wi]. In my analysis, the vowels [i] and [u] are specified as [+high] in their underlying representation. Following what we have said in this section regarding rising diphthongs whose constituents share a feature value, we would expect the diphthongs [ju] and [wi] to exhibit stress-triggered alternations similar to those of {je} and {wo}. As we have seen, this prediction is not borne out in diphthongs formed from high vocoids.

However, although we know for a fact that [wi] and [ju] do not monophthongize in unstressed syllables, we are not certain of a number of crucial facts. First of all, in stressed syllables, the rising diphthongs [ju] and [wi] alternate with [iw] and [uy]. Therefore, we cannot say with certainty that unstressed diphthongs with high vocoids have stressed variants that are rising diphthongs. A related difficulty comes from the fact that we do not have any knowledge of what kind of representation is assigned to tautosyllabic sequences of high vowels in unstressed syllables. As Navarro Tomás points out, in unstressed syllables it is impossible to tell whether the sequences [iu] and [ui] are realized as rising or falling diphthongs. My guess is that the difficulty involved in telling what kind of diphthong results from such sequences stems from the fact that both vowels have the same sonority value. In an unstressed syllable, this makes it difficult to establish any one vowel as the head. When stress is available, the vowel that bears the accent will be perceived as the head of the structure. This does not mean, however, that a high vowel sequence that is perceived as a rising diphthong will necessarily have the structure that is characteristic of rising diphthongs. All that is needed for such a sequence to be perceived as a rising diphthong is that the second high vowel be pronounced with greater stress than the first. The high-vowel sequences in (31) are bi-skeletal diphthongs. In structure they resemble falling diphthongs rather than rising diphthongs. In terms of perception, however, it is stress, rather than structure, which determines which high vowel will be judged to be more sonorous.

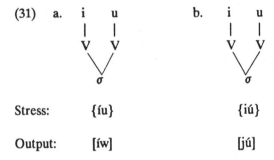

Item (31a) is perceived as a falling diphthong because the stressed vowel precedes a tautosyllabic high vocoid. On the other hand, (31b) is perceived as a rising diphthong because the stressed vowel is to the right of a tautosyllabic high vocoid.

The point of this discussion is that a sequence of two tautosyllabic high vowels can be perceived as a rising diphthong even though it does not have the structure of a rising diphthong. The reason why this can happen is that in the absence of a sonority difference, only the location of stress will determine whether the first or the second vowel is considered the head of the syllable.

Crucially, the existence of unstressed diphthongs consisting of two high vowels should not force us to abandon the hypothesis that monophthongization is a repair strategy that applies to all rising diphthongs that violate the maximum number of association lines allowed in unstressed syllables. In view of the absence of compelling evidence against it, I will maintain the strongest claim regarding the restriction that triggers the alternations of Spanish: The sharing of feature specifications between segments that are anchored to the same V-slot violates the maximum number of associations allowed in unstressed syllables. Segments that violate this limit are subject to monophthongization.

I have now provided an account of the monophthongization of unstressed {je} and {wo}. This still leaves us with the task of explaining what happens to stressed {wo}.

5 From {wo} to {we}. The kind of constraint that rules out the sequences [ow] and [wo] is rather different from that which applies to unstressed {je} and {wo}. While the latter is sensitive to stress and structure, the former rules out all tautomorphemic [-cons, +round, +back] segments regardless of their stress or structure. I will not investigate here the specific nature of the constraint that rules out the diphthongs [ow] and [wo]. I will simply assume that in Spanish there is a surface constraint against diphthongs whose constituents are [+round]. This is a separate and different constraint from that which applies to unstressed {je} and {wo}.

I propose a prohibition against the following autosegmental configuration. (32) depicts two root nodes that share the value of the features round and back. This configuration applies to falling and rising diphthongs in tautomorphemic environments.

(32)   * o o (Root tier)
              \/
         [+round]
              |
         [+back]

The structure in (32) depicts a single melodic matrix linked to two elements on the root tier. The reason why the prohibition above does not apply to heteromorphemic {wo} and {ow} is that across morpheme boundaries we find two instances of [+round]. It is also important to point out that the constraint above will not become operative until the postcyclic phonology since it targets the feature [round].

What happens to segments that violate this constraint? My analysis of the alternating diphthongs commits us to saying that stressed {wo} is changed to [we]. This result can be achieved if we assume that the violation incurred by {wo} is resolved by eliminating the place of articulation features of the nuclear vowel. Once this has taken place, the structure is no longer in violation of (32). The unspecified vowel is subsequently given the feature values of the default vowel. The process is illustrated in (33):

(33)

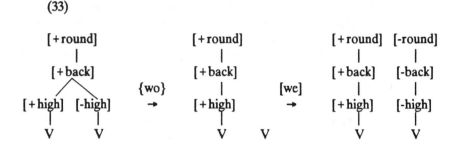

It is my hypothesis, then, that the diphthong {wo} changes to [we] due to a ban against the configuration in (32). The repair strategy invoked in dealing with this diphthong is very different from that which applies to unaccented {je} and {wo} at earlier levels of the phonology. The latter undergo monophthongization while the former retain their structure but change the segmental composition of the diphthong in violation. This difference in repair strategies reflects a difference in the nature of the offense incurred by the structures in question. Unstressed {wo} and {je} exceed the number of association lines allowed on single V's. Monophthongization repairs such a structure by deleting an association line. The solution adopted for {wo} in a noncyclic level of the lexical phonology is one which preserves the bisegmental character of the structure but substitutes feature values that do not violate the restriction against [+round, -cons] segments. The feature values that are inserted are those of the default vowel of Spanish.

The relationship between {wo} and [we] is well attested in Spanish. Navarro Tomás (1977) claims that in certain dialects of Spanish spoken in Asturias words like *p[w]érta* alternate with *p[w]órta*. Penny (1978: 31) makes a similar claim: 'Se diría que, tras [w], los sonidos [e] y [o] son variantes libres de /e/, e.g. [nwora] 'nuera', [fwora] 'fuera'. This lends support to my claim that the source of the [we]/[o] alternation is {wo} and that this diphthong is transformed to [we]. We know that in the change from Latin to Spanish the tense vowel [o] diphthongized to [wo] before becoming the modern [we]: Lat. rota > r[w]eda, bono > b[w]eno (see Menéndez Pidal 1980). Thus, the analysis proposed closely follows the historical development of the alternating diphthongs.

My proposal that {wo} is changed to [we] as a result of a ban against the configuration in (32) also defines a process that is found in other languages. Yip (1988) discusses a ban in La-mi, a Cantonese secret language, which rules out more than one labial segment per word. The repair strategy that is invoked for structures in violation of this constraint is one which deletes the place of articulation features of one of the offending segments. If the segment is an /m/, the repair strategy turns it into [n]. Assuming that [n] is the least marked of the nasal segments, we see that rules of default supply the unspecified segment with place of articulation features. This situation is analogous to that of Spanish. Instead of eliminating a segment, the repair strategy used in both languages deletes the offending features from one of the segments. Subsequently, default rules supply this segment with the missing values. It has been my claim that the nature of the repair strategy used on the sequences [wo] and [ow] is a function of the type of violation incurred by such sequences. The La-mi data support this conclusion. The ban in La-mi which triggers the process illustrated above is similar to that proposed for Spanish in (32). Both are examples of feature cooccurrence restrictions. The repair structures invoked on sequences that violate these restrictions affect the melodic content of one of the segments but leave the prosodic structure of such segments intact. The ban that triggers monophthongization in {je} and {wo} does not impose any restriction on specific features. Instead, such a ban targets a structural configuration that is ruled out in metrically weak positions. Monophthongization destroys this offending structure but preserves the melodic quality of the original configuration.

In sum, the [we]~[o] alternation is regulated by two different kinds of constraints. The ban on feature-sharing among segments that share a V position triggers monophthongization of unstressed {wo}. Stressed {wo} surfaces as [we] as a result of a ban on tautomorphemic sequences of [-cons, +round, +back] segments.

Having proposed an account of the change from {wo} to [we], my analysis of the alternating diphthongs of Spanish is now complete. Before concluding this section, however, it is important to say a word about how (32) affects the diphthong [ow]. Following the line of reasoning in this section, we expect all tautomorphemic instances of {ow} to surface as [ew]. That is, we should expect the same kind of repair strategy that applies to {wo} to also apply to {ow}. Unfortunately, there is no evidence to this effect in the phonology of modern Spanish. This is because the kind of change we are proposing is one which transforms all existing {ow} to [ew]. Therefore, my claim that all instances of tautomorphemic {ow} are changed to [ew] makes it impossible to find corroborating evidence. Although this is an undesirable property of my analysis, it is not one which affects the alternating diphthongs.

The derivations in (34) illustrate the conditions that give rise to the alternations of Spanish (a period signals a syllabic boundary):

(34)   a.

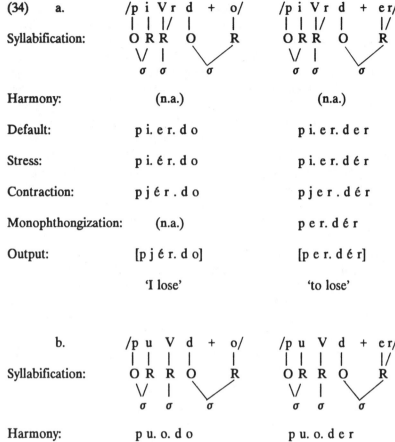

	/p i V r d + o/	/p i V r d + er/
Syllabification:		
Harmony:	(n.a.)	(n.a.)
Default:	p i. e r. d o	p i. e r. d e r
Stress:	p i. é r. d o	p i. e r. d é r
Contraction:	p j é r. d o	p j e r. d é r
Monophthongization:	(n.a.)	p e r. d é r
Output:	[p j é r. d o]	[p e r. d é r]
	'I lose'	'to lose'

b.

	/p u V d + o/	/p u V d + er/
Syllabification:		
Harmony:	p u. o. d o	p u. o. d e r
Stress:	p u. ó. d o	p u. o. d é r
Contraction:	p w ó. d o	p w o. d é r
Monophthongization:	(n.a.)	p o d. é r
Rule (33):	p w é. d o	(n.a.)
Output:	[p w é. d o]	[p o. d é r]
	'I am able to'	'to be able to'

Of the steps given in (34), the repair structure invoked for structures in violation of (32) is the only process for which we have no independent evidence elsewhere in the grammar of Spanish. This rule, however, enables us to explain the relationship that exists between [we] and [wo] in certain dialects of Spanish. Finally, the proposal regarding the change from {wo} to [we] finds an analogue in La-mi.

All other steps involve processes that must exist in the phonology independent of the question of the alternating diphthongs. We have seen that harmony applies between a syllable-final nasal and a following consonant. The change from {wo} to [o] is evidenced in nouns such as *acto* and *punto*. These words require that we posit a rule of monophthongization. Contraction, stress, and syllabification are processes that are independently motivated.

6 The alternations of Italian. A desirable property of a solution to a problem in a particular language is that it extend with minimum modifications to languages that exhibit a similar phenomenon. This is especially true when the languages in question are closely related and resemble each other in many other relevant aspects. Such is the case for Spanish and Italian. The striking similarities between these languages bear testimony to their common ancestry: Latin. The similarities in syllable structures, stress, and morphology often make it possible for phonological solutions that apply to one language to be extended to the other.

The intention of this presentation is to show that the proposed analysis for Spanish extends with minor modifications to Italian. As a result, I will not engage in a detailed discussion of Italian phonology.

Italian exhibits an alternation of diphthongs that closely resembles that of Spanish. The diphthongs that alternate are [je] and [wo]. These undergo monophthongization in unstressed environments, becoming [e] and [o], respectively.

(35) l[j]éve ~ levitá   l[y]éto ~ letízia   t[j]épido ~ tepóre
      c[w]óre ~ coratélla   f[w]óco ~ focóso   n[w]óvo ~ novitá

As is the case for Spanish, the diphthongs that alternate (i.e., [je] and [wo]) are restricted in their distribution to stressed syllables. There are, however, a few differences between the two languages. First, while in Spanish it is the diphthong [wé] that alternates with [o], in Italian the alternation is [wó]~[o]. Second, the effect that suffixation of certain morphemes has on the alternation varies between the languages. Thus, while in Spanish the diminutive suffixes -*it*V, -*cit*V do not induce monophthongization of the root, Italian -*(u)olino*, and *(u)oletto* yield monophthongal forms (see Marotta 1988).

Another position where the monophthongal variant is favored is in closed syllables, e.g. *muó.ve.re/mo̲.vi.mén.to/mós.si* 'to move'/'movement'/'I moved.'

In Spanish, the diphthongal forms can appear in closed syllables (*p[j]érna*, *p[w]énte*). These differences between the two languages are easily expressed in terms of parametric variations in the syllable structure and the lexical phonology of Spanish and Italian.

Recall from the discussion of Harris (1985) that an analysis based on epenthesis cannot work for Italian because neither one of the monophthongal forms behaves as an epenthetic vowel in Italian. The analysis we have provided for Spanish, on the other hand, can transfer to Italian with very minor modifications.

First of all, since the diphthong [wó] appears in root morphemes we must assume that the restriction against [+round, -cons] diphthongs does not hold in Italian. This means that [jé] and [wó] have completely parallel derivations. They undergo monophthongization in unstressed syllables and in checked syllables, and surface intact in stressed open syllables. Thus, the analysis is considerably simpler and more uniform for Italian than for Spanish. The difference in the behavior of the diminutive suffixes can be accounted for in terms of where in the phonology the destressing induced by the suffixation of the diminutive morphemes takes place. In Spanish the destressing occurs at a time when the restriction against unstressed rising diphthongs that agree in the value of the feature [back] is no longer operative. For this reason, the diphthongs [je] and [we] are allowed to appear unstressed in words that have undergone diminutive formation, e.g., *v[j]ejecíto*, *p[w]eblíto*. In Italian the destressing that is triggered by the suffixation of the diminutive takes place while the above restriction is still operative. Hence, monophthongization applies to nouns that have the diminutive suffix.

The difference in the effect that closed syllables have on the alternations can also be accounted for without the need to revise the main thrust of the analysis. In Italian, the monophthongs are favored over the diphthongs in closed syllables. In Spanish, the presence of a tautosyllabic postnuclear consonant does not induce monophthongization.

(36) *Spanish:*   *Italian:*
     c[w]érpo   corporál   c[w]ócere   cótto
     'body'   'bodily'   'to cook'   'cooked'

     m[w]érdo   mordér   m[w]óvere   mósso
     'I bite'   'to bite'   'to move'   'moved'

As we have seen, Contraction in Spanish creates a 'light' diphthong. Thus, GVC rhymes are possible because they do not exceed the maximum size of the rhyme in Spanish. If we assume that Italian rising diphthongs are 'heavy', then we can explain monophthongization in closed syllables as a process that repairs a structure which violates the bi-skeletal limit on rhymes. In other words, if we accept that it is possible for languages to exhibit parametric variation on the structure of their prevocalic glides, and we assume that Italian differs from Spanish in that it has heavy rising diphthongs, then monophthongization in checked syllables can be viewed as a repair strategy.

Evidence in favor of the proposal that rising diphthongs in Italian are 'bi-skeletal' comes from a lengthening process that affects Italian vowels in open syllables. Vogel (1977b: 601) reports that stressed vowels in word-internal open syllables are always long. She posits the rule in (37):

(37) $$V$$
$$|$$
$$[+stress] \rightarrow [+long] \ / \ \underline{\hspace{1cm}} CV$$

(e.g.: *pane* 'bread' = [páːne])

In an autosegmental model where a long vowel is represented as a single segmental matrix linked to two positions on the skeletal tier, the process illustrated in (37) can be expressed in the following way: Insert a V-slot lacking any features in an open syllable that is stressed as in (38a), and spread the feature values of the preceding vowel onto this slot, as in (38b) (V' = a vowel associated to no features):

(38) a. $\emptyset \rightarrow V' \ / \ V \ \underline{\hspace{0.5cm}}]_\sigma$ b. [α high, β back, ...]
$$|$$
$$[+stress]$$

$$V \qquad V'$$

Stressed VC syllables are not subject to this process. The reason for this is that they are 'bi-skeletal' structures. Lengthening, therefore, would create a rhyme that is too long. Stressed vowels that are preceded by a glide pattern are like stressed VC rhymes in that they do not lengthen. If rising diphthongs were mono-skeletal in structure, we would expect them to pattern like V rhymes in lengthening in stressed syllables. Since they behave like VC rhymes in failing to lengthen, it is logical to assume that they too are bi-skeletal.

Of course, if Italian rising diphthongs are heavy, then the constraint that triggers monophthongization of unstressed [je] and [wo] must target shared feature values among tautosyllabic vowels regardless of whether they form a falling or rising diphthong. This being the case, we expect falling diphthongs as well as rising diphthongs to be subject to stress-triggered alternations whenever there's a shared feature matrix.

A survey of the inventory of Italian diphthongs reveals only two types of tautomorphemic falling diphthongs: [aw] and [ew]. These appear in lexical items like *a[w]tomóbile* 'automobile', *cawsále* 'causal', *E[w]rópa*, 'Europe' and *ne[w]tróle* 'neutral'. Of these two types of falling diphthongs, only the behavior of [aw] will concern us since the components of [ew] share no feature values. The existence of nonalternating falling diphthongs as in *cá[w]sa/ca[w]sále* is not necessarily a problem for my analysis. Recall from an earlier discussion that the vowel /a/ is uniquely specified as [+low]. It is not until the postcyclic phonology that this segment acquires the specification [+back]. By then, of course, the ban on shared feature matrices is no longer operative. Thus, the fact that at the surface level the diphthong [aw] is composed of segments that share the feature value [+back] should not trigger monophthongization.

In sum, the analysis sketched here for Italian is minimally different from that which has been proposed for Spanish. The differences between the diphthongal alternations in the two languages are easily expressed in terms of parametric variations in the syllable structure and the lexical phonology of Spanish and Italian.

8   Conclusions. I have presented an analysis of the alternating diphthongs which offers several advantages over previous analyses. In accounting for the alternations of Spanish, I have explained the systematic absence of unstressed [je] and [we] from certain environments. Second, we have related the alternations [je]/[e] and [we]/[e] to general processes that rule out [wo] and [ow]. A third advantage of the proposed analysis is that it explains why only rising diphthongs are subject to stress-triggered alternations. The structure of rising diphthongs is such that any shared feature matrix in unstressed position exceeds the number of association lines allowed. Finally, the proposed analysis extends with minor modifications to Italian. Putting it all together, we have a maximally simple analysis which goes much further than its immediate goal of explaining the behavior of [je] and [we].

References

Alarcos Llorach. 1967. Fonología española. Madrid: Gredos.
Archangeli, D. 1984. Underspecification in Yawelmani Phonology and Morphology. Doctoral dissertation, MIT, Cambridge, Mass.
Archangeli, D. 1985. Yokuts Harmony: Evidence for Coplanar Representation in Nonlinear Phonology. Linguistic Inquiry 16, 335-372.
Carreira, M. (forthcoming) The Structure of Rising Diphthongs in Spanish. Proceedings of LSRL XIX, 1989.
Carreira, M. 1990. The Diphthongs of Spanish: Stress, Syllabification, and Alternations. Doctoral dissertation, University of Illinois at Urbana.
Chung, R. 1988. On the Representation of Kejia Diphthongs. Unpublished ms., University of Illinois, Urbana.
Clements, G. N. 1985. The Geometry of Phonological Features. Phonology Yearbook 2, 225-52.

Harris, J. 1983. Syllable Structure and Stress in Spanish: A Nonlinear Analysis. Cambridge, Mass.: MIT Press.

Harris, J. 1985. Spanish Diphthongization and Stress: A Paradox Resolved. Phonology Yearbook 2, 31-45.

Hayes. 1989. Compensatory Lengthening in Moraic Phonology. Linguistic Inquiry 20, 253-306.

Kaye, J. 1985. On the Syllable Structure of Certain West African languages. In D. L. Goyvaerts, ed., African Linguistics: Essays in Memory of M. W. K. Semikenke. Philadelphia: John Benjamins.

Kaye, J., J. Lowenstamm, and J. R. Vergnaud. 1985. The Internal Structure of Phonological Segments: A Theory of Charm and Government. Phonology Yearbook 2, 305-328.

Malkiel Y. 1966. Diphthongization, Monophthongization, Metaphony: Studies in Their Interaction in the Paradigm of the Old Spanish -ir Verbs. Language 42, 430-472.

Morgan, T. 1984. Consonant-Glide-Vowel Alternations in Spanish: A Case Study in Syllabic and Lexical Phonology. Doctoral dissertation, University of Texas at Austin. (Available through University Microfilms, Ann Arbor, Mich.).

Navarro Tomás, T. 1977. Manual de pronunciación española. Madrid: CSIC.

Penny, R. J. 1969. El habla pasiega: ensayo de dialectología montañesa. London: Tamesis Books.

Real Academia Española. 1973. Esbozo de una nueva gramática de la lengua española. Madrid: Espasa-Calpe.

Roca, I. 1988. Theoretical Implications of Spanish Word Stress. Linguistic Inquiry 19, 393-423.

Sagey, E. 1986. The Representation of Features and Relations in Non-Linear Phonology. Doctoral dissertation, MIT, Cambridge, Mass.

Selkirk, E. 1984. On the Major Class Features and Syllable Theory. In M. Aronoff and R. Oehrle, eds., Language Sound Structure. Cambridge, Mass.: MIT Press, 107-136.

Steriade, D. 1984. Glides and Vowels in Romanian. Proceedings of the Tenth Annual Meeting of the Berkeley Linguistics Society 10. Berkeley, California, 47-54.

Steriade, D., and B. Schein. 1984. Geminate Structure-dependent Rules. Proceedings of the West Coast Conference on Formal Linguistics 3, Stanford University, 263-91.

Steriade. 1987. Redundant Values. In A. Bosch, B. Need, and E. Schiller, eds. Papers from the Parasession on Autosegmental and Metrical Phonology. Chicago Linguistic Society, Chicago, Il., 339-362

Vogel, I. 1977. Length Phenomena in Italian: Support for the Syllable. Proceedings of the Tenth Annual Meeting of the Berkeley Linguistics Society 3. Berkeley Linguistics Society, Berkeley, Calif., 600-615.

Yip, M. 1988. The Obligatory Contour Principle and Phonological Rules: A Loss of Identity. Linguistic Inquiry 19, 65-100.

With respect to metrical constituents in Spanish

James W. Harris
Massachusetts Institute of Technology

1 Introduction. This study is concerned with the formal mechanisms whereby stress contours are associated with the segmental content of utterances. At the lowest level of detail, I argue that the computation of stress grids involves only left–headed binary feet in some dialects of Spanish but both left–headed binary and right–headed unbounded feet in other dialects. At the highest level of generality, I argue that certain universal constraining principles that guarantee 'respect' for metrical constituents (Halle and Kenstowicz 1991, hereafter 'HK91') receive qualified empirical support from the analysis I propose for the assignment of accentual constituents in Spanish.[1]

Chomsky (1986, and other works) has argued with great force that the astonishing rapidity and uniformity of language acquisition by all normal members of the human species on the basis of fragmentary and degenerate experience is made possible by the fact that the learner approaches the task equipped with a genetically determined language faculty of a particular character. This acquisitional mechanism must be so specific and restrictive that it leads learners to the correct internalized representations despite the impoverished nature of the relevant triggering data. The central goal of linguistic theory, then, is to develop a correspondingly specific and restrictive explanatory model of this language faculty.

Of the several components that evidently comprise human linguistic competence, phonology occupies our attention here, in particular, the accentual (metrical) subcomponent. The Chomskian view underlies and guides our argumentation in the following way. The metrical HK91 'respect' principles are explanatory in that they restrict the set of possible language–particular grammars. A grammar consistent with these principles-- call it G_C--is thus *a priori* more highly valued than one that is not--call it G_N-- all other things being equal. Therefore, in order to establish the explanatory superiority of G_C over G_N it is necessary to demonstrate only that G_C captures all relevant generalizations expressed by G_N; it is not necessary to demonstrate additionally some descriptive failure of G_N. I propose a set of accentual rules

---

[1] The writing of HK91 and of the present paper was done over approximately the same period of time in the same building at MIT by authors who share their ongoing research with one another. The reader can therefore understand that the two papers have influenced each other and the final versions cross reference each other.

for Spanish that both capture all the accentual generalizations accounted for in certain published alternative proposals (discussed below) and also are more closely consistent with the 'respect' principles than are these alternatives. The proposal developed here thus attains a higher degree of explanatory value, corresponding to the increase in restrictiveness demanded of metrical descriptions by the line of research presently culminating in HK91. In order to qualify for serious consideration as a description of Spanish accentual structure, any analysis that requires violation of the HK91 metrical 'respect' principles must assume the burden of proof to show that the extra theoretical latitude is empirically warranted. This challenge has not yet been accepted by any study that I am aware of.

The most fully articulated theory of the universal schematism wherein the accentual facts of natural language must be learned, stored, and processed by the speaker is that of Halle and Vergnaud's *Essay on Stress* (1987, hereafter 'EOS'). The stress system of Spanish has been investigated in some depth in this general framework (see references). While there is a great amount of consensus in these investigations, there are also at the moment--not surprisingly--circumscribed areas of disagreement and numerous loose ends.

One of the latter is the focus of the present study, namely, the nature of the mechanisms whereby Spanish determines the location of subsidiary rhythmic stresses from a fixed reference point, the primary word stress. Our point of departure is Roca's 'Secondary Stress and Metrical Rhythm' (1986, hereafter 'R86'), the best treatment of the topic that I know of. The present study aims to build on this foundation, extending and refining it in a principled way.

The body of this essay is organized as follows. Section 2 provides theoretical grounding by illustrating relevant postulations of EOS and introducing certain subsequent developments, including the HK91 metrical 'respect' principles. Section 3 examines in detail the assignment of secondary stress in Spanish and its relationship to the 'respect' constraints. Section 4 discusses two recent analyses of primary word stress in Spanish that violate these constraints and shows how one of the analyses can be modified so as to entail no violation and no loss of generalization. Section 5 contains a summary and final conclusions.

2 Preliminaries

2.1 General. I assume that the reader is familiar with EOS, or will soon become so. In any event, I will sketch some background assumptions in order to highlight certain discrepancies between EOS and earlier, more familiar versions of 'Lexical Phonology', to introduce certain details of the framework assumed here that have been developed subsequent to EOS, and to clarify certain points of confusion that have arisen in the literature. (The careful reader should of course consult the original sources.)

I show in (1) a block diagram of the overall model of syntax/morphology/
phonology interaction that I assume:

(1)   DS = D-structure, SS = S-structure,
        LF = Logical Form, PF = Phonological Form

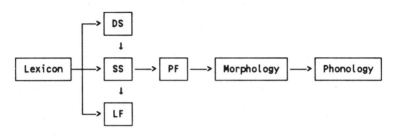

Following Marantz (1988), I assume a set of principles that convert
mobile-like (hierarchically nested, linearly unordered) trees of S-structure
to linearly ordered constituent trees in Phonological Form that serve as the
input to the morphology. Morphology is an autonomous component of the
grammar that provides input to the phonological component. That is,
affixation processes and other rules of word formation are not interleaved
among the rules of phonology as proposed in 'classical' Lexical Phonology.[2]
    The internal organization of the phonological component is shown in (2):

(2)

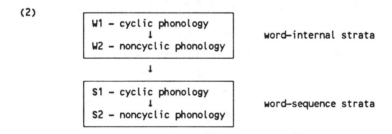

Phonological rules are organized into four ordered strata: W1, W2, S1,
S2. The rules in the first pair of strata apply word internally, while those in
the second pair apply to sequences of words. Within each of the two pairs,
the first stratum is cyclic and the second is noncyclic. The rules in the cyclic
stratum W1 apply to each cyclic constituent of a word in turn, in the familiar
fashion, subject to strict cyclicity and other conditions. The rules of the
noncyclic stratum W2 apply after all passes through W1 are completed; and
they apply exactly once to the entire word, regardless of the number of
noncyclic affixes in the word, including the case of words with no noncyclic

---

[2] Cf. Pesetsky (1979), Kiparsky (1982, 1985), and much related work.

affixes.

The representation of stress in the EOS model is illustrated in (3), as a first approximation:

```
(3)    de.mo.cra.ti.co
       (*   *) (*   *)<*>    line 0
       (*   ·   *) ·   ·     line 1
        ·   ·   *   ·   ·    line 2
```

The example is of course the Spanish word *democrático* 'democratic'; for the moment, however, it can be taken as a hypothetical form provided for the sake of illustration. For convenience, syllable boundaries are indicated by periods in the sequence of consonants and vowels. Stress contours are represented by the grid of asterisks and dots below (or above) this sequence. (Dots will usually be omitted henceforth.) Such grids are constructed on the 'stress plane' of multiplanar (autosegmental) representations; the stress plane intersects with other autosegmental planes at the 'prosodic skeleton' or X–tier.[3] (The line of consonants, vowels, and syllable–marking periods in (3) is thus the X–tier onto which segmental and other information has been collapsed as a space–saving convenience.) Degree of stress is relative to the number of asterisks in a particular column. Thus (3) represents the word *democrático* as having primary stress on the syllable *crá* and secondary stress on the syllable *de*. The asterisks on line 0 of the grid identify all and only the stressable elements in a particular system--syllable 'nuclei' or 'heads' in the case at hand. Angle brackets '< >' indicate that a particular stressable element--the head of the word–final syllable in (3)--is extrametrical, that is, invisible to prosodic rules and processes that would otherwise take it into account. The asterisks on lines 0 and 1 are gathered into headed constituents whose boundaries are indicated by parentheses; the head of a given constituent is identified by aligning with it an asterisk in the next higher numbered line. Line 0 constituents are commonly called 'feet', a term I adopt here. The head of the line 1 constituent (identified by the asterisk on line 2) marks the location of the primary word stress.

Many languages employ bounded (binary) feet as a device to measure distances in the calculation of stress contours (among other computations) yet do not exhibit at particular levels of derivation every line 1 asterisk associated with the head of a line 0 constituent. In this case, the line 1 asterisks in question are removed by the operation of Conflation. An informal statement of Conflation as proposed in EOS is given in (4a), and the effect of conflating lines 1 and 2 of (3) is shown in (4b).

---

[3] Cf. Clements (1985), Sagey (1986), EOS, Gorecka (1989), Halle (1989), and much related work.

(4)   a.   *Conflation*: Remove asterisks on line *n* in columns that have no asterisk on line *n+1* (=leave only the heads of the constituents constructed on line *n*).

b.   de.mo.cra.ti.co
```
*  *  (*  *)<*>    line 0
.  .  (*) .  .     line 1
.  .   *  .  .     line 2
```

Special note should be taken of the fact that Conflation leaves some elements unmetrified or 'free'--that is, members of no metrical constituent--at certain derivational stages. (The unmetrified status of these elements follows directly from the definition of 'headed constituent', whereby the constituent ceases to exist if its head ceases to exist--as may happen when asterisks in the lower numbered of two conflated grid lines are erased.) This fact is crucial in the argumentation below.[4]

2.2 Stress 'rules.'   Stress grids must conform to language–particular rules and to the language–particular values of a universal set of parameters.[5] To provide a concrete example, I present now an illustrative subset of the stress rules of Spanish.

Consider this minimal set of data in (5):

(5)   *C-final*   *V-final*
   a.   *General case*
         contról   'control'   contróla   '(he) controls'
         cantár   'to sing'   cantára   'sang' (past subj.)

   b.   *Special case*
         apóstol   'apostle'   epístola   'epistle'
         ámbar   'amber'   cántaro   'pitcher'

   c.   *Systematically disallowed*
         *ápostol   *épistola

---

[4] Roca (1990: 146, notes 12 and 13) refers to Conflation as 'artifactual'/ 'an artifact'. This evaluation would have substance if it were accompanied by successful reanalysis without Conflation of all the cases in the literature in which Conflation has been argued to play a crucial role. Since Roca has not provided such reanalysis, his evaluation must be regarded as conjectural.

[5] In informal discourse, both the parameter values and the rules are referred to indiscriminately as 'rules.' I follow this normal practice here, but the reader should keep the technical distinction in mind.

The immediately salient characteristics of (5) are these: (i) the right edgeof the word evidently serves as reference point for the computation of stress placement, (ii) stress is located at most three syllables leftward of this reference point, (iii) stress is found one syllable nearer the end in consonant-final than in corresponding vowel-final words, and (iv) most words are stressed on the final syllable if they end in a (noninflectional) consonant and on the next-to-last syllable if they end in a vowel (5a). Statement (iv) covers the vast majority--perhaps up to 90%--of the lexical items of Spanish; it thus in some way embodies the basic stress rule of the language.

We ask now what generalizations a learner equipped with the universal human language acquisitional mechanism internalizes on the basis of data of which (5) is a tiny but representative sample. The statements in (6) are an informal bridge to the EOS formalism, which I take to be the best available theory of metrical representations:

(6) a. Stressable elements are vowels (syllable nuclei).
     b. A word-final vowel is invisible (extrametrical).

The notion of metrical invisibility allows us to capture formally the regularity expressed in (iii): the final vowels of *contróla*, *cantára* (5a) and *epístola*, *cántaro* (5b) are invisible to prosodic rules (notation: *contról<a>*, *cantár<a>*, *epístol<a>*, *cántar<o>*). *Contról*, *cantár*, *apóstol*, and *ámbar*, on the other hand, have no invisible element since their rightmost vowel is not word final but rather followed by a consonant. Given invisibility, *contróla* is prosodically identical to *contról*, *epístola* is prosodically identical to *apóstol*, and so on. Consequently, all of the forms in (5) reduce to one general case (5a) and one special case (5b), and statement (iv) covering the former can be recast as (7):

(7) Place stress as far to the right as possible; i.e., accent the rightmost (visible) vowel.

The learner equipped with the mechanisms of EOS needs to learn very little more than (6) and (7) in order to deal with the remaining facts in (5), including the special case (5b). The only measuring device provided by the theory is the bounded (binary) foot. Therefore in stress systems that measure the location of stress from the right edge of the word, as Spanish obviously does, the left-headed binary foot determines the greatest leftward displacement of stress allowed by the theory. This is exactly case (5b), where primary word stress falls on the next-to-last visible syllable: *apóstol*, *epístol<a>*, etc., as illustrated in (3). What the learner must recognize about the residual class of words illustrated in (5b) is thus essentially that they are lexical exceptions to rule (7), which regularly applies to the vast majority of words.

We can now integrate (6) and (7) into the more formally stated set of parameters/rules given in (8):

(8)   a.   Stressable elements: syllable nuclei (rhyme heads).[6]
     b.   Extrametricality: right.[7]
     c.   The rightmost (visible) stressable element in line 0.
        heads a foot (i.e. has * associated in line 1).
     d.   Line 0 (feet): binary, left-headed, right to left.[8]
     e.   Line 1 (primary stress): unbounded, right-headed.
     f.   Conflation: 1/2.

I show step by step in (9) how grids of the type illustrated in (3) are constructed for the examples *contróla* (5a) and *epístola* (5b) so as to uniquely meet the specifications of (8):

(9)

	con.tro.la		e.pis.to.la
(8a)	* * *	line 0	* * * *
(8b)	* * <*>	line 0	* * * <*>
(8c)	* * <*> *	line 0 line 1	(lexical exception)
(8d)	(*) (*)<*> * *	line 0 line 1	(*)(* *)<*> * *
(8e)	(*) (*)<*> (* *) *	line 0 line 1 line 2	(*)(* *)<*> (* *) *
(8f)	* (*)<*> (*) *	line 0 line 1 line 2	* (* *)<*> (*) *

---

[6] Available options include all [−consonantal] segments, all members of the rhyme constituent of the syllable, and perhaps others.

[7] This parameter need only select the left or the right edge of its domain; rules of extrametricality are universally limited to affect a single element per rule, adjacent to the chosen edge.

[8] Line 0 and line 1 constituents may be either binary (bounded) or unbounded and either left-headed or right-headed. Binary feet are constructed by either left-to-right or right-to-left iteration. The marginal possibility of ternary feet is discussed in EOS, pp. 25-28.

Of the statements in (8), all except (8c) give the Spanish settings of universal parameters. These settings are indispensable and irreducible in the sense that the full specification of the accentual system of any natural language requires the setting of a value for each of the parameters in (8) as a necessary (though perhaps not sufficient) core of information that must be supplied in one way or another. Statement (8c), on the other hand, is a language–particular rule whose effect is this: since line 0 constituents are left–headed in Spanish, the rightmost foot assigned to *control<a>* can contain only the 'accented' syllable *tro*. Since language–particular rules often have idiosyncratic (lexically marked) exceptions, it is not surprising that (8c) has arbitrary exceptions--i.e. the class of words illustrated in (5b)--despite its status as a general rule of the language.[9] On the other hand, we do not expect parameter settings like the remainder of (8) to be subject to idiosyncratic variation among individual lexical items.

2.3 The alterability of prosodic constituents. A longstanding concern in the study of metrical constituency is this: Under what conditions, and to what extent, can structure already assigned be altered in the course of a derivation? Or conversely: Under what conditions, and to what extent, must existing metrical structure be 'respected'? Two cases are illustrated in (10) in which virtually all investigators have assumed without comment that existing structure is not altered.

(10) a. <u>Final output of stratum n</u> → <u>input to stratum n+1</u>

        line 0   * * * * (* *)   X * * * * (* *) Y
        line 1   (*)   (*)
        line 2   *   *

      b.   (σ = unstressed syllable; Σ = stressed syllable)

         $\sigma\ \sigma\ \sigma\ \sigma\ \sigma$ → $(\Sigma\ \sigma)\ \sigma\ \sigma\ \sigma$ → $(\Sigma\ \sigma)(\Sigma\ \sigma)\ \sigma$ → $(\Sigma\ \sigma)(\Sigma\ \sigma)(\Sigma)$

Case (10a) illustrates the fact that if a representation R is the final output of some stratum, then exactly R appears unaltered in the input to the

---

[9] Roca (1990: 145) asserts that a rule like (8c) 'amounts to the statement that Spanish regular stress is exceptional.' It is difficult to understand this assertion since the reasoning that supports it (if I have grasped Roca's point) would lead to the conclusion that, say, the rule that laxes vowels before the suffix *-ic* in English is a statement of exceptionality and all the words that undergo this rule are exceptions to the (regular?) pattern manifested in a minority of words like *scenic, phonemic*, and so on. Indeed, it seems that by Roca's reasoning all language–particular rules would be statements of exceptionality and all forms that undergo such rules would be exceptions. I know of no precedent in linguistics, or elsewhere, for such use of the term 'exceptional.'

following stratum, along with any new material--the X and Y in (10a)--that becomes available.[10] In (10b), as Prince (1985) observes, left–to–right iteration of a rule of left–headed binary foot formation in a single cycle is always assumed to have the effect illustrated, not $\sigma\,\sigma\,\sigma\,\sigma\,\sigma$ → $(\Sigma\ \sigma)\,\sigma\,\sigma\,\sigma$ → $(\Sigma)(\Sigma\ \sigma)\,\sigma\,\sigma$ → $(\Sigma)(\Sigma)(\Sigma\ \sigma)\,\sigma$, etc., as would be the case if each iteration did not respect the output of the previous one.[11]

Other cases are intuitively less accessible and less securely established. Extending Prince (1985), Steriade (1988), Poser (1989), and related work, Halle (1990) and HK91 identify the three situations illustrated in (11), in which rules that create a particular metrical structure S 'respect' instances of S that already exist.

(11)   a.   'opacity'

```
     [[1 2  3 4  5] 6 7]      ≠      *[1 2  3  4 5  6 7]
      (* *)(* *)<*> * *               (* *)(*)(* *)(* *)
       *     *                         *     *  *     *
```

       b.   'closure'

```
     [[1 2  3] 4]      ≠      *[1 2  3 4]
      (* *)(*) *                (* *)(* *)
       *    *                    *     *
```

       c.   'crossover'

```
     [1 2 [3 4] 5 6]      ≠      *[1 2  3 4  5 6]
      * * (* *) * *                (* *)(* *)(* *)
            *                       *     *     *
```

Assume in (11a) that the metrical structure in the inner (bracketed) morphological constituent is assigned by a rule R that generates left–headed binary feet from right to left. In the next cycle, when elements 6 and 7 become available and 5 thereby loses its extrametricality, R cannot generate a foot *(45), since element 4 is already incorporated into the foot (34). The only possible output of reapplication of R to (12)(34)567 is (12)(34)(5)(67). HK91 calls this inaccessibility of metrified elements the 'opacity' effect.

In (11b), the degenerate foot formed on element 3 in the first cycle cannot expand to form *(34) when element 4 becomes available in the next cycle, even though (34) would be pattern–conforming (binary left–headed).

---

[10] Of course, extrametricality of some element e disappears if newly available material makes e nonperipheral.

[11] Steriade (1988) points out the analogous assumption regarding syllable structure: left–to–right iteration of a rule creating (C)V syllables on, say, /uia/ gives $(wi)a$ then $(wi)(a)$, not $(wi)a$ then $(u)(ja)$.

The foot (3), once generated, is inalterable; the only possible output is (12)(3)(4), even though (12)(34) would be legitimate had elements 3 and 4 been available for incorporation simultaneously. HK calls this inability ofestablished constituents to expand the 'closure' effect.[12]

Case (11c) illustrates that existing metrical structure is 'respected' in the sense that iterative rules are forbidden to cross it. The feet (12) and (56) cannot both be generated in successive applications of one iterative rule in a single stratum if (34) is present. Possible metrifications are (12)(34)56 by rightward propagation and 12(34)(56) by leftward propagation. HK calls this inability of structure–building rules to propagate over an established constituent the 'crossover' effect.

When CAN an existing metrical constituent be altered or crossed? Three cases have been identified with reasonable clarity. First, the Conflation operation can destroy constituents by decapitating them, as explained just below (4). Second, metrical structure can be altered by processes whose very formulation guarantees that this is their only function--for example, rules of rhythmic reversal, clash removal, resyllabification, and grid–oriented operations for which constituency is irrelevant--as opposed to rules, like foot–erecting operations, whose function is to form constituents out of metrically 'free' elements. Finally, metrical structure is eradicated by the Stress Erasure Convention, which operates between successive passes through the rules assigned to the cyclic word–internal stratum W1, but not elsewhere. Consequently, the only accentual structure carried forward into W2 is that generated in the last pass through W1. I will say no more about this Convention now, but we return to it in section 4.[13]

3 Secondary stress in Spanish. It is well known that the languages of the world exhibit different relationships between primary word stress and subsidiary stresses. In some languages, one syllable is singled out for primary stress from among those already assigned stress; the latter syllables are said to have 'secondary' stress. In other languages, primary word stress must be assigned first, and is then used as a point of reference for positioning

---

[12] If the same conditions hold for syllable structure, the explanation for the syllabification of [sub [lunar]] as *sub.lu.nar*, for example, may be that the syllable *lu* formed in the inner cycle cannot expand to include unsyllabified *b* of the prefix even though *bl* is an allowable onset. It would obviously be highly desirable to unite all aspects of metrical constituency, syllabic as well as accentual, under the same notion of 'respect.' Cf. note 11.

[13] The role of the Stress Erasure Convention in Spanish is discussed at length in Halle, Harris, and Vergnaud (1991).

subsidiary or 'secondary' stresses. Modern Spanish is the second kind of language. The examples in (12) illustrate that subsidiary stresses can be placed on alternating syllables to the left of the primary word stress:[14]

(12) na.tù.ra.lì.za.ción   nà.tu.rà.li.zár
      còns.tan.tì.no.pò.li.tá.no   cons.tàn.ti.nò.po.lì.ta.nís.mo

R86 studies the assignment of subsidiary stresses in Spanish in considerable detail. The primary concern of the investigation is whether such stresses are assigned 'lexically' or 'postlexically.'[15] A compelling argument is given that they cannot in general be assigned in the same stratum in which primary word stress is assigned, as Harris 1983 had mistakenly proposed. Instead, primary stress is assigned lexically whereas secondary stress is assigned postlexically in the terms of R86. Reduced to essentials, the reasoning is this: because of the effect of obviously postlexical syllable–reduction processes, lexically assigned feet do not always correspond to the secondary stresses that actually appear in surface representations; the latter must then be computed postlexically.[16] I accept this conclusion here; it is a valuable contribution to our understanding of Spanish accentual structure.

R86 regards the precise formulation of the Spanish 'rule' for primary stress as 'orthogonal' to the main concern of that study and considers it sufficient 'to say that primary stress can be assigned independently of secondary stress, and that the appropriate rule must be lexical' (p. 350). We understand now, however, that primary and secondary stress assignment cannot be divorced so cleanly. In section 2.3, we have seen that because of the effects of 'opacity', 'closure', and 'crossover' (11a-c), the metrical constituency associated with primary stress may well play a role in the assignment of secondary stress: if the rules that assign secondary stress are subject to these effects, then only elements left 'free' in the assignment of primary stress constituency can be incorporated into secondary stress constituents. We are thus obliged to pay due attention to lexically assigned

---

[14] Subsidiary stresses in Spanish are often not perceptually salient, and native judgments about them are typically not robust. The latter do converge, however, with much greater than chance frequency. Except as noted, the data in this study are taken from or based directly on R86.

[15] R86 did not envision the elaboration of strata into word–internal and word–sequence pairs shown in (2).

[16] It is therefore not surprising that certain feet are erased by Conflation (8f) lexically (i.e. in the word–internal strata) only to be reassigned postlexically (i.e. in the word–sequence strata).

accentual structure as we investigate secondary stress. The following sections focus on those aspects of the assignment of secondary stress in Spanish that bear on the HK91 principles of 'respect' for accentual constituents.

3.1 Secondary stress; posttonic syllables. R86 provides the following rules for the postlexical assignment of secondary stress in Spanish:[17]

(13)   a. Stressable elements are rhymes (equivalently for our purposes here, [+syllabic] segments).
       b. Line 0 constituents are right–headed.
       c. On line 0 construct bounded constituents from right to left.

R86 notes in the explication of (13) that it 'is at odds with Halle and Vergnaud's (1985: 14) statement of the 'Alternator Rule' for Spanish, as follows' (p. 353):[18]

(14)   a. Line 0 constituents are left–headed.
       b. On line 0 construct from right to left bounded constituents.

We note that (13) and (14) agree on right–to–left iteration. The reason is clear. Left–to–right assignment would give, for example, *(natù)(ralì)zár with right–headed feet and *(nàtu)(ràli)(zà)ción with left–headed feet. The results are still bad if the 'clashing' pretonic secondaries are removed-- *(natù)ralizár, *(nàtu)(ràli)zación--because the 'internal dactyls' –tùrali– and –ràliza– are 'illegitimate' (R86, p. 359).

The argument R86 offers in favor of (13) over (14) rests on the well–known fact (Trager 1939, Stockwell, Bowen, and Silva–Fuenzalida 1956, Navarro Tomás 1917: 385) that in some dialects, words like *cántaro* 'pitcher' and *cántalo* 'sing it', whose normal primary stress is antepenultimate as shown, may be pronounced with some degree of stress on the final vowel. In the case of *cántalo*, R86 interprets this final stress as primary and attributes it to an unformulated process of 'enhancement' due to 'primary stress shift' (p. 354).[19] R86 asserts that the fact that stress can be 'shifted' onto the final syllable 'can be taken as evidence that the formulation in (30) [=(13) above] (in particular, the direction of headedness) is indeed correct' (p. 354). The intermediate representations, consistent with (13), to which 'primary stress

---

[17] Rule (13) is identical to (30) in R86, p. 353.

[18] Rule (14) is identical to (31) in R86, p. 353; it is also equivalent to parameter (8d) above.

[19] R86 hedges this point a bit, having noted that the facts are 'somewhat uncertain' (p. 353). The conclusions that matter both to R86 and to the present study are unaffected by whether the stresses in question are primary or secondary in surface representations.

shift' applies are shown in (15):[20]

```
(15)  a.  can ta ro   'pitcher'              b.  can ta lo   'sing it'
          (*) (*  *)          line 0            (*) (*  *)
           *   ·  *           line 1             *   ·  *
           *   ·  ·           line 2             *   ·  ·
```

Since R86 does not provide an algorithm for assigning primary stress, we do not know exactly how these representations are generated, but let us assume, as R86 obviously intends, that only the constituent (*cán.*) in each word is assigned lexically, so that the unmetrified strings accessible to postlexical rules are *ta.ro* and *ta.lo*. We now ask how the derivation continues. In particular, what properties of the 'enhancement' process (p. 354) can be empirically motivated?

At least two properties of this process in the dialect described in R86 are clear and crucial to an understanding of the assignment of secondary stress. First, it is clear that the 'enhancement' of stress on clitics occurs only phrasefinally. For example, *cántalo hóy* 'sing it today' cannot be uttered with primary (or any other) stress on the clitic *-lo* (i.e. as *càntaló hóy*) if the two words *cántalo* and *hóy* constitute a single intonational phrase, that is, if *hóy* follows the cliticized verb in the intonational phrase. One might speculate that the illformedness of *càntaló hóy* is due to the 'stress clash' (discussed below) created by the adjacent primaries in the string *-ló hóy*. Comparison with well-formed cases like *càntará hóy* '(s)he will sing today', however, demonstrates that clash is not the problem. The fact is that 'stress-enhanced' clitics as in *càntaló* are normal in the dialect of R86 only in absolute final position in the intonational phrase.

The second property of 'enhancement' in the dialect of R86 is illustrated in (16), where rightmost position in the intonational phrase is assumed. For maximum clarity, the clitic string is separated from the verb host by a hyphen.

(16) a. cànta–ló   'sing it'
      b. cànta–meló   'sing it for me'
      c. cantàndo–semeló   'it being sung for me'

These examples demonstrate that the phrase-final target of the 'enhancement' process can be separated from primary word stress by an arbitrary number of syllables: one in (16a), two in (16b), and three in (16c).[21]

---

[20] Item (15) is identical to (32) in R86, p. 354.

[21] Examples with four or more intervening syllables cannot be constructed: the three-clitic cluster *se-me-lo* in (17c) is already marginal, and the verb forms to which clitics may be attached cannot have primary stress farther to the left than the penult.

In other words, the formulation of any rule responsible for the final stresses in (16) as a BOUNDED process cannot be empirically motivated. So far as I can see, there is no evidence in R86 against the assignment of phrase-final stress by rule (17), which gathers posttonic syllables into an UNBOUNDED right-headed constituent:

(17)   Line 0 (feet): unbounded, right-headed

Rule (17) applies to cases like those in (16) as illustrated in (18), where phrase-final position is again assumed:

```
(18)  a.  cantalo      →   cantalo         b.  cantamelo    →   cantamelo
          (*) * *          (*)(* *)            (*) * * *        (*)(* * *)
           *                *   *               *                *     *

      c.  cantandosemelo   →   cantandosemelo
          * (*) * * * *        * (*)(* * * *)
             *                    *   *
```

Obviously, it is necessary to reconsider R86's claim that 'stress shift' onto the final syllable 'can be taken as evidence that the formulation in [(13)] . . . is indeed correct' (p. 354). More specifically, examples like (15) and (16) do not support (13c), which asserts that stress feet are bounded (binary).

This conclusion is reinforced by additional data. Those familiar with a variety of Spanish dialects recognize that many speakers allow no stress on the last syllable of proparoxytones in phrase-final position. Rather, words like *cántaro* and *cántalo* are pronounced with a sharp posttonic decrescendo in this context. In these dialects, even maximally long strings of posttonic syllables, e.g. *cantándosemelo*, can bear no stress at all.[22]

These dialects, in addition to lending no support to (13), raise the question of WHY no stress can appear between primary word stress and the right edge of an intonational phrase. Speakers of such dialects must internalize some mechanism M for distributing secondary stress over pretonic syllables (as described in section 3.2) and they must learn that the effects of this mechanism are never manifested between primary word stress and phrase end. The logically simplest analysis of these dialects, then, allows M to apply freely (subject, of course, to relevant universal constraints) and then eliminates any overapplication with the straightforwardly formalizable rule 'Erase all subsidiary stresses to the right of the rightmost primary stress in the intonational phrase.' Alternative (and in fact, more interesting) descriptions are available, but I do not discuss them since the real usefulness of 'nonenhancing' dialects for our study is exhausted at this point: they cannot

---

[22] Cf. Stockwell, Bowen, and Silva-Fuenzalida (1956: 657).

provide further direct evidence distinct from that provided by the dialect type on which R86 is based.

To clarify my proposals regarding R86–type dialects, I give an illustrative derivation in (19):[23]

```
(19)     { {cantando } se me lo }
         { * (*)<*>}
           (*)
            *                          output of W1 and W2
         ————————————————————————————————————————————————————
         {  * (*) *   * * * }          input to postlexical strata
            (*)
             *
         ————————————————————————————————————————————————————
         {  * (*)[*   * * *]}          rule (17)
            (*)          *
             *
         ————————————————————————————————————————————————————
         {  * (*)[*   * * *]}          'enhancement'
            (*)          *
             *           *
```

Only the verb *cantándo* is stressed in the word–internal (lexical) strata W1 and W2; the clitics *se, me, lo* are first attached in the syntax, i.e. post-lexically, yielding the input representation *can (tán) dosemelo*, in which *do* loses its extrametricality because it is no longer peripheral. Rule (17) forms a single constituent that contains all the syllables to the right of *(tán)*. To complete (19), I tentatively propose, pending further study, that what we have referred to atheoretically as 'stress shift' and/or 'enhancement' is nothing other than the effect of the independently required rule of 'main' phrasal stress, which 'builds a further layer of prominence' on the rightmost accented syllable in the 'focus phrase' (R86, p. 342-ff.).[24] The focus phrase is typically rightmost in the sentence but it may be elsewhere; this could well be the factor that underlies the apparent optionality of 'enhancement'.[25]

In any event, the contrast in enhanceability manifested by examples like those in (15)--*càntaló* but **càntaró*--has a straightforward explanation under the proposals illustrated in (19). The rules in (8) produce the lexical output *(cánta) <ro>*; extrametricality of *<ro>* is carried over to the postlexical strata

---

[23] For maximum clarity--but with no theoretical import--morphological/ syntactic constituent boundaries are written as { }, lexically generated foot boundaries as ( ), and postlexically assigned accentual boundaries as [ ].

[24] Perhaps main phrasal stress should expand the grid by creating an additional line 3 on which to place its asterisk. In this case a line–2 asterisk in the same column would be supplied by convention where appropriate. The issue is immaterial to present concerns.

[25] Contreras (1976) contains extended discussion of the syntax and semantics of focus in Spanish. Meredith (1990) contains recent discussion of the general theory of the phonology of focus.

in phrase–final position, with the result that this syllable remains immune to (17) and main phrasal stress. In phrase–internal position, <*ro*> loses its extrametricality and is thus available for footing, e.g. (*cánta*) [*rò de*] (*bá*)<*rro*> 'clay pitcher.' On the other hand, the clitic –*lo* 'it' in *cántalo* 'sing it', like the clitics in (19), is targeted for footing only postlexically where it is not extrametrical and thus may undergo (17) and 'enhancement'.

3.2 Pretonic syllables. The distribution of pretonic subsidiary stresses, unlike that of posttonic syllables, leads directly to the conclusion that the associated feet are binary—but not that they are right–headed. The first point is illustrated clearly enough in (12) above: such alternating stresses are precisely the signature of binary feet. And, to be sure, some examples are consistent with right-headed binary feet assigned from right to left, as illustrated in (20):

(20)   [na.tù.][ra.lì.](za.ción)   [nà.][tu.rà.](li.zár)

A problem arises, however, in cases of the very simple type shown in (21):[26]

(21)   [para [ti]]   'for you'
        line 0   (*)
        line 1   (*)
        line 2   *   output of lexical strata

        line 0   * * (*)   input to postlexical strata
        line 1   (*)
        line 2   *

        line 0   [* *] (*)   final output
        line 1   *   (*)
        line 2   *

Since the pronoun *ti* is monosyllabic, there is no alternative to the lexical output shown. There are exactly two syllables available for postlexical metrification, those of the preposition *para*. Algorithm (13) inexorably yields the incorrect representation *[pa.rà] (tí)* instead of correct [pà.ra] (tí). Two otherwise unmotivated mechanisms are then required: one, a new process of clash deletion (distinct from the rule I will propose in (23)) to remove the offending secondary on –*rà*; two, some additional device to place the correct secondary on *pà–*.

It is important to note that (21) illustrates not simply an isolated case but rather a problem for (13) in principle, which arises with any word with initial

---

[26] I am unable to find an example of this kind in R86.

primary stress preceded postlexically by unstressed syllables, e.g. *pàra còn el níño* 'in relation to the child', to which (13) assigns the contour **[parà][con èl] níño*. As in (21), otherwise unmotivated mechanisms must be invoked in order to yield the correct output.

It is also important to note the relevance to (21) of the universal principles illustrated in (11) that demand 'respect' for existing metrical structure. These close off two logically conceivable escape routes for (13). First, postlexical feet cannot be assigned that overlap with and/or include the lexically assigned constituent, as in **[pà] [ra (tí)]*--cf. (10). Second, the lexically assigned foot cannot expand postlexically to take in the rightmost unmetrified syllable as a nonhead element, as in **[pà] (ra tí)*--cf. (11b), the 'closure' effect. Since the 'respect' principles significantly restrict the set of possible grammars, analyses consistent with them are *a priori* more highly valued than those that are not. The fact that (13) is inconsistent with these principles, then, counts as a serious liability. Indeed, we must consider (13) to be ruled out by universal grammar until compelling evidence is offered that it is necessary to abandon the restrictive notion of 'respect' for metrical constituency.

It will be obvious that the examples under discussion are not problematic for (14): left-headed feet are assigned to the pretonic syllables (*[pàra], [pàra] [còn el]*) when they become available postlexically. Nothing else is required. Furthermore, (14) covers all of the cases of pretonic subsidiary stresses given in R86. A few transparent examples are shown in (22):

(22)
[còn.los.][còns.tan.][tì.no.][pò.li.]tá.nos   'with Constantinopolitans'
[còns.tan.][tì.no.][pò.li.][zà.cio.]nís.mo   'constantinopolizationism'
[là.cons.][tàn.ti.][nò.po.][lì.za.]ción   'constantinopolization'

Incorrect results appear in one class of cases, namely, those with an odd number of syllables to the left of primary stress, e.g. **[lòs.][còn.stan.][tì.no.]-[pò.li.]tá.nos* 'the Constantinopolitans', **[còns.][tàn.ti.][nò.po.][lì.za.]ción* 'constantinopolization.' These cases are straightforwardly rectified by a clash-removal rule with the effect shown in (23):[27]

(23)   Clash Removal:

        line 0   (*)   →   *
        line 1   *   .
        line 2   .   .

---

[27] Clash removal does not affect main stresses: *yó sé* 'I know', *Fidél Cástro*, etc. This is reflected in (23) by the requirement that the affected element have no * in line 2.

As formulated, (23) beheads degenerate feet with no primary stress, thus correcting *[còns.][tàn.ti.][nò.po.][lì.za.](ción) to cons.[tàn.ti.][nò.po.][lì.za.]- ción), and so on. Appeal to clash removal is independently motivated and not a liability for (14) vis-à-vis (13), since the analysis espoused in R86 requires an analogous rule (p. 354-ff.).[28]

For the sake of completeness, I will demonstrate that (14) also covers some data that I have not yet introduced. As is well known,[29] in a somewhat less deliberate and/or artificial stylistic register than that illustrated in (12), phrase-initial syllables can be assigned secondary stress. Of the examples in (12), cònstantìnopòlitáno and nàturàlizár come out the same in the colloquial style, but secondary stresses in the other words are distributed as shown in (24):[30]

(24)   nà.tu.ra.lì.za.ción   còns.tan.ti.nò.po.lì.ta.nís.mo

R86 (p. 358) postulates the optional postlexical rule of Initial Shift to account for this pattern:[31]

(25)   Initial Shift (IP = Intonational Phrase):

```
        ┌ *    *  line 0
        │ '  ← *  line 1
     IP └
```

Initial Shift is a grid operation that ignores constituency and changes representations like (26a) to the form (26b) after all secondary stresses are assigned and Clash Removal (23) has applied:

```
(26)  a.  natura lizacion      →    b.  naturalizacion
          *[* *][* *](*)                * * *[* *](*)
          *    *    *                   *    *    *
               *                             *
```

In short, Initial Shift (25) plays the same supplementary role in both (13) and (14) in the derivation of contours like those in (24), and both algorithms appeal to a process of clash removal. Consequently, the colloquial register data do not alter our current assessment of the relative merits of the two: the

---

[28] The maximally simple formulation of (23) cannot handle the cases like *[parà] tí and *[parà][con èl] níño discussed just above, whose offending secondaries are in nondegenerate feet.

[29] Cf. Stockwell, Bowen, and Silva-Fuenzalida (1956), Harris (1983: 85-86), R86, p. 356-ff.

[30] The admissible dactyls nàtura- and cònstanti- in (24) differ from the 'illegitimate' ones mentioned just below (14) in being initial rather than internal.

[31] Rafael Núñez-Cedeño informs me (personal communication) that Initial Shift is apparently obligatory in several dialects he has observed.

distribution of posttonic subsidiary stresses is neutral with respect to (13) and (14), while the distribution of pretonic subsidiary stresses favors (14) over (13), which is outside the bounds of universal grammar. I proceed under the assumption that this assessment is correct.[32]

3.3 Pre- and posttonic syllables together. Up to now we have investigated only cases in which all syllables without primary stress are grouped together in a single string at one or the other edge of an intonational phrase. We will now examine metrical 'sandwiches', in which unstressed syllables appear on both sides of primary stress and/or primary stresses appear on both sides of unstressed syllables.

First consider simple one-word phrases in which a primary stress is internal, e.g. *preparándomelas* 'preparing them for me', *resilabifícalo* 'resyllabify it.' The inputs to the word-sequence strata are *prepa(rán)domelas* and *resilabi(fí)calo*, whose unstressed syllables are broken into discontinuous strings by the lexically assigned feet (*rán*) and (*fí*). These strings can be stressed and 'enhanced' to produce the familiar contours *prèpa(ràn)domelás* and *rèsilàbi(fí)caló*. Recall now the discussion of (11c) in section 1, the 'crossover' effect, whereby metrical structure-building rules cannot cross existing constituents. In view of this constraint, we must ask how interrupted strings like *prepa...domelas* and *resilabi...calo* can be incorporated into metrical structure.

An easy answer is available in the case of dialects of the type illustrated in (19): two separate footing rules apply, (17) to posttonic strings (giving ...[*domelàs*], ...[*caló*], etc.) and (14) = (8d) to pretonic strings (giving [*prèpa*]..., [*rèsi*] [*làbi*]..., etc.). Neither rule crosses an existing constituent.

The answer is less obvious in the case of more complex examples, however. Valuable information in R86 allows us to construct a contrast that guides us directly to the heart of the matter:

(27)
a. quejàndoseme   'complaining to me'
b. quejándosème pòr Constáncia   'complaining to me for Constance'

Example (27a) adheres to the generalization governing 'clitic phrases said in isolation' (i.e. that constitute a single intonational phrase), namely, that enhancement is undergone by the last in a sequence of clitics' (p. 354), while

---

[32] Diligent readers are encouraged to work through all of the data in the remainder of this study and in R86—or any other source—to verify that none of it tips the descriptive balance in favor of (13).

(27b) shows that in 'the appropriate syntactic collocation ... penultimate stress is indeed possible in clitic constructions' (p. 367, note 17).

It is easy to see that (27b) does not reflect the accentual constituency of the two separate intonational phrases *que (jàn) [dosemé]* and *[pòr Cons] (tán)* *<cia>*. Rather, stress on the clitic *–se–* in (27b) is possible only if it is an element in the string *–[sè.me.] [pòr.Cons.] (tán.)–*. This must be the case since (a) *–se–* is not 'the last in a sequence of clitics' and (b) it is only in the string *–[sè.me.] [pòr.Cons.] (tán.)–* that *–se–* is an even number of syllables to the left of a primary stressed syllable. Consequently, this string must be metrified by successive iterations of (14) = (8d) in a single pass, whether or not the component phrases are covered separately at an earlier stage of derivation. In sum, the import of (27) is that it securely establishes the conclusion in (28):

(28) Intertonic strings are metrified in a single pass.

Now let us give Constancia an ordinary last name, Valenzuela. Conclusion (28) insures that in the phrase *pòr Constáncia Vàlenzuéla* the entire intertonic string *–cia [Vàlen]–* is scanned in a single pass. Now, if each of the intertonic strings *–do [sème][pòr Cons]–* and *–cia [Vàlen]–* is metrified as required by (28), then it follows as a matter of simple logic that these two strings must be scanned together in a single pass in *que (ján) do [sème] pòr Cons] (tán) cia [Vàlen] (zué) <la>* since it is only in this superstring that either intertonic string occurs intact. It follows as a further deduction that the foot–building rule that metrifies the intertonic strings--presumably (14) = (8d)-- must cross the existing constituent *(tán)* in its right–to–left sweep over these strings.

Summarizing, our investigation of Spanish has verified all of the cases discussed in section 1 in which 'respect' for existing metrical constituents is required--except for the 'crossover' effect (11c). It should be noted that the other 'respect' effects are well documented in a variety of languages. The 'no crossing' constraint, on the other hand, is supported only by one of two descriptive options considered in a tentative analysis of certain data from the Austronesian language Manam (HK91, section 3.3) and by a more secure analysis of data from Lebanese Arabic (HK91, section 6). The case from Spanish, which rests on the extensive and meticulous data of R86, is hardly less secure, however. A possible resolution, noted by HK91, is that the 'crossover' constraint holds in word–level phonology but not at the phrase level. This distinguishes correctly between the Arabic case, where the 'crossover' effect is observed within the word, and the Spanish case, where the effect does not constrain the construction of accentual constituents at the phrase level. Clearly, more research is needed to confirm the correctness of this suggestion.

4 Implications for primary word stress. As noted in section 1, the recent published and unpublished literature contains a fair number of studies of Spanish stress formulated in the EOS framework or some close relative. These studies contain lengthy and sometimes discordant discussion of numerous complex issues. With no thought whatsoever of a comprehensive review, I will now examine a subset of these works that involve a clear violation of what I take to be the most firmly founded and widely accepted of the 'respect' principles illustrated schematically in (10) and (11), namely, the impossibility of invading an existing constituent to kidnap one of its elements for incorporation into a new constituent (cf. (10b) and (11a)). The analyses in question are Harris (1989b) (henceforth 'H89') and Roca (1990) (henceforth 'R90'). I will discuss the former in just enough detail to show that an alternative is available which (a) does not undermine the central contribution of the study and (b) involves no violation of the metrical 'respect' principles. Crucially, both (a) and (b) are accomplished with a gain rather than a loss in descriptive generality. This result invites reconsideration of the basic premises of R90, which I do not undertake here.

The stress rules of H89 (pp. 250-251) are given in (29), unaltered in content but renumbered and reworded for expository convenience:

(29) a. Stressable elements: syllable nuclei (rhyme heads)
      b. Extrametricality: right
      c. Line 0 (special case): binary, left–headed, right to left
      d. Line 0 (general case): unbounded, right–headed
      e. Line 1 (main stress): unbounded, right–headed
      f. Conflation: 1/2

These rules apply in both the cyclic and noncyclic word–internal strata W1 and W2. The analogous rules of R90 (pp. 146-ff.) are given in (30), with innocuous editing as in (29):

(30) a. Stressable elements: syllable nuclei (rhyme heads)
      b. Extrametricality: right
      c. Line 0: unbounded, right–headed

Excluding all extraneous considerations, we focus on the fact that (29) and (30) agree in assigning right–headed unbounded feet in the normal case in the lexical strata, with the result that both analyses generate representations essentially like (31):[33]

(31) constantinopolita no   naturalizacion
      (* * * * * * *)<*>   (* * * * * *)
                        *   *

The problem with such representations is that the binary feet needed in order to account for the alternating secondary stresses in *cònstantìnopòlitáno* and *natùralìzación* cannot be built without invading the unbounded foot constructed lexically for the primary word stress, in the absence of additional mechanisms.[34]

I will now show that H89 can straightforwardly dispense with (29d).

For the most part, the location of primary stress in verb forms does not differ from that of segmentally identical nouns and adjectives with the same stem. This is illustrated in (32):

(32) *Noun/Adjective*   *Verb*
      arrúga   'wrinkle'   arrúga   'he wrinkles'
      precísa   'precise'   precísa   'he makes precise'

In cases like those illustrated in (33), on the other hand, the nouns and adjectives in such cognate sets have antepenultimate stress while the verbs are stressed on the penult:

(33) *Noun/Adjective*   *Verb*
      práctica 'practice, practical'   practíca 'he practices'
      contínua 'continuous'   continúa 'he continues'

Ever since cases like (33) were brought to the attention of investigators over two decades ago (Harris 1969: 120-ff.), they have generally been taken as solid evidence that verb forms cannot be assigned stress by the same rules that apply to other categories. The contribution of H89 is to show that this

---

[33] I am not sure whether or not Roca (1988) follows suit. This study proposes to "build right-headed (possibly unbounded, but see below) constituents at the foot level" (p. 414). It is not clear, however, where the resolution lies 'below'. In any event, the issue is academic since the distinctive proposals of Roca (1988) are evidently superseded by those of R90.

[34] R90 suggests such a mechanism (though not in anticipation of the problem pointed out here), namely, that "secondary stress will be assigned in a separate, rhythm plane" distinct from the plane on which primary stress is registered (p. 146, note 13). The postulation of multiple accentual planes, however, vastly expands the expressive potential of the grammar, with corresponding loss of explanatory power. Such an *a priori* undesirable move would therefore be made only as an act of desperation, whose necessity has not been demonstrated.

evidence has been misunderstood: the stress rules in (29) in fact handle all cases at issue, including those in (33).

This contribution relies on two basic elements that modulate the effect of stress assignment rules: an understanding of the morphological structure of the forms in question and the Stress Erasure Convention of Universal Grammar.[35]

Though the members of each verb–nonverb pair in (32) and (33) are segmentally identical, they do not have the same morphological structure. In the nouns and adjectives, the final vowel is a so-called 'word marker', which signals declensional class. In the verbs, on the other hand, the final vowel is the 'theme vowel', which forms the base to which inflectional and derivational suffixes are attached. The word marker is a noncyclic affix but the theme vowel is a cyclic affix.

The rules in (29) apply in both the cyclic and noncyclic word–internal strata W1 and W2. Given (29) and the cyclic/noncyclic status of 'theme vowels' and 'word markers', the correct stress patterns are derived as illustrated in (34) with the stem *practic-*. For maximum clarity I use [ ] to enclose cyclic constituents and normal square brackets ⌈ ⌉ to enclose noncyclic constituents.

(34)	Noun/Adjective	Verb	
	⌈[PRACTIC] a⌉	[[PRACTIC] a]	
line 0	(*　*)	(*　*)	W1, first pass
line 1	*	*	(29a, c, e–f)
		practic　　a	W1, second pass
line 0		*　*　　*	input
line 0		(*　*) <*>	(29a–b, d–f)
line 1		*	
	PRACTIC　a	practic　　a	input to W2
line 0	(*　*)　*	(*　*) <*>	
line 1	*	*	

The stem *practic-* is lexically marked--flagged typographically with upper case in (34)--to undergo the special rule (29c), whose application automatically preempts (29d). Thus the output of the first pass through the cyclic rules of stratum W1--that is, the stem cycle--is *(práctic)-* for the verb as well as for the noun and the adjective. Now, since only the verb has a cyclic affix, only the verb is subject to a second pass through the cyclic stratum W1. At the beginning of this pass, the Stress Erasure Convention erases constituent

---

[35] Cf. EOS; Halle (1990); HK91; Halle, Harris, and Vergnaud (1991). The last study contains extensive discussion of the role of the Stress Erasure Convention in Spanish.

structure and stress assigned in the previous cycle. Thus the verb enters the second cycle as a metrical *tabula rasa*, in particular, without the information that a left-headed metrical constituent was associated with the stem in the first cycle. The head of the current cycle, namely, theme vowel -*a*, is not exceptional in any way; thus all the rules in (29) except (29c) apply as expected, producing the output (*practí*) < *ca* >. The Stress Erasure Convention does not operate at the beginning of the noncyclic stratum W2, whose inputs are thus (*práci*)*ca* for the noun and adjective and (*practí*) < *ca* > for the verb. Reapplication of (29) in W2 is effectively vacuous: in the Noun/Adjective *práctica* the word-final vowel is marked extrametrical and no further change is possible since all remaining syllables are already incorporated into metrical structure, as they are also in Verb *practíca*.

In sum, (34) summarizes an attractive solution to the heretofore unexplained and seemingly intractable contrast illustrated in (32-33). Rule (29c), however, is not crucial to this solution: exactly the same results are obtained with rule set (8). This is shown in (34'):

(34')	Noun/Adjective		Verb		
	[[PRACTIC] a]		[[PRACTIC] a]		
line 0	(* *)		(* *)		W1, first pass
line 1	*		*		(8a, d-f)
line 0			practic a		W1, second pass input
			* * *		
line 0			* (*) <*>		(8a-f)
line 1			*		
	PRACTIC a		practic a		input to W2
line 0	(* *) *		* (*) <*>		
line 1	*		*		

In (34') the stem *practic*- is lexically marked as an exception to the general rule (8c), and the derivation proceeds exactly as in (34), *mutatis mutandis*. The pair of rules (8c-d) is the precise functional equivalent of (29c-d); the forms lexically marked as idiosyncratically exempt from the general rule (8c) are exactly those lexically marked to idiosyncratically undergo the special rule (29c). Data of the sort illustrated in (32) and (33), then, are neutral with respect to supporting (29) of H89 versus (8) of the present study.[36] The considerations involved in (29)–(31), on the other hand, decisively favor (8), which generates lexical representations of the sort

---

[36] The same is true, so far as I can see, of the other, less problematic, apparent accentual discrepancies between verbs and other categories discussed in H89. Detailed demonstration would be tedious and unrewarding.

illustrated in (3), (4b), (9), and so on, where no constituent boundaries isolate the syllables that must be metrified postlexically for the proper assignment of subsidiary stresses.

5 Concluding remarks. Underlying the present study is a particular point of view regarding what is often referred to as 'linguisic theory', as supposedly distinct from 'linguistic description' or (more distantly?) 'linguistic data.' My view is that such distinctions are not very meaningful or useful. Physics provides an instructive analogy. Researchers who call themselves theoretical physicists do not conceive of their work as the study of data plus the added frill of theory construction: for physicists, 'physics' and 'theoretical physics' are synonymous. Linguistics, phonology in particular, should be no different. In the foregoing sections we have paid careful attention to certain data that are absolutely meaningless in and of themselves--like meter readings in the physics laboratory. There is no reason why anyone should give them a second thought, except insofar as they acquire significance in the enterprise that we call 'phonological theory.'

The presentation of the phonological subtheory of accentuation (stress) found in EOS, with further elaboration in HK91 and other work, is unrivaled at present in terms of factual coverage, explicitness of formulation of first principles, and restrictiveness of descriptive possibilities--hence explanatory value. While these characteristics by no means bestow on the EOS paradigm the status of immutable holy writ, they do make it 'the best show in town' in phonology, the one that sets the standards of descriptive discourse and defines the issues of current interest. We have taken up here the issue introduced in section 2.3, the limits on alterability of metrical structure in the course of a derivation. The theory of metrical 'respect' developed in HK91 imposes quite specific and strict constraints on metrical alterability, thus significantly narrowing the range of options available to the linguist and, more relevantly, to the language learner (see section 1).

The factual and descriptive foundation on which this study rests is R86. R86 makes a substantial contribution to Spanish accentology in its determination of the stratal allocation of the stress rules, but its proposals regarding the nature of the constituents formed by these rules do not withstand scrutiny. The postulation of binary right-headed feet (13) is not empirically supported: binarity (but not right-headedness) is falsified by the distribution of posttonic secondary stress, as is right-headedness (but not binarity) by the distribution of secondary stress in pretonic position.

Why should anyone care about the headedness and/or binarity of stress feet in Spanish? The result that emerges from our study is that the empirically supported set of stress rules for Spanish, which eschews right-headed binary feet, is also the set that is maximally consistent with the maximally restrictive theory of the construction of metrical constituents. In

this context, the investigation of such technical minutiae as we have engaged
in here may acquire some broader significance.

References

Chomsky, N. 1986. Knowledge of Language: Its Nature, Origin, and Use. New York: Praeger.
Clements, G. N. 1985. The Geometry of Phonological Features. Phonology Yearbook 2,
223-252.
Contreras, H. 1976. A Theory of Word Order with Special Reference to Spanish.
Amsterdam: North-Holland.
Den Os, E., and R. Kager. 1986. Extrametricality and Stress in Spanish and Italian. Lingua 69,
23-48.
Gorecka, A. 1989. Phonology of Articulation. Doctoral dissertation, MIT, Cambridge, Mass.
Halle, M. 1989. The Intrinsic Structure of Speech Sounds. Unpublished ms., MIT, Cambridge,
Mass. (Paper presented at the Conference on Feature and Underspecification Theories,
MIT, October, 1989).
Halle, M. 1990. Respecting Metrical Structure. Natural Language and Linguistic Theory 8,
149-176.
Halle, M., J. W. Harris, and J.-R. Vergnaud. 1991. A Reexamination of the Stress Erasure
Convention and Spanish Stress. Linguistic Inquiry 22, 141-159.
Halle, M., and M. Kenstowicz. 1991. The Free Element Condition and Cyclic vs. Non-Cyclic
Stress. (To appear in Linguistic Inquiry 22).
Halle, M., and J.-R. Vergnaud. 1985. Stress and the Cycle. Unpublished ms., MIT, Cambridge,
Mass. (Paper presented at the colloquium Phonologie Pluri-linéaire, Lyon).
Halle, M., and J.-R. Vergnaud. 1987. An Essay on Stress. Cambridge, Mass.: MIT Press.
Harris, J. W. 1969. Spanish Phonology. Cambridge, Mass.: MIT Press.
Harris, J. W. 1983. Syllable Structure and Stress in Spanish. Cambridge, Mass.: MIT Press.
Harris, J. W. 1987. The Accentual Patterns of Verb Paradigms in Spanish. Natural
Language and Linguistic Theory 5, 61-90.
Harris, J. W. 1988. Spanish Stress: The Extrametricality Issue. Unpublished ms., MIT,
Cambridge, Mass.
Harris, J. W. 1989a. The Stress Erasure Convention and Cliticization in Spanish. Linguistic
Inquiry 20, 339-363.
Harris, J. W. 1989b. How Different is Verb Stress in Spanish? Probus 1, 241-258.
Harris, J. W. 1989c. Narrowing the Stress Window in Spanish. Unpublished ms., MIT,
Cambridge, Mass. (Paper given at University of Massachusetts, Amherst, May, 1989).
Hochberg, J. G. 1988. Learning Spanish Stress. Language 64, 683-706.
Kiparsky, P. 1982. Lexical Phonology and Morphology. In Y.-S. Yang, ed., Linguistics in the
Morning Calm. Seoul: Hanshin, 3-91.
Kiparsky, P. 1985. Some Consequences of Lexical Phonology. Phonology Yearbook 2, 85-138.
Marantz, A. 1988. Clitics, Morphological Merger, and the Mapping to Phonological Form. In
M. Hammond and M. Noonan, eds., Theoretical Morphology. Berkeley: Academic Press.
Meredith, S. E. 1990. Issues in the Phonology of Prominence. Doctoral dissertation, MIT,
Cambridge, Mass.
Navarro Tomás, T. 1917. Cantidad de las vocales inacentuadas. Revista de Fonología
Española 4, 371-388.
Núñez Cedeño, R. A. 1985. Análisis métrico de la acentuación verbal en español. Revista
Argentina de Lingüística 1, 107-132.
Otero, C. P. 1986. A Unified Metrical Account of Spanish Stress. In M. Brame, H. Contreras,
and F. J. Newmeyer, eds., A Festschrift for Sol Saporta. Seattle: Noit Amrofer, 299-332.

Pesetsky, D. 1979. Russian Morphology and Lexical Theory. Unpublished ms., MIT, Cambridge, Mass.

Poser, W. J. 1989. The Metrical Foot in Diyari. Phonology 6, 117-146.

Prince, A. 1985. Improving Tree Theory. In M. Niepokuj, M. van Clay, V. Nikiforidou, and D. Feder, eds., Proceedings of the 11th Annual Meeting of the Berkeley Linguistics Society, University of California, Berkeley, 471-490.

Roca, I. 1986. Secondary Stress and Metrical Rhythm. Phonology Yearbook 3, 341-370.

Roca, I. 1988. Theoretical Implications of Spanish Word Stress. Linguistic Inquiry 19, 393-423.

Roca, I. 1990. Diachrony and Synchrony in Word Stress. Journal of Linguistics 26, 133-164.

Sagey, E. C. 1986. The Representation of Features and Relations in Nonlinear Phonology. Doctoral dissertation, MIT, Cambridge, Mass.

Steriade, D. 1988. Greek Accent: A Case for Preserving Structure. Linguistic Inquiry 19, 271-314.

Stockwell, R. P., J. D. Bowen, and I. Silva-Fuenzalida. 1956. Spanish Juncture and Intonation. Language 32, 641-665.

Trager, G. L. 1939. The Phonemes of Castilian Spanish. Travaux du Cercle Linguistique de Prague 8, 217-222.

On Spanish syllabification·

José Ignacio Hualde *
University of Illinois at Urbana-Champaign

0 Introduction. This paper deals with syllabification in Spanish. Both the nature of the syllable–building mechanisms and the morphological and syntactic domains in which these mechanisms apply are examined. Syllabification, Spanish syllabification in particular, is a topic that has received a certain amount of attention in the last decade. There is no radical break between the ideas presented here and previous work on the syllable structure of Spanish. The purpose of this paper is, rather, to propose certain refinements in the analysis. Harris (1983, 1989a) and Hualde (1989b) are taken as point of departure. The reader will notice a number of discrepancies at the purely descriptive level between Harris (1983, 1989a) and the present paper. Some of these disagreements are due to factual differences between the dialects that are considered in each case. Others arise from differences of opinion about the importance and relevance of certain data.

1 Syllabification rules. I will adopt here a rule-based approach to syllabification (Steriade 1982), employing the formalism of Levin (1985), in which the syllable is conceived as a maximal projection (N") of the nucleus (N node), with coda segments attached under an intermediate N' node and onset segments attached directly under the N" or syllable node.

1.1 Nuclei. The first step in syllable–building is the identification of those segments that are syllable heads. These are the vowels in Spanish, as in (1):

(1)   N   N   N   N
         | | | |
      m e   d i   θ i   n a   'medicine'

From each N node N' and N" nodes are projected, as shown in (2):

---

*For comments on an earlier version of this paper I want to thank Jennifer Cole, Iggy Roca, and, especially, James Harris, who convinced me to change its focus substantially.

(2)
```
      N"    N"    N"    N"
      |     |     |     |
      N'    N'    N'    N'
      |     |     |     |
      N     N     N     N
      |     |     |     |
   m  e  d  i  θ  i  n  a
```

The initial syllable-building operation can thus be stated as in (3):

(3) Node projection: Mark vowels as syllable–heads, i.e., create N nodes, and project N' and N" nodes.

A complicating factor in the identification of syllable nuclei is given by the existence of glides [w, j], which contrast with high vowels only in syllabicity. High vowels are syllable nuclei and glides are not. The status of glides in Spanish has long been controversial (cf. Harris 1969: 20–37, 122–123, Cressey 1978: 75–82). I will assume that there is an underlying difference between glides and vowels. Glides and high vowels contrast in the same environment in many Spanish dialects. Whether a sequence of two vocoids, one of which is high, can be pronounced in hiatus (in two separate syllables) or must be pronounced as a diphthong is a lexical property of individual items (cf. Real Academia Española 1973: 47–58, Cressey 1978: 79–80, Harris 1969: 27, fn. 15, 122–127, Harris 1989a: 161). As pointed out by these authors, there is considerable variation among speakers on individual items. Nevertheless, speakers' intuitions about which words allow a hiatus are generally very strong and clear. The examples in (4) reflect the shared intuitions of five speakers from Spain, including this author:[1]

(4)

V . V		G V	
mi.ásma[2]	'miasma'	Ma.riá.no	(name)
ti.ára	'tiara'	me.ri.diá.no	'meridian'
pi.áno	'piano'	li.viá.no	'light'
esti.á.je	'draught'	San.tiá.go	(name)
am.pli.ár	'to broaden'	cam.biár	'to change'
di.á.blo	'devil'	a.ciá.go	'fateful'
di.á.rio	'daily'	me.dián.te	'by means of'

---

[1] We could not agree on *viaje* 'trip', *viajante* 'traveling salesman', *vianda* 'food', *viola* 'viola', *piara* 'herd', and *Luarca* (toponym). I expect other speakers to differ in some other items. The point is that many, if not all, speakers have a lexical distinction between words that allow a hiatus and words that do not.

[2] Stress marks are added when not supplied in the standard orthography.

hi.á.to	'hiatus'	yá.te	'yacht'
li.á.na	'vine'	come.dián.te	'comedian'
zu.á.vo	'Zouave'	suá.ve	'soft'
		cuár.ta	'fourth'
cli.én.te	'client'	tié.rra	'land'
ri.én.te	'laughing'	dién.te	'tooth'
li.é.mos	'we tie, subj.'	piér.na	'leg'
bi.é.nio	'biennium'	vié.jo	'old'
		sié.rra	'saw'
		fié.ra	'wild beast'
du.é.to	'duet'	dué.lo	'mourning'
		bué.no	'good'
		mué.ca	'grimace'
		nué.ra	'daughter-in-law'
i.ón	'ion'	gra.ció.so	'funny'
bi.óm.bo	'screen'	pa.trió.ta	'patriot'
ma.ni.ó.bra	'manoeuvre'	pió.let	'ice-ax'
bi.ó.lo.go	'biologist'	ra.dió.lo.go	'radiologist'
li.ó.so	'confusing'	ra.bió.so	'rabid'
ri.ó	'he laughed'	diós	'god'
gui.ón	'script'	ac.ción	'action'
bri.ó.so	'vigorous'		
qui.ós.co	'kiosk'		
je.su.íta	'Jesuit'	cuí.da	'takes care'
hu.í.mos	'we fled'	fuí.mos	'we were'
flu.í.do	'fluid'	ruí.do	'noise'

The fact that speakers have very strong intuitions about syllabification in these cases is rather remarkable: first, because, as mentioned, there are idiosyncratic differences among speakers in the treatment of particular items; but especially, because all words that have a pronunciation with a sequence in hiatus can also be pronounced with a diphthong. The distinction is between words that allow a hiatus as a possibility and those that do not.

One may try to derive these contrasts in syllabification from stress facts. In a possible analysis, words of the mi.ás.ma type would have penultimate stress, whereas in the Ma.riá.no type stress would be assigned to the antepenultimate, in an initial representation where all vocoids are syllabic /ma.rí.a.no/. Then a rule of coalescence or syllable merger would merge the two vocoids in one syllable, with syllable-internal stress shifting to the most sonorant of the two vocoids and gliding of the high vocoid: Ma.rí.ano → Ma.riá.no (cf. Roca 1986 and this volume).

An advantage of such a proposal is that it would explain why in Spanish surface antepenultimate stress is impossible when the penultimate contains a glide. The impossibility of the stress pattern that *Máriano* illustrates would be reduced to the 'three-syllable window' for stress assignment in Spanish, i.e. the generalization that stress must fall on one of the three last syllables (cf. Roca, this volume).

This analysis would also explain the fact that the contrasts illustrated in (4) are not found with sequences of the type /ai/, i.e. in sequences of two vocoids where the second one is high. To be sure, we find contrasts such as *ca.í.da* 'fall' with two vowels in hiatus versus *vái.na* 'sheath' with a falling diphthong, *o.í.do* 'ear' versus *bói.na* 'beret', or *sa.ú.co* 'elder tree' versus *sáu.ce* 'willow tree'. But these pairs contrast on the element that receives stress. In *mi.ás.ma* and *Ma.riá.no*, on the other hand, stress falls on the same place.[3] What we do not find is hypothetical *vá.i.na* contrasting with *vái.na*. In the case of falling diphthongs, then, we can safely assume the application of a coalescence rule.

This explanation, however, is highly problematic in the case of /ia/ sequences, i.e. sequences of two vocoids, the first of which is high. For one thing, we have a three–way contrast here, as among *río* 'river/I laugh', *rió* 'he laughed' and *dió* 'he gave'. The two first words are bisyllabic and differ in the position of the stress. The third example, which presents the same configuration of vocoids, is monosyllabic. Contrasting with both *mi.ás.ma* and *Ma.riá.no*, we find *e.gip.cí.a.co* 'Egyptian'. And contrasting with both *li.ó.so* and *ra.bió.so*, we find *pe.rí.o.do* 'period'.[4] It should thus be clear that a difference in the position of the stressed element cannot produce these contrasts and that all glides are not derivable from underlying vowels.

A strong argument for the phonemicity of glides is found in the stress patterns of verb forms. In the present indicative (and most other forms), stress falls unexceptionally on the penultimate syllable. Spanish lacks irregularly stressed proparoxytonic verb forms like those found in Italian, e.g. It. *ábita*, Sp. *habíta* 'he dwells'. Given unexceptional penultimate accentuation, the contrast between *amplía* 'he enlarges' and *cámbia* 'he changes' can only be due to an underlying vowel/glide contrast (Harris 1969: 122-124, 1989a: 161). Moreover, as Harris remarks, this same argument leads us to conclude that glides in falling diphthongs are also underlying, in spite of the facts mentioned above. Only in this way can we explain the contrast between verb forms such as *a.ú.lla* 'he howls' and *cáu.sa* 'he causes'. Given the stress rules in verbs, we cannot possibly have *cá.u.sa* at some point in the derivation in a present tense form.

---

[3] Actually, in *Mar[já]no* both glide and vowel are stressed (cf. section 1.2).

[4] *E.gip.ciá.co* and *pe.rió.do* are also possible pronunciations for these two words.

Another argument for underlying glides is that in words like *sáu.rio* 'saurian' or *áu.re.o* 'golden' we would violate the three-syllable window if glides were underlyingly syllablic /sá.u.ri.o/ (Harris 1969: 31, but see Roca this volume).[5]

Finally, the contrast illustrated in (4) also extends to unstressed syllables for some speakers. For instance, I have *vi.a.duc.to* 'viaduct' versus *via.ján.te* 'traveling salesman'.

1.2 Prevocalic glides. After syllable nuclei have been identified, the next syllabification operation is to join a consonant in onset position. In Spanish, however, before the incorporation of onset consonants, we must deal with prevocalic glides. Prevocalic glides, if not syllable–initial, as in *pierde* 'he loses', *rabia* 'rage', are part of the nucleus in Spanish. A couple of arguments for considering that noninitial prevocalic glides are part of the nucleus, rather than being in the onset, are given in Harris (1983: 9-14). Interesting confirming evidence for this position is found in Montañés (Cantabrian) Spanish dialects which have stress–sensitive vowel harmony. In the Montañés dialects spoken in Tudanca and Montes de Pas, mid vowels are raised to high if the stressed syllable contains a high vowel or a (high) prevocalic glide (Penny 1969, 1978, McCarthy 1984, Hualde 1989a). Postvocalic glides, on the other hand, do not trigger harmony. The examples in (5) are from Penny (1969):

(5) [kuxiría]   cogería   'I would take' (136)
     [kuxjéra]   cogiera   'I took' (subjunctive) (136)
cf. [koxeré]   cogeré   'I will take' (136)
     [afloxájs]   aflojáis   'you-plural loosen' (122)

     [mi lu djó]   me lo dió   'he gave it to me' (58)
cf. [me lo kompró] me lo compró 'he bought it for me' (58)

Since this process singles out stressed elements as triggers of harmonization, it must be the case that prevocalic glides bear stress. Under the assumption that stress is assigned to syllable nuclei (Harris 1989b), prevocalic glides must be part of the nucleus. Postvocalic glides would be part of the rime, but not part of the nucleus, since they do not trigger rising when

---

[5] Roca (this volume) develops an analysis in which glides are underlyingly high vowels. I find this proposal difficult to evaluate since: (a) he describes a dialect that totally lacks the contrasts illustrated in (4), and (b) he does not examine verb forms.

they are found in the stressed syllable. Prevocalic glides are part of the unit that receives stress (the nucleus), postvocalic glides are not.

Thus, we need a rule (6), to incorporate prevocalic glides to the nucleus, before the syllabification of onset consonants:

(6) Complex Nucleus: Adjoin a prevocalic glide under the N node.

```
        N
       /|
  p  r  j  e  (t  o)
```

The rule in (6) will produce the correct results for an example like *prieto* 'compact, dark', where the glide is preceded by a consonant, but not for *mayo* 'May' or *yegua* 'mare'. If syllable-initial, glides are consonantized and become the onset of the syllable, as in *yegua* and *mayo*.[6] We could obtain these results by adding to (6) the stipulation that there must be a consonantal segment to the left of the glide for the rule of incorporation to the nucleus to apply (cf. Harris 1989a). In a word like /majo/ [ma.ŷo], the glide would not be adjoined to the nucleus of the second syllable, since it is preceded by a vowel, and would be incorporated as onset by a later rule of syllabification. However, there is independent evidence that suggests that all prevocalic glides are initially syllabified as part of the nucleus. If syllable-initial, they are moved from nucleus to onset by a subsequent process. The reason for maintaining this analysis is that many prevocalic glides arise from the diphthongization under stress of certain underlying mid vowels /E/, /O/ (cf. Harris 1969: 24, 1985b). For these segments, I will assume an underlying representation with two skeletal slots, following Harris (1985b). Consider now the syllabification of a word such as *hielo* /Elo/ [ŷelo] 'ice', with a syllable-initial diphthongizing vowel.[7] The underlying /E/ must be syllabified as nucleus of the syllable. But, then, after diphthongization, the resulting prevocalic glide must be consonantized and moved to onset position. Since this syllable-internal resyllabification process is required for words like *hielo*, we may extend it to words like *mayo*, where the glide is not the product of diphthongization. Then the rule in (6) can be left as it has been formulated.

I am thus proposing to understand the process of consonantization of syllable-initial glides as a rule whereby a glide is moved from a nucleus position to a position directly under the N" node, acquiring consonantal

---

[6] See section 1.2.

[7] The diphthong of this word is alternating, cf. *helar* 'to freeze', *helado* 'ice-cream'.

features as a result of this.[8] The syllabification of the prevocalic glide in *hielo* and *mayo* is illustrated in the representations in (7) and (8):

(7)

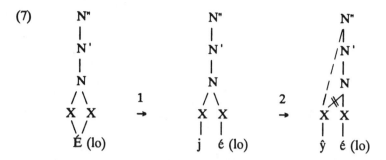

1. Diphthongization
2. Consonantization

(8)

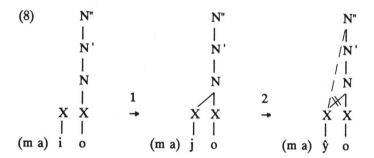

1. Complex Nucleus
2. Consonantization

Thus, all prevocalic glides will be initially syllabified in the nucleus. If not in syllable-initial position, as in *prieto* and *rabia*, they will remain in the nucleus. If syllable-initial, they will be consonantized and moved to the onset, as in *hielo* and *mayo*.

1.3 Onsets. Once we have taken care of prevocalic glides, the universal rule (9) applies to adjoin a consonant to the left of the nucleus as its onset (cf. Steriade 1982):

---

[8] Holly Nibert points out to me that the causality could be the opposite: Syllable-initial glides, which are first syllabified as part of the nucleus, receive consonantal features by rule. Being consonantal, they cannot remain in the nucleus of the syllable because of sonority requirements and are automatically moved to onset position.

(9)   CV rule: Adjoin a consonant to the left of the nucleus
       under the N" node.

This rule corresponds to Itô's (1986) Universal Core Syllable Condition.
In some languages, such as Arabic and Farsi, the CV rule is obligatory, so
that, if there is no consonant that could provide an onset to the syllable, a
glottal stop is inserted. In Spanish, a CV sequence is always tautosyllabic, but
there can be syllables without an onset, as in the first syllable of *apto* 'apt'.[9]

An onset in Spanish can have a maximum of two segments. There must
then be an operation allowing the adjunction of a second consonant under the
N" node. Permissible onset clusters are only those formed by a stop or /f/
plus a liquid, except that */dl/ and */tl/ are not possible. Some speakers
allow /tl/ in word-medial position. In Mexican Spanish, /tl/ is possible also
word-initially:[10]

(10)   Complex Onset: Adjoin a second consonant under the N"
       node if the result would be a permissible onset cluster
       (stop or /f/ + liquid, except: */dl/ and (*)/tl/).

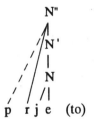

---

[9] An exceptional language for which it has been claimed that a consonant-vowel sequence is
heterosyllabic in most cases is Barra Gaelic (Kisseberth and Kenstowicz 1979: 262-264, Clements
1986).

[10] /θr/ is not found at all, but it sounds perfectly possible as an onset group. Speakers of
Castilian Spanish show agreement in this. All speakers consulted declared that they would not
be surprised to find out that hypothetical *Alazraque* [a.la.θrá.ke] was the name of a village in La
Mancha. Hypothetical /θl/, on the other hand, seems rather difficult.

In Spanish, when a segment could be syllabified either as onset or as coda, giving in both cases well-formed syllables, it is unexceptionally syllabified as onset. For instance, the word *copla* 'verse' is divided in syllables as *co.pla* 'verse' not as **cop.la* , even though *cop* is a well formed syllable, cf. *cop.to* 'Coptic'.[11] That is, onsets are maximized. In the approach adopted in this article, onset maximization follows from the relative order of the rules of syllabification. This means that rules (9) and (10) apply before any rule that incorporates segments into a coda.

1.4 Codas. Only once onsets have been maximized, are codas created. A first coda rule (11) adjoins an unsyllabified segment to the right of the nucleus:

(11) Coda Rule: Adjoin a segment to the right of the nucleus under N '.

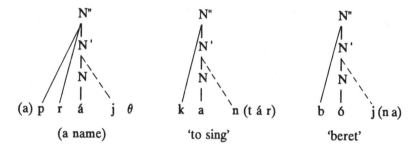

      (a) p ɾ á j θ   k a n (t á r)   b ó j (n a)

      (a name)   'to sing'   'beret'

The segment that is adjoined by this rule can be a glide or a consonant. All consonants are in principle syllabifiable immediately after the nuclear vowel, although a number of neutralization rules apply in different dialects. Harris (1989a) excludes [x] and [č] from this position. In the dialect under consideration, [x] appears both word-finally, as in *reloj* [r̄e.lóx] 'watch', *boj* [bóx] 'box (bush)' and in word-internal rimes, as in *dignidad* [dix.ni.dáθ] 'dignity'. The affricate [č], on the other hand, only appears in the pronunciation of Catalan names ending in 'ch', such as *Domenech*.[12]

Under some very limited circumstances a second nonsyllabic segment can be added to the coda. After a postvocalic glide, /s/, /θ/, or /n/ can appear as the second element in a coda cluster, as in *dais* [dájs] 'you-pl. give', *cambiéis* [kam.bjéjs] 'you-*pl.* change-*subj.*', *beísbol* [béjz.βol] 'baseball', *veinte* [béjn.te] 'twenty', *aunque* [áwŋ.ke] 'although', *aun* [áwn] 'even', *clown* [kláwn],

---

[11] But see below for violations of this principle in certain morphological contexts.

[12] Actually, the digraph 'ch' in Catalan names stands for [k]. *Domenech* is pronounced [dumə́nək] in Eastern (Barcelona) Catalan. But the pronunciation that follows the spelling rules of Spanish is general outside of Catalonia, even by people who bear such Catalan names.

Urtain [ur.tájn], *Beriain* [be.rjájn], *Apraiz* [a.prájθ]. In foreign names other consonants can appear in this position as well, as in *Puig* [pújx][13] *Cruyff* [krújf].[14] We may then postulate a rule of adjunction after a glide:

(12) Complex coda: Adjoin a consonant to the right of a glide under N'.

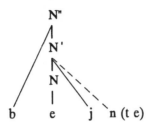

Only /s/ can appear in a rime after another consonant. In a word-final rime, /s/ may follow any consonant, as in *vals* [báls] 'waltz', *bíceps* [bí.θeps], *tórax* [tó.raks], *Ferradans* [fe.r̄a.ðáns], *yens* [ŷéns]. In word-internal syllables, on the other hand, /s/ can normally appear only after /r/ in the dialect under discussion, as in *perspectiva* [pers.pek.tí.βa] 'perspective'.[15] Coda clusters of nasal plus /s/ are possible only in the most careful styles, e.g. *transportar* [tras.por.tár]. Clusters of obstruent plus /s/ present in the spelling are consistently simplified, e.g. *abstracto* [as.trák.to], *excelente* [es.θe.lén.te], *exterior* [es.te.rjór] (cf. Navarro Tomás 1977: 140-141). It is possible to speak of an active rule of cluster simplification in these cases, since there are morphophonological alternations, e.g. *ex-alumno* [ek.sa.lúm.no] vs. *ex-presidente* [es.pre.si.ðén.te], *ex-portero* [es.por.té.ro] 'ex-goalie'. The question is why it is the first consonant in the sequence and not the second that is left unpronounced. Employing our syllabification algorithm, we could always syllabify the first consonant after the nucleus. If a consonant in a cluster of two ought to be left unsyllabified (and therefore unpronounced), it should be the second one, the /s/ in these cases. In other cases of consonant deletion, an approach to syllabification that uses ordered rules seems to produce the correct result. Thus, Harris (1983: 35) notices that from a word such as *esculp-ir* 'to sculpt', we should derive **esculp-tor*. However, we find *escultor* 'sculptor'. Harris argues that the second consonant in the cluster, the /p/, could not be syllabified either as coda of the preceding syllable or as

---

[13] The correct Catalan pronunciation of this name is [púč]. There is a castilianized version of this family name: *Puche*.
[14] Name of a famous Dutch player with the Barcelona soccer team.
[15] I have not been able to find any examples of word-internal /lsC/.

onset of the following syllable and, for this reason, it is deleted. Applying the same reasoning, in an example such as /eks-presidente/, it should be the /s/ in the /kspr/ cluster that is left unpronounced, if any, since the /k/ can be incorporated by our coda rule (11). The simplification that obtains in /CsC/ clusters should then be treated in a different manner. Given the fact that /s/ is pronounced in these /CsC/ clusters, we must allow its syllabification in the rime. We must have a rule like (13):

(13) /s/-Adjunction: Adjoin /s/ under N'.

This rule will create the groups illustrated in (14) and (15):

(14)

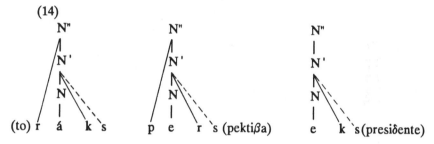

(to) r á k s   p e r 's (pektiβa)   e k 's(presiδente)

After the incorporation of /s/, another rule (15) will apply to simplify illicit sequences:

$$(15) \quad \left\{ \begin{array}{l} [\text{-cont}] \\ [\text{-son }] \end{array} \right\} \text{ s C}$$
$$\downarrow$$
$$\emptyset$$

This rule will produce the simplification of the cluster in *ex-presidente*.

1.5 Resyllabification. A well-known fact about Spanish syllabification is the existence of resyllabification of CV sequences across word boundaries. This is shown in (16):

(16)
club abierto	[klú.βa.βjér.to]	'open club'
chef honesto	[čé.fo.nés.to]	'honest chef'
pez azul	[pé.θa.θúl]	'blue fish'
más osos	[má.só.sos]	'more bears'
boj enorme	[bó.xe.nór.me]	'enormous box bush'
azul oscuro	[a.θú.los.kú.ro]	'dark blue'

In presenting this process of resyllabification, Spanish differs from a language like English, where CV sequences are not grouped in the same syllable across word boundaries, as in *take aim*, or even across a compound boundary, as in *cat album* (Goldsmith 1989: 122). Harris (1983: 43) proposes a rule of resyllabification across word boundaries for Spanish, formulated as in (17):

(17) Resyllabification:
$$[+\text{cons}] \rightarrow [+\text{cons}] \,/\, \underline{\hspace{1cm}} \# \text{ V}$$
$$\;\;\;\;\;\; | \;\;\;\;\;\;\;\;\;\;\;\; |$$
$$\;\;\;\;\;\; \text{R} \;\;\;\;\;\;\;\;\;\;\; \text{O}$$

In fact, a special, language-specific, rule of resyllabification is not needed to account for these facts. Instead, I will assume that resyllabification is the result of a second, postlexical, application of the universal CV rule. This second application of the CV rule will alter previously built structures. I will show that the CV rule reapplies, not only across word boundaries, but also within certain morphologically complex words.

The Complex Onset rule does not reapply postlexically. There is no resyllabification of CC clusters that would constitute well-formed onsets:

(18) club latino   [klúβ.la.tí.no]   *[klu.βla.tí.no]   'Latin club'
     chef latino   [čéf.la.tí.no]   *[čé.fla.tí.no]   'Latin chef'

1.6 Summary. In the preceding subsections, it has been argued that syllabification in Spanish comprises the set of ordered operations shown in (19):

(19) Node projection
     Complex nucleus (i.e. adjunction of prevocalic glides)
     Consonantization (movement of initial glides from nucleus to onset)
     CV rule
     Complex onset
     Coda rule
     Complex coda
     /s/-Adjunction

One of these operations, the CV rule, has a second, structure-changing application. In addition, it has been shown that there is a rule simplifying CsC clusters.

2 Domain of syllabification. In this section, I examine the domain in which the syllable-building rules examined above apply. It will be shown that these rules apply in a domain which may be smaller than the word. In particular, productive prefixes are separated from the rest of the word for syllabification purposes and the members of a compound also constitute separate domains. In this regard, Spanish presents a similar situation to that found in other European languages. In languages such as English or Dutch, the domain of syllabification is also smaller than the syntactic word (cf. van der Hulst 1984). Productive prefixes also seem to constitute separate domains of syllabification in German and Polish (Rubach 1990: 84, fn.1). In Spanish, however, there are facts that complicate the situation. Consider the syllabification of the words in (20):

(20) sublime   [su.βlí.me]   'sublime'
      sublunar   [suβ.lu.nár]   'sublunar'
      subalterno [su.βal.tér.no] 'subordinate'

The word *sublime* is syllabified according to the rules proposed in section 1. In *sublunar*, on the other hand, the /b/ is syllabified in the rime of the first syllable (cf. Navarro Tomás 1977: 177, Real Academia Española 1973: 46), violating the principle of onset maximization. The explanation for this fact is that the prefix *sub-* is syllabified independently from *lunar*.

The contrast in syllabification between these two words is thus due to the fact that in *sublime*, which is monomorphemic, we have a single domain of syllabification, whereas in *sublunar*, which carries a productive prefix, we have two: [sub] [lunar]. The prefix-final /b/ is not visible at the moment when the onset rules apply in the domain of the stem. Now, if the prefix *sub-* constitutes an independent domain of syllabification, as examples such as *sub.lu.nar* would seem to show, we should also expect that a word such as *subalterno* would be syllabified as *sub.al.ter.no*. But, as shown in (20), the correct syllabification is *su.bal.ter.no*. The explanation that I will propose for this is that *sub.al.ter.no* is indeed the initial result of the rules of syllabification; but this result is later modified by the reapplication of the CV rule. Intermediate *sub.al.ter.no* presents an input for this second application of the CV rule, since it contains a heterosyllabic CV sequence. An example such as *sub.lu.nar*, on the other hand, does not present an input for the application of this rule, since here we find a CC sequence and, as shown in 1.5, the Complex Onset rule does not have a second, structure-changing, application. The derivation of the three examples in (20) is given in (21):

(21)	[sublime]	[[sub] [alterno]]	[[sub] [lunar]]
Syllabification	[su.bli.me]	[[sub] [al.ter.no]]	[[sub][lu.nar]]
Prefixation	(n.a.)	[sub.al.ter.no]	[sub.lu.nar]
CV rule	(n.a.)	[su.bal.ter.no]	(n.a.)
Other rules	[su. βlí. me]	[su. βal. tér. no]	[suβ. lu. nár]

In between syllabification and the structure-changing reapplication of the CV rule, other phonological rules may apply. In a language closely related to Spanish, such as Catalan, there is in fact a rule that applies at that stage in examples that are similar to those just considered. In Catalan, as in Spanish, compounds and words bearing productive prefixes present two separate domains of syllabification. Catalan has a rule whereby stops are devoiced syllable-finally (or in a rime) if not followed by a voiced consonant. So, in word-final position, we find alternations of the type *llop* [λóp] 'wolf', *lloba* [λóβə] 'she-wolf' (cf. Mascaró 1976, Wheeler 1979, Hualde forthcoming). Interestingly, this rule also affects the final consonant of the prefix *sub-*. This consonant will appear syllabified in onset position if followed by a vowel, but will be devoiced. So, *subaltern* is pronounced [su.pəl.tɛ́rn] and *subindex* is [su.pín.dəks] (cf. Bonet 1989). Similarly, a compound like *sudest* 'southeast' is pronounced [su.tɛ́st] and can be compared with *sudenc* 'southern' [suδɛ́ŋ]. The derivation of these last two words is given in (22):

(22)	[[s u d] [ɛ s t]]	[[s u d] [ɛ n k]]
Suffixation	(n.a.)	[s u d ɛ n k]
Syllabification	[[s u d] [ɛ s t]]	[s u d ɛ n k]
	σ σ	σ σ
Syll.-final Devoicing	t	(n.a.)
Compounding	[s u t . ɛ s t]	(n.a.)
CV Rule	[s u t ɛ s t]	
	σ σ	
Other rules	[s u . t ɛ́ s t]	[s u . δ ɛ́ ŋ]

Some Spanish dialects also have phonological rules affecting rime consonants which are ordered before the reapplication of the CV rule. These will be examined below.

Another process that takes place in the domain that we are considering for syllabification is the strengthening of initial rhotics (cf., for instance, Harris 1983: 64, for a formulation of this rule). The rule that strengthens word-initial rhotics in Spanish must operate before prefixes are joined with the stem, since it applies in *pre*[r̄]*ománico* 'pre-romanesque' or *sub*[r̄]*egión* 'subregion', and before the two stems are put together in compounds such as hombre-[r̄]*ana* 'frogman', *peli*[r̄]*ójo* 'redhead' or *mata*[r̄]*atas* 'rat poison' (lit. 'rat-killer'), where the rhotic is not, strictly speaking, word-initial. On the other hand, suffix-initial rhotics are not strengthened, e.g. /kom-e-ria/ *come*[r]*ía* 'I/he would eat', not **come*[r̄]*ía*.

In sections 2.1 and 2.2, I will consider some processes in Spanish that make direct reference to syllable structure and that offer evidence for the domains of syllabification that I have proposed.

2.1 Consonantization of syllable-initial glides. As was mentioned above, most Spanish dialects have a process whereby syllable-initial glides become consonantal segments. Dialects differ in the segments that result from the consonantization of syllable-initial glides. In particular, syllable-initial /j/ may be realized as a palatal or prepalatal fricative, affricate, or stop, and is partially or totally devoiced in some dialects. I will use [ŷ] and [ŵ] as cover symbols for the (pre)palatal and the labiovelar consonantal segments, respectively. As argued, this rule affects syllable-initial glides, moving them into onset position. This operation effectively blocks the incorporation of a consonant as onset in a glide-initial syllable by the postlexical reapplication of the CV rule. Thus, there is no resyllabification across the word boundary in phrases such as *más hielo* [máz.ŷélo] 'more ice' (*[má.sjé.lo]) or *más huesos* [máz.ŵé.sos] 'more bones' (*[ma.swé.sos]). This is because, at the point where the CV rule applies, there is a C.C sequence in these examples. Identical effects are obtained word-internally in words bearing a prefix like *des-*, as in *deshielo* [dez.ŷé.lo] 'thawing' (*[de.sjé.lo]), which contrasts with *desierto* [de.sjér.to] 'desert', and *deshuesa* [dez.ŵé.sa] 'he debones' (*[de.swé.sa]), which contrasts with *resuena* [r̄e.swé.na] 'it resounds'. The existence of these contrasts has long been recognized (cf. Saporta 1956, Bowen and Stockwell 1956, Stockwell, Bowen, and Silva-Fuenzalida 1956, Alarcos Llorach 1965, Cressey 1978, Harris 1969). What these contrasts illustrate is that at the point when the consonantization of the glide applies, the prefix is not visible, i.e. that in a word like *deshielo*, *des-* and *hielo* constitute separate domains of syllabification. Were the prefix visible, its final consonant would be incorporated as onset of the second syllable, thus preventing the consonantization process, which only affects syllable-initial glides, as it is prevented in *desierto* or *resuena*. The derivation of monomorphemic *desierto* and bimorphemic *deshielo* and *desarme* 'disarmament' is given in (23) (after stress assignment and diphthongization have applied):

(23) Initial syllabification:

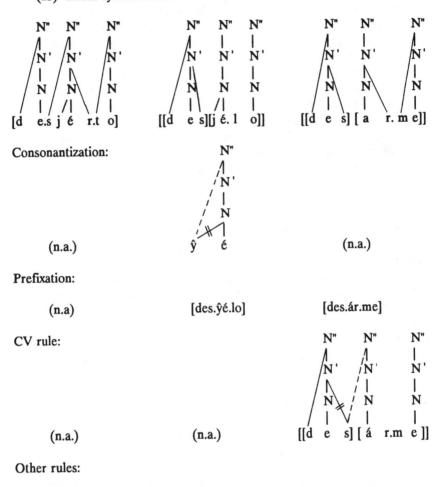

Consonantization:

Prefixation:

   (n.a)   [des.ŷé.lo]   [des.ár.me]

CV rule:

   (n.a.)   (n.a.)   [[d e s] [á r.m e]]

Other rules:

   [de.sjér.to]   [dez.ŷé.lo]   [de.sár.me]

In *deshielo*, the CV rule does not apply between prefix and stem because it finds a C.C sequence.

The consonantization of glides does not apply to suffix-initial glides in postconsonantal position, as for example in *quisiera* /kis-jera/ [ki.sjé.ra] 'he wanted, subjunctive' not *[kiz.ŷé.ra] (cf. *creyera* /kre-jera/ [kre.ŷé.ra] 'he believed, subjunctive', where the glide is syllable-initial).

2.2 Aspiration and velarization. Further evidence for the separation of prefixes and the members of a compound at the stage when syllabification takes place is found in certain Spanish dialects that possess rules that affect consonants in coda position, such as the velarization of nasals and the aspiration of /s/ and other consonants. Harris (1983: 45-47), crediting Guitart for the observation, notes that these rules may affect word-final consonants which appear in onset position, as in *más animales* [má.ha.ni.má.leh] 'more animals' and *son animales* [só.ŋa.ni.má.leh] 'they are animals'. Harris concludes that the resyllabification of word-final consonants across word boundaries must take place after the application of the rules of aspiration and velarization.

In certain Peninsular Spanish dialects, prefix-final /s/ and /n/ are also affected by aspiration and velarization, respectively, even when they appear in an onset, as the examples in (24) from the Granada dialect show:[16]

(24)
[e.heh.pe.ráo]	desesperado	'desperate'
[de.har.máo]	desarmado	'unarmed'
[no.hǫ́.trǫ]	nosotros	'we'
[bu.hǫ́.trǫ]	vosotros	'you-plural'
[i.ŋu.má.no]	inhumano	'inhuman'
[bje.ŋeh.tá]	bienestar	'well-being'

These facts receive the same explanation as similar situations across word boundaries. The segments affected by aspiration or velarization are in coda position at the point where those rules apply. Only a later application of the CV rule places them in onset position:

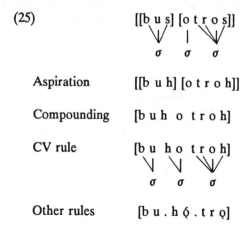

(25)

[[b u s] [o t r o s]]

Aspiration   [[b u h] [o t r o h]]

Compounding   [b u h o t r o h]

CV rule   [b u h o t r o h]

Other rules   [b u . h ǫ́ . t r ǫ]

---

[16] I want to thank my Granadino informant, José Luis Suárez. This phenomenon was also examined in Hualde (1989a).

I have assumed until now that the reapplication of the CV rule takes place only once, postlexically. From this assumption one would expect all dialects with the aspiration or the velarization rule to give results like those illustrated in (24). However, this does not seem to be the general situation. Many dialects do not velarize or aspirate prefix-final consonants. This shows that the CV rule must reapply with each operation of concatenation, at least in some dialects. The aspiration and velarization rules could be ordered before the concatenation (and resyllabification) of prefixes in some dialects, before the concatenation of compounds but after the concatenation of prefixes in other dialects, and after all morphological concatenation operations in yet other dialects. In the first case, we would obtain the situation illustrated in (24), where prefix-final and stem-final consonants in compounds are affected by velarization and aspiration. In the second case, these rules would apply inside compounds, but not to prefix-final consonants. Finally, in the third case, only strictly word-final consonants would be affected. Each of the two rules of aspiration and velarization could also apply at a different stage in the same dialect.

3 Conclusion. In this paper, the process of syllabification in Spanish has been examined in some detail and a set of ordered operations has been proposed. It has been shown that syllabification takes place in a domain that may be smaller than the word. In particular, prefixed and compound words present two domains of syllabification. This is a fact that is often obscured by the application of a rule that makes a domain-final consonant the onset of a following vowel-initial syllable, modifying previously created structures. Evidence for the independence of productive prefixes in syllabification has been offered from the application of rules that are sensitive to the position of the target within the syllable.

References

Alarcos Llorach, E. 1965. Fonología española. Madrid: Gredos.
Bonet, E. 1989. What Syllabification Tells Us About the Organization of Phonology: Evidence from Catalan. Unpublished ms., MIT, Cambridge, Mass.
Bowen, J. D., and R. Stockwell. 1956. A Further Note on Spanish Semivowels. Language 32, 290-292. Reprinted in M. Joos (ed.), 1963.
Clements, G. N. 1986. Syllabification and Epenthesis in the Barra dialect of Gaelic. In K. Bogers, H. van der Hulst, and M. Mous, eds., The Phonological Representation of Suprasegmentals: Studies Offered to John M. Steward on his 60th Birthday. Dordrecht: Foris, 317-336.
Cressey, W. 1978. Spanish Phonology and Morphology. Washington D. C.: Georgetown University Press.
Goldsmith, J. 1989. Autosegmental and Metrical Phonology. New York: Blackwell.
Harris, J. W. 1969. Spanish Phonology. Cambridge, Mass: MIT Press.

Harris, J. W. 1983. Syllable Structure and Stress in Spanish: A Nonlinear Analysis. Cambridge, Mass: MIT Press.

Harris, J. W. 1985. Spanish Diphthongization and Stress: A Paradox Resolved. Phonology Yearbook 2, 31-45.

Harris, J. W. 1989a. Our Present Understanding of Spanish Syllable Structure. In P. Bjarkman, and R. Hammond, eds., American Spanish Pronunciation: Theoretical and Applied Perspectives. Washington D. C.: Georgetown Univ. Press, 151-169.

Harris, J. W. 1989b. Spanish Stress: The Extrametricality Issue. Unpublished ms., MIT, Cambride, Mass.

Harris, J. W. 1989c. The Stress Erasure Convention and Cliticization in Spanish. Linguistic Inquiry 20, 339-364.

Hualde, J. I. 1989a. Autosegmental and Metrical Spreading in the Vowel Harmony Systems of Northwestern Spain. Linguistics 27, 773-805.

Hualde, J. I. 1989b. Silabeo y estructura morfémica en español. Hispania 72, 821-831.

Hualde, J. I. Forthcoming. Catalan. Croom Helm Descriptive Grammar Series. London: Routledge.

Hulst, H. van der. 1984. Syllable Structure and Stress in Dutch. Dordrecht: Foris.

Itô, J. 1986. Syllable Theory in Prosodic Phonology. Doctoral dissertation, Univ. of Massachusetts at Amherst.

Joos, M. 1963. Readings in Linguistics, 3rd ed. New York: American Council of Learned Societies.

Kenstowicz, M., and Ch. Kisseberth. 1979. Generative Phonology. New York: Academic Press.

Levin, J. 1985. A Metrical Theory of Syllabicity. Doctoral dissertation, MIT, Cambridge, Mass.

Mascaró, J. 1976. Catalan Phonology and the Strict Cycle. Doctoral dissertation, MIT, Cambridge, Mass. Distributed by Indiana University Linguistics Club.

McCarthy, J. 1984. Theoretical Consequences of Montañés Vowel Harmony. Linguistic Inquiry 15, 291-318.

McCarthy, J. 1986. OCP Effects: Gemination and Antigemination. Linguistic Inquiry 17, 207-264.

Navarro Tomás, T. 1977. Manual de pronunciación española. 19th ed. Madrid: Consejo Superior de Investigaciones Científicas.

Penny, R. 1969. El habla pasiega: ensayo de dialectología montañesa. London: Tamesis.

Penny, R. 1978. Estudio estructural del habla de Tudanca. Beihefte der Zeitschrift für Romanische Philologie 167. Tübingen: Niemeyer.

Real Academia Española. 1973. Esbozo de una nueva gramática de la lengua española. Madrid: Espasa-Calpe.

Roca, I. 1986. Secondary Stress and Metrical Rythm. Phonology Yearbook 3, 341-370.

Roca, I. This volume. Stress and Syllables in Spanish.

Rubach, J. 1990. Final Devoicing and Cyclic Syllabification in German. Linguistic Inquiry 21, 79-94.

Saporta, S. 1956. A Note on Spanish Semivowels. Language 32, 287-290.

Steriade, D. 1982. Greek Prosodies and the Nature of Syllabification. Doctoral dissertation, MIT, Cambridge, Mass.

Stockwell, R., J. D. Bowen, and I. Fuenzalida. 1956. Spanish Juncture and Intonation. Language 32, 241-265. Reprinted in M. Joos, ed., (1963).

Wheeler, M. 1979. Phonology of Catalan. Oxford: Blackwell.

The insert/delete parameter, redundancy rules, and neutralization processes in Spanish

Fernando Martínez-Gil *
Georgetown University

0 Introduction. Recent developments in phonological theory suggest that the range of possible phonological operations can be reduced to one of two basic types: rules may either insert or delete content (features) or structure (association lines). For any given rule, the choice is viewed as function of the *insert/delete parameter* (Archangeli and Pulleyblank 1986). The insertion of feature content is generally executed by redundancy rules. Spreading rules insert structure by extending association lines from one autosegment to another. Deletion of both content and structure is the realm of delinking rules. Most common phonological processes, such as assimilation, dissimilation, and neutralization rules in general, can be readily stated under the insert/delete parameter. (Several illustrations are provided later in this paper). Whether other residual 'garden–variety' of processes (e.g., metathesis rules) can also be formally expressed in terms of this parameter is an open question, and remains for feature research.[1]

The insert/delete parameter is coupled with a universal feature hierarchy, which encodes the internal structure of phonological segments.[2] The range of possible insertion and deletion operations is severely restricted, since only constituents in the hierarchy can be affected (i.e., individual features and natural classes of features, including whole segmental roots). Operations on feature structure interact in various ways with the universal markedness theory. This component provides a battery of redundancy rules which supply default specifications, both to underlying forms and to the output of delinking rules. Such default rules constitute an essential ingredient of the most rudimentary underspecification theory. Given these basic assumptions, the description of a wide variety of phonological rules, customarily conceived as feature–changing operations in linear frameworks, can be more insightfully

---

* I am grateful to María Carreira, Jim Jarris, José Hualde, Carlos Otero, and Tom Walsh for valuable comments and criticism. They are not responsible for any deficiencies in my analysis.

[1] See McCarthy (1989: 76–77) for some discussion on the problems that arise in attempting to state Yawelmani metathesis in this way. Archangeli and Pulleyblank (1986: 129) suggest that processes such as metathesis and feature copying in reduplication involve a complex of mechanisms, rather than a simple one.

[2] See Clements (1985), Sagey (1986), Steriade (1987a), McCarthy (1989), and much related work.

recast as particular instantiations of the insert/delete parameter and subsequent application of default rules. Cases of contextual and absolute neutralization of underlying distinctions are perhaps the most conspicuous; the former are normally associated with synchronic alternations; the latter generally correspond to historical merger of underlying distinctions.

One of the fundamental differences of autosegmental theory and previous frameworks involves the formal expression of assimilation rules. In the linear model of phonology articulated in Chomsky and Halle (1968), such rules are stated as feature-changing operations. According to the strongest version of an autosegmental theory, assimilation rules are to be represented exclusively by spreading of association lines.[3] Archangeli and Pulleyblank (1986: 176) refer to this assumption as the Spreading Hypothesis, and state it as follows:

(1)   *Spreading Hypothesis*
       Phonological processes of assimilation are accomplished uniquely by the spreading of autosegments.

Sagey (1986) remarks that autosegmental spreading, in conjunction with hierarchical representations, entertains two clear advantages over the feature-changing mechanism. First, it excludes a large number of impossible assimilation rules, namely, those in which 'the target takes on a feature that is not present in the trigger, a type of assimilation which doesn't occur' (Sagey 1986: 9). And second, it has successfully overcome a vexing problem of linear descriptions: the common lack of reciprocity between rule simplicity and rule naturalness. Thus an objection commonly raised against a feature-changing framework is that the expression of some highly natural assimilation rules (e.g., homorganic nasal assimilation) require great complexity, while many formally simple rules can be written but they do not correspond to processes actually attested in human language.[4] Assimilation by spreading involves the linking of two given autosegments by extension of a connecting association line. This implies that, all other things being equal, the whole set of possible assimilation rules becomes equally simple, independent of whether the process involves one feature or a subset of features, as in partial assimilation, or the whole segmental melody, as in total assimilation.

By greatly reducing the class of possible assimilation rules, hierarchical feature representation and autosegmental spreading virtually dispel an undesirable residue of arbitrariness in phonological descriptions. It must be clearly understood, however, that an autosegmental theory of assimilation does not exclude the possibility of expressing assimilation phenomena as feature-

---

[3] See Hayes (1986b), Sagey (1986: 9-11).
[4] For a more detailed discussion, see Hyman (1975) and Kaye (1989).

changing operations. In fact, in much of the autosegmental literature on assimilatory processes written in the last fifteen years or so, the assumption is made, whether implicitly or explicitly, that spreading proceeds indeed in a feature-changing fashion, by inducing automatic delinking of the target's specification(s).[5] Some cases presumably could be reformulated as simply the acquisition of specifications by spreading (by assuming some version of the underspecification theory), that is, when it can be shown that the target lacks a specification at the point the spreading rule applies. In many other cases they cannot be reanalyzed this way, primarily because either the target's specification is needed underlyingly, or there is clear evidence that such specification must have been assigned by rule prior to the spreading in question. While there is nothing inherently wrong or inelegant in describing assimilation processes in an autosegmental feature-changing manner, whether or not this is an adequate formalization of such processes is ultimately an empirical question, and bears directly on the characterization of linguistic competence. On the other hand, some phonologists have taken the more radical view that spreading operations may only affect unspecified targets (Mascaró 1988, Avery and Rice 1989, Rice and Avery 1991). In order for this condition to hold, all relevant specifications must be delinked prior to spreading. In this approach, there is no ambiguity as to the identity of delinking and spreading: both operations are clearly distinct.

This essay has two primary concerns. The first is to investigate the interaction of redundancy rules and the insert/delete parameter in a number of historical and synchronic processes in Spanish phonology. The second is to examine these data in the light of the claims of the two approaches to assimilation just outlined. Additional data will be presented from Galician, a Romance language spoken in the northwest of Spain. My discussion will proceed by showing, first, that delinking rules have an independent status in phonological theory, a claim substantiated by both dissimilation rules and absolute neutralization processes in historical change. The application of redundancy rules to the output of delinking operations is shown to be crucial in accounting for some diachronic facts of Spanish. Second, it is suggested that such autonomy is additionally supported in cases of contextual neutralization, either because delinking must be ordered prior to spreading, or vice versa. In discussing various types of assimilation rules, I argue that certain generalizations would be missed if feature delinking is characterized as the automatic consequence of spreading. Furthermore, I show that delinking-by-spreading and the condition that spreading is restricted to unspecified targets are untenable in view of a wide range of empirical data.

---

[5] See, for example, Goldsmith's (1981) analysis on Spanish nasal assimilation.

This paper is organized as follows. In section 1 some relevant aspects of the theoretical background are first reviewed, including syllable structure, the feature hierarchy, and the underspecification theory. In section 2, I discuss some details of two prevalent approaches to the expression of assimilation rule. In section 3, I examine two types of types of neutralization rules involving exclusively the delinking-and-default procedures: Old Spanish dissimilation and Proto-Spanish lowering of high lax vowels. I propose that the assignment of default features proposed for the lowering process can be naturally extended to account for the neutralization of lax mid vowels in Proto-Spanish metaphony. In section 4, I examine cases of partial and total assimilation processes, and investigate the interaction of delinking, spreading, and default assignment: vowel rounding in Galician, co-articulation of coda nasals in Galician and Spanish velarizing dialects, Proto-Spanish Palatalization, Spanish voicing assimilation, and consonant gemination in several Spanish dialects. Finally, in section 5 I present some concluding remarks.

1   Theoretical background

1.1   Syllable structure. I follow Levin (1985) in assuming an X-bar theory of the syllable.[6]   The categories N", N', and N are the formal equivalent of the traditional labels 'Syllable', 'Rhyme', and 'Nucleus', respectively. A simple illustration of the types of representations generated by this model is shown for the Spanish word *sol* 'sun' in (\$2):

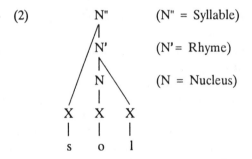

(2)   N"   (N" = Syllable)

            N'   (N' = Rhyme)

             N   (N = Nucleus)

        X   X   X

        s   o   l

1.2   The feature hierarchy. The   first   aspect   of   phonological representation relevant to our purposes is related to the organization of phonological features. In this paper I assume a version of the articulator–based model of feature organization. Succinctly, this model maintains that phonological features are hierarchically arrayed, forming higher

---

[6] Examples of this theory applied to Spanish data can be found in Harris (1889a, 1989b) and Hualde (1989a, this volume).

constituents (the Class nodes) which determine internal dominance relations within the Root node, the formal correlate of a phoneme–sized segment (Clements 1985, Sagey 1986, and much related work).

Although many phonologists today accept a universal feature hierarchy, there is some disagreement on just how many members it should contain, and the particular location of some features/nodes. Some of Clements' original proposals regarding major constituents in the hierarchy have prevailed in most later versions, including the branching of roots into the Laryngeal and the Supralaryngeal nodes (but cf. Iverson 1989), as well as the distinction of various articulator nodes under the Places node. The precise number and location of manner features are somewhat controversial.

In this paper I assume the following version of the feature hierarchy:

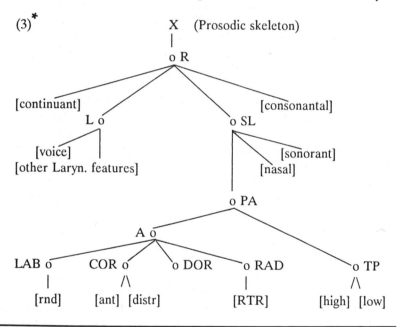

$(3)^*$

*Here and in subsequent examples, the following abbreviations are used: R = Root; L = Laryngeal node; SL = Supralaryngeal node; PA = Place node; A = Articulators node; TP = Tongue Position node; COR = Coronal node; DOR = Dorsal node; RAD = Radical node; [RTR] = Retracted Tongue Root.

As shown in (3), the Root node is directly linked to the prosodic skeleton or sequence of timing units, an intermediate level in which segmental structure intersects with higher (suprasegmental) units of representation (Levin 1985). The first branching of the Root corresponds to the division between the

Laryngeal and Supralaryngeal articulators. Laryngeal features account for vocal fold vibration and other states of the glottis. Following Pulleyblank (1988) and Archangeli and Pulleyblank (1989), I assume that some stricture features, such as [consonantal] and [continuant], are directly attached to the Root (see also Sagey 1986), while [nasal] and [sonorant] are dominated by the Supralaryngeal node.

Some recent research on the feature hierarchy has raised considerable debate on the proper characterization of Place features.[7] As shown in (3), I follow Lahiri and Evers (1991: 87) in assuming that the Place node is organized into two constituents: (i) the Articulators node, which comprises four articulators corresponding to the lips (Labial node), the tongue tip/blade (Coronal node), the tongue dorsum (Dorsal node), and the tongue root (Radical node); and (ii) and the Tongue Position which comprises the tongue body features [high] and [low]. On the basis of a various pieces of evidence from assimilation rules, Lahiri and Evers argue for the integration of primary and secondary articulation features in both consonants and vowels. Thus in contrast with other models, front vowels now have a Coronal articulator (cf. Keating 1991). Furthermore, the feature [back] is disposed of, its function being taken over by the Dorsal node, which is both monovalent and has no feature dependents; it characterizes both back vowels and velar consonants.[8]

Class nodes are monovalent: for any given representation of a certain segment they are either present or absent altogether. On the other hand, whether all terminal features are binary or privative is a matter of controversy.[9] I follow Steriade (1987b) in assuming that the feature [round] is monovalent for vowels. If a vowel has a Labial node it will also contain [round] as a dependent. This reflects the fact that labiality is a natural consequence of lip rounding in vowels. In consonants, on the other hand, labiality is independent of rounding, as suggested by the unmarked status of labial consonants (in contrast to the less common labialized ones). Therefore, the distinction between labial and labialized consonants is that the former have a Labial node with no dependent, while the latter are specified for roundness. The reader will also have noticed that [RTR] (Retracted Tongue Root) is used in (3) instead of the more traditional [ATR]. This move can be

---

[7] See, for example, Archangeli and Pulleyblank (1986, 1987), Steriade (1987a), McCarthy (1989).

[8] The reader is referred to Lahiri and Evers' (1991) original essay for further discussion. It should be added that their primary concern is to achieve a more adequate formulation of palatalization processes. The hierarchy they propose is admittedly tentative, and many details and predictions of such model, as compared to other models, are not fully explored.

[9] In Clements (1985), Sagey (1986), and many others, all terminal features are binary. More recently, some phonologists have proposed that all features are monovalent (Avery and Rice 1989, Hulst 1989). Eclectic positions also exist (Steriade 1987b, Rice and Avery 1991).

motivated on markedness grounds. In three and five triangular vowel systems (apparently the least marked ones; cf. Crothers 1978, Maddieson 1984) tongue root advancement is the default specification for non-low vowels, while low vowels are generally [RTR]. Moreover, although underlying [RTR] distinctions among mid vowels are relatively common, the presence of such contrasts among low vowels is highly exceptional. In high vowels, [RTR] contrasts are relatively rare and typically unstable, as attested by the historical evidence from the Romance languages. Consequently, I consider tongue root retraction the marked option. Hence, parallel to Labial and [round], only [RTR] vowels are specified for a Radical node.

As a simple illustration, consider the Proto–Spanish vowel system at the stage prior to the diphthongization of mid lax vowels (cf. Otero 1988), which exhibits [RTR] distinctions among mid vowels:

(4)		Front	Back unrounded	Back rounded
High		i		u
Mid	non-[RTR]	e		o
	[RTR]	E		O
Low			a	

According to the feature hierarchy in (3), the Proto-Spanish vowel system can be characterized as follows ('[H]' and '[L]' stand for [high] and [low], respectively):[10]

(5)

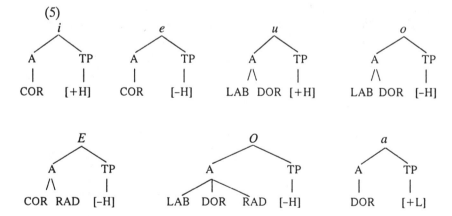

In section 1.3 I present a maximally underspecified version of (5).

---

[10] Here and in subsequent examples, irrelevant nodes and structure will be omitted in rules representations, unless required for clarity. [RTR] vowels are represented by upper case letters.

1.3 Underspecification. In this paper, I follow the theory of radical underspecification put forth in Archangeli (1984, 1988) and Archangeli and Pulleyblank (1986). The basic assumption of this theory is that only idiosyncratic, unpredictable properties are stored in underlying forms, in accordance with the Feature Minimization Principle (Archangeli 1984: 56):

(6) *Feature Minimization Principle*
A grammar is most highly value when underlying representations include the minimal number of features necessary to make different the phonemes of the language.

Radical underspecification theory requires that for every contrastive feature only one value (the marked one, all other things being equal) may be present in underlying representations. Central to the framework is a universal markedness theory which contains a set of redundancy rules, termed 'default rules', stating which features and feature combinations are supplied by Universal Grammar.[11] In addition, the assumption is made that for every feature that plays a distinctive role in a language, only one value is marked underlyingly. The opposite (complementary) value is supplied by default. In general, default rules may reflect absolute restrictions derived from anatomical constraints (high vowels must necessarily be [-low], and conversely, low vowels must also be [-high]); or they may express universal markedness principles (e.g., in the unmarked case, low vowels are [-round]).[12]

In addition, many languages contain a default vowel, which commonly shows up in epenthesis rules. I assume that the default vocalic features of Proto–Spanish are those of /e/.[13] Therefore, the underlying representation of this vowel will only contain a Root node specified as [-consonantal], as shown in (7); all other features remain unspecified:

---

[11] Archangeli (1984) and Archangeli and Pulleyblank (1986) make the distinction between 'default' and 'complement' rules. The former supply universally unmarked values, while the latter supply a marked value whenever the phonemic distribution in a language requires the unmarked specification to be present in underlying representations. In this paper I simply maintain a distinction between universal default rules and language-specific default rules.

[12] Radical underspecification has been challenged by some phonologists (Steriade 1987b, Mester and Itô 1989), who maintain that all contrastive features must be specified for both values in underlying forms. See Archangeli (1988) and Mohanan (1991) for further discussion.

[13] Some Romance scholars have pointed out that the epenthetic vowel in Proto–Romance was [i], as shown by the graffiti at Pompeii and other evidence (cf. Väänänen 1968). However, most Western Romance languages insert [e] (e.g., Catalan, French, Portuguese, and Spanish), which strongly suggests a dialectal split between Western and Eastern (Italic) dialects.

(7)
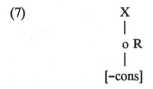

```
            X
            |
           o R
            |
         [-cons]
```

As for the remainder of Proto–Spanish vowels, the minimally–specified versions of the hierarchical representations in (5) are given in (8):

(8)
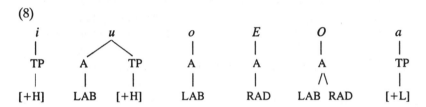

The missing specifications are supplied by the set of redundancy rules stated in (9):[14]

(9)
i.	[ ]	→	[o TP, -high]
ii.	[ ]	→	[o TP, -low]
iii.	[o LAB]	→	[round]
iv.	[+low]	→	[o RAD]
v.	[ ]	→	[o COR] / [__ oTP, -low]
vi.	[+low]	→	[o DOR]
vii.	[rnd]	→	[o DOR]
viii.	[o RAD]	→	[RTR]

In section 3.2, I return to the representations and rules in (8)-(9) as critical for my analysis of vowel neutralization and metaphony in Proto-Spanish.

Let us assume that /i/ is the universal default vowel (cf. Chomsky and Halle 1968: 405, Archangeli and Pulleyblank 1986: 16). With the exception of (9i), which is a specific default rule of Proto–Spanish, all the other redundancy rules in (9) define unmarked properties of vowels. I assume that such default rules may insert redundant features, as in (9i–iii) and (9viii), or redundant nodes, as in (9iv–vii).

---

[14] In (9) and thereafter, [o N, αF] (N = a node, and F = a terminal feature) will be used as a simple notational equivalent to the hierarchical representation:

```
   o N
   |
  [αF]
```

The recognition of monovalent features, such as [round], is required in order to account for asymmetries in vowel harmony systems. An obvious advantage in assuming privative specifications is that rules and representations can be simplified. For example, a rule whose structural description does not refer to [round] would apply to all vowels that do not bear this specification, while in a binary feature theory, the same effect can only be obtained if the rule explicitly mentions the value [−round]. Such simplification can be further enforced if phonological statements are subject to the Linking Constraint (Hayes 1986a), which restricts rule application to those strings that satisfy the tupe of linking explicitly stated in its structural description. However, by excluding the possibility of referring to the absence of a given specification, a model allowing monovalent features would appear to introduce an undesirable consequence in markedness theory, since additional constraints are now required to exclude an otherwise unmarked structure. Thus, as it stands, (9v) wrongly predicts front round vowels in this system. The problem here clearly stems from [round] being universally monovalent. If [−round] is not a possible specification, there is only one way of preventing (9v) from incorrectly supplying a Coronal node to round vowels, namely, a negative condition prohibiting the co-occurrence of the Labial and Coronal nodes on the same vowel. Following Archangeli and Pulleyblank (1986), we may propose the negative configuration constraint in (10):[15]

(10)

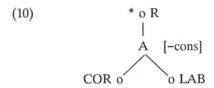

The underspecification theory makes use of structure-building rules such as (9) to reflect redundant distributional properties of segmental inventories. The function of configuration constraints such as (10) is to preserve these properties throughout the lexical phonology of a language. In fact, the presence of such constraints constitutes the empirical basis for the principle of Structure Preservation and, by implication, for the distinction between a lexical and a postlexical component in phonology (Kiparsky 1982a, 1985, Mohanan 1986). Structure Preservation states that lexical rules must respect such configuration constraints. They may be violated, however, at the

---

[15] Some scholars suggest that if configuration constraints such as (9) are needed to capture general restrictions on feature co-occurrence, structure building rules (such as those in (8)) represent an unnecessary duplication (Calabrese 1988, Mohanan 1991).

postlexical level, in which Structure Preservation does not necessarily hold (Archangeli and Pulleyblank 1986: 31). Redundancy rules are subject to three general conditions. First, they must be intrinsically ordered, a property which follows from the Default Ordering Principles (Archangeli and Pulleyblank 1986: 11–15), and the Elsewhere Condition (Kiparsky 1982a, 1985). Second, they apply whenever their structural description is met, in accordance with the Redundancy Rule Ordering Constraint (a principle already implicit in the concept of 'linking' in Chomsky and Halle 1968). And third, they are subject to the Distinctiveness Condition. According to this condition, redundancy rules can only fill in unspecified values. Archangeli (1984: 46) provides the following definition:

(11)   *Distinctness Condition*
        The input to a redundancy rule is not rendered distinct
        from the output by application of the redundancy rule.

where the notion 'distinct' is understood in the familiar sense of Chomsky and Halle (1968: 336). According to the Distinctness Condition, redundancy rules *may not* change feature values, whether such values are present in underlying representations or they have been assigned by phonological rules. This condition will be critical in the discussion of some issues which will be addressed later in this paper.

Finally, I assume with Archangeli and Pulleyblank (1986: 73-79) and Avery and Rice (1989: 183) that whenever feature content is inserted by redundancy rules, all the required higher nodes in the hierarchy are generated by convention. Thus if a redundancy rule assigns, say, [-high] to a vowel unspecified for Place features, the Node Generation Convention will automatically create the higher nodes Tongue Position, Place, and so on.

2   Delinking, spreading, and redundant feature assignment. In order to present a modicum of theoretical context for my analysis of the data in subsequent sections, a brief excursus is in place. It is generally assumed that phonological segments are fully specified at the phonetic level. Suppose we derive this requirement from some version of the Well–Formedness Condition (cf. Goldsmith 1976, Clements and Ford 1979) in the sense that for each member of the universal set of phonetic properties contained in the feature hierarchy (whatever these turn out to be), segmental melodies have to be associated to at least one specification in surface representations. Maximally unspecified underlying segments will acquire full content through two channels: by spreading from available units (subject, of course, to general well–formedness principles), or by default assignment of features, whether on a universal or on a language–specific basis.[16]   Thus if through a delinking operation a given segment becomes unspecified for some feature/node in the hierarchy, full specification will proceed by spreading, provided a legitimate trigger is available.   By 'legitimate trigger' I mean a unit which contains the specification missing in the target at that point in the derivation, and spreading does not violate other relevant well-formedness principles (e.g. the Crossing Constraint, Locality, and so on), or other language-specific conditions.[17] If such requirements are not met, full specification is assigned by default.

We observe further that among the conditions that determine most consonantal neutralizations cross–linguistically, a common one arises through restrictions on consonantal feature content in syllable rhymes (a type of constraint often referred to as 'prosodic licensing'; Itô 1986, Goldsmith 1990). When a certain combination of features (i.e., a consonant or a class of consonants) is not licensed, delinking of the offending features from syllable structure typically ensues. Segments unaffiliated to syllable structure are generally subject the universal Stray Erasure Convention (Itô 1986: 48ff., Harris 1983: 35, 1985), and therefore do not receive any phonetic interpretation.   A rather systematic class of exceptions to this prohibition occurs when an otherwise unlicensed consonantal melody is linked simultaneously to a rhyme and to a following onset, a type of configuration readily identifiable with geminates. This type of structure–dependent licensing is quite widespread; it can be found, among other languages, in Italian, Finnish, and Japanese (Itô 1986). Such cases of total assimilation can be captured by means of a rule that delinks the association between the segmental melody of the unlicensed consonant and the prosodic tier. The skeletal unit rendered available by the delinking operation may reassociate to a following consonant by the application of a structure–inserting rule. Or, alternatively, it may link to the preceding vowel. In both cases, the delinking-and-spreading mechanism yields a geminate structure results, as a result of compensatory lengthening.

The theory of prosodic licensing can be naturally extended, *mutatis mutandis*, to account for partial delinking of segmental melody; that is, disassociation of a feature or a subsegmental node.   For example, in many languages coda consonants may not bear an autonomous specification of place of articulation features, a constraint commonly termed the 'Coda Condition'

---

[16] But cf. Keating (1988) who contends that occasionally secondary feature values found in simple consonants in phonetic structure are not acquired by either phonological or redundancy rules, but rather by interpolation from other specified values.

[17] Notice, however, that although an unspecified target is a sufficient condition for feature spreading, it is by no means a necessary one, as amply shown in this paper.

(Steriade 1982, Itô 1986, Yip 1991).[18] In Spanish, nasals contrast in place of articulation underlyingly. However, when assigned to a rhyme in preconsonantal position, they acquire the place of articulation of a following consonant. Syllable structure is to a large extent redundant in Spanish, and thus is absent from underlying representations. When a nasal is assigned to a rhyme, its place of articulation features are delinked. Neutralization takes two basic forms. A nasal lacking place features may become available for linking to a following consonant, an operation perfomed by a spreading rule (Goldsmith 1981, Harris 1984a, 1984b, Hualde 1988, 1989c). However, in non-assimilating environments, rhyme nasals in many dialects consistently surface as coronal, clearly a prosodically–licensed specification in Spanish. This can be no accident, since coronal is the universally unmarked place of articulation for this class of segments.[19] The assignment of default features in non-assimilating environments is carried out at no cost by a universal redundancy rule. Minor details aside, such characterization essentially sums up the analysis by Harris (1984a, 1984b). This type of contextual neutralization bears a striking resemblance to the total assimilation scenario just depicted; too striking, one may add, to be a matter of mere coincidence. Here again, the descriptive generalization seems to be that nasals may be linked to place features only if they also 'share' such specification with a following (prosodically–licensed) onset consonant. The formal identity of the two processes can be identified, in its most relevant details, with a violation of prosodic licensing resolved by delinking of the 'offending' specification, and subsequent reassociation to the specified constituent of a licensed segment. On the other hand, the residual cases of nasal neutralization in non-assimilating environments would simply follow from the well–formedness requirement of full surface specification. Such requirement is satisfied cost–free by Universal Grammar through a redundancy rule that assigns coronal as the default place of articulation. The vast literature describing phonological systems of human languages abundantly attests to cases of total and partial assimilation exhibiting general properties similar to those just mentioned, and further examples could be added ad libitum.

---

[18] Incidentally, the Coda Condition provides a principled explanation for the fact that rules involving regressive assimilation in consonants are overwhelmingly more frequent than those involving progressive assimilation. This is predicted if we assume that: (a) violations of of feature content in syllable rhymes are by delinking rules; and (b) spreading is enforced by the Well-Formedness Condition when there is an available specified trigger (e.g., a following onset consonant).

[19] In fact, a substantial body of empirical evidence suggests that a coronal place of articulation is unmarked for consonants in general (see, for example, the collection of articles in Paradis and Prunet 1991). I return to the behavior of nasals in other Spanish dialects later in this paper.

It has become increasingly clear in recent research that the formal mechanisms involved in a substantial corpus of neutralization processes can be most insightfully expressed in terms of the delinking-and-spreading and delinking-and-default procedures. A further illustration is provided by two familiar instances of segmental neutralization, this time narrowed down to a single feature. Many languages (e.g., Catalan, Dutch, German, Russian, and Turkish) exhibit underlying voicing distinctions among obstruents, but these contrasts are neutralized in syllable rhymes. Neutralization arises in two already familiar fashions. The target obstruent may undergo assimilation in voicing to a following consonant; in the absence of an assimilating environment, voiced obstruents become voiceless.[20] Reformulated in terms of prosodic licensing, we may assume that in these languages a [+voice] autosegment cannot be linked to an obstruent in rhyme position, unless it is also linked to a following (prosodically licensed) onset consonant. Assimilation or, in its absence, default assignment of [−voice] (the universally unmarked value for obstruents) proceeds much like in Spanish nasal neutralization. The statement of many common instances of absolute neutralization in diachronic change is straightforward assuming a delinking–and–default mechanism. In this instance, however, prosodic licensing does not appear to a relevant factor. Rather, involved here is the context–free obliteration of an underlying contrast, typically through the loss of a marked specification in a given class of phonological segments, an event that ultimately leads to lexical reanalysis. A familiar example is the devoicing of the Old Spanish sibilants /z, d^z, ž/ in the 14th and 15th centuries, thus merging with their voiceless counterparts /s, t^s, š/.[21] The statement of this and many other types of phonological merger can be naturally captured by a rule that delinks the marked feature, followed by the redundant assignment of the universally unmarked value.[22]

---

[20] This is a slight simplification which does not invalidate the point at hand. Devoicing may interact in different ways with syllable structure rules in particular languages. In Catalan, for example, when the obstruent is both syllable- and morpheme-final, devoicing occurs prior to morpheme concatenation, and subsequent resyllabification, to a following vowel-initial root or suffix (cf. Mascaró 1976, 1988, Hualde this volume). In Turkish, resyllabification to a following vowel across word-boundaries is ordered before devoicing (Rice 1989). And in German, devoicing is dependent on cyclic assignment of syllable structure (Rubach 1990). For a detailed study of similar effects in various languages, see Mascaró 1988).

[21] See Martinet (1951), Joos (1952), Alonso (1955), Harris (1969: 189ff.), Lloyd (1987: 328ff.), and references therein.

[22] Of course, if it could be demonstrated beyond reasonable doubt that absolute neutralization arises in the course of language acquisition, then a delinking rule would be no longer required. According to this scenario, we might speculate that the marked feature is never incorporated into the underlying representations that the child acquires in the first place. Instead, such learning would be superseded by the child's reanalysis of the data in accordance with innate principles contained in Universal Grammar (cf. King 1968: 71ff.).

In the preceding paragraphs, I have outlined some of the basic ingredients of an integrated approach to neutralization rules, taking as a point of departure the parametric proposals of Archangeli and Pulleyblank (1986). Having established that the range of delinking and spreading operations is partly determined by the number of constituents in the universal feature hierarchy (and partly, of course, by other principles of phonological theory), a specific question arises as to whether there is an intrinsic relationship between both procedures. This question is ultimately related to the more general one: under what formal conditions does feature spreading take place? The autosegmental literature abounds in accounts of assimilation stated as spreading and concurrent delinking of features. As a simple illustration of this approach, consider the usual statement of an assimilation rule in (12) (where N = a node, and F = a dependent node or a feature, and both N_1 and N_2 are dependents of the same superordinate node in the feature hierarchy):

(12)

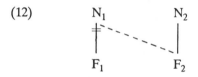

I will refer to the mechanism in (12) as the 'Spreading-cum-Delinking' approach to assimilation (henceforth SCD). According to this formalism, spreading rules induce simultaneous delinking of a certain feature/node specified in the rule's target. Both operations are conceived as occurring in a cause–effect procedure: when a given autosegment specified as, say, $[\alpha F]$ spreads onto a target T, delinking of $[-\alpha F]$ from T follows automatically (see, for example, Goldsmith's 1981 analysis of Spanish nasal assimilation). The very same assumption is explicitly or implicitly made in many analyses of assimilatory processes to the present day. In sum, although the autosegmental model undoubtedly changed the letter of phonological representations, the *modus operandi* inherent to the SCD approach essentially retains the spirit of its segmental predecessor; radical reforms in notational machinery should not obscure the fact that the SCD mechanism ultimately characterizes assimilation rules as feature–changing rules.

Archangeli (1987) demonstrates that SCD has undesirable theoretical consequences in that it unduly expands the power of autosegmental theory, by predicting many scenarios which are never found in natural languages. On the other hand, under the SCD approach it would be difficult to explain the enduring opacity effects of prespecified vowels, as is often the case in vowel harmony. It is true that the universal feature hierarchy greatly restricts the

SCD types of feature-changing operations on segmental structure since, by implication, phonological rules may not manipulate the hierarchy. Nevertheless, as Archangeli points out, this approach still predicts rules such as (13a-b), in which spreading of F to N_1 induces delinking of G (where N is, say, the Coronal node, and F and G are two dependent features, e.g., $[\alpha$ ant] and $[\beta$ distributed]) or, for that matter, of another constituent not directly dependent from N_2, among other logically possible scenarios. To the extent that such rules do not occur in natural language, they would have to be ruled out by some special stipulation.

(13)   a.

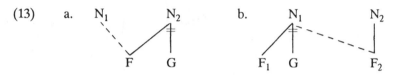

Suppose further that a statement along the lines of (12) is selected to formulate the voicing assimilation rule mentioned earlier. An additional statement would be required in order to account for devoicing in non-assimilating environments:

(14)   [–son]   →   [–voice] /___ #

The problem is that (14) unnecessarily duplicates the statement of obstruent neutralization, and it further introduces a feature which is wholly predictable by independent principles of markedness. Similar objections could be raised if, instead, a delinking rule is posited in addition to (12), because the delinking operation would have to be stated twice in the grammar. Neither solution, then, can capture the essentially unitary nature of neutralization as the direct consequence of one single delinking rule, whose motivation, as suggested earlier, can often be related to language-specific conditions related to prosodic licensing. It should be clear that the issue here is not simply a matter of notation; at stake here is the proper characterization of neutralization processes, including the formal conditions that grammars impose on the targets of spreading rules.

Perhaps the strongest argument in favor of the SCD procedure is that it seems to be required to explain general properties of lexical phonology. Suppose that a lexical rule spreads a certain feature onto a specified target, where such specification is ensured either by assignment at the underlying level or by prior application of another rule. It has been proposed that when such a situation arises, feature spreading induces principled delinking when otherwise the resulting structure (quite generally, a contour or a complex segment) is missing from the class of linkings that function distinctively in the language (Pulleyblank 1986: 221-222). The principle involved is Structure Preservation: no lexical rule may generate segments which are absent from underlying representations (Kiparsky 1985). However, since Structure Preservation apparently need not be respected postlexically, as already mentioned, the question arises as to whether (i) delinking operations are also the automatic consequence of spreading rules in the postlexical component, or (ii) some other principle is at work. This question, it seems to me, is relevant, since postlexical rules (and especially assimilation rules) are generally identifiable with phonological phenomena that have a clear phonetic motivation. Faced with the facts of postlexical assimilation rules discussed later in this papers, SCD runs into immediate difficulties. In fact, the SCD mechanism can be readily falsified by determining that in a certain assimilation process, disassociation of features is required independently of spreading. A similar conclusion would be reached by showing that a spreading rule applies but there is no concomitant delinking in the target, in which case the outcome is a contour structure. I return to this point later, showing that such contour segments occur in Galician and Spanish velarizing dialects, and here they are the direct result of assimilation of nasals which have already been assigned the default Place features. Clearly, such types of phenomena provide *prima facie* evidence against SCD.

In other instances, most visibly in vowel harmony processes, assimilation typically proceeds in a feature–filling fashion, by spreading of a specified harmonic property. Consider the example of Akan, in which tongue root advancement is an underlying property of whole root morphemes—rather than individual vowels (Clements 1981). Thus the feature [ATR] establishes two broad morphological classes of words: those whose vowels harmonize in [+ATR] and those that exhibit [-ATR] harmony. In essence, Clements' proposal is to mark each root morpheme with its corresponding [ATR] specification in the lexicon. Universal association conventions will map the harmonic feature onto the leftmost vowel in a word, and then spread it onto other available [ATR]–bearing units from left to right. However, many words in Akan exhibit disharmonic patterns. In these cases, rightward spreading of [+ATR] is stopped, generally by the presence of a root–final low vowel /a/. The low vowel not only blocks [+ATR] harmony, but it also spreads its [-ATR] value onto following suffixes, thereby defining a harmonic domain to its right. Clements' crucial assumption is that the opaque vowel blocks spreading of the harmonizing feature by virtue of being prelinked to [-ATR] in lexical representations.[23] However, SCD would predict spreading of the

---

[23] Other languages exhibiting a type of vowel disharmony akin to that of Akan are Turkish (Clements and Sezer 1982), and Vata (Kaye (1982).

harmonic feature onto this vowel with simultaneous delinking of its [ATR] specification, therefore removing the barrier to propagation of the harmonic feature onto available vowels beyond the opaque one. In short, in an SCD framework, root and word disharmony in Akan and opacity effects in vowel harmony systems in general would be regarded as an odd accident of particular grammars. If, on the other hand, feature prespecification acts as a general constraint on linking, blocking of a spreading property could be made to follow from an independent principle of phonological representation.

In recent work, some phonologists have attempted to place a highly specific condition on targets of assimilation rules, by requiring that the receiving node be unspecified for the spreading constituent (Mascaró 1988, Avery and Rice 1989, Rice and Avery 1991). I refer to such a constraint as the 'Spreading Condition' (henceforth SC). In this view, an autosegment A may link to another autosegment B if and only if B is unspecified for A at the point the spreading occurs. Rice and Avery (1991: 106) formulate this condition as follows:

(15)   *Spreading Condition*

    a. Spreading can only occur if the spreader is spreading to the same node that dominates it, that is, a structural target must be present.

    b. A feature or node can spread only to an empty position.

The SC provides a principled account of the blocking effects of opaque segments in vowel harmony processes. Thus the fact that the vowel /a/ inhibits spreading of the harmonic feature in Akan can be explained in a straightforward manner by assuming that the specified content blocks spreading. Clause (15b) will prevent the harmonic feature from attaching to the opaque unit; further spreading beyond this unit onto other available targets is ruled out, given the prohibition against crossing of association lines. By contrast, the existence of opacity effects is a serious problem for the SCD hipothesis, since nothing would prevent the spreading of a harmonic feature onto the opaque vowel, simultaneously delinking the blocking feature, and further propagating to available targets. Again, under SCD, the fact that languages like Akan exhibit root disharmony would have to be considered a peculiar idiosyncrasy.

An interesting theory-internal consequence of the SC is the requirement that feature content specified on a given node must be delinked prior to spreading. Otherwise, such a node cannot be an elegible target. Thus, confined to the lexical domain, the structure-preserving effects of the

Spreading Condition are in general equivalent to those produced by an SCD mechanism.[24]

There is evidence, however, that clause (15b) is too strong in that it limits the set of possible anchors of spreading operations to those unspecified for the spreading unit. Examples abound in which contour melodies are formed by either spreading or reassociation of a strayed (floating) element, even when the host unit is demonstrably specified. Consider the example of Terena. In this language, nasality spreads from left to right onto any number of segments but it is stopped by an obstruent. However, when the blocker is a (non–glottal) stop, it surfaces as a prenasalized consonant (Durand 1990: 255), in clear contravention of (15b). The emergence of contour structures created by postlexical assimilation rules demonstrates that the Spreading Condition may be irrelevant in the postlexical level. As we shall see in the Galician data examined in section 4.2, nasal consonants in preconsonantal position end up doubly–linked to both a Dorsal node (by application of a default rule) and to another articulator node (by spreading of Place features from a following consonant).

Consider the following three scenarios:

(16)   a. A delinking rule applies to a target in the absence of concomitant spreading.

      b. A spreading rule applies to a target but there is no concomitant delinking.

      c. Both delinking rule and spreading apply to the same target independent of each other, either because the former must precede the latter in the derivation or vice versa.[25]

In the following sections I examine an array of phonological processes that illustrate the interaction of the insert/delete parameter and redundancy rules. In section 3 I establish, in support of (16a), that delinking rules have an autonomous role in phonology, and independent of spreading operations.

---

[24] They differ, however, in one important respect. Unlike the SCD, as qualified by Pulleyblank (1986: 221-222), the Spreading Condition incorrectly predicts that lexical rules may not generate a contour of the type [αF, -αF] ([F] = a feature), even if such a contour is found in underlying representations. Since Structure Preservation is clearly irrelevant in these cases, and some other principle would have to be invoked.

[25] A particularly strong argument for this case could be provided by showing that some other rule intervenes between both operations. In section 4.2, I claim that an adequate account of the nasal co-articulation facts in Galician and Spanish velarizing dialects requires such an analysis.

Further evidence of the autonomy of delinking rules is furnished in section 4, where I analize various assimilation rules illustrating (16b-c). Against SCD, it will be argued that these rules do not operate in a feature-changing fashion. In addition, instances of (16b) provide evidence that spreading rules may in fact apply to specified targets, in contradiction of the SC.

3 Dissimilation and phonological merger

3.1 Old Spanish nasal dissimilation. Among the various types of phonological processes that support (16a), dissimilation rules are perhaps the most compelling. In this section I present an analysis of Old Spanish nasal dissimilation. Crucial for my analysis is the familiar constraint that phonological rules obey locality; that is, both trigger and target must be adjacent at some relevant level of representation (Cole 1987). For any given phonological unit undergoing a rule, adjacency is defined in terms of the 'Locality Condition.' Archangeli and Pulleyblank (1986: 83) define this condition as follows:

(17) α is adjacent to β iff

(i) α and β are on the same tier (content or structure), and

(ii)   there is no γ on tier x such that γ follows α and precedes β, or vice versa.

Locality requirements are universally determined in accordance with the *maximal/minimal parameter* (Archangeli and Pulleyblank 1986, 1987). In a maximal rule adjacency is scanned at either of two levels: the prosodic skeleton or the Rhyme node in syllable structure. Recall that Spanish nasals, when located in a rhyme, assimilate in Place features to a following consonant. Clearly, the rule's trigger and target must satisfy locality in the prosodic skeleton; otherwise, nasal assimilation is blocked. For example, the nasal assimilates to the following /p/ in *trampa* 'trap, snare', and so it surfaces as a labial: [trám.pa], but assimilation does not apply because /s/ intervenes in /transpirar/ 'to perspire', which does not become *[trams.pirar]. Prosodic adjacency may also be satisfied at the rhyme level, in which a feature is spread only to syllable heads, as in many vowel harmony processes. Minimal rules, on the other hand, scan tiers of intrasegmental representation, both features and class nodes.

I would like to argue that Old Spanish nasal dissimilation is a minimal rule. We first observe that Early Old Spanish underwent a process of vowel syncope which applied to non-low vowels in the syllable following main stress in proparoxytonic words.[26] In a large number of lexical items, the process resulted in the creation of nasal clusters, quite generally *m–n* (Menéndez Pidal 1968: 309–310). Subsequently, the second member was dissimilated to /r/.[27] I present evidence, however, that this vowel (or some reduced alternant) was still pronounced in Early Old Spanish.[28] The immediate effect of the dissimilation is a sequence of sonorants whose sonority differential is too small to constitute an admissible onset. In Old Spanish (much as in the modern language) nasal–flap sequences did not satisfy a minimal syllable–edge sonority distance. The conflict was resolved by the insertion of an intrusive stop between the two members of the cluster, its Place features being determined by the preceding consonant, and its stricture features by universal default rules (cf. Wetzels 1985, Clements 1987, Martínez–Gil 1991).[29] Some representative examples of regular correspondences produced by these changes are illustrated in (18):

(18)	*Latin*	*Early Old Sp.*	*Mod. Sp.*	
	femina	femna/femra	fembra	'female'
	homine	omne/omre	hombre	'man'
	lumine	lumne/lumre	lumbre	'fire'
	famine	famne/famre	hambre	'hunger'
	nomine	nomne/nomre	nombre	'name'

Nasal dissimilation can be formally expressed by delinking of a nasal specification from the second member in a sequence of two nasals. A first approximation would be as in (19):

---

[26] Old Spanish vowel syncope must be clearly distinguished from a much older Proto–Romance rule of post-tonic vowel syncope rule, which converted /-min-/ into /-mn-/ sequences, thus merging with the original /-mn-/ Latin clusters. Here, the first member of the cluster underwent total assimilation to the following nasal, producing a geminate whose historical reflex is a palatal nasal [ñ] in Old Spanish (e.g., *dominu > domnu > donno > dueño* 'lord'), while its more recent counterpart is the dissimilated /-mr-/ cluster (cf. example (18).

[27] In the earliest records we find both the dissimilated and undissimilated outcomes, sometimes even in the same document (Menéndez Pidal 1968: 309ff.). On the other hand, it is interesting to note that although the dissimilation sequence has its mirror image *n–m*, in both cases it is the least marked nasal (i.e., a coronal) that dissimilates: *minimare > mermar* 'to diminish'; in other cases, dissimilation yields a lateral: *anima > alma* 'soul' (cf. Old French *arme*).

[28] Some spellings from as late as the 12th century still contain an unsyncopated vowel (Menéndez Pidal 1968: 161–168).

[29] A similar process also took place in Old French (Walker 1978, 1981, Morin 1980, 1987, Wetzels 1985).

(19)   OSp. nasal dissimilation (preliminary version)

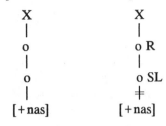

However, as stated, rule (19) contains some irrelevant information. Specifically, reference to two adjacent X-slots in the prosodic skeleton would give dissimilation the status of a maximal rule. However, there is aboundant evidence that the rule was minimal. First, prior to the stage of intrusive consonant formation, the items in (18) were consistently spelled *femna/femra*, *omne/omre*, etc., which indicates that the cluster in each case was heterorganic. Clearly, the fact that the first nasal does not assimilate in these items cannot be attributed to scribal practice; nor can it be due to the (nasal) nature of the second member, as seems to be the case in Modern Spanish *alumno* 'student', *columna* 'column', etc. (Harris 1984b). The presence of unassimilated nasals ceases to be striking when confronted with systematic spellings of the same type in other lexical items exhibiting nasal–obstruent sequences: *comde* (< *comite*) 'nobleman', *limde* (< *limite*) 'boundary', and many others. Second, syllable-final /m/ does not occur otherwise at any stage of Old Spanish, except when it is followed by a homorganic labial.

   Menéndez Pidal (1968) has argued forcefully that the presence of such unexpected heterorganic nasal–consonant clusters in Old Spanish is to be attributed to an intervening vowel at this stage.[30] He suggests that the syncopated vowel was still 'a living memory' in the speech of the period, and he speculates that syncope was completed in a gradual process, from a full vowel, to a reduced vowel (he suggests a schwa), to complete deletion.[31] Menéndez Pidal's insight can be recast in our theoretical context by interpreting that the vowel in question was still present in underlying

---

[30] See pp. 163–166, 309, 313–314, and especially 318–320.

[31] 'En casos como *comde, limde, semdero* la nasal no se ha asimilado aún al punto de articulación de la consonante siguiente; ambas se articulan con entera dependencia una de otra, mediando un hiato o espacio entre ambas, o dando a una y otra consonante la mayor duración de cuando van intervocálica. Esta larga y bien distinta pronunciación de ambas consonantes *obedece al recuerdo vivo que aún subsiste de la vocal postónica perdida,* y que la escritura de entonces representaba a veces con una vocal indiferente, que debemos suponer relajada o muda: *comide,* que se pronunciaría *comede* o **comode....* Otras veces la exageración en la articulación de la *m* se manifiesta en su desnasalización final, surgiendo después de ella una b: limbde; esta consonante de transición se olvidará cuando la asimilación de las consonantes originarias se haya generalizado e impuesto completamente' (1968: 319) [my emphasis].

representations at the stage in which the nasal dissimilation rule was added to the grammar. This assumption would also account for the blocking effect on nasal assimilation in items such as *comde, limde.*

There are four pieces of evidence in favor of positing an underlying vowel. First, in Hispano–Romance a flap is strengthened into trill both in word–initial and postconsonantal positions.[32] The process is well attested in early medieval spelling practice: a double grapheme *rr* always represents a trill, while a single *r* usually stands for a flap. The simplest interpretation of spellings such as *omre, femra* in (18) is that *r*–strengthening was blocked by the intervening vowel. It is interesting to note that *r*-strengthening in fact applied to some of these forms, as witnessed by Galician–Portuguese and western Leonese *xen[r̄]o* (< *gen(e)ru*).[33] Second, in Old Spanish vowel syncope applied optionally to the object pronouns *me* 'me' and *le* 'to him/her' in proclitic position. Significantly, when syncope results in a nasal-liquid sequence the appropriate environment for intrusive consonant formation is created, and the rule also applies in these cases.[34] Thus in the *Poema de Mio Cid* the clitic sequence *ni me la* (lit. 'neither from me it-fem.') becomes *nimbla* (through intermediate *nim'la*), as in: *nimbla messó fijo de mora nin de cristiana* (v. 3286).[35] Third, there are scores of verbs in Old Spanish in which the stressed theme vowel of second and third conjugation verbs alternates with zero in the simple future and conditional tenses, where the vowel no longer bears stress. Here too, intrusive consonant insertion is triggered under the appropriate conditions, namely, when after syncope a 'bad' syllable contact is created: *doler/doldrá/doldría* 'to hurt/it will hurt/it woud hurt', *fallesçer/fallestrá/ fallestría* 'to die', *salir/saldrá/saldría* 'to leave', *yaçer/yazdrá/yazdría* 'to lie, rest'(Martínez-Gil 1991). And fourth, in some documents from the 11th and 12th centuries many words preserve the post-tonic vowel (e.g. *comide, limide*), while in later documents such words were invariably subject to syncope (Menéndez Pidal 1968: 163ff.). In some cases the syncopated and the unsyncopated forms are variably used by the same scribe. These arguments clearly support intrusive consonant formation as a synchronic rule at some historical stage in Old Spanish.

---

[32] Cf. Lloyd (1987: 244). A similar rule is motivated for Modern Spanish in Harris (1983: 62-ff.).

[33] Latin *honorare* 'to honor' yielded *ondrar* in some Old Spanish varieties (by regular dissimilation and intrusive consonant formation), but *onrrar* in others, in which the spelling leaves no doubts about the effect of *r*-strengthening (cf. Modern Spanish *hon[r̄]ra* 'honor').

[34] In the *Poema de Mio Cid* (Michael 1980), for example, we find examples such as 'Ascóndese de Mio Cid, ca *nol'* [= no le] ozan dezir nada' (v. 30), and 'Ya mugier doña Ximena, *nom'lo* [= no me lo] aviedes rogado' (v. 1763).

[35] '*Neither* has the child of a Moor or a Cristian ever pulled *it from me*' (El Cid boasts about the fact that no one had ever dared 'pull his beard', an idiom that in medieval times presumably had connotations beyond the obvious physical denotation).

Following Menéndez Pidal's suggestion, I assume a first stage in which the vowel was reduced to a schwa. The process can be captured by a rule that delinks the vowel's Supralaryngeal features. The result is a vocoid specified as [-consonantal], the phonological structure that some have ascribed to a schwa (cf. Anderson 1982, Montreuil 1989), as in (20a). Vowel syncope involves further delinking of the remaining melodic specification, as in (20b). The result is a floating X-slot (*X'* in the output of (20b)), the prosodic unit to which the intrusive consonant will attach (Martínez-Gil 1991):

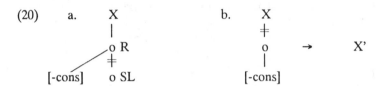

(20)   a.   X   b.   X

I assume further that nasal assimilation was ordered before vowel syncope at this stage. This assumption can be motivated as follows: (i) aside from the apparently exceptional cases we have mentioned, there is absolutely no evidence suggesting that nasal assimilation ever failed to apply at any historical stage in Spanish since Latin times; and (ii) in the unmarked case, sound changes are added to a grammar at to the end of the phonological component (King 1968, Kiparsky 1982b).

Further evidence for the claim that nasal dissimilation cannot be a maximal rule is provided by a few lexical items in which similar transparency effects are obtained. Here, however, in addition to a vowel, dissimilation also applies across an intervening consonant, such as /d/ and /g/ in (21):[36]

(21) | *Latin* | *Early Old Sp.* | *Old Sp.* | |
|---|---|---|---|
| glandine | landne | landre | 'bubo' |
| *lendine | liendne | liendre | 'nit' |
| sanguine | sangne | sangre | 'blood' |
| *inguene | ingne | ingle | 'groin' |

Since nasal assimilation is a maximal rule and therefore requires strict adjacency of trigger and target in the prosodic tier, the blocking effects on nasal assimilation can now be given a natural and simple explanation. Following Yip (1989) I interpret the dissimilatory operation as triggered by the Obligatory Contour Principle (OCP), which prohibits identical adjacent

---

[36] Notice that dissimilation yields [l] in *ingle*, clearly an idiosyncratic development.

elements in the same tier. Nasal dissimilation can now be formalized as follows:

(22)   *OSp. nasal dissimilation (final version)*

```
    o              o SL
    |              ‡
 [+nas]          [+nas]
```

In order to obtain the dissimilated segment, we need only invoke a universal redundancy rule which states that non–nasal sonorants are [–lateral] continuants in the default case, precisely the feature values of [r]:

(23)   [+son, –nas]   →   [–lat, +cont]

Assuming that the intervening segments are not specified for [nasal], dissimilation applies to the intermediate forms [ómǝne], [sángǝne] because at the relevant level of scansion (the nasal tier) both nasals are adjacent and thus no violation of locality occurs (recall that the intervening reduced vowel in (24) does not have a Supralaryngeal node):

(24)   a.   *o   m   ǝ   n   e*

```
         |            |
         o            o SL
         |            ‡
      [+nas]        [+nas]
```

         b.   *s   a   n   g   ǝ   n   e*

```
              |     |            |
              o     o            o SL
              |                  ‡
           [+nas]              [+nas]
```

Dissimilation (22) and default assignment (23) will then apply to both items in (24). Subsequent application of subject vowel deletion and intrusive consonant formation yields the Modern Spanish forms [ómbre] and [sáŋgre].

Being a maximal rule, nasal assimilation requires strict adjacency of trigger and target in the prosodic skeleton. The presence of the syncopated vowel at the point the rule applies would bleed assimilation, thus explaining the blocking effects on in (18) and (21), as well as in items such as *comde*, *limde*, as shown in the following sample derivation (the order of nasal assimilation and vowel reduction is not crucial, but the former must precede vowel syncope):

(25)	/femina/	/sangine/	/limide/
Vowel reduction (20a):	femǝna	sangǝne	limǝde
Nasal assimilation:	(n.a.)	saŋgǝne	(n.a.)
Nasal dissimilation (22):	femǝra	saŋgǝre	(n.a.)
Vowel syncope (20b):	femra	saŋgre	limde
Consonant intrusion:	fembra	(n.a.)	(n.a.)
Output	[fembra]	[saŋgre]	[limde]

There is a less abstract alternative analysis to items in (18) and (21) which does not appeal to the maximal/minimal distinction. In fact, suppose that nasal dissimilation is maximal and thus requires strict adjacency of both nasals. Under this analysis, no underlying vowel is required. Therefore both vowel reduction and vowel syncope can be dispensed with, and the derivation would simply proceed from underlying /femna/, presumably by lexical restructuring of former /femina/. This would also entail the underlying form /sangne/. Notice, however, that we still need to explain the spelling *ng* in *sangne*, since tautosyllabic /ng/ does not constitute a well-formed rhyme at any stage of Spanish. We might propose that it represents a velar nasal [ŋ]. Since intrusive consonant formation copies the Place features of the first nasal, [ŋ] can only have two sources: /ŋ/ or /ng/. At stake here is the ultimate source of the /g/ intervening between the nasal and the rhotic in Modern Spanish *sangre*; namely, whether it was preserved from the original Latin root, or whether it derives from intrusive consonant formation. The first option is untenable, since underlying velar nasals do not occur otherwise at any stage in the history of Spanish. As for the second option, one needs to postulate an underlying representation /ng/ by two crucially ordered rules: (i) nasal assimilation (/sangne/ → [saŋgne]); and (ii) *g*-deletion ([saŋgne] → [saŋne]). The output of (ii) would then be subject to dissimilation ([saŋne] → [saŋre]) which, in turn, feeds insertion of the intrusive consonant [g]. This alternative presents two shortcomings. First, the preservation of the etymological /g/ in a coda would be quite unlikely, since historically coda stops were either vocalized or deleted, the latter being the usual outcome when the stop is the second member of a cluster of tautosyllabic consonants. Notice, furthermore, the derivation of [saŋgne] from /sangne/ would require deletion of the velar stop only to be inserted immediately by intrusive consonant formation. Second, and most important, the fact that nasal assimilation does not apply in (18), as well as in items such as *comde*, *limde*, would be left unaccounted for. Of course, the latter problem can be circumvented if we posit an underlying vowel. This would allow for a statement of Old Spanish dissimilation maintaining the strict adjacency hypothesis, as in (19), provided that the rule is ordered after vowel syncope, although it would still have to apply prior to nasal assimilation, in order to obtain the blocking effects on the latter rule.

But such a move would be beside the point; there is overwhelming empirical evidence that dissimilation rules obey the minimal parameter, and thus should be expressed within this formal context; this notwithstanding the presence of other phonological properties which may sometimes conspire to convey a resemblance of maximality. Indeed, an analysis that requires strict adjacency would attribute an exceptional character to the Old Spanish dissimilation facts, thus obscuring its phonological relationship to similar, abundant dissimilatory phenomena found in the historical development of Spanish and other Romance languages, in which adjacency is clearly irrelevant. If these observations are correct, there is nothing surprising about the dissimilatory process shown in (24). Indeed, at some historical stage, almost every Romance language (including Spanish) has undergone similar types of long–distance dissimilation, traditionally ascribed to the class of 'sporadic' (i.e., irregular) sound changes. Dissimilation occurred most frequently in sequences of liquids and nasals, but is not by any means confined to this class (Grammont 1895, Posner 1961). The following are illustrative examples (most of them from Posner 1961):

1. Nasal dissimilation: Spanish (also Tuscan) *Antolin* (name) (< *Antoninu*), *Coromina(s)* (name) (< *condominiu* 'shared property, land'), *delante* 'in front of (< *de in ante*), *caramelo* 'candy' (< *cannamelle*) *montaraz* 'wild, mountain–like' (< *montanaz*), *comulgar* 'to take communion' (< *communicare*); Argentine Spanish *bayonesa* (< French *mayonnaise*), *desboronar* (< MSp. *desmoronar* 'to collapse'); Old Leonese *calonigo* 'canon' (< *canonicu*); Portuguese *lembrar* 'to remember' (< memorare), *abstilencia* (< *abstinentia* 'abstinence'); Catalan *Barcelona* (name) (< *Barcinona*); Provençal *corlamuso* 'bag–pipe' (< French *cornemuse*), *camparol* 'mushroom' (from *Campania*); south–west French proto–form **verenu* (< *venenu*); French *orphelin* 'orphan' (< *orphaninu*); Walloon *bargamer* 'to combine' (< *amalgamare*); Corsican *timurella* 'aperture where the propeller works' (< timonella); Corsican and Sicilian *riformu* 'uniform' (< *uniforme*); Old Campidian *muristeri* 'monastery' (< *monasteriu*); Italian *meliaca* 'apricot' (< *armeniaca*), *scheranzia* 'quinsy' (< Greek *kynankhe* 'dog–collar'; cf. OSp. *esquilencia*), *gonfalone* 'banner'(< West Germanic **gundfano*; cf. MSp. *confalón*, Provençal *gonfairó*); Calabrian *vignanu* 'terrace' (< *maenianu*); Sursilvan *abuldonza* 'abundance' (< *abundantia*); Rumanian *irimă* 'soul' (< *anima*).

2. Liquid dissimilation: OSp. *almario* 'cupboard' (< *armariu*; cf. Catalan *almari*, Old French *almaire*); MSp. *árbol* 'tree' (<*arbore*; cf. Italian *albero*), *fraile* 'friar' (< *fratre*; cf. French *frère*), *cárcel* (<*carcere*), *taladro* (< *taradru*), *Guillermo* (name) (< *Guillelmo*), *mármol* 'marble' (< *marmore*); dialectal MSp. *celebro* 'skull'(< *cerebru*); Leonese *colambre* 'pelt'(< *coriamine*); Portuguese *lobo cerval* 'wolf'(< *lupu cervariu*); Catalan *aladre*

'plough' (< *aratru*); Old French *alondre* (< from *arondne* < *harundine* 'reed'), French *flairer* 'to smell' (< *fragrare*), *rossignol* 'nightingale' (< **lusciniolu*), *remoulache* (from Middle French *ramorache* < *armoracea*) ; Middle French *coronel* 'coronel' (for *colonel*); Troyes French *épleindre* 'to squeeze out' (< *exprhymere*); Lombard *lavarin* 'gold finch' (der. of *rapu* 'turnip'), *martol* 'silly' (< *martyr*); Vulgar Latin *fragellu* (< *flagellu* 'whip'), *grandula* (< *glandula* 'small acorn'); Italian *mercoledí* 'Wednesday' (< *Mercuri Die*), *groviglio* (< *globellu* 'small globe'); North Italian versions of the proto–form **curtellu* 'knife' (<*cultellu*); Cerignola *kelumbre* 'first fruit of fig–tree' (< *columbula* 'little dove'); Friulian *ladros* 'topsy–turvy'(< *retrorsu* 'backwards'); Pirano (Istria) *zerbelajo* 'type of net' (< *cerberariu*); Venetian *Malgeri* (name) (< *Margarita*); Vegliot *saraula* 'sister' (< *sorore*); Irpinian *leggistro* 'records'(< *registru*); Engadine *coriandel* 'coriander' (< *coriandru*); South Tyrol *algordar* 'to recall' (< *recordare*); Romagnol *litrat* (< *retractu* 'withdrawn, distant').

Finally, a well–known example of liquid dissimilation is discussed in Steriade (1987b: 351–352). Old Latin underwent a historical rule of long–distance dissimilation affecting /l/ in the adjectival suffix /–alis/ > /–aris/. Steriade observes that the process took place when the suffixal /l/ was preceded by another lateral in the stem, independent of the number of intervening segments. Since vowels and non–liquids do not bear any specification in the lateral tier, adjacency of both laterals is met, and so dissimilation obtains: /sol+alis/ > /sol+aris/ 'solar', /Latia+lis/ > /Lati+aris/ 'of Latium', /milit+alis/ > /milit+aris/ 'military.' However, dissimilation was blocked when the non–lateral liquid /r/ intervenes: /sepulchr+alis/ 'funereal', /floral+lis/ 'floral', /litor+alis/ 'of the shore' (cf. */sepulchr+aris/, etc.). Steriade argues that since the intervening /r/ is specified as [–lateral] in Latin, adjacency of both laterals in these items no longer obtains, and thus the rule is blocked.

The facts discussed in this section illustrate the interaction of delinking rules and universal redundancy principles, bringing out some interesting connections with other synchronic facts of Old Spanish which otherwise would not be immediately obvious. Finally, features and subsequent application of universal default rules appear to be the appropriate mechanism to capture dissimilation rules. In the case of nasal dissimilation in Old Spanish, the only available alternative a would be feature-changing rule that states the change as /n/ → [r] is hardly an illuminating solution, since the fact that the outcome is almost invariably a sonorant or a homorganic obstruent, and not some arbitrary segment, would be considered an accident.

3.2 Vowel lowering and metaphony in Proto-Spanish.
The commonly held view in Romance scholarship is that the vowel systems of Late Latin and Early Romance exhibited lax/tense contrasts among non-low vowels (in our terms, [RTR]/non-[RTR]). It is also the general opinion that this scenario

came about through the historical loss of vowel length distinctions in the system of Classical Latin (but cf. Klausenburger 1975). Although [RTR] distinctions apparently existed in Classical Latin, they were redundant and wholly predictable from vowel length in high and mid vowels. As a result of the loss of vowel length, the tenseness/laxness attribute, formerly dependent on the long/short distinction, now became phonemic. Thus the non-[RTR] vowels /i, u/ (from long /iː, uː/ contrasted with [RTR] /I, U/ (from short /e, o/) and non-[RTR] /e, o/ (from Latin long /eː, oː/) were opposed to [RTR] /E, O/ (from Latin short /e, o/). In a subsequent shift, believed to have taken place by the second or third centuries A.D., high [RTR] vowels merged with their mid non-[RTR] ones at the Proto Western-Romance stage. Such was the system of Proto-Spanish prior to the diphthongization of mid [RTR] vowels, and it has been preserved in most Western-Romance varieties Of course, the modern reflexes of the original proto-vowels in particular languages may not coincide due to other historical changes, such as mid-vowel diphthongization (or lack thereof), metaphony, and so on.[37] The three historical stages are shown in (26):

(26)

	Classical Latin		Late Latin		Proto-Spanish	
i/iː:	u/uː:	i	u	i	u
e/eː:	o/oː:	I	U	e	E
	a/aː:	e	o	E	E
		E	O		a
			a		

Primarily as a consequence of this merger, [RTR] distinctions among high vowels have not survived in the Romance languages. Some illustrative correspondences between Latin and Modern Spanish are given in (27) (the relevant Latin vowel is shown in boldface for clarity):

(27) a. /e, I/ > /e/:   b. /o, U/ > /o/:

Latin	Sp.		Latin	Sp.	
rete	red	'net'	totu	todo	'all'
plenu	lleno	'full'	flore	flor	'flower'
pilu	pelo	'hair'	cubitu	codo	'elbow'
silva	selva	'forest'	bucca	boca	'mouth'

In accordance with the feature hierarchy in (3) and the underspecification theory assumed in this paper, the underlying representations of high [RTR] vowels in Late Latin in (26) would be as in (28):

---

[37] See Menéndez-Pidal (1980), Lloyd (1987), Otero (1988), Penny (1991).

(28)

The neutralization of high [RTR] vowels can be captured by means of two rules, delinking [+high] and the Radical node, respectively:

(29) *High and Radical Delinking*:

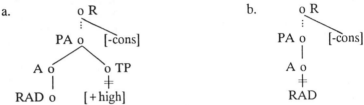

The output of (29) becomes now available for assignment of the default specifications for Proto-Spanish vowels, stated earlier in (9), which produces the non-[RTR] mid vowels /e, o/. The two relevant redundancy rules are repeated in (30) for convenience.

(30) *Default Assignment*

a.   [ ]   →   [o TP, -high]   (= (9i))
b.   [ ]   →   [o TP, -low]   (= (9ii))

Notice that the particular organization of the Place node in the hierarchy in (3) requires the postulation of two delinking rules. The same effect could be achieved by one single rule delinking the Place node, since this constituent immediately dominates the Articulators and Tongue Position nodes. However, this possibility is excluded by the fact that delinking of Place features would wipe out the Labial node in /U/. Subsequent application of (30) would wrongly predict */e/ as the historical reflex of this vowel.

Proto-Spanish vowel metaphony is a rather complex issue, and I will not attempt to review all its details here.[38] My discussion will focus exclusively on non-verb forms. Put succinctly, the metaphony process consists of a restricted (bounded) kind of vowel harmony whereby stressed non-low vowels are raised by one degree by assimilation to a 'yod' or palatal element contained in a high front glide in the last syllable of a word. In many

---

[38] Cf. Alarcos Llorach (1974), Craddock (1980), Menéndez Pidal (1980), Lloyd (1987), Penny (1991) and references therein. See Malkiel (1966) and Harris (1975) for detailed studies of metaphony in verb forms.

instances, this yod was created by desyllabification of a front vowel. Under certain conditions which need not concern us here, it underwent deletion at some later stage. These comprise the cases that Menéndez Pidal (1980: 44-ff.) includes in the domain of the second and third yods.[39] By raising the lax mid vowels /E, O/, metaphony bled many potential targets of Proto-Spanish dipthonguization. The correspondences in (31a-d) are representative of the metaphonic changes. As illustrated in (31e), the low vowel /a/ fails to undergo metaphony.

(31)

a. /E/ > /e/

Latin	Old Sp.	
pulegiu	poleo	'pennyroyal'
nerviu	nervio	'sinew'
mediu	meyo	'half'
ingeniu	engeño	'invention'

b. /O/ > /o/

Latin	Old Sp.	
fovea	foya	'pit'
podiu	poyo	'bench'
folia	foja	'leaf'
spoliu	(d)espojo	'booty'

c. /e, I/ > /i/

Latin	Old Sp.	
vendemia	vendimia	'harvest'
sepia	xibia	'cattle fish'
fastidiu	fastío	'boredom'
vitreu	vidrio	'glass'

d. /o, U/ > /u/

Latin	Old Sp.	
vitoneu	viduño	'vine'
terroneu	terruño	'soil'
rubeu	ruyo	'blond'
muliere	mujer	'woman'

---

[39] Menéndez Pidal distinguishes four types of yods. The first one is irrelevant here since it does not have any metaphonic effect on vowels. The forth yod has two sources. The first source is the reflex of a vocalized syllable-final velar stop or a lateral: *lacte* → *la[j]te* → *leche* 'milk'; *nocte* → *no[j]te* → *noche* 'eight', *multu* → *mu[j]tu* → *mucho* 'plenty' (cf. Galician *leite, noite, muito*). The second source is the regular metathesis of /-VCjV-/ into /-VjCV-/ sequences: *altariu* → *alta[j]ru* → *otero* 'hill'; *caseu* → *ca[j]su* → *queso* 'cheese' (cf. Galician *outeiro, queixo*). Although most scholars also include these cases under metaphony, there are compelling reasons to believe we are dealing with a very different kind of phenomenon (let us call it 'vowel raising'). The first is historical: the diphthong /aj/, for example, is still found in 12th-century Mozarabic forms, such as *pandáyr* (< *pandairu* < *pandariu*) 'tambourine', *febráyr* (<*febrairu* < *februariu*) 'february', etc. (Menéndez Pidal 1964: 90), while metaphony triggered by the second and third yods is well attested in Vulgar Latin. The two other are phonological: in vowel raising the glide is tautosyllabic with the target vowel, while in metaphony the glide it is invariably located in the following syllable. In addition, while the low vowel /a/ was almost unfailingly affected by the fourth yod, it remained impervious to metaphony, as illustrated in (31e). Although the fourth yod did raise lax mid vowels at an early stage in many Proto-Spanish words, thereby bleeding diphthonguization in *noche, ocho*, etc., raising did not occur in other Hispano-Romance varieties, in which lax mid vowels diphthongize regularly (cf. Old Leonese and Old Aragonese *nueite, ueito*; Zamora Vicente 1979: 150, 242). This topic deserves more space than can be granted here. Instaed, my analysis will focus exclusively on the harmonic effects of the second and third yods.

e. /a/

Latin	Old Sp.	
exagiu	ensayo	'attempt'
radiare	rayar	'to scratch'
palia	paja	'straw'
aranea	araña	'spider'
fagea	faya	'beech tree'

Metaphony is illustrative of one of the classical problems in generative phonology: the impossibility of formally expressing in a unitary fashion rules which, as in the case of Proto-Spanish, can be informally stated as the 'raising of vowels height by one degree' (cf. Contreras 1969, Hyman 1988).[40]   In autosegmental terms, the only viable solution, so it would seem, is to posit two spreading rules: (i) a first rule of [+high] harmony, applicable to [+ATR] vowels: /e, o/ → [i, u]; and (ii) a second rule of [+ATR] harmony, whose targets would be [-ATR] vowels: /I, U/ → [i, u] and /E, O/ → [e, o].   Of course, the order of these two rules is irrelevant, provided that they apply to their specified targets.   I have assumed, however, that tongue root retraction is a monovalent feature; since non-[RTR] front vowels lack a Radical node, there is simply no Tongue Root feature available for spreading.   I would like to argue, however, that only one rule is involved, namely one of high harmony. In fact, one may argue that the mid vowel shift along the height parameter is the expected result once certain facts concerning the interaction of universal and language-specific principles are adequately examined.   Suppose we state the metaphony rule as in (32) (N' = a non-head position; notice that tongue position features are unspecified in mid vowels):

(32) *High Harmony:*

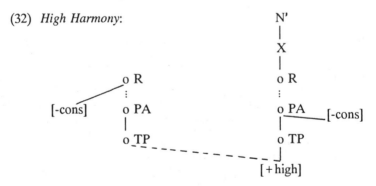

---

[40] This is a consequence of the fact that only three degrees of height can be registered in terms of the feaures [high] and [low]. Accordingly, the feature [tense] or, alternatively, [ATR] has been traditionally used to establish a fourth height distinction in vowels. It should be pointed out, however, that this problem does not stem from assuming any particular version of the feature hierarchy known to me. Rather, it seems to be a shortcoming of general phonetic theory.

The effect of (32) is to raise /e, o/ to [i, u], and /E, O/ to [I, U]. The latter will then meet the structural description of the neutralization rules (27)-(29), which will turn them into [e, o], a common kind of telescoping effect. We still have to account for the [i, u] reflexes of the high [RTR] vowels in the relevant items in (31c-d). If the representations of these words were to contain the [RTR] vowels /I, U / at the stage in which (32) applies, they would not have been affected by high harmony (i.e., the rule would have applied vacuously to them), since these vowels are already [+high]. Therefore, the prediction is that they would have followed the harmonic pattern of /E, O/, not that of /e, o/. This assumption, however, lacks any justification, since we have established that the grammar of Proto-Spanish contains the rules (29)-(30), which are independently needed in order to account for the neutralization of underlying high [RTR] vowels. The logical conclusion is that the high [RTR] vowels in items such as *fastidiu, rubeu*, etc. in (31c-d) had already undergone lowering, thus merging with /e, o/ at the point high harmony became applicable. The observation that metaphony treated /I, U/ and /e, o/ alike simply follows from the existence of the neutralization rules (29)-(30) in the grammar of Proto-Spanish.

Our next task now is to determine whether high harmony (32) applied in an SCD fashion. I would argue that it did not, provided we make certain reasonable assumptions, which in any event are justified independently by general principles of underspecification theory. Recall that the default values for Proto-Spanish vowels are those of /e/. The relevant redundancy rule here is (30a) (= (9i)), which assigns [-high] as the default value for mid vowels. In accordance with the principle that redundacy rules apply as late as possible in the derivation (Archangeli and Pulleyblank 1986: 13), we simply need to assume that high harmony applies at a stage in which the underlying set of mid vowels /e, o, E, O/ are still unspecified. The same assumption can be extended to those instances of /I, U/ undergoing high harmony. My point is that although the latter are subject to the delinking rules in (29), default assignment of [-high] by (30a) was superseded by high harmony. In short, at the point (32) applies all target vowels are unspecified for the [high], and receive [+high] by spreading from the target yod. Sample derivations are shown in (33) for items containing [RTR] vowels (boldfaced **I** and **U** represent the neutralized high [RTR] vowels resulting from the application of the delinking rules in (29)):

(33)	/mOdiu/	/fOlia/	/fastIdiu/	/rUbeu/
Desyllabification:	mOdju	fOlja	fastIdju	rUbju
Delinking (29):	(n.a)	(n.a.)	fastIdiu	rUbju
Metaphony (32):	mUdju	fUlja	fastidju	rubju
Default assignment (30):	modju	folja	(n.a.)	(n.a.)
Output (Proto-Sp. stage)	modju	folja	fastidju	rubju

Finally, we can provide a straightforward explanation for the failure of /a/ to undergo high harmony, by simply assuming (i) that this vowel is underlyingly specified as [+low] (cf. (8) in section 1.3), and (ii) that high harmony is not feature-changing. The application of high harmony would produce a vowel that contains two contradictory specifications (i.e. [+low] and [+high]), a structure which is universally disallowed.

I conclude that two redundancy rules, independently needed to account for the neutralization of high [RTR] vowels, interact in a subtle--but nevertheless crucial--way with the metaphonic process. It may well be that other processes involving changes along the four-degree parameter of vowel height are ultimately amenable to an underspecification analysis. Hyman (1989), for example, has proposed a solution along these lines for Esimbi, a language whose alternation patterns in vowel height far exceeds in complexity and detail those of Proto-Spanish.

4. Partial and total assimilation.
4.1 Vowel rounding in Ferrol Galician. A compelling piece of evidence against both the SCD and the SC mechanisms is found in the Ferrol dialect of Galician. The facts on vowel rounding in this dialect also provide support for the hypothesis that [round] is a monovalent feature.

The underlying vowel system of Galician is identical to Proto–Spanish in (4). Therefore it is subject to the configuration constraint in (10), which prohibits front round vowels from the lexical phonology. In the Ferrol variety, there is a postlexical rule that rounds a unstressed mid vowel in contact with a labial consonant (Porto Dapena 1977: 21, 112). Some correspondences between standard Galician and the Ferrol variety are shown in (34):

(34)	Underlying	Standard Gal.	Ferrol Gal.	
	/fErOl/	[fEról]	[föról]	(Name)
	/lebar/	[leβár]	[löβár]	'to carry'
	/abelaiña/	[aβelaíña]	[aβölaíña]	'moth'
	/memoria/	[memórja]	[mömórja]	'memory'

If [round] were to be characterized as a binary feature, we would obtain the Place configurations of [b] and [ö] shown in (35):

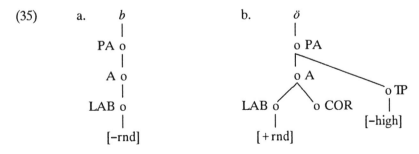

Clearly, mid-vowel rounding involves spreading of the Labial node from an adjacent labial consonant to the left. If this node were to contain the specification [−round], as in (35), no such rule can be stated, because the output would not be a round vowel. If on the other hand [round] is privative, the rule can be easily stated as follows:

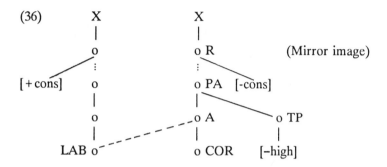

(36) X   X
      | |
      o   o R   (Mirror image)
     ⟋ ⋮   ⋮ ⟍
[+cons] o   o PA [−cons]
      | |⟍
      o   _o A   `o TP
      | ⟋ | |
LAB o⟋   o COR   [−high]

Since vowels contaning a labial node are predictably [round], a specification is supplied at no cost by the universal default rule (9iii).

Vowel rounding in Ferrol Galician provides a first illustration of an assimilation rule whose target contains a specified segment. Rule (36) spreads the Labial node but, crucially, the Coronal specification must not be delinked by the spreading operation, since the outcome would be a back vowel, not a front one. On the other hand, the SC would outrule linking because the target's Articulators node is already specified. Thus both approaches would characterize vowel rounding as an unlikely rule.

4.2   Nasal co-articulation in Galician and Spanish. A further argument against the SCD and SC hypothesis is found in common assimilatory processes, such as nasal assimilation. Underlying contrasts among nasals in all Spanish dialects are confined to three points of articulation: labial /m/, alveolar /n/, and palatal /ñ/ (e.g., *cama* 'bed' ~ *cana* 'grey hair' ~ *caña* 'cane'). As already mentioned, when assigned to a rhyme, nasals assimilate in Place features to a following consonant. However, in non-assimilating environments syllable-finally, nasals acquire a uniform Place specification. For example, in standard dialects they consistently surface as an alveolar [n]. In order to account for this dialectal group, Harris (1984a, 1984b) proposes a delinking rule to the effect of (37a), which disassociates the Place features of a nasal when located in a rhyme; rule (37b) illustrates the spreading of Place features in nasal assimilation:

(37) a.

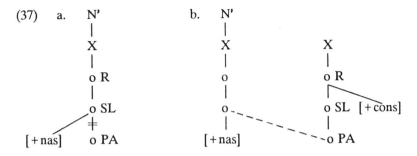

Harris argues that if assimilation (37b) were to be stated as simultaneous spreading and delinking (e.g., as in Goldsmith 1981), an unnecessary complexity would be added to the formulation of the rule, since (37a) is needed independently of assimilation in order to account for rhyme neutralization in non-assimilating environments. In other words, an analysis in terms of the SCD mechanism concedes no formal relationship between delinking in (37a) and delinking in assimilation. As a consequence, the same delinking process would have to be stated twice in the grammar of Spanish, an ostensible candidate for Occam's razor.

I follow Harris in assuming that nasals are not specified for Place features at the point where assimilation applies, as shown in (37b); nasals acquire their surface alveolar features by a universal redundancy rule, which I state as follows:

(38)   *Default Assignment (Spanish)*

[+nas] → [o Cor, +ant]

However, in a considerable number of Spanish dialects the neutralized nasal consistently surfaces with a velar point of articulation: [ŋ]. The same phenomenon is also found in Galician. The interesting aspect of Galician is that nasal velarization by default also applies in assimilating environments. Articulatorily, they are produced with two simultaneous occlusions: one produced by raising the tongue dorsum towards the velum, and the other determined by with the point of articulation of the following consonant. In short, a nasal is dorsolabial before a labial, a dorso–dental before a dental, dorso–palatal before a palatal, and so on. As expected, there is simply one velar articulation before a velar consonant.[41] Examples of the whole range

---

[41] The co-articulatory process is overlooked by most recent descriptive grammars and dialectal studies of Galician, although all of them include some brief reference to nasal velarization (Veiga Arias 1976, Porto Dapena 1977, Carballo Calero 1979, Alvarez et al. 1986, Fernandez Rei 1990). There is no systematic phonetic study comparable to Navarro Tomás' (1977) unequalled manual on Castilian Spanish.

of nasal co-articulations in the dialect I am describing are illustrated in (39) for the word *can* /kan/ 'dog':[42]

(39) *Underlying*   *Surface*

/kan # parbo/	[kám̩ párβu]	'silly dog'
/kan # ferido/	[kám̩ firídu]	'wounded dog'
/o+kan # de+Ela/	[ukáṇ̩ déla]	'her dog'
/kan # tolo/	[káṇ̩ tólu]	'crazy dog'
/kan # san/	[káṇ̩ sáŋ]	'healthy dog'
/o+kan # noso]	[ukáṇ̩ nósu]	'our dog'
/kan # ruin/	[káṇ̩ ruíŋ]	'mean dog'
/kan # šОben/	[káṇ̩ šóβiŋ]	'skilfull dog'
/kan # čino/	[káṇ̩ čínu]	'Chinese dog'
/din+ʝe # o+kan/	[dĩ̯ʝu káŋ]	'I gave him the dog'
/kan # xordo/	[káŋ xórdu]	'fat dog'
/kan # katibo/	[káŋ katíβu]	'small dog'

What at first sight would appear a peculiar aspect of Galician phonology becomes less surprising when we inspect carefully some observations by Spanish phoneticians and phonologists.

In the Peninsular Spanish dialects described by Navarro Tomás (1977), non-assimilated rhyme nasals are always alveolar. Navarro Tomás' manual, however, contains several explicit references to co-articulation. For example, he indicates that before labials, a nasal may be articulated with overlapping alveolar and labial closures.[43] Partial articulatory overlapping before palatals also occurs in the style that Navarro Tomás describes as a somewhat slow and deliberate pronunciation, resulting in a simultaneous alveolar and palatal closure.[44] Furthermore, Menéndez Pidal (1980: 97) explicitly describes the preconsonantal nasal in *compañero* 'friend, companion' as involving a simultaneous dorsal and bilabial occlusion. Since velarized nasals in non-assimilating environments are well attested in dialectal studies, both in

[42] In the dialect I am describing there is a rule that raises tense mid vowels in unstressed position. The notation [ŋ̩] in (39) denotes a 'centro-domal' or 'fronted dorso-velar' point of articulation in Hockett's terms (1955: 37).
[43] 'Suelen darse asimismo, según la rapidez con que se habla, formas intermedias de assimilación en que la *n*, sin perder enteramente su articulación alveolar, resulta en parte cubierta por la oclusión de los labios' (p. 89; see also p. 113).
[44] Thus he states: 'La pronunciación lenta y silabeada puede hacer que la *n* mantenga en estos mismos casos [i.e., rhyme-final before a palatal; FMG] su forma ápico-alveolar, más o menos palatalizada, sin asimilarse por completo al modo de articulación de la palatal siguiente' (p. 133).

Peninsular and in American Spanish, one is led to speculate that nasal co-articulation may be much more widespread in Spanish velarizing dialects than the paucity of available descriptions would suggest.[45] In fact, a co-articulatory phenomenon similar to that of Galician has been sporadically attested in Spanish velarizing dialects, as for example, in Cuban (Harris 1969: 15–16, Guitart 1976: 22–23), and in Asturian (Cadierno and Prieto 1989).[46]

Underlying Galician nasals are restricted to the same three points of articulation they exhibit in Spanish: velar nasals do not function contrastively in the language (Veiga Arias 1976: 105–107).[47] Extending our analysis of Spanish to Galician nasals, neutralization can be captured by rule (37a), which delinks Place features in when the nasal is assigned to a rime. The universal default rule (38) obviously does not apply here. Instead, I propose the language-specific default rule (40) for Galician and Spanish velarizing dialects:

(40)   *Default Assignment*

[+nas]   →   [o DOR]

This rule expresses the generalization that velar is the default point of articulation for nasals in Galician, as shown in the tokens [sáŋ], [ruíŋ], [šóβiŋ], and [káŋ] in (39).[48] Because the difference in rules (40) and (38) correlates with a marked vs. unmarked status, respectively, default assignment in non-velarizing dialects is cost-free, whereas in velarizing ones it has to be considered a learned rule.

The crucial question now is: why do nasals still acquire their default value in cases where they are available for homorganic assimilation to a

---

[45] See, for example, Alonso, Zamora Vicente, and Canellada (1950: 226), R. Hyman (1956), Alvar (1959), Malmberg (1965: 4–5), Cedergren (1973), Terrell (1975), Poplack (1979), Zamora and Guitart (1982: 115ff.), and Salvador (1987), among many others.

[46] Guitart (1976), in referring to Harris' observation, confirms a strong tendency to nasal velarization in rhyme position in Havana Spanish: 'every nasal is velarized, *regardless of the consonant that follows.* . . although assimilation also takes place, resulting in a sort of co-articulation where a dorsal element is always present. . .' [emphasis added].

[47] It is curious for the record of phonological systems that in Galician /ŋ/ is contrastive in just *one* lexical item, the indefinite article *unha* 'one-fem.' syllabified as [ú.ŋa], its derivatives (*algunha* [al.xú.ŋa] 'some-fem.' *ninghuna* [niŋ.gú.ŋa], 'none-fem.'), and preposition plus article contractions (*c'unha* [kú. ŋa] 'with one', *d'unha* [kú. ŋa] 'of one'). It would appear that, historically, this would be accounted for by restructuring of /una/ into /ú.ŋa/ by analogical formation with the masculine *un* [uŋ]. Although minimal pairs exist in the language (cf. *una* [ú.na] 'I unite-sub.' *uña* [ú.ña] 'nail' and *cuña* [kú.ña] 'wedge'), the existence of this oddity does not grant /ŋ/ phonemic status in Galician, since with the exception of cases of resyllabification to a following vowel, discussed later in this paper, a velar nasal can only occur in rhyme position.

[48] Notice that Tongue Position specification by (40) is not required since all dorsal consonants are redundantly [+high] in Galician, as they are in Spanish.

following consonant? The simplest possible way to interpret this fact is to assume that both default assignment (40) and homorganic assimilation (37b) have applied to forms in (39), thus producing the complex segments in (39). Consider the following Supralaryngeal node representation of the dorsocoronal complex [ⁿ̩], as in the phrase [káⁿ̩ sáŋ] in (39) above (in (41) *1* indicates the specification inserted by (40), and *2* the association promoted by coronal spreading in homorganic assimilation):

(41)

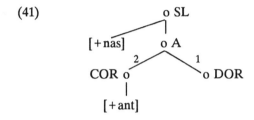

Having assumed that the co-articulatory effects in Galician are to be attributed to the application of rules ((37b) and (40)), the crucial part of this analysis is to establish in what ordering relation both rules stand. In order to assess three logical alternatives, some further facts need to be explored about the interaction of default assignment with other morpho–phonological domains.

Harris (1983, 1984a), and later Hualde (1989a, this volume) have shown that there are two stages of resyllabification in Spanish. The first applies at the lexical level after plural suffixation: a root–final consonant is delinked from its rhyme position and is resyllabified to the initial vowel of the plural allomorph /–es/. In many dialects, there is an optional rule that turns onset–initial glides into obstruents (*hielo* [é.lo] → [ĵélo] 'ice', *huevo* [wéβo] → [gʷéβo] 'egg'). Thus glide obstruentization applies optionally to a root–final glide resyllabified as an onset, as in the plural of *rey* [réj] 'king', which may surface as [re.ĵes] (cf. Harris 1983: 58–62). Further evidence for lexical resyllabification is provided by the alveolar vs. palatal alternations in forms such as *don.ce*[l] 'lad', *don.ce.*[l]*es* (plural) vs. *don.ce.*[ʎ]*a* 'lass', and *des.dé*[n] 'disdain', *des.de.*[n]*es* (plural) vs. *desde*[ñ]*es* 'you disdain–subj.', *des.de.*[ñ]*oso* 'disdainful.' Harris (1983: 50–55, 1984a: 73) postulates a rule that depalatalizes, in each case, laterals and nasals in rhyme position.[49] He observes that depalatalization must apply after a first stage of syllabification in which the target root–final sonorant is assigned to a rhyme by core syllabification. Affixation of the plural morpheme feeds resyllabification, and the depalatalized consonant will carry over as such onto its new onset position. By contrast, in gender and verb inflection, as well as in derivational affixation,

---

[49] For criticisms of Harris' proposal and further discussion, see Hualde (1989a).

syllabification applies in one single pass to the whole word. The second stage of resyllabification is postlexical: a word–final consonant and a word–initial vowel are combined into a syllable, as in *en abril* /en # abríl/ → [e.na.βríl] 'in April', or *el amigo* /el # amigo/ → [e.la.mí.ɣo] 'the friend.'

Recall that the delinking rule (37a) is sensitive to syllable structure. With regard to nasals, postlexical resyllabification in Galician operates essentially in the same fashion as in Spanish: rules applicable to rhyme nasals will take effect prior to their shift to onset position. However, unlike in the depalatalization examples in Spanish, lexical resyllabification in Galician applies in prefixation (Veiga Arias 1972: 105) and compounding, much as in the non-standard Spanish varieties discussed by Hualde (1989a, this volume), but not in inflectional suffixation, (the only exception being *unha* and its derivatives; see fn. 47). Consider examples (42a–d), in which a velar nasal surfaces in onset position after both stages of resyllabification:[50]

(42) *Underlying*   *Surface*

a. /in + umano/   [i.ŋu.má.nu]   'inhuman'
    /en + ebrar/   [e.ŋe.βrár]   'to thread'

b. /bEn + estár/   [bE.ŋis.tár]   'well–being'
    /kastElan + araxones/ [kas.tE.la.ŋa.ra.xu.nés] 'Castilian–Aragonese'

c. /kon # aseite/   [ku.ŋa.séj.ti]   'with oil'
    /sEn # Oras/   [sE.ŋÓ.ras]   'one hundred hours'

d. /korason/   [ku.ra.só.ŋi]   'heart'
    /aleman/   [a.li.máŋi]   'German'

e. /san + a/   [sána]   'healthy–fem.'
    /langran + a/   [laŋgrána]   'big woman'

    (cf. *[sáŋa] *but* [sáŋ] 'healthy–masc.'
          *[laŋgráŋa] *but* [laŋgráŋ] 'big man')

---

[50] The application of delinking, default assignment, and subsequent resyllabification of prefix–final nasals is subject to a great deal of variability in Galician. To mention some examples from my own dialect, the prefix–final nasal in *en-*, *in-* resyllabifies as a velar in *enherbar* 'to cure livestock with herbs', *eneixar* 'to install a cart's axels', *enarbolar* 'to hoist', *inimaxinable* 'unimaginable', *inhabilidade* 'inability', *inhibido* 'inhibited', *inalterable* 'unchangeable', and *inaceitable* 'unacceptable', but as an alveolar in *enemistade* 'enmity', *enamorado* 'in love', *enervar* 'to enervate', *inimigo* 'enemy', *inicial* 'initial', *inútil* 'useless', and *inocente* 'innocent.' José Hualde (p.c.) suggests that most words in the first set are analizable as prefix plus stem, and hence they are subject to cyclic syllabification, following the pattern in *inhumano*, while most of those in the second set are not readily decomposable in this manner.

f. /pan+adeiro/   [pa.na.déj.ru]   'baker
    /lambon+ada/   [laŋm.bu.ná.da]   'tidbit/delicacy'
(cf. *[pa.ŋa.déj.ru] but [paŋ] 'bread'
      *[laŋm.bu.ŋá.da] but [laŋm.bóŋ] 'greedy')

In (42a–b), morphological structure acts as a barrier to initial syllabification. Clearly, delinking (37a) and default assignment (40) apply lexically in a stratum in which core syllable structure is assigned individually to prefixes and members of compounds. The delinking rule applies at a point in which the target nasal, located in a rhyme at the end of a prefix or a first member of a compound, is deprived of its Place features by (37a), thereby becoming available for default assignment. By contrast, examples (42e–f) indicate that lexical insertion of inflectional and derivational suffixes occurs prior to the first stage of syllabification (see Hualde 1989a). Examples in (42c) illustrate the familiar postlexical resyllabification across word boundaries. In (42d) a word-final nasal is resyllabified to [i] ([e] in other dialects), inserted optionally via a postlexical rule of vowel epenthesis. Sample derivations are given in (43) (*N* in (43) represents a nasal deprived of Place features as a result of delinking; square brackets indicate morphological composition):

(43) LEXICAL:	[in[umano]]	[[sEn][Oras]]	[[pan]adeiro]
Stratum 1			
Suffixation	(n.a.)	(n.a.)	[panadeiro]
Syllabification	[in.[u.ma.no]	[[sEn].[O.ras]]	[pa.na.dej.ro]
Delinking (37a)	[iN.[u.ma.no]	[[sEN].[O.ras]]	(n.a.)
Default (40)	[iŋ.[u.ma.no]	[[sEŋ] [O.ras]	(n.a.)
Stratum 2			
Prefixation	[iŋ.u.ma.no]	(n.a.)	(n.a.)
Resyllabification	[i.ŋu.ma.no]	(n.a.)	(n.a.)
POST-LEXICAL:			
Resyllabification	(n.a.)	[sE.ŋO.ras]	(n.a.)
(Other rules)	[i.ŋu.má.nu]	[sÉ.ŋÓ.ras]	[pa.na.déj.ru]

We are now in a position to inquire how default assignment and nasal assimilation are combined to yield the complex segment in (41). Homorganic nasal assimilation is clearly a postlexical rule. In accordance with the corollary that lexical rules apply before postlexical ones, two logical possibilities are excluded: (i) that default assignment and assimilation apply simultaneously;

and (ii) that assimilation applies prior to default assignment. Moreover, the latter ordering is also disallowed by the Distinctness Condition, which would prohibit a redundancy rule from supplying Place features already assigned by nasal assimilation. The only viable solution is then to order default assignment prior to nasal assimilation. Here again, it is critical that spreading of Place features does not proceed in an SCD manner, because automatic delinking of Place features assigned by default would predict a fully assimilated nasal. Moreover, spreading applies in spite of the fact that the nasal's Place features have already been assigned by default, which in turn argues against the SC.

Finally, notice that the data on nasal velarization seem to contradict Structure Preservation. As mentioned, this principle precludes the introduction of non-contrastive features by lexical rules. If a rule makes reference to such features, then it must be postlexical (Kiparsky 1985). The velar point of articulation is non-distinctive among nasals, both in Galician and Spanish velarizing dialects. However, I have argued that default assignment of the Dorsal node must take place prior to lexical resyllabification after prefixation and compounding, two lexical operations. This suggests that Structure Preservation is too strong and must be relaxed in some way in order to accommodate such apparent violations.[51]

4.3 Proto-Spanish palatalization. I turn now to the analysis of Proto-Spanish palatalization, a process that cannot be adequately characterized by assuming either an SCD mechanism or the SC, and lends further support to the autonomy of spreading and delinking operations.

Many Proto-Romance dialects underwent consonantal palatalization during the last centuries of the Roman empire. As in metaphony, the phonetic conditioning of this sound change is a front vocoid containing a palatal component or yod. In most medieval Hispano-Romance varieties, the historical outcomes of palatalized velar and dental stops are the affricate sibilants /tˢ/ and /dᶻ/. Labials show a strong resistance to the process: labial stops palatalize in some instances; /m/ does not palatalize at all (see Otero 1971, Menéndez Pidal 1980). Among the several types of palatalization that emerged in the historical development of Spanish, here I will focus exclusively on what is generally considered the oldest one: palatalization of velar and dental stops.

Most scholars agree that Proto-Romance palatalization of velar stops should be broken up into three general stages: (i) gemination and fronting (through the addition of a secondary articulation by assimilation to front

---

[51] See Archangeli and Pulleyblank (1986: 30-35) for furhter discussion.

vowels and glides); in a subsequent sound change, these consonants underwent a process of affrication; (ii) degemination and yod 'absorption' (Otero 1971, 1976, Menéndez Pidal 1977, Calabrese 1991); and (iii) assibilation of the palatal affricates produced in stage (ii), which yielded the Old Spanish laminodental affricates: /t^s/, /d^z/. I will suggest, however, that these changes in some varieties of Hispano-Romance may have stopped at the palatalizing stage (ii), a supposition that is strongly confirmed by the existence of numerous doublets in Old Spanish ehibiting either the palatal reflex or the sibilant reflexes. The three stages are schematically shown in (44):[52]

(44)   i.   /ke/, /ki/ > /kk^j/ > /čč^j/
           /ge/, /gi/ > /gg^j/ > /ɟɟ^j/

       ii. /čč^j/ > /č/
           /ɟɟ^j/ > /ɟ/

       iii. /č/ > /t^s/
           /ɟ/ > /d^z/

The following are some representative Latin–Old Spanish correspondences:[53]

(45) | Latin | Old Spanish | |
       |-------|-------------|--|
       | centu | [t^s]iento | 'hundred' |
       | vicinu | ve[d^z]ino | 'neighboring' |
       | calceu | cal[t^s]a | 'type of shoe' |
       | racemu | ra[d^z]imo | 'bunch' |
       | aciariu | a[d^z]ero | 'steel' |
       | fascia | fa[t^s]a | 'bandage' |
       | lancea | lan[t^s]a | 'spear' |
       | corticea | corte[d^z]a | 'bark' |
       | spargere | espar[d^z]er | 'to scatter' |
       | argilla | ar[d^z]illa | 'clay' |

Dental stop–front glide sequences were also affected by gemination and affrication, and toward the end of stage (44i) they merged with their velar counterparts, thus following an identical fate:

---

[52] I use 'assibilation' for lack of a better term, since palatalization also involves assibilation.

[53] As examples (45)–(47) clearly show, assibilation exhibits a proclivity to voicing variations, an issue that need not concern us here.

(46) | Latin | Old Spanish | |
|---|---|---|
| capitia | cabe[tˢ]a | 'head' |
| platea | pla[tˢ]a | 'square' |
| pigritia | pere[dᶻ]a | 'laziness' |
| ratione | ra[dᶻ]ón | 'reason' |
| puteu | po[dᶻ]o | 'well' |
| gaudiu | go[dᶻ]o | 'joy' |
| viridia | ver[tˢ]a | 'cabbage' |
| hordeolu | or[tˢ]uelo | 'snare, trap' |

Of special interest to the study of the Old Spanish dialectal complex is the existence of a sizable number of lexical items exhibiting either the palatal or the sibilant outcome. In some instances they have survived in the modern language. It is reasonable to assume, then, a dialectal split between palatalizing and assibilating dialects, a scenario also found in the development of Italian varieties (Calabrese 1991). The following correspondences are illustrative (in (47) *OSp-P* and *OSp-A* stand for palatalizing and assibilating Old Spanish dialects, respectively; cf. Menéndez Pidal 1980: 148):[54]

(47) | Latin | OSp-P | OSp-A | |
|---|---|---|---|
| cappaceu | capa[č]o | capa[tˢ]o | 'pannier' |
| ruptiare | ro[č]ar | ro[tˢ]ar | 'to grub' |
| badiu | ba[ɟ]o | ba[dᶻ]o | 'spleen' |
| *radia | ra[ɟ]a | ra[tˢ]a | 'sunray' |
| jungere | u[ñ]ir | un[dᶻ]ir | 'to yoke' |
| frangere | fra[ñ]er | fran[dᶻ]ir | 'to break' |
| ringella | re[ñ]illa | ren[dᶻ]iella | 'quarrel' |
| verecundia | vergüe[ñ]a | vergüen[dᶻ]a | 'shame' |

---

[54] For the change /ng/ > /ñ/, see Lloyd (1987: 255–258) and references therein. In addition to the items in (47) we find: *cistella* 'little box' > *chistera* 'fisherman's basket' vs. *çestilla* 'small basket', *cimice* 'bug' > *chisme/chinche* vs. *çisme/çimçe*, *schisma* 'schism' > *chisme* 'gossip' vs. *çisma* 'dissension', apprehension', *subputeare* (from *puteus* 'well, pit') > *chapuçar* vs. *çapuzar* 'to splash, to duck (someone) under water', and *socculu* > *choclo* vs. *çoclo* 'clog, galosh' (examples from Menéndez Pidal 1980: 121; see also 132, 139, 148, and 164–165). It should be noted that the common outcome of intervocalic /bj/ and /gj/ in both dialects is a palatal: *habeam* > *haya* 'I have, subj.', *fovea* > *hoya* 'hole, pit', *rubeu* > *royo* 'reddish, blond' *fagea* > *haya* 'beech tree', *exagiu* > *ensayo* 'essay, test.' In postconsonantal position, the outcome is generally a sibilant: *grandia* > *grança* 'type of plant', *hordeolu* > *orçuelo* 'trap, snare.' On the other hand, although the predecessor of Modern Spanish certainly was an assibilating dialect, in some instances the palatalized item (*raya*) ultimately prevailed over its sibilant counterpart (*raça*), while in others, both alternatives have survived (e.g., *bayo* and *baço*). Finally, in some /dj/ sequences, only the palatal outcome is attested, presumably due to an early loss of the voiced dental: *podiu* > *poyo* 'balcony', *modiu* > *moyo* 'wine measure'.

The first step in (44i) involves the addition of a secondary place of articulation, which yielded palatalized velars. Following Lahiri and Everts (1991: 91), I assume that the process is one of assimilation to the coronality of the following glide, and not to the feature [−back], as in other frameworks. As mentioned earlier, front vowels in this model have a Coronal node further specified as [−anterior]. This naturally accounts for the Place articulator of the resulting palatal. As Lahiri and Evers indicate, spreading of [−back] would yield the right results for velars, but this operation cannot be extended to account for palatalization of dentals, alveolars, and labials, which are themselves already [−back]. On the other hand, spreading of [+high] would account for the palatalization of anterior consonants, but it would not work for velars, which are already specified as [+high]. This option would partially fail to capture palatalization induced by front vowels, a fairly common phenomenon (Bhat 1978), since mid and low front vowels are obviously [−high]. In sum, the trigger conditions of many palatalization processes, stated in terms of the traditional tongue body features, would have to be formally expressed by the curious disjunction 'either [+high] or [−back].' The assumption that front vowels contain a Coronal node specified as [−anterior], as Lahiri and Everts suggest, permits a straightforward account of most palatalization processes.

Ignoring gemination for present purposes, I formulate palatalization of velar stops as the spreading of the Coronal node, as shown in (48). The result is a dorso–coronal stop (the intermediate palatalized velars /kkʲ/ and /ggʲ/ of stage (44i)):

(48)

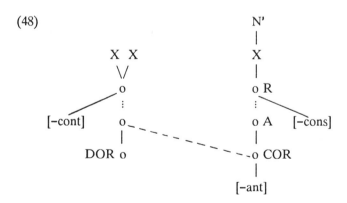

The addition of a secondary point of articulation to velar stops (the intermediate stage in (44i)) arose by assimilation to the palatality of a following front vocoid, a rather common type of process.[55] Assuming the general correctness of this intermediate stage, spreading of the coronal node here must not induce delinking of the Dorsal node, also a dependent of the Articulator node, since the result is a palatal, not a palatalized velar. The final stage can be captured by a rule that delinks the Dorsal node of the palatalized velar, as in (49a). On the other hand, as Lahiri and Evers point out, stridency is unmarked in palatal affricates, and therefore the specification [+strident] is to be assigned by default. Similar considerations apply to Tongue Position features: a non–anterior coronal is predictably [+high]. Both generalizations are captured by the redundancy rule in (49b):

(49)   a.

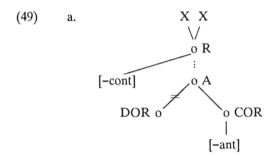

        b.   [o COR, –ant] → [+strid; o TP, +high]

In the hierarchical model, affricates are sequentially linked to the '–' and '+' values of [continuant] (Sagey 1986). An issue of some debate is how the [+continuant] specification is assigned in the final affrication stage in (44i). Lahiri and Evers (1991: 91) argue that [+continuant] should be assigned by default, since non–anterior coronals are predictably affricates. This statement, however, entails a violation of the Distinctness Condition, which prohibits default rules from supplying a redundant feature to a node already specified for that feature. Therefore, I assume that the [+continuant] specification is spread from the glide at a subsequent stage, as in (50) (which, incidentally, simply recasts the hypothesis that assibilation is, in part, the consequence of

---

[55] Alonso (1967: 151) reports that the passage from a dorsopalatal consonant [kʲ] to a fully palatal one [č] has actually been recorded within living memory in the variety spoken in Lerín, a town in Navarre. According to Alonso, the pronunciation of *quiosco* 'kiosk' was first [kjosko] (with devoicing of the front glide), and subsequently (i.e., at the time of Alonso's observation) it had become [čosko], a scenario that bears a striking resemblance to that proposed here for Proto-Spanish.

assimilation to the continuancy of the 'yod', as commonly held by traditional historians):

(50)

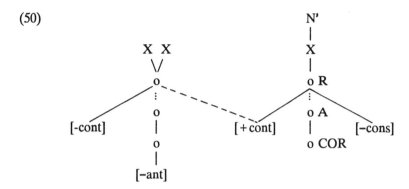

Stage (44ii) involves degemination and yod deletion. Both presumably entail disassociation from syllable structure, along the lines of the parametric option presented later in section 4.5. Obviously, the sequence of [−continuant] and [+continuant] specifications stay with the newly created affricate.

Most interesting is the assibilation process that came about in stage (44iii). Here, what at first sight might resemble a somewhat drastic change (i.e., /č/ → /tˢ/, and /ǰ/ → /dᶻ/), can be simply stated by delinking of the feature [−anterior], as in (51):

(51)

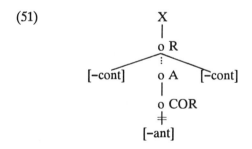

Disassociation of [−anterior] triggers, in turn, the application of a redundancy rule that assigns [+anterior] as the unmarked value for coronal consonants, as in (52a). In addition, the default assignment of [−high] to anterior coronals is principled, as in (52b). Since these rules supply the universal default values to coronals, they do so at no cost in the grammar of assibilating dialects. The output of (52) are the Old Spanish alveolar affricates /tˢ/, and /dᶻ/.

(52)   a.   [o COR]   →   [+ant]

         b.   [o COR, +ant]   →   [oTP, −high]

In this analysis, the relevant processes that ultimately account for Proto-Spanish palatalization are remarkably simple: two spreading operations (the fronting rule (48) and affrication (50)), and two delinking rules (disassociation of Dorsal in (49a) and of [-anterior] in (51)). The ensuing changes in palatalizing and assibilating dialects are the expected result, given the application of the universal redundancy principles (49b) and (52), in each case. Here again, an adequate characterization of the historical steps involved in palatalization not only supports the autonomy of spreading and delinking rules, but also—and most crucially—requires that both types of operations not be applied in an SCD fashion. Only in this way is the intuitive simplicity of the process matched with an equally simple descriptive apparatus. Finally, palatalization is of special interest because it illustrates the role of universal redundancy principles in historical change.

4.4 Obstruent voicing assimilation. The data I have presented so far illustrate some of the three general scenarios that argue against SCD and the SC. In this section, further evidence is provided from obstruent voicing assimilation in Castilian Spanish, in which spreading of Laryngeal features occurs without concomitant delinking, thus resulting in voicing contours. For the most part, my discussion will be restricted to the Castilian dialects described by Navarro Tomás (1977: 83-141). I will focus primarily on more casual registers, roughly corresponding to Harris' (1969) *Andante* and *Allegretto* styles.[56]

Consider the underlying set of consonants in these dialects:

(53)	Obstruents:	p		t		č	k
		b		d		ǰ	g
		f	θ	s			x
	Sonorants:	m		n		ñ	
				l		(λ)	
				r, r̄			

As shown in (53), there is an underlying voiced–voiceless contrast among plosive obstruents, but no such distinction is present in the set of fricatives. Since [+voice] is the universally marked value for obstruents, the principles of radical underspecification require that voiceless non-continuants be unspecified for [voice] underlyingly. However, voicing is contrastive in the set of plosives. Hence rule (54a) will apply lexically as a complement rule to

<hr>

[56] Although described in much less detail, similar data can be found in Harris (1969: 29, 40–46) for Mexican Spanish. See also Hooper (1972: 530–531), and Lozano (1979).

voiceless stops. Moreover, the default value for Laryngeal specifications in sonorants is [+voice], as stated in (54b):

(54)   *Default assignment for [voice]*

    a. [–son] → [–voice]

    b. [+son] → [+voice]

Notice that (54a) is also a default rule that supplies [–voice], the default value for obstruents, to underlying fricatives. Structure Preservation prevents the default statements in (54) from supplying non–contrastive features to underlying continuant obstruents and sonorants in the lexicon (see Kiparsky 1985), and therefore they should apply to both sets postlexically.

    Voicing assimilation is clearly a postlexical rule: it applies both within words and across word boundaries. Traditional grammars and segmental generative studies of Spanish postulate that syllable–final obstruents assimilate in voicing to the following consonant. The rule has been customarily stated along the following lines (cf. Harris 1969: 44, Cressey 1978: 74):

(55)   [–son] → [α voice] /___ (#) $\begin{bmatrix} +\text{cons} \\ \alpha \text{ voice} \end{bmatrix}$

    A typical autosegmental reformulation of (55) would be a rule that spreads the Laryngeal node of a consonant onto a preceding obstruent, delinking its laryngeal features as in (56) (of course, this rule applies vacuously when both consonants agree in the value for [voice]):

(56)

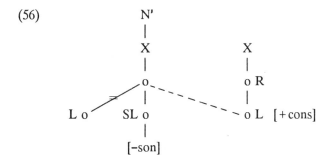

    Although a rule similar to (56) applies in a consistent fashion in many languages (Catalan, German, Russian), it has at best a doubtful status as a descriptive generalization in most Spanish dialects/styles, because it conveys the illusory impression of a regular process of voicing assimilation. In fact, a cursory look at Navarro Tomás' phonetic study of Castilian Spanish shows that such a generalization does not hold, at least in what he terms 'ordinary conversation.' He observes, for example, that in this style the word *absurdo* 'absurd' surfaces as [aββsúrðo], in which [ββ] represents a *partially* devoiced bilabial (1977: 86–87). Navarro Tomás contains abundant and unequivocal statements on partial voicing of obstruents in preconsonantal position.

One of the commonplace criticisms of autosegmental phonology against segmental rules such as (55) is its inability to express the internal structure of complex segments, such the sonority contour involved in a partially devoiced obstruent. Rule (56) does not fare any better, because automatic delinking would wrongly rule out such a contour. There is no doubt, however, that voiceless obstruents are not completely voiced before voiced consonants in casual styles. In addition to Navarro Tomás, Harris (1969: 29) and Hooper (1972: 530) also report that in certain varieties of American Spanish, voiceless fricatives in this environment are only partially voiced. Curiously, Navarro Tomás (1977: 108) does not mention such partial voicing in his description of /s/, and thus he transcribes *mismo* 'same, self' as [mizmo]. He gives some indication, though, that voicing of /θ/ may be partially or totally arrested in slow or deliberate speech (p. 95).[57]

Spanish voiced obstruents, whether underlying or derived by voicing assimilation, undergo a rule of continuancy spreading (traditionally known as 'spirantization'). I assume as essentially correct Mascaró's (1984) proposal that underlying voiced obstruents are unspecified for the feature [continuant] and they assimilate their surface value by spreading from the preceding segment.[58] I state spirantization as follows:

(57)

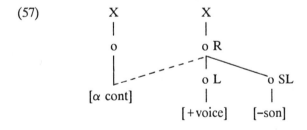

In some dialects/styles spirantization of voiced obstruents in rhyme position may optionally fail to apply; my discussion focuses on the most common case,

---

[57] My own impression is that, independent of style, the /s/ in *mismo* is not fully voiced; clearly it is not identical to its (fully voiced) English counterpart in, say, *plasma* [plæzma], and there is general agreement about this point among other Spanish speakers I have consulted.

[58] See Harris (1984c) and Hualde (1988) for different analyses of spirantization.

namely, on spirantized obstruents that either exhibit voicing contours or are devoiced altogether.[59]

It would be useful to state some generalizations regarding syllable final spirantized obstruents. From Navarro Tomás' observations, two general patterns emerge in regard to voicing assimilation. For expository convenience I will term them *A* and *B* dialects. Dialect A corresponds to standard Castilian; in most relevant respects it does not differ substantially from the educated Mexican variety described in Harris (1969). Dialect B can be found across a number of Castilian varieties:[60]

(58)   a.   *Underlying voiced obstruents*
They almost invariably surface as spirants in both dialects.

Dialect A: They are voiced before voiced consonants and partially devoiced before voiceless consonants. They are either voiced or voiceless word–finally.

Dialect B: They surface as voiceless, both word–medially and word–finally, irrespective of the following consonant.

    b.   *Underlying voiceless stops*
(When pronounced at all) they are voiceless stops before voiceless consonants.[61]

Dialect A: They are partially voiced spirants before voiced consonants.

Dialect B: They are voiceless spirants before voiced consonants.

The following data are representative of A dialects (orthographic *j*, *qu/c*, and *z* = /x/, /k/, and /θ/, respectively):

---

[59] For further details, see Harris (1969: 37–38), Navarro Tomás (1977), and Lozano (1979). Here, I draw mainly from Navarro Tomás (1977).

[60] The Valladolid and Salamanca provinces are cited by Navarro Tomás (1977: 101). It should be noted that this work was first published in the first quarter of this century. My own observation is that pattern B is much more widespread in northern and central Spain. See also Hualde (1989b).

[61] The occurrence of syllable–final voiceless stops is severely restricted in Spanish, and they generally undergo various reduction processes. Except for a very small number of loans, word–final voiceless stops do not occur before voiced obstruents. There is a relatively large number of learned words in which voiceless stops are followed by a voiceless obstruent *optional* 'optional', *actuar* 'to act', etc.) but they are deleted in many dialects. Finally, according to Navarro Tomás, before voiceless consonants underlying voiceless stops may sometimes surface either as (i) unreleased stops (p. 83); or (ii) as voiced spirants (pp. 87, 140–141), a realization also found in American dialects (see, for example, Dalbor 1980). Voicing before a voiceless consonant clearly defeats any explanation in terms of phonetic conditioning; of course once the consonant is voiced, spirantization is the expected outcome.

(59) *Underlying voiced obstruents*

a. /___[+voice]

a[β]dicar	'to abdicate'
clu[β] malo	'bad club'
su[β]glotal	'subglottal'
a[δ]vertir	'to notice/warn'
a[δ]mirar	'to admire'
amí[γ]dalas	'tonsils'
i[γ]norante	'ignorant'

b. /___ [−voice]

a[β$^\phi$]solber	'to absolve'
clu[β$^\phi$] caro	'expensive club'
su[β$^\phi$]terráneo	'subterranean'
a[δ$^\theta$]quirir	'to acquire'
a[δ$^\theta$]juntar	'to enclose'
vo[δ$^\theta$]ca	'vodka'
zi[γ^x]zag	'zigzag'

c. /___##

clu[β]	(or: clu[φ])	'club'
verda[δ]	(or: verda[θ])	'truth'
ciuda[δ]	(or: ciuda[θ])	'city'
zigza[γ]	(or: zigza[x])	'zigzag'
iceber[γ]	(or: iceber[x])	'iceberg'

(60) *Underlying voiceless stops*

a. /___ [+voice]

é[θ$^\delta$]nico	'ethnic'
a[θ$^\delta$]mósfera	'atmosphere'
fú[θ$^\delta$]bol	'soccer'
ri[θ$^\delta$]mo	'rhythm'
fra[x$^\gamma$] grande	'large tuxedo'
coña[x$^\gamma$] malo	'bad brandy'

b. /___ [−voice

a[p]to	'apt'
ecli[p]se	'eclipse'
e[t]cétera	'et cetera'
a[k]tuar	'to act'
fra[k] chico	'small tuxedo'
coña[k] francés	'French brandy'

c.

ceni[t]	(cf. *ceni[θ])	'zenith'
sovie[t]	(cf. *sovie[θ])	'soviet'
fra[k]	(cf. *fra[x])	'tuxedo'
coña[k]	(cf. *coña[γ])	'brandy'
anora[k]	(cf. *anora[x])	'anorak'

Before voiced consonants, underlying continuants follow a pattern of voicing assimilation essentially similar to voiceless stops in (60a). Within this set, there is some variability which appears to be determined by speech tempo: voicing is arrested in slower and moreemphatic styles (Navarro Tomás 1977: 108). As mentioned, Navarro Tomás only reports a voiced allophone [z] of /s/, and he adds that the articulatory gesture is characteristically 'brief and smooth.' He does mention, however, that voicing of /θ/ may be partially arrested in more careful styles (p. 95). I interpret Navarro Tomás' remarks as an indication of partial voicing in this environment. This interpretation is consistent with the descriptions by Harris (1969: 29) and Hooper (1972: 530) for American varieties:

(61)

a. / ___ [+voice]		b. / ___ [−voice]	
a[fʸ]gano	'Afghan'	na[f]talina	'naphthalene'
ha[θᵟ]llo	'do it!'	há[θ]selo	'do it for him!'
jue[θᵟ] nuevo	'new judge'	jue[θ] famoso	'famous judge'
ati[sᶻ]bar	'to watch'	ra[s]par	'to scrape'
de[sᶻ]de	'from'	e[s]te	'this one'
ra[sᶻ]gar	'to tear'	ra[s]car	'to scratch'
a[sᶻ]no	'donkey'	e[s x]igante	'it is gigantic'
mi[sᶻ]mo	'same'	a[sθ]ender	'to rise'
i[sᶻ]la	'island'	fó[s]foro	'phosphorus'
bo[xʸ] nuébo	'new boxwood'	bo[x] caro	'expensive boxwood'

In dialect B there is a devoicing rule that applies to voiced obstruents in rhyme position, and the result is invariably a spirant (cf. Hualde 1989b). Representative examples in this dialect for some of the tokens in (59a–c) are given in (62a–c). In addition, underlying voiceless stops also surface as voiceless spirants; thus items in (60a) surface as in (62d):[62]

(62)

a. a[φ]dicar	b. a[φ]solver	c. clu[φ]	d. é[θ]nico
a[θ]vertir	a[θ]juntar	verda[θ]	a[θ]mósfera
a[θ]mirar	a[θ]quirir	ciuda[θ]	fú[θ]bol
i[x]norante	zi[x]zag	iceber[x]	do[x]mático

We saw above that rules (55) and (56) fail to capture the contour segments in dialect A. With regard to dialect B, a further inadequacy becomes apparent: if voicing assimilation is posited in terms of either of these two rules, an ordering paradox emerges. Recall that the spirantization rule (57) applies only to *voiced* obstruents, not to voiceless ones. Among other reasons, this assumption is required in order to explain why the items in (59c) undergo spirantization (and further devoicing) but those in (59b) and (60b–c) do not: there is simply no stage of the derivation in which the latter bear [+voice]. Consider now how the surface allophones in (62) can possibly be generated. The paradox emerges because in order to obtain voiceless spirants from underlying voiceless stops in (62d), voicing assimilation must precede spirantization. However, the voiceless spirants in (62b) can be derived only

---

[62] As pointed out, I am not claiming that the devoicing pattern is exclusive of B dialects. My impression is that in A dialects it is less systematic and seems to be determined by stylistic and other external factors. I have been unable to find any systematic dialectal or sociolinguistic work on this kind of variation, in spite of its immediate interest to the study of sound change in present-day Spanish.

if voicing assimilation applies after spirantization. Sample derivations for the dental obstruents in the words *étnico* in (62d) and *adjuntar* in (62b) are given in (63) (for clarity, here and in subsequent examples, the symbols D/T are used to represent voiced/voiceless dentals, respectively, not specified for the feature [continuant]):

(63)	a.	/etniko/	/aDxuntar/
Voice Assim. (56)		d	T
Spirantization (57):		ð	(n.a.)
Devoicing:		θ	(n.a.)
		eθniko	*aTxuntar[63]

	b.	/etniko/	/aDxuntar/
Spirantization (57)		(n.a.)	ð
Voice Assim. (56):		d	θ
Devoicing		t	(n.a.)
Output:		*etniko	aθxuntar

As shown in (63), voicing assimilation feeds spirantization in the derivation of *étnico* in (63a), but it bleeds spirantization in the derivation of *adjuntar*, by virtue of producing a voiceless dental to which the latter rule can no longer apply. Therefore, no independently motivated rule of Spanish will turn it into the expected [θ]. Conversely, if the order in (63b) is assumed, the surface [θ] in *étniko* cannot be derived. Clearly, this dilemma cannot be resolved even if devoicing is ordered prior to either rule (or to both of them) without ad hoc stipulations. Of course, the fundamental flaw of both (55) and (56) should now be apparent: the voiced/voiceless allophones are generated by voicing assimilation *at the same (intermediate) stage* of the derivation. Once this assumption is made, there is no way of escaping the ordering paradox. I will show, however, that such problems dissapear if three reasonable assumptions are made. The first is that spreading of Laryngeal features does not induce delinking; this accounts naturally for the voicing contours in dialect A. Second, a [+voice] specification is the necessary and sufficient condition for spirantization, independently of Laryngeal node structure; that is, any obstruent specified as [+voice] will meet the structural description of the rule, both when this is the only specified value (as in (59a)), and when it is part of a voicing contour, as in (59b) and (60b). And third, a devoicing rule which ultimately accounts for the voiceless allophones in both dialects applies at a later point of the derivation, after both assimilation and spirantization. This

---

[63] Presumably, the voiceless dental in the output of *adjuntar* in (63a) would receive the unmarked specification [–voice], since no other rule applies, yielding *[atxuntár].

process has two stages formally identical to those we have already seen in nasal neutralization: (i) delinking of the Laryngeal node from the target obstruent; and (ii) default assignment of the default Laryngeal value ([–voice] for obstruents), a rule we introduced in (54b).

Let us explore these assumptions in more detail. Accounting for the data in dialect A is straightforward if we assume, contrary to (56), that spreading of Laryngeal features does not induce automatic delinking on the target obstruent, as in (64):

(64)   *Voicing assimilation*

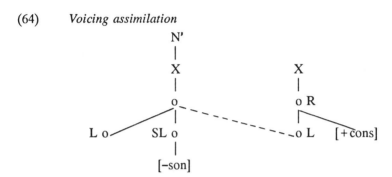

Of course, rule (64) does not apply to items in (59a), (60b), and (61b) (or does so vacuously). Word–final obstruents in (60c) and (61c) are not affected either, because they do not meet its structural description. The emergence of contour structures in the remaining examples (i.e., partially devoiced obstruents in (59b) and partially voiced ones in (60a) and (61a)) simply follows from the assumption that rule (62) does not induce delinking of the target's Laryngeal features. The result will be, in each case, an obstruent whose Root is doubly linked to two Laryngeal nodes, each dominating, in turn, two opposite [voice] specifications, a type of configuration that closely resembles that of an affricate. The operation of (62) is shown in (65) for the items *étnico* in (60a) and *adjuntar* in (59b) ('[V]' = [voice]):

(65)   a.   *e t   n i k o*   b.   *a D   x u n t a r*

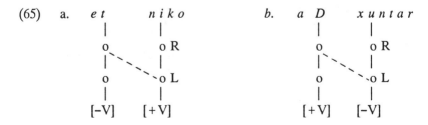

Spreading of the Laryngeal node from the trigger will result in an obstruent whose Root is linked to two Laryngeal nodes. The doubly–linked structure is automatically readjusted by the OCP which merges the two identical nodes in the same tier into one.[64] The outputs of (65) and the OCP–induced merger are shown in (66):

(66)   a.

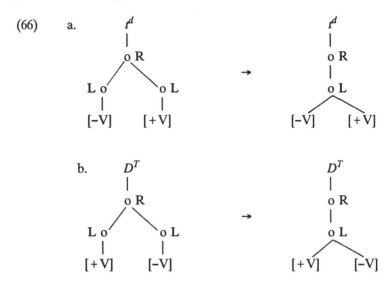

b.

It should be evident that the creation of contour segments can only be achieved by spreading without delinking. In addition, the structures generated by (64) provide a simple phonological formalism that closely reflects the Laryngeal events involved; namely, these structures can be naturally interpreted as representing the activation/deactivation or vice versa, in each case, of vocal cord vibration within the duration of a single timing unit. Thus (66a) embodies a lag in voice onset time, a kind of voicelessness interlude between the vowel preceding the obstruents and the voiced consonant following it. On the other hand, (66b) naturally represents the cessation of voicing within the obstruent's phonation span.

There is, however, an alternative phonetic interpretation of how the contour segments in (59)–(61) are generated. In an earlier framework, Harris (1969: 40–45) proposed a characterization of the process as involving, in part, an assimilation to supraglottal tension/laxness of the triggering consonant. This view is based on a model in which voicing distinctions are determined by certain glottal adjustments (e.g., constriction, degree of opening, subglottal pressure, etc.) in conjunction with the relative tension of supraglottal gestures. Thus the production of a partially devoiced segment, as in (59b), would

---

[64] A particular instantiation of this principle is the Shared Features Convention proposed in Steriade (1982).

resemble a voiceless obstruent in that the glottal gesture involved inhibits Laryngeal vibration, while at the same time it lacks enough supraglottal tension, a condition that allows a sufficient amount of airflow through the glottis, typical of voiced obstruents. Conversely, the production of a partially devoiced obstruent, as in (60a) and (61a), involves a Laryngeal configuration that favors vocal fold vibration in voiced obstruents, but phonation is accompanied by an increased tension of the supraglottal muscles, a condition that contributes to arresting Laryngeal vibration in voiceless ones. Presumably, these and other considerations led Harris to define the former as [–voiced, –tense], and the latter as [+voice, +tense] (p. 41). However, phonetic research suggests that the most critical parameter in determining voicing distinctions, both physically and perceptually, is the control of the timing of Laryngeal and Supralaryngeal gestures, rather than their specific combination (Ladefoged 1971, Lisker and Abramson 1971, Keating 1984), which is in line with the account given in (64)–(66). Given an adequate representation of voice onset timing, the function of other contributing features, such as tensity, constriction, and so on, may be regarded as entirely redundant.

We may turn now to our second assumption that the target conditions of spirantization are satisfied when a rhyme obstruent contains a [+voice] specification, even if this property is a component of a voicing contour. The merged representations in (66) will then be subject to spreading of [+continuant] from a preceding vowel. The result is precisely a spirant with a voicing contour, as in (67):

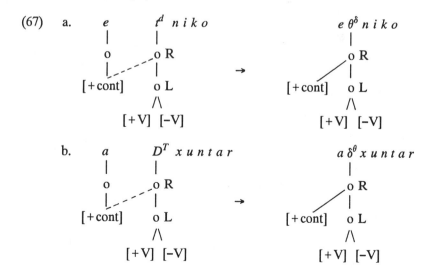

Deriving the surface voiceless continuants found in dialect B, as well as those that are stylistically determined in dialect A, is straightforward. As in our account of nasal neutralization, the appropriate mechanism appears to be a rule that delinks the Laryngeal node of the output spirants as in (68a), followed by redundant assignment of [–voice] by rule (54a) (repeated here for convenience as (68b)):

(68)   a. *Delinking*   b.   *Default Assignment*

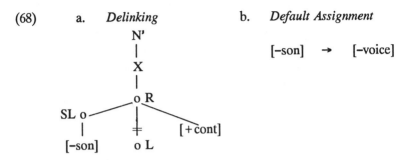

In this account, the voiceless spirants in, say, (62b) do not arise through assimilation, but rather through the operation of an independent principle of markedness which supplies the default value to obstruents. The output is a continuant temporarily unspecified for voicing, which now becomes available for default assignment (68b). Sample derivations for the relevant items are shown in (69):

(69)	/aDmirar/	/aDxuntar/	/etniko/	/seD/
Voicing Assim. (62)	(n.a.)	D^T	t^d	(n.a)
Spirantization (57)	δ	$δ^θ$	$θ^δ$	δ
Output (dialect A):	aδmirár	$aδ^θ$xuntár	$éθ^δ$niko	séδ
Devoicing (68):	aθmirár	aθxuntár	éθniko	séθ

Finally, it would not be unreasonable to speculate that dialect B is an innovative variety of dialect A in the following way. Optional (stylistic) devoicing of rhyme obstruents in dialect A has become practically categorical in dialect B. This process resembles a well–attested type of sound change, namely, rule simplification (King 1969: 58ff., Kiparsky 1982b: 16ff., among others). Rule simplification involves the removal of some restricting condition from the structural description of a rule, so that it applies to either a wider class of segments or to a wider class of environments.

The analysis just presented brings out some striking parallelisms with the nasal neutralization facts discussed earlier, most of which are not immediately obvious in a SCD type of analysis. Notice, first, that the assignment of default features for both rhyme nasals in non–velarizing dialects ([o COR, –ant]) and for obstruents in (68) ([o Laryngeal, –voice]) are supplied by independent principles of Universal Grammar. Second, in both processes underlying distinctions have been neutralized and, arguably, the simplest mechanism to express neutralization rules is delinking and default. This allows us to express phonological neutralization unitarily, as a function of the delete parameter, which is then motivated independently of spreading operations, as suggested by syllable–final devoicing of obstruents. By contrast, assuming SCD, the emergence of word–final voiceless spirants from underlying voiced obstruents cannot be formally related to those occurring word–medially: the former would have to be accounted for by a devoicing rule; the latter would arise through assimilation. This shows that neutralization cannot be unitarily expressed in a SCD analysis, since the context of devoicing–by–spreading and word–final devoicing would have to be stated separately, in spite of the obvious generalization that both take place in the same domain: a syllable rhyme. Finally, once more, the SC is contradicted by the emergence of contours in voicing assimilation, as amply shown in this section.

4.5 Consonant gemination. We have already mentioned that Universal Grammar restricts the range of possible phonological operations to two basic types: insert or delete. The deletion function, as argued in this paper, is formally expressed by delinking rules. The output of delinking operations may be subject either to spreading or to default rules, which supply surface specifications. Delinking rules may refer to: (i) one feature, as in we saw in Old Spanish nasal dissimilation; (ii) a Class node, as in neutralization of rhyme nasals in Spanish (delinking of the Place node), or aspiration of rhyme /s/ in many Modern Spanish varieties (delinking of the Supralaryngeal node; Goldsmith 1981, Hualde 1989c); and (iii) the whole segmental melody (i.e., the Root node, as in some aspirating dialects which further delete /s/ altogether; cf. Goldsmith 1981).

A most compelling argument could apparently be raised against the Spreading Condition in (41) by total assimilation processes (i.e., gemination). An illustrative type of consonantal gemination is the change from Latin *septem* to Italian *sette* 'seven' (see Weinrich 1958). In the autosegmental literature, such processes are almost invariably characterized as spreading of the Root node of an onset consonant onto the prosodic slot of a preceding rhyme consonant, thereby delinking all the segmental features of the latter, as in (70) ('σ' = syllable):[65]

(70)

$$
\begin{array}{cccccc}
\sigma & \sigma & & \sigma & \sigma \\
| & | & & | & | \\
X_1 & X_2 & \rightarrow & X_1 & X_2 \\
\Vert & | & & & \\
o\,R_1 & o\,R_2 & & o\,R_2 &
\end{array}
$$

---

[65] Cf. Steriade (1982), Sagey (1986), Schein and Steriade (1986).

Obviously, the operation in (70) would be prohibited by the SC, which requires that X_1 be unspecified for R_1 prior to spreading of node R_2. On the other hand, an SCD mechanism must be rejected if delinking of R_1 in (70) can be shown to apply prior to the spreading operation that accounts for gemination.

Since a large number of delinking rules are prosocdically conditioned, it would be useful to review briefly some of the postulates of the theory of prosodic licensing (cf. Itô 1986). This theory assumes the template approach to syllable structure. Syllabification proceeds by mapping segmental units onto a given template, a unit determined in part on a language–specific basis, and which essentially contains information on the number and feature content of possible syllable constituents. Syllable structure is assigned in one single pass: a consonant that does not satisfy the template conditions is prosodically unlicensed, and therefore it never has the chance of being incorporated into syllable structure. Thus most consonantal deletions seem to affect coda consonants which are not prosodically licensed (see Itô 1986).

Although the notion of prosodic licensing is a useful one, there are empirical arguments against the template theory and in favor of a rule–approach to syllabification. First, there are instances in which prosodic licensing seems to be a matter of degree rather than of categorical restriction. Thus many Spanish speakers delete syllable–final stops in more casual styles (/septimo/ → [sé.ti.mo]), but they may be licensed in careful speech ([sép.ti.mo]). A second argument is provided by epenthesis rules applying to rescue prosodically unlicensed consonants. In Spanish an underlying /s/ cannot be parsed as an onset if it is followed by another consonant at the beginning of a word (Harris 1980, 1983, 1985). When this happens, an epenthetic [e] is inserted, thus providing the unsyllabifiable consonant with a syllabic support: /spirar/ → [es.pi.rár] 'to breath out'. Such a procedure is not needed when the stem is preceded by a vowel–final prefix, since /s/ makes a perfectly acceptable coda: /in+spirar/ → [ins.pirár] 'to breath in' (Harris 1983). The same argument applies to prosodically unlicensed coda consonants. Harris (1989b) demonstrates that e–epenthesis also applies in order to 'rescue' unlicensed word–final consonants: /padr/ → [pá.ðre] 'father', /tripl/ → [trí.ple] 'triple.' Clearly, this result would be surprising under a template–based approach: in both cases, the consonants at issue are unlicensed, since they cannot be mapped onto any imaginable Spanish template. The prediction is made, then, that they would be deleted. This conclusion is inescapable because (crucially in this model) segment–to–template mapping takes effect in one single pass. Otherwise, the only phonological motivation for *e*-epenthesis, namely, that it applies to prosodically unlicensed consonants, would be lost.[66]

In a rule-based approach, syllables are built up in successive steps. It is generally agreed that consonants are incorporated into syllable structure first, in accordance with the Onset Maximization Principle, and remaining consonants are then adjoined to syllable rhymes. This basic operational device is repeated through the derivation whenever syllable structure readjustments take place (cf. Steriade 1982, Harris 1983, 1989a, 1989b, Levin 1986).

Suppose now that we interpret prosodic licensing in the following sense. In underlying representations each (non-geminate) segmental Root is linked to a prosodic slot. If a rhyme consonant does not meet some licensing condition, the feature content of the offending consonant is generally delinked. The offending consonant will not survive in phonetic structure. This type of deletion has two distinct and well-documented general effects: either the offending consonant is delinked from syllabic structure, together with its associated mora (i.e., its skeletal slot), or it is delinked from prosodic structure, leaving a mora deprived of segmental melody. In other words, the distinction involves deletion that leaves no trace at all, and deletion that induces a structural change in some adjacent segment.

When a timing unit is not linked to segmental material, its survival in surface representations may be insured in two ways: (a) it may receive the language's default features (Harris 1985a); or (b) it links to the Root of an adjacent (prosodically licensed) segment, for example, a following onset consonant, and the result is a geminate. The formal relatedness between neutralization and segmental deletion can now be identified. Just as contextual neutralization is characterized as *partial* delinking of consonantal features in a syllable rhyme, as in Spanish and Galician coda nasals, consonantal deletion involves an extreme case of neutralization: delinking of *complete* segmental melody.

These observations motivate a formal distinction on the level of representation referred to by rules delinking consonants in syllable rhymes, which I view as a function of the Rhyme Consonant Deletion Parameter (RCDP). Thus such rules may select from two parametric options: (i) delinking from syllable structure, i.e., disassociation of the syllabic and prosodic tiers ($RCDP_1$), as in (71a); and (ii) delinking from prosodic structure, i.e., disassociation of the prosodic and melodic tiers ($RCDP_2$), as in (71b):

---

[66] This argument was first brought to my attention by James Harris in 1986, during a summer course at the University of Barcelona.

(71) a. *RCDP₁*   b. *RCDP₂*

N'   N'   (syllabic tier)

╪ |

X   X   (prosodic tier)

| ╪

o Root   o Root   (melodic tier)

As already mentioned, a segmental unit must be associated to a syllabic constituent in order to receive phonetic interpretation; otherwise it is subject to the Stray Erasure Convention (Itô 1986, Harris 1983: 35, 1985). Selection of RCDP₁ entails that the delinked units (a Root node and its mora) will not surface in phonetic representations. Hence, in many Spanish dialects/styles only coronal sonorants and continuants are licensed in rhymes; any other consonants are deleted along with ttheir associated mora (/akto/ → [á.to] 'act', /opθional/ → [o.θjo.nál] 'optional', /doktor/ → [do.tór] 'doctor', /robot/ → [ro.βó] 'robot', /aktibo/ → [a.tí.βo] 'active'), and this also occurs when the coda in question contains the extraprosodic consonant /s/, in which case the restriction extends to any consonant except /r/ and /l/ (/transformar/ → [tras.for.már] 'to transform', /transmitir/ → [trasᶻ.mi.tír] 'to transmit, to broadcast', /eksportar/ → [es.por.tár] 'to export', /substituir/ → [sus.ti.tu.ír] 'to substitute'.[67] Other dialects which also contain a similar prosodic restriction select option RCDP₂, leaving a prosodic unit deprived of its segmental melody which then links to the following consonant, in a typical case of compensatory lengthening: /akto/ → [át.to], /oktubre/ → [ot.tú.βre] 'october', /opθional/ → [oθ.θjo.nál] 'optional', /teknika/ → [tén.ni.ka] 'technique', /submarino/ → [sum.ma.rí.no] /'submarine'.[68] This clearly shows that both options of the RCDP may be found within dialects of the same language. An illustration of the two delinking options is given in (72) for the word *acto*:

(72) a. RCDP₁: /akto/ → [á.to]

N'   N"   N"

╪ | |

X   X   →   X

| | |

o   o R   o R

a   *k*   *t*   *o*   *a*   *t*   *o*

---

[67] See Malmberg (1965), Navarro Tomás (1974, 1977), Zamora Vicente (1979), Dalbor (1980), among many others.
[68] Thus in these dialects, there is a phonetic distinction in consonant length between, say, [át.to] (*acto* 'act') and [á.to] (*hato* 'provisions, belongings').

b. RCDP$_2$: /akto/ → [át.to]

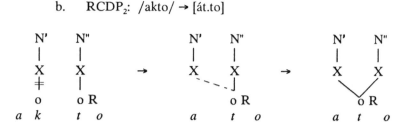

An analysis in terms of the RCDP$_2$ option is also required by the total assimilation process that gave rise to Proto–Italian geminates, as in *septem > sette*. Thus while in Classical Latin most consonants could appear in rhyme position (cf. Devine and Stevens 1977), in Modern Standard Italian only sonorants and /s/ are licensed (Basbøll 1974, Itô 1986). There is a unique set of systematic exceptions: other consonants may occur in a rhyme but only when they are also the beginning of the following syllable; that is, when they are geminates. Itô (1986) observes that this situation is typical in a number of languages (Attic Greek, Finnish, Japanese): a type of segmental melody, which otherwise is banned in coda position, is prosodically licensed because it is also linked to a following onset, a position which lacks such restrictions on feature structure. The crucial point is that at the historical stage in which Proto–Italian introduced a prosodic constraint on coda consonants, deletion is motivated independently of the gemination process itself, compensatory lengthening being a consequence of selecting option RCDP$_2$ (cf. Ingria 1980, and Saltarelli 1983). In essence, the same argument can be extended to the analysis of the data on consonantal gemination in the Spanish dialects briefly discussed above. Quite generally, compensatory lengthening, as the term is understood in autosegmental phonology, involves the reassociation of a prosodic unit which has been previously delinked from melodic structure. Different languages may implement delinking and subsequent reassociation in various ways. The basic principle is still the same: a selection of RCDP$_2$ entails the emergence of an available timing unit. Whether this unit associates to a following consonant or to a preceding vowel appears to be determined on a language-specific basis.[69]

---

[69] See de Chene and Anderson (1979), Ingria (1980), Hock (1986), Hayes (1989). Thus although in many languages deletion of all segmental material from a coda induces compensatory lengthening of a following consonant, as in Proto–Italian, in other languages the prosodic unit is attached to the preceding nuclear element, resulting in a long vowel (see, for example, Ingria 1980 for Ancient Greek, Anderson 1984 for Scandinavian languages, and Sezer 1985 for Turkish). There are still other languages, such as Tiberian Hebrew (Lowenstamm and Kaye 1985) and Luganda (Clements 1985), in which both vowels and consonants may be subject to compensatory lengthening.

There is a second example of consonantal gemination in Spanish, but this one is not related to prosodic licensing in any obvious fashion. It occurs in a sizable number of dialects that aspirate and optionally delete syllable–final /s/ (e.g., /mas/ → [máh] or [má] 'more'). Two patterns of gemination are attested both in southern Peninsular and in American Spanish (for convenience, I will use the terms *A* and *B*, respectively).[70] In pattern A, when the aspirated /s/ is followed by a voiceless obstruent, the sequence surfaces as a preaspirated geminate.[71] The term 'geminate', however, should not lead to confusion. Close inspection of the process indicates that involved here is gemination of Supralaryngeal features, not complete assimilation. This can be determined by observing the behavior of the following consonant. If such consonant is a voiceless obstruent, the result is a preaspirated voiceless geminate, as in (73a). However, if it is a sonorant, the result is a partially voiced geminate, as shopwn in (73b). This is a clear indication that the Laryngeal features of the aspirated segment are preserved. On the other hand, in dialects exhibiting pattern B, the outcome in both cases is a plain geminate:[72]

(73)

	Underlying	Pattern A	Pattern B	
a.	/kaspa/	[káʰp.pa]	[káp.pa]	'dandruff'
	/esfera/	[ęʰf.fé.ra]	[ęf.fé.ra]	'sphere'
	/mas θera/	[máʰθ.θé.ra]	[máθ.θéra]	'more wax'
	/mas xente/	[maʰx.xéɳ.te]	[máx.xéɳ.te]	'more people'
	/susto/	[súʰt.to]	[sút.to]	'fright, scare'
	/moska/	[móʰk.ka]	[mók.ka]	'fly (insect)'
b.	/mismo/	[mím̥.mo]	[mím.mo]	'same, self'
	/asno/	[áɳ̥.no]	[án.no]	'donkey'
	/isla/	[íḷ.la]	[íl.la]	'island'
	/los reyes/	[lǫṛ.r̄ę́.ɟęʰ]	[lǫr.r̄ę́.ɟęʰ]	'the kings'

---

[70] Data on both patterns of gemination can be found, among others, in Lenz (1940: 127–134), Rodríguez–Castellano and Palacio (1948), Alonso, Zamora Vicente, and Canellada de Zamora (1950), Salvador (1957), Mondéjar (1970), , Navarro Tomás (1974: 71–73), Oftedal (1985: 51ff.), Zamora Vicente (1979: 320–321), Lapesa (1981: 504–506), Zamora and Guitart (1982: 109), and Hualde (1989b, 1989c), who draws primarily from the data in Salvador (1957). The list of references is by no means exhaustive.

[71] It is interesting to note that in Peninsular dialects containing an underlying /θ/, this consonant is also aspirated in syllable–final position. Therefore, it triggers gemination in a fashion similar to /s/ (see Salvador 1957: 222, Hualde 1989b).

[72] Strengthening of /r/ is predictable after a closed syllable and in word–initial position (cf. Harris 1983, Hualde this volume).

In the autosegmental framework, aspiration is usually captured by a delinking of the target's Supralaryngeal node (Goldsmith 1981, Clements 1985, Hualde 1989b, 1989c). The resulting structure will bear Laryngeal specifications, as well as other Root-dependent features. The delinking operation involved in aspiration is illustrated in (74a) for the word *más*; the output is shown in (74b):

(74)   a.   b.

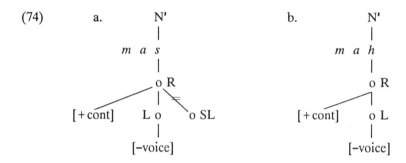

Although a number of *s*-aspirating dialects lack the described gemination patterns shown in (73), the resulting segment in (74b) is still affected by the preceding vowel, to which it assimilates in point of articulation (see Goldsmith 1981). This process is generally captured by a rule that spreads the Supralaryngeal node from a preceding vowel onto the Root node of the aspirate:[73]

(75)

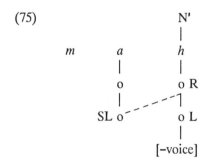

---

[73] It is doubtful whether this type of assimilation should be stated as a language-specific rule since is wholly predictable. In fact, an /h/ type of consonant will always take on the point of articulation of either a preceding or a following vowel, a fact presumably due to anatomical restrictions. The direction of assimilation seems to be completely determined by the position of the aspirate in syllable structure. Thus in a language allowing /h/ both in onset and rhyme positions, it will always be homorganic with the closest tautosyllabic vowel. Thus in the hypothetical sequences [a.hi] and [ah.ti], [h] takes on the Supralaryngeal features of [i] in the first and those of [a] in the second.

The structure illustrated in (75) is precisely the input to the process that generates preaspirated geminates in pattern A. The latter, as suggested in Hualde (1989b, 1989c), involves spreading of the Supralaryngeal node from a following consonant. Its effect on the item *caspa* ([kaʰp.pa] in (73)) is shown in (76):

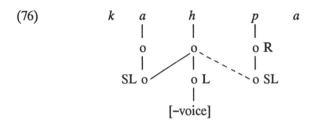

(76)   k   a   h   p   a

SL o   o L   o SL

[-voice]

The Root node of the aspirated segment will now be sequentially linked to both the Supralaryngeal nodes of the preceding vowel and those of the following consonant. As a consequence, the Supralaryngeal features of the latter will also be doubly linked to two Root nodes, namely, its own and that of the aspirated consonant. The outcome is a preaspirated geminate.

The next question is how capture complete gemination in pattern B, and whether it is formally related to pattern A. Hualde (1989b) proposes that pattern B involves Supralaryngeal gemination only. This would work for gemination before voiceless stops, because trigger and target bear the same Laryngeal specification (i.e., [-voice]). However, this analysis accounts only for the partially-voiced sonorants in pattern A, not for the sonorant geminates found in pattern B. The latter must be captured by delinking the Root node of the aspirated segment. I motivate this move as follows. First, the two patterns are not attested outside the dialectal domain of /s/-aspiration, nor do they appear in all aspirating varieties; therefore, they should be regarded as an innovative development within the /s/-aspirating group. Second, deletion of the aspirated segment is optional in most aspirating dialects, independently of whether they exhibit or not either geminating pattern (or both). Third, given the optionality of /s/-deletion, in terms of phonological and phonetic plausibility total gemination in pattern B is arguably a further innovation of dialects that exhibit preaspirated geminates, rather than vice versa. Preaspirated geminates, as we have seen, involve both aspiration (delinking of the Supralaryngeal node) and spreading of the Supralaryngeal features from the following consonant. The emergence of plain geminates follows from the optional deletion of the aspirated segment (delinking of the Root node) and subsequent spreading of the all segmental features from the following consonant. On the other hand, both Supralaryngeal and Root delinking are independently needed to account for *s*-aspiration and deletion in non-geminating environments (e.g. word-finally in prepausal position, and before a vowel in the following word). Salvador (1957) mentions three facts of particular relevance for a Root delinking analysis in pattern B. First, in the dialects he describes, aspirated /s/ is commonly deleted, especially in word-final position; noun plurality and second person marking in verbal morphology are taken over by vowel laxing (see also Hooper 1976, Zubizarreta 1979). Second, when an aspirated /s/ is followed by a lateral, there is a strong tendency to produce a fully voiced geminate, as in /isla/ → [il.la] (Salvador 1957: 206, 224; see also Mondéjar 1979: 51). Scattered examples of this outcome before other sonorants are also attested in Andalusian (Alonso, Zamora Vicente, and Canellada 1950: 228-229, Mondéjar 1979: 52, Lapesa 1981: 504), in Chilean (Lenz 1940: 134), and in Puerto Rican (Navarro Tomás 1974: 72).

These observations suggest that *h*–deletion must be stated in terms of option RCDP$_2$ in (71b); that is, by a means of a rule that delinks the Root node of the aspirated segment, leaving its timing unit available for spreading of the Root node to its right. In fact, the mere selection of this parameter already predicts compensatory lengthening (of the following consonant, in the particular case at hand). I formalize Root delinking and compensatory lengthening as in (77a) and (77b), respectively:

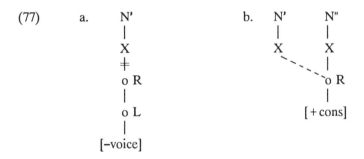

(77)   a.   N'   b.   N'   N"

The application of the rules in (77) is illustrated schematically in (78) for the word *caspa*:

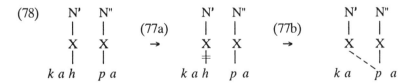

(78)

There is a compelling piece of evidence for Root delinking in terms of the RCDP$_2$ option. In many dialects, when the aspirated /s/ is deleted in non-geminating environments (word-finally), the preceding vowel is both laxed and lengthened (Navarro Tomás 1939: 161).[74] Thus the item *más* in these dialects may surface as [mǽʰ] (laxing and aspiration) or [mǽ:] (laxing, Root deletion, and compensatory lengthening). The latter outcome follows automatically if we assume Root delinking in a RCDP$_2$ fashion, and rightward spreading of the vowel's Root node onto the mora unaffiliated to any segmental material; the outcome is a long vowel. Since vowels universally bear the peak of sonority within the syllable, the linking of the incorporated mora is subsequently shifted from a rhyme to a head position by universal convention. A sample derivation is shown in (79) ((a) = Root delinking; (b) = compensatory lengthening; and (c) = syllable-structure readjustment):[75]

(79)
```
     N    N'          N    N'          N    N'           N
     |    |    (a)     |    |    (b)    |    |    (c)      /\
     X    X    →       X    X    →      X    X     →      X   X
     |    |            |    ǂ           L--⌐             L/
     m    a    h       m    a    h      m    a            m    a
```

---

[74] Rodríguez–Castellano and Palacio (1948: 589) state: 'la vocal anterior experimenta cierto alargamiento, cuyo grado está en razón inversa al de la conservación del sonido aspirado. Esto es, a mayor cantidad de aspiración final menor alargamiento de la vocal precedente; y, viceversa, cuanto más reducida sea la aspiración, mayor es el alargamiento de esa vocal.' And Salvador (1957: 174) also indicates the extreme opening and lengthening of the preceding vowel: 'la extraordinaria abertura y duración de este sonido. . . le dan una cierta resonancia característica.' Crucially, however, there is no indication of vowel lengthening in preconsonantal position, which suggests that compensatory lengthening of consonants takes precedence over vowels (i.e., there is priority of regressive over progressive gemination).
[75] Within the framework of moraic phonology (McCarthy and Prince 1986, Hayes 1989) such syllable structure readjustments in compensatory lengthening are captured by the convention of 'Parasitic Delinking': 'Syllable structure is deleted when the syllable contains no overt nuclear segment' (Hayes 1989: 268). An alternative derivation to (79) in this model would be the following ((a) = Root delinking; (b) = Parasitic delinking; and (c) = compensatory lengthening):

Moraic phonology appears to be more explanatory than other prosodic models in describing compensatory lengthening processes in languages in which moraic structure is contrastive serves to establish underlying length distinctions (Hayes 1989). This is clearly not the case in the Spanish dialects I am describing. As mentioned, the morphological information conveyed by word-final /s/ (or its aspirated variant) has been undertaken by vowel laxing, not by vowel length (Mondéjar 1970, Hooper 1976, Zubizarreta 1979). At present, I do not know of any evidence showing that the moraic model would enjoy a descriptive edge over the framework adhered to in this paper.

So far, my discussion of the data on gemination in (73) has deliberately ignored the contexts in which the aspirated /s/ is followed by a voiced obstruent. The reason is that these cases contain an additional complexity. Recall that voiced obstruents are subject to the spirantization rule (57) introduced earlier. Here, instead of the expected voiced spirant geminates, we obtain voiceless ones:[76]

(80)   *Underlying*   *Surface*
        /resBalar/   [r̥e̞ɸ.ɸalár]   'to slip, slide'
        /es Bino/   [é̞ɸ.ɸíno]   'it's wine'
        /DesDe/   [dé̞θ.θe]   'from'
        /los Dos/   [lo̞θ.θó̞:]   'the two (of them)'
        /los Gatos/   [lo̞x.xáto̞:]   'the cats'
        /musGo/   [múx.xo]   'moss'

In Hualde (1989b), the process is captured by a rule that spreads the [–voice] specification from the output segment in (74b) onto the spirantized voiced obstruent. I have argued, however, that gemination should be stated as Root spreading, as in (77b). This rule produces intermediate voiced spirant geminates (which are are simultaneously linked to a rhyme and to the following onset), and thus they meet the structural description of two rules we have already discussed in (68), namely, Laryngeal delinking and default assignment of [–voice]. These rules account for the voiceless spirant geminates in (80). A sample derivation for the item *musgo* in (80) is given in (81):

(81)   /musGo/
Spirantization (57):   musɣo
Aspiration (74b):   muhɣo
Gemination (77b):   muɣɣo
Delinking and default (68):   muxxo   (output)

In addition to *s*-induced gemination, some aspirating dialects have extended the geminating effects of /s/ to syllable-final liquids. Thus when

---

[76] Rodríguez-Castellano and Palacio (1948: 581–583), Salvador (1957: 225–226), Zamora Vicente (1979: 320), Lapesa (1981: 519). In some Andalusian and Chilean dialects, instead of [r̥e̞ɸ.ɸalár], [é̞ɸ.ɸíno], we find a geminate strident: [re̞f.falár], [é̞f.fíno] (cf. Hualde 1989b). This suggests the application of a redundancy rule that assigns [+strident] to labial fricatives, the labiodental articulation being an automatic phonetic consequence of such specification. My personal observation is that in some southeastern Andalusian varieties (e.g., Almería, Granada, Málaga), the phonetic realization of 'it's wine' in (79) ([é̞f.fíno]), is phonetically indistinguishable from *es fino* 'it's fine.'

syllable–final /r/ and /l/ are followed by a coronal sonorant, the latter may optionally surface as either an aspirated or a plain geminate, matching the pattern in (73): *carne* /karne/ → [kán̺.ne] or [kán.ne] 'meat', *codorniz* /kodorniθ/ → [co̯ðo̯n.ní] or [co̯ðo̯n.ní] 'quail', *comerlo* /komer+lo/ → [komé l̺.lo] or [komél.lo] 'to eat it', *el niño* /el niño/ → [en̺.ní.ño] or [en.ní.ño] 'the child', *el ratón* /el raton/ → [er̺.r̄atón] or [er.r̄atón] 'the mouse.'[77] To judge from the data available in the literature, the process appears to be more variable and unstable than obstruent. Furthermore, in the absence of gemination, both [r] and [l] are apparently interchangeable (i.e., in free variation) in syllable–final position, a curious type of neutralization that has been amply documented in many aspirating dialects (see fn. 65 for references). Crucially, syllable–final /r/ and /l/ may be aspirated and optionally deleted in these dialects, following the pattern observed for /s/ (Lenz 1940: 112, Rodríguez–Castellano and Palacio 1948, Alonso, Zamora Vicente, and Canellada 1950, Salvador 1957, Mondéjar 1970: 49–51, 67, Lapesa 1981: 505).

The data examined in this section falsify the SCD analysis in (70) because the delinking operation built into the spreading rule is not a formal property of spreading *per se*. On the other hand, such an analysis entails an unnecessary duplication, since additional delinking rules would be required in order to account for deletion in non–geminating environments. I have argued that there are two types of gemination in Spanish. The first seems to respond to matters of prosodic licensing; as such, it reflects general constraints on syllabic structure, and therefore its scope extends to phonological facts beyond the gemination process itself. The second (*s*–induced gemination) has been shown to arise as a consequence of delinking Supralaryngeal and Root features. In sum, the consonant gemination facts discussed here suggest that spreading rules may in fact arise as a consequence of delinking. Thus, although the same result would also be reached by SCD, a close inspection of the data suggests that the mechanism involved is just the opposite.

---

[77] Syllable–final liquids induce a somewhat similar type of gemination in Havana Spanish. But here the environment is more inclusive (it occurs before any consonant), and there are two concurring operations: spreading of retroflexion from the liquid to coronal consonant to its right, and spreading of [continuant] from the consonant leftwards onto the liquid. It appears, however, that in liquid–stop obstruent sequences the process involves gemination of Supralaryngeal features, and not Laryngeal ones: cf. /kurBa/ → [kúb.ba] 'curve', /GorDo/ → [góḍ.ḍo] 'fat' /el BoBo/ → [eb.bó.bo] 'the fool' vs. /ser pobre/ → [séb.pó.bre] 'to be poor', /el pobre/ → [eb.pó.bre] 'the poor one', /palko/ → [pág.ko] 'stage', etc. There are further complexities that require more space than can be granted here; see Harris (1985b) for an incisive study of this dialect.

5 Conclusion. In this paper I have discussed a variety of neutralization processes in Spanish, both synchronic and historical, illustrating how they can be interpreted as instances of the insert/delete parameter. I have shown that delinking is an autonomous mechanism in several types of segmental neutralization, and it interacts with redundancy principles and linking operations in principled ways. Furthermore, I have examined several types of assimilation rules that falsify two putative mechanisms of feature spreading. The data examined argue against the two prevalent approaches to assimilation rules. First, the evidence suggests that spreading rules are not feature changing. In the relevant cases, delinking operations have been motivated independently of assimilation. And second, the emergence of complex and contour segments in postlexical assimilation rules shows that the Spreading Condition that requires feature unspecification on the targets of spreading does not hold in many cases either. What are, then, the general conditions determining the application of assimilation rules? From the discussion presented here it would seem that there is a conjunction of factors, such as prosodic restrictions on content, the kind of feature content specified in targets, relative ordering relations among rules, and so on. The data presented in this paper, however, clearly show that the formal conditions on feature spreading in assimilation do not include target unspecification.

References

Alarcos Llorach, E. 1974. Fonología española (4ª edición). Madrid: Gredos.
Alonso, A. 1955. De la pronunciación medieval a la moderna en español. Madrid: Gredos.
Alonso, A. 1967. Estudios lingüísticos. Temas hispanoamericanos. Madrid: Gredos.
Alonso, D., A. Zamora Vicente, and M. J. Canellada. 1950. Vocales andaluzas. Nueva Revista de Filología Hispánica 3, 209–230.
Alvar, M. 1959. El español hablado en Tenerife. Madrid: CSIC.
Alvarez, R., et al. 1986. Gramática galega. Vigo, Spain: Galaxia.
Anderson, S. R. 1982. Schwa in French, or How to Get Something for Nothing. Language 58, 534–574.
Anderson, S. R. 1984. A Metrical Interpretation of Some Traditional Claims about Quantity and Stress. In M. Aronoff and R. T. Oehrle, eds., Language Sound Structure. Cambridge, Mass.: MIT Press, 83–106.
Archangeli, D. 1984. Underspecification in Yawelmani Phonology and Morphology. Doctoral dissertation, MIT. Cambridge, Mass.
Archangeli, D. 1987. Feature Organization: Implications of the Maximal/Minimal Parameter. Ms., University of Arizona.
Archangeli, D. 1988. Aspects of Underspecification Theory. Phonology 5, 183–207.
Archangeli, D., and D. Pulleyblank. 1986. The Content and Structure of Phonological Representations. Ms., University of Arizona and University of Southern California. (To be published by MIT Press, Cambridge, Mass.)
Archangeli, D., and D. Pulleyblank. 1987. Maximal and Minimal Rules: Effects of Tier Scansion. Proceedings of NELS 17, 16–35.

Archangeli, D., and D. Pulleyblank. 1989. Yoruba Vowel Harmony. Linguistic Inquiry 20, 173-218.

Avery, P., and K. Rice. 1989. Segment Structure and Coronal Underspecification. Phonology 6, 179-200.

Basbøll, H. 1974. Structure consonantique du mot italien. Revue Romane 9, 27-40.

Bhat, D. N. S. 1978. A General Study of Palatalization. In J. H. Greenberg et al., eds., Universals of Human Language, vol. 2. Stanford, Ca.: Stanford University Press, 47-92.

Cadierno, T., and P. Prieto. 1989. Asturian Nasal Assimilation and the Structure of Complex Segments. In B. Lawton and A. J. Tamburri, eds., Romance Languages Annual, vol. 1. West Lafayette, Indiana: Purdue Research Foundation, 653-660.

Calabrese, A. 1988. Towards a Theory of Phonological Alphabets. Doctoral dissertation, MIT. (Distributed by MIT Working Papers in Linguistics, Cambridge, Mass.)

Calabrese, A. 1991. On Palatalization Processes. Ms., Harvard University.

Carballo Calero, R. 1979. Gramática del gallego común. Vigo, Spain: Galaxia.

Cedergren, H. 1973. The Interplay of Social and Linguistic Factors in Panama. Doctoral dissertation, Cornell University.

Chomsky, N. G., and M. Halle. 1968. The Sound Pattern of English. New York: Harper & Row.

Clements, G. 1981. Akan Vowel Harmony: A Non-Linear Analysis. Harvard Studies in Phonology 2. Bloomington: Indiana University Linguistics Club, 108-177.

Clements, N. G. 1985. Compensatory Lengthening and Consonant Gemination in LuGanda. In L. Wetzels and E. Sezer, eds., Studies in Compensatory Lengthening. Dordrecht: Foris, 38-78.

Clements, G. N. 1985. The Geometry of Phonological Features. Phonology Yearbook 2, 224-254.

Clements, G. N. 1987. Phonological Feature Representation and the Description of Intrusive Stops. In A. Bosch, B. Need, and E. Schiller, eds., Papers from the 23rd Annual Meeting of the Chicago Linguistics Society. Chicago: Chicago Linguistics Society, 29-50.

Clements, G. N. 1988. Towards a Substantive Theory of Feature Specifications. Proceedings of NELS 18, 79-93.

Clements, G. N., and K. Ford. 1979. Kikuyu Tone Shift and its Synchronic Consequences. Linguistic Inquiry 10, 179-210.

Clements, G. N., and E. Sezer 1982. Vowel and Consonant Disharmony in Turkish. In H. van der Hulst and N. Smith, eds., The Structure of Phonological Representations, vol. 2. Dordrecht: Foris, 213-255.

Cole, J. S. 1987. Planar Phonology and Morphology. Doctoral dissertation, MIT, Cambridge, Mass.

Contreras, H. 1969. Simplicity, Descriptive Adequacy, and Binary Features. Language 45, 1-8.

Craddock, J. R. 1980. The Contextual Varieties of Yod: An Attempt to Systematization. In E. L. Blasnitt and R. V. Teschner, A Festschrift for Jacob Ornstein. Studies in General Linguistics and Sociolinguistics. Rowley, Mass.: Newbury House, 61-68.

Cressey, W. W. 1978. Spanish Phonology and Morphology: A Generative View. Washington, D. C.: Georgetown University Press.

Crothers, J. 1978. Typology and Universals of Vowel Systems. In J. Greenberg et al., eds., Universals of Human Language, vol. 2. Stanford University Press, 93-152.

Dalbor, J. 1980. Spanish Pronunciation: Theory and Practice (2nd ed.). Chicago: Holt, Rinehart, and Winston.

De Chene, B., and S. R. Anderson. 1979. Compensatory Lengthening. Language 55, 505-535.

Devine, A. M., and D. Stephens. 1977. Two Studies in Latin Phonology. Studia Linguistica et Philologica, vol 3. Saratoga, Ca.: Anma Libri.

Fernández Rei, F. 1990. Dialectoloxía da lingua galega. Santiago de Compostela, Spain: Edicións Xeráis de Galicia.

Goldsmith, J. 1976. Autosegmental Phonology. Doctoral dissertation, MIT, Cambridge, Mass. (Published 1979, Garland, New York).

Goldsmith, J. 1981. Subsegmentals in Spanish Phonology: An Autosegmental Approach. In W. W. Cressey and D. J. Napoli, eds., Linguistic Symposium on Romance Languages IX. Washington, D. C.: Georgetown University Press, 1-16.

Goldsmith, J. 1990. Autosegmental and Metrical Phonology. Cambridge, Mass.: Basil Blackwell.

Grammont, M. 1895. La dissimilation consonantique dans les langues indo–européennes et dans les langues romanes. Dijon, France.

Guitart, J. 1976. Markedness and a Cuban Dialect of Spanish. Washington, D. C.: Georgetown University Press.

Harris, J. W. 1969. Spanish Phonology. Cambridge, Mass.: MIT Press.

Harris, J. W. 1975. Diphthongization, Monophthongization, Metaphony Revisited. In M. Saltarelli, and D. Wanner, eds., Diachronic Studies in Romance Linguistics. The Hague: Mouton, 85-97.

Harris, J. W. 1980. Non–Concatenative Phonology and Spanish Plurals. Journal of Linguistic Research 1, 15-31.

Harris, J. W. 1983. Syllable Structure and Stress in Spanish: A Non–Linear Approach. Cambridge, Mass.: MIT Press.

Harris, J. W. 1984a. Autosegmental Phonology, Lexical Phonology, and Spanish Nasals. In M. Aronoff and R. T. Oehrle, eds., Language Sound Structure. Cambridge, Mass.: MIT Press, 67-82.

Harris, J. W. 1984b. Theories of Phonological Representation and Nasal Consonants in Spanish. In Ph. Baldi, ed., Papers from the 12th Linguistic Symposium on Romance Languages. Philadelphia: John Benjamins, 153-168.

Harris, J. W. 1984c. La espirantización en castellano y la representación fonológica autosegmental. Universitat Autònoma de Barcelona, Estudis Gramaticals 1, 149-167.

Harris, J. W. 1985. Spanish Diphthongization and Stress: A Paradox Resolved. In: Phonology Yearbook 2, 31-46.

Harris, J. W. 1989a. Our Present Understanding of Spanish Syllable Structure. In P. C. Bjarkman and R. M. Hammond, eds., American Spanish Pronunciation. Washington, D. C.: Georgetown University Press, 151-169.

Harris, J. W. 1989b. Sonority and Syllabification in Spanish. In C. Kirschner and J. Decesaris, eds., Studies in Romance Linguistics. Philadelphia: John Benjamins, 139-153.

Hayes, B. 1986a. Inalterability in CV Phonology. Language 62, 321-352.

Hayes, B. 1986b. Assimilation as Spreading in Toba Batak. Linguistic Inquiry 17, 467-500.

Hayes, B. 1989. Compensatory Lengthening in Moraic Phonology. Linguistic Inquiry 20, 253-306.

Hock, H. 1986. Compensatory Lengthening: in Defense of the Concept of Mora. Folia Linguistica 20, 431-460.

Hockett, C. F. 1955. A Manual of Phonology. Baltimore: Waverley Press.

Hooper, J. B. 1972. The Syllable in Phonological Theory. Language 48, 525-540.

Hooper, J. B. 1976. An Introduction to Natural Generative Phonology. New York: Academic Press.

Hualde, J. I. 1988. A Lexical Phonology of Basque. Doctoral dissertation, University of Southern California, Los Angeles.

Hualde, J. I. 1989a. Silabeo y estructura morfémica en español. Hispania 72, 821-831.

Hualde, J. I. 1989b. Procesos consonánticos y estructuras geométricas en español. Lingüística ALFAL 1, 7–44.

Hualde , J. I. 1989c. Delinking Processes in Romance. In C. Kirschner and J. Decesaris, eds., Studies in Romance Linguistics. Philadelphia: John Benjamins, 177–193.

Hulst, H. G. van der. 1989. Atoms of Segmental Structure: Components, Gestures, and Dependency. Phonology 6, 253–284.

Hyman, R. 1956. /n/ as an Allophone Denoting Open Juncture in General Spanish-American Dialects. Hispania 39, 293-299.

Hyman, L. 1975. Phonology: Theory and Analysis. New York: Holt, Rinehart and Winston.

Hyman, L. 1988. Underspecification and Vowel Height Transfer in Esimbi. Phonology 5, 255-274.

Ingria, R. 1980. Compensatory Lengthening as a Metrical Phenomenon. Linguistic Inquiry 11, 465–495.

Itô, J. 1986. Syllable Theory in Prosodic Phonology. Doctoral dissertation, University of Massachusetts at Amherst.

Iverson, G. 1989. On the Category Supralaryngeal. Phonology 6, 285–304.

Joos, M. 1953. The Medieval Sibilants. Language 28, 222-231.

Kaye, J. 1982. Harmony Processes in Vata. In H. van der Hulst, and N. Smith, eds., The Structure of Phonological Representations, vol. 2. Dordrecht: Foris, 385-452.

Kaye, J. 1989. Phonology: A Cognitive View. Hillsdale, NJ: Laurence Erlbaum Associates.

Keating, P. 1984. Phonetic and Phonological Representation of Stop Consonant Voicing. Language 60, 286–319.

Keating, P. 1988. Underspecification in Phonetics. Phonology 5, 275–292.

Keating, P. 1991. Coronal Places of Articulation. In C. Paradis and J.-F. Prunet, eds., The Special Status of Coronals (Phonetics and Phonology, vol. 2). New York: Academic Press, 29–48.

Kiparsky, P. 1979. Metrical Structure Assignment is Cyclic. Linguistic Inquiry 10, 421–441.

Kiparsky, P. 1982a. Lexical Morphology and Phonology. In I. S. Yang, ed., Linguistics in the Morning Calm. Seoul: Hanshin Publishing Co., 3-92.

Kiparsky, P. 1982b. Explanation in Phonology. Dordrecht: Foris.

Kiparsky, P. 1985. Some Consequences of Lexical Phonology. Phonology Yearbook 2, 85-138.

Klausenburger, J. 1975. Latin Vocalic Quantity to Quality: A Pseudo Problem? In M. Saltarelli and D. Wanner, eds., Diachronic Studies in Romance Linguistics. The Hague: Mouton, 107–117.

Ladefoged, P. 1971. Preliminaries to Linguistic Phonetics. Chicago: University of Chicago Press.

Lahiri, A., and V. Evers. 1991. Palatalization and Coronality. In C. Paradis and J.-F. Prunet, eds., The Special Status of Coronals (Phonetics and Phonology, vol. 2). New York: Academic Press, 79–100.

Lapesa, R. 1981. Historia de la lengua española (9ª ed.). Madrid: Gredos.

Lenz, R. 1940. Estudios chilenos. (Spanish version of Chilenische Studien, translated by A. Alonso and R. Lida). Buenos Aires: Imprenta de la Universidad de Buenos Aires.

Levin, J. 1985. A Metrical Theory of Syllabicity. Doctoral dissertation, MIT.

Lisker, L., and A. S. Abramson. 1971. Distinctive Features and Laryngeal Control. Language 47, 767-785.

Lloyd, P. M. 1987. From Latin to Spanish. Philadelphia: American Philosophical Society.

Lowenstamm, J., and J. Kaye. 1985. Compensatory Lengthening in Tiberian Hebrew. In L. Wetzels and E. Sezer, eds., Studies in Compensatory Lengthening. Dordrecht: Foris, 97–132.

Lozano, M. del Carmen. 1979. Stop and Spirant Alternations: Fortition and Spirantization Processes in Spanish Phonology. Doctoral dissertation, Univ. of Indiana, Bloomington. Distributed by Indiana University Linguistics Club.

Maddieson, I. 1984. Patterns of Sounds. New York: Cambridge University Press.

Malkiel, Y. 1966. Diphthongization, Monophthongization, Metaphony: Studies in their Interaction in the Paradigm of the Old Spanish -ir Verbs. Language 42, 430-472.

Malmberg, B. 1965. Estudios de fonética hispánica. Madrid: CSIC.

Martínez-Gil, F. 1991. Old Spanish Intrusive Consonants. Ms., Georgetown University.

Mascaró, J. 1976. Catalan Phonology and the Phonological Cycle. Doctoral dissertation, MIT. Distributed by Indiana University Linguistics Club, Bloomington, Indiana (1978).

Mascaró, J. 1984. Continuant Spreading in Basque, Catalan, and Spanish. In M. Aronoff and R. T. Oehrle, eds., Language Sound Structure. Cambridge, Mass.: MIT Press, 287-298.

Mascaró, J. 1988. A Reduction and Spreading Theory of Voicing and Other Sound Effects. Ms., Universitat Autònoma de Barcelona.

McCarthy, J. J. 1986. OCP Effects: Gemination and Antigemination. Linguistic Inquiry 17, 207-264.

McCarthy, J. 1989. Linear Order in Phonological Representation. Linguistic Inquiry 20, 71-100.

McCarthy, J., and A. Prince. 1986. Prosodic Morphology. Ms., University of Massachussets at Amherst and Brandeis University. (To be published by MIT Press, Cambridge, Mass.)

Menéndez Pidal, R. 1968. Orígenes del español (6ª ed.). Madrid Espasa-Calpe.

Menéndez Pidal, R. 1980. Manual de gramática histórica española (16ª ed.). Madrid: Espasa Calpe.

Mester, A., and J. Itô. 1989. Feature Predictability and Underspecification: Palatal Prosody in Japanese Mimetics. Language 65, 258-293.

Mohanan, K. P. 1986. The Theory of Lexical Phonology. Boston: D. Reidel.

Mohanan, K. P. 1991. On the Basis of Radical Underspecification. Natural Language and Linguistic Theory 9, 285-325.

Michael, I. (ed.). 1980. Poema de Mio Cid. Madrid: Catalia.

Mondéjar, J. 1970. El verbo andaluz: formas y estructuras. Madrid: CSIC.

Montreuil, J.-P. 1989. On Assimilation through Schwa. In C. Kirschner and J. Decesaris, eds., Studies in Romance Linguistics. Philadelphia: John Benjamins, 261-272.

Morin, I. Ch. 1980. Morphologization de l'épenthese en ancien français. CJL/RCL 25, 204-225.

Morin, I. Ch. 1987. De quelques propriétés de l'épenthese consonantique. CJL/RCL 32, 365-375.

Navarro Tomás, T. 1939. Desdoblamiento de fonemas vocálicos. Revista de Filología Hispánica 1, 165-167.

Navarro Tomás, T. 1974. El español en Puerto Rico. Río Piedras, Puerto Rico: Editorial Universitaria.

Navarro Tomás, T. 1977. Manual de pronunciación española (19ª ed.). Madrid: CSIC.

Odden, D. 1986. On the Role of the Obligatory Contour Principle in Phonological Theory. Language 62, 353-383.

Odden, D. 1988. Antigemination and the OCP. Linguistic Inquiry 19, 451-475.

Oftedal, M. 1985. Lenition in Celtic and Insular Spanish: The Second Voicing of Stops in Gran Canaria. (Monographs in Celtic Studies from the University of Oslo, vol. 2). Oslo: Universitetsforlaget.

Otero, C. P. 1971. Evolución y revolución en romance, vol 1. Barcelona: Seix Barral.

Otero, C. P. 1976. Evolución y revolución en romance, vol. 2. Barcelona: Seix Barral.

Otero, C. 1988. From Latin to Romance: The Vowel Systems. In C. Duncan-Rose and Th. Vennemann, eds., On Language: Rethorica, Phonologica, Syntactica. London: Routledge, 233–256.

Paradis, C., and J.-F. Prunet. 1991. Asymmetry and Visibility in Consonant Articulations. In C. Paradis and J.-F. Prunet, eds., The Special Status of Coronals (Phonetics and Phonology, vol. 2). New York: Academic Press, 1–28.

Paradis, C., and J.-F. Prunet, eds. 1991. The Special Status of Coronals (Phonetics and Phonology, vol. 2). New York: Academic Press.

Penny, R. 1991. A History of the Spanish Language. New York: Cambridge University Press.

Poplack, Sh. 1979. Function and Process in a Variable Phonology. Doctoral dissertation, University of Pennsylvania.

Porto Dapena, J. A. 1977. El gallego hablado en la comarca ferrolana. Verba, anejo 9. Santiago de Compostela, Spain: Universidade de Santiago de Compostela.

Pulleyblank, D. 1986. Tone in Lexical Phonology. Dordrecht: Reidel.

Pulleyblank, D. 1988. Vocalic Underspecification in Yoruba. Linguistic Inquiry 19, 233–270.

Rice, K. 1989. On Elliminating Resyllabification into Onsets. Proceedings of WCCFL 8. Stanford, Ca.: Stanford Linguistics Association, 331-346.

Rice K., and P. Avery. 1991. On the Relationship between Laterality and Coronality. In C. Paradis and J.-F. Prunet, eds., The Special Status of Coronals (Phonetics and Phonology, vol. 2). New York: Academic Press, 101–124.

Rodríguez-Castellano, L., and A. Palacio. 1984. El habla de Cabra: contribución al estudio del dialecto andaluz. Revista de Tradiciones Populares 4, 387–418, and 570–599.

Rubach, J. 1990. Final Devoicing and Cyclic Resyllabification in German. Linguistic Inquiry 21, 79-94.

Sezer, E. 1985. An Autosegmental Analysis of Compensatory Lengthening in Turkish. In L. Wetzels and E. Sezer, eds., Studies in Compensatory Lengthening. Dordrecht: Foris, 227–250.

Schein B., and D. Steriade. 1986. On Geminates. Linguistic Inquiry 17.691-744.

Sagey, E. C. 1986. The Representation of Features and Relations in Non-Linear Phonology. Doctoral dissertation. MIT, Cambridge, Mass.

Saltarelli, M. 1983. The Mora Unit in Italian Phonology. Folia Linguistica 17, 7–24.

Salvador, G. 1957. El habla de Cúllar-Baza. Revista de Filología Española 41, 161–252.

Salvador, G. 1987. Estudios dialectológicos. Madrid: Paraninfo.

Schein, B., and D. Steriade. 1986. On Geminates. Linguistic Inquiry 17, 691-744.

Steriade, D. 1982. Greek Prosodies and the Nature of Syllabification. Doctoral dissertation, MIT.

Steriade, D. 1987a. Locality Conditions and Feature Geometry. Proceedings of NELS 17, 595–617.

Steriade, D. 1987b. Redundant Values. In A. Bosch, B. Need, and E. Schiller, eds., Papers from the 23rd Annual Meeting of the Chicago Linguistics Society. Chicago: Chicago Linguistics Society, 339–362.

Terrell, T. 1975. La nasal implosiva y final en el español de Cuba. Anuario de Letras 13, 257–271.

Väänänen, V. 1968. Introducción al latín vulgar. Madrid: Gredos.

Veiga Arias, A. 1976. Fonología gallega. Valencia, Spain: Editorial Bello.

Walker, D. C. 1978. Old French Epenthesis, Boolean Algebra and Syllable Structure. CJL/RCL 23, 66-83.

Walker, D. C. 1981. Old French Epenthesis Revisited. CJL/RCL 26, 78-83.

Wetzels, W. L. 1985. The Historical Phonology of Intrusive Stops: A Non-Linear Description. CJL/RCL 1, 3-54.

Weinrich, H. 1958. Phonologische Studien zur romanischen Sprachgeschichte. Münster Westfalen: Aschendorff.

Yip, M. 1988. The Obligatory Contour Principle and Phonological Rules: A Loss of Identity. Linguistic Inquiry 19, 65-100.

Yip, M. 1991. Coronals, Consonant Clusters, and the Coda Condition. In C. Paradis and J.-F. Prunet, eds., The Special Status of Coronals (Phonetics and Phonology, vol. 2). New York: Academic Press, 61-78.

Zamora, J., and J. Guitart, 1982. Dialectología hispanoamericana. Salamanca, Spain: Almar.

Zamora Vicente, A. 1979. Dialectología española (2ª ed.). Madrid: Gredos.

Zubizarreta, M. L. 1979. Vowel Harmony in Andalusian Spanish. In K. Safir, ed., Papers on Syllable Structure, Metrical Structure, and Harmony Processes. MIT Working Papers in Linguistics, vol. 1, 1-11.

Headship assignment resolution in Spanish compounds

Rafael A. Núñez Cedeño *
University of Illinois at Chicago

1 Introduction. In their analysis of French compounds, Di Sciullo and Williams (1987; hereafter DS&W) claim that the members of the nominal compounds in (1) could not be the nucleus or head of their respective words 'because neither one is a noun,' except for those in (1a) whose right members may be construed as the nuclei (here, and in subsequent examples, the following abbreviations are used for expository convenience: V = Verb; N = Noun; A = Attributes (adjectives and adjective-functioning nouns); P = Preposition; Adj = Adjective; Adv = Adverb).

(1) a. V + N
    essui-glace   'windshield wiper'
    attrape-nigaud   'trickster'
    rabat-joie   'kill-joy'

   b. V + A
    gagne-petit   'cheap-jack'
    sent-bon   'perfume'
    pense-bête   'reminder'

   c. V + A
    couche-tard   'nightowl'
    leve-tôt   'earlyriser'
    passe-partout   'masterkey'

   d. V + P
    frappe-devant   'sledge-hammer'
    saute-dessus   'leap-frog'

They analyze (1) as syntactic phrasal categories lacking morphological forms though displaying the properties of words, namely, that they are X^os insertable in syntax into N positions. According to DS&W, these types of forms are accounted for by rule (2), which essentially says that in this language any syntactic category can be analyzed as one of the noun types shown in (3):

(2)   N → XP

---

*I am most thankful to Heles Contreras, Jim Harris, and José Ignacio Hualde for their valuable comments. The usual disclaimer applies.

(3)

```
      N           N           N           N
      |           |           |           |
      VP          AP          PP          NP
     / \         / \         / \         / \
    V  NP       A  PP       P  NP       N  PP
```

Based on this assumption, DS&W claim that Spanish, like French, lacks compounding altogether. Though DS&W are partially correct as far as a certain type of Spanish compounds is concerned, their claims cannot apply to all compound combinations. In 1985 Contreras had convincingly demonstrated that many compounds are left-headed. There are, however, many other compounds that are right-headed. In this study I will argue against both DS&W's headless analysis and Contreras's head-initial only hypothesis, and instead will propose that Spanish may be characterized as having total headlessness and a mixture of left- and right-headedness. It will be shown that the latter can be predicted by a single unitary statement which takes into account the semantic and morphological relationship holding between the members of the compound. In a sense, this statement is a modified version of Lieber's (1983) Convention IV.

In order to facilitate the discussion, I have organized the exposition in the following way. In section 2, I examine adverb-formation with -*mente* and conclude that this type of compounding supports DS&W's arguments. In section 3, I digress somewhat to present as a background to headship   a general overview of the theory of lexical structure that will guide our discussion of right-headedness in derivational forms and in compounds. Section 4 summarizes Contreras's arguments for left-headed compounding. In this section I also introduce additional Spanish data which question Contreras's hypothesis. While reviewing in section 5 Di Sciulo and Williams's hypothesis, I will demonstrate that some morphological operations, i.e., pluralization and diminutive formation, totally contravene their non-morphological word-creating rule. Section 6 presents a solution to the various headship parameters and shows that these can be reduced to one with a generalized single statement.

2 Headless compounds. DS&W (1987) argue that compounds are reanalyzed phrases. They distinguish between what they call, on one hand, syntactic words, and on the other hand, syntactic phrases. Syntactic words are basically a class of phrasal objects displaying the general characteristics of X°s but lacking morphological forms as in the structures presented in (3). Because they lack morphological form, they are considered marked objects presumably found in the periphery of the grammar. These will be discussed below with examples from Spanish. Syntactic phrases differ from the former in that they are phrasal idioms listed in the lexicon and are further characterized as not having compositional meaning. Examples of these are phrases such as:

meterse en camisas de once varas
to get oneself into shirts of eleven yards
'to get oneself into deep trouble'

In this idiom, the subject (the underlined in the ensuing sentences is the subject) may appear between the verb and the rest of the phrase. Thus the phrasal sentence *Juan se metió en camisas de once varas* alternatively can be *se metió Juan en camisas de once varas* 'John got himself into deep trouble,' which is exactly what one would expect in a regular syntactic construction. Notice, for instance, that the sentence:

los muchachos lo hicieron en el campo
the boys it did in the country
'the boys did it in the country'

can also be:

lo hicieron los muchachos en el campo
it did the boys in the country

with the same meaning.

Another crucial difference between the two is that syntactic words are inserted into X^0s whereas syntactic phrases are insertable only into X^{max} positions. Of paramount importance for the argument in this paper will be the compounds of the X^0 type. The data in (4) support DS&W's argument for headlessness in Spanish compounds.[1]

(4)   a.   P +   Adv or Adj

parabién	(para	+	bien)		'compliment'
	'for'		'well'		
parapoco	(para	+	poco)		'numbskull'
	'for'		'little'		
pormenor	(por	+	menor)		'detail'
	'by'		'minor'		

---

[1] In what follows I center my attention on the following headed combinations: V+N, N+N, N+Adj, Adj+N, P+N, and N+V. Except for the last one, the rest appear to be quite numerous in Spanish. There are other combination types such as Adj+Adj, V+Adv, P+Adv not studied here; the latter two (V+Adv and P+Adv) are very rare. Also, I am assuming that something like Lieber's Argument Linking Principle (1983) applies in Spanish. In general, this principle predicts what kinds of compounds should be the most productive and which ones should be less than fully productive or totally nonexistent.

b. Adj + N (*mente* 'mind')

gentilmente	(gentil + mente)	'gently'
estúpidamente	(estúpida + mente)	'stupidly'
arrogantemente	(arrogante + mente)	'arrogantly'
humildemente	(humilde + mente)	'humbly'
sinceramente	(sincera + mente)	'sincerely'

Now, the data in (4) show conclusively that neither of the two elements forming the compound heads the whole. Note that if headship is fixed either on the right or on the left, the net result is a compound whose major category is diametrically different from those categories containing it: all items in (4a) are nouns and those in (4b) adverbs. Though (4a) corresponds to a limited set (I have just been able to collect these three), those in (4b) are quite abundant and productive. Incidentally, the combinations in (4b) reflect accurately their diachronic structure and have been elegantly argued for in Zagona (1989). Thus the compounds (4), present prima facie evidence for headlessness in Spanish. In order to account for the existence of the more abundant ones in (4b), the language needs the marked rule (5), which simply says that an adjective and the noun *mente* 'mind' are together analyzed as an adverb. Since this combination is a headless X°, it follows that the features of its members are not percolated.

(5)   Adv → [Adj + mente]$_N$

Another class of compounds which seems to support the headless hypothesis belongs to the N+A type. However, we must be careful with the analysis of this type of combination because the right member could be construed as the head. Observe the class in (6), drawn from Narváez (1970) and Montes Giraldo (1983) (the abbreviations *f.*, *m.*, and *u.* stand for feminine, masculine, and unmarked for gender, respectively).

(6)   N + Adj

lengualarga	(lengua, f. + larga, f.)	'foul-mouthed'
	tongue long	
paticojo	(pata, f. + cojo, m.)	'lame'
	leg lame	
ojialegre	(ojo, m. + alegre, u.)	'with happy eyes'
	eye happy	
almanegra	(alma, f. + negra, f.)	'a coffee bean disease'
	soul black	

pelirrojo	(pelo, m. + rojo, m.)	'redhead'
	head red	
carirredondo	(cara, f. + redondo, m.)	'round-faced'
	face round	
barbilampiño	(barba, f. + lampiño, m.)	'beardless'
	beard hairless	

This adjective-deriving combination is generally considered exocentric and could be compared to the English *redhead, longlegs* type. As Selkirk notes, *pace* Bloomfield (1984: 233), a *redhead* is not a head that is red but someone having that special characteristic. Similarly, Spanish *carirredondo* does not mean a face that is round but rather someone having a round face. Notice in this example, and in the last one in (6), that the first element is feminine and the second one is masculine, thus clearly indicating that the latter could not be modifying the former, for otherwise the expected agreement would show. Since *redondo*, an adjective, is modifying something or someone other than *cara*, and furthermore, since the function of adjectives is to determine or describe nouns in some way (thus showing that adjectives need to agree with nouns in number and gender), it follows that they can only stand in a nonhead relationship to that someone or something which may turn out to be their head. The N+A combinations, or for that matter, the A+A types, such as *claroscuro* (*claro*, adj. 'clear' + *oscuro*, adj. 'dark') 'chiaroscuro,' or *sordomudo* (*sordo*, adj. 'deaf' + *mudo*, adj 'mute') 'deafmute,' are adjectival exocentric compounds which lend support to DS&W's position. Therefore, in the absence of a clearly distinguishable nucleus, which in these cases is being referred to by implication or metaphor, (6) must be considered a headless compound with adjectival functions (though I should point out that not all types of N+A compounds are headless, as we will see shortly). The data in (6), in addition to the A+A combination, are generated by the marked rule (7). Again, these are headless X^0s and the features of their members are not percolated.

(7) $\quad A \rightarrow \left\{ \begin{array}{c} Adj \\ N \end{array} \right\} A$

Aside from the data listed in (4) and (6), there exists no further support for DS&W's claims. On the contrary, the vast majority of compounds seems to have a fixed head, either on the right or on the left. Contreras (1985), in responding to Lieber's (1983) theory of lexical structure, has presented the most cogent argumentation for left-headedness. There is also evidence for right-headedness but before studying this, it is worth reviewing Contreras's arguments; so in order to do this, let us first put the issue of headship in its appropriate perspective, that is, by giving an overview of headship in derivations.

2 Headship in a larger context. Structurally, Spanish nonverbs are composed of a derivational base which may end with the coronal consonants /d, l, r, n, s/ or may be followed by a predictable terminal vowel or word marker signalling in general gender distinctions; for a more extensive discussion, see Harris (1985). So, when speaking of 'word,' I assume that in nonverbs it is a stem followed by a word marker, if there is any. Essentially, a word is an X°, as in X-bar syntax. However, I should call attention to the fact that the vowel immediately following the stem in verbs is not a word marker but a theme vowel which may or may not appear in derivations. Its absence is conditioned by a number of factors that are not relevant to the present discussion (see Núñez Cedeño, forthcoming). This contrasts with the behavior of word markers which never appear inside the stem when suffixes are attached to it.[2]

Assuming then that suffixes invariably attach to derivational stems in non-verbs, with the above proviso for verbs, this attachment entails (recursive) changes to the category of its derivational stem. Ultimately, the last suffix added assigns its category and subcategory to the whole word. The examples in (8) show what normally occurs in Spanish derivations.

(8)　　$[[\text{libert}]\text{o}]_A$　　　　　　　'free'
　　　　$[[\text{libert}]_A\text{in}]\text{o}]_A$　　　　'dissolute'
　　　　$[[\text{libert}]_A\text{in}]_A\text{aj}]_N\text{e}]_N$　　'libertinism'
　　　　$[[\text{periferi}]\text{a}]_N$　　　　　'periphery'
　　　　$[[\text{periferi}]_N\text{ic}]\text{o}]_A$　　　'peripheric'
　　　　$[[\text{periferi}]_N\text{ic}]_A\text{idad}]_N]_N$　'peripheriality'
　　　　$[[\text{afianz}]\text{ar}]_V$　　　　　'to fasten'
　　　　$[[\text{afianz}]\text{a}]_V\text{mient}]_N\text{o}]_N$　'fastening'
　　　　$[[\text{constitu}]\text{ir}]_V$　　　　'to constitute'
　　　　$[[\text{constitu}]_V\text{cion}]_N$　　　'constitution'
　　　　$[[\text{constitu}]_V\text{cion}]_N\text{al}]_A$　　'constitutional'
　　　　$[[\text{constitu}]_V\text{cion}]_N\text{al}]_A\text{idad}]_N$　'constitutionality'

It is evident that suffixes generally determine the category of the newly formed word. This suggests that Spanish derivations are preferentially right-headed, though some suffixes seem to behave exceptionally. For example, diminutive,

---

[2] It is the case, for instance, that in order to derive *periférico* 'peripheric' from *periferia* 'periphery,' the ultimate result must be the former and not **periferiaco*. Note that the *-a* of the inner base is gone in the derivation.

6pejorative, and augmentative suffixes do not change category; rather, the latter is inherited from its inner base. This fact would indicate that these affixes bear no category type. Lieber's Convention III given in (9) would account for this.

3.1 Lieber's theory of lexical structure. The lexical structure theory of Lieber (1983) provides us with the basic structural principles for deriving words and assigning headship. The basic mechanism for derivation works as follows. Morphemes and affixes are listed in the lexicon with their unpredictable categories and subcategories which signal the kind of lexical items they must attach to. Additional unpredictable information that must be specified for each lexical item are its: (1) category and conjugation class, (2) phonological representation, (3) semantic representation, (4) diacritic specification, and (5) frames of insertion. In Spanish, for instance, the suffix -*ez* '-ness' is a nominal suffix that must attach to adjectives only. Its phonological representation for Spanish American Spanish is /-es/ and for Castilian /-eθ/; it has an abstract interpretation of 'quality of', and it is generally restricted to polysyllabic bases (Núñez Cedeño, op. cit.).

Notwithstanding their subcategorization restrictions, morphemes are inserted into unlabeled binary-branching trees which ar ventually labeled by means of Feature Percolation Conventions.

(9) Feature Percolation Conventions (Lieber 1983: 252):

a. Convention I:
All features of a stem morpheme, including category features percolate to the first nonbranching node dominating that morpheme.

For example:

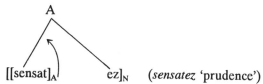

[[sensat]_A ez]_N   (*sensatez* 'prudence')

b. Convention II:
All features of an affix morpheme, including category features, percolate to the first branching node dominating that morpheme.[3]

---

[3] Convention I fails to apply to prefixes such as *contra, sobre, des*, etc. because they seem to be categoryless. The fact that prefixes attach to bases without causing any categorial changes is sure proof of their categoryless status. For example, the prefix *des* denotes the opposite of its base and may attach to nouns, adjectives or verbs, yet the resulting word bears exactly these

For example:

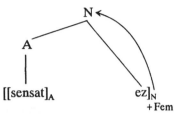

$$[[sensat]_A \qquad ez]_N$$
$$+Fem$$

    c. Convention III:
    If a branching node fails to obtain features by Convention II,
    features from the next lowest labeled node automatically percolate
    up to the unlabeled branching node.

This applies to suffixation with diminutives lacking category features. A derivation for the diminutive *camita* 'little bed' is provided:

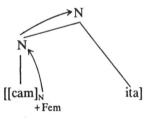

    d. Convention IV:
    If two stems are sisters (i.e., they form a compound), features from
    the right-hand stem percolate up to the branching node dominating
    the stems.

For example:

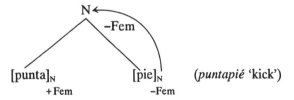

(puntapié 'kick')

The first three Conventions are said to be universal and the fourth one is language-specific (i.e. for English and Spanish) since there are languages, like Thai and Vietnamese, that label compounds with the features of the leftmost element. Conventions I-II and IV have the effect of labeling the

---

same categories: [des[acierto]$_N$]$_N$ 'blunder,' [des[leal]$_{Adj}$]$_{Adj}$ 'unfaithful,' [des[hacer]$_V$]$_V$ 'to undo.' Convention II obviously must apply here.

highest branching node with the category and features of the rightmost affix or word. Convention III is exceptional in the sense that the lowest morpheme down, on the left, provides the tree with its category and features. This only occurs when the affix in question is unspecified for the relevant features, as shown above. The first three Conventions then have the general effect of providing a basic structure to Spanish derivations and of determining right-headedness in a principled way. If this right-hand parametrization holds for derivations, there are reasons to believe that it is equally applicable to compounds, hence Convention IV. However, the exocentric combinations of the V + Comp type and other combinations seem to pose a serious problem to Convention IV as stated. It is precisely the former types that led Contreras (1985) to reject Convention IV, and propose instead that compounding is left-headed. Let us examine his arguments briefly.

4 Contreras's framework. Contreras discusses and rejects Lieber's Convention IV and proposes that Spanish must be parametrized so as to assign the features of the left-hand element. He argues that if Convention IV were allowed to apply with right-hand parametrization it would make incorrect predictions for Spanish. Consider, for instance, the words *tocadiscos* 'record player' and *tapaboca* 'slap on the mouth'. According to Convention IV, the following should occur.

(10)   a.   b.

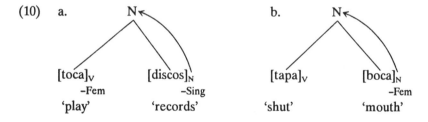

The problem with (10a) is that the noun on the right is plural and therefore when the features percolate up the noun should become plural, but the fact is that it remains singular. An example of this would be the phrase *este tocadiscos* 'this record player', which shows the adjective *este* in singular. In (10b) Convention IV incorrectly assigns the feminine gender to the whole word which is patently masculine; notice, for instance, that in a phrase with a definite article, *tapaboca* must be preceded by *el* 'the, masc.' and never by *la* 'the, fem.,' i.e., one must say *el tapaboca*. Since a generalized left-hand parametrization à la Lieber would allow for additional incorrect predictions, in *tocadiscos*, for example, Convention IV would wrongly assign the features of the verb to the word, thus making it a verb and not the expected noun. Contreras argues further, that there is a universal rule which generates both exocentric compounds and relative clauses. He therefore proposes that these compounds, admittedly the most productive type in Spanish, are structured as in (11):

(11)

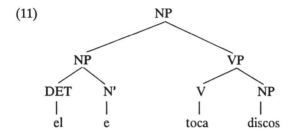

The presence in (11) of a null subject is determined by the rich inflectional system of Spanish (the verb, for instance, is in the third person singular) and it is licensed by the determiner *el* 'the'. Contreras points out that the structure in (11) follows a historical progression whereby one generation structures it as indicated and the next one simply interprets them as unanalyzed nouns. As the Convention IV does not apply in this type of compounds, Contreras provides a reinterpretation of X-bar theory that would account for automatic left-headedness in all compounds and relative clauses without further stipulations. This is accomplished with the following schemata which is applicable to other languages, hence its purported universality:

(12)   NP → NP X^{max}

Schemata (12) will also account for the nominal compounds illustrated in (13):

(13)   a. V + N

ganapán	(gana + pan, m.) win bread	'messenger'
comemierda	(come + mierda, f.) eat shit	'dumbshit'
limpiasaco	(limpia + saco, m.) clean jacket	'apple-polisher'
picaflor	(pica + flor, f.) pick flower	'Casanova'
vendepatria	(vende + patria, f.) sell fatherland	'traitor'
comelibros	(come + libros, m.) eat books	'bookworm'
matasanos	(mata + sanos, m.) kill healthy people	'quack'

portaaviones	(porta + aviones, m.)	'plane carrier'
	carry planes	
salvavidas	(salva + vidas, f.)	'lifeguard'
	save lives	
rascacielos	(rasca + cielos, m.)	'skyscraper'
	scratch skies	

b. N + N

hombre rana, m.	(hombre, m. + rana, f.)	'frogman'
	man frog	
camión cisterna, m.	(camión, m. + cisterna, f.)	'water-tank truck'
	truck water-tank	
cochecama, m.	(coche, m. + cama, f.)	'sleeping car'
	car bed	
pejemujer, m.	(peje, m. + mujer, f.)	'manatee'
	fish woman	
oración modelo, f.	(oración, f. + modelo, m.)	'model sentence'
	sentence model	
falda pantalón, f.	(falda, f. + pantalón, m.)	'culottes'
	skirt trousers	

c. N + Adj

lengua santa, f.	(lengua, f. + santa, f.)	'Hebrew'
	language saint	
aguas negras, f.	(aguas, f. + negras, f.)	'sewage water'
	water black	
aguardiente, f.	(agua, f. + ardiente, u.)	'spiritous liquor'
	water burning	
aguja magnética, f.	(aguja, f. + magnética, f.)	'compass needle'
	needle magnetic	
lengua viperina, f.	(lengua, f. + viperina, f.)	'evil-tongue'
	tongue viperine	
camposanto, m.	(campo, m. + santo, m.)	'cemetery'
	field sacred	

These examples undoubtedly support Contreras's thesis but they simultaneously countenance DS&W's, for it is clear that the head is the left-most element. Compounds of the type found in (13a) have been discussed in Contreras (1985) along the lines summarized above. For our purposes, the forms in (13b) are more to the point. Here, head assignment is particularly evident in the first four forms. Note that they are formed with masculine elements on the left and feminine ones on the right, but that the compound is masculine. The next two are a mirror-image of the first four: the first element in each is feminine and the second is masculine, but the whole is feminine. The items in (13c) differ from those in (4) in that the former are truly endocentric compound, whereas the latter, as discussed above, are headless. For instance, the compounds *lengua santa* and *aguas negras* designate a subset of the meaning of the elements contained or designated by the respective nouns *lengua* and *aguas* (cf.Selkirk 1983: 26). When speaking of *aguas negras*, in fact, there is a sense that *aguas* properly, and not something or someone outside the compound, has acquired the characteristic of blackness; therefore, the qualified element *aguas* must be the compound head.[4]. The same interpretation cannot apply to (4).

In a nutshell then, in Contreras's analysis it is argued that the 'exocentric' compounds in (13a) must be parametrized so as to receive the left-hand features of an empty NP. This is accomplished by means of the rule schemata (12), which by extension applies equally to all nouns I have introduced above; in other words, this rule states in general that Spanish compounds are head-initial. Other linguists have echoed a similar analysis, among them, Zagona (1989), Wong-opasi (1987), and Varela (1990). The common assumption underlying these analyses is that Spanish compounds manifest the internal structure of affix-derived verbs and non-verbs but with a distinct fixed parameter for left headhood.

Contreras's approach is illuminating to the extent that it shows there is headship assignment in Spanish. Yet, his discussion was restricted to one class of compounds and did not consider other possible productive combinations. A more in-depth probe unearths sufficient data showing that headedness is not limited to initial position but is permitted in final position as well. This, of course, would mean that Lieber's head-final parametrization (Convention IV) cannot be dispensed with lightly.

4.1 Counterevidence to the head-initial parameter. Let us consider some of the types of endocentric compounds not treated in previous generative analyses.[5]

---

[4] It would be an enormous enterprise to characterize fully the semantics of each compounds in (13b-c). For now, it suffices to say that each one forms a single semantic unit, and furthermore, that one of the element is the 'head.' Thus, for example, *buqueescuela* 'training ship' is a ship that functions as a school. There is a sense that somehow the second element, *escuela*, defines the first, thus semantically endowing the former with the attributes of headship. I will examine this in section 6.

[5] The compounds *piepaloma* and *gallocresta* are listed here as endocentric although they could be considered exocentric in the sense that their meaning is referential, that is, it is drawn from metaphorical comparisons to external objects or animals. However, unlike the exocentric forms in (6) whose referential nucleus is always outside of the compound, these two, having

(14)   N + N

puntapié, m.	(punta, f. + pie, m.) tip foot	'kick'
piepaloma, f.	(pie, m. + paloma, f.) foot pigeon	'type of yucca'
canaricultura, f.	(canario, m. + cultura, f.) canary breed	'canary breeding'
caficultura, f.	(café, m. + cultura, f.) coffee growth	'coffee growing'
maricultura, f.	(mar, m. + cultura, f.) sea breed	'breeding in the ocean'
carbodinamita, f.	(carbono, m. + dinamita, f.) carbon dynamite	'carbodynamite'
carricuba, f.	(carro, m. + cuba, f.) car barrel	'sprinkling van'
vasoconstricción, f.	(vaso, m. + constricción, f.) vessel constriction	'vessel dilation'
gallocresta, f.	(gallo, m. + cresta, f.) cock comb	'wild sage'
baciyelmo, m.	(bacía, f. + yelmo, m.) basin helmet	'a barber's helmet-like basin'
madreclavo, m.	(madre, f. + clavo, m.) mother clove	'spice clove'
claviórgano, m.	(clave, f. + órgano, m.) key organ	'string organ'
aguaviento, m.	(agua, f. + viento, m.) water wind	'driving rain'
aguaají, m.	(agua, f. + ají, m.) water greenpepper	'green-pepper soup'
arquibanco, m.	(arca, f. + banco, m.) chest bench	'bench with drawers'

In each of the examples in (14) above, the category of the whole does not seem to be determined by the noun on the left, for otherwise one would

---

internalized the totality of semantic features of that something to which they are being compared, would ultimately have to be considered headed compounds. Recall that *carirredondo* 'round-faced', for instance, refers to a person with those facial features and that its nucleus is outside. In *hombre carirredondo* 'a round-faced man', the nucleus is *hombre* and the phrase is perfectly acceptable. A similar reasoning cannot apply to *planta gallocresta* 'a wild sage plant' (the exact Spanish equivalent to the English translation would be *planta de gallocresta*) because it does not seem that the compound is modifying anything.

expect as a result a compound bearing its subcategory features, and this does not occur. In fact, by following Contreras's analysis one must conclude that the leftmost noun c-commands the rightmost one, much in the manner of (13). If this were so, then it would follow that the latter must be the head. Such a conclusion is not borne out by the facts presented above. On the contrary, these facts show that Convention IV still seems to be fully operative.

The A+N or the rare N+V combinations, which derive nouns and verbs respectively, are yet another type of compound that show right-headedness, countenancing again not only DS&W's approach but also Contreras's. The data can be accounted for with Convention IV. Observe example (15):

(15) a. Adj + N

malalengua, n.	(mala, f. + lengua, f.) bad tongue	'evil tongue'
bajorrelieve, m.	(bajo, m. + relieve, m.) low relief	'bas-relief'
altorrelieve, m.	(alto, m. + relieve, m.) high relief	'high relief'
fisicoquímica, f.	(físico, f. + química, f.) physical chemistry	'physical chemistry'
mediodía, m.	(medio, m. + día, m.) half day	'noon'
mediozapato, m.	(medio, m. + zapato, m.) half shoe	'a kind of shoe'
vanagloria, f.	(vana, f. + gloria, f.) vain glory	'conceit'
salvoconducto, m.	(salvo, m. + conducto, m.) safe conduct	'safeconduct'

b. N/Adv + V

maniatar	(mano, f. + atar, v.) hand to tie	'to handcuff'
caramarcar	(cara, f. + marcar, v.) face to mark	'to put on make-up'
malcriar	(mal, n. + criar, v.) bad to raise	'to spoil'

In each of the compounds above, the right element determines the feature taken on by the whole. In (15a), the items become nouns with all of their accompanying features; they certainly are not adjectives. In (15b), they become verbs and not nouns or adverbs. In each of the instances, headship is unquestionably assigned on the right, thus severely undermining DS&W's headless arguments and Contreras's formulation. The latter would generate incorrectly adjectival, nominal, and adverbial compounds. Convention IV, on the other hand, predicts that the right element will denote the whole compound.

Still, by further adhering to Contreras's hypothesis we cannot account for the fact that in a Preposition+Noun sequence the lexical output is systematically headed by N and not by the preposition on the left.[6] These same facts, illustrated in (16), erode further the 'syntactic atoms' hypothesis because there is an unquestionable head.

(16) P + N

sinrazón, f.	(sin + razón, f.) without reason	'unreasonableness'
sinsubstancia, f.	(sin + substancia, f.) without substance	'frivolous'
sinjusticia, f.	(sin + justicia, f.) without justice	'injustice'
sinvergüenza, f.	(sin + vergüenza, f.) without shame	'scoundrel'
sinsabor, m.	(sin + sabor, m.) without flavor	'sorrow'
sinnúmero, m.	(sin + número, m.) without number	'a great number'
sobrefalda, f.	(sobre + falda, f.) over skirt	'overskirt'
sobreclaustro, m.	(sobre + claustro, m.) over cloister	'apartment over cloister'
sobrepaño, m.	(sobre + paño, m.) over linen	'topcloth'
traspié	(tras + pie, m.) after foot	'stumble'

---

[6] There are numerous compounds of this type preceded by the words *contra* 'against' and *sobre* 'over'. Montes Giraldo (1983:57) lists them as combinations of prepositions and nouns. However, if we take a cursory look at the dictionary, we will notice that these two words do not generally denote their regular prepositional meanings when adjoined to nonverbs. In *sobreabundancia* 'superabundance,' for instance, *sobre* has the meaning 'excessive', whereas in *sobrearar* 'to replow' it means to 'repeat'. Notice, though, that in (16) *sobre* has its usual meaning. As far as *contra* is concerned, it is more difficult to discern its function clearly. I will follow tradition by claiming that it is used as a prefix in compounds (RAE 1984). On the other hand, *sobre* has a twofold function: (1) when it behaves properly as a preposition, and (2) when it is simply a prefix. It would be marked in the lexicon accordingly.

It is obvious in (16) that in each entry the compound adopts the features of the element on its right, clearly signalling right-headedness. This is noticeable in the gender feature of the right element which is transmitted to the compound. Again, Contreras's rule would wrongly generate a prepositional class of compounds rather than the expected nominal compounds.

To sum up, the evidence presented so far show that Spanish compounds are headed. This is particularly noticeable when gender is assigned to the whole compound. We have seen that in compounds formed with elements of different genders, the whole takes on the gender of one of the two elements. Such was the case for the compound $[[falda]_N \ [pantalón]_N]_N$, and others. This refutes DS&W's claims that Spanish lacks compounding. We have provided additional data showing that Spanish compounds can also be parametrized on the right, which contradicts Contreras's head-initial only parametrization hypothesis. In section 5, I will present morphological rules which by virtue of being operative in compound-internal position severely undermine DS&W's claims about Spanish.

5   Morphological operations in compounds. Recall that DS&W's hypothesis is that Spanish compounds must be considered reanalyzed phrases. We saw that (4) indeed lends partial support to this claim. But let us consider the facts (17), extracted from Narváez (1984: 39-42), a couple of which were presented in (13b). Notice that in some of these left-headedness is signalled by the gender subcategory of the first member which ranges over the entire compound.

(17)

niño héroe, m.	(niño, m. + héroe, u.) child hero	'child hero'
visita relámpago, f.	(visita, f. + relámpago, m.) visit lightning	'short visit'
avión espía, m.	(avión, m. + espía, u.) plane spy	'spy plane'
nudismo relámpago, m.	(nudismo, m. + relámpago, m.) nudism lightning	'streaking'
biblioteca piloto, f.	(biblioteca, f. + piloto, m.) library pilot	'experimental library'
manuscrito fuente, m.	(manuscrito, m. + fuente, f.) manuscript source	'original manuscript'
hombre hora, m.	(hombre, m. + hora, f.) man hour	'man hour'
fecha clave, f.	(fecha, f. + clave, f.) date key	'key date'

barco-factoría, m.	(barco, m. + factoría, f.)	'factory-ship'
	ship factory	
ministro clave, m.	(ministro, m. + clave, f.)	'key minister'
	minister key	

The morphological operations that the compounds in (17) may undergo make them all the more damaging to DS&W's claims. If these words indeed are reanalyzed syntactic phrases which can be inserted in X° positions, one should expect pluralization to take place at the X° level, that is, for Spanish it should only be at the right edge of the word, as illustrated with the simple nonverbs in (18) (the plural marker -*s* generally attaches to bases ending in vowels; -*es* attaches to bases ending in consonants or stressed vowels).

(18) Singular Plural
[muchacho]$_N$ [[muchacho]$_N$s] 'boy(s)'
[hotel]$_N$ [[hotel]$_N$es] 'hotel(s)'
[inteligente]$_A$ [[inteligente]$_A$s] 'intelligent'
[loco]$_A$ [[loco]$_A$s] 'mad'

Since the pluralization process takes place at the end of words, we should expect this to hold in (19). This is not the case, however. Observe the plurals for some forms.

(19) Plurals: or:
aviones espía aviones espías
bibliotecas piloto bibliotecas pilotos
niños héroe niños héroes
hombres-hora hombres horas
oraciones modelo oraciones modelos
horas pico horas picos

In (19) the plural marker is affixed either to the first element of the compound or to both, thus making it difficult to identify inflection association with a particular parametrized head (cf. Selkirk 1983:21). The occurrence of an internal marker suggests that these are nonlexicalized compounds consisting of two X°s. Viewed in this light, each X° would then be susceptible to the effects of pluralization rules.[7] Now, unlike the plural marker in the

---

[7] While referring to the forms in (19) as nonlexicalized compounds, I am claiming, in effect, that there must be other type of compounds, namely, lexicalized compounds. These belong to the overwhelming majority of the V + Comp type, as presented in (13a), or to the type given in (13b). I should point out, however, that although the morphological operations referred to above

English compound *parks commissioner*, which does not necessarily signal plurality, for the compound carries a singular interpretation, the internal -*(e)s* in Spanish ranges over the whole compound with a transparent plural meaning. It is rather unusual, though, to find an optional plural marker in just one member of the compound, especially when Spanish is known for its agreement in gender and number.[8] Independently of the constraints that may be allowing or preventing the occurrence of the plural marker in the second noun, DS&W's hypothesis permits plural assignment only at the extreme right of the compound; therefore, each plural in (19) is ruled out in their formulation.

In addition to forming plurals on either element of the compounds above, diminutives, which behave much like plurals by generally being attached at the end of words (Jaeggli 1980), can also occur in the first position of (17), though finding this kind of suffix simultaneously in both elements is highly improbable. One can form *camita* ('bed + dim.'), *litera* ('bunk') 'small bunk-bed' and *oracioncita* ('sentence + dim.'), *modelo* ('model') 'short model sentence', but I find *cama literita* (*cama litera* + 'dim.') questionable with the intended meaning given above (*oración modelito* is totally unacceptable) or worse yet, *camita literita* (*cama* + 'dim.' *litera* + 'dim.') that, in my opinion, is outright nonsensical. Interestingly, in these nonlexicalized forms diminutive or augmentative suffixes are affixed on the head noun. But it would be risky to suggest that this is a kind of head-triggered affixation, for one would encounter serious problems with lexicalized compounds. Notice that in the so-called exocentric V+N types, as in *paraguas* (*para* + *aguas*, lit. 'stop rains') 'umbrella', the noun *aguas* is an internal (nonhead) argument of the verb *para*; nonetheless the diminutive is *paraguitas* (*para* + *agua* + 'dim. + pl.').

Since Di Sciulo and Williams's syntactic atoms do not permit internal

---

do take place internally in nonlexicalized compounds, no grammatical or modifying constituents (i.e. adjective, quantifiers, etc.) can occur between the two elements. In lexicalized compounds, no morphological operations can apply internally. In other words, affixation is restricted to the right edge of the word, which means that their structure representation must be $[X + Y]_Z$ where Z is an X^o. With respect to stress, they behave differently: lexicalized compounds show a secondary stress in their first member whereas their counterparts show primary stress in both, i.e., *limpiasáco* vs. *oración modélo*. In any case, lexicalized compounds show the effects of earlier rules (the ones we have been considering) operating in compound formation. Structured as suggested, then, it is not difficult to explain why internal affixation cannot occur.

[8] In order to account for this lack of agreement, one could conceivably posit an optional morphophonological rule that would copy -*(e)s* onto the second element. But whatever its structural description, it would be a highly idiosyncratic rule restricted in its application to nonlexicalized N+N compounds because in nonlexicalized N+Adj combinations the plural marker appears obligatorily in both members. For the respective compounds *reactor atómico* 'atomic reactor' and *platillo volador* 'flying saucer', the plural is *reactores atómicos* and *platillos voladores*, whereas *reactores atómico and *platillos volador are considered ungrammatical.

occurrences of the plural morpheme or of diminutive suffixes in nonlexicalized compounds (because structurally they are not X°s), it stands to reason, then, that their structure must be along the lines of (20) or perhaps as in (12) for the V+Comp combinations. Both possibilities would be generated by (25).

(20)

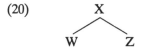

In (20), X is the lexical category N, V, or Adj, and W and Z represent one of these categories. Such a structure cannot be parametrized entirely within the framework of the X-bar theory (or, for that matter, with Contreras's rule schemata) because by doing so we would assign headship on the left member of the compounds only, and this would obviously not account for heads in rightmost positions.

6 A solution. Evidently, we are facing a threefold situation, First, there is total headlessness, a fact that has been exemplified by the vast productive pattern of adverb formation (cf. (4b)); second, Spanish opts preferentially for left parametrization (cf. (13)); and third, right-headedness, which is also a major characteristic of derivations, is yet another viable alternative to the preceding two (cf. (14)). The fact that parametrization can occur one way or the other is an unequivocal indication that DS&W's approach cannot hold. On the other hand, this mixture of headedness permits us to question a one-sided parameter setting. If we were to follow the grammatical principles of the X-bar schema or Contreras's modified schemata, and fix a parameter on the left, we would fail observationally because we would miss both headless and right-headed compounding; if parametrization were to occur on the right, via Lieber's Convention IV, we would encounter a similar problem but in reverse. This indeterminacy in headship leads us to propose not that there is a need to settle on any particular parameter but rather that Spanish must be allowed freedom in choosing its headship. This apparent freedom must be stated as a language-specific property of the grammar of Spanish.

But there remains an unresolved problem: if a choice of headship is said to exist in Spanish, then we must discover a (principled) way of knowing under what conditions left- or right-headedness obtains without having to appeal to two independent parameters; that is, we must construct one single, unitary statement that would account for both parameters. The easiest expedient for remedying the problem would be to mark the lexicon indicating the parameter-fixing principles that apply to a given form: either Contreras's head-initial hypothesis or Convention IV. This is obviously an ad-hoc move with no explanatory power and as such it must be rejected. Still, we could go further and invoke phonology but this would be to no avail because there are no known rules, processes, or principles that would justify splitting the lexicon. A morphosyntactic analysis would work, as we saw, with the so-called *exocentric* compounds but it would leave many endocentric forms untouched: we still could not tell whether a form is headed in one direction or in another. We come to a full circle because whichever of these solutions is chosen, we would end up with two parameters, albeit restricted in their applications to a given module. The semantics of these compounds is a third possibility that may prove to be a most promising avenue of analysis.

Let us trace our steps and reconsider the compounds in (13b) and (13c). Recall that I have said that the key characteristic of these compounds is that the elements on the right stand in a modifier-like relationship to the ones on the left; in other words, the right member semantically qualifies the left one. When speaking of N+N combinations, as in *hombre rana* 'frog man', it means that a man receives the attributes of a frog or acts like one. Similarly, in the N+Adj types, as in *camposanto* 'cemetery', there is a sense that the left hand member, *campo*, receives certain sacred qualities from the adjective on its right. Or in the Adj+N types of (15), the right member is modified by the adjective on its left. This is the case for *malalengua* 'evil tongue', which literally translates as a tongue that is bad.

It is precisely this idea that I would like to pursue next, namely, that in these types of compounds modification expresses some sort of conjunction. Borrowing from Higginbotham (1985: 563), I propose that when adjective-functioning nouns and adjectives combine with a noun, then the former are 'taken as grading with respect to the attribute given in the N'. Consequently, all three representative examples quoted above would have the interpretation given in (21).

(21) a. This is a man that resembles or acts like a frog.
      b. This is a field, and it is sacred.
      c. This is a tongue, and it is bad.

Such an interpretation could be encoded into the compound if we were to assume that lexical items have a thematic grid as part and parcel of their lexical representations. Let us say that nouns are lexically represented as in (21a) with a single θ-role and that adjectives have two θ-roles, as in (21b), because they serve both as modifiers and as predicates (cf. *camposanto* with *el campo es santo* 'the field is sacred'). Furthermore, since a noun may also occur as an attribute (note that *modelo* in *la oración es modelo* 'it is a model sentence' serves as a predicate), I assume that in this instance it would be potentially identifiable with two positions as well which would be acquired by virtue of its association with another noun.

(22) a. campo, oración, etc.,   -V +N, <1>
      b. santo, mala, modelo, etc., -V -N, <1, 2>

In (22b), position 1 would assign identity with the noun so that a θ-identification is established; with position 2, θ-marking occurs. This is accomplished with the following statement:

(23) a. The position 1 of N is identified with position 1 of A(ttribute);
      b. A(ttribute) autonymously θ-marks N, through position 2.

In (23), Higginbotham recognizes explicitly two new thematic discharges which he calls, respectively, θ-identification and autonymous θ-marking, meaning by the latter that the θ-marked N is itself the value rather than having the θ-marker acquire the value. The application of (23) is displayed arboreally in (24):

(24)

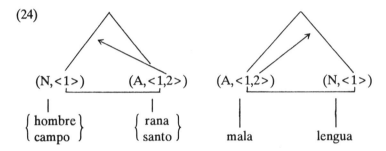

(N,<1>)   (A,<1,2>)   (A,<1,2>)   (N,<1>)

{ hombre }   { rana }
{ campo }   { santo }   mala   lengua

The solid lines assign θ-identification under government between the attributes and N; and the arrows discharge the θ-marking of Attributes (i.e., adjectives and adjective-functioning nouns) on N.

The rules in (23) then permit us to accomplish a qualifying relationship, both morphologically and semantically, between the members of the compound. Having done that, headship could be obtained automatically without fixing parameters in any direction. A modified version of Convention IV will yield correct results:

(25) Convention IV modified (preliminary version):
      In a configuration of modification, the features
      of N percolate up to the branching node.

For (25) to apply, it would first have to be fed by rule (23). The net result of (25) is to label the branching node with the lexical category and thematic grid of N.

(26)

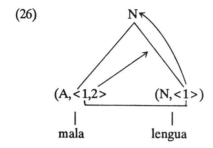

$$(A, <1,2>) \qquad (N, <1>)$$

| | |
| mala | lengua |

Notice again that by assuming (23) followed by the application of the modified Convention in (25), it becomes unnecessary to invoke directions since the features of N will percolate up, regardless of the position it occupies in the compound. It is also at this time that Higginbotham's (1985: 565) semantic algorithm would apply so as to capture the external attributes expressed in the upper N. A slightly modified notation of the algorithm is provided in (27).

(27) $v(x, N') \;<\text{----}>\; v(x, N) \;\&\; v(x, {}^\wedge N, A)$

(where N' = upper N, and $^\wedge$N refers to the attribute)

The notation (27) accompanies (26) with the intended interpretation provided in (21). For example, (27) applied to *hombre rana* says that *hombre rana* is someone who is a man and who acts like a frog. Thus (27) sums up the fact that the qualified constituent is expressed as a conjunction.

Now, the V+Comp compounds can also be analyzed and interpreted along the lines discussed above. That is, I would like to suggest that in V+Comp something is predicated about a tacit someone. In this sense, the whole V+Comp is the attribute of N^e, i.e., the attribute of *rompehuelgas*, namely, being a scab, is assigned to N^e. This is not inconsistent with the proposal if an assumption is made to the effect that *rompehuelgas* would have two positions acquired by virtue of its functioning as an adjective. Compare, for example, *el rompehuelgas trabajó* 'the scab worked' with *el es un rompehuelgas* 'he is a scab'. Roughly, after applying rules (23) and Convention (25), its structural display would be as in (28):[9]

---

[9] This hypothesis will apply equally to cases where the first element is considered a deverbal noun and the second its complement (Varela 1989). But Varela's analysis predicts headship on the left and it therefore misses all right headships studied here. This observation also applies to Clements (1989, ms.) who nevertheless considered compounds with nucleus on the right but treated them either as lexical exceptions or as Latinate calques. His proposal is still quite problematic in that it fails to account for left headship in the vastly productive Verb+Comp types and, furthermore, it must invoke unmotivated hypothetical rules. In addition, the study wrongly assumes that the N+Adj compounds (i.e., *pelirrojo* 'redhead') is headed by the member

(28)

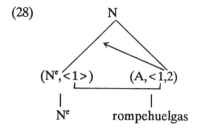

N^e rompehuelgas

Though Convention (25) accounts for compounds when their members stand in a modifying relationship, there are still many compounds that escape its effects. Consider (14) again. Do all of its members stand in a modifying relationship? I believe they do not. Take for instance *puntapié* 'kick with the foot'. It is not the case here that one could interpret *pie* 'foot' as having adopted the characteristics of *punta* 'tip.' In fact, it seems that *pie* receives objective case, probably transmitted by a tacit preposition, presumably *de* 'of'. Its structural representation would be, roughly speaking, *punta* [p del pie]$_{PP}$ 'tip of the foot' which coincides with its meaning. Since it is structurally different, it follows that the interpretive conjunction (21) does not apply. A similar structural representation and interpretation applies to *piepaloma* 'type of yucca'. Thus the second element seems to be the object of a preposition and is not immediately qualifying the first element. It so appears that when the elements are not in a qualifying relationship, there is a distinct assignment of right headship.

What about the remaining thirteen forms in (14)? None of the elements on the right is the object of a preposition because *baciyelmo* 'helmet-like basin', for example, cannot be interpreted as a *bacía de yelmo, nor can either member modify the other semantically: *yelmo* simply does not receive the attributes of *bacía* nor vice versa, and the compound cannot be interpreted along the lines of (21). What we seem to have here is the sum total of two elements in a coordinative fashion producing a compound with compositional meaning: that is, the independent meaning of both elements is recoverable in the whole. Viewed this way, these compounds would be represented and interpreted roughly as '[[X]$_N$ *y* [Y]$_N$]$_N$.' So, when compounds stand in an additive (coordinative) nonqualifying relationship, headedness is again assigned on the right.[10]

---

of the left which is said to be an adjective. We have already demonstrated with *carirredondo* 'round-faced' that the nucleus is found outside. These liabilities outweigh the benefits that can be gained with the principles proposed by Clements.

[10] I am assuming there are two morphophonological rules that optionally delete the word marker in the context of the conjunction *y* and the conjunction itself; compare, for example, *carricuba* with *gallocresta*. It appears that the vowel *i* in coordinate compounds is not the same vowel that surfaces in *carirredondo*, which might have been derived by analogy to Latin sources

Having treated (14), let us review the P+N combinations in (16). The elements on the right are objects of prepositions and they obviously do not modify these prepositions, so an interpretive conjunction would not apply. The right element is once again the head. But even if we arbitrarily chose to assign headship on the left, that would still be impossible because doing so would open up the possibility of making numerous prepositional compounds out of a rather closed class: one simply cannot produce prepositional compounds in the same manner one can with other combinations (cf. Lieber 1983). The default is naturally right headship.

The picture seems to be clear: when the members of compounds are not semantically qualifying each other, there is an invariable assignment   of headship on the right. Recall, though, that headship cannot be assigned with (25). Perhaps a supplementary statement would be needed to capture the fact that in compounds whose members are in a nonmodifying relationship, parametrization is strictly on the right. To reflect this, I would propose the addition of a second Convention to (25), expressed in (29):

(29)   In a configuration of nonmodification, the features of
       the right-hand element percolate to the branching node.

To illustrate its application, consider the representation of *arquibanco* 'bench with drawers' (cf. (14)) in (30).

(30)

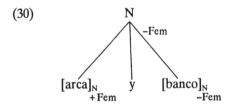

Both (25) and (29) can be collapsed into one single statement, applied conjunctively.

(31)   Modified Convention IV (final):
       In a configuration of (non)modification, the features
       of (the right) N percolate to the branching node.

___

(see Montes Giraldo 1977: 54). The vowel in this form does not denote the adjective interpretation which is conveyed by the *i* in the previous two compounds.

Again, the shortest version presupposes (23) and (25). The important claimmade by (31) is that, in effect, there is only one headship assignment: on the right, which serves to establish a perfect symmetry with headship assignment in regular derivations. The left or right parametrization via the shortest version of (31) is basically a cost-free solution to the grammar. Convention (31), then, has the heuristic effect of accounting for headship in a principled manner. Its predictive power is, by all counts, superior to past formulations: assuming the application of (23) in the required cases, it achieves its purposes in one full swoop.[11]

7 Summary. To conclude, if we accept (31) the majority of Spanish compounds are endowed with morphological structure, This in turn means that it must be part of the core grammar and, in addition, that it is subject to the parametrization stated therein. Convention (31) embodies a large empirical generalization, and furthermore, it provides a principled explanation as to why in some cases a given parameter holds when a converse parametrization was the expected result. But also by including rules (2), (5), and (7), which de facto leave no room for freedom in headship choice, we are thereby relegating them to the periphery of the grammar. Since they are marked rules, the learner has no choice but to memorize their outputs.

---

[11] Convention (31) makes correct predictions even in those combinations whose features are practically of no use in helping us to identify headship, i.e., compounds of the same gender and lexical category. Take for instance group (i). It seems that their members are in a nonqualifying relationship, in which case headship should be on the right. That this must be so is shown in the composition of *arquimesa* vis-à-vis *arquibanco*, where the left member for both is the feminine noun *arca*. Recall, however, that in (14) it was noted that *banco* is masculine and that the derived compound bears precisely this feature.

(i)
salipimienta, f.	'salt and pepper'
ajoqueso, m.	'garlic and cheese'
ajiaceite, m.	'garlic and oil sauce'
arquimesa, f.	'writing desk'
bocamanga, f.	'cuff'
hojalata, f.	'tinplate'

In (ii), the short version (33) predicts left-headedness and once again this is borne out by the compound *casa hogar* 'boarding house'. Compared to *casa cuna*, one can see in the former that the whole compound does not show the masculine gender of *hogar* but the feminine one of *casa*.

(ii)
casatienda, f.	'shop and house combined'
casa cuna, f.	'day care center'
puercoespín, m.	'porcupine'
noticia bomba, f.	'bombshell news'

References

Bloomfield, L. 1984. Language. Chicago: University of Chicago Press.
Clements, C. 1989. Lexical Category Hierarchy and 'Head Compound' in Spanish, ms. Bloomington: Indiana University.
Contreras, H. 1985. Spanish Exocentric Compounds. In F. Nuessel (ed.), Current Issues in Hispanic Phonology and Morphology. Bloomington: Indiana University Linguistics Club, 14-27.
Di Sciullo, A. M., and E. Williams. 1987. On the Definition of Word. Cambridge, Mass.: MIT Press.
Harris, J. W. 1985. Spanish Word Markers. In F. Nuessel (ed.), Current Issues in Hispanic Phonology and Morphology. Bloomington: Indiana University Linguistics Club, 34-54.
Higginbotham, J. 1985. On Semantics. Linguistic Inquiry 4, 547-594.
Jaeggli, O. 1980. Spanish Diminutives. In F. Nuessel, ed., Contemporary Studies in Romance Languages. Bloomington: Indiana University Linguistics Club, 142-158.
Lieber, R. 1983. Argument Linking and Compounds in English. Linguistic Inquiry 14, 251-285.
Montes Giraldo, J. J. 1977. Un tipo de composición nominal y el español del Atlántico. Boletín del Instituto Caro y Cuervo 23, 653-659.
Montes Giraldo, J. J. 1983. Motivación y creación léxica en el español de Colombia. Bogotá: Publicaciones del Instituto Caro y Cuervo.
Narváez, R. A. 1970. An Outline of Spanish Morphology. Saint Paul, Minnesota: EMC Corporation.
Narváez, R. A. 1984. Morfología flexional del español. Minn.: Arteric International.
Núñez Cedeño, R. A. Forthcoming. Morfología derivacional de la sufijación española. Bogotá: Instituto de Filología Caro y Cuervo.
Real Academia Española. 1984. Diccionario de la lengua española. Madrid: Espasa-Calpe.
Selkirk, E. O. 1983. The Syntax of Words. Cambridge, Mass.: MIT Press.
Varela, S. 1989. Spanish Endocentric Compounds. In C. Kirschner and J. Decesaris (eds.), Studies in Romance Linguistics. Amsterdam: John Benjamins, 397-412.
Varela, S. 1990. The Organization of the Lexical Component: Noun-Compounds in Spanish. Acta Lingüística, 206-215.
Wong-opasi, U. 1987. Lexical Phonology and the Spanish Lexicon. Doctoral dissertation, University of Illinois at Urbana. (Distributed by Indiana University Linguistics Club, 1989).
Zagona, K. 1989. *Mente* Adverbs, Compound Interpretation, and the Projection Principle. Probus 2, 1-30.

Stress and syllables in Spanish·

Iggy Roca *
University of Essex

1 The three–syllable window. Perhaps the most incontrovertible fact about Spanish stress is the existence of Three–Syllable Window effects at least in nonverbals (cf. Roca 1990b for a discussion of verbals). Specifically, as is well known, the stress of such words cannot be placed more than three syllables from the right edge. This distributional restriction has the interesting consequence of inducing stress shift upon suffixation, so that the appropriate distance from the edge is maintained, as shown in (1) (whenever relevant, stress is shown in the space immediately preceding the vowel that bears it; otherwise, the standard orthographic conventions are used):

(1) tel'egrafo   'telegraph'   telegr'afico   'telegraphic'
     s'ilaba   'syllable'   sil'abico   'syllabic'
     bi'ologo   'biologist'   biol'ogico   'biological'
     hip'erbole   'hyperbole'   hiperb'olico 'hyperbolic'
     ap'ostol   'apostle'   apost'olico   'apostolic'
     an'ecdota   'anecdote'   anecd'otico   'anecdotal'

The adjectival suffix *-ico* can usefully be construed as stressless. As can be seen, it nonetheless affects the location of stress in the base noun inasmuch as it affects the distance between the stressed syllable and the right word edge.[1] The same effect can be observed in other similar (i.e. bisyllabic and stressless) suffixes (cf. e.g. *p'urpura* 'purple' (N) → *purp'ureo* 'purple' (A)).

---

* A paper under this title was hyperbolically announced as 'in preparation' in Roca (1988a). A better description then would have been 'in the process of ideation.' As is now apparent, over two years of further quiet gestation and the challenge of Héctor Campos and Fernando Martínez-Gil's kind invitation to contribute to a volume on Spanish linguistics were needed in order for the present materialisation to emerge. I am grateful to François Dell, Jim Harris, José I. Hualde, and Rafael Núñez Cedeño for comments on a previous version, and I also want to thank Morris Halle, with whom I had lengthy discussions on many of the ideas that follow back in 1984. I of course am alone responsible for the defects. (The following works, specifically drawn to my attention by some of the above named, were not available to me at the time of writing: M. Carreira, *The Diphthongs of Spanish: Stress, Syllabification and Alternations*, doctoral dissertation, University of Illinois at Urbana-Champaign, 1990; J. Harris, 'Narrowing the Stress Window,' ms., MIT; U. Wong-Opasi, *Lexical Phonology and the Spanish Lexicon*, IULC, 1989).

[1] The stresslessness of this suffix must therefore be given a different formal account than that of such 'level 2' English suffixes as *-ness*, which are simply ordered in a stratum subsequent to that where the stress rule applies.

The connection between shift and the Three–Syllable Window is brought out by the examples in (2):

(2) diarr'ea   'diarrhea'   diarr'eico   'diarrheic'
     apote'osis   'apotheosis'   apote'osico   'apotheosic'
     gran'ito   'granite'   gran'itico   'granitic'
     volc'an   'volcano'   volc'anico   'volcanic'
     higi'ene   'hygiene'   higi'enico   'hygienic'

Here, the addition of -*ico* to the stem causes no violation of the Three–Syllable Window, and thus no rightward stress shift ensues.

Formally, the Three–Syllable Window effects follow automatically from the interaction between the universal constraints on foot construction, specifically the fact that heads must be terminal,[2] and the grammar of Spanish stress, specifically the fact that in this language the construction of feet is exclusively algorithmic. In particular, there is no Three–Syllable Window in systems where unbounded feet are built on freely distributed preexisting heads. For instance, in Khalkha Mongolian the leftmost syllable containing a long vowel is stressed, regardless of its distance from the edge (cf. Hayes 1980/81: 63, Halle and Vergnaud 1987: 71).

While in Spanish there are no known violations of the Three–Syllable Window, it is not the case that the configuration provided by the window is fully exploited under all circumstances. In particular, the more stringent constraints in (3) have been mentioned in the literature:[3]

(3) a. No antepenultimate stress with a closed penult.
     b. No antepenultimate stress with a closing diphthong in the penult.
     c. No antepenultimate stress with an opening diphthong in the penult.
     d. No antepenultimate stress with an opening diphthong in the ultima.
     e. No antepenultimate stress with a closed ultima.
     f. only final stress with a closing diphthong in the ultima.

---

[2] This statement abstracts away the possible existence of ternary feet, which according to Halle and Vergnaud (1987) must in any event be bounded, thus yielding the same effects as regards the Three–Syllable Window. Throughout this paper I am assuming familiarity with Halle and Vergnaud's (1987) stress theory, in which framework the present analysis is couched.

[3] Post-Harris (1983) Spanish stress bibliography includes den Os and Kager (1986), Halle, Harris, and Vergnaud (1991), Harris (1989a, 1989b, 1989c), Núñez Cedeño (1985), Otero (1986), and Roca (1986, 1988a, 1990a, 1990b). The reader is referred to these works for background to the present discussion where appropriate.

In effect, thus, Spanish has two-syllable windows in addition to the standard Three–Syllable Window: a one syllable window, covering case (3f), and a two syllable window, covering the rest of the restrictions in (3). While the Three–Syllable Window falls out of Universal Grammar, as explained above, the other two windows per se are language-specific, in that they do not appear to follow from more general principles. Two strategies can, in principle, be adopted for their integration in the formal description of Spanish stress. First, we could assume that the syllables in question already bear a stress mark prior to the operation of the stress algorithm, the output of which will accordingly be narrowed. Second, we could attempt to derive the three surface windows from an identical underlying source, viz. from the Three–Syllable Window itself. It is obvious that, unless indicated otherwise by the evidence, the second solution will be more highly valued. In what follows, we first examine the first, more complex, strategy. After showing that there are independent reasons not to follow it, the second solution is explored and adopted.

2 Quantity sensitivity. In much of the literature (e.g. Harris 1983, and thereafter den Os and Kager 1986, Otero 1986) the narrowing of the window is attributed to syllable weight and the concomitant accenting of the corresponding stress bearer. Specifically, it has been suggested (Harris 1983: 85, den Os and Kager 1986: 37, Otero 1986: 312) that Spanish basically keeps the stress rule of Latin, which, as is well known, makes decisive use of quantity sensitivity, a penultimate heavy syllable preventing antepenultimate stress. According to this line of thinking, the constraints in (3a-c) would therefore follow from the accenting of Spanish heavy syllables, very much along the lines of Latin.[4]

There are serious observational problems with this analysis, which have been spelled out in some detail in Roca (1990a). Thus, on the one hand, the Three–Syllable Window appears inviolable at all levels: synchronic, diachronic, acquisitional. By contrast, the two syllable window responsible for (3a) admits of violations (at least one native place name, *Fr'omista,* and, quite freely, foreign names of Germanic flavour, such as *W'ashington*). This is in contrast with (3b) and (3c), where there are no contraventions.[5]

---

[4] The Latin stress algorithm first accents heavy syllables, and then builds leftheaded bounded feet from right to left, the rightmost of which will bear the word stress. The domain of the algorithm does not include the last syllable, which is extrametrical in all cases (see Roca 1988a, 1988b, 1990a for some discussion).

[5] This statement appears to be contradicted by *al'icuota* 'aliquot,' already mentioned in Harris (1969), which seemingly violates (3c) (and similarly for *ventr'ilocuo* 'ventriloquist' and (3d)). Two comments must be made in this connection. First, as I have had the occasion to observe, both in acquisition and in ordinary speech the two forms in question are subject to a tendency towards stress shift: *alicu'ota, ventril'ocuo.* Second, it is interesting that in both cases the offending sequence is [kwo]. This fact can be related to Harris's (1969) analysis of such [kʷV]

Moreover, accenting of heavy syllables is insufficient to account for the distribution in (3d–f). In particular, if heavy syllables were automatically accented, as they were in Latin, all word-final closed syllables in words with no desinence would be expected to carry the stress (final syllables are not automatically extrametrical in Spanish, as they are in Latin), contrary to fact. If, on the other hand, such syllables are exempted from receiving accent by some means,[6] then the constraint in (3e) becomes mysterious. Closer examination further reveals that there are common violations of (3e) (e.g. *r'egimen* 'régime'), again in sharp contrast with (3b-d), which are exceptionless (cf. fn. 5). Also, if, say, the word-final mora were discounted for weight purposes,[7] then there would be no way of accounting for (3f) either, which, moreover, is also claimed to be exceptionless. Clearly, thus, an alternative account of the window restrictions is in order.

3 The identity of the stress bearers. In our examination of the restrictions listed in (3) we found that these obey two different degrees of strength. On the one hand, the restrictions in (3a) and (3e) are met with a variety of exceptions. On the other, the remaining restrictions can reasonably be said to be absolute, and thus exceptionless (again, abstracting away the two forms referred to in fn. 5). Crucially for our present purposes, the criterion dividing the two groups concerns the nature of the segment responsible for the heaviness of the syllable. Thus, when heaviness is attributable to the presence of consonants in the coda, the narrowing of the window is only a tendency, which can otherwise be related to specific historical processes (cf. the discussion in Roca 1990a). By contrast, complex nuclei, i.e. nuclei comprising at least two vocoids,[8] exceptionlessly create narrower windows.

---

strings as underlying /kʷ/, for which he provides justification independent of stress (cf. also Harris 1983: 148, fn. 10). Note that from a more up-to-date perspective it may be possible to reinterpret /kʷ/ as simply /w̥/, i.e. as a voiceless back rounded glide, which will undergo (obstruent) strengthening in a manner parallel (though of course not identical) to its voiced counterpart [gʷ] in, e.g. *huerto* 'garden.'

[6] Harris (1989a: 43) suggests that the final consonant is not syllabified until the word-level is reached, thus echoing the position of Itô (1986: 100), while stress assignment would be cyclic, exception made of a limited set of suffixes (cf. Halle, Harris, and Vergnaud 1991 for discussion). In the absence of specific evidence, however, it is not evident that Itô's procedure is relevant to Spanish, where morpheme-final sequences of TWO consonants of the appropriate sonority must be syllabified with the following vowel: [[[ca.br]e.r]o] 'goat keeper.'

[7] This is in effect the suggestion in Harris (1989a: 44-ff.). However, in the face of the arguments against the direct computation of stress on a mora tier put forward in Roca (1988a, 1988b), an analysis which does not make use of this device is to be preferred. It is the purpose of the present paper to present precisely such an analysis.

[8] I deliberately choose this term, as a neutral term between 'vowel' and 'glide' in the SPE sense. Note that the SPE use is equivalent to the lexical marking of syllable nuclei, since a segment will be [+syllabic] if and only if it is associated with the nucleus. In many of the world's

Such strength differences should not be approached as accidental. Naturally, the likelihood of chance will diminish even further if it were to turn out that the robust narrower windows can in fact be analysed on the same footing as the Three–Syllable Window. As we shall now see, this is indeed the case.

Let us first consider (3d), as exemplified by the proper name *Mac'ario*. The crucial (negative) datum is the impossibility of **M'acario*. Now, note that in the surface both forms are consonant with the Three–Syllable Window, which we wish to maintain as the only constraint limiting the distribution of stress in Spanish. The reason that **M'acario* also complies with the Three–Syllable Window is of course the fact that the last two vocoids form a diphthong, and thus the stressed syllable of this hypothetical form would still fall within the space defined by the window: *M'a.ca.rio* (N.B.: the syllable boundaries are represented by the dots). If, on the other hand, *i* and *o* were assigned to different syllables, we would need to search no further for an explanation for the impossibility of **M'acario* and the grammaticality of *Mac'ario*. Suppose then that, as a first approximation, we indeed postulate such a syllable division underlyingly: *Ma.ca.ri.o*. The assignment of stress to this form is perfectly straightforward, in accordance with the procedure in Roca (1990a) (or its equivalents elsewhere). Simply, the final syllable corresponds to the desinence[9] and is thus made extrametrical. Stress is therefore assigned to the rightmost syllable in the stem, *ri*, from which it is retracted to *ca* by the appropriate mechanism, which in Roca (1990a) is identified as stress-bearer deletion:[10]

```
(4)    Ma ca ri  o          Ma ca ri  o          Ma ca ri  o
       (*   *  *)<*>    →    (*   *  ')<*>    →    (*   *) '<*>    L0
             *                      *                    *        L1
```

According to this approach, therefore, the derivation of *Mac'ario* is identical

---

languages, however, nucleus formation is (at least partially) predictable from the sonority relations between the elements in the melody. Consequently, indiscriminate lexical specification of nuclei would be at odds with the aims of underspecification, which in fact underpin the whole edifice of phonology (and of linguistics in general), and which can be seen as the formal expression of the simplicity criterion, in turn anchored in the more general Occam's razor. In the present paper I therefore assume that, whenever possible, the assignment of nucleus status to segments is rule-governed, and it is in this context that the term (and the construct) 'vocoid' will be found particularly useful (I am grateful to François Dell for having made this suggestion to me in the course of a discussion of an earlier version of this paper).

[9] See Roca (1990a) for presentation and justification of this term.

[10] The formulation of this rule in Roca (1990a: 147) is as follows:

(28) *) → ' / in especially marked forms   (level 0).

to that of, e.g. *esp'arrago* 'asparagus'.

Before investigating further the details of the proposed mapping, it will be useful to show that the analysis also accounts for the restriction in (3f), and in particular for the difference between (3f), which entails a one syllable window, and (3d), which corresponds to a two syllable window. Thus, consider for instance *conv'oy* 'convoy.' All we need to assume is that the final [i] (represented by *y* in the orthography) falls inside the stem, i.e. does not constitute a desinence. Independent evidence for this analysis comes from the behaviour of such nonce derivatives as *convoyito* or *convoicito* (crucially, not *convoíto*), or *convoyista* (not *convoísta*), which keep the [i] (which segment will of course occupy the onset and be consonantalised where appropriate, along the lines mentioned in fn. 5), contrary to what would happen if it constituted the desinence, as desinences are characteristically absent from derivatives word-internally (cf. Harris 1985b: 39, Roca 1990a: 135). Now, if there is no desinence in *convoy*, this string will be coextensive with the domain of stress. If, moreover, each vocoid is analysed as an underlying syllable, there will be no way of assigning stress any further to the left than the *o*. In particular, there are two possible situations. Suppose first that the word contains no lexical marking for retraction. If so, stress will fall on the final vocoid, as in (5):

(5)   con.vo.i
        (*   * *)
              *

Although rare, this is indeed a possible configuration (cf. *ah'i* 'there'; the letter *h* has of course a purely orthographic value in Spanish). If, on the other hand, the item is marked for retraction, the following derivation will ensue as a result of rule (28) in Roca (1990a) (cf. fn. 10 above):

(6)   con vo i   con vo i   con vo i
        (*   * *)   →   (*   * ')   →   (*   *)'
              *   *   *

This matches more closely the actual surface form of *conv'oy*, where the *o*, rather than the *i*, is stressed. Crucially, given the proposed morphological constituency, no other stress pattern is possible.[11]

---

[11] Rafael Núñez Cedeño informs me that *convoy* happens to have initial stress in his dialect: *c'onvoy*. This seems to suggest treatment as an unassimilated loan, along the lines of, e.g. *D'isney*, which was discussed in Roca (1988a: 416). Note that such words do not create a problem for our approach, given the possibility of analysing the final *i* as a desinence:

    D i s n e i   D i s n e i   D i s n e i
    (*   *) <*>   →   (*   ')<*>   →   (*)   · ·
          *   *   *

4 Syllable merger. As it stands, the analysis eschews the fact that in both *Macario* and *convoy* the surface manifestation of the [i] is not syllabic. This obviously points to a distinction between underlying and surface syllabification, such that vocoid sequences which are heterosyllabic in the former become diphthongs in the latter. Before completing our examination of the list of restrictions above, we must therefore address this important question.

In essence, I am maintaining that vocoids which are syllabic in underlying representation may surface as nonsyllabic, i.e. lose their syllabicity in the course of the derivation. The evidence for syllabicity loss is in fact very strong in Spanish, as we shall now see.

4.1 Across words. Consider the data in (7):

(7) a.

			b.		
bisturí	'scalpel'		metrópoli	'metropolis'
colibrí	'humming bird		confeti	'confetti'
jabalí	'boar'		taxi	'taxi'
zulú	'Zulu'		tribu	'tribe'
canesú	'camisole'		espíritu	'spirit'
ambigú	'foyer'		ímpetu	'impetus'

These words contain a syllabic high vocoid in final position, either stressed (7a) or stressless (7b). When followed by another vocoid, its syllabicity is normally lost (for the reader's convenience, I underline the vocoids affected

---

There is of course nothing extraordinary with allotting the second of two adjacent vocoids to the desinence (cf. *Macario, navío* 'vessel,' and thousands of others). Less usual is the adoption of this parsing in cases of falling sonority like the ones at hand, but this is hardly surprising given the scarcity of high vocoid desinences in general (note that e.g. *-u* in *espíritu* 'spirit' must be analysed as a desinence to get the antepenultimate stress), and of high vocoids in final position in general. We should naturally be able to muster independent support for the proposed parsings [[convo]y], [[Disne]y] in the appropriate dialects, and an attempt is made in Roca (1988a: 416) as regards the latter word. Note that the crucial fact is that such forms cannot accept stress any further to the left, thus contrasting with their counterparts with a final closed syllable. Thus, while *r'egimen* is possible (and existing), **c'uribay* is not (the form *curibay* is given in the dictionary of the Real Academia Española). Likewise, a word like *Maracaibo*, to be discussed below in some detail, could never have stress on the first or the second syllable, since these are followed by three vocoids, and such stress would therefore violate the Three–Syllable Window. Note in particular that the stress-retraction strategy we followed in *D'isney* of parsing the final *-i* as a desinence is not open to us here, since desinences must be word-peripheral, and the *i* in *Maracaibo* is word-internal.

and enclose the relevant syllable within square brackets):[12]

(8) un bistu[rí a]filado   'a sharp scalpel'
     un coli[brí en]cantador   'a charming humming bird'
     un jaba[lí or]gulloso   'a proud boar'

     un zu[lú in]teresante   'an interesting Zulu'
     un cane[sú es]cotado   'a low-cut camisole'
     un ambi[gú a]barrotado   'a crowded foyer'

(9) una metrópo[li ul]trajada   'an offended metropolis'
     un confe[ti o]riginal   'an original confetti'
     un tak[si a]veriado   'a broken-down taxi'

     una tri[bu a]fricana   'an African tribe'
     un espíri[tu hon]rado   'an honest spirit'
     un ímpe[tu ex]traordinario   'an extraordinary impetus'

It is of course possible to prevent desyllabification by lengthening the first of

---

[12] A very important caveat must be made here. Practically all the facts of syllabicity between adjacent vocoids in Spanish are heavily dialect-dependent, and frequently idiolect-bound. Confronted with this fact, the researcher has a number of alternatives. First, he can abandon the enterprise as hopeless. Second, he can adopt the data which have been reported in the literature. If so, however, he will face a further choice, since these data will almost certainly not be isomorphic with each other. Third, he can survey and analyse all the dialects of Spanish. Fourth, he can try to create an abstract, internally consistent superdialect. Fifth, he can opt for describing a particular set of data with which he is deeply acquainted. Ideally, the fourth alternative is to be preferred, since it would by definition be the simplest one consistent with all varieties of Spanish. Clearly, however, at our present stage of knowledge such a goal is plainly unreachable. Next desirable will be alternative three, which at least has the virtue of completeness. Such a mammoth task is, however, patently beyond the reach of any one ordinary mortal. Consequently, I have decided for the last strategy and based my description on my own intuitions, which I have been examining on and off for a period of some six years, and which I have checked against such classics as Robles Dénago (1905) and Navarro Tomás (1959), who I assume are dealing with dialects similar (though not identical) to mine. I am of course fully aware that these intuitions will not necessarily correspond with those of others (they certainly do not exactly coincide with those of the authors cited, who also don't entirely agree with each other), and it will be interesting to compare the results reported here with those stemming from a different (but, crucially, unitary) database. Note also that, even within any particular idiolect, syllabicity is dependent on a variety of factors, some of them internal to language (e.g. morphological structure) and others external to it (e.g. degree of speaker excitement). So much must be obvious to any careful observer of the matter, and can easily be gleaned from comments which can be found in the classics. All this makes this area a lush garden of Eden for the dialectologist, historical linguist and sociolinguist alike, as well as a hornet's nest for the descriptivist and the theoretician.

the two vocoids, or by inserting a pause after it, but this behaviour is confined to very slow or artificial speech, and in normal styles there is merger of the two syllables.

The reality of syllable merger is captured by the poetic device of synalepha, by which abutting syllable heads are counted as one by the poetic meter. The suspension of synalepha by the means just mentioned, known as hiatus, is exceptional and artificial, brought in solely as a poetic licence.[13]

Syllable merger also takes place when a high vocoid follows, rather than precedes, a lower vocoid, again irrespective of stress:

(10) una ma[má in]geniosa   'an ingenious mum'
      un aima[rá u]niversal   'a universal Aymara'
      un ac[né i]noportuno   'an inopportune acne'
      un quin[qué hur]tado   'a stolen oil lamp'
      un frican[dó i]nusitado   'an unusual fricassee'
      un ca[pó u]sado   'a second-hand bonnet'

(11) un juerguis[ta in]veterado   'an inveterate reveller'
      una car[ta ur]gente   'an urgent letter'
      un geren[te in]teligente   'an intelligent manager'
      un estudian[te u]niversitario 'a university student'
      un casamien[to his]tórico   'an historical wedding'
      un cronóme[tro u]sado   'a second-hand stop watch'

So far, at least one of the vocoids undergoing the merger has been high. The action of syllable merger extends, however, to nonhigh vocoids, thus showing that heterosyllabic vocalic sequences are strongly disfavoured in Spanish:

(12) un qui[zá e]vasivo   'an evasive perhaps'
      una heri[da ho]rrible   'a terrible wound'

      un lan[ce a]moroso   'a love affair'
      un chimpan[cé o]rejudo   'a big-eared chimpanzee'

      un cam[po a]rado   'a ploughed up field'
      un encuen[tro e]mocionante   'a moving encounter'

---

[13] Cf. e.g. Quilis's (1984: 50) comment that synalepha is a common and practically constant phenomenon in speech (N.B. 'casi un hecho de norma lingüística'), hiatus being therefore exceptional. Spanish thus contrasts with such languages as German or English, where the identity of the two syllables must be preserved. German typically resorts to the glottal stop to keep the vocoids apart, while English also uses such devices as *r*-intrusion or glide insertion to achieve the same aim.

There is one specific circumstance under which syllable merger is prevented. Consider the sequences in (13):

(13) un tabú ético   (*ta[bú é]tico)   'an etical taboo'
      un frenesí hondo   (*frene[sí hon]do)   'a deep frenzy'
      un capó único   (*ca[pó ú]nico)   'a unique bonnet'
      un chimpancé indio   (*chimpan[cé in]dio)   'an Indian chimpanzee'

In order to understand the conditions blocking syllable merger here, we must refer to the claim in Roca (1986) that in Spanish the prominence peak of the intonational phrase is carried by the last primary-stressed syllable, as in (14) (the syllable with the intonational peak is given in capitals):[14]

```
(14)        *     *
        ya lleGO
        'he already arrived'

        *     *     *
        ya llegó a CAsa
        'he already arrived home'

        *     *     *        *
        ya llegó a casa de su aMIgo
        'he already arrived at his friend's'

        *     *     *        *     *
        ya llegó a casa de su amigo PEdro
        'he already arrived at his friend P.'s'

        *     *     *        *     *     *
        ya llegó a casa de su amigo Pedro MarTInez
        'he already arrived at his friend P. M.'s'

        *     *     *        *     *     *     *
        ya llegó a casa de su amigo Pedro Martínez con su PErro
        'he already arrived at his friend P. M.'s with his dog'
```

In terms of the theory of stress put forward by Halle and Vergnaud (1987), such a syllable would simply be assigned an asterisk at the grid level corresponding to the intonational phrase, as in (15) (here as elsewhere, irrelevant grid levels are omitted for simplicity):

---

[14] According to Roca (1986), therefore, the position of 'phrasal accent' in Spanish is fixed, thus contrasting with such languages as English, where effectively any word in the phrase (in fact, any syllable!) can in principle be assigned accent. The expression of focus in Spanish will consequently be syntactic or lexical, whereas in English it is primarily intonational (more precisely, accentual).

(15)   *   Intonational Phrase Level
     *   *   *   *   Word Stress Level
     ya llegó a casa de su amigo

Now, in the data given above with no merger, one of the abutting vocoids is the carrier of sentence stress, and this obviously prevents the merger of the two syllables:

(16)   *
              *   *
     un tabu etico

Note that phrasal stress blocks merger even if the first of the two abutting vocoids is stressless:

(17)   *
     *   *
     este hombre   (*es[te_hom]bre)   'this man'

On the basis of all the data considered, the rule of Syllable Merger in (18) can therefore be proposed, somewhat updating the formalism in Roca (1986: 351-352):

(18)   N   N   N
        | | →   / \
        V   V   V V

Condition: V does not bear phrasal stress

Because in all the cases examined the merger takes place across word boundaries, it will not be necessary to specify in (18) which of the two vocoids blocks the rule according to the condition, since phrasal stress will of necessity fall on the second, given the already mentioned observation in Roca (1986) that phrasal stress is assigned to the rightmost primary stressed vocoid in the phrase. Note also that the output of the rule leaves the headedness of the resulting complex nucleus unspecified, as headedness assignment will be automatic, simply a function of sonority, as we shall see below.

The formulation in (18) provides for sequences of more than two vocoids also to be brought together, as corresponds to fact:

(19)   [lo ha in]sultado   'he has insulted him'

If the abutting syllables already contain diphthongs, it is possible to string up as many as five vocoids tautosyllabically:

(20)   se lo cam[bia Eu]sebio   'E. will change it for you'
        se lo [dio a Eu]sebio   'he gave it to E.'

The mechanics of syllable merger will be examined in more detail in section 8. At this point, it is important to note that all the vocoids affected by merger mentioned so far are in different words, and consequently Syllable Merger (18) must be included in the word-sequence module.[15] In order to determine whether Syllable Merger applies cyclically or in one swoop to the maximal string available in the intonational phrase domain, we must next examine the fate of similarly abutting vocoids word-internally.

4.2 Word-internally. Consider the data in (21) (Pej. = pejorative):

(21) a. [rí]o   'river'   b. [ria]chuelo   'river-Pej.'
         mo[hín]   'grimace'   a[mohi]nado   'sulking'
         pa[ís]   'country'   [pai]sano   'fellow-countryman'
         [ví]a   'track'   [via]ducto   'viaduct'

In the forms in (21a) the high vocoid *i* carries the word stress (which in isolated words naturally also corresponds to phrasal stress) and constitutes a separate syllable from its adjacent vocoid. In the forms in (21b), however, where both abutting vocoids are stressless, diphthongisation takes place, as predicted by Syllable Merger (18). As before, this outcome is independent of the height of the vocoids, again in apparent agreement with Syllable Merger:

(22) a. [le]al   'loyal'   b. [leal]tad   'loyalty'
         [le]ón   'lion'   [leo]nino   'leonine'
         [bo]ato   'pomp'   [boa]tillo   'pomp-Pej.'
         [po]eta   'poet'   [poe]tastro   'poet-Pej.'

All the data so far therefore suggest that Syllable Merger is noncyclic postlexical. In particular, given this ordering all sequences of vocoids which do not include the intonational head will be tautosyllabic.

Consider, however, sequences of vocoids which are heterosyllabic when the word is pronounced in isolation, as in *río*. In particular, the question arises of what the syllabic fate of these sequences is after syntactic

---

[15] I am assuming with Halle and Vergnaud (1987) that the phonology is organised in two modules, one corresponding to morphological domains up to the word, and the other to domains formed by syntactic concatenation, to be referred to by the labels 'word-internal' and 'word-sequence,' respectively. Within each such module the rules can apply in one of two modes, viz. cyclic or noncyclic, also organised in two successive blocks.

concatenation makes them compatible with Syllable Merger (for clarity, the relevant words in (23) have been underlined):

(23) un río muy caudaloso   'a very large river'
      un mohín muy simpático   'a very friendly grimace'
      un país maravilloso   'a wonderful country'
      la vía del ferrocarril   'the railway track'

      su leal amante   'his/her loyal lover'
      un león muy cariñoso   'a very affectionate lion'
      un boato sin ton ni son   'a pomp without rhyme or reason'
      un poeta dieciochesco   'a seventeenth–century poet'

In Roca (1986) it is suggested that forms such as these are also subject to Syllable Merger. This is undoubtedly so in fast casual speech, but in slower or more careful registers heterosyllabicity tends to be preserved. Moreover, the conditions for such preservation appear to be heavily particularised (cf. the comments in Navarro Tomás 1959: 148). For instance, word stress on high vocoids strongly disfavours merger, as brought out by the pair in (24):

(24) una ganzúa muy práctica   'a very useful picklock'
      atormentado por suaves celos 'tormented by sweet jealousy'

When the words *ganzúa* and *suave* are pronounced in isolation, *u* and *a* are heterosyllabic in the dialect under consideration,[16] but in the phrasal collocation above *ganz'ua*, with a stressed *u*, is much more resistant to desyllabification than *su'ave*, where the *u* is stressless. In the face of this and similar facts, it will be wise to adopt a conservative attitude and prevent the application of Syllable Merger word-internally if one of the vocoids bears word-stress. This can be accomplished straightforwardly by assigning Syllable Merger to both the word-internal and the word-sequence modules, but giving it different cyclic status in each of them. In particular, word-internally Syllable Merger will be applied noncyclically. Consequently, it will be operative in, e.g. *lealtad* or *paisano*, since in each case neither of the two adjacent vocoids is stressed (equivalently, bears the maximum height in the metrical grid) at word level, but it will be blocked in *leal* or *país*, where one of the vocoids is thus stressed. On the other hand, by making postlexical (i.e. word-sequential)

---

[16] Following on from fn. 12, the importance of dialect variation as regards Syllable Merger cannot be overemphasised. Put at its simplest, Spanish has been undergoing throughout its history a process of extension of Syllable Merger to all contexts. Different dialects are, however, at different stages in this evolution.

application of Syllable Merger cyclic, it will be blocked by strict cyclicity from applying internally to these words, but it will be free to apply to sequences of vocoids arising as a result of syntactic concatenation. In fast casual speech (and in the appropriate dialects), we simply allow the postlexical application of Syllable Merger also to be noncyclic, thus accounting for its generalised effects.[17]

It should now be clear how the existence of Syllable Merger facilitates the analysis of adjacent vocoids as underlyingly heterosyllabic. Thus, returning to *Mac'ario*, which exemplifies (3d) above, neither *i* nor *o* is a carrier of word stress, and consequently they will automatically be merged by Syllable Merger in its noncyclic word-internal application. If the analysis being proposed is adopted, the two-syllable window can therefore simply be assimilated to the Three–Syllable Window, as desired, at no additional cost.

The case of the one-syllable window in, e.g. *convoy*, appears less manageable, since here one of the two abutting vocoids carries the stress, and Syllable Merger should therefore be blocked. This difficulty, however, is only apparent. Thus consider the groups of words in (25)(verb forms are provided in brackets where nonverbals with the desired melody are scarce):

(25)   a.   cacao   'cocoa'   b.   oboe   'oboe'
            sarao   'soirée'   (roe)   'he gnaws'
            bacalao   'cod'   (corroe) 'he corrodes'

            (cae)   'he falls'   correo   'mail'
            (recae)   'he relapses'   fideo   'noodle'
                                                 Macabeo   'Maccabee'

The sequences in (25a) are tautosyllabic, despite the fact that the *a* is stressed, whereas those in (25b) are heterosyllabic. The difference between both classes lies in the sonority difference between the two vocoids, which is zero in (25b).[18] Consider now the words in (26):

---

[17] Note that this obviously makes noncyclic word-internal application redundant. This formal simplification corresponds well with the less complex nature of the process, as desired.

[18] Recent research on syllable structure makes widespread use of the notion of a sonority scale, although there is as yet no overall consensus about the details of the ranking (for a useful, if still incomplete, discussion, see Selkirk 1984). For our purposes here, the following gross classification will be sufficient:

low vocoid [a]   more sonority
mid vocoids [e], [o] |
high vocoids [i], [u]   ↓
consonants   less sonority

(26) Samoa   ———
       canoa   'canoe'
       anchoa   'anchovy'

       marea   'tide'
       polea   'pulley'
       platea   'orchestra box'

Clearly, the greater sonority must correspond to the first of the two vocoids. Consider further the forms in (27):

(27) Mahón   ———
       faraón   'pharaoh'

       (caer)   'to fall'
       Jaén   ———
       jaez   'harness'

Here, the existence of the same sonority difference as in (25a) is insufficient to create tautosyllabicity, because the stress falls on the second abutting vocoid. Obviously, thus, in addition to the sonority difference, tautosyllabicity requires stress to be borne by the first of the two vocoids. This suggests that the condition on Syllable Merger (18) must be qualified as in (28):

(28) Unless V_1 bears the stress peak and is more sonorous than V_2

For convenience, the full formulation of the revised Syllable Merger is now given in (29):

(29)   N   N   N
        | | →   / \
       V_1 V_2 V_1 V_2

        Condition: either *a* or *b*
        a. neither V bears the stress peak
        b. V_1 bears the stress peak and is more sonorous than V_2

Clearly, Syllable Merger will now be applicable to *convoy* and similar words, thus producing the correct results. Thus, here too, the apparent one-syllable window has been found to be reducible to the Three–Syllable Window, which is in fact a two–syllable window on the stem, given the extrametricality of the desinence.

5 Stress-bearer status and syllable peakness. There is still an apparent difficulty with the derivation of *convoy*. We said earlier that the surface form can be obtained regardless of whether or not this word is lexically marked as a stress retractor. Given the formulation of Syllable Merger above, however, merger can only occur when stress is carried by V_1, i.e. by the *o*, and this suggests that words in this category are all retractors, exception made of such forms as *ahí*, which are few and far between. While workable, this solution thus arguably inverts the markedness hierarchy, since it is reasonable to approach *ahí* as marked, and *convoy* as unmarked.

Suppose therefore that we formalise *convoy* as a nonretractor. Can the surface tautosyllabicity still be obtained? Notice that if we can show that it can, we will have placed our analysis in a very strong position, since we will be deriving final stress regardless of retractor status, thus matching the compulsory oxytone contour of these forms.

In order to arrive at a solution, we must return to the words in (7a). As shown, in isolation the last vocoid of these words is high and bears primary stress, and the question therefore arises of the fate of this stress after merger with a lower vocoid, as in (8).

Not surprisingly, in Spanish the syllable head position must correspond to a sonority peak,[19] and therefore in the phrase *bisturí afilado* the head of the merged nucleus *ia* will be the *a* (in (30) and thereafter the nucleus head is indicated by the vertical line):

(30)   N
          / |
          i a

As the result of such head assignment, there will be a mismatch in prosodic strength between the syllable plane and the stress plane, i.e. between the syllable headedness of the stressless [a], and the stressfulness of the headless [i]:

(31)   / | syllable plane
            i a
            * *   L0
            *   L1   stress plane

There are two logically possible ways of resolving the conflict, viz. either by inverting the headedness relation, or by moving the stress to the syllabically stronger vocoid. Factually, only the second solution is possible in Spanish.

---

[19] If the two vocoids have equal sonority, syllable headedness is assigned by position, and the second will be the head; cf. Navarro Tomás (1959: 67).

The desired shift can be implemented most naturally by assuming that after desyllabification [i] loses its stress bearer status and the concomitant movement of the stress mark is constrained by syllable constituency.[20] Given these assumptions, the derivation will proceed as in (32):

(32)

```
   |  | |              |  | /| | | |              |  | /| | | |
  bisturí        →   bisturí afilado      →    bisturí afilado
   *  * *             *  * ' * * *<*>            *  * ' * * *<*>
        *                   *     *                    *   *
```

Direct evidence for the loss of stress bearer status comes from the assignment of secondary stress, discussed in Roca (1986). Specifically, such desyllabified vocoids as [i] in *bisturfi alfilado* are not included in the syllable count responsible for the creation of feet,[21] thus suggesting the ordering Syllable Merger > Secondary Stress. This ordering follows automatically if stress bearers are identified with syllable heads, and Spanish secondary stress construed as the postlexical footing of surface syllables, since it is Syllable Merger that is finally responsible for the number and identity of such syllables.

6 Further instances of desyllabification. We must now consider the two remaining cases in the list in (3), viz. (3b) and (3c), which can be exemplified by *Maracaibo* and *Venezuela*, respectively. The extension to (3b) of the approach proposed is straightforward. Thus, suppose that we postulate that *a* and *i* in *Maracaibo* are heterosyllabic in underlying representation. If so, two possibilities exist for the surface form, which parallel those we just saw for *convoy*. First, if *Maracaibo* is marked in the lexicon as a stress retractor, the penultimate stress on the *i* will be moved to the *a* by the normal procedure

---

[20] This is apparently at variance with the prediction in Halle and Vergnaud (1987) that the direction of stress shift will be determined by the direction of foot headedness (cf. e.g. their discussion on Russian, Vedic, and Winnebago on pp. 29-ff.). The contrast with Vedic is particularly striking, since here too movement is induced by vocoid desyllabification. Note however that, on the basis of the information made available by Halle and Vergnaud (1987), the Vedic data are in fact compatible with the Spanish account, since stress is moved to the new syllable head also in Vedic. There thus appear to be two classes of cases. In one, represented by Russian and Winnebago in Halle and Vergnaud's (1987) discussion, there is deletion or insertion in the melodic tier. In the other, represented by Vedic and Spanish, there is only resyllabification. My tentative proposal is that in the latter case the movement of the stress mark is constrained by the syllable boundaries. This naturally suggests that the domain of movement is the minimal prosodic domain which includes the mark undergoing the process.

[21] Interestingly, this suggests that stress retraction in proparoxytones ought not to be formalised as stress bearer deletion (cf. fn. 10), since here the supposedly erased stress bearer does apparently take part in the secondary stress count. A plausible alternative is Line 0 bracket metathesis, i.e., *) →)*. This matter is tangential to the subject of the present paper, and will consequently not be taken further.

(following on from fn. 21, I henceforth informally assume that stress retraction does not involve stress bearer deletion):

(33)

```
        *              *
 * * * * *       * * * * *
 Maraca ibo  →   Maraca ibo
```

Given this configuration, Syllable Merger (29) will merge the two abutting vocoids and yield the desired surface form, as (34) shows:

(34)

```
       | |              |\
 Maraca ibo   →   Maraca ibo
 * * * * *        * * * ' *
      *                *
```

If, on the other hand, *Maracaibo* were not a stress retractor, the form *Maraca'ibo* would result, in the obvious way (note in particular that Syllable Merger will be inapplicable here). While this structure is not ruled out in Spanish (cf. e.g. *vah'ido* 'swoon'), the predictions of the model run into the same difficulties we experienced with *convoy*, i.e. markedness reversal. Consequently, we would like the configuration in *Marac'aibo* to be derivable regardless of the retractor status of this form, as was also the case with *convoy*. In order for this result to be achieved, underlying heterosyllabicity must be destroyed even when the [i] bears the stress. Let us therefore provisionally assume that there exists a rule to this effect, independent of Syllable Merger (29), which clearly cannot be thus extended. Such a rule, which we will refer to provisionally as rule *R*, will produce the desired output, in the obvious way.[22] Marked forms such as *vahído* will simply be specified as lexical exceptions to *R*. Note that it would be desirable to extend the application of *R* to the *convoy* cases, since this would allow such marked forms as *ahí* also to be formalised as exceptions to *R*, thus bringing them into line with *vahído*, a natural result.[23]

---

[22] Rule *R* is strongly reminiscent of Harris's (1969: 31) rule (39), which creates 'glides' out of high vocoids adjacent to other vocoids regardless of stress, in the same way that Syllable Merger cannot fail to remind one of his rule (28c) (p. 24), where desyllabification is further contingent on stresslessness. The conclusion we will reach in this paper is that both *R* and Syllable Merger are necessary, and that, contrary to the view expressed in Harris (1969), this result is not paradoxical. The actual formalisation and roles of *R* and Syllable Merger are, however, significantly different from those of their counterparts in Harris (1969).

[23] There is an important additional advantage to severing the syllabification of these forms from Syllable Merger. Specifically, as formulated in (29), this rule contains an obvious asymmetry, brought on by the condition in (28) (where, moreover, V_2 can possibly be confined to high vocoids in some dialects). Consequently, it would be desirable to leave open the possibility of restricting Syllable Merger to the more general case (18), and give independent formalisation to the syllabification embodied in condition (28). Future research will hopefully

The introduction of rule *R* provides a straightforward account of the *náufrago* 'castaway' class, which Harris (1969:31) effectively regarded as a potential counterexample to the Three–Syllable Window, since, although such words comply with the window in the surface (*n'au.fra.go*), stress is borne by the preantepenultimate vocoid, thus possibly corresponding to *n'a.u.fra.go* underlyingly. We can now see that *náufrago* can be assimilated to *Maracaibo* in a natural way. Simply, stress will first be assigned to the antepenultimate vocoid *u*, with no violation of the window. After the application of rule *R* and the consequent desyllabification of *u*, it will automatically move to the new head of the still antepenultimate syllable, *a*, as in (35):

(35)
```
    | |              |\               |\
  na ufrago    →   na ufrago    →   na ufrago
  * * * *           * '  * *          * '  * *
    *                 *                *
```

7 Moras vs. syllables. Before examining in detail the mechanics of rule *R*, we must complete our survey by turning to (3c), exemplified by *Venezuela*. It is clear that the approach we are adopting will yield the desired results here also. Specifically, whether or not such forms are lexically marked as retractors, stress cannot be assigned further to the left than the vocoid sequence, which *R* will turn into a diphthong, with the accompanying effects as regards syllable headedness and stress placement. Thus, even if the form were to be marked as a retractor, stress would eventually fall in the desired place, as in (36):

(36)
```
      | |                  /|                 /|
  Venezu ela     →     Venezu ela     →    Venezu ela
  * * * * *             * * ' *             * * ' * *
      *                     *                   *
```

Again, such words as *per'iodo* will be marked as exceptions to *R*, and thus will not be subject to desyllabification or stress movement.[24]

It is obvious by now that rule *R* plays a crucial role in the derivation of (3b), (3c), and perhaps also (3f), and it is therefore imperative further to investigate the identity of this rule. Clearly, *R* is a rule of syllabification, not of stress. Less obviously as yet, its domain of application is purely morpheme-

---

shed light on this interesting, if rather subtle, matter.

[24] Interestingly, the stress (and syllabification) pattern of *período* and other similar words (*cardíaco*, etc.) is undergoing change in the direction of *Venezuela*. The approach adopted here formalises this change in the most natural way, i.e., as loss of the lexical marking.

internal, as we shall now see. The forms in (37) have been subjected to the operation of *R*, as expected:[25]

(37)	*i*V	V*i*	*u*V	V*u*	
	Javier	reina	Manuel	neutro	V = e
	siempre	peine	duelo	feudo	
	tiempo	veinte	fuente	Abreu	
	Diego	seis	asueto	Pentateuco	
	embrión	estoico	cuota	bou	V = o
	acción	boina		Bouzas	
	idiota	convoy		Souza	
	idioma	Eloy			
	aciago	aire	Juan	claustro	V = a
	Santiago	gaita	ajuar	fausto	
	Aviaco	mosaico	aplauso		
	magiar		centauro		

Some of the diphthongal combinations in (37) are more typically Spanish (and thus come in more abundance) than others, but they are all pronounced unhesitatingly by native speakers.

The tautosyllabicity exhibited by the vocoid sequences in these forms, which contain no obvious stem-internal structure, must be contrasted with the heterosyllabicity of the forms in (38), where the vocoid sequence straddles

---

[25] I give the glosses separately, so as not to interfere with the visual symmetry of the table in (37):

Xavier	queen	Emmanuel	neutral
always	comb	duel	feud
time	twenty	fountain	---
---	six	time off	Pentateuch
embryo	stoic	quota	trawler
action	beret		---
idiot	convoy		---
language	---		
ill-fated	air	John	cloister
---	bagpipes	trousseau	magnificence
---	mosaic	applause	
magyar		centaur	

two morphemes:[26]

(38)

patri. 'ota	bilba. 'ino	peru. 'ano	bacala. 'ucho
esti. 'aje	hero. 'ina	padu. 'ano	trofe. 'ucho
chipri. 'ota	mana. 'ito	individu. 'al	pigme. 'ucho
mani. 'obra	ego. 'ismo	monstru. 'oso	ancho. 'ucha
barri. 'ada	mama. 'ita	anu. 'ario	jale. 'ucho
ali. 'anza	canape. 'ito	amanu. 'ense	caca. 'ucho
resfri. 'ado	canesu. 'ito	obitu. 'ario	barbaco. 'ucha
vali. 'oso	fricando. 'ito	afectu. 'oso	fide. 'ucho

Syllable Merger (29) is of course inapplicable to these forms, given the fact that the second of the two consecutive vocoids is stressed in all cases. Note that, in any event, the only function of Syllable Merger is to create diphthongs out of heterosyllabic sequences, and thus the fact that Syllable Merger fails to apply here does not explain why the sequence is heterosyllabic in the first place. Such heterosyllabicity would, however, be readily explainable if we were to assume that underlyingly all the relevant vocoids are originally syllabic, and that rule R, which affects the distribution of syllabicity among vocoids, has no extramorphemic effects.

One obvious way of formalising the difference between the two groups of forms is as follows. Suppose that rule (39) is made responsible for the formation of Spanish nuclei:

(39)

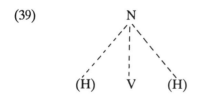

---

[26] Glosses ('Dim.' = diminutive):

patriot	from Bilbao	Peruvian	cod-Pej.
low water	heroin	from Padua	trophy-Pej.
Cypriot	manna-Dim.	individual	pygmy-Pej.
manoeuvre	selfishness	monstrous	anchovy-Pej.
neighborhood	mum-Dim.	yearbook	racket-Pej.
alliance	canapé-Dim.	amanuensis	cocoa-Pej.
cold	camisole-Dim.	obituary	barbecue-Pej.
valuable	fricassee-Dim.	affectionate	noodle-Pej.

In the semi-informal notation adopted, V represents any vocoid, and the (optional) H a high vocoid. In turn, a vocoid is defined as a segment carrying the specification [-consonantal] (cf. the discussion in fn. 8). The rule is intended simply to associate the nucleus node to the specified segmental string. Note that rule (39) basically identifies syllable heads with sonority peaks, and thus is maximally natural.

Suppose, moreover, that this rule applies in a structure–building mode in two steps. In the first step, V takes on a sonority value greater than H, i.e. the rule is applied to vocoids whose sonority exceeds that of high vocoids. In the second step, however, this constraint is removed, and so any high vocoids which still remain free will also be designated heads.[27] Now, if we apply this procedure cyclically, the desired results will ensue, as exemplified in (40) with *Manuel*, which is monomorphemic, and *bilbaíno*, polymorphemic:[28]

(40)

a. [Manuel] → [Manu el]   only cycle

b. [[[bilba] in] o] → [[[bilba] in] o]   1st cycle

   [[[bilba] in] o] → [[[bilba] in] o]   2nd cycle

   [[[bilba] in] o] → [[[bilba] in] o]   3rd cycle

Both derivations are straightforward. Crucially, in the second cycle of *bilbaíno*, the structure carried over from the first cycle is not tampered with, as corresponds to the structure–building status of the nucleus formation rule (39), which we now identify with rule *R*. This respect of rule (39) for its own output is thus the source of the heterosyllabicity of the sequence *a.i* in *bilbaíno*.

There are of course morpheme–internal heterosyllabic sequences (as follows from fns. 12 and 16, the existence of considerable lexical variation

---

[27] Staged application of syllabification rules contingent on sonority can be found, e.g. in Dell and Edmelaoui (1985).

[28] It would appear that right to left directional application is required in order to account for the syllabification of, e.g. *cacahuete* as *ca.ca.hue.te*, rather than **ca.cahu.e.te*, but this presents problems for the class of data referred to in fn. 19. As will be shown in section 8, such directionality is equivalent to a stipulation to maximise the pre-head material, and is in fact unnecessary in the context of the reanalysis to be carried out here.

across dialects here as elsewhere does not invalidate the point being made):[29]

(41)   *i*V   V*i*   *u*V   V*u*
     tri.unfo   su.ave
     vi.aje   su.izo
     di.ablo   cru.el
     pi.ojo   ru.ina

     gavi.ota   va.hído   Litu.ania   a.úpa
     ari.ete   a.hí   adu.ana   bara.únda
     boni.ato   coca.ína   Noru.ega   Ara.újo

Some of these exceptions can in fact be reduced to rule. For instance, the first group of forms illustrates a tendency of word-initial sequences to heterosyllabicity. In the second group, some of the forms could perhaps be analysed as suffixal derivatives (e.g. *cocaína* < *coca+ina*, *boniato* < *boni+ato*), thus having their heterosyllabicity fall out of the structure–building status of rule (39). Clearly, however, such reductionist strategies cannot be extended to all cases, and there will therefore be a remnant of genuine exceptions to morpheme-internal diphthongisation. A straightforward formalisation of this situation consists in providing the corresponding high vocoids with a lexical syllabic nucleus, thus preventing their association to the nucleus of the adjacent vocoid, again because of the structure–building status of the nucleus formation algorithm *R* (cf. Guerssel 1986 for a similar approach with regard to some troublesome facts of Ait Seghrouchen Berber).

The proposed algorithm creates an immediate problem for our stress assignment procedure, which I have deliberately been ignoring so far, but which we must now address. Specifically, the direct creation of morpheme-internal diphthongs by the algorithm does not appear compatible with the analysis of all underlying vocoids as syllable heads, and thus as stress bearers, which is essential to the interpretation we have been putting forward for the

---

[29] Glosses:

triumph   soft
journey   Swiss
devil   cruel
louse   ruin

sea-gull   swoon   Lithuania   up
battering-ram   there   customs   racket
sweet potato   cocaine   Norway   ----

window constraints in (3).

There are two logical solutions to this problem, each of them apparently requiring the abandonment of one of our proposed procedures. First, if we insist on granting all lexical vocoids syllabic status, we must obviously reform the syllabification algorithm R. Specifically, in this case a stage must be allowed for where there still has not been any diphthongisation, at which point the stress algorithm will apply, in the manner indicated earlier. Second, if we decide that diphthongisation indeed occurs simultaneously with nucleus formation, another analysis must be sought for the window effects already discussed.

Let us explore the first strategy. This strategy implies that in the first step the syllabification algorithm declares all vocoids syllable heads. As noted, this will allow the application of stress in the fashion explained above. After stress assignment, diphthongisation must occur, i.e. a rule R_i, the counterpart of rule R, must apply. The obvious role of rule R_i will be to associate high vocoids to adjacent nuclei, as (42) shows:

(42)   N   N

           H   V   (mirror image)

The question is how the application of R_i (42) can be limited to the morpheme-internal domain. Thus, suppose that we apply R_i to the stem before any suffixation has taken place, so as to prevent diphthongisation in such cases as *pe.ru.a.no*, while enforcing it, e.g. in *Ma.ra.cai.bo*. This would appear to imply structure-changing cyclic application to underived forms, in violation of Strict Cyclicity. Moreover, it is difficult to see how the derivation of, e.g. *pe.rua.no* would indeed be blocked, since rule R_i ought to apply again in the second cycle, in the obvious way. Clearly, we would have to resort to a sort of Anti-Strict Cyclicity condition, whose effect would be the exact reverse of the standard Strict Cyclicity, a paradoxical result. Consequently, the first of our two strategies does not appear viable.

Suppose that we adopt instead the second strategy and thus that syllabification does take place as encapsulated in (39). What will the results be for stress assignment? Simply, the stress bearers will no longer be identifiable with the syllable heads, as we have been assuming throughout. But then, why should they have to be? Specifically, given the parametrisation of stress bearer status, different languages may opt for different settings of this parameter. Suppose therefore that in Spanish we declare all vocoids stress bearers, regardless of whether or not they are heads of syllables.[30] Clearly, this will allow stress to be assigned in the correct position, in exactly the manner indicated above. Consequently, the assumption that all vocoids are stress bearers is consistent with the observed distribution of stress, and in particular with the constraints in (3). The problem, however, will once more be the relationship between stress and syllables. In particular, how does stress end up realised in the nucleus head in such words as *n'aufrago, Marac'aibo* or *conv'oy* if it is in fact assigned to its mate (i.e. *na'ufrago, Maraca'ibo, convo'y*)?

The paradox we are now facing is that, on the one hand, we need to identify stress bearer status with nucleus head status in order to assign stress to the appropriate element in the nucleus, while at the same time this identification must be prevented in order to make stress assignment compatible with the windows. On closer examination, however, the paradox turns out to be only apparent, since both assignments are valid, albeit at different levels. Thus, in underlying representation all vocoids must be treated as stress bearers, as corresponds to the window distributions, while in surface representation only syllable nuclei can be, as corresponds to the fact that only syllable nuclei may carry the phonetic stress.

The formalisation of this situation is in fact straightforward. Thus, remember that syllable-induced stress shift must be included in the word-sequential module, given the fact that it must follow Syllable Merger, which is also postlexical. If so, we can LIMIT such shift to this module, i.e. prevent shift from occurring in the word-internal module. A natural implementation of this ordering consists in stipulating that the constraint that only syllable heads can be stress bearers is only operative postlexically. This amounts to countenancing two settings for the stress bearer parameter, viz. one per module. The resulting division of labour allows us to enjoy the best of both worlds without incurring any loss. On the one hand, the location of the stress mark will be constrained by the underlying distribution of vocoids, as corresponds to the factuality of the windows,[31] while, on the other, such a

---

[30] This situation is sometimes referred to in the literature as mora stress. The ambiguity of the term (and the construct) 'mora,' however, makes its use ill-advised (cf. Roca 1988b for some discussion), notwithstanding the title of this section, chosen for effect.

[31] The ensuing formal compatibility of diphthongs with multiple stress bearers circumvents a problem glossed over in the discussion above for ease of exposition. Specifically, it has been suggested (Harris 1985a, García-Bellido 1986) that such diphthongs as *ue* in *Venezuela* (and *ie* in *tierra* 'earth') are given in underlying representation (with the *e* melody underspecified). If so, and if stress bearers were identified with syllable nuclei, the diphthong would count as a single stress bearer at the stage where stress applies, thus allowing for the violation of (3c) (**Ven'ezuela*). No such violation is possible, of course, if all vocoids are given stress bearer status in underlying representation, as I am proposing.

mark will eventually come to be associated with the appropriate melodic element, as corresponds to the surface manifestation of stress.

8 Refinements in the syllabification procedure. Having shown the basic independence of stress and syllabification and ascribed the interaction between
the two levels to the stress bearer parameter of the metrical algorithm, we must now return to the two proposed syllabification rules and examine their operation more closely.

The formulation of Syllable Merger in (29) is now repeated in (43) for convenience:

(43)   N   N   N
         | | →   / \
         V_1 V_2 V_1 V_2

Condition: either *a* or *b*
a. neither V bears the stress peak
b. V_1 bears the stress peak and is more sonorous than V_2

Syllable Merger has been seen to be a structure-changing rule, and to apply noncyclically in the word-internal module, and cyclically or noncyclically in the word-sequence module, in normal and fast casual speech, respectively.

In (20) we saw that Spanish allows for as many as five vocoids in the same nucleus. The formation of such a maximum constituent necessarily involves both Nucleus Formation (39) and Syllable Merger (43), and we shall focus on the latter rule for the moment.   In order for the five–vocoid sequence in *se lo dio a Eusebio* to become tautosyllabic, Syllable Merger must obviously apply more than once, since the input defined in (43) is limited to two vocoids. At present, nothing prevents Syllable Merger from applying simultaneously to all the eligible segments, in line with the usual SPE convention (SPE: 344):

(44)   N   N   N

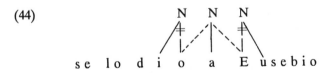

          s e   l o   d i   o   a   E u s e b i o

As shown in (44), Syllable Merger applies to the three heteromorphemic abutting vocoids *oae* and encompasses them under one nucleus. As a result of this process, the high vocoids *i* and *u* are left stranded in their original nuclei, as in (45):

(45)

se lo d i o a E usebio

We naturally want these vocoids also to be included in the newly formed nucleus. Two strategies are available in principle to attain this result. First, we could assume that by convention merger affects the entire nucleus, rather than simply the strictly adjacent vocoid. Alternatively, we could assume that Syllable Merger will reapply to the configuration in (45), intramorphemic application having been made compatible with Strict Cyclicity by the change effected in the syllables in question by the first application of Syllable Merger. Either strategy will yield the desired configuration, represented in (46):

(46)

se lo d i o a E u sebio

Consider now the slight, but crucially distinct, variant *se lo doy a Eusebio* 'I give it to E.', which has the structure in (47) on entry to the word-sequence module:

(47)

se lo d o i a E usebio

Here, the target syllabification excludes the initial *o*: *se lo [do][iaeu]sebio*. The reason for the failure of such *o* to undergo merger is well known (cf. e.g. Navarro Tomás 1959:150). Simply, the string of vocoids in the nucleus must obey the Sonority Sequence Generalisation (cf. e.g. Selkirk 1984: 116), nucleus-internal sonority troughs being therefore disallowed. It is obvious that if the sequence *oiaeu* in (47) were syllabified as one nucleus, the *i* would constitute a sonority trough, and consequently the *o* cannot undergo merger.

Two questions arise. First, how is the *o* excluded from the domain of Syllable Merger? Second, granting that the *o* remains outside the scope of Syllable Merger, how come the *i* is syllabified with the *a*, rather than with the *o*, particularly in view of the fact that these two vocoids indeed are tautosyllabic on exit from the word-internal module?

In order to prevent the *o* from undergoing merger, a sonority-related condition must be included in the rule of Syllable Merger. Suppose that we replace (43) with (48) (the new clause in the condition is given in italics):

(48)

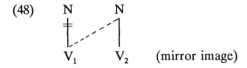

V_1 V_2 (mirror image)

Condition: either *a* or *b*
a. neither V bears the stress peak *and V_1 is not more sonorous than V_2*
b. V_1 bears the stress peak and is more sonorous than V_2

In the phrase in (47) all the abutting vocoids comply with the first part of condition (a) in (48), since the phrasal stress is carried by the syllable *se*. Let us therefore proceed to the second part of this condition. Given the new formulation of Syllable Merger as a mirror image rule, we must first examine the first branch of the rule, as given in (48). The condition that V_1 not be more sonorous than V_2 is met by the pair *ia*,[32] but not by *oi*. Going next to the mirror branch of the rule, the condition is met by both *ae* and *eu*. The resulting syllabification will accordingly be *[o][iaeu]*, as desired. This is illustrated in (49) for greater clarity:

(49)

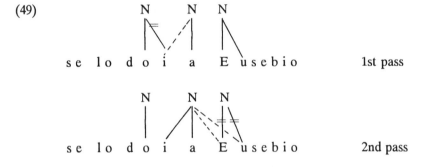

se   lo   do   i   a   E   u s e b i o   1st pass

se   lo   do   i   a   E   u s e b i o   2nd pass

We are now in a position to adjudicate between the two alternative blocking

---

[32] The reason for this particular formulation is that, as referred to in fn. 19, two vocoids of equal sonority also undergo merger, the second vocoid being the head of the resulting nucleus:

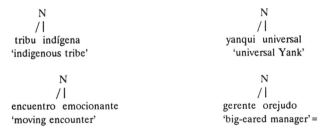

N
/|
tribu indígena
'indigenous tribe'

N
/|
yanqui universal
'universal Yank'

N
/|
encuentro emocionante
'moving encounter'

N
/|
gerente orejudo
'big-eared manager' =

strategies mentioned above. Clearly, if Syllable Merger were to apply in one swoop, it would have to be allowed to apply to whole nuclei, rather than to two strictly adjacent vocoids, and the corresponding sonority condition would either need to look ahead at the output, and block the rule if a sonority trough would be generated, or be unnecessarily complicated by including a righthand, as well as a lefthand, environment. Consequently, we conclude that the appropriate blocking procedure makes use of multiple application, as in Z(49).

We must next turn to the rule of Nucleus Formation (39), repeated here as (50) for convenience:

(50)

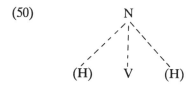

This rule is ordered in the word-internal module and applies cyclically in a structure-building mode. It clearly feeds Syllable Merger, and thus must precede it in the ordering. Both syllabification rules crucially interact with the rules of stress assignment, both primary stress assignment (including stress movement) and phrasal stress assignment. (For detailed discussion of the stress rules, the reader is again referred to Roca 1986, 1988, 1990a, 1990b, and the references therein.)

It will be interesting to note at this point the similarity between the new rule of Syllable Merger (48) and our previous rule R_i (42), subsequently dismissed as an alternative to Nucleus Formation (50). Specifically, (48) and (42) embody an identical syllabification process, the two rules differing only in the conditions under which such (re)syllabification takes place. We mentioned in fn. 22 the discussion of two similar rules in Harris (1969), only one of which was adopted by this author on the grounds that their noted similarity militated against granting them both independent status.

Our argument against R_i (42) hinged on the fact that Nucleus Formation must be structure-building, whereas R_i is by definition structure-changing. Note, however, that this argument does not prevent us from restating (50) as (51):

(51)

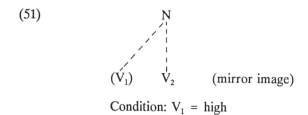

Condition: V_1 = high

The mirror image status of (51) will guarantee its application in the same environments as (48).[33]

Interestingly, the formulation in (51), unlike that in (50), brings out a strong parallelism with Syllable Merger (48), very much along the lines of (42). Thus, the processes encoded in Nucleus Formation (51) and Syllable Merger (48) are in fact identical. The two rules differ, however, in two respects. First, their mode of application is opposite: structure-building in (51) and structure-changing in (48). Second, the conditions attached to the rules are different in various ways, as summarised in (52):[34]

(52)   Conditions on (re)syllabification

	Sonority		*Metrical*
(51)	$V_1 = H$		
(48)	$V_1 \leq V_2$	*and*	V has no metrical peak
	or:		
	$V_1 > V_2$	*and*	V_1 has the metrical peak

In view of the noted similarities, I shall make the tentative proposal that (51) and (48) are in fact the same rule. It has been known for some time that it is possible for a rule to be assigned to more than one stratum (cf. Kiparsky 1983 for a particularly illuminating discussion). If so, the mode of application of the rule will vary, in line with the requirements associated with each level (e.g. in Kiparsky's model it applies cyclically in the lexical stratum and noncyclically postlexically; note that our own rule (48) has been proposed to apply differently in each of our two modules). This suggests a separation

---

[33] Strictly speaking, (51) is not isomorphic with its mirror image branch, which will instead have the following configuration:

In particular, the head is constructed in the pass through the first branch, and thus the action of the mirror branch is limited to the possible adjunction of a sister. Such a difference is, however, an artifact of the operation of the rule itself, and therefore cannot be regarded as a problem for the present formulation.

[34] A third difference between (51) and (48) resides in the optionality of V_1 in the former, but not in the latter. Note, however, that nothing prevents us from considering V_1 in (48) as also optional: in the absence of V_1, the application of (48) will simply be vacuous.

between a rule as such and the conditions under which it operates.

A rule per se is simply the expression of a phonological process. Thus, the Spanish syllabification procedure of which (51) and (48) are specific instantiations simply creates nuclear structures. These structures are maximally natural in that (i) they are headed by vocoids which constitute sonority peaks in the segmental chain, (ii) they are algorithmically binary and thus strictly comply with locality, (iii) they replicate the generalisation captured in the universal principles of Onset Maximisation and CV Syllable Formation, of adjoining the material to the left of the head prior to the post-head material. Note that the application precedence of the first branch dispenses with the need for directionality referred to in fn. 28.

In turn, the conditions attached to rules can usefully be regarded as assigning specific values to a set of universal parameters. Thus, it seems reasonable to regard the high vocoid constraint on (51) as one of such parameters. In particular, it is usual in the world's languages for high vocoids to be nonsyllabic in the appropriate circumstances, a fact which can be made partly responsible for the SPE stand of creating a special class of 'glides' separate from ordinary vocoids or 'vowels'. Similarly, the various metrical constraints on (48) and their related sonority conditions appear as plausible candidates for parametrisation, since, again universally, stress and syllabicity interact in (at least partially) predictable ways. The interpretation being suggested is very much in the spirit of much current research in generative linguistics (for phonology, cf. e.g. Archangeli and Pulleyblank 1986). The precise specification of these matters lies outside the scope of the present paper, however, and accordingly I decline to take the discussion further.

9 Exemplification and conclusion. We shall now examine a few derivations to exemplify the overall procedure.

Consider first the words *hoy* 'today' and *continua* 'continuous' in isolation. These words will originally be syllabified as in (53), in accordance with the Nucleus Formation rule (51):

(53)   o i   c o n t i n u a
          |/ | | | |

In particular, rule (51) will apply in its maximal expansion to *hoy*, which only has only one cycle, but minimally to *continua*, which has two cycles, one on the stem [continu], and the second on the desinence]a].

Acting on these configurations, the stress pattern of these words will be *h'oy* and *cont'inua*, respectively, after application of all the appropriate rules:

(54)   *   *
          o i   c o n t i n u a
          |/ | | | |

In *hoy*, the stress mark is originally assigned to the stem-final vocoid *i*, in accordance with the general stress rule:

(55)
```
        *
      o i
      |/
```

On entry to the postlexical level the constraint that only syllable heads be stress bearers will come into operation, and stress will automatically move to the more open vocoid *o*:

(56)
```
    *           *           *
  * *         * ·         * ·
  o i    →    o i    →    o i
  |/          |/          |/
```

In *continua*, stress is first assigned on the stem-final vocoid *u*, and then moved leftfwards by idiosyncratic stress retraction:

(57)
```
              *                     *  ·
    *    *  * *           *    *   * *
  c o n t i n u a   →   c o n t i n u a
  |    |   | |           |    |   | |
```

The as yet heterosyllabic vocoid sequence *u.a* complies with condition (a) of Syllable Merger (48), and thus will be merged:

(58)
```
            *
  c o n t i n u a
  |    |   \|
```

Suppose now that we concatenate the two words under analysis in the phrase *¿continua hoy?*, which can question the availability of a continuous showing in the local cinema today (*continua* thus abbreviating *sesión continua* 'continuous showing'). On exit from the word-internal module, the (simplified) metrical and syllabic representation will be as in (59):

(59)
```
            *           *
  c o n t i n u a     o i
  |    |   \|         \|
```

As before, *o i* will automatically become *o i* as a result of the stress bearer constraints:

(60)
```
            *           *
  c o n t i n u a     o i
  |    |   \|         \|
```

This string will next undergo the rule of phrasal stress assignment, which will construct a higher level of prominence on the rightmost stressed syllable *oi*:

(61)
```
                         *
          *              *
c o n t i n u a      o i
|   |    \|       \|
```

At this point there is a sequence of four adjacent vocoids, *uaoi*. While strict cyclicity will limit the possibility of syllable merger to the heteromorphemic *ao*, if these two vocoids were to merge, they would obviously drag along their syllable mates *u* and *i*, respectively, and this would result in the creation of a unique syllable for the whole sequence. As it happens, however, Syllable Merger (48) is inapplicable, since the second of the two abutting vocoids carries phrasal stress (cf. in particular condition (b)). Consequently, the stress and syllabification pattern of the phrase will remain as in (61).

Suppose, however, that we add the adverb *también* 'also'. If so, the phrasal stress will be removed from the vocoid sequence *uaoi*:

(62)
```
                                          *
          *              *                *
c o n t i n u a      o i    t a m b i e n
|   |    \|       |/     |     \|
```

The sequence *uaoi* now meets the conditions of Syllable Merger (48), since neither *a* nor *o* bear the phrasal stress. Consequently, resyllabification will take place, as in (63) (the details will be clear in light of the discussion in section 8, and are accordingly omitted):

(63)
```
                                  *
          *       *               *
c o n t i n u a o i    t a m b i e n
|   |   |          |    \|
```

The structure in (63) is illegitimate, however, because in the new syllable *nuaoi* the stress is not borne by the head *a*, in contravention of the restriction of stress bearers to syllable heads in the word-sequence module. Accordingly, we must replace (63) with (64), which complies with the restriction:

(64)
```
                                  *
          *    *                  *
c o n t i n u a o i    t a m b i e n
|   |   |          |    \|
```

thus (64) is the definitive accentual and syllabic representation for the phrase under analysis.

Let us next substitute the verb *continúa* 'continues', with stress on the penultimate vocoid, for the adjective *continua*, with stress three vocoids from the end. In isolation the stress and syllabification pattern of this word will be as in (65) (for a detailed discussion of stress in verb forms, see Roca 1990b):

(65)
```
              *
    c o n t i n u a
    |     |   | |
```

Consider now the phrase *continúa hoy* 'carry on today', which we represent in (66) after the assignment of phrasal stress:

(66)
```
                      *
                *     *
    c o n t i n u a   o i
    |     |   | |     |/
```

As before, the merger of *a* and *o* will be blocked by condition (b) of (48). Moreover, the merger of the sequence *ua* will be blocked by strict cyclicity in the normal style, in which Syllable Merger (48) applies cyclically in the word-sequence module. In fast casual style, however, Syllable Merger will apply noncyclically, and *ua* will merge:

(67)
```
                      *
                *     *
    c o n t i n u a   o i
    |     |   \|      |/
```

Note that resyllabification automatically causes the movement of the stress mark onto the new syllable head, as explained above.

Suppose, finally, that we add the intensifier *mismo* 'right' to the phrase under scrutiny:

(68)
```
                              *
                *       *     *
    c o n t i n u a   o i   m i s m o
    |     |   | |     |/    |     |
```

As before, there are two possibilities. In normal speech resyllabification will only occur across words, and therefore *a* will merge with *oi*, while *u* will remain heterosyllabic, as (69) shows:

(69)
```
                              *
                *   *         *
    c o n t i n u a o i   m i s m o
    |     |   | |         |     |
```

On the other hand, in casual speech total merger will take place:

(70)
```
                              *
                *             *
    c o n t i n u a o i   m i s m o
    |     |   |           |     |
```

As we have now had occasion to observe in some detail, the mechanics of the rules we have proposed are straightforward. Moreover, the predictions represented in the respective outputs are in agreement with the intuitions being tested, and we must consequently conclude that the analysis we have been putting forward enjoys a high degree of descriptive plausibility as regards at least this one variety of Spanish. It will be useful to note the simplicity of the analysis, and the fact that it provides further empirical substantiation for such theoretical devices as the stress cycle and its associated Strict Cyclicity Condition, or the distinction between structure-changing and structure-building rules, the latter exempt from Strict Cyclicity.

As regards the theory of the syllable, our findings confirm the overall predictability of syllabicity, which must consequently not be approached as a primitive, but rather as an artifact of the linear sonority relationships. In this connection, it is interesting to note that the incorporation of the syllable into the general theory after Kahn's (1976) thesis has not always been accompanied by a dismissal of the feature [± syllabic], whose introduction and defence in SPE obviously predate the syllable in Generative Phonology. Thus, for instance, the CV theory of the syllable made use of in Steriade (1984) is underpinned by the association of V slots to [+syllabic] segments. Likewise, Harris's (1983) description of the Spanish syllable assumes the availability of lexical [± syllabic] markings, and in subsequent work this same author goes so far as to suggest that 'explicit specification of underlying *non-syllabicity* is empirically well motivated in Spanish' (Harris 1989d: 149; my emphasis, IMR). The discussion above leads us to the very opposite conclusion. Specifically, the facts of Spanish examined here support the goal of predicting syllabification from the segmental feature content, as made explicit in such works as Levin (1985), Dell and Elmedlaoui (1985), and Guerssel (1986). The only proviso to be made refers to the availability in Spanish of marked syllabicity, which is, however, subject to stringent constraints, derivable from the limitation of syllabicity marking to the provision of nuclei in the lexicon, along the lines suggested in these works. We have also seen how the facts of Spanish syllabicity can be taken to be consistent with parametrisation, and in particular with the factoring out of conditions in rules.

A theoretical innovation given strong empirical support here concerns the possibility of a differing setting for the stress bearer parameter at different derivational levels, specifically as between the word-internal and the word-sequence modules. As we have been showing in some detail, this simple switch in the theory allows a maximally simple account of a set of otherwise considerably complex facts, and it is therefore reasonable to conclude that such a modest degree of setting variability must indeed be made available.[35]

---

[35] Note that also in syntax the original internal uniformity of parameter setting has been found to need relaxing. One step in this direction has been Wexler and Manzini's (1987) 'Lexical Parameterisation Hypothesis.'

References

Archangeli, D., and D. Pulleyblank. 1986. The Content and Structure of Phonological Representations. Unpublished ms. University of Arizona and University of Southern California. (To appear in MIT Press, Cambridge, Mass.).

Chomsky, N., and M. Halle. 1968. The Sound Pattern of English. New York: Harper and Row.

Dell, F., and M. Elmedlaoui. 1985. Syllabic Consonants and Syllabification in Imdlawn Tashlhiyt Berber. Journal of African Languages and Linguistics 7, 105-130.

den Os, E., and R. Kager. 1986. Extrametricality and Stress in Spanish and Italian. Lingua 69, 23-48.

García-Bellido, P. 1986. Lexical Diphthongisation and High-Mid Alternations in Spanish: An Autosegmental Account. Linguistic Analysis 16, 61-92.

Guerssel, M. 1986. Glides in Berber and Syllabicity. Linguistic Inquiry 17, 1-12.

Halle, M., and J. R. Vergnaud. 1987. An Essay on Stress. Cambridge, Mass.: MIT Press.

Halle, M., J. W. Harris, and J. R. Vergnaud 1991. A Reeexamination of the Stress Erasure Convention and Spanish Stress. Linguistic Inquiry 22, 141-159.

Harris, J. W. 1969. Spanish Phonology. Cambridge, Mass.: MIT Press.

Harris, J. W. 1983. Stress and Syllables in Spanish. Cambridge, Mass.: MIT Press.

Harris, J. W. 1985a. Spanish Diphthongisation and Stress: A Paradox Resolved, Phonology Yearbook 2, 31-45.

Harris, J. W. 1985b. Spanish Word Markers. In F. Nuessel (ed.), Current Issues in Spanish Phonology and Morphology. Bloomington, Ind.: Indiana University Linguistics Club.

Harris, J. W. 1989a. Spanish Stress: The Extrametricality issue. Unpublished ms., MIT, Cambridge. Mass.

Harris, J. W. 1989b. How Different is Verb Stress in Spanish? Probus 1, 241-258.

Harris, J. W. 1989c. The Stress Erasure Convention and Cliticization in Spanish. Linguistic Inquiry 20, 339-363.

Harris, J. W. 1989d. Sonority and Syllabification in Spanish. In C. Kirschner and J. Decesaris (eds.), Studies in Romance Linguistics. Philadelphia: John Benjamins, 139-153.

Hayes, B. 1980. A Metrical Theory of Stress Rules. Doctoral dissertation, MIT, Cambridge. Mass. (Distributed in 1981 by the Indiana University Linguistics Club, Bloomington, Ind.).

Kahn, D. 1976. Syllable-Based Generalizations in English Phonology. Doctoral dissertation, MIT, Cambridge. Mass.

Kiparsky, P. 1983. Word Formation and the Lexicon. In F. Ingemann (ed.), Proceedings of the 1982 Mid-America Linguistics Conference. Lawrence, Kansas: University of Kansas. 3-29.

Levin, J. 1985. A Metrical Theory of Syllabicity. Doctoral dissertation, MIT, Cambridge. Mass.

Navarro Tomás, T. 1959. Pronunciación española. Madrid: CSIC.

Núñez Cedeño, R. 1985. Stress Assignment in Spanish Verb Forms. In F. Nuessel (ed.), Current Issues in Hispanic Phonology and Morphology. Bloomington, Ind.: Indiana University Linguistics Club, 55-76.

Otero, C. P. 1986. A Unified Metrical Account of Spanish Stress. In M. Brame, H. Contreras, and F. J. Newmeyer (eds.), A Festschrift for Sol Saporta. Seattle: Noi Amrofer, 299-332.

Quilis, A. 1984. Métrica española. Barcelona: Ariel.

Robles Dégano, F. 1905. Ortología clásica de la lengua castellana. Madrid: M. Tabares.

Roca, I. M. 1986. Secondary Stress and Metrical Rhythm. Phonology Yearbook 3, 341-370.

Roca, I. M. 1988a. Theoretical Implications of Spanish Word Stress. Linguistic Inquiry 19, 393-423.

Roca, I. M. 1988b. Constraining Extrametricality. Paper read at the 6th International Phonology Meeting at Krems, Austria. (Forthcoming in Phonologica 1988, Cambridge University Press.

Roca, I. M. 1990a. Diachrony and Synchrony in Word Stress. Journal of Linguistics 26, 133-164.

Roca, I. M. 1990b. Verb Morphology and Stress in Spanish. Probus 2, 321-350.

Selkirk, E. O. 1984. On the Major Class Features and Syllable Theory. In M. Aronoff and R. Oehrle (eds.), Language Sound Structure, Cambridge, Mass.: MIT Press, 107-136.

Steriade, D. 1984. Glides and Vowels in Romanian. Berkely Linguistic Society 10, 47-64.

Wexler, K., and R. Manzini. 1987. Parameters and Learnability in Binding Theory. In T. Roeper and E. Williams (eds.), Parameter Setting. Dordrecht: Reidel, 41-76.